PUBLIC POLICY

For Mary, Ben and John

PUBLIC POLICY

An introduction to the theory and practice of policy analysis

WAYNE PARSONS

Professor of Public Policy and Head of the Department of Politics
Queen Mary, University of London, UK

Edward Elgar
Cheltenham, UK • Northampton, MA, USA

Published by
Edward Elgar Publishing Limited
Glensanda House
Montpellier Parade
Cheltenham
Glos GL50 1UA
UK

Edward Elgar Publishing, Inc.
136 West Street
Suite 202
Northampton
Massachusetts 01060
USA

Cased edition reprinted 2001
Paperback edition reprinted 1997, 1999, 2001, 2003, 2005

British Library Cataloguing in Publication Data
Parsons, D.W.
    Public Policy: Introduction to the Theory
    and Practice of Policy Analysis
    I. Title
    320.6

Library of Congress Cataloguing in Publication Data
Parsons, D.W.
    Public Policy: an introduction to the theory and practice of
policy analysis / Wayne Parsons.
    Includes bibliographical references and index.
    1. Policy sciences. I. Title.
    H97.P373 1996
    320'.6—dc20

                                                   95—10756
                                                    CIP

ISBN 1 85278 553 5 (cased)
    1 85278 554 3 (paperback)

Typeset by Manton Typesetters, 5-7 Eastfield Road, Louth, Lincolnshire LN11 7AJ
Printed and bound in Great Britain by MPG Books Ltd, Bodmin, Cornwall

Civil knowledge is conversant about a subject which of all others is most immersed in matter, and hardliest reduced to axiom.

Francis Bacon

There is no art that hath been more canker'd in her principles, more soyl'd and slubber'd with aphorising pedantry than the art of policie.

John Milton

Contents

Figures

Table

Preface

This book has evolved out of some fifteen years of teaching public policy at an undergraduate and postgraduate level. However, its real origins are to be found in my own undergraduate education. As a student I was fortunate to have as a teacher Michael Watson, at the University College of Wales, Aberystwyth, whose courses on public policy managed to bring some very dry stuff on planning and organizational rationality alive and relate such ideas to a broader intellectual context. In those days there was all too often a chasm between politics, government, political theory and public administration. Mike's genius was to create courses in which 'public admin' was exciting and challenging. His use of philosophy, public policy, economics and political theory, and administrative and organizational analysis in the early 1970s was years ahead of its time and was, I believe, a model of the integrative capacities of the policy approach. A lasting influence from those years was my encounter with the work of Dewey, Keynes and Harold Lasswell, as well as that of Simon, Lindblom, Etzioni, Dror, Galbraith and Vickers. Lasswell – as the reader will discover – has been especially important in forming my ideas about policy analysis as an approach. If this book has any merits as an introduction to public policy, then it is due in large measure to that early undergraduate experience of public policy as a fascinating field of inquiry for which I shall always be exceedingly grateful: thanks again, Mike. I was then doubly fortunate in later being apprenticed to Trevor Smith, when I was appointed as a lecturer in the Department of Economics (and later Politics) at Queen Mary and Westfield College, University of London. As a lecturer I was allowed great freedom to teach courses which examined the 'theory and practice' of politics and government. Out of this experimentation were to emerge several courses which endeavoured to explore ideas and government, including the theory and practice of modern government; contemporary political thought; the methodology of social science; organization theory; political psychology; and comparative public policy.

xiv PUBLIC POLICY

Over the last few years two colleagues have had a formative influence on my approach: Ken Young, and Andrew Massey who worked with me in setting up a master's programme in public policy. As a teacher, my debt to the authors of some of the earliest texts in the field was, and remains, immense: they include Jones, Anderson, Richardson and Jordon, William Jenkins, and later Hogwood and Gunn, and Ham and Hill. I am happy to record my thanks and appreciation to all these scholars for providing such admirable works for both teacher and student alike.

As this book is essentially the outcome of lectures and seminars, my greatest thanks must go to members of the MSc. in Public Policy team (Ken Young, Andrew Massey, Anne Kershen, Tolis Malakos, Helen Leigh-Phippard, Shamit Saggar, Stephen Thake and Keith Aldred) and all those undergraduate and postgraduate students at QMW, the University of Essex, the University of Maryland and elsewhere, whose interest, enthusiasm and feedback on the evolving text have been a constant source of motivation to finish a project which just kept on growing. Now at last they can buy the book to treasure with their handouts! Thanks also go to Tony Barker, who was so very kind and gave me plenty of advice (on advice) during my year at Essex. External examiners have also been helpful in the development of the teaching on which this book is based, and I should like to thank Geoffrey Alderman, Mike Goldsmith and Stephen Wilks for their evaluation of the various courses which have led to this volume.

I must record my deep gratitude to Trevor Smith and Andrew Massey for their unwavering friendship and encouragement at some of the more interesting times we have shared over the years; my publisher, Edward Elgar, who has been all that a good publisher should be, and more; and my editor, Julie Leppard, for all her help in completing this project.

Finally, my greatest debt is owed to my wonderful wife Mary and our sons John and Ben (not forgetting Bertie the dog!) for all their love, laughter and music.

Introduction

'Policy studies' have become an important aspect of the academic publishing industry, as is evidenced by the growing number of titles concerned with 'policy' and the fact that it forms a significant component in many a course and programme of study in numerous disciplines. So rapid has the expansion been that many of us involved in teaching and researching the subject now feel that it is becoming more and more unmanageable. Not the least of the reasons that public policy has proved so unwieldy is that it is the property of everyone and no one. The disciplines required to understand public policy cut right across the old academic lines of demarcation. Indeed, it is this interdisciplinary quality which makes the approach so interesting for both student and teacher alike. But the flipside of such a splendid single market of ideas and techniques wherein all the borders between disciplines and sub-disciplines are breached is that the subject is always verging on complete fragmentation. This becomes very evident when public policy is taught.

Public policy and policy analysis

Public policy focuses on what Dewey (1927) once expressed as 'the public and its problems'. It is concerned with how issues and problems come to be defined and constructed and how they are placed on the political and policy agenda. But it is also the study of 'how, why and to what effect governments pursue particular courses of action and inaction' (Heidenheimer et al., 1990: 3) or, as Dye puts it, with 'what governments do, why they do it, and what difference it makes' (Dye, 1976: 1). This study of 'the nature, causes, and effects of public policies' (Nagel, 1990: 440) requires that we avoid a 'narrow' focus and draw on a variety of approaches and disciplines. Policy analysis is an approach to public policy that aims to integrate and contextualize models and research from those disciplines which have a problem and policy orientation. Thus, as Wildavsky defines it: 'Policy analysis is an applied sub-field whose content cannot be determined by disciplinary boundaries but by whatever appears appropriate to the circumstances of the time and the nature of the problem' (Wildavsky, 1979: 15).

The policy orientation therefore may be summed up in Harold Lasswell's terms as being:

- multi-method;
- multi-disciplinary;
- problem-focused;
- concerned to map the contextuality of the policy process, policy options and policy outcomes;
- and whose goal is to integrate knowledge into an overarching discipline to analyse public choices and decision-making and thereby contribute to the democratization of society (see Lasswell, 1951a, 1968, 1970, 1971).

In the book we mix two kinds of approach which are often separated out in textbooks: the analysis of the policy process, and the use of analytical techniques and knowledge for and in policy-making. Thus in considering different frames of analysis in the four parts of the book we are employing two broad categorizations:

- *analysis of the policy process*: how problems are defined, agendas set, policy formulated, decisions made and policy evaluated and implemented;
- *analysis in and for the policy process*: this encompasses the use of analytical techniques, research and advocacy in problem definition, decision-making, evaluation and implementation.

The book aims to introduce students to the various frameworks and approaches which may be employed to analyse policy problems and policy processes. The frameworks which we discuss do not represent a complete or definitive set of approaches used in the 'policy sciences'. Dror (1989: 320–6), for example, lists some 23 disciplines to be included in the policy disciplines. Here we take a more modest selection. In addition to political science, public administration and political theory, we draw on several other key policy disciplines, including sociology, psychology, economics and management. This is by no means an exhaustive selection from policy-orientated fields of inquiry, but as this book is intended as an introduction, I feel justified in keeping to a fairly limited range of disciplines.

Using the book

The book does not follow a purely 'stagist' format. The common approach is to divide the policy process into phases and stages, beginning with policy formation and ending with evaluation and termination. In reality, of course, phases and stages tend to blur, overlap and intermingle. At the same time, the arrangement of such phases tends to exclude consideration of the fact that there is a multiplicity of ways of looking at policy-making and policy analysis. However, the book does not entirely dispense with the policy cycle concept, notwithstanding its drawbacks. As we explain in Part One, the reason for this adherence to the 'normal science' paradigm is that, as Lasswell's work (as a whole) amply demonstrates, the idea of 'stages' must be expanded to include a wider contextualization of different frameworks and methods or approaches. Thus there can be no one definition of policy analysis (Wildavksy, 1979: 15), and no one theory or model can capture or explain the complexity involved in what Easton once termed the 'web of decisions' (Easton, 1953: 130) which comprise public policy.

Although the book is divided into parts, there is no reason to read them sequentially. The parts are not designed to be read as a set of stages, so much as a guide to how different frameworks approach policy analysis and the policy process. Thus instead of ten or so chapters devoted to stages of the policy process, we group them into three broad and overlapping levels or dimensions of analysis. (If readers are unfamiliar with the idea of a policy cycle then they could well begin by looking at the ideas in 1:10.)

In using the book, therefore, the method should be iterative rather than linear. That is to say, the reader should follow up references to other parts of the book and other texts, going backwards and forwards, rather than starting at the first page of Part One and ending at the last page of Part Four. For, as critics of the policy cycle model all too readily point out, in the real world there are no defined or distinct phases.

I would strongly recommend that the book be used in conjunction with case study material relevant to the particular problem or policy concern of the reader or course. In general terms, texts such as Harrop (ed.) (1992) and Heidenheimer et al. (1990) are ideal. Texts and articles have been chosen to provide a point of entry into other studies chosen by the instructor or student which have a more specific context within a given course. Some texts serve as case studies of actual policies, others develop ideas in a more tangential manner.

As a reading strategy to supplement the book, I recommend that students familiarize themselves with the core work of some of the founding figures in the field such as Lasswell, Simon, Lindblom, Etzioni, Dror and Wildavsky. Begin at the beginning with Lasswell's 'The policy orientation' (1951b) and some of the more recent reviews of his contribution such as Torgerson (1985). Next, instead of reading about Simon, read his book *Administrative Behavior* (1976). Two key texts are Lindblom's book on the policy-making process (Lindblom and Woodhouse, 1993) and his *Inquiry and Change* (1990). Still the best introduction to Etzioni is *The Active Society* (1968), although his more recent works help to place his ideas in a wider context. Dror's *Public Policy Making Re-examined* (1989) remains an excellent starting point to explore Dror's work. Finally, Wildavsky's book on the 'art and craft' of *Speaking the Truth to Power* (1979) is essential reading.

There is no substitute for the study of the texts which have shaped the field, and the student should not rely on this or any other textbook to provide them with anything more than an introduction to these and other major works. Having read the 'masters', students should be in a better position to understand textbooks such as Hogwood and Gunn (1984); Rossi and Freeman (1993); Weiss (ed.) (1992); and Heineman *et al.* (1990). To 'round off', students should study recent contributions, such as Bobrow and Dryzek (1987); Fischer and Forester (eds) (1993); Kooiman (ed.) (1993); and Sabatier and Jenkins-Smith (eds) (1993). The impact of management on public policy also requires that students become familiar with the main ideas and developments in this field. Three excellent sources of material are the OECD annual surveys; Massey (1993); and Hughes (1994).

PART ONE

Meta Analysis

Analysing analysis

1.1   Introduction

> Any serious human activity begets 'meta-activity', individual brooding or talk among a group. This is as true about hunting or gambling or house-building as it is about politics; and such talk always 'feedsback' in some sense into the original activity itself.
> *(W.J.M. Mackenzie, cited in Gregor, 1971: 1)*

When we engage in meta analysis we are considering the methods and approaches used in the study of public policy and the discourse and language which it employs. This 'meta' analysis 'feedsback', as Mackenzie notes (above), into the practice of policy analysis. Meta analysis is analysis concerned with the activity of analysis. In another sense, meta analysis is concerned with understanding the idea that the analysis of public policy proceeds by employing *meta*phors: we analyse by describing something in terms of something else. Public policy, as other forms of political analysis, uses metaphors or models as devices to explore the 'unknown' (Landau, 1961: 353) and possibly unknowable world of politics. The choice is, as Landau observes, not between models and no models, but an open and 'hygienic' use so as to form a critical awareness of their assumptions, origins, and signifi-cance.

With this aim in mind, in this part of the book we discuss the idea of 'public' policy and look at what may be understood by the notion of a public sphere, and how the changing conceptualization of public and private has shaped the study of 'public' policy. We then examine the idea of 'policy' and how this concept has changed over time and discuss its modern usage (1.2). In the following section the book ac-counts for the development of public policy and policy analysis as a subject or field of inquiry (1.3), and then examines the kinds of policy analysts, where they are, and what they do (1.4). As there are different kinds of analyst, so there are different kinds and types of analytical 'framework'. Section 1.5 reviews the major frameworks or approaches which are used by policy analysts. Section 1.6 looks at the key 'philo-

1

sophical' frameworks which have had an influence on the normative, ethical, and methodological approaches to the theory and practice of public policy. A major concern in the study of policy is the actual 'process' of policy-making. In section 1.7 we consider some of the main approaches to the study of policy-making and policy analysis. At this point we need to address wider methodological issues. Having used terms such as 'frameworks', 'metaphors' and 'models', we must consider what these concepts mean and how change and 'shifts' occur between different frameworks or 'paradigms' (1.8). The penultimate section (1.9) applies the idea of shifts in paradigm shift to account for the changing focus of policy analysis in the period from the 1950s to the present. The final section (1.10) considers how the policy process has generally been 'mapped' into stages and cycles, and outlines the approach taken in the remainder of the book.

1.2   'Public' and 'policy' as concepts

The starting point for a discussion of public policy must be to consider what we mean by the idea of 'public', and to account for the development of the concept in theory and practice. This is particularly important in view of the fact that the idea of the 'public' has undergone considerable change in recent years in the Anglo-Saxon world as elsewhere.

❖ Key texts

Three useful texts for the analysis of the idea of 'public' are:

S.I. Benn and G.F. Gaus (eds), *Public and Private in Social Life*, 1983: on the ideas of public and private.

J. Habermas, *The Structural Transformation of the Public Sphere*, 1989: on the development of the public sphere.

J.A.W. Gunn, 'Public Opinion', 'Public Interest', 1989: on 'public opinion' and 'public interest'. ◆

Let us begin with some terms in common use:

- public interest
- public opinion
- public goods
- public law
- public sector
- public health

- public transport
- public education
- public service broadcasting
- public accountability
- public toilets
- public order
- public debt

We could argue that 'public policy' has to do with those spheres which are so designated as 'public', as opposed to a similar list we could make of expressions which involve the idea of 'private'. The idea of public policy presupposes that there is a sphere or domain of life which is not private or purely individual, but held in common. The public comprises that dimension of human activity which is regarded as requiring governmental or social regulation or intervention, or at least common action. Does this sphere of the public require a different form of analysis to that of the private, or of the business world? What is the relationship of the public to the private? What should be public and what should be private? To any student of modern politics these questions are all too familiar. However, the relationship of the 'public' and the 'private' is an enduring theme which we may trace back to the beginnings of civilization. In this section we shall briefly outline some of the main features of the development of the concepts in Western society and endeavour to show how a knowledge of the history of the ideas provides an essential background for the student of public policy in the late twentieth century. As we shall see, there has always been a tension or conflict between what is held to be 'public' and what 'private', and it is vital that in studying 'public' policy we set our present arguments in this wider historical context.

A suitable starting point is that of ancient Greece and Rome. It is from the Romans that we derive our concept of public and private: they defined the two realms in terms of *res publica* and *res priva*. The Greek idea of public and private may be expressed in the terms *Koinion* (roughly, public) and *Idion* (equally roughly, private). Hannah Arendt's analysis of the Greek dichotomy of public and private may be summarized in the following set of opposites (cited in Saxonhouse, 1983: 380):

- public   private
- polis   household
- freedom   necessity
- male   female
- equality   inequality

- immortality   mortality
- open   closed

However, as Saxonhouse notes, this is a somewhat over-simplified characterization of the boundaries or lines of demarcation between the two realms. In theory and practice the relationship was more complex and reflected the 'tragic' interdependence of the two spheres. Indeed, Saxonhouse argues that there was no unified conception of the relationship between the two, and a study of the literature of ancient Greece suggests that at least seven quite distinct conceptualizations of the tension between the conflicting demands of the public and the private may be discerned. It is in the work of Aristotle that we find the earliest attempt to find some kind of resolution to the conflict between the public and private in the idea of the 'polis' as the highest form of human association. This search for some arrangement whereby the tension between the public and the private may be resolved or mediated was to echo down the history of political thought to the present day. In the nineteenth century this resolution between the public and private spheres found its most powerful formulation in the ideas of the political economists. It is this formulation of the 'problem' of the relationship of the public and private spheres which continues to predominate in contemporary arguments about the role of 'public' policy.

For the political economists the trick of resolving the tension as between public and private in terms of 'interests' was in the deployment of their idea of markets. As Habermas argues in the early nineteenth century, the 'public sphere' developed in Britain out of a very clear demarcation between public power and the realm of the 'private' (Habermas, 1989). Through market forces the maximization of individual interest could best promote the 'public interest'. The free functioning of individual choice and freedom could, it was argued, advance both the interests of individuals, and the public good and welfare. The role of the state and politics was thus to create the conditions in which the public interest could be so secured. Government was consequently best when it did the least. For the political economists this did not mean that the state should not be involved in the provision of 'public' facilities, but that the crucial line of demarcation was economic freedom. The public interest in this sense was most likely to be served when the interests of economic freedom and the market were facilitated by the state, rather than being constrained or regulated. Order was essentially a spontaneous outcome of private choices. Public intervention was primarily desired so as to secure a framework of law, rights and order, rather than to interfere with the natural equilibrium which was the outcome of self-interest. Private interests were convergent with the public interest.

The quintessential statements of this view may, of course, be found in the writings of Adam Smith's *Wealth of Nations* (1776) and James Mill, Torrens, McCulloch and their popularizers (Parsons, 1989). This notion of the public as essentially a space which did not involve the interference in economic and business activities, and in which there was a well-defined boundary between the public and private spheres was, as Habermas shows, in contrast with the continental European tradition of the public as encompassing business and trade and 'private' life to a far greater extent than that which developed in Britain and America. In France and Germany, for example, the relationship between the state and business and trade was to be markedly different to that of the US and Britain.

However, the liberal idea(l) of a clear distinction between the public and private began to collapse from the late nineteenth century onwards. The penetration of the public policy into what the political economists would have regarded as private took place in almost all areas of 'social life'. Education, health, welfare, housing, urban planning were all to become subjected to regulation and/or state interference (see Heidenheimer *et al.*, 1990: *passim*). This process of collectivization in the public domain took place at different times in various industrial nations, but always for the reason that certain kinds of problems were no longer seen as purely 'private'. J.S. Mill had, in the mid-nineteenth century, provided the essential criterion for this shift of boundary: harm. The private was that sphere which did no harm to others (Mill, 1968). The problem was, of course, that the notion of what counted as 'harm' changed and expanded as more and more information about social and other problems legitimated concerns about the public consequence of private actions and supported arguments for reform. The utilitarianism of Mill and Bentham also provided another important test for determining public policy: the greatest happiness of the greatest number (see below: 1.6). By the early twentieth century, the liberal conception of the 'public' and the 'private' was undergoing a profound change. The 'new liberalism' as expressed by Dewey in America, and Hobhouse and Keynes in Britain took issue with the idea that the market could any longer bring about a convergence in 'public' and 'private' interests, or left to itself could promote a spontaneous order. For both Dewey and Keynes it was knowledge – organized intelligence, as Dewey termed it – which could now provide the means by which private and public spheres and interests could be balanced and advanced: *laissez faire* had had its day. A more knowledgeable form of governance was, from the standpoint of this new liberalism, the key to resolving the conflict between the claims of the private and the public. This was, of course, no new idea: Plato had long ago also come to the conclusion that philosophers would make the best of kings.

It was in the context of this 'new liberalism' as articulated by Dewey and Keynes (and others), and expressed in the practice of Roosevelt's New Deal and war-time administration and reform, that the 'public policy' approach was to develop. As Lasswell notes, the policy sciences as developed after the Second World War were but an 'adaptation of the general approach to public policy that was recommended by Dewey and his colleagues' (Lasswell, 1971: xiii–xiv). In the post-war era liberal ideas about the purpose of public policy-making were predicated on the belief that the role of the state was to manage the 'public' and its problems so as to deal with those aspects of social and economic life which markets were no longer capable of solving. The key to this brave new world was the development of a policy process and decision-making which was more informed by knowledge than it had been in the past.

The 'old' liberalism was by no means dead, but it showed little signs of life until the 1970s. The claim that knowledgeable governance could better 'solve' or mediate the relationship between public and private interests began to sour in the era of stagflation. 'Keynesian'-inspired economic management and liberal welfare reforms seemed to be creating more problems than they solved. At this point Adam Smith's invisible hand clenched its fist and struck back. The champions of the 'new [sic] right' were Hayek and Friedman. They argued, to great effect, that this attempt to use public policy to promote the 'public interest' was flawed. For, as the political economists of the nineteenth century had showed, the public interest could only be advanced through allowing private interests a free hand. The answer they and others in the 'new right' camp argued, was to contract the 'public sector' and expand the use of the market mechanism to better ensure that, where there was a public sector, it functioned in a way that corresponded to market, or 'private sector', principles of 'management'.

One of the consequences of the growth of the state as a means of reconciling public and private interests was the development of 'bureaucracy' as a more rational form of organization (see Weber, 1991: 196–252). 'Public administration' evolved as a means by which the 'public interest' could be secured through a neutral class of civil servants whose task it was to carry out the will of those elected by the people. Public bureaucracy was, therefore, different to that which existed in the private sector (business, commerce and industry) because it was motivated to secure the 'national interest', rather than private interests. Thus, whereas for the political economists (and the new right) only markets could balance private and public interests, the 'new liberalism' was based upon a belief that public administration was a more rational means of promoting the public interest.

It was in the 1880s, when Woodrow Wilson formulated the essential theory for this conceptualization of bureaucracy as a defender of the 'public interest', that he posited that there was an important distinction to be made between politics and administration (Wilson, 1887). Public administration as a framework for the analysis of bureaucracy in liberal democratic political systems thrived in this period when the civil servant was viewed as a functionary involved in the rational pursuit of public interests as defined by the political process. The idea of a rational, hierarchically arranged non-political form of administration was central to the idea of liberal democracy (see, for example, Mill, 1968) The division of the state into a political realm and a 'rational' or bureaucratic realm paralleled the demarcation between the public and private spheres. As the division of public and private began to to appear more and more imperceptible, the state laid claim to a legitimacy based upon its capacity to ameliorate a growing range of problems defined as 'public'. It was in this period – roughly 1950s–1970s – that public policy really began to take off, and public administration began to move into a state of decline which was to accelerate in the 1980s.

Central to this change in orientation was the notion of rationality. Weber had shown that the growth of bureaucracy was due to the process of 'rationalization' in industrial society. The bureaucrat was the rational functionary who served the public interest. The rational public interest argument began to erode from the late 1940s onwards. It took three main directions:

- Studies which posited that bureaucratic rationality (as set out by Weber) was a theory which needed re-examination. In both theory and practice it was demonstrated that bureaucracies exhibited a large measure of 'irrationality', or at least 'bounded' rationality (see Simon, 1945; Lindblom, 1959).
- Studies which argued that in reality bureaucrats did not function in the 'public interest', but displayed the capacity to have distinct goals of their own (see Mueller, 1989).
- Research which questioned the distinction between policy and administration (see Appleby, 1949).

By the late 1970s the lines of demarcation between public and private and policy and administration were looking increasingly less well-defined. Thus as a leading comparative study of bureaucracy was to observe: 'The last quarter of this century is witnessing the virtual disappearance of the Weberian distinction between the roles of the politician and the bureaucrat, producing what may be labelled a "pure hybrid"' (Aberbach et al., 1981: 16). The 'new' liberal 'solution' to managing the relationship between the public and private interests through the state was looking less defensible in the light of the 'failures' of 'public policy' in so many areas. Two ideas of 'public' were questioned: the 'public' interest motivation of bureaucrats and professionals in the public service; and the relationship between the public (*qua* state) and private (*qua* market) spheres.

It was undoubtedly the 'new right' (or 'old' liberals) who shaped much of the agenda for this debate. Returning to the position as set out by Adam Smith and the political economists of the nineteenth century, Hayek, Friedman and others asserted that the relationship between the public and the private was something which was best defined through the market and freedom of choice rather than by the state operating in the 'public interest'. During the 1980s and 1990s this argument that the demarcation between the public and private spheres should be left to the market has formed the dominant framework within which the theory and practice of public policy has taken place. This shift from the 'new' liberalism to the 'new right' in public policy may be discerned most clearly in the rise of the 'public-sector management' approach and the demise of 'public administration'.

❖ The new liberalism and the public and private realms

Several key texts provide the background to the new approach to the role of the state in seeing to public problems and interests:

J.M. Keynes, 'The End of *Laissez-faire*', in *Essays in Persuasion*, 1926; and *The General Theory of Employment*, 1936.
J. Dewey, *The Public and its Problems*, 1927.
W.H. Beveridge, *Full Employment in a Free Society*, 1944.

Keynes's essay on the end of *laissez-faire* is, perhaps, the most concise expression of the view that the state – armed with new knowledge and 'wisdom' – should seek to have a more interventionist role in social and economic problems. In the essay he surveys the development of liberalism from the seventeenth century onwards and argues that it was the economists who provided the 'scientific pretext by which the practical man could solve the contradiction between egoism and socialism which emerged out of the philosophy of the eighteenth century' (Keynes, 1926: 277). In the twentieth century Keynes thought that economists would have the leading role again, but that this time their theories would point towards a new kind of balance of interests. Progress, he believed, now lay in the path towards recognizing semi-autonomous bodies within the state 'whose criterion of action within their own field is solely the public good as they understand it, and from whose deliberations motives of private advantage are excluded' (Keynes, 1926: 288). The chief task, he argued, was to distinguish between those services which are 'technically social' from those that are 'technically individual'. Government should not do those things which individuals can do already, but address those aspects of society and economy which cannot be 'technically' done by individuals.

The seed of modern policy analysis is to be found in the notion that society should aim to improve the 'techniques' of governing a capitalist system, so as to make it 'more efficient' through 'wise management'. Whereas Dewey (1927) was to argue that experiments could provide the way to discover such new techniques, Keynes believed that it should come through 'thought', or the 'elucidation of our feelings', a 'candid examination of our own inner feelings in relation to the outside facts' (Keynes, 1926: 294).

On this point Keynes's idea of 'policy analysis' is closer to Lasswell and Vickers than to the tradition of experimentalism and scientism, which may be traced back to Dewey. ◆

❖ What are the differences between the public and private sectors?

Are the lines of demarcation between the two spheres as well marked as once they were?

W.F. Baber (quoted in Massey, 1993: 15) argues that the public sector has ten key differences from the private sector:

- it faces more complex and ambiguous tasks;
- it has more problems in implementing its decisions;
- it employs more people with a wider range of motivations;
- it is more concerned with securing opportunities or capacities;
- it is more concerned with compensating for market failure;
- it engages in activities with greater symbolic significance;
- it is held to stricter standards of commitment and legality;
- it has a greater opportunity to respond to issues of fairness;
- it must operate or appear to operate in the public interest;
- it must maintain minimal levels of public support above that required in private industry.

This focus on the 'profit' characteristics of the public sector and the 'non-profit' sector such as schools, universities, voluntary organizations, hospitals, etc., suggests to Anthony and Herzlinger that the line of demarcation is that: 'In nonprofit organizations, decisions made by management are intended to result in providing the best possible services with the available resources; and success is measured primarily by how much service the organizations provide and by how well the services are rendered' (Anthony and Herzlinger, 1980: 31). The 'non-profit' sectors thus are measured more by social welfare criteria than by financial profits. The authors argue that the non-profit sector may be characterized by:

- the absence of a profit measure;
- the tendency to be service organizations;
- the greater constraint in the goals and strategies they can develop;
- their greater dependence on clients for financial resources;
- their greater domination by professionals;
- their accountability, which is different to a private/profit organization;

- top management not having the same responsibilities or the same financial rewards;
- the accountability of public-sector organizations to electorates and the political process;
- their lack of a tradition of management control.

However, as we shall see in section 1.5 below and in Part Four, the distinctions between public and private and profit and non-profit organizations is something which has undergone considerable change, due to reforms made within the public/non-profit sectors to make them more like the private/profit sectors.

Against this view of a gradual convergence between sectors is the reminder offered by the Cabinet Office (1988, para. 1.5):

> Comparison with the private sector has to be treated with caution. In the private sector there is a direct relationship between commercial success ... and the standard of customer service. The public sector position is more complicated and in many instances distinctly different. In general, the reasons for providing a service in the first place, the nature of that service and the manner in which it is delivered, are not dictated by markets. In these circumstances the balance between public expectations and the level of service to be provided is decided on the basis of political judgements about economic and social priorities. All that said, those who execute public service functions have a professional responsibility to do so to the highest standards of service possible, within the given level of resources, and this is what civil servants want to achieve. ◆

❖ But what is the public sector, exactly?

One of the main frameworks for considering this question is provided by economists, who argue that we can analyse the public and the private in terms of 'goods'.

A public good is a 'good' or service which is available to all. Pure public goods are those which are produced by the state, rather than by the market. Pure private goods are those which are consumed by choice and only those who pay for them may consume them. Samuelson (1954) suggests that the main characteristic of public goods is that they are indivisible, namely that they are available for all, and that they are non-excludable, unlike private goods which are, by definition exclusive. Public goods are paid for by taxes and borrowing, and their price may be expressed in the level of taxation required to finance their production. Private goods are paid for through a price system operated in a market.

In broad terms it is possible to say that public choices do indeed involve decisions about 'public' or 'private goods'. In some countries, for example, health policy takes place in a largely public domain, where care is available to all citizens; and in others it is dominated by private care and personal health insurance. In some countries public transport is heavily subsidized; in others it is the case that public transport is practically non-existent, or the user has to pay a high price for his ticket. So up to a point the public/private good dichotomy has some utility in tackling the question of what is the public sector. However, what counts as a public good has long been (since the 1960s) a matter of considerable dispute amongst economists. Buchanan (1968), for example, questioned the purity of public goods as set out by Samuelson in 1954, and suggested that there were many goods that could not be so neatly pigeon-holed. Some public goods could have 'excludable' benefits. Buchanan suggested that 'clubs' may exist which exclude members of the public through a mechanism such as a toll or charge. Club theory emerged as an important aspect of the public–private debate, which pointed towards the fact that, in both theory and practice, the 'pure' public good was subject to (growing) impurity. From the point of view of the purity of public goods, public policy is really about defining what counts as public, who provides, who pays, how they pay, and who they pay. It does not follow that, because we admit that a service is 'public', it should be provided by the state, or that it should be open to all. In socialist China, for example, comrades pay for a variety of health and educational services. A public good may be privately provided, and consumed after a charge – or user fee – has been paid. A tank, for example may be ordered by the army, but manufactured by a private company. Furthermore a 'public' good may conform to the kind of criteria set out by Samuelson, but it may be available to people depending on criteria laid out in a policy: benefits which can only be distributed to defined groups or types of people. So-called 'merit' goods will exclude parts of the public on the grounds that they do not meet a set qualification or condition (Musgrave, 1959). In other words, the public and private sectors, when considered from the point of view of a theory of goods, reveal themselves as overlapping and interacting, rather than as well-defined categories. The public sector is a mix of public and private and of public goods which are rationed through a toll or by a criterion of merit.

What determines this mix of public and private goods? Frey (1978) argues that there is a cycle in the demand for public goods which means that the public/private sector will over time change in response to the interaction of voters, government, civil service and producers (see Figure 1.1).

Figure 1.1   The cycle in the demand for public and private goods

Rise in disequilibrium

Dissatisfaction with existing supply
of public/private goods

Articulation of demand
Demands for a new
distribution

Reaction to demand
Government reacts to demands

Supply of goods
A new mix of goods

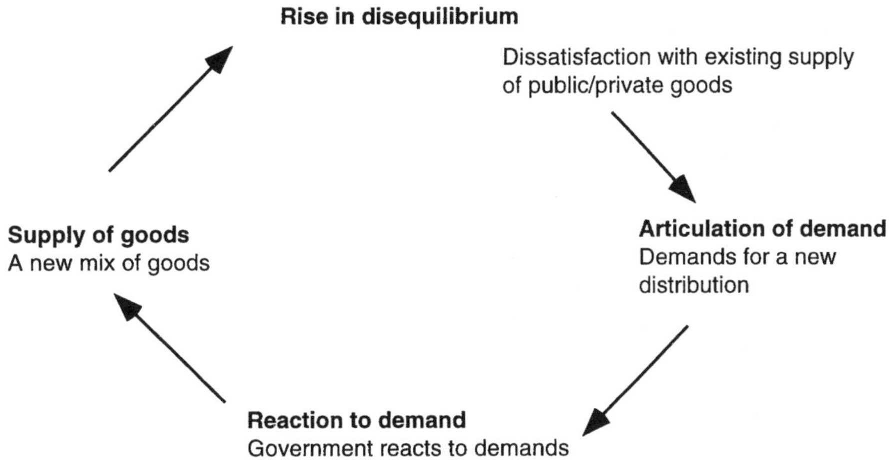

Source: Adapted from Frey (1978: 116–21)

At some periods there were will be dissatisfaction with the way in which a public good is supplied or with its price. Government responds by changing the way in which a public good is supplied or the size or scale of its provision. This new mix provides the source of later dissatisfaction. Is this what happened in the 1980s: a demand (from voters/capitalists for more 'private' goods as against 'public' goods, a new supply (more 'club' goods, a reduction in 'pure' public goods)? Will the 1990s be about redefining the public/private mix? ◆

❖ Whose public? Have men defined the 'public' sphere?

Since the 1970s and 1980s feminist critiques of public policy have argued that policy-making has largely been framed by what men regard as the public domain.

Carole Pateman, 'Feminist Critiques of the Public/Private Dichotomy', 1983

> The dichotomy between the private and public is central to almost two centuries of feminist writing and political struggle; it is, ultimately, what the feminist movement is all about ... Liberal feminism has radical implications, not least in challenging the separation and opposition between the private and public spheres that is fundamental to liberal theory and practice. The liberal contrast between private and public is more than a distinction between two kinds of social activities. The public sphere, and the principles that govern it, are seen as separate from, or independent of, the relationships of the private sphere ... Feminists argue that liberalism is structured by patriarchal as well as class relations, and that the dichotomy between the private and public obscures the subject of women to men within an apparently universal, egalitarian and individualist order.
> (pp. 281–3)

Kristie Beuret, 'Women and Transport', in Mavis Maclean and Dulcie Groves (eds), *Women's Issues in Social Policy*, 1991

Using data on travel methods, the age and sex of travellers, car ownership and use, the author argues that the lack of good public transport is a considerable disadvantage to the employment opportunities of women, and a factor which greatly limits their family and leisure activities. She concludes that women need to shape public transport agendas and policies if they are to improve economic and social opportunities. Beuret advocates a range of policies to this end, including: policies which improve the safety of public transport; better access to cars; travel schemes which make public transport cheaper and better geared to the needs of women; and more radical strategies to reduce the necessity of women to travel.

The authors in Maclean and Groves's book point out that the boundaries of the public sphere have been constructed in such a way that the private problems which women as a whole face in transport and in other areas of social and economic life have been excluded from consideration as a 'public' issue', with the consequence that those areas which affect women more than men are poorly resourced and have low visibility and a low profile in the public sphere.

Jan Pahl (ed.), *Private Violence and Public Policy*, 1985

This book examines the way in which 'public' policy in western societies has excluded the family from the public sphere. The result has been that violence against women in domestic circumstances has been a neglected area of policy-making. The issue illustrates the problem of defining public and private domains, and the relationship between public policy and individual privacy. Pahl concludes that the way in which the private is defined (by men) tells us a great deal about power and powerlessness in society as whole.

E. Meehan and S. Svenhuijsen (eds), *Equality Politics and Gender*, 1991

This is an excellent selection of papers dealing with the politics and policy of gender equality in a number of European countries. Several contributors discuss the impact that the public/private sphere dichotomy has had on the issue. ◆

The idea of 'policy'

Words change their meaning. Like the notion of 'public', the idea of policy is, as Heclo (1972) argues, not a precise or self-evident term:

> To suggest in academic circles that there is general agreement on anything is to don a crimson in the bullpen, but policy is one term on which there seems to be a certain amount of definitional agreement. As commonly used, the term policy is usually considered to apply to something 'bigger' than particular decisions, but 'smaller' than general social movements. Thus, policy, in terms of level of analysis, is a concept placed roughly in the middle range. A second and essential element in most writers' use of the term is purposiveness of some kind.
> (*Heclo, 1972: 84*)

Despite this agreement, however, he notes that there are differences about whether policy is more that an 'intended' course of action. A policy may also be something which is not intended, but is none the less carried out in the practice of implementation or administration. In some languages, such as English, such distinction between 'policy' and 'administration' is well defined, in others it is not. The *Oxford English Dictionary* offers definitions of policy, covering: 'Political sagacity; statecraft; prudent conduct; craftiness; course of action adopted by government, party, etc.'. One dictionary of synonyms and antonyms offers the following: 'Policy, statesmanship, administration, wisdom, plan, role, action, tactics, strategy, sagacity'. And its antonym? Aimlessness. Dror notes that the notion of 'policy-making' as a 'conscious awareness of choice between two main alternatives for steering societies' (Dror, 1989: xiii) may be found in Greek and Renaissance political theory, but it is not so evident in Roman civilization. Policy in the sense of choosing between options is, he suggests, an idea which may also be discerned in mercantilist writings on trade. Heidenheimer (1986), in a study of the policy concept in Europe, records that from the late eighteenth century onwards, professorial chairs in 'Polizey' science were established in an effort to systematize knowledge about administration and social welfare. The word's Anglo-Saxon notion of 'policy' does not travel well. In many European languages there are problems over distinctions to be made between 'policy' and 'politics'. As Ostrom and Sabetti observe: 'Policy as used in English is not easily rendered into French, German, Italian and Spanish.' Lerner and Lasswell's *The Policy Sciences in the United States* (1951) had to be translated into French as *Les Sciences de la politique aux Etats-Unis* (Ostrom and Sabetti, 1975: 41).

The modern meaning of the English notion 'policy' is that of a course of action or plan, a set of political purposes – as opposed to 'administration' (Wilson, 1887). Above all, the modern meaning of the word, dating from the post-Second World War period in particular, is that of policy as a rationale, a manifestation of considered judgement. Imagine, for example, politicians admitting that they do not have a policy on *x*? A policy is an attempt to define and structure a rational basis for action or inaction.

As the state changes its mode of legitimating discourse, so the function of 'policy' has altered. The modern liberal democratic state, post-Second World War, was to be a system which sought to define its legitimacy in terms of policy. Hogwood and Gunn (1984: 13–19) specify ten uses of the term 'policy' in this modern sense:

- as a label for a field of activity;
- as an expression of general purpose or desired state of affairs;
- as specific proposals;
- as decisions of government;
- as formal authorization;
- as a programme;
- as output;
- as outcome;
- as a theory or model;
- as a process.

The meaning of the word policy must also be understood in a more historical context. For, like the concept of public, the changing meaning of policy tells us much about the change in policy in practice. In English, 'policy' has a rich and complex meaning. In Shakespeare, for example, we may find four distinct uses: prudence, a form of government, affairs and administration, and as 'Machiavellianism' (see below: 1.6). Policy encompassed the arts of political illusion and duplicity. Show, outward appearance and illusions were the stuff of which power was made. Shakespeare employed the terms of Machiavellian philosophy that were well known at the time. Power cannot be sustained purely with force. It needs, in a Machiavellian sense, *policy*: and 'policy sits above conscience', as the bard tells us in *Timon of Athens*.

❖ Policy as craftiness

It is perhaps in the work of Shakespeare's great contemporary, Marlowe, that we may see one of the most interesting illustrations of the use of a Machiavellian notion of policy. In Marlowe's play *The Jew of Malta* the notion of policy has a central role; the word itself appears many times in the text. A knight, for example, refers to it as 'simple policy', to which Barabas adds later, 'Ay, policy, that's their profession, And not simplicity as they suggest.' Policy has a duality of meaning: simple and scheming. Policy involves creating a plausible story which secures the purposes of the plotter: policy is acting a part. And, as Ithamore says, 'The meaning has a meaning.' By his policy Barabas gets 'no simple place' as the Governor of Malta. He plays off Turk against Christian and thus makes a 'profit' from his policy.

Fiction is often stranger than fact

In *Yes Prime Minster*, by Jonathan Lynn and Antony Jay (1987), we find an interesting illustration of the way in which a policy may be little more than elaborate window-dressing. Sir Humphrey, discussing a plan for reducing unemployment, observes that in reality the PM is 'only trying to look as if he is trying to reduce unemployment. This is because he is worried that it does not look as if he is trying to look as if he is trying to reduce unemployment' (p. 26). ◆

As we shall see (1.6) Francis Bacon, a contemporary of Shakespeare and Marlowe, also defined policy in terms of rational cunning. However, over time this notion of policy as politics and of politics as policy is replaced by the idea of policy as political whilst carrying it out, or implementation as 'administration' or 'bureaucracy'. With the development of industrial society in national states and its consequent administrative forms, bureaucracy, as Max Weber demonstrated, became the expression of the rational component of the state, whose function it was to carry out the will of its political – elected – masters.

Bureaucracy derived its legitimacy from its claims to being non-political, whilst politicians claimed that their authority rested on the approval of their policies or 'platforms' by electorates. Policy therefore as a term becomes an expression of political rationality. To have a policy is to have rational reasons or arguments which contain both a claim to an understanding of a problem and a solution. It puts forward what is and what ought to be done. A policy offers a kind of theory upon which a claim for legitimacy is made. With the development of modern electoral and party systems in industrial societies policy discourse became the main mode through which electorates engaged with 'politics' and rival political elites. The politician is expected to have 'policies' as a shop is expected to have goods to sell. In the Schumpeterian 'realistic' sense of democracy, the 'policy' or 'plank' was the essential currency of democratic exchange:

> the democratic method is that institutional arrangement for arriving at political decisions in which individuals acquire power to decide by means of a competitive struggle for the people's vote ... all parties will of course, at any given time, provide themselves with a stock of principles or planks and these principles or planks may be the characteristic of the party that adopts them and as important for its success as the brands of goods a department store sells are characteristic of it and important for its success ... Party and machine politicians are simply the response to the fact that the electoral mass is incapable of action other than a stampede ... The psycho-technics of party management and party advertising, slogans and marching tunes, are not accessories. They are the essence of politics.
> (*Schumpeter, 1974: 269–83*)

(On the role of party management and advertising, see Franklin, 1994, and section 2.3.2 in this volume.)

The idea of policy as a 'product' or 'plank' consequently developed a neutral connotation, far removed from the Machiavellian sense displayed in Shakespeare or Marlowe. Policy and politics now (in English at least) become quite distinct terms. The language and rhetoric of 'policy' thus became the main instrument of political rationality. As Lasswell observed:

> The word 'policy' is commonly used to designate the most important choices made either in organized or in private life ... 'policy' is free of many of the undesirable connotations clustered about the word *political*, which is often believed to imply 'partisanship' or 'corruption'.
> (*Lasswell, 1951b: 5*)

In liberal democratic systems, political elites have to give rational reasons for what they propose or what they have done. Peter the Great had only to say that he did not like beards for beards to be shaved off. In regimes which operate under a code of religious beliefs, it may well be enough that an edict or decision is justified in accordance with a religious precept for it to be considered legitimate. In societies that are not so informed by religious values, politicians as policy-makers have to claim that they are doing something after rational consideration of the facts: in other words, we expect governments to have 'a policy'.

1.3   The development of the policy approach

The development of policy analysis must be placed in the context of this rationalization of the state and politics as a 'policy-making' activity. The emergence of the methods of natural science provided the essential framework within which the study of society and 'public administration' was to grow in the nineteenth and twentieth centuries. As Trudi Miller notes:

> Natural science represents the approach to public administration and political science that has prevailed for most of the twentieth century ... The implicit assumptions of this nature-focused approach are that (1) the laws that govern human behaviour exist independent of human control, and (2) the units of analysis in social systems are highly similar over time and space. The conventional quantitative methods of social science reflect these implicit empirical assumptions.
> (*Miller, 1984: 253*)

As we shall see later (4.5) this was to prove especially true in the case of analysis deployed to measure/evaluate the 'performance' of organizations, people and policies in an 'assumptive world' (Young, 1977, 1979: see 3.7.7) of 'reliable relationships and measurable phenomena' (Kirlin, 1984: 161).

The Enlightenment notion that the world was full of puzzles and problems which, through the application of human reason and knowledge, could be 'solved' forms the background to the growth of the policy approach. What Newton had done to the laws of planetary motion became a model for what it was possible to do with knowledge of human society. Thus we may chart the development of the policy sciences in terms of the desire for knowledgeable governance, that is, the acquisition of facts and 'knowledge' about 'problems' so as to formulate 'better solutions'. As Max Weber showed, the growth of industrial civilization brought about a search for more rational forms of organization for the state, commerce and industry (Weber, 1991: 196–252). Out of this was to emerge the kind of separation of policy-making as a political function from administration as a bureaucratic function. At the same time, the desire for a more rational approach to social and other 'problems' was manifested in the growth in the capacity of the state to acquire and store information, and in the development of empirical research such as social surveys (see 2.2.1).

Later, in the early twentieth century, this idea that government could, by making policies 'solve' problems, not least those of 'the economy', meant that the social sciences began to establish a new relationship to politics and government. In the 1930s social scientists, the most famous of whom was the economist John Maynard Keynes, could claim that, if government was to have any chance of dealing with the problems of the day, it had to recognize the need for a more informed, theoretically driven approach to governing. In the future, he predicted, it would be the ideas of economists rather than political interests which would shape decision-making (Keynes, 1936).

Other 'policy'-focused forms of inquiry were to develop in the period between the wars and up to the 1950s and early 1960s. For the greater part of the period fields such as sociology, psychology, political science, social administration, management, and natural sciences with policy implications remained related, but in no sense formed a common approach. It was in America where moves towards a more unified approach to the study of public problems and policy really began in the work of Harold Lasswell (see, for example, Lasswell, 1930a, 1948b), which culminated in the publication of Lerner and Lasswell's volume on the 'policy sciences' (1951).

❖ Lasswell and the idea of policy sciences and the role of the policy analyst

Sciences are policy sciences when they clarify the process of policy-making in society, or supply data needed for the making of rational judgments on policy questions ... If we get rid of the standoffishness that has kept men of knowledge apart in our civilization, we can more conveniently come together in research teams that are capable of contributing the knowledge needed by the democratic polity ... Today we are living in a world of ever-deepening shadow, in which basic democratic values are challenged as never before and in which even the survival of the human species is at stake. Under these circumstances it makes sense to develop a strategy of using our limited intellectual resources for the defense and extension of our values. The term 'policy' is used to indicate the need for clarifying the social ends to be served by a given allocation (including self-allocation) of scientific energy.
(*Lasswell, 1948b: 122*)

The policy sciences includes (1) the methods by which the policy process is investigated, (2) the results of the study of policy, and (3) the findings of the disciplines making the most important contribution to the intelligence needs of our time.
(*Lasswell 1951b: 4*)

We can think of the policy sciences as the disciplines concerned with explaining the policy-making and policy-executing process, and with locating data and providing interpretations which are relevant to the policy problems of a given period. The policy approach does not imply that energy is to be dissipated on a miscellany of merely topical issues, but rather that the fundamental and often neglected problems which arise in the adjustment of man in society are to be dealt with. The policy approach does not mean that the scientist abandons objectivity in gathering or interpreting data, or ceases to perfect his tools of inquiry. The policy emphasis calls for the choice of problems which will contribute to the goal values of the scientist, and the use of scrupulous objectivity and maximum technical ingenuity in executing the projects undertaken. The policy frame of reference makes it necessary to take into account the entire context of significant events (past, present, and prospective) in which the scientist is living ... It is probable that the policy science orientation ... will be directed toward improving the knowledge needed to improve the practice of democracy. In a word, the special emphasis is upon the policy sciences of democracy, in which the ultimate goal is the realization of human dignity in theory and practice.
(*Lasswell, 1951b: 14–15*). ❖

❖ **Harold D. Lasswell, 'The Emerging Conception of the Policy Sciences', 1970**

Lasswell's article set out the state of the policy sciences in 1970 in the first number of the journal *Policy Sciences*. He introduced the idea of knowledge of the policy process and in the policy process, and argues that the distinctive outlook of the policy science is that it is problem-orientated. This problem focus means that the subject aims to be multidisciplinary and involved in the synthesis of ideas and techniques. What the policy scientist brings to the analysis of problems is a creativity in which there is a 'creative rearrangement', and an enlargement of the conceptual map which defines the problem as perceived by specialists:

> The contemporary policy scientist perceives himself as an integrator of knowledge and action, hence as a specialist in eliciting and giving effect to all the rationality of which individuals and groups are capable at any given time. He is a mediator between those who specialize in specific areas of knowledge and those who make the commitments in public and private life ... Both the intellectual community and the community at large are beginning to acknowledge the indispensable place of the integrator, mediator, and go-between ...
> (*Lasswell, 1970a: 13–14*)

The policy sciences were, therefore

- contextual;
- multi-method;
- problem-orientated.

A major feature of this orientation towards policy as a knowledge process was the designation of stages and functions within policy-making (see 1.10).

Policy analysis as public therapy

> We cannot fear the policy scientist because, unlike the politician, the policy scientist is not a driven personality. As Lasswell discusses him we get the impression that sooner or later political conflicts must yield to the policy scientist's implacable logic and empirical data, just as in the therapeutic situation, the patient's personal conflicts gradually yield to the analyst's expert ministrations ... We cannot escape the parallel here between the function of policy science for the political scientists and the function of the training for the fledgling psychothera-pist. The training analysis arms the young therapist with insight into his or her own deepest motives, thus preventing the projection of the therapist's conflicts onto patients and the consequent perpetuation rather than curing of illness. Similarly, learning to be a policy scientist is self-therapy, for it obliterates the social scientist's lust for power. Thus, policy science is therapeutic and pragmatic: the social physician heals himself while learning to heal the polity.
> (*Merelman, 1981: 496*) ◆

The policy sciences soon settled into two main approaches which, as Lasswell suggested, could be defined in terms of knowledge in the policy process and knowledge of the policy process (Lasswell, 1970a):

- 'policy analysis': concerned with knowledge in and for the policy process;
- the analysis of the policy process: concerned with knowledge about the formation and implementation of public policy.

Policy analysis may be traced back to the war years, in particular to the introduction of OR (operations research), and techniques of economic analysis. Among the first kinds of policy analysis, therefore, was that which took place in economic policy-making and defence. However, later in the 1960s in the US and elsewhere governments increasingly required more information and analysis about education, transport, urban planning, health, and so on. In America this expansion of government as a problem-solver became associated with the Kennedy–Johnson 'New Frontier' and 'Great Society' programmes. These programmes called forth a new kind of applied methods of investigation whose primary goal was to analyse 'problems' and to develop options or alternatives which could ameliorate or solve them. Meltsner (1976: 2) notes that the modern terms 'policy analysis' and 'policy analyst' began to be used frequently in the 1960s by Dror (1967), in various government papers (US Congress, 1969) and, Meltsner believes, was probably first used by Charles Lindblom, in 1958. This kind of policy analysis (what Wildavsky (1979) terms 'speaking the truth to power') was in all essentials a belief in social science as a form of engineering or medicine. Knowledge of society could provide a way of making it better. Furthermore, this growth of analysis for government was allied to the export from the defence sector and the business world ideas about how decision-making as a process could be made more effective. One major source of these ideas was operational or operations research, a method of analysis which had been developed in Britain and America during the Second World War. The other main influence over policy analysis in government were theories and techniques borrowed from management in the private and corporate sector. As we shall see later, these two influences were to come together via the personification of 1960s' analysis: Robert McNamara, President Kennedy's Defense Secretary. The approach to policy analysis which emerged in these years was in a relatively short time to percolate through to other policy sectors and departments in the US and elsewhere.

By the 1960s, more and more was going into the black box of the policy-making 'system'. Liberal-democratic governments were increasingly being called upon to take responsibility for a growing range of social, economic and other problems. In the USA it is a period closely identified with the Kennedy–Johnson years. Typical of the literature which was to emerge in the 1960s was the volume edited by Bauer and Gergen, *The Study of Policy Formation* (1968), which contained chapters reviewing the then state of the art. The book contained an approving foreword from Robert C. Wood, then Under-secretary at the Department of Housing and Urban Development. Wood commends the book for the way in which it assists practitioners such as himself in the task which President Johnson expressed as 'knowing as well as doing what is right'. Policy analysis therefore evolved in an era in which government was seen as a 'problem-solver' and the political system as a problem-processor. As Keith Hope observed of American politics at this time:

> The typical American word for an unsatisfactory social state is 'problem', something, that is, which can be solved and thereby disposed of; and the typical word for ameliorative social action is 'program', something, that is, which has a pre-ordained beginning, middle and end. Thus it is that social scientists in the United States frequently talk as if it were possible to jump to the goal of the 'Great Society', without first passing though a period of a welfare state ...
> *(Hope, quoted in Sharpe, 1975: 16)*

The other kind of analysis – which developed *pari passu* with the problem focus in the 1960s – was the analysis of the policy process as an alternative focus to the study of constitutions, legislatures and interest groups, and public administration. This policy focus in political science is most closely associated with the contribution of four people: Harold Lasswell, Herbert Simon, Charles Lindblom and David Easton. Their ideas will feature prominently throughout this book, and there is no better starting point for the study of policy-making and the role of policy analysis than to read their early works and follow the development of their thought.

Lasswell, perhaps, stands out as the pre-eminent moving spirit behind the growth of a policy approach. His writings on public policy may be dated back to the 1930s, when he was inspired by the Chicago School to be concerned with problems and to take a multidisciplinary approach. In the 1940s, for example, he was instrumental in setting up an early 'think-tank', the American Policy Commission, whose aim was to 'close the gap between knowledge and policy' by fostering a constructive dialogue between social scientists, businessmen, and policy-makers (J.A. Smith, 1991: 105). He was also closely involved with one of the most important 'think-tanks', the RAND corporation (as chairman of the board of trustees of the RAND graduate school; on RAND, see 2.8.2). Lasswell (1956) was one of the early attempts to formulate a set of 'stages' in the policy process (see 1.10).

Herbert Simon's contribution to the development of the policy approach has been without doubt more far-reaching than any other single theorist. Given the multidisciplinary nature of public policy, the fact that Simon's work has impacted on a range of social sciences – including economics, psychology, management, computer science, sociology and political science – means that wherever the student turns, there he is. His concern with human decision-making has centred on the idea of rationality as 'bounded' but capable of improvement. This theme he has explored both theoretically and experimentally. Simon's idea of examining decision-making in terms of a sequence of rational stages: intelligence, design, and choice, has formed a central element of policy analysis. Simon will figure prominently throughout this book, particularly in 3.4.2 and 3.7.4.

The third key contributor to the development of policy analysis as concerned with the 'process' of making policy is Charles Lindblom, who is best known for his advocacy of an alternative to Simon's rational approach in the form of 'incrementalism'. His article on the 'science of muddling through', published in 1959, is a classic text in the literature of policy studies. It remains as perhaps the single most important contribution to the formation of a theory of the policy-making process. Over the years Lindblom's thought has evolved beyond his original argument – some might argue to the point where there are two different kinds of Lindblom. We shall examine his ideas more fully in Parts Two and Three. In criticizing the 'rational' model as expounded by Simon and others, Lindblom also rejected the idea that thinking in terms of 'stages' or 'functional' relationships (see Easton, below) was of any real value to the study of the policy process. The models which owe their inspiration to Lasswell, Simon and Easton were viewed by Lindblom as thoroughly misleading. Instead, Lindblom (1968) proposed a model which took account of power and interaction between phases and stages. As he explains in the most recent edition of his textbook on the policy process: 'Deliberate, orderly steps ... are not an accurate portrayal of how the policy process actually works. Policy-making is, instead, a complexly inter-active process without beginning or end' (Lindblom and Woodhouse, 1993: 11). Lindblom suggests that in studying the policy process we should take account of elections, bureaucracies, parties and politicians, and interest groups, but also of 'deeper forces' – business, inequality, and the limited capacities of analysis – which structure and distort the policy process.

❖ Lindblom's framework

C.E. Lindblom and E.J. Woodhouse, *The Policy-making Process*, 3rd edn, 1993

- What are the limits of analysis in the policy process?
- What is the role of analysis in a democracy?
- Conventional government and politics and policy:
  the imprecision of voting;
  the impact of elected functionaries;
  bureaucracy and policy-making;
  interest groups and policy-making.
- The broader influences:
  the role of business;
  political inequality;
  impaired inquiry.
- How can policy-making be improved (given the above)? ◆

Figure 1.2   The Eastonian 'black box' model

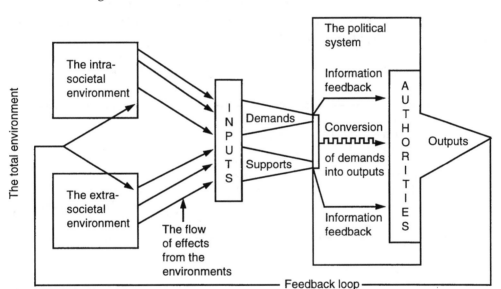

Notes:
The intra-societal environment:

- ecological system
- biological system
- personality system
- social system

The extra-societal environment:

- international political systems
- international ecological systems
- international social systems

Source: Adapted from Easton (1965: 110)

Finally, the work of David Easton (1953, 1965), although not regarded as primarily 'public policy', has made as vital a contribution to the establishment of a policy approach as the other scholars we have mentioned, in that it provided a model of the political 'system' which greatly influenced the way in which the emerging study of policy (outputs) in the 1960s began to conceptualize the relationship between policy-making, policy outputs and its wider 'environment' (see Figure 1.2).

The main characteristics of the Eastonian model is that of viewing the policy process in terms of received inputs, in the form of flows from the environment, mediated through input channels (parties, media, interest groups); demands within the political system (withinputs) and their conversion into policy outputs and outcomes (see figure 1.3). The frameworks which have dominated the field from the 1960s onwards derive from the combination of the 'stages' approach set out by Lasswell, Simon and Easton's 'political system' model. The text-books which, in Kuhn's sense (see 1.8), provided the 'normal science' of policy analysis were, for the most part, derived from the fusion of Lasswell, Simon and Easton's models of decision-making and the po-litical 'system'. (See, for example, Jones, 1970; Frohock, 1979; Dye, 1972; Sharkansky, 1970.)

Figure 1.3   The policy process as inputs and outputs

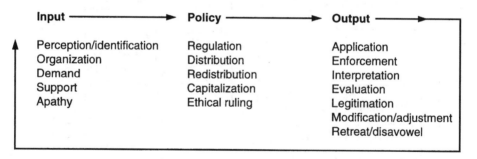

Input	Policy	Output
Perception/identification	Regulation	Application
Organization	Distribution	Enforcement
Demand	Redistribution	Interpretation
Support	Capitalization	Evaluation
Apathy	Ethical ruling	Legitimation
		Modification/adjustment
		Retreat/disavowel

Sources: Frohock (1979); Jones (1970)

The combination of rational stages and systems approaches thus af-forded a more dynamic model of policy-making, and a basis for un-derstanding policy in terms other than institutional and constitutional arrangements; although from Lindblom's point of view the models which developed have served more to obscure than to illuminate the policy process. Along with Easton's a number of other structural func-tional or 'systems' models had an important role in the development of new models of the policy process in the 1960s. Chief amongst them were those of G.A. Almond and Karl Deutsch (on Deutsch, see 3.7.6). The most comprehensive introduction to Almond is Almond and Powell (1966 and later editions) and Almond *et al.* (1993). The latter sets out a model of the political system as composed of inputs (inter-est articulation), process functions (interest aggregation, policy-mak-ing, policy implementation and adjudication), and policy function (extraction, regulation and distribution). Policy output is fed back into the political system, which is located in a domestic and international environment. This (1993) version acknowledges that it has sought to take more account of the role of institutions than in the past, when political scientists were hell bent on ignoring the fact that institutions, rules and constitutions do actually matter (see, for example, March and Olsen (1989); and 2.11.6, 3.6)

The theorists who had most influence on the development of models for analysing the policy-making process were American, but there were a few exceptions to the dominance of American policy science. A British theorist – and practitioner – whose work was important but had far less influence on the way in which the policy approach evolved was Sir Geoffrey Vickers. We shall examine his ideas in 3.7.5. Vickers's work stressed the importance of analysing the interaction of value judgements and reality judgements and was a major synthesis of psychological, cybernetic and political ideas, as well as an extensive administrative experience. It is to be hoped that with the rise in interest in the role of values in the policy process his work will find a new relevance for the study of public policy in the 1990s.

❖ Sir (Charles) Geoffrey Vickers (1894–1982)

Born in Nottingham, he went up to Merton College, Oxford in 1913 to read classics. During the war he was awarded the V.C. and the croix du guerre. On leaving the army he returned to Oxford to complete his degree and qualified as a solicitor. During the Second World War he was put in charge of economic intelligence in the Ministry of Economic Warfare. He joined the new National Coal Board and became Board member in charge of personnel and training in 1948 and retired in 1955. Vickers became involved in voluntary work in support of medical research especially in psychiatric and mental illness. His retirement gave him the opportunity to pursue his ideas, resulting in ten books and many papers, articles and lectures. His work became widely known and respected in the US and Canada. Nevil Johnson records that:

The problem which chiefly preoccupied Vickers was how individuals can best fulfil the requirements of social cooperation in conditions of accelerating economic and scientific change. He came to reject moral and economic individualism and argued that institutions are necessary conditions of satisfactory social coexistence. Influenced by Michael Polanyi he saw the achievement of an adequate understanding of institutions as an epistemological challenge: individuals have to grasp how their actions always involve the regulation of relationships with others, and this occurs only through the exercise of judgement. Consequently much of his work is devoted to the analysis of judgement in terms of what he called 'appreciative behaviour'. Though appreciation and judgement express individual capacities, Vickers never saw the individual as isolated or sovereign, but rather as defined by the relationships he has. He believed that social institutions are best analysed in terms of systems and his published work ... made far-reaching contributions to systems thinking in its

applications to human society. These themes, refined, developed and set within various organizational contexts, recur in all his mature works.
(Johnson, 1990: 400) ◆

Another exception to the early American dominance of the field was the Israeli political scientist Yehezkel Dror. Although agreeing with Lindblom that policy-making was far too complex to be captured in any model, he was opposed to Lindblom's incrementalist position and advocated a modified form of rationalism (see 3.8.8). Dror drew from systems analysis, policy analysis and the behavioural sciences in an attempt to develop a 'scientific' approach and *Public Policy-making Re-examined* (1968) was widely adopted as a text in the late 1960s and 1970s. It remains as an important source of the policy approach and the later edition (1989) greatly benefited from practical experience in the Israeli government. From the Middle Eastern perspective Dror was more sensitive to the limitations of policy analysis for the devel-oping world than had been the case in American and European texts (Dror, 1989: 105–19). This deficiency is still a matter of concern: few texts since have sought to address the problems of policy analysis in the context of the developing world (see Bertsch *et al.*, 1992; Younis (ed.), 1990: 117–38; Wildavsky, 1986).

❖ The development of the policy approach

The early growth of academic courses

Public Administration Bulletin published two articles in April 1978, at a time when interest in the public policy was growing apace:

- Le Roy Graymer, 'Profile of the Program at the Graduate School of Public Policy, University of California at Berkeley'.

The author describes how a public policy programme was set up in 1969 at the University of California, Berkeley, and discusses how the school was multidisciplinary and how it came to develop a curriculum which enabled graduates to use a broad range of skills in the analysis of problems and policies.

- Aaron Wildavsky, 'Principles for a Graduate School of Public Policy'.

Wildavsky's paper is an important source for understanding how the subject developed in an institutional context. The experience of the Berkeley programme was to be influential in the development of policy programmes in the US and elsewhere and provides an excellent intro-duction to the 'twilight world' (*sic*) of policy analysis.

A number of texts emerged from the experience of teaching public policy in the 1970s; in the UK these include Jenkins (1978) at the University of Kent; Rhodes (1979) at the University of Essex; Hogwood and Gunn (1984) at Strathclyde University; and Ham and Hill (1984) at the School for Advanced Urban Studies, University of Bristol. ◆

❖ Key readings and texts

The starting point for the study of the policy approach includes Lasswell (1951, 1970, 1971); Simon (1947); Lasswell (1959); Easton (1965); Lindblom (1968); Almond and Powell (1966); Deutsch (1963); and Vickers (1965).

The 1960s
Two early textbooks which express very different viewpoints as to the rationality of policy-making are Lindblom (1968) and Dror (1968). Other texts which were also published in 1968 include Bauer and Gergen (eds) and Ranney (ed.).

The 1970s
The policy approach took off in textbook terms in this period. Several books served as key texts on many a new policy course. These included Jones (1970); Dye (1972); Anderson (1975) and Jenkins (1978). Of special importance was the study of the Cuban missile crisis by Graham Allison (1971) which, although a study of foreign policy, was rapidly adopted as a core text of courses in decision-making in the context of 'public policy'. Also at this time a series of books came out of the Policy Studies Organization. They aimed at promoting the 'application of political science to important policy problems'. Two of these are of general importance to the student as they provide excellent surveys of the state of the art in the mid-seventies: (Nagel (ed.), 1975a and b). The mid-seventies also witnessed the publication of texts in comparative public policy, most notably Heidenheimer (*et al.*, 1975) and Hayward and Watson (1975). In 1979 a major contribution appeared in the form of Wildavsky's *Speaking the Truth to Power*; it appeared outside the US as *The Art and Craft of Policy Analysis* (Wildavsky, 1980).

The 1980s
The decade saw the extensive development of the policy approach in textbooks. They are too numerous to list, but amongst the most widely used were Burch and Wood (1983); Peters (1982); Hogwood and Gunn (1984); Ham and Hill (1984); Hill and Bramley (1986); Jordan and Richardson (1987); and Richardson and Jordan (1979/1985).

Policy analysis for and in the policy-making process
Analysis which sought to employ rational techniques for decision-making and policy evaluation also resulted in the development of a range of textbooks. Key readings in this field include: Campbell and Stanley (1966); Suchman (1967); Rivlin (1971); Rossi and Williams (1972); Quade (1976); Weiss (1977b); Stokey and Zeckhauser (1978); Rossi and Freeman (1979); and Carley (1980). ◆

The growth of public policy as a distinct field of academic activity may be dated to the late 1960s when, as a result of a meeting held under the auspices of the American Social Science Research Council, two conferences resulted in a collection of papers edited by Austin Ranney (Ranney, 1968). In 1972 the Policy Studies Organization was founded and this was followed by other 'policy' focused associations and several journals (Henry, 1990: 6) But perhaps more significant than these formal – and largely political science dominated – developments, the subject of policy and problems commanded the attention of a wide range of academic interest. Policy and problems cut across the lines of demarcation and the growth of policy studies was to be a feature of all social sciences. For this reason policy analysis emerged in the 1970s as an approach which offered the possibility of a unified or integrated social science which could bridge the boundaries of academic disciplines. The prospects of policy analysis as an integrative field of inquiry prompted a lively symposium under the auspices of the American Academy of Political and Social Science in 1971 (Charlesworth, 1972). The contributors to this debate were, for the most part sceptical of the search for such an integrated social science via policy science. The subsequent history of the social sciences in the 1970s and 1980s was to confirm their doubts. In the universities in particular there was little sign that boundaries were coming down, or that an interdisciplinary approach was taking place. Even so, in the 1970s and 1980s numerous textbooks were published aimed at undergraduate and postgraduate courses which were concerned with the analysis of policy-making, and the role of analysis in decision-making. Perhaps, however, it is significant that one of the most important developments in policy analysis has taken place outside the halls of academe. The 1970s and 1980s witnessed a veritable explosion of think-tanks and research institutions in which interdisciplinary approaches to policy thrived. The production incentives for academics still remained tied to the research agenda of their respective disciplines, rather than the 'policy agenda'. Think-tanks, on the other hand, have provided the kind of problem and policy-focused environment which has been conducive to the renewal of the 'policy orientation' which was first promoted by Lasswell (see 2.8.2).

In the 1980s and 1990s one of the most distinctive features of the public policy field is the extent to which it has spread beyond America to other countries. Indeed, some the most innovative thinking and new approaches are now coming out of Europe. This is an important development because, for the greater part of the history of the subject, it has tended to be dominated by American material and ideas. A number of texts should be consulted to give an idea of the scope of the European contribution in recent years:

J. Kooiman and K.A. Eliassen (eds), *Managing Public Organizations*, 1987.

J. Kooiman (ed.), *Modern Governance*, 1993.

M.J. Hill (ed.), *New Agendas in the Study of Policy Process*, 1993.

J.-E. Lane, *Institutional Reform*, 1990.

J.-E. Lane, *The Public Sector*, 1993.

1.4   Kinds of policy analysts and policy analysis

Prince Metternich once described Italy, then composed of a dis-aggregated collection of regions, as little more than a 'geographical expression'. Such a viewpoint has some relevance to policy analysis. It is a field which is composed of a patchwork of disciplines, theories and models. As Wildavsky puts it: 'Policy analysis is an applied subfield whose contents cannot be determined by disciplinary boundaries but by whatever appears appropriate to the circumstances of the time and the nature of the problem' (Wildavsky, 1979: 15). Policy and problems provide a common focus for social science as well as in areas of scientific activity and research which have become more aware of the political context within which they operate. This common focus has meant that the analysis of policies and problems has increasingly taken on a multidisciplinary character. In this book we include a variety of academic disciplines under the remit of policy analysis. These include political science and philosophy, economics, psychology, sociology. However, in addition to these approaches the analysis of policy also requires that we have an understanding of the historical, legal, anthropological and geographical contexts of public policy. The impact of quantitative techniques and computer science on the formation, implementation and evaluation of policy must also be regarded as falling within the domain of policy analysis. Policy analysis necessarily needs to maintain a multiframework approach. The student of a particular policy or problem must, above all, be aware of the different frameworks or lenses which may be brought to the interpretation of information and data.

Who are 'policy analysts' and what do they do?

There are varieties of people who are involved in policy analysis. Some might be happy with the description of their work as 'policy analysis', others would not. But they have a number of common and overlapping concerns:

- they are concerned with 'problems' and the relationship of public policies to these problems;
- they are concerned with the content of public policies;

- they are concerned with what the decision-makers and policy-makers do or do not do. They are interested in the inputs and processes of a policy area;
- they are concerned with the consequences of policy in terms of outputs and outcomes.

Harold Lasswell's conception of the policy analyst/scientist encompassed a number of roles and types. Merelman (1981: 492) has characterized these in terms of:

- the physician to the political personality (see Lasswell, 1948a: ch. 6);
- the social engineer (see Lasswell, 1963, 1971);
- the intelligence gatherer (see Lasswell, 1935: 134–5);
- the policy advocate (see Lasswell, 1948a: 186–7);
- the student of public administration (see Lasswell, 1930a).

It is the latter three which have emerged as the dominant 'types' of policy analyst. The psychological/psycho-analytical and experimentalist or 'prototyping' aspects of policy analysis have been far less well developed (see 3.7, 4.5.2).

Institutional settings: where can you find them?

- Universities: academics who are interested in policy and problem areas and in the policy process. They are involved in personal research and competing for funds from grant-giving bodies.
- Independent research institutions and 'think-tanks': these may have full-time and contract staff who are involved in specialist research.
- In-house policy units: analysts who are responsible for research and intelligence in government, governmental agencies and public bodies.
- Pressure and lobby groups: interest groups which seek to influence policy engage in monitoring policy as well as developing alternative ideas and proposals.
- Political parties: will have departments/units or groups involved in policy research and development to support party activities and interests.
- Freelance consultants: people who engage in research on the basis of contracts and fees.

What are their professional backgrounds and academic orientations?

Although they have shared concerns and may be part of a policy network or community (see 2: 10) analysts differ in their professional setting. Those who work in the field of public policy have a wide range of academic fields. Economics, law, political science, sociology, geography, environmental science, transport studies and so on.

What kinds of policy arenas, fields, communities and networks are they involved in?

Public policy is a field which tends to be defined by policy areas or sectors, and it is largely in this setting that interdisciplinary and inter-institutional interaction may take place. They also provide the context of comparative studies. Some of the key areas of public policy include:

- health;
- transport;
- education;
- the environment;
- social policy;
- housing;
- economic policy;
- race;
- urban planning.

Within each of these areas there exist specialized research networks and communities which address problems and policies and advocate ideas. (For reviews of research in such fields on a comparative level, see Heidenheimer *et al.*, 1990; Harrop (ed.), 1992.)

What kinds of phases in the policy process do analysts focus on?

Analysts focus on different stages of the policy process, have particular relationships with the policy process, and different ideas, beliefs and assumptions about it. Some, for example, will be interested in the role of interest groups in shaping policy, others in the impact of bureaucracy on decision-making, or the role of professionals in policy delivery. Analysts may also be concerned with different stages: such as policy formulation, implementation, or evaluation.

1.5   Varieties of analytical frameworks

Given the wide range of institutional settings, academic orientations, policy interests and relationships to the policy process, it is not unexpected that the theoretical frameworks which analysts employ manifest a similar pluralistic pattern.

❖ Using 'frames'

The idea of thinking in terms of 'frames' which structure and provide a 'discourse' of analysis came into use in the 1970s and 1980s. Frames may be thought of as modes of organizing problems, giving them a form and a coherence. A frame involves the notion of constructing a boundary around reality which is shared, or held in common by a group or community. Conflict may occur within the frame or between different frames. When we study public policy we must be aware of how different frames of analysis define and discuss problems, and how these frames clash, converge, and shift around (see Rein and Schön, 1993). ◆

In one of the most perspicacious classifications of the field, Bobrow and Dryzek (1987) suggest that the policy analysis may be considered as comprising five main fames of analysis:

• welfare economics;
• public choice;
• social structure;
• information processing;
• political philosophy.

Welfare economics and public choice are frameworks derived from economics; social structure from sociology; information processing encompasses the largest selection of disciplines, including psychology, organizational behaviour, artificial intelligence and information science; political philosophy is also a broad category of interest including normative and ethical philosophy as well as methodology.

For the purposes of this book we can add a further three additional frameworks:

• political process;
• comparative politics;
• management.

In this section we shall consider the main analytical frameworks as suggested by Bobrow and Dryzek, with the inclusion of our additional frameworks. The 'philosophical' framework will be considered in more detail in 1.6. The point to stress about these frameworks is that they are not necessarily exclusive or incommensurate. Policy analysis tends to range across them and to draw upon them, rather than remain locked into one specific framework. Indeed, some of the most important contributions to the study of public policy have been made by those who have had the greatest ability to work across different frameworks. As Wildavsky notes, policy analysis requires both art and craft: 'analysis is imagination', involving 'experiments in thought' and creativity (Wildavsky, 1979: 16–17). Brian Hogwood (1984: 25) suggests that the policy analyst must therefore aim to be a 'JOAT', or 'jack of all trades', that is:

> someone with a good training (or self-education) in a wide range of approaches and techniques, not necessarily an expert in any one of them ... but with an ability to identify potentially relevant techniques, if not the ability to carry them out, an awareness of their strengths and weaknesses, and a strong emphasis on the problems of decision makers.

Frameworks are the tools of the JOAT's trade.

Welfare economics

In a direct descent line from the utilitarianism of Mill and Bentham (see below, 1.6), welfare economics constitutes a core component of policy analysis for and in the policy process. Numerous books on policy analysis portray the subject as the dominant paradigm of policy analysis. Broadly it involves the application of the theories and models of welfare economics to improving the rationality and efficiency of decision-making. Texts which review or employ welfare approaches include:

E.S. Quade, *Analysis for Public Decisions*, 1976.
E. Stokey and R. Zeckhauser, *A Primer for Policy Analysis*, 1978.
H. Jenkins-Smith, *Democratic Politics and Policy Analysis*, 1990.
M. Carley, *Rational Techniques in Policy Analysis*, 1980.

Policy analysis as a form of 'rational technique' derived from the postulates of welfare economics will be considered in 3.8, 3.9, 4.5 and 4.7.

Public choice

A leading textbook on the subject defines the approach in the following terms:

> Public choice can be defined as the economics of non-market decision-making, or simply the application of economics to political science. The subject matter of public choice is the same as that of political science: the theory of the state, voting rules, voter behaviour, party politics, the bureaucracy, and so on. The methodology of public choice is that of economics, however.
> (*Mueller, 1979: 1*)

Key exponents of this framework that are discussed in this book include:

W.A. Niskanen, *Bureaucracy and Representative Government*, 1971.
A. Downs, *An Economic Theory of Democracy*, 1957.
A. Downs, *Inside Bureaucracy*, 1967.
P. Dunleavy, *Democracy, Bureaucracy and Public Choice*, 1991.

The public choice approach will be reviewed in 3.5.1.

Closely related to the public choice approach is economic institutionalism, or the 'new institutionalism', which is concerned with analysing market and organizational behaviour and development in terms of rational choices and economic theories of the firm. We shall consider the relevance of these theories to the analysis of public policy in 2.11.6 and 3.6.3.

Key texts for the institutionalist approach include:

T.M. Moe, 'New economics of organizations', 1984.
L. Kiser and E. Ostrom, 'The three worlds of political action', 1982.
J.E. Stiglitz, 'Principal and agent', 1987.
B.R. Weingast, 'The political institutions of representative government', 1989.
D.C. North, *Institutions, Institutional Change and Economic Performance*, 1990.

Social structure

Social structure approaches include the analysis of public policy in terms of sociological theory. In this book the contribution of sociology to the development of policy analysis may be viewed in several areas.

The contribution of sociology to the analysis of social problems is of special significance (see 2.2.1/3). Key texts for this include:

R.C. Fuller and R.R. Myers, 'The natural history of a social problem', 1941.
C.W. Mills, *The Sociological Imagination*, 1959.
H.S. Becker, *Outsiders*, 1963.
H. Blumer, 'Social problems as collective behaviour', 1971.
M. Spector and J.I. Kitsuse, *Constructing Social Problems*, 1977.
R.L. Henshel, *Thinking about Social Problems*, 1990.

The 'lifecycle' approach to social problems also forms an important source of the 'stagist' model of the policy process (see Fuller and Myers, 1941). Sociologists have contributed much to our understanding of power in society (3.3); in organizations (3.6.2, 4.3.7); in institutions (2.11.6); and about the sociology of knowledge (2.2.1). At a broader level, 'functionalist' sociology (Parsons, 1937, 1951) has been a predominant influence on the 'systems' approach to the study of the policy process (for example, Easton, 1953, 1965; Almond and Powell, 1966). The impact of sociological approaches at a policy level has also been significant, both in terms of 'direct' and 'indirect' influence (Bulmer, 1990).

Information processing

As Bobrow and Dryzek observe, this framework has an extensive reach into a range of academic disciplines. It is perhaps the most diverse of all analytical frameworks. Analysts who operate within this frame: 'share an interest in how individuals and organisations ... arrive at judgments, make choices, deal with information, and solve problems' (Bobrow and Dryzek, 1987: 83). It uses approaches which include:

• cognitive psychology;
• social psychology;
• decision science;
• information science;
• artificial intelligence;
• organizational behaviour.

Key texts for this framework include:

H.D. Lasswell, *Psychopathology and Politics*, 1930.
———, *Power and Personality*, 1948.

H.A. Simon, *Models of Man*, 1957.

———, *The New Science of Management Decision*, 1960.

———, *The Sciences of the Artificial*, 1969.

———, 'Human nature in politics', the dialogue of psychology with political science', 1985.

C.E. Lindblom, 'The science of muddling through', 1959.

———, *The Intelligence of Democracy*, 1965.

———, 'Still muddling through', 1979.

——— and D.K. Cohen, *Usable Knowledge*, 1979.

A. Newall and H.A. Simon, *Human Problem Solving*, 1972.

J.G. March and H.A. Simon, *Organizations*, 1958.

G. Vickers, *The Art of Judgment: a study of policymaking*, 1965.

———, *Value Systems and the Social Process*, 1968.

R.M. Cyert and J.G. March, *A Behavioral Theory of the Firm*, 1963/1992.

K.W. Deutsch, *The Nerves of Government*, 1963.

D.T. Campbell, 'The social scientist as methodological servant of the experimenting society', 1973.

———, 'Experiments as arguments', 1982.

H.L. Wilensky, *Organizational Intelligence*, 1967.

C. Argyris and D.A. Schön, *Organizational Learning*, 1978.

C. Argyris, *Strategy, Change and Defensive Regimes*, 1985.

I.L. Janis, *Groupthink*, 1972/1982.

——— and L. Mann, *Decision Making*, 1977.

R. Jervis, 'Hypothesis on misperception', 1968.

J.S. Carroll and E.J. Johnson, *Decision Research, A Field Guide*, 1990.

This framework will be examined in 3.7 and will be encountered in other sections (for example, 3.4; 4.6.4).

❖ Psychology and policy analysis

The contribution of psychology to the policy sciences has been significant, and to some extent has been overshadowed by economics, especially public choice theory. The contribution of psychology (of William James) to the development of symbolic interactionism was of major importance to the study of social problems (see 2.2.2). Lasswell was the first to systematically apply psychology and psychoanalysis to the study of politics. In the 1930s he argued, for example:

> The ideal of a politics of prevention is to obviate conflict by the definite reduction of the tension level of society ... The achievement of the ideal of preventive politics depends less upon changes in social organization than upon improving the methods and the education of social administrators and social scientists. The preventive politics of the future will be intimately allied to general medicine, psychopathology, physiological psychology, and related disciplines ...
> (*Lasswell, 1930: 203*)

Simon in the 1960s was to make key contributions to cognitive approaches. The development of evaluation research owes much to early pioneers such as Campbell and others (see 4.5; Stier, 1975: 107). If we also include the contribution of the human relations school of management theory, then the psychological contribution offers a far more sophisticated and empirically founded view of human behaviour than the notion of self-interest as advanced by economists. In the 1970s the contribution of psychology to the understanding of group decision-making of Janis (1972/1982) and Janis and Mann (1977) provided new insights into the policy-making process (see 3.7.3).

In a more general way psychology has also helped to frame the stagist approach to policy analysis by the development of approaches to decision-making which break it down into a number of stages. This is evident in Simon's work, in cognitive psychology (see Carroll and Johnson, 1990) and in social psychology (see Mann, 1969).

Mann, for example, distinguishes between three stages: predecision; decision; post-decision. (Mann, 1969: 133–52). Although these are logical stages, Mann and other social psychologists use such frames to show how decision-making is a process which is far removed from some rational ideal.

Carroll and Johnson (1990: 16) distil a good deal of research in cognitive psychology (including Simon's) to set out a useful framework for an empirical study:

- *Recognition*: Who notices the problem? What had to happen for this to be labelled as a decision problem?
- *Formulation*: Who was involved in defining the problems? How was it distinguished from other problems? What goals and whose goals emerged?
- *Alternative generation*: Where did alternatives come from? Why was the search for alternatives stopped?
- *Information search*: How much information was collected, by whom? What kind of information was searched for? How was it used?
- *Evaluation/choice*: What kind of judgements were used, by whom, and what kinds of knowledge were used? What assumptions were made?
- *Action/feedback*: What happened after the decision was made? Who gets the feedback? ◆

Public policy in a managerial framework

The influence of management ideas and techniques on the development of the theory and the practice of policy analysis has been extensive. To begin with, the development of policy analysis in the US under McNamara in the 1960s inaugurated an era in which management ideas – such as corporate planning – had a major influence on government in the US and elsewhere. In the 1970s this gave way to the notion that public administration was fast evolving into a form of public 'management'. A growing literature sought to apply management approaches to the study of public administration and was also used as a critique of the deficiencies of bureaucracy. By the late seventies and early eighties, under the rising pressure on public finances, the management approach developed rapidly in theory and practice and offered an alternative to the long-established public administration tradition (Rainey, 1990). The demise of the public administration paradigm and the rise of public policy as public management accelerated in the 1980s and 1990s (Metcalfe and Richards, 1992; Lane, 1993; Flynn, 1990; OECD, 1990, 1991, 1992; Osborne and Gaebler, 1992; Hughes, 1994).

The focus of the management approach is the improvement of the efficiency, effectiveness and economy of the public sector by the utilization of techniques which were once regarded as purely appropriate to the private/profit sector. The sources of this framework are somewhat eclectically drawn from a number of disciplines, including: scientific management approaches; economics; social and occupational psychology; management accounting; and management auditing. The figure whose ideas were very influential in this shift towards a managerial framework was Peter Drucker: the man who is credited with developing MBO (Management by Objectives). A key text, or rather the bible of this framework in the 1980s, was the study by Peters and Waterman (1982) which examined leading 'excellent' (*sic*) companies; it offered a checklist of the characteristics of excellence, which was taken to heart by reformers, especially those on the 'right' who were convinced of the case made by the public choice framework against Weberian 'public interest' (self-serving) administrative hierarchies and in favour of a shift towards greater market-driven 'management' (see Part 4, *passim*).

Critics of managerialism as either a tool of control or as an ideology (Massey, 1993; Politt, 1990) challenge the idea that the concepts and methods of private-sector management are fitted to the administration of the public sector in a liberal democratic society. However, such academic arguments have not detracted from the appeal of the framework to policy-makers working in the context of ever-tighter constraints on public finances. The impact of this framework has been widespread (OECD, 1991, 1992) and must now be considered to constitute the dominant framework in the practice, if not in the theory, of the modern public sector.

The impact of managerialism has been extensive and is a theme which will be encountered throughout the book. We examine it more specifically in 4.3.5 and 4.5.3.

Key texts for this framework include:

P. Drucker, *The Practice of Management*, 1954.

——, *Managing for Results*, 1964.

——, *The Age of Discontinuity*, 1969.

T. Peters and H. Waterman, *In Search of Excellence*, 1982.

J.L. Perry and K.L. Kraemer (eds), *Public Management*, 1983.

D. Osborne and T. Gaebler, *Reinventing Government*, 1992.

C. Pollitt, *Managerialism and the Public Sector*, 1990.

N. Flynn, *Public Sector Management*, 1990.

L. Metcalfe and S. Richards, *Improving Public Management*, 1992

A. Massey, *Managing the Public Sector*, 1993

Political/policy process

This framework consists of various approaches to how the political context of policy-making may be explained. We can discern six main approaches:

- *Stagist approaches*: which view the policy-making process as composed of a series of steps or sequences, derived from Lasswell, Simon and Easton, and Almond (for example, Jones, 1970; Anderson, 1975; Hogwood and Gunn, 1984). This approach analyses policy in terms of a process beginning with 'agenda-setting' and concluding with policy evaluation and termination (see 1.3, 1.9, 1.10).
- *Pluralist-elitist approaches*: which focus on power and its distribution amongst groups and elites (iron triangles) and the way they shape policy-making (eg: Dahl, 1961; Lindblom, 1977; Lindblom and Woodhouse, 1993; Shattschneider, 1960; Cobb and Elder, 1972; Bachrach and Baratz, 1962, 1963, 1970; Crenson, 1971; Lukes, 1974; Gaventa, 1980) (see 2.4, 2.6, 3.3).
- *Neo-Marxist approaches*: which are concerned with the application of Marx and Marxist ideas to the explanation of policy-making in capitalist society (Miliband, 1982; O'Connor, 1973; Poulanzas, 1978; Cockburn, 1977; Offe, 1985; see, in general, Dunleavy and O'Leary, 1987) (see 2.7, 3.3.3).
- *Sub-system approaches*: which analyse policy-making in terms of new metaphors such as 'networks', 'communities' and 'sub-systems' (Heclo, 1978; Richardson and Jordan, 1979; Rhodes, 1988; Atkinson and Coleman, 1992; Smith, 1993; Baumgartner and Jones, 1993; Sabatier and Jenkins-Smith (eds), 1993) (see 1.9, 2.10).
- *Policy discourse approaches*: which examine the policy process in terms of language and communication. It draws on the work of French and German critical theorists, such as Foucault and Habermas, as well as Toulmin and Wittgenstein (Fischer and Forester (eds), 1993; Edelman, 1967, 1977, 1988) (see 2.7.3, 2.9.2).

- *Institutionalism*: which has been less well developed than the others, but is emerging as an important new set of approaches to the policy process (see 2.11.6, 3.6; and Almond *et al.*, 1993: 132–54). Key texts include: Skocpol (1985) and Hall (1986) (see 2.11.6, 3.6.4); and Weaver and Rockman (eds) (1993) (see 2.11.6).

Comparative public policy

Comparative public policy is, as Feldman observes, a method of studying public policy (Feldman, 1978) by adopting a comparative approach to policy processes and policy output and outcomes. As one of the leading texts in the field maintains: 'Comparative public policy is the study of how, why, and to what effect different governments pursue a particular course of action or inaction' (Heidenheimer *et al.*, 1990: 3). In asking these questions the frameworks use a number of approaches. These may be set out in several main ways (see ibid.: 7–9). Such approaches are, of course, not exclusive to comparative public policy or exclusive of one another. In this book we shall introduce a number of them through the use of a number of key texts:

- *socio-economic approaches*: which look at how public policy is the outcome of economic and social factors (Wilensky, 1975; Hofferbert, 1974);
- *party government approaches*: which study how party competition and partisan control of government 'matters' to policy (Castles, 1982);
- *class struggle approaches*: which explain public policy in terms of the political forms of the class struggle in different capitalist countries (Offe, 1984);
- *neo-corporatist approaches*: which focus on the influence of organized interests in determining public policy (Lehmbruch and Schmitter, 1982);
- *institutionalist approaches*: which address the role that state and social institutions have in defining and shaping public policy (Hall, 1986; Weaver and Rockman (eds), 1993).

The comparative approach tends to use three main methods (see Harrop (ed.), 1992): single case studies of one policy area in one country (Parsons, 1988); statistical analysis of several case studies and countries (Castles (ed.), 1989; Wilensky, 1975; Heidenheimer *et al.*, 1990); or a more focused comparison of a policy area or sector between a selected number of comparable countries (e.g.: health policy, industrial policy, law and order amongst G5 countries: see Harrop (ed.), 1992).

The book makes specific use of the comparative politics approach in 2.11, 3.6.4, and 4.7.

1.6   Philosophical frameworks

The contribution of the philosophical (ethical, normative, methodological) dimension of the analysis of public policy is immense. Indeed, one could construct the story of political philosophy to show how concern with 'policy' and 'problems' has been a central aspect of political theory since ancient times (see Nagel, 1990: 422–3). However, for the purposes of this section of the book we shall content ourselves with seven groups of philosophers (or social theorists) whose work has had – or is having – a formative influence on public policy and policy analysis:

- Machiavelli and Bacon;
- Bentham and Mill: the utilitarian contribution;
- James and Dewey: pragmatism and the development of the policy sciences;
- Rawls and Nozick: two theories of justice;
- Karl Popper and the piecemeal engineering model;
- Hayek's case for markets and individual choice;
- Etzioni's case for 'communitarianism';
- Habermas and communicative rationality.

Machiavelli and Bacon

Machiavelli (1469–1527) was concerned with relating theories of government to what he had experienced at first hand about the actualities of politics and had studied in history. Machiavelli believed that it was necessary for those in power to understand how power worked, but he was also convinced, as a diplomat, of the need for good-quality information and proper interpretation of that information. Furthermore, he believed that it was possible to make general conclusions about the nature of human behaviour and the influence of institutions and structures. In short, he thought that government was a craft, and its study could approximate to a science. Machiavelli was interested in the craft of the state ('statecraft'): his belief was that, through knowledge of the reality of politics and power, decision-makers could better control affairs and have a greater capacity to deal with problems. And, as *The Economist* more recently commented, the concerns of Machiavelli have a curious resonance in the modern world of statecraft:

When Machiavelli sat down to write *The Prince*, he was feeling anxious. Unemployed after many years' government service, he wrote his handbook of advice to new rulers in an attempt to win a job with the incoming Medici administration. The Machiavelli problem would be recognisable to hordes of would-be and once-were government officials in today's world: 'policy intellectuals', as Americans call them ... Today [Machiavelli] would sit in a think tank, cosseted by secretaries and flattered by a stream of calls from talk show producers. The 'policy intellectuals' still strive to present their conclusions as impartial expertise. But, like Machiavelli, they are for ever tugging the sleeves of politicians.
(*The Economist*, 25 May 1991)

Machiavelli was fascinated by power and outcome, with the use of policy to obtain whatever were the objectives of power-holders. He believed that he had discovered the fundamental forces which shaped policy and politics in a world which was subject to continual change. Above all, he was concerned with the relationship of ends and means and their context in processes of change that are beyond the rational control of men: *fortuna*. The effective politician (prince) is one who can make best use of the times and circumstances. Machiavelli believed that there was a kind of knowledge which could facilitate knowledgeable governance.

The Prince still has a very modern feel to it. Policy analysis, and the analysis of policy in the twentieth century emerged for similar kinds of Machiavellian reasons: the desire to understand what actually happens in government and how governmental performance measures up to its promises. Success, performance, getting results, are ultimately the criteria by which we have come to judge those in government. Policy is the strategy by which goals are reached. Whether a policy is right or wrong does not come into it, what matters in the end is that which the policy is designed to achieve. Therein lies the only real source of legitimacy as effectiveness.

❖ **James Burnham, *The Machiavellians: Defenders of Freedom*, 1943**

Burnham's book, *The Managerial Revolution* (1941) was an important contribution to debate about what was happening to capitalism in an era in which power was shifting towards managers. Burnham argued that economic conditions had resulted in a revolution in which the owners of capital were replaced by a new managerial elite. To what extent was 'scientific' governance possible? The conclusions of a Machiavellian perspective suggested the following to Burnham:

It should not be imagined that even the most thoroughly scientific procedures on the part of a ruling class could 'solve' all the problems of society ... Scientific action could ... make a difference only within the framework of general patterns. Many important social problems ... are very probably insoluble. It is in general ... exceedingly difficult for men to be scientific or logical about social and political problems ... A dilemma confronts any section of the elite that tries to act scientifically. The political life of the masses and the cohesion of society demand the acceptance of myths. A scientific attitude toward society does not permit belief in the truth of myths. But the leaders must profess, indeed foster, belief in the myths, or the fabric of society will crack and they be overthrown. In short, the leaders, if they themselves are scientific, must lie. It is hard to lie all the time in public but to keep privately an objective regard for the truth ... The programmes which they profess, as well as those upon which they act, are devoid of reality ...

Antony Jay, *Management and Machiavelli*, 1987
This book, first published in 1967, is amongst the best-known books about management, having sold over one and a quarter million copies world wide. Jay was later to become known as the joint author of the BBC series *Yes Minister* and *Yes Prime Minister*. Jay argues that management science is in fact a continuation of older arts of government:

> when you study management theory side by side with political theory ... you realise that you are studying two very similar branches of the same subject.

It was Machiavelli who, he says, brought this home to him, and in his book he applies Machiavelli's method to the study of management issues and problems with some effect: 'Machiavelli is in fact bursting with urgent advice and acute observations for all top management ...' (pp. 15–16)

Machiavelli as patron saint
Watching over the work of the Efficiency Unit in the Cabinet Office is a framed extract from the works of the master:

> It must be considered that there is nothing more difficult to carry out, nor more doubtful of success, nor more dangerous to handle, than to initiate a new order of things.
> (*Metcalfe and Richards, 1992: 211*) ◆

If Machiavelli was the philosopher of policy as cunning and deception, Francis Bacon (1561–1626) was the man who may be said to have examined policy in its more modern sense, as a rational course of action predicated on knowledge. A contemporary of Shakespeare (indeed, there is one theory that argues that Bacon wrote Shakespeare's plays), Bacon's idea of policy was that of the pursuit of the middle way – *res mea*. Good policy was essentially realizing that the exercise of power required the ability to sustain authority and legitimacy by building up support and agreement rather than antagonism: advice which King James was not wholly to embrace. Power was the exercise of knowledge. And, in the words of Bacon's famous dictum, knowledge was power. For Bacon, *policy* was the use of knowledge for the purposes of governance.

Both Bacon and Machiavelli were men deeply involved in the politics and government of their day, and both suffered the disgrace of losing their place at court. In Machiavelli's view, policy was an activity of sustaining power; for Bacon it was an activity of sustaining balance and authority. For Machiavelli the policy adviser was there to help the Prince to lie, cheat and murder effectively. Bacon, on the other hand, envisaged a role for advisers which was far more elevated and powerful – as is portrayed in his *New Atlantis* (published after his death, in 1627) wherein he describes a world in which scientists have the real power in a new social order.

This, of course, is to be a central theme of 'positivist' social thought from Bacon, Comte and St Simon onwards. However, it is true to say that in style and method Bacon was highly Machiavellian. As a philosopher he sought to organize the scientific knowledge and inductive method of his day, and as a political theorist he endeavoured to define and distil political insight and learning. In essence, he argued that progress depended on the organization of scientific knowledge, and governance on the organization of policy knowledge. Government involved a complex art of the application of judgement and knowledge.

As for Machiavelli, his notion of policy was embedded in the idea that it was possible to acquire knowledge to make better policy. The difference between the Baconian idea of policy and that of Machiavelli is largely one of historical context. Bacon was writing at a time when policy needed to be framed with consent and agreement in mind. For Bacon, the king needed to be aware of the necessity of building that consent, and policy involved what in modern language we might express as legitimacy. Policy was the activity wherein the decisions of the king facilitated a balance in political forces. When combined with his inductivism and his belief in science, Bacon may be said to represent the genesis of the modern idea of policy as the product of rational consideration and science (Bell, 1976).

❖ Francis Bacon

Bacon was the son of Sir Nicholas Bacon, Elizabeth's Lord Keeper. He was educated at Trinity College, Cambridge, and became a lawyer and a Member of Parliament. He was knighted in 1603 and became Solicitor General in 1612, Privy Councillor in 1616 and Keeper of the Great Seal, or Lord Chancellor, in 1617. He was charged with accepting bribes in 1621 and fell from favour. From thence onwards he dedicated himself to writing.

Bacon was a leading politician of his day, and nursed considerable ambitions which were, in the end, only partly realized. He sought advancement in a political career, and came to the belief that the successful polity and political order was one in which governance was informed by learning. Like Machiavelli, whose work he greatly admired and which influenced his own ideas, Bacon had a plan for his country. Machiavelli's was Italian unity, effective government and a political morality distinct and separate from ordinary ethics. Bacon's plan was the fusion of knowledge and power in a new political order. Machiavelli addresses the Prince of the Medici; Bacon dedicated his writings to the powerful men of his time: King James I and the Duke of Buckingham. As Johnson notes:

> Having seemingly failed to obtain the preferment he hoped for in his political career, Bacon hoped to attract the king by his plans for a regeneration of the world of learning. He is not suggesting that learning should be the occupation of a few men withdrawn from active affairs, but that men of affairs in the state should set learning as the highest and most practical of their aims. Bacon wants a good society, well governed, orderly, religious, chaste, courageous and rich, and he believes that only a society that sets learning as its goal can achieve these things.
>
> (*Bacon, 1973, p. x*)

In his book *New Atlantis* Bacon describes a Utopian island founded by a King Salomon, whose philosophy is that knowledge is the foundation of a good society. The king establishes a house of scientific research – Salomon's House – one of whose tasks is to gain knowledge from all over the world. This house of learning provides the foundation of the peace and prosperity of the land, and underpins the maintenance of the power and authority of the king. Radical in his vision of scientific progress and discovery, Bacon was highly conservative in political terms. Knowledge was, he believed, destined to be the mainstay of a rational political order. The New Atlantis is such an orderly place in which everybody knows where they are in the social hierarchy; and knowledge, though it benefits the welfare of all, ultimately has a political function in terms of upholding the power of the state. Bacon's vision was of a new Britain in which the power of knowledge was harnessed to the power of the state. The New Atlantis is a place wherein policy is informed by knowledge, truth, reason, facts, rather than by what he calls elsewhere (*Novum Organum*, 1620) the 'idols of the mind': idols of the tribe, of the cave, of the market place, and of the theatre. Bacon's ideas inspired the development of universities and learned societies from the late seventeenth century onwards and served as an inspiration to the French Encyclopaedists. ◆

Bentham and Mill: the utilitarian contribution

Utilitarianism, of which Jeremy Bentham (1748–1832) and James Mill (1773–1836) were amongst the leading exponents, declared that the principle of utility – the greatest happiness for the greatest number – should serve as the foundation of individual actions and government policies. Good decisions should thus lead to good consequences. Utilitarianism's belief that it was possible to make calculations about pleasures and pains and compare the actions on the basis of their consequences naturally lent itself to the development of theories which sought to quantify and model human welfare. The case for reform in public policy often takes the form of a utilitarian argument as to the promotion of greater social welfare and individual freedom. As a theory it has been subjected to much criticism on the grounds that, for example, such calculus ignores moral issues and questions of equity or fairness. Nevertheless, the centrality of utilitarianism to the growth of public policy and policy analysis continues despite its philosophical shortcomings.

If we define policy analysis in terms of a 'set of techniques with which to evaluate public policy options and select amongst them' (Jenkins-Smith, 1990: 1), then the contribution of Bentham and Mill and other utilitarian philosophers defines core elements of the analytical paradigm: the notion that the calculation of human welfare is possible and desirable. Out of this premise economists could lay claim to devising methods of setting costs against benefits and defining levels of efficiency.

James and Dewey: 'pragmatism' and the development of the policy sciences

William James (1842–1910) trained as a doctor, and became interested in psychology and philosophy. Along with Dewey he is known as the father of modern 'pragmatism' (James, 1970): a philosophy first advanced by Charles S. Pierce. James believed psychology had to be founded on empirical biological knowledge, rather than introspection. As a philosopher he argued that truth is something which happens to ideas. Ideas become true, or are made true by events. Ideas are, in a biological sense, the activity which enables human beings to modify their environment in order to survive and develop. James liked to distinguish between 'tough-minded' philosophers, who were alive to empirical knowledge, and the 'tender-minded', who derived their ideas from abstract thinking. The idea of tough-mindedness imbued the emerging social reformers, social scientists and politicians eager to change US public policy in the interwar era. James's brand of 'radical empiricism' was a source of inspiration to a generation of people who believed that it was possible to improve and adapt policies and processes so as to advance the progress of mankind.

John Dewey (1859–1952) was a long-lived and prolific author and reformer. Pragmatism for Dewey was a method of social experiment, a form of trial and error learning (Dewey, 1927, 1963). Democracy as he understood it was an investigative activity in which ideas were exchanged, and society solved problems through learning and testing. He was an enthusiastic advocate of the development of new 'political technologies' which could make a more scientific approach to problem-solving methods of democracy. Lasswell argues:

The policy sciences are a contemporary adaptation of the general approach to public policy that was recommended by John Dewey and his colleagues in the development of American pragmatism.
(*Lasswell, 1971: xiv*)

In recent decades Dewey's ideas about democratic decision-making as a mode of communication and experimentation has been developed in the work of critical theorists such as Richard Rorty, Jürgen Habermas (see below, and 1.9, 2.7.3, 3.9, 3.10.5) and Raskin (Raskin, 1973) as well as in social experimentalists such as Campbell (see 4.5.4).

The pragmatic inheritance of Dewey and James was a call for action and for social science to become involved in the betterment of society and government. This call to a focus on problem-solving was to be a core belief of the policy approach as it was to develop in the post-war period, both in the US and elsewhere.

Rawls and Nozick: two theories of justice

Just when it was felt that it was safe to get back in intellectual waters free from philosophers and largely composed of empirical social science, two philosophers were to create waves across many a think-tank. Rawls and Nozick have provided the greater part of the philosophical discussion about public policy since the 1970s. John Rawls's *A Theory of Justice* (1971) took up the utilitarian interest in welfare and posited a model of justice which involved fairness. Differences could only be accepted if social and economic inequalities were such that they maximized benefits to the least advantaged. Rawls's world demands fairness in outcomes and also in equality of opportunity. People of similar ability should have similar life chances. Critics have seen in Rawls the essence of what lies at the centre of the folly of state intervention, whilst advocates of Rawls's model contend that it provides a philosophical underpinning for better public policy.

Nozick's *Anarchy, State and Utopia* (1974) has been an influential text for the 'new right' in that it provided a powerful critique of the theory and practice of Rawlsian policy-making. Against Rawls's notion of justice as having to do with the distribution of outcomes in a 'fair' way, Nozick argues that distributive justice does not hold much water theoretically or in the real world. Nozick bases his attack on the idea of 'entitlement' and of individual rights. In Nozick's philosophy justice has to do with what people are entitled to, rather than what is fair: a distribution may be just, as everyone is entitled to what they have, but it may not be fair in a distributive sense. Individuals and markets are the only way in a free world in which a society can be organized so as to attain justice. This was a thesis not lost on those who wished to see less public policy and more individual freedom of choice. The Rawls–Nozick argument has in part been responsible for a revival of philosophy which has an application to public policy stretching back to the utilitarians and Dewey. Theorists whose work has also addressed policy issues include Ronald Dworkin, Thomas Nagel, T.M. Scanlon and Bernard Williams.

Karl Popper and the piecemeal engineering model

Popper's contribution to the philosophy of public policy has been twofold. First, at a methodological level he challenged the validity of the Baconian idea of science as induction: the observation of facts from which theories or general laws may be deduced. Secondly, he advocated a method of public policy which aimed to make political decision-making approximate to the scientific approach to problem solving (Popper, 1957; 1976: 72).

Scientific method, he reasoned, did not comprise the logical process of proof, based on the accumulation of 'facts' and evidence, so much as the setting out of conditions in which theories could be falsified. Furthermore, the idea that facts existed independent of theories was also doubtful. Problems, he argued, exist within a structure of knowledge. Thus, he refuted the notion that positivists – such as Bacon – believed: that 'facts' exist separately to existing perceptions, values, theories and solutions.

❖ Which came first?

The problem 'which came first, the hypothesis (*H*) or the observation (*O*)', is soluble; as is the problem, 'Which comes first, the hen (*H*) or the Egg (*E*)'. The reply to the latter is 'An earlier kind of egg'; to the former, 'An earlier kind of hypothesis'. It is quite true that any particular hypothesis we choose will have been preceded by observations ... But these observations, in their turn, presupposed the adoption of a frame of reference: a frame of expectations: a frame of theories.
(*Popper, 1963: 47*) ◆

The implications for empirical social science – and the natural sciences – of this argument were immense. Scientific theories were those which could be 'disproved'. This left social science with a questionable kind of scientific status. Marxism in particular was singled out for criticism on this score because it advanced a theory of history which could not set out those conditions under which it could be shown to be false. General theories of this kind, Popper argued, were dangerous to an open society in that it made claims to having reached a final truth, or knowledge. However, for Popper, knowledge was above all never final. All theories are tentative, and it is of the nature of knowledge to be conjectural. Knowledge progresses by a process which gives rise to tentative theories, subjected to tests of falsifiability, out of which new problems emerge.

$$P_1 \rightarrow TT \rightarrow EE \rightarrow P_2$$

where P = initial problem; TT = tentative theory/trial solution; and EE = error elimination.

Applied to society, what this model suggested to Popper was that social progress did not take place as a result of big or total changes, so much as a cycle of trial and error experimentation: what he terms, following Roscoe Pound, 'piecemeal social engineering' (Popper, 1969: 46, 69, 83). As a model of policy-making it has proved as influential in practical politics as in the philosophy of science. Instead of trying to find laws of society or develop large-scale programmes of reform, politics should be concerned with understanding the limitations of knowledge and human institutions. Popper believed a liberal society (an open society) to be one in which rational argument and adjustment provides the method of governing, rather than Utopian grand schemes, whose record in history is, he argues, invariably tragic and violent.

Figure 1.4   The Popperian 'piecemeal engineering' model

Knowledge of society
is inadequate, imperfect,
tentative
↓
Consequences are unknowable
↓
Consensus is lower the
more comprehensive the
scheme/policy/plan
↓
Thus, small steps: piecemeal
engineering
↓
Learn from
small mistakes

Policy-making as scientific problem-solving therefore had to be infused with a critical, open, experimenting spirit. In policy analysis the leading exponents of this 'Popperian' approach are Donald Campbell and Alice Rivlin. The Popperian method of learning from experience, in a step-by step way, is also a theme of decision theories which emphasize the 'iterative' nature of 'trial and error' approaches (figure 1.4) (see Collingridge, 1992). For critiques of Popper, see Magee (1973: 74–107); Parekh (1982: 124–53); Bobrow and Dryzek (1987: 136–48). On experimentalism, see Rossi and Freeman (1993: 297–329).

Hayek's case for markets and individual choice

The influence of Hayek's theories on public policy has been extensive. However, for the greater part of his life Hayek's reputation was more in the realm of ideas than in policy-making. During the heyday of the 'Keynesian era' his writings on the role of government were somewhat marginal to the way in which policies – in economic and other spheres – were formulated and problems defined. Works such as *The Road to Serfdom* (1944) and *The Constitution of Liberty* (1960), which applied his philosophy and economic theory to politics and government, did not enter into the mainstream of the policy agenda until the late 1970s, in conditions which saw the apparent end of the Keynesian era (Skidelsky, 1977). During this period Hayek became (along with Nozick) one of the leading, if not *the* leading, source of ideas for the emergent 'new right' (Levitas, 1986; Smith, 1979). Another major contribution of Hayek to the policy field was his appreciation of the politics of ideas, and the importance of promoting ideas through organizations. He founded one of the first 'think-tanks' (the Mont Pelerin Society, 1947) and was an inspiration behind the establishment of several influential think-tanks, most notably the Institute of Economic Affairs.

Like Popper, Hayek's framework derived from early work on knowledge. Hayek rejected the logical positivism of his native Vienna, and was critical of the idea that empirical 'objective' knowledge existed or could serve as the basis from which to deduce laws or plan society in a 'scientific' way. Human knowledge was, he argued, so very limited and fragmented that the belief in the ability of the state, government or bureaucracy to aggregate or co-ordinate all the infinite amount of information required to make social decisions or decisions which interfered in the free functioning of individual choice and markets was both erroneous and dangerous. Society is, Hayek argues, not a product of human design, but a spontaneous order. The idea therefore that it is possible, by the application or imposition by government of a theory or policy, to make this order 'better', more efficient or more just, is both epistemologically incorrect and morally wrong. In its extreme form the belief in the capacity of government to acquire knowledge sufficient to direct society and the economy was made manifest in the evils and inefficiency of fascism and communism (Hayek, 1944). However, democratic countries were also easy prey to the belief that public agencies could plan and solve problems. Hayek forecast that, in labouring under the delusion that individuals and markets were incapable of regulating and co-ordinating human decision-making, liberal democracy faced the prospect of being undermined and ultimately destroyed. With the onset of rising inflation and unemployment, and with state spending seemingly out of control in the 1970s, the stage was set for Hayek's theories to have a central part in shaping 'new' policies and redefining 'old' problems.

Perhaps the most important implication of the Hayekian framework for public policy is the notion that government, or policy-makers, cannot 'solve' problems or improve on what would spontaneously arise from the interaction of free individuals and free markets. The role of public policy is therefore viewed as limited to ensuring that this spontaneous order in society and the economy should be allowed to take place without any interference or reduction in free competition. The state should aim to promote personal liberty and free markets, enforce the rule of law so to do, and defend its citizens. The role of public policy is therefore to promote the conditions in which the spontaneous order can function to the advantage of all individuals. Policy-making ought not to be seen as a problem-solving activity, so much as an activity which facilitates personal freedom within the rule of law. And, where policy-making does involve the state, it should not do so by creating a monopoly of provision, but stimulate competition and create the conditions in which market forces can most effectively and efficiently allocate (but not redistribute) resources (on Hayek's ideas, see Gray, 1986; Kukathas, 1989; Plant, 1991).

Etzioni and communitarianism

If the 1960s and 1970s saw the rise and decline of the Rawlsian framework of public policy concerned with fairness of outcomes, and the 1980s the triumph of Hayekian individualism and the market, the latest framework which has come to the fore in the 1990s has been 'communitarianism'. Amongst the major exponents of this philosophy are Walzer (1983), Sandel (ed.) (1984) and Taylor (1985). In the 1990s the arguments of these theorists for a renewal of the idea of community has provided a source for an alternative to the individualism of the 1980s. Reporting on the rise of the idea, Seumas Milne notes:

> Communitarianism can be summed up in two essential ideas. Modern, atomised societies, its supporters argue, have lost a sense of community and social solidarity. The vital social fabric between the state and the individual – everything from voluntary associations and geographical communities to schools, families, churches and trade unions – has withered under the impact of rampant market individualism. It must be protected or rebuilt. In a related ethical thrust, the communitarians believe that selfish liberalism has created an alienated social wasteland, shifting the balance between rights and duties too far in the direction of rights. A new emphasis on individual and mutual responsibility is needed to right the balance, they think, along with a sharper sense of morality and an end to fashionable embarrassment over the distinction between right and wrong ... [It] has the great selling point of being a flexi-philosophy. For the 'modernising' left, it is about solidarity, fraternity and a revival of non-statist 19th century labour movement traditions of mutual self-help, friendly societies, coops and utopian socialism. For the right ... it has its own allure as a new moralising credo, hot on civic pride, social obligation and tradition. ... and the rhetoric of moral education, traditional family values and cracking down on crime ...
> (*The Guardian, 7 October 1994*)

The idea of the 'community' as a response to state centralism and free-market individualism is, of course, by no means new. It has, as Plant observes, frequently been invoked as a critique of liberalism (Plant, 1991: 325). T.H. Green, Bosanquet, Tawney and Raymond Williams, for example, have all emphasized the role of 'community' in counteracting the effects of what Tawney once termed the 'acquisitive society' (Tawney, 1921). Indeed, Nisbet (1974) argues that we may read the development of political and social thought since Greek and Roman times as being preoccupied with the 'search' or 'quest' for community. Thus the concept is by no means the property of the 'left' or 'right'. At a time when industrialized polities confront the problem of finding new forms of governance for more complex 'post-modern' societies, it is not entirely surprising that policy-makers should have recourse to the 'new' rhetoric of 'community'. It has a rich and varied body of theories which look likely to provide a mine of ideas for agenda-setters in the 1990s.

At the forefront of advocating communitarianism as an approach to public policy is Amitai Etzioni (1968, 1993a, 1993b, 1994), whose contribution to the development of the policy approach will be noted elsewhere in this book (see 3.4.4, 3.10.2, 4.4.3, 4.4.8). His formulation of communitarianism as a framework for policy-making has widely influenced thinking in America and Europe. Its appeal lies in pointing towards a middle way between the excesses of state regulation and control, on the one hand, and the reliance on pure market forces on the other. As he explains:

As communitarians see it, a strong but scaled-back core of the welfare state therefore should be maintained. Other tasks, currently undertaken by the state, should be turned over to individuals, families and communities. The philosophical underpinning for this change requires the development of a new sense of both personal and mutual responsibility. But how do we work out which activities should be dealt with at which level of society? By applying the principle of subsidiarity. This says that responsibility for any situation belongs first to those who are nearest to the problem. Only if a solution cannot be found by the individual does responsibility devolve to the family. Only if the family cannot cope should the local community become involved. Only if the problem is too big for it should the state become involved.
(*Etzioni, 1994*)

What this means in policy terms is that there are lines of responsibility: the person at hand; the family; the community; society at large. Public policy, he maintains, should aim to promote and revive those institutions which stand between the individual and the state: family; voluntary organizations; schools; churches; neighbourhoods and communities. Policy-makers must endeavour to change policies so that greater emphasis is placed on personal responsibility, rather than on rights. In particular, he has stressed the role of the family, making divorce harder, and presenting community service and a return to moral values as policies to counteract the growing fragmentation of modern society.

Habermas and communicative rationality

Although an interdisciplinary field, policy analysis has, until comparatively recently, been somewhat narrow in terms of its ideas about the role of reason in human affairs. That is to say, it has been dominated by a belief in the possibilities of rationality in 'solving' problems. This may be observed in its most vivid form in the development of 'rational' utilitarian techniques such as cost-benefit analysis and various forms of operational research and systems analysis (see 3.8). However, this view of rationality has been a focus of concern in the work of German critical theorists, such as Habermas, and French deconstructivists, such as Foucault, who criticize the use of rationality as forms of control and oppression. Such ideas have become an increasingly important source of critical approaches to public policy and policy analysis (see de Haven-Smith, 1988; Hawkesworth, 1988). Habermas in particular has been seen as having a special relevance to the development of a critical policy analysis. In place of the instrumental rationality which is encapsulated in rational analytical techniques, Habermas proposes an alternative model of 'communicative rationality'. As Patsy Healey notes, this idea is seen as offering

a way forward though a different conception of human reason as an informing principle for contemporary societies ... [since] Habermas argues
that far from giving up on reason as an informing principle for contemporary societies, we should shift perspective from an individualized, subject–object conception of reason to reasoning formed within intersubjective
communication. Such reasoning is required where 'living together but
differently' in shared space and time drives us to search for ways of
finding agreement on how to address our collective concerns ... The effort
of constructing mutual understanding as the locus of reasoning activity
replaces the subject-centred 'philosophy of consciousness' which, Habermas
argues, has dominated Western conceptions of reason since the Enlightenment.
(*Healey, 1993: 238–40*)

Reason, in Habermas's sense, is not a logical process concerned with
objective proof or falsifiability, but one which is about 'reaching understanding in a social context' (de Haven-Smith, 1988: 85). Habermas's
ideas have far-reaching implications for both the theory and practice
of public policy. At the theoretical level it suggests the need for a
greater attention to language, discourse and argument. At a practical
level Habermas's theories – such as the 'ideal speech situation' – have
prompted the search for new analytical methods and institutional
processes which may serve to promote an intercommunicative approach to formulating and delivering public policy (see Fischer and
Forester, 1993; Dryzek, 1987, 1990, 1993; and 1.9, 2.7.3, 2.9.2, 3.10.5 and
4.5.4). For the impact of Habermas on public administration and organization theory, see Denhardt (1981a, 1981b); Denhardt and Denhardt
(1979); and Degeling and Colebatch (1984) and 4.5.3 on domination in
organizations.

The 'discovery' of Habermas by students of public policy should (hopefully) lead to a renewed interest in the work of Harold Lasswell,
whose ideas on the role of the policy sciences have much in common
with Habermas's theories (see Bobrow and Dryzek, 1987: 172–4).

1.7   Analysis and the policy process

Analysis has different objectives and relations to the policy process.
Etzioni, who we discussed above, for example, has (successfully) sought
to influence the policy-making process through research and arguments which advocate an analysis not only of the 'problems', but also
what the policy options – or 'solutions' – should be. We may think of
kinds of policy analysis as comprising a range of activity on a spectrum of knowledge in the policy process; knowledge for the policy
process; and knowledge about the policy process. Gordon *et al.* (1977)
definitively set out the varieties along such a continuum (figure 1.5).

Figure 1.5   *Varieties of policy analysis*

Analysis of Policy			Analysis for Policy	
1 Analysis of policy determination	2 Analysis of policy content	3 Policy monitoring and evaluation	4 Information for policy	5 Policy advocacy

Source: Adapted from Gordon et al. (1977)

Analysis of policy

This includes:

- *policy determination*: this is analysis which is concerned with how policy is made, why, when and for whom;
- *policy content*: this may involve a description of a particular policy and how it developed in relation to other earlier policies, or it may be informed by a theoretical/value framework which seeks to offer a critique of policy.

Policy monitoring and evaluation

The focus of such analysis is to examine how policies have performed against policy goals and what impact a policy may have had on a given problem.

Analysis for policy

This encompasses:

- *policy advocacy*: which involves research and arguments which are intended to influence the policy agenda inside and/or outside government;
- *information for policy*: a form of analysis which is intended to feed into policy-making activities. This may take the form of detailed internal/external research or advice of a judgemental or qualitative nature. It may give help in sorting out options or may suggest policy options.

As a term 'policy analysis' is most closely associated with the use of a variety of techniques to improve – or make more rational – the decision making process. Quade (1976: 21), for example, expresses the view that its main purpose is to: ' help a decision-maker make a better choice than he would otherwise have made. It is thus concerned with the more effective manipulation of the real world.' In order to do this analysis proceeds through three stages:

> First, the discovery, attempting to find an alternative that is satisfactory and best among those that are feasible; second acceptance, getting the findings accepted and incorporated into a policy or decision; third, implementation, seeing that the policy decision is implemented without being changed so much that it is no longer satisfactory.
> (Quade, 1976: 254)

Hank Jenkins-Smith (1990) argues that cost-benefit analysis (or CBA: see 3.8.6) constitutes a 'dominant paradigm' of modern policy analysis which:

> makes use of techniques developed in the fields of economics, mathematics, statistics, operations research and systems dynamics, among others to provide decision makers with advice on the formulation of public policy. In applying those techniques, the analyst may draw on knowledge from fields such as sociology, political science, welfare economics, law, organisation theory, physical and biological sciences, and elsewhere ... Despite the apparent cacophony of activities involved in policy analysis, the logic of analysis imposes an order on these activities and bends them to a uniform purpose: to determine which policy (if any) provides the largest net gains in social welfare.
> (Jenkins-Smith, 1990: 11)

Policy analysis in this 'orthodox' sense is therefore concerned with improving the methods by which problems are identified and defined, goals are specified, alternatives evaluated, options selected and performance measured. As such it is a field which focuses on what Bobrow and Dryzek (1987: 16) term 'knowledge based interventions in public policy making'. As students of policy analysis we are concerned with what they define as knowledge: content; production; dissemination; and interpretation. We may translate these into four kinds of question about beliefs or values: who, what, when, and how? *Who* secured *what* values through *what* institutions, and *when* and *how* did it come about?

- **Whose** knowledge is being used? Is it produced by a bureaucracy? Does it come from a research institute? Is it the result of an official inquiry or commission? Is it a form of policy advocacy from a think-tank? Is it knowledge which is produced by experts? Who is using this knowledge? Who is propagating this knowledge (beliefs/ideas/ideology)? Who is constructing knowledge? Whose interpretation/definition won out and whose lost out and whose was not even considered? Who is doing the monitoring and evaluation of policy? Who is doing the informing and disseminating?

Who is included and who is excluded from the policy process? *Whose values predominate?*

- **What** kind of knowledge does it claim to be? Is it presented as a scientific or 'objective' 'fact'? What kind of language is employed? What kind of knowledge is it: qualitative or quantitative? What kinds of experts are involved? What kinds of values, beliefs, ideas, ideologies underpin or inform policy knowledge? What kind of claims are being made for the knowledge? What kind of assumptions about the policy-making process inform those who produce, use and disseminate policy knowledge? What kinds of institutions and elites are involved? *What values predominate?*

- **When** does knowledge come to be produced, propagated and used/ abused or ignored? When was knowledge about a problem constructed? When was a problem 'discovered'? When did knowledge impact on policy-making? When was it made public knowledge? When did it matter? When did the mass media get involved? When did it influence public opinion? When was it used/abused by policy-makers? When do beliefs change? *When do a given set of values predominate?*

- **How** is knowledge used in the policy process? How is it produced? How is knowledge organized in policy communities/networks? How is knowledge organized in government? How is it commissioned? How is it propagated? How does policy advocacy take place? How do arguments win and lose? How is policy determined? How does it impact on public opinion? How do beliefs change? *How do a given set of values predominate?*

To put it another way: *a primary task for the student of public policy is to understand and clarify the discourse or frameworks which structure the analysis of policy problems, content and processes.*

1.8   Models, maps and metaphors

In analysing public policy we need to be able to organize our ideas and concepts. The world is a complex place, and in order to understand this complexity we need to simplify. When we simplify in order to comprehend the multiplicity of factors and forces which shape problems and social processes, we construct models, maps, or think in terms of a metaphor. These constitute frameworks within which and through which we can think and explain. Frameworks may be viewed as having different aims or purposes, although in practice these may be somewhat confused and may overlap:

- *explanatory frameworks* endeavour to show how something happens the way it does. On the one hand, it may claim to be a 'heuristic' model/theory/map; that is, it aims to provide a framework which may be used to explore, a method by which we can learn or investigate a complex problem or process. The notion of policy stages, or a policy cycle itself, is an example of an important 'heuristic' model in policy analysis. On the other hand, a model may lay claim to being 'causal': that it would predict or hypothesize that if x happens, then y will occur. This causal model may be deductive, based upon a series of propositions which may be validated or falsified by evidence; or it may claim to have an inductive basis: that is the theory derives from the empirical study of a given phenomenon;

- *'ideal-type' frameworks* set out the defining characteristics of a phenomenon, by which we can recognize something as belonging to a group of phenomena which share the same properties or criteria. The most famous of the ideal-type frameworks is that advanced by Max Weber when he proposed that we can understand bureaucracy in terms of a set of structural and organizational features;

- *normative frameworks* set out what conditions or arrangements ought to exist if given goals are to be attained. The normative framework is therefore concerned with what ought to be, rather than what is.

When we deploy a framework, therefore, we are imposing a way of thinking about the world; we are creating an order out of what does not have an objective order in itself. As Popper argued, the facts exist in the context of theories, values, beliefs, not independently of them. We begin with theories, models, mental maps, metaphors; and to think analytically about public policy we have to be sensitive to the existence of 'reality' as a construction within a multiplicity of frameworks. The activity of theorizing about public policy is, therefore, like drawing a map: 'they embody what we know and carry us forward toward what we don't know' (Judson, 1980: 109). A map of London, however accurate, is not London. And a map of the policy 'process' (a metaphor) can only ever be a representation of a reality which cannot be 'proved' or 'disproved' in an 'objective' sense. Our frameworks construct what 'problems' or social, economic and political 'processes' mean. The danger is that we are often convinced that our map is 'real' because lots of other people share the same perception (McCaskey, 1991: 139). Witness, for example, a recent statement on one of the more enduring problems of history:

Mona Lisa Atrophy
Two doctors in search of the truth to Mona Lisa's smile said in Lyon yesterday that the person posing for the portrait suffered from muscular atrophy. – AP
(*Guardian*, 26 April 1991)

No doubt had they been chiropodists they would have diagnosed athletes' foot! Antony Jay gives another instance of seeing what you are looking for in a nursery rhyme that we all know and love:

'Pussycat, pussycat, where have you been?'
'I've been to London to see the Queen.'
'Pussycat, pussycat, what did you there?'
'I saw a little mouse under a chair.'

To which Jay observes:

why had the cat not seen the Queen? It might be, of course, that the Queen was not there. But it might be that the Queen was there all the time, sitting on the chair, but the cat, being only a cat, saw nothing except the mouse. After all, if you are only a cat, your eyes are not looking at where the Queen might be, and anyway, your mind is not capable of comprehending anything so great and splendid even if your eyes saw it.
(Jay 1987: 153)

Figure 1.6   The London underground map: the surface of a complex system

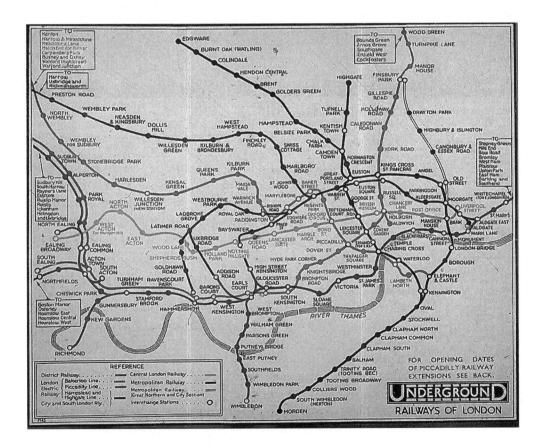

Reproduced by permission of The London Transport Museum

Figure 1.7   The London underground map: Beck's model

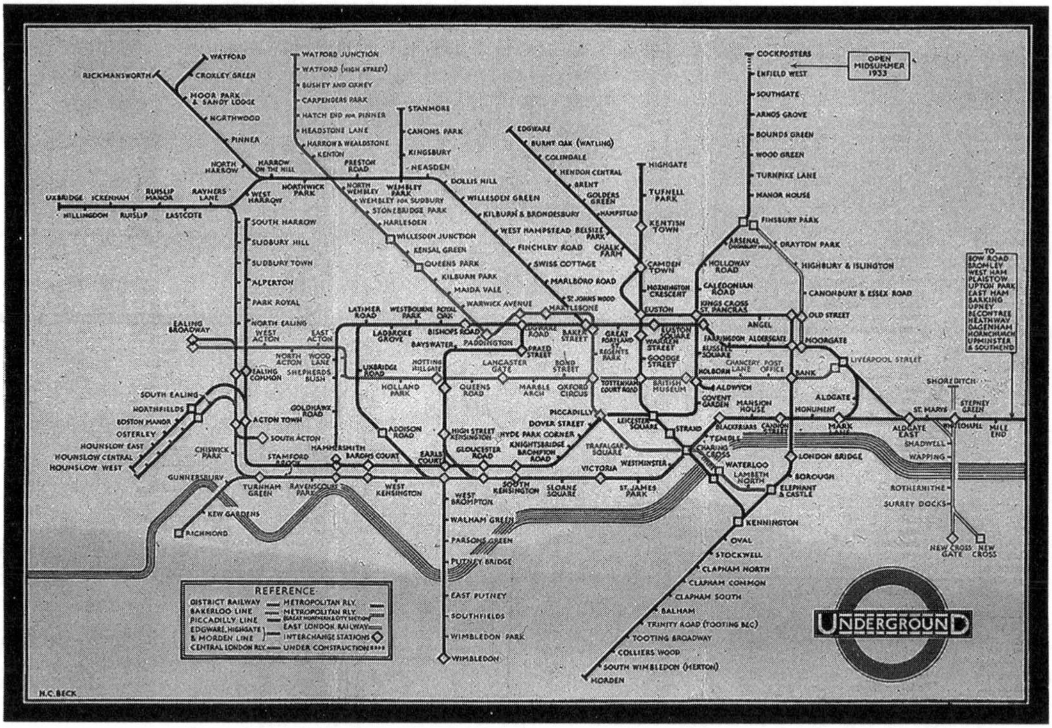

Reproduced by permission of The London Transport Museum

Another illustration will suffice. The cat, no doubt being an environ-mentally friendly cat, used public transport. To find his way to the palace he would have consulted his map of the London Underground. In so doing our cat would be using a very powerful framework for understanding one of the world's largest urban transport systems (see figures 1.6 and 1.7).

London first opened an underground railway system in 1900. By 1910, as the system grew, it became apparent that passengers needed a map so that they could use the system efficiently. The early maps were geographical, that is they showed where the lines actually ran, and the location of the stops (figure 1.6). However, as London Under-ground grew, so the complexity of the system called for a measure of simplification. It was Henry C. Beck, a temporary draughtsman, who realized that the map had to be less realistic and more diagrammatic. At first his sketch was rejected by his superiors, but in 1933 it was decided to give his idea a trial: figure 1.7). The public liked it, and thereafter London's Underground map attained its present form, which has served as a model for other systems all over the world. (Beck, by the way, received only five guineas for his efforts.)

The London Underground map is an example of constructing a map which enables us to use this highly complex system. However, it is more than that. For many, including the author, the map has come to form a mental image of London. It is a useful tool of exploration, but it is not very reliable in terms of facilitating an understanding of the actual system from the point of view of locating tube stations on the surface. The danger for tourist and resident alike is that Beck's map becomes our image of London.

Models and maps in policy-making carry with them the same danger. As Albert Hirschman notes: 'without models, paradigms, ideal types and similar abstractions we cannot even start to think. But cognitive style, that is, the kinds of paradigms we search out, the way we put them together, and the ambitions we nurture for their powers – all this can make a great deal of difference' (Hirschman, 1970a: 338). In seeking to understand the world of policy-making and policy analysis we need ways of thinking, or models. But we must be aware of the danger which the philosopher Alfred North Whitehead expressed as the 'Fallacy of Misplaced Concreteness' (Whitehead, 1925). That is, in trying to make sense of the abstract or of notions we tend to see them as real concrete things when in truth they are derived from human experiences. The way we see and interpret the policy world, as with any other, depends on the kinds of models and frameworks we employ, and with policy analysis we have to be keenly aware of the way in which the mapping of social, economic and other territory takes place: how it comes that people share a map; how and why they hold different maps; the process whereby one map replaces another, and so on. At the same time, a map may claim to be one thing – an explanatory framework – but it may be heavily prescriptive or normative. Its picture of what is, is drawn to deduce a model of what ought to be; or, a normative theory may lay claim to being based upon an empirical investigation.

❖ Using models

Models of decision-making: Graham Allison

One of the most important contributions to the analysis of decision-making was made by Graham Allison in a study of the 1962 Cuban missile crisis: *The Essence of Decision* (1971). Since its publication the book has continued to have a place in the reading lists of students of both public policy and international relations. Allison's study seeks to show how different 'lenses' provide very different kinds of interpretation of the events which brought the world to the edge of nuclear war. He suggests that we view the crisis through three models or lenses:

- *Rational actor*: This lens focuses on decision-making by 'national government' as about goals, options, consequences and choice.
- *Organizational process*: The organizational lens focuses on the organizations which compose national government, and how these organizations perceive and deal with problems.
- *Bureaucratic politics*: This lens focuses on national government as composed of players with goals, interests, stakes and stands. Decision-making is framed in terms of the power relations and bargaining processes which take place.

These lenses provide three 'cuts' through the crisis which illustrate that each paradigm provides a different version of why events took place in the way they did. They provide more than simple 'angles of vision':

> Each conceptual framework consists of a cluster of assumptions and categories that influence what the analyst finds puzzling, how he formulates his question, where he looks for evidence, and how he produces an answer.
> (*Allison, 1971: 245*)

The choice of framework, or lens, produces 'different explanations of the same happenings' and different judgements about what is important and what is not important (ibid.: 25)

Allison's book has been widely criticized on methodological and empirical grounds (Bendor and Hammond, 1992; Steve Smith, 1981). Not the least of these criticisms relates to the issue of the assumptions which frame each of the models, the logical consistency of the models, and the conclusions which he derives from the models. Clearly, in analysing the Cuban missile crisis in terms of just three models Allison was over-simplifying what was a highly complex decision-making process. Furthermore, as Weiss points out, the Cuban missile crisis is not perhaps the best case study from which to analyse even more complex circumstances:

> The image of decision-making represented ... in the Cuban missile crisis is inappropriate to most of daily bureaucratic life. Much more commonly, each person takes some small step ... that has seemingly small consequences. Over a period of time, these small steps foreclose alternative courses of action and limit the range of the possible. Almost imperceptibly a decision has been made, without anyone's awareness that he or she was deciding.
> (*Carol Weiss, quoted in Lindblom, 1990: 276*)

Nevertheless, the continued use of Allison's book by teachers and researchers in many fields is indicative that the real strength of the study is in showing how the analysis of decision-making involves an awareness of the frames which are employed to interpret events. Reality is not just out there. The analysis of decision-making involves an awareness of the way in which a decision process exists in the context of a variety of contending interpretations.

Metaphors of organization: Gareth Morgan
Morgan (1986) is a more recent example of the use of frameworks – or metaphors – to explore and understand organizations. He makes the point that organizations are many things at the same time, and given the metaphor we employ, our understanding of organizations will vary considerably:

We use metaphor whenever we attempt to understand one element of experience in terms of another ... By using different metaphors to understand the complex and paradoxical character of organizational life, we are able to manage the design of organizations in ways we may not have thought possible.
(*Morgan, 1986: 13*)

Morgan suggests that we can imagine organizations as:

* machines;
* organisms;
* brains;
* cultures;
* political systems;
* psychic prisons;
* flux and transformation;
* instruments of domination.

Models of organization: markets, hierarchies and networks
A frequently used framework is that of viewing organizations in terms of three models: markets; hierarchies or bureaucracies; and networks or communities. These define three different approaches to the study of 'social co-ordination' (Thompson *et al.*, 1991: 3). Colebatch and Larmour (1993) prefer to use the terms 'bureaucratic' for hierarchy, and 'community' to include the concept of 'network'. They argue that the organizing principles of each model are:

* incentives, and prices for the 'market' model;
* rules, authority and hierarchy for the 'bureaucratic' model;
* norms, values, affiliations and networks for the 'community' model.

Figure 1.8   Thinking in terms of organizational models

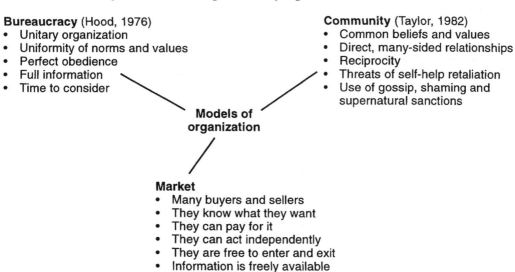

Bureaucracy (Hood, 1976)
* Unitary organization
* Uniformity of norms and values
* Perfect obedience
* Full information
* Time to consider

Community (Taylor, 1982)
* Common beliefs and values
* Direct, many-sided relationships
* Reciprocity
* Threats of self-help retaliation
* Use of gossip, shaming and supernatural sanctions

Models of organization

Market
* Many buyers and sellers
* They know what they want
* They can pay for it
* They can act independently
* They are free to enter and exit
* Information is freely available
* No costs in making and keeping agreements

Source: Adapted from Colebatch and Larmour (1993: 23)

They put forward a framework which we have adapted in figure 1.8.

In order to illustrate how these models may be applied, they select three policy areas: youth homelessness; HIV/AIDS; and broadcasting. They show how each of these may be approached both analytically and normatively or prescriptively from the standpoint of the three models. In the case of youth homelessness, for example, they show how each model generates different definitions of what the problem 'is' and how the problem may be approached at an organizational level.

The concepts may also be used to account for changing forms of policy-making and governance. We may, for instance, read the development of public policy-making in terms of 'bureaucracy' as a response to market failure, and the growth of 'market'-based public policy as a response to the percieved failure of bureaucratic modes of public policy-making and implementation. Network forms may be interpreted as a manifestation of a 'post-modern' capitalism, and of growing complexity in patterns of policy-making. 'Community' forms of organization may be seen as alternatives to both market and hierarchical forms of public policy.

Readings
On bureaucracy, see: G. Thompson, *et al.* (eds), *Markets, Hierarchies and Networks*, 1991.
H. Colebatch and P. Larmour, *Markets, Bureaucracy and Community*, 1993.
J. Kooiman (ed.), *Modern Governance*, 1993.
S.R. Clegg, *Modern Organisations*, 1990.
M. Weber, *From Max Weber*, 199).
C.C. Hood, *The Limits of Administration*, 1976.
D. Beetham, 'Models of bureaucracy', 1991.

On policy networks and communities, see 1.9; 2.10.

On the mixing of models, see 4.4.1.

On Hayek and Etzioni (markets and community), see 1.6.

On community and the voluntary sector, see 4.4.3. ◆

Choosing and evaluating

Public policy is a field rich in different approaches, academic disciplines, models (heuristic and causal), metaphors and maps. What is involved in choosing, evaluating or 'testing' frameworks?

The first point to make is that the policy orientation, as it developed from Lasswell onwards, is one which accepts that public policy and the problems with which it is concerned do not exist in neat, tidy, academic boxes. The problems which confront us as citizens or as policy makers or shapers exist as many things at once. Unemployment, for example, is an economic issue, a sociological issue, a psychological issue, a geographical issue, a medical issue, and so on. In analysing the causes, effects and policy options for this issue, academic disciplines and boundaries bring specialist knowledge and expertise on what is a whole problem. Therefore, the aim of the policy approach is not to pull these issues apart, so much as to recognize how problems come to be addressed and structured by the way in which knowledge is organized and deployed. The policy focus recognizes the multidimensionality and multidisciplinary nature of problems, and that consequently and inevitably the study of policy-making and policy analysis is essentially multiframed.

The primary task therefore of policy analysis is, as Lasswell defined it, to understand how problems and processes may be contextualized. As we have seen earlier, from a Popperian viewpoint social knowledge is not 'falsifiable' in a 'scientific' sense. In public policy we confront knowledge about problems or the policy process which cannot be 'disproved': social 'facts' are bundles of values. For Bacon and other positivists the matter was, of course, much simpler: given enough facts, figures and theories could change the world. What Popper demonstrated was that inductivism was an inadequate basis for both science and social reform.

When it comes to evaluating theories, therefore, there are a range of approaches on a continuum:

- we can choose between theories on the basis of testing them against empirical evidence or research (a positivist or behaviouralist position); or
- we can argue that there is no possible way of choosing one theory or another; all theories are equal in that they are social constructions (a relativist position).

Along this continuum we can plot various positions relative to these extremes. We may, for example, argue that the behaviouralist position is such that it only takes account of what can be observed, or empirically studied. Thus, although a behaviouralist (such as Dahl) might argue that empirical research demonstrates the validity of his hypothesis about power, anti-behaviouralists (such as Bachrach and Baratz) might claim that all research has done is to use evidence about power that can be seen, measured, observed. This ignores the fact that there are other aspects of power which cannot be so readily observed. At the other end of the continuum, if we argue that all theories are equal, we are left with the problem of how to make a choice. We cannot say every theory is right when they argue very different, opposite or incommensurate cases.

One answer to this dilemma is provided by Rein (1976), who argues that theories may be understood as being like 'stories'. We can compare theories in terms of how 'plausible' we think the story told by a theory is, either in itself or in comparison with rival stories. In Rein's view we could look at the extent to which the story of a problem or a process is believable. A story may, like a metaphor, work well in one context or situation, but not in another. Or we may consider that a theory is plausible in parts, but does not tell the whole story. We may consider that a story-teller is plausible up to a point at which the account no longer provides a satisfactory picture of what a social or any other problem is about, or how a decision was made. In this way we might envisage different theories as tools rather than as total explanations. For example, the story told by public choice theory may have plausibility, but its account of human motivation as interest maximization through budget size may be less plausible than other stories of human motivation. A framework is adopted, but parts of the story are modified in accordance with a more plausible version of how bureaucrats behave (see, for example, Dunleavy, 1991).

The problem with this idea of plausible stories is that we need to have some criteria of plausibility. Paris and Reynolds (1983), for instance, offer an account of theory choice as something which involves the analysis of 'rational ideologies' – a term neatly capturing the notion that theories are frames of values and beliefs which claim to be the result of rational inquiry. They suggest that the criteria by which we can evaluate a theory are:

- coherence;
- congruence;
- cogency.

Greenaway et al. (1992: 214) propose a similar list of things to check out:

- coherence;
- consistency;
- comprehensiveness;
- parsimony.

In other words, we may evaluate a model, theory, metaphor or map in terms of the quality of its arguments. The evaluation has greater similarity to the way in which we judge a case or evidence submitted in a court of law than to a test done in a laboratory (see 2.7.3). Our focus is not 'proof' or 'truth', so much as how arguments are used or the case is made. We might ask of a model:

- Does it make sense?
- Does it hold together?
- Is it consistent with available evidence?
- How much does it explain?
- Does it convince us?
- Does it add to our understanding?
- Does it say anything different to any other existing theory?

Having said that our models, maps and metaphors are not testable in a Baconian way, and that choosing between rival approaches or theories is fraught with difficulties, the question may arise as to why we should study public policy by the use of frameworks in the first place. Why not simply content ourselves with an historical approach? It is true that historical approaches to public policy have great strengths; not least, the way in which a detailed picture of what happened and why can be built up. Examples abound of where historical accounts provide comprehensive, coherent explanations of a problem or a policy (see Castles (ed.), 1989; Parsons, 1988; Vinovskis, 1988). Furthermore, as Fee and Fox (1988: 1–2) point out, the study of problems and policy from a historical perspective can throw great light on present issues and policy options. However, policy analysis is predicated on the idea that problems and policies need contextuality (Lasswell, 1951b). Theories are a vital dimension of this contextuality. As Popper argued, to see facts existing outside frameworks of values and beliefs is to commit the same error as crude Baconian inductivism. We do not start with facts, we start with theories: 'without theories we cannot even begin' (Popper, 1976: 59). Although the models and metaphors of public policy are not testable in a 'scientific' sense, they provide a way in which the values, assumptions and beliefs which frame the analysis of problems and processes can be made clear and open to critical understanding. However, and this is a big however, as Kuhn argues (p. 69) the danger is that our models do not provide us with paths to better theory and practice, but with narrow, confining prisons.

1.9 Paradigms lost and found: shifts in the focus and frameworks of policy analysis

The focus of the 'policy orientation' has shifted over the years to the extent that nowadays, as is the case with most areas of academic research and teaching, the subject is far more methodologically and philosophically diverse than it was in the past. Three key aspects of this changing approach to the theory and practice of policy analysis may be noted: the disillusionment with positivism and the behavioural approach; an enthusiasm for markets and management ideas and techniques; and the development of new models of the policy process.

The disillusionment with positivism

❖ Background notes

The Enlightenment inheritance
This is the notion which predominated in western society from the age of Newton and Bacon and the French Enlightenment that there was something called 'facts' out there which could be studied empirically. It was possible to know the world in an objective sense and to change it.

Positivism
A movement which began with the French philosopher Auguste Comte (1798–1857); and earlier, in the ideas of Bacon, who believed in the application of science to human affairs. What was real was held to be what could be subjected to empirical investigation. Positivism was highly influential in the development of social science in the nineteenth and twentieth centuries.

Logical positivism
In the 1920s a group of philosophers based in Vienna propounded the theory of logical positivism. Beliefs, they maintained, should only be founded on what could be firmly established by empirical method.

Key texts
For reviews of positivist and post-positivist influences on public policy and policy analysis, see:

B. Fay, *Social Theory and Political Practice*, 1975.
M. Hawkesworth, *Theoretical Issues in Policy Analysis*, 1988.
L. de Haven-Smith, *Philosophical Critiques of Policy Analysis*, 1988. ◆

The early development of the policy approach was rooted in the assumptions of positivism. As Amy argued in 1984:

> positivist methodologies continue to dominate in policy analysis despite the fact that their intellectual foundations were undermined at least a decade ago. Positivism survives because it limits, in a way that is politically convenient, the kinds of questions that analysis can investigate. Moreover, the aura of science and objectivity that surrounds positivist policy analysis adds to the image of the policy analyst as an apolitical technocrat. (*Amy, quoted in Heineman* et al., *1990: 23*)

A particularly important source of criticism of the positivism which has dogged policy analysis came from the arguments which emerged regarding the nature of scientific investigation and theoretical change. As we noted earlier, Karl Popper's ideas about scientific knowledge and the 'open society' laid the basis for the idea that, at best, policy-making could approximate to 'piecemeal social engineering'. Popper argued that science was essentially not defined by its capacity to test theories by proving them, so much as by falsifying them. In 1962 Thomas Kuhn, although agreeing with Popper's critique of positivism as not comprehending facts as forms of value, took issue with the idea of falsifiability as the hallmark of scientific method. Kuhn suggested that, far from science being an activity in which scientists sought to falsify their theories, the scientific community exhibited in practice a deep reluctance to relinquish theories until a crisis forced them to switch or shift 'paradigms'. The real world of science did not go about trying to disprove theories, as Popper maintained. In the real world, theories were not subjected to falsification so much as to a normal science of puzzle-solving. Theories were in many senses ideologies. Scientists were prone to be prisoners of their frameworks, until a revolution set them free.

❖ Kuhn's approach to understanding theoretical change

In the course of instructing non-scientists in the theory and practice of scientific research, Kuhn became fascinated by the relationship between the theory – or ideal – of research and its actual practice. His book *The Structure of Scientific Revolutions* (1962) was to have a massive influence on how people talked about theories and theoretical change in practically every academic subject. His main argument was that all theories are 'paradigms'. The study of knowledge could be approached by looking at how these frameworks of thinking and research come to dominate an area and establish a 'normal science'. The normal science structures thought and how we see problems, until a crisis leads us to abandon the framework and move into another paradigm.

Thus understanding the growth of knowledge involves the analysis of:

PARADIGM → NORMAL SCIENCE → REVOLUTION → PARADIGM

For Kuhn, although he disagrees with Popper over the nature and logic of scientific revolutions, shares his view of observation being embedded in theories. Kuhn sees science as an activity driven by paradigms which dominate how observations and research are conducted. Such paradigms are essentially a community of researchers which largely determines the 'normal science'. Some consider him to be saying that science is in this sense ideological. Theories are accepted because of the power of the paradigm and the scientific consensus. A revolution occurs when there is a crisis in the paradigm, and then a shift from one to another takes place. He has characterized this process as akin to a Gestalt: we see a rabbit then we see a duck!

See T.S. Kuhn, *The Structure of Scientific Revolutions*, 1962. ◆

The impact of this theory on the policy sciences in general was profound and prompted many to rethink what was involved in theories and models: could they be disproved, in an 'objective', 'positivist' sense? Were theories in social science theories in a Popperian sense, since we could not 'falsify' them? Or could theories, models and frameworks exist in relation to one another in ways which meant that, as social scientists, we confront a reality which 'exists' in the context of a multiplicty of frames or paradigms? Were all frames simply relative? On what basis could we say one paradigm was 'right' and another 'wrong'? Furthermore, if social knowledge was not composed of 'facts' so much as versions of reality, what role should/could analysis of poverty, health, unemployment and so on, have in the political process? Was all knowledge equal, and simply 'an argument' within a given framework?

The ideas of Popper, Kuhn and others regarding the nature of science and knowledge signal the dawn of a post-positivist era in which the old certainties about the uses and status of facts and theories began to look less and less sustainable. Several commentators expressed doubts about policy analysis as offering a basis of more 'rational'/'scientific' decision-making. On the one hand, the Popperian idea that experimentation should be the basis of policy-making, rather than big unscientific/non-falsifiable theories was developed in Campbell's metaphor of the 'experimenting society' (1969, 1973, 1981, 1982). On the other hand, students of public policy more influenced by the position adopted by Kuhn – and subsequently Habermas – developed an approach which emphasized how reality had to be conceptualized as being framed by competing paradigms (Landau, 1977; Rein, 1976; Rein and Schön, 1993; Rein, 1983; Fischer and Forester, 1993; Stone, 1988) (see 2.7).

Another important influence on the shift away from a positivist view of public policy was 'constructivism', important sources of which are to be found in the so-called 'constructivist' approach to social problems (Becker, 1963; Spector and Kitsuse, 1977; Henshel, 1990) (see 2.2.1) and the exposition of the theory that reality is socially constructed, rather than an 'objective reality', that was developed by sociologists Berger and Luckman in 1966. Subsequently, due to the impact of the theories of the French philosopher Foucault and German critical thought, most notably that of Habermas, public policy was increasingly informed by theories which stressed the need to analyse politics and policy as modes of discourse which structure reality. A leading exponent of this view in public policy, whose work is highly accessible, is Murray Edelman (1964, 1977, 1988) (see 2.9).

Guba proposes that we may understand the current state of social science inquiry in terms of four paradigms.

❖ Paradigms of inquiry

Egon G. Guba (ed.), *The Paradigm Dialog*, 1990

Guba sets out four main 'paradigms' employed in social inquiry:

- positivism;
- post-positivism;
- critical theory;
- constructivism.

He contrasts (a) their ontology (what is regarded as the nature of 'reality'); (b) their epistemology (what is the relationship between knowledge and the knower) and (c) their methodology (how knowledge should be found out).

Positivism
(a)   Reality exists and is driven by laws of cause and effect which we can know.
(b)   Inquiry can be free of value.
(c)   Hypotheses can be empirically tested

Post-positivism
(a)   Reality exists, but cannot be fully understood or explained. There is a multiplicity of causes and effects.
(b)   Objectivity is an ideal, but requires a critical community.
(c)   It is critical of experimentalism, and stresses qualitative approaches, theory and discovery.

Critical theory
(a)   Reality exists, but cannot be fully understood or explained. There is a multiplicity of causes and effects.
(b)   Values mediate inquiry.
(c)   Proposes the elimination of false consciousness and facilitates and participates in transformation.

Constructivism
(a)   Realities exist as mental constructs and are relative to those who hold them.
(b)   Knowledge and the knower are part of the same subjective entity. Findings are the result of the interaction.
(c)   Identifies, compares and describes the various constructions that exist (hermeneutical and dialectical). ◆

In the light of this situation in which policy analysis no longer is seen as a simple 'positivist' business, where does this leave our notion of knowledge? Yvonna Lincoln (1990: 84–5) argues that what needs to be abandoned is the view that knowledge about social and other problems is like a collection of building blocks:

> It is quite possible that knowledge is more circular or amoebalike, or that knowledge exists in clumps of understanding, with different kinds of knowledge taking different shapes ... We simply do not have the metaphors we need for conceiving of knowledge in any other way but hierarchic, pyramidal, or taxonomic ... It may be that, if some forms of knowledge exist in clumps, or in non-hierarchic organization, we ought to be talking not about 'building blocks of science' but about extended sophistication, or the artistic and expressive process of creatively conjoining elements in ways that are fresh and new.

Lincoln believes that this requires linking and bridging between areas of knowledge. And this theme of the need for an intermediate or linking level of analysis is a common one in policy studies, where the number of knowledge 'clumps' is larger than in many other fields of inquiry. In Part Two of the book ('Meso analysis') we shall examine a variety of ideas which provide links and bridges between different approaches to the definition of problems and the formation of policy agendas.

If we accept the arguments of post-positivists and post-modernists, big theories and meta languages exist as multiple versions of reality. In which case, it could be argued, we should abandon the use of paradigms, models and theories and recognize that we do not know anything. However, this carries with it many dangers. As Harvey (1992: 116–17) observes:

> Post-modernist philosophers tell us not only to accept but even to revel in the fragmentations and the cacophony of voices through which the dilemmas of the modern world are understood. Obsessed with deconstructing and delegitimating every form of argument they encounter, they can end in only condemning their own validity claims to the point at which nothing remains of any basis for reasoned action. Post-modernism has us accepting the reifications and partitionings, actually celebrating the activity of masking and cover-up, all the fetishisms of locality, place or social grouping, while denying that kind of meta theory which can grasp economic processes ... that are becoming ever more universalising in their depth.

A post-positivist interpretation of policy analysis, if taken to the point of saying that we can dispense with paradigms, results in actually ignoring political and economic realities. In using theories and articulating different ways of seeing policy-making and policy outcomes this book is acknowledging that there is fragmentation in public policy;

there are many schools of thought; but in so recognizing this pluralism we also recognize the necessity of making the paradigms and
viewpoints clearer.

Contemporary views of scientific theories which derive from Popper
are therefore radically different from the simplistic Baconian worldview
in which facts and values, observation and theory were clearly and
boldly defined and bricks of knowledge could be laid on top of each
other. The impact of new discoveries in particle physics, following on
from those of quantum mechanics, give us a very different picture
framework for the use of theories in the social sciences. The ideas of
Geoffrey Chew, for example, suggest that there are no fundamental
laws or constants in the universe, and that everything exists in an
interrelated web. No one theory is adequate to explain such complex
processes, and thus we have to accept a more pluralistic approach to
models and theories. Chew argues that 'bootstrapping' is the process
in which we hold on to models and theories with which we disagree
as well as those with which we agree. 'A physicist who is able to view
any number of different partially successful models without favourit-
ism is automatically a bootstrapper' (Chew, 1970: 27; see also Chew,
1968; Capra, 1985). What is significant to the bootstrapper is understanding the differences which exist between and within approaches,
because the world is far too complex to be pressed into one explanatory box.

In this book we consider policy analysis to be essentially a bootstrapping activity. No one theory or model is adequate to explain the
complexity of the policy activity of the modern state. The analyst
must accept the pluralistic nature of the inquiry, both in terms of the
interdisciplinary quality of investigation and the need for a hermeneutic
tolerance of diversity. The analysis of public policy therefore involves
an appreciation of the network of ideas, concepts and words which
form the world of explanation within which policy-making and analysis takes place. This book is written within the context of post-positivist and constructionist conceptions of policy analysis. That is to say, it
considers policy analysis as made of multiple constructions of the
policy process and of the problems that policy-makers address. When
we analyse public policy we are seeking to understand the modes of
thinking and 'maps' which structure analysis of and for 'processes'
and 'problems'.

The world of policy analysts is now composed of a variety of different
attitudes and beliefs about what knowledge for the policy-making
process or knowledge about policy-making actually means. For example, those who are involved in the use of so-called rational policy

analysis may well be highly 'positivist' in their concept of knowledge: the world is a knowable place; facts are 'out there'; costs and benefits can be calculated; performance can be measured. At the other end of the spectrum, policy analysts working in the context of a 'critical' or 'post-modern' framework may take the view that there are no such things as objective 'facts' 'out there', and measurement and calculation of costs and benefits and performance are highly suspect. At the level of policy advocacy, analysts who believe themselves to have knowledge of a whole problem or society as a whole, may campaign for large-scale, comprehensive change. However, those who do not believe that such knowledge of a 'holistic' kind is possible may argue for policy which is piecemeal and experimental. An analyst working in the context of critical theory of knowledge (derived from Habermas) may advocate a model of intervention which involves a clash of different constructions and frameworks so as to realize a more 'ideal speech situation'. However, this said, there is a real danger that in acknowledging 'post-modern' critiques of knowledge we end up in adopting an attitude towards the public and its problems which is wholly negative and defeatist. As Popay and Williams argue (1994a: 10):

> Those who spend time pondering the contours of 'high modernity' ... may smile, shrug their shoulders, and murmer, 'C'est la vue post-moderne'. Those who spend their working lives at the intersections of theory, research, policy and practice have no such escape. And amongst those for whom the closure of a ward, an accident emergency department, or a whole hospital means something more than the deconstruction of a discursive practice, these questions will have continuing and urgent relevance.

As we shall see, critical theories do not have to lead into such a dead end. A number of policy analysts have, in recent years, shown how the ideas of Habermas, Foucault and others can be deployed to devise an approach to public problems which although it rejects the positivist inheritance, believes that knowledge can serve to improve and ameliorate the human condition – but not in the way suggested by positivist social science. (see, for example, Fischer and Forester, 1993; Dryzek, 1990).

The changing focus of policy analysis in large part has been to do with the changing status of 'positivist' ways of thinking and the change in attitudes towards the nature and value of 'empirical' approaches. In the post-war era, public policy grew out of a highly positivistic ethos. To know was to govern, or reform. This was an attitude which had come to the fore in various nineteenth-century reformist movements (such as the Fabians in Britain), and in John F. Kennedy's Camelot, when the possibilities of using knowledge and expertise to govern rationally and solve problems was, when allied to the spectacular growth in information technology and science in the post-war era, a powerfully attractive idea. The emergence of the 'policy sciences' in the 1960s was the most manifest demonstration of a new-found faith in science as offering the basis for solving all those problems which had defied the wit of previous generations. However, notwithstanding all the knowledge which was available to policy-makers, governments in industrial societies seemed to be no better as 'problem-solvers' than their predecessors. Indeed, in seeking to solve problems armed with new knowledge, many argued, especially on the 'new right', that policy-makers were just making matters worse. As the belief in experts and government faltered in the 1970s, so a new faith in the old-time religion developed.

The enthusiasm for markets and management

Policy analysis and management have had a close affinity since the 1960s when, as we observed earlier, the Kennedy–Johnson period witnessed the growing influence of management techniques in government. During the 1960s the focus of both policy analysis (concerned with making government more rational) and the study of the policy process (which was also concerned with how rational policy-making was, or could be) was decision-making. That is to say, the focus was on how decisions come to be made – by an elite, or pluralistically, rationally or incrementally – and how decision-making could be improved through the deployment of new techniques.

In the 1960s, the primary focus was undoubtedly the issue of power; on the one hand this involved the study of how decision-making took place; on the other, it was a focus which was framed by the belief in improving the capacity of government to do things and 'solve' problems. Thus at one level it was concerned with the equality or lack of equality in the input side of the political process (the debate about pluralism/elitism: see 3.3.1/2) and at another it involved a debate about the rational capabilities of government (the Simon–Lindblom argument: see 3.4.3/4).

In the 1970s, however, the focus of analysis began to shift, as the problems of so-called 'overloaded' government became apparent, and the failure to implement policy became more evident. The decisional/input paradigm gave way to a new focus on the implementation/withinput issues. The decisional/input paradigm was concerned about such questions as: Who had power? What was power? Who was involved in decision-making and who was excluded? and, Could decision-making be more rational, or was it doomed to be incrementalist? The implementation/withinput paradigm which developed in the 1970s, on the other hand, became more concerned with such questions as: Why was implementation so difficult? How do bureaucrats and professionals behave? Was top-down implementation more effective than bottom-up? and, How could implementation be improved? Although the issues which these paradigms addressed were different, it might be argued that they were really part of the same paradigm: a framework which believed that public policy involved problem-solving by government.

In the 1980s, however, a radical challenge to these approaches was to have a formative impact on the theory and practice of public policy. It came in two forms: the first was that of public-choice economics which posited that public policy *qua* state or bureaucratic intervention made problems worse, rather than actually solving them. By interfering in markets and by allowing bureaucrats to have too much power, policy-makers only served to make matters worse. This anti-statist argument found its most famous champions in the Reagan and Thatcher administrations, but was also taken up by governments of a variety of ideological predispositions (see Martin, 1993).

This shift in economic orientation is associated with the so-called 'supply-side' and 'monetarist' revolutions in which 'government was best which governed least', and the belief that markets were more efficient at making decisions than bureaucrats and politicians. The rise of public-choice theory as justification – if not an explanation – of cutting back government and expanding markets was such that in the 1980s and 1990s it became a core public policy theory (Self, 1993). In addition to this, students and practitioners of public policy also became enamoured of using models and techniques developed in the private sector to analyse and reform the public sector. Thus, alongside the growth of market-orientated approaches to the role of government in relation to society and the economy, there also took place a shift towards viewing public administration as a form of public management (Rainey, 1990; Massey, 1993).

New models of the policy process

The belief that bureaucratic pyramidical hierarchies were no longer adequate to the task of policy-making in modern society has not been confined to those who advocate normative theories of markets as more effective and efficient than government. Those who wished to develop models which sought to explain how modern policy-making actually worked were equally disenchanted with so-called 'iron-triangle' conceptualizations of policy-making in modern society as something which should be studied in terms of the relationship between government and administration, legislatures and interest groups. Thus one of the features of approaches to policy-making in the 1980s and 1990s has been the attempts to break away from the Eastonian black box and the iron triangle and formulate models whose new metaphors are those of policy 'networks' and 'communities' (see, for example, Heclo, 1978; Benson, 1982; Rhodes, 1988; Sabatier and Jenkins-Smith (eds), 1993). On the other hand, the 'new' models have also incorporated an older approach. As we noted above in respect of Gabriel Almond *et al.* (1993), for the greater part of the post-war period the role of institutions in political science, sociology and economics was somewhat neglected by model-builders. However, in the 1980s a growing interest developed in the way in which institutions shape policy-making and policy outcomes (see 2.11.6, 3.6).

The new network metaphors and the rediscovery of institutions conveys much of the nature of the change in public policy over the last decade and more: it is an infinitely more diverse, multiframed field than in it was in the period from Lasswell (1951b) to the late 1970s.

1.10   Stages and cycles: mapping the policy process

Despite the fact that there has been a growing unease with the dominant framework of policy analysis, rational decision-making, the policy

Figure 1.9   The policy life cycle

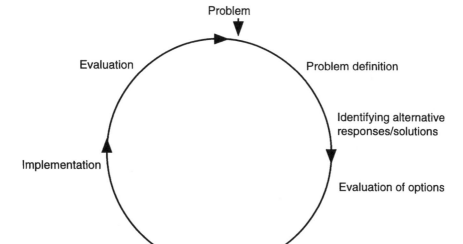

cycle or stagist approach continues to be the basis for both the analysis of the policy process and of analysis in/and for the the policy process. By the 1970s and 1980s a variety of stages were put forward to map the policy process which involved the kind of formulations represented in figure 1.9.

In the late 1970s the concept of the policy cycle was reviewed in a collection of papers edited by May and Wildavsky (1978). This volume constitutes a main source for those who wish to examine the concept in more depth. In the box below we set out some of the cycles which have served to structure the analysis of the policy process.

❖ Policy/decision stages defined

H.A. Simon, *Administrative Behaviour*, 1947.

- Intelligence
- Design
- Choice

H.D. Lasswell, *The Decision Process*, 1956.

- Intelligence
- Promotion
- Prescription
- Invocation
- Application
- Termination
- Appraisal

R. Mack, *Planning and Uncertainty*, 1971.

- Deciding to decide: problem recognition
- Formulating alternatives and criteria
- Decision Proper
- Effectuation
- Correction and Supplementation

R. Rose, 'Comparing public policy', 1973.

- Public recognition of the need for a policy to exist
- How issues are placed on the agenda of public controversy
- How demands are advanced
- The form of government involved in policy-making
- Resources and constraints
- Policy decisions

- What determines governmental choice
- Choice in its context
- Implementation
- Outputs
- Policy evaluation
- Feedback

W. Jenkins, *Policy Analysis: A Political and Organisational Perspective*, 1978.

- Initiation
- Information
- Consideration
- Decision
- Implementation
- Evaluation
- Termination

B.W. Hogwood and L.A. Gunn, *Policy Analysis for the Real World*, 1984.

- Deciding to decide (issue search or agenda-setting)
- Deciding how to decide (issue filtration)
- Issue definition
- Forecasting
- Setting objectives and priorities
- Options analysis
- Policy implementation, monitoring and control
- Evaluation and review
- Policy maintenance, succession, and termination ◆

The 'stagist' model or the 'textbook approach' (Nakamura, 1987) is not without its critics (Stone, 1989; Nakamura, 1987; Lindblom and Woodhouse, 1993; Sabatier and Jenkins-Smith (eds), 1993) who argue that it creates an artificial view of policy-making. The real world, critics maintain, is far more complicated and not composed of tidy, neat steps, phases or cycles. The idea of dividing up policy-making in such a way greatly overstates the rational nature of policy-making and gives a false picture of a process which is not a conveyor belt in which agenda-setting takes place at one end of the line and implementation and evaluation occurs at the other. Sabatier and Jenkins-Smith (1993: 1–4) set out five major criticisms which may be made of the heuristic approach used in the textbook paradigm:

- it does not provide any causal explanation of how policy moves from one stage to another;
- it cannot be tested on an empirical basis;

- it characterizes policy-making as essentially 'top-down', and fails to take account of 'street-level' and other actors;
- the notion of a policy cycle ignores the real world of policy-making which involves multiple levels of government and interacting cycles;
- it does not provide for an integrated view of the analysis of the policy process and analysis (knowledge, information, research) which is used in the policy process. Policy analysis does not just take place in the 'evaluation' phase.

The present author shares the concerns of such criticisms of the stagist 'policy cycle' approach. As a heuristic device the policy cycle enables us to construct a model with which we can explore public policy. But, as with all heuristic models, it must be treated with caution. Like the case of the Underground map of London, we must be wise to the fact that such maps have grave limitations and may distort our understanding. Frogs may have a life-cycle, and living things may be regarded as 'systems', but to imagine that public policy can be reduced to such over-simplified stages has more methodological holes than a sack-load of Swiss cheese. However, the idea of analysing policy-making and policy analysis in terms of a 'stagist' framework is not without its advantages and it should not be abandoned lightly.

This book adheres to the stagist approach because, given the sheer range of frameworks and models which are available as analytical tools, we need some way in which this complexity can be reduced to a more manageable form. (On the cognitive limits of the human mind and the importance of reducing complexity, see Simon, 1957: 198; Newall *et al.*, 1979; see also 3.4.2, 3.7.4). Those who advocate abandoning the stagist model argue for a different framework to take its place (see, for example, Lindblom and Woodhouse, 1993: 11–12). However, what needs to be accepted is that contemporary policy analysis is a multiframed activity. The strength of the stagist approach is that it affords a rational structure within which we may consider the multiplicity (Cook, 1985) of reality (see 4.5.4). Each stage therefore provides a context within which we can deploy different frames.

If we put aside the stagist model the choice is either a bewildering array of ideas, frameworks and theories, or the acceptance of another alternative model. In broad terms, therefore, the stagist framework does allow us to analyse complexities of the real world, with the proviso that, when we deploy it as a heuristic device, we must remember that it has all the limitations of any map or metaphor. And, unlike maps of Africa or America, we have no way of knowing if (in the words of Walter Lippman, 1922) the 'world out there' is really the same as the 'picture in our heads'. The idea of breaking down the making of public policy into phases, which begin with defining problems and setting agendas and end with implementing and evaluating policy, may well be to impose stages on a reality that is infinitely more complex, fluid and interactive; but, to adopt a cyclical metaphor, it is not necessarily an unreasonable or unrealistic way of looking at what happens when public policy is made. What is important, however, is that we realize that understanding and explaining this complexity is a matter which involves appreciating that reality exists within the context of a multiplicity of frameworks.

Here it is well to emphasize that Lasswell's approach involved far more than simply setting out stages: public policy, in Lasswell's sense, went beyond consideration of the 'stages' of policy-making towards the mapping of the wider contexts of problems, social process, values and institutions within which policy-making and policy analysis took place. In Kuhnian terms, the dominant paradigm may be regarded as requiring adaptation or modification, rather than a revolution. Indeed, one might argue that the Lasswellian approach, far from being hopelessly out of date, needs to be considered afresh as offering the foundations of a contextual and more critical and post-positivist form of policy analysis (Torgerson, 1985). This analytical framework, which is far wider than a list of stages at first suggests, is revealed in Lasswell's ideas for 'decision seminars' to provide a new tool for policy analysis (see Lasswell, 1960; and 3.10.5).

In this book, therefore, whilst mindful of the limitations of 'stagism' as it is used and abused in 'textbook' policy analysis, we are not prepared to abandon its heuristic (and hermeneutic) usefulness. However, on its own the simple policy cycle is as inadequate a tool as its critics suggest. This is particularly so because of the way in which the stagist framework naturally lends itself to a 'managerialist', 'top-down' approach to the policy process and to a view of the role of policy analysis as a form of elite resource, rather than as involving wider social enlightenment. In this book, therefore, we aim to retain the stagist approach, allied to the kind of multidisciplinary, contextual focus which was central to Lasswell's idea of the policy sciences. Given the existence of a complex policy reality framed by a range of theories, models, explanations, values and ideologies, the problem is not with the policy cycle *per se* as with the need to incorporate or include models and approaches which are or may be deployed in policy analysis.

1.11   The arrangement of Parts Two, Three and Four

Each 'stage' of the policy cycle may be seen through a variety of different frameworks and approaches.

Part Two: Meso Analysis

Meso analysis is the way in which issues and problems are defined and policy agendas set. 'Meso' – or a level of analysis which cuts across or through the various phases of the policy process – explores approaches which link the input side of the policy-making process with the policy/decision-making and output process by focusing on the relationship between the 'pre-decisional' dimensions of policy-making and its decisional and post-decisional contexts. Meso-level analysis encompasses 'deciding to decide', problem recognition, and formulating alternatives (Mack, 1971); public recognition, the placing of issues on the agenda, advance of demands (Rose, 1973); initiation and information (Jenkins, 1978); and issue search, filtration and definition (Hogwood and Gunn, 1984). But it also recognizes that problems and agenda formulation take place in a domain framed by existing and earlier policies, decisions, implementation, evaluation and policy analysis.

Part Three: Decision Analysis

This part of the book deals with the analysis of how decisions are taken and policies are made and how analysis is used within the decision-making process. It is concerned with action and inaction, decisions and non-decisions. We consider frameworks for analysing the decision-making process and frameworks which are used as forms of rational policy analysis. These modes of analysis encompass decision proper (Mack, 1971); consideration and decision (Jenkins, 1978); involvement of government, resource constraints, policy decisions, determinants of government choice, and the context of choice (Rose, 1973); forecasting, setting objectives and options analysis (Hogwood and Gunn, 1984).

Part Four: Delivery Analysis

The analysis of how policies are administered, managed, implemented, evaluated and terminated is covered here. The analysis of policy delivery covers effectuation, correction and supplementation (Mack, 1971);

implementation, evaluation and termination (Jenkins, 1978); implementation, outputs, policy evaluation, feedback (Rose, 1973); implementation, monitoring, control, evaluation and review, policy maintenance, succession and termination (Hogwood and Gunn, 1984).

As a classification it is perhaps closest to that suggested by Lynn's concept of the 'games' which take place at different levels of the policy cycle: high, middle and low (Lynn, 1981: 146–9; Hoppe, 1993: 82–3). The 'high game' involves ideology-formation and agenda-setting and corresponds to our 'meso' classification. Thus, meso analysis (Part Two) involves models and theories which seek to explain what is going on when problems are defined and agendas are being set. But it will also include the activities of those who seek to bring an analysis of problems to influence and shape the perception of the problems. Reports by think-tanks, academics, government studies and so on, are all analysis which is involved in the business of the production of knowledge and information.

Lynn's 'middle game' is concerned with the design of policies and their adoption. This phase, which we encompass in 'decision analysis' (Part Three), is concerned with explaining the hows and whys of decision-making, but also with how the analysis of problems is used to structure and inform the decision-making process. Decision analysis is consequently concerned with the knowledge of the decision process and the use of knowledge in that process.

The 'low game' Lynn sees as involving an interaction of implementation, evaluation, adjustment and maintenance. This part of the cycle, which we have classified as 'delivery analysis' (Part Four), also focuses on this interaction between the analysis of how policy is implemented and evaluated, and how knowledge is produced to structure the practice of implementation and evaluation. In turn the evaluation of policy must be viewed as comprising an important dimension of how issues, problems and agendas are formulated.

PART TWO

Meso Analysis

The analysis of problem definition, agenda-setting and the formation of policy

2.1 Introduction

Meso (from the Greek 'mesos': middle, or intermediate) analysis is a middle-range or bridging level of analysis which is focused on the linkage between the definition of problems, the setting of agendas and the decision-making and implementation processes. The policy approach is a problem-focused inquiry, and in this part of the book we are concerned with how problems are formed and framed, and how they become – or do not become – items or issues on the policy agenda. However, although 'problem' recognition and definition, the search for information, the framing of agendas, and alternatives are 'early' stages in the policy process (*qua* model or map) these activities/stages are not logical sequences which culminate in decision and implementation. Policy-making in this sense may be viewed as a form of 'collective puzzlement on society's behalf; it entails both deciding and knowing' (Heclo, 1974: 305). This puzzlement in the form of defining problems and framing agendas continues – like a core or thread – throughout the policy process. Consequently, the ideas, theories, concepts and frameworks in this part of the book must be seen as having as much relevance to 'evaluation' as to the stage at which a 'problem' is initially 'recognized'.

We begin by examining one of the earliest contributions to the study of policy in terms of 'problem': the so-called 'social problem' approach, whose origins we may date back to the ideas and ideals of reformers and social researchers in the nineteenth century and, later, to the theories of social problems as 'constructions' which developed as a critique of these early ideas, and later functionalist frameworks (2.2). The next approach to the study of problems and political agendas grew out of a different – but related – concern with the study of public opinion and the mass media. The origins of this may be seen in the writings of Walter Lippman in the 1920s, and subsequently with the ideas of Harold Lasswell. From this point of view the main focus has been on how public opinion and the mass media interact with policy-makers to define agendas and problems (2.3). The next approach has addressed the way in which problems and agendas are shaped in the institutional setting: how parties, interest groups and policy-makers interact so as to determine what counts as being a political issue and what is excluded from the political arena (2.4). How a problem is politicized may, of course, depend on what kind of issue it is, as well as the way in which the political process has dealt with it. As Lowi argues, different 'types' of problem may consequently give rise to different kinds of politics (2.5).

Much of the thinking about policy-making in these sections of Part Two have been framed by a highly pluralistic set of assumptions about politics and the making of policy problems. However, as the analysis presented in 2.4 by Schattschneider, and Cobb and Elder argues, the political process may not be so open as to allow all problems to be brought to political attention. The agenda-setting process may be heavily biased and loaded against certain problems and interests. In 2.6 we examine an important contribution to agenda analysis by theorists who argue that real power in the policy process is the power to make non-decisions; that is, the capacity of one group to prevent the ideas, concerns, interests and problems of another group getting 'on' the agenda in the first place. Furthermore, this position may be extended to say that, if we want to understand how problems are defined and agendas are set, we have to go much deeper than the surface relations of power, into the way in which the values and beliefs of people are shaped by forces which cannot be observed in an empirical or behavioural way (2.7). Two key concerns of this critical (anti-behavioural) approach have been the role of knowledge and of language in framing political 'reality'. In the following sections (2.8 and 2.9), therefore, we examine the role of knowledge and language in the construction of problems, the terms of political debate and the formation of the policy agenda.

At this point in the story the book enters into a more synthetic mode in focusing on approaches which advance what might be termed 'macro' accounts of the policy process. First, we review a number of frameworks which endeavour to provide models of policy-making in an industrial society, which incorporate many of the themes and issues that have been dealt with in earlier sections by employing new metaphors of the policy process, including networks, streams, advocacy coalitions and punctuated equilibrium (2.10). Following this, we then consider approaches which set the process of problem definition and agenda-setting in the context of wider social, economic, institutional and other boundaries or parameters, such as national economic and social conditions, and historical and institutional experience (2.11). Finally, we consider the idea that policy-making does not take place in isolation from global and international pressures and influences (2.12).

2.1.1   The analysis of problem definition and agenda-setting

The genesis of a policy involves the recognition of a problem. What counts as a problem and how a problem is defined depends upon the way in which policy makers seek to address an issue or an event. As James A. Jones nicely expressed this in the context of social problems: 'whosoever initially identifies a social problem shapes the initial terms in which it will be debated' (Jones, 1971: 561).

Consider, for example, the following sequence:

$$\text{ISSUE} \quad \rightarrow \quad \text{PROBLEM} \quad \rightarrow \quad \text{POLICY}$$
(people sleeping on the streets)   (homelessness)   (more housing)

We may all agree what an issue is but disagree as to what exactly the problem is, and therefore what policy should be pursued. If we see people sleeping on the streets as a problem of vagrancy, then the policy response may be framed in terms of law enforcement and policing. The early analysts of social problems believed, rather na-ively, that 'the facts would speak for themselves': the evidence of a problem would lead to action to 'solve' it. However, facts are things which never speak for themselves; they require an interpreter. And, even when a condition is so recognized, it does not follow that it becomes a public matter. As reformers in the nineteenth century learnt, a problem tends to exist in the political sense when it affects and threatens some other group.

How may we explain this process wherein problems are defined and positioned on the political agenda?

Although the various approaches to agenda-setting are different, and in many respects may well be considered as incommensurate, they also overlap, complement and supplement one another. However, in practice, the analysis of the agenda process tends to take place within these parameters and academic paradigms rather than between them.

Even though they are of differing analytical contexts, the approaches to agenda setting ask very similar questions, the answers to which often run in parallel and may actually intersect at some points. All have a common concern with how issues and problems come to be – or not to be (that is the question) – political or public things.

Underpinning much of the analysis of agenda-setting and problem definition is that of the controversy surrounding the idea of an objective, knowable world being 'out there'. The question of when an issue becomes a political or policy problem turns upon the idea of the objective versus the subjective nature of reality.

A problem has to be defined, structured, located within certain boundaries and be given a name. How this process happens proves crucial for the way in which a policy is addressed to a given problem. The words and concepts we employ to describe, analyse or categorize a problem will frame and mould the reality to which we seek to apply a policy or 'solution'. The fact that we may share the same data, or at least believe that we share the same data, does not mean that we see the same thing. Values, beliefs, ideologies, interests and bias all shape perceptions of reality. As Popper and Kuhn argued (see 1.6 and 1.8), reality is perceived through a theory or framework, and the theory we choose determines the problem we see. From the same sensory data, some may see a rabbit and others a duck! (The best-known illustration of this point is the famous drawing by W.E. Hill of 1915, which shows an old woman and a young woman at one and the same time.)

Problems involve perceptions, and perceptions involve constructions. The main characteristic of policy problems, as opposed to other kinds of problems such as in mathematics or physics, is that they are of an ill-defined nature. As we shall see later, policy analysts could be said to be in the business of problem-structuring and ordering so as to facilitate problem-solving by decision-makers. Politics arises because we do not share perceptions of what the problems are, or if we do, what follows from the definition in terms of what can be or should be done. *A definition of a problem is part of the problem.* The act of observation is, as quantum theory in physics maintains, something which affects the object of study. When we consider the question of 'problems' we are therefore conscious of being in a post-Baconian world: observation and definition are forms of participation. In Tom Stoppard's play *The Real Inspector Hound*, a critic sitting in the audience is annoyed that no one on the stage is answering the phone. He jumps up on the stage and picks it up: it is for his colleague, whose wife is phoning him at work. The actors return on stage and the critics become caught up in the play. Problem definition is not unlike this situation. In defining a problem, analysts and policy-makers jump into the problem like Stoppard's critic jumps into the play. Analysis is participation in a problem, not simply observing a problem. The phone rings, we get up and answer it, and we become involved in the drama and the spectacle.

The difficulty with 'policy' problems is compounded by their complexity and ill-definition. And, as Simon argues in respect of ill-defined problems (see 3.7.4), they require problem-solvers to contribute to the problem definition. Although problems are ill-structured, government is highly structured. This fact means that all problems have an organizational or governmental context which has a major influence on the way in which problems come to be structured. As we shall see in decision analysis (Part Three), this kind of argument about 'problem solving' in situations of ill-structuredness has given rise to a literature on the possibility of constructing techniques to improve decision-making in conditions of poor definition and complexity. For the moment, however, we simply observe that 'political problems' are of a different order of complexity to problems in natural science or mathematics. Ill-structured as they are, public issues are not clearly demarcated: we do not know where one problem begins and another ends. They overlap, intersect and bump into one another.

❖ Case 1: Poverty

Ruth Lister, writing on changing concepts of poverty, argues that, for example, the way in which we define poverty has had a crucial impact on policy responses. Some writers, she notes, have articulated the idea of an 'underclass', a concept which she thinks is particularly dangerous since:

> It is used freely by the media, often as if it were synonymous with poor people generally. It is, I would argue a dangerous concept. People tend to use it to mean what they want it to mean … The language one uses in conceptualising poverty is important because it conveys images which can shape attitudes towards poor people and which can shape poor people's own attitudes and self image … People in poverty themselves do not want to own the word. The ambivalence has been cleverly exploited by some politicians … It is [she concludes] important that conceptions of poverty have built into them a dynamic element that does not deny the individuality and agency of people in poverty.
> (*Lister, 1991*)

Case 2: Urban riots

In the autumn of 1991 there were riots in a number of British cities. Explanations from 'underclass' to 'law and order' were advanced by police, politicians, church leaders and academics.

The Sunday Times (15 September 1991) reported:

as the wreckage is cleared away, the theorising starts – will politicians, the police and 'society' take the rap, or will the car thieves, arsonists and vandals belatedly be brought to book?

Digby Anderson commented in the same paper:

The list so far is: poverty, or better 'hopeless' unemployment, social strain (whatever that may be), 12 years of Conservative government, bad housing, the male ego, 'lack of infra-structure', 'alienated youth' and boredom. And who is responsible? Why, the government, or anyone except the rioters.

On the front page the newspaper headline read: 'Ministers to target 6 year olds in bid to fight lawlessness'. The government initiative, it observed, had an added urgency in the wake of the urban violence in Handsworth, Cardiff, Oxford and Newcastle upon Tyne. 'Many of those arrested were children.'

Case 3: A plausible story

Just imagine what would happen if, for some reason, pigs did fly or Martians did land. What kind of issue would it become? How would governments handle the situation? Who would handle it? How would the issue/ problem be constructed?

First of all, the media would need experts:

'In the studio tonight we have Professor Heinz Krieger, an astronomer who is an expert on Mars. Professor, what kind of people – or should I say creatures – are these Martians?' 'Well, Mr Sage, I think that, given what we know about the planet, they may be a cross between the Swiss, with their mountain culture, and the Bedouin. It is a very dry planet you know.'

Meanwhile, in government departments all over the world, policy-makers are trying to work out who should deal with it.

'It seems to me, minister, that it is very much a defence issue, with health and environmental implications. We should set up an inter-departmental committee.'

Years pass. They settle down, work hard, get mortgages and attract considerable research interest and several journals of Martian studies. A confectionery company endows the MMRI, the Mars© Mars Research Institute at the University of Warwick. The Martian Problem has become a fully developed research industry.

As Zork Mottelfunjer, the Snickers© Professor of Martian Studies later explained:

'When we first arrived I think we Martians were an unknown quantity. Humans did not know how to relate to us. But, as we say in Martian, 'Gurrsed iy 'uy i jus thungth berufff fanhg!!' We are still not happy with the way in which our community has been sterotyped, and politicians and the media don't exactly help in defining what the real problems are. I know that if you prick us we don't bleed, but that is not the point at issue here. The sooner we see the end of ARAP (Alien Resettlement on Another Planet Agency) the more we shall be convinced that the so-called 'Martian Problem' is not seen as one of how to get rid of us. We are here to stay! And I think that the significant thing is that public opinion is going our way: 67% of people now think that living next door to a Martian is no different from living next door to anyone else. Politicians who try to make an issue out of the Martian question had better remember that public opinion is more pro than anti, and that Martians have the vote as well.'

Case 4: Another plausible story

What if pigs could fly? As a result of mad pig disease, pigs develop an ability to fly. What kind of issue would it become, and how would the problem (or would it be a problem?) be defined?

Health: Pigs flying about and depositing large quantities of fertiliser over the place could be the main issue.
Air safety: Flying pigs may cause accidents. After all, it is bad enough sucking a sea gull into an engine, much more, a saddleback.
Agriculture policy: Farmers may find that they no longer have a monopoly on pigs. Such might be the pressure from the powerful agri-business lobby that the government is forced into introducing some method of ensuring that foreign pigs do not fly over from other countries and flood the domestic market.
Economy: The price of bacon may go through the roof!

Or ... it may be a green issue. Animal campaigners could make the pig issue into one of animal rights. Pigs, they might argue, should be allowed to fly free, and the hunting of pigs by men in red coats be castigated as a 'barbaric relic'.

Different countries may frame the issue and construct the problem in different ways: the British as animal rights; the French as a culinary matter; Israel as a religious controversy, and so on...

Case 5: Nuclear energy

Jasper (1992) examines the ways in which nuclear energy decisions were framed in the USA, Sweden and France. He shows how the different social and political preoccupations of each country led to differing constructions within which decision-making took place:

> American politicians debated the price controls and markets and ownership of uranium plants, French politicians were concerned with private profits, the health of industrial work-ers, the implementation capacities of the state, Swedish political leaders over Social Demo-cratic hegemony and then over 12 versus 13 reactors. Swedes rarely raised issues of ownership or state capacities. Americans seldom asked about the capacities of the state or precise numbers of reactors. The French never questioned government interference in markets. Existing partisan frames were too strong.
> (*Jasper, 1992: 107*)

As to the influence of experts, such as scientists and economists, decision-makers accepted the arguments that suited their frames, rather than those which challenged them. And, in turn, decision-makers largely framed the public debate (in the media) in terms that suited their policy. ◆

2.2   Social problem approaches

2.2.1   The positivist approach

The concern for social problems which developed in the nineteenth century may be said to mark the beginning of modern policy analysis. The enlightenment had led to a reformulation of the human condition. The problems which beset mankind were no longer seen as inescapable or inevitable. The application of intelligence and knowledge could, it was believed, solve problems and improve the lot of humanity. The work of social reformers and the development of an empirical analysis of social problems such as poverty, child labour, health, prisons, and so on, form the positivist foundation of social policy research. Victorian social reformers were deeply committed to the idea that the production of knowledge was the engine of improvement. Facts were powerful political forces. People such as Henry Mayhew, Sir Edwin Chadwick, Florence Nightingale, Octavia Hill, William Beveridge, Beatrice and Sidney Webb and above all Charles Booth (and in America, Jane Adams) were highly optimistic about the possibility of scientific empirical data being able ultimately to solve problems. As Florence Nightingale famously observed; 'facts are everything – doctrines are nothing' (Harris, 1990: 389). However, how much this pure unadulterated positivism was realized in practice is in some doubt, for as Harris (1990: 389) notes:

> The ubiquitous Victorian 'social science' societies purposefully sought to ground public policy on a basis of empirical data. Yet recent studies of these societies have shown that their work was almost wholly taxonomic, rather than analytic or genuinely prescriptive; for all their amassing of detail, they by and large failed to generate coherent explanations of pathological social conditions.

As she comments, the facts may well have been simply a substitute for thought and action. Facts frequently followed policy, rather than preceding it as positivists advocated. And policy many times bore little relation to the actual data that was available (ibid.: 391). The argument that social policy was shaped by social facts is therefore a difficult thesis to sustain in the light of a good deal of historical scholarship, which shows that facts did not have the kind of impact which the social science reformers believed they would achieve. Nevertheless, the analyst as reformer, and vice versa, was an important phase in the history of the application of 'science' to social problems.

From their work was to stem a tradition of social research focused on 'problems' and their amelioration and solution (Bulmer *et al.*, 1991). It was a phenomenon which was not confined to Britain and America. In Germany, for example, there was also a tradition of social surveying that was most clearly manifested in the 1870s and 1880s when Bismarck's social welfare legislation derived from fact-finding reports. But it was undoubtedly in Britain that the impact of the empirical study of social problems was to be most influential in shaping policy and opinion. Mitchell (1968: 129) argues that this was due to a number of factors:

> Partly this was because of the established tradition of appointing Royal Commissions to investigate specific subjects which, of course, depended upon the cross-examination of witnesses, but partly also, it must be admitted, because academic prejudices in Britain were not as effective as in Germany; the number of graduates in the country being small, amateur politics was therefore more down to earth and empirically orientated. Moreover, in Britain the social survey movement was initiated by wealthy philanthropists, and philanthropists cannot with good conscience be spurned; reports based on surveys were treated with respect by upper and middle class people because they were carried out by their own kind.

❖ The social survey tradition

Charles Booth (1840–1916)

Booth was a Liverpool shipowner and is best known for his seventeen-volume *Life and Labour of the People of London* (1899–1903) in which he set out to analyse the causes of poverty and their consequences. Booth used his research to campaign for reform and legislation. Kershen notes:

> Charles Booth's voice did find the ear of policy makers and helped persuade them to change direction ... Booth's scientific approach to the problems of poverty within society sprang from his early enthusiasm for Positivism and his examination of the works of Auguste Comte. Charles Booth set out, as the young Mayhew had, to use science to solve social problems ... He may not have been 'one of the clever ones', but his conscientious and steady work was of great value in defining, locating and proffering solutions to improve the condition of the disadvantaged ... Unlike Henry Mayhew, whose findings were forgotten for almost a century, Booth's work resulted in an almost instantaneous 'watershed in the history of British social policy'.
> (*Kershen, 1993: 115*)

Booth's influence in America was also significant. His work was a major early influence on the development of the Chicago School of sociology and was the inspiration behind social surveys in the late nineteenth and early twentieth centuries (Hull House Maps and Papers, 1895; Pittsburgh Survey, 1909–14) (see Sklar, 1991; Bales, 1991; Lerner, 1975).

Seebohm Rowntree (1871–1954)

Rowntree was a manufacturer and a great philanthropist. Like Booth, he set out to inform public debate as to the nature and extent of poverty in his native York. His main books were: *Poverty: A Study of Town Life* (1901); *The Human Needs of Labour* (1937); *Poverty and Progress* (1941); *Poverty and the Welfare State* (1951); and *English Life and Leisure: A Social Study* (1951). His criteria of poverty were more robust that Booth's and were based on consultations with British and American food experts. He defined poverty as primary and secondary and set out a 'poverty line'. Although his work, like Booth's, is open to methodological criticism, Rowntree's research made policy makers and public opinion aware of the 'social problem'.

The professionalization of social analysis: American fact-finding and its political impact

Although social problems in America were to attract the attention of the amateur reformers (Jacob A. Riis and Lincoln Steffens), the main feature of the study of social problems in the US was that it was conducted by professional social scientists. The most significant was headed by Paul N. Kellog: the Pittsburgh Survey of 1909–14. It covered 'Wage Earning', 'Women and Trades', 'Homestead', 'The Household of a Mill Town', 'Work Accidents and the Law', and 'Steelworkers'.

It is significant, however, that the study did not have the kind of political impact that Booth and Rowntree were to have in Britain. No legislation can be identified as being prompted by the survey. However, the Pittsburgh survey did inspire the tremendous growth in social surveying in the inter-war period: by 1928 some 2,800 had reported.

The German social survey tradition

Social surveys were also a feature of the development of empirical social science in Germany from the late nineteenth century onwards. The activities of the research institutes came to an end (1933–6) under the National Socialist government (see Gorges, 1991). ◆

2.2.2   The study of social problems: sociological approaches

---

❖ The sociology of social problems

Key texts

Three general introductions are pre-eminent in this field:

M. Spector and J.I. Kitsuse, *Constructing Social Problems*, 1977.
J.W. Schneider and J.I. Kitsuse (eds), *Studies in the Sociology of Social Problems*, 1984.
R.L. Henshel, *Thinking about Social Problems*, 1990.

Also in connection with social problems the work of Murray Edelman is of great importance, providing as it does a 'constructivist' approach based on theories of language (see 2.9.2). See Edelman (1964, 1977, 1988).

Early contributions to the field provide a core part of reading:

R.C. Fuller, 'The problem of teaching social problems', 1938.
R.C. Fuller and R.R. Myers, 'The natural history of a social problem', 1941.
R.K. Merton and R. Nisbet (eds), *Contemporary Social Problems*, 1961.
H.S. Becker, *Outsiders*, 1963.

For a review of the 'stages' approach, see Hazelrigg (1985). Loney *et al.*, (1991) provide excellent material on social policy which can be used to explore how problems become defined and politicized. The collection covers issues such as old age, sexual abuse of children, and the family. ◆

The reformers of the nineteenth century, such as Booth, were convinced positivists. Problems were 'facts', they could be measured and dealt with in a 'scientific' manner: to analyse causes was to solve problems. A variant of this notion of problems as 'objective facts' was the functionalist approach, which saw problems as essentially dysfunctions in the smooth 'functioning' of society as a 'system'. Problems in this sense were 'analysable' in terms of their origins in social conditions. Having identified the conditions which gave rise to the dysfunctionality, policy-makers could deal with the manifest or latent 'problems'.

There were two sources of this approach: Emile Durkheim and Talcott Parsons. Durkheim viewed problems – or deviance – as 'functional' in the 'social system'. From a Durkheimian perspective social problems were inevitable and necessary: those who depart from common expectations of 'normal' behaviour serve to define what is acceptable and non-acceptable – good or bad. The recognition of these deviances can serve to promote change as well as to reinforce prevailing notions of acceptable behaviour. The problem for Durkheim was how to keep the level of deviancy to a scale which does not threaten the social order. Thus, kept within bounds deviancy can actually benefit society by setting out the limits of what is deemed to be 'normal' and enabling us to have some criteria of what is a problem. Deviance from the norm was not the result of moral sickness, sin or psychological illness, but an integral part of the smooth functioning of a modern society. Social problems in this sense were 'social solutions'.

The influence of Durkheim on the analysis of social problems as forms of deviancy has been profound. Above all, it gave social scientists a sense of mission. Social problems required the development of forms of social analysis which could lead to the effective control of the level of deviant behaviour. The influence of Durkheim on thinking about social problems must also be viewed alongside the impact of two anthropologists, Margaret Mead and Bronislaw Malinowski. Their studies of West Samoa and the Trobriand Islands claimed that individuals were products of their culture and society, rather than of biology or psychology. The school of social science which they founded emphasized that societies had to be understood as self-maintaining, unchanging 'systems'. Problems in this sense were the product of how those systems operated and how the cultures framed and conditioned reality for individuals. It was a model of society and individual behaviour which was at odds with a conflict/change model of the Marxists and the focus on the individual psychology of Freud. The impact of this 'structural-functionalist' view was widespread. As Badcock (1988: 146) notes:

> Almost immediately, the views of Mead, Malinowski and others of similar outlook became part of the Western cultural mythology ... Since culture, rather than nature, was now believed to determine everything, cultural causes were now believed to determine everything ... Now criminals were seen as products of bad housing, unemployment, incorrect socialization or even arbitrary social 'labelling'; insanity was generally caused by society and primarily by the family; suicide by too little or too much social solidarity ... Any fact which did not fit the expectations of the theory could be conveniently explained away as having some hidden or 'latent' social function ... Society as a whole was imagined to be the product of itself so that, for a while, every problem seemed to have social causes and every answer was looked for in society itself.

Talcott Parsons was the most important source of the functionalist approach to social problems in the post-Second World War era. Parsons analysed societies as tending towards equilibrium: from this perspective social problems constituted adjustments and possible 'dysfunctions' within the social 'system'. The main text for this functionalist approach to social problems was Merton and Nisbet (eds) (1961). Merton and Nisbet saw problems as having an objective and a subjective dimension. Social problems could be analysed in terms of objective knowledge: social problems, as social disorganization (inadequacies in meeting one or more of the functional requirements of the system: Merton and Nisbet, 1971: 820) and deviant behaviour – or departures from accepted and institutionalized social norms. The main source of criticism of the functionalist approach came from the so-called 'symbolic interactionists' who were influenced by the pragmatism of James, Dewey and Mead.

❖ Symbolic interactionism

This was a school that developed in Chicago in the inter-war period and which was informed by the pragmatism of John Dewey, William James and G.H. Mead. The study of society in this approach involves the examination of the way in which symbols are employed in communication. The Chicago School was particularly concerned with the sociology of urban problems and the way in which social identities were constructed. Blumer (1969: 2–6) argues that the approach has three central premises:

- human beings act on the basis of the meanings that things have for them;
- meanings are the outcome of social interaction;
- meanings are modified and handled through an interpretative process that is used by individuals in dealing with the 'signs' he or she encounters.

The interactionist image of human beings thus may be said to be framed by the belief that:

> the individual and society are inseparable units ... a complete understanding of either one demands a complete understanding of the other ... Society is to be understood in terms of the individuals making it up, and individuals are to be understood in terms of the societies of which they are members ... Since much of the environment's influence is experienced in the form of social interaction, behaviour is constructed and circular, not predetermined and released.
> (*Meltzer* et al., *1975: 2–3*)

Note: There are two other 'Chicago Schools': in economics and in law. The Chicago School of economics developed in the 1950s through the close association of the Department of Economics with the ideas of Hayek. Its chief exponents were Milton Friedman and George Stigler. The former was to have a considerable impact on the policy agenda in the 1970s as a prophet of 'monetarism' (*sic*) and, along with 'public choice' theory, laid much of the foundation for 'new right' policies (see Parsons, 1989). The Chicago law school is associated with the law department's equally right-wing ideas on liability law and the application of 'cost-efficiency' analysis to cases involving damages. ◆

Among the first notable critics of the functionalist framework of social problems to advance an interactionist or constructivist analysis was Richard Fuller. In the late 1930s he argued that:

> The hypothesis of a smooth-functioning social order is not only artificial, but dangerous ... We must abandon the notion that social problems represent human behaviour which is a departure from an unquestioned and smooth-running cultural status quo ... when and where do we sociologists find this nice equilibrium of forces (social organization) from which we are supposed to be slipping into a morass of confusion (social disorganization)?
> (*Fuller, 1938: 433–4*)

Fuller posited that a social problem involved fundamentally subjective judgements, as well as objective conditions. In themselves the existence of an objective condition (which was dysfunctional) was not sufficient for it to be regarded as a social problem. Fuller and Myers put forward an alternative to the functionalist model in 1941, in a paper which looked at the stages (or life-cycle) of a social problem. This paper provided an influential model by which a problem could be seen as moving through a stage of awareness, policy determination and reform.

❖ A natural history approach to social problems

Richard C. Fuller and Richard R. Myers, 'The natural history of a social problem', 1941
The authors took the view that a social problem is a condition of deviance from a widely held social norm and it has an objective and a subjective dimension. The former can be observed, but the fact that it may be held to exist does not mean that it is considered to exist: subjective factors come into play. Given this, a social problem is always in a dynamic state of becoming a problem. To examine this idea they studied a trailer park 'problem' in Detroit. They show how the problem moved through three distinct stages:

- awareness: when values are seen as threatened;
- policy determination: debates over policy options;
- reform: putting formulated policy into action.

They concluded:

In the search for temporal sequences in the 'becoming' of a social problem, the student does not take the problem conditions for granted, as objective 'evils' caused by 'evils'. He seeks to explain social problems as emergents of the cultural organisation of the community, as complements of the approved values of the society, not as pathological and abnormal departures from what is assumed to be proper and normal.
(*Fuller and Myers, 1941: 329*)

J.H.S. Bossard's stages in the life-cycle of problems

1 recognition of the problem;
2 discussion of its seriousness;
3 attempts at reform: usually intuitively arrived at, often ill-advised, promoted by the 'well let's do something, folks' approach;
4 suggestions that more careful study is needed – 'what we need is a survey';
5 here follows some change in personnel among interested people;
6 emphasis on broad basic factors;
7 dealing with individual cases;
8 another change in personnel;
9 programme inductively arrived at;

10 refinements of techniques of study and treatment;
11 refinements of concepts;
12 another change in personnel.

See Bossard (1941).

Anthony A. Vass, *Aids a Plague in US: A Social Perspective*, 1986
In this detailed account of the development of Aids as a social problem, Vass employs Fuller
and Myers's model to explore the making of a contemporary medical/social condition. Although
he finds the model valid for Aids he has some reservations:

> it is useful because it makes many events appear intelligible and somewhat orderly. It helps
> to clarify issues and to analyse them ... However, the analysis failed to support the proposi-
> tion that social problems develop in a clear-cut developmental – progressive – manner ...
> Rather, the developmental stages of a social problem are often difficult to classify and
> identify into distinct identifiable stages. Stages are interrelated and interconnected, and no
> stage on its own can exist, or be understood, without the continued existence and support
> offered by other stages. Stages do not progress in an inevitable way ... they develop in a
> circular manner and they have a tendency to move forward (progressively) to a new stage
> and backward (regressively) to an earlier stage as part of their gradual maturity on becoming
> engrained in the social structure. Finally, social problems do not follow a path of constant or
> consistent velocity but, rather, they experience loops and temporary diversions and gaps
> called null periods, in their development.
> (*Vass, 1986: 150–1*) ◆

The idea of exploring the natural history of problems in 'stages' was
developed by a commentary on the paper by Bossard in the same
number of the *American Sociological Review*, enlarging his simple three-
stage model into a twelve-stage version (see above). Thus by the 1940s
we may discern two broad lines of development in the study of social
problems: positivist/functionalist and phenomenological.

- The positivist/functionalist approach saw social problems as 'facts'
  to be measured, and as having a 'functionality' to the maintenance
  of society. The role of social science in this approach was to identify
  those conditions that were dysfunctional to society, develop knowledge about problems so as to analyse their 'causes' and offer remedies. Social scientists were the 'conscience and protector of society' (Spector and Kitsuse, 1971: 37). In the post-war period the
  leading exponents of this approach were Merton and Nisbet (1961,
  and later editions).
- The phenomenological approach which derived from the symbolic
  interactionist school saw problems as essentially subjective social
  constructions. Here the role of social science was to clarify defini-

tions and assumptions, show whose definitions were operating, what alternative points of view existed and identify points of intervention (Becker (ed.), 1966: 23–6).

It was the latter approach which was to have an important influence on the formation of the 'life-cycle' framework and thence to several other theories and models. In order to understand this line of development, five texts are of special importance to the study of public policy:

C. Wright Mills, 'The professional ideology of social pathology', 1943.
——, *The Sociological Imagination*, 1959.
Howard Becker, *Outsiders*, 1963.
Howard Becker (ed.), *Social Problems*, 1966.
P.L. Berger and T. Luckman, *The Social Construction of Reality*, 1975.

C. Wright Mills was amongst the first of the post-war generation to attack the idea that problems could be approached as objective conditions and causes. In his seminal work *The Sociological Imagination* he argued that it was necessary to distinguish between 'troubles' and 'issues'. It is such an important statement of the anti-positivist position that it merits being quoted at length:

> Troubles occur within the character of the individual and within the range of his immediate relations with others; they have to do with his self and with those limited areas of social life of which he is directly and personally aware. Accordingly, the statement and the resolution of troubles properly lie within the individual as a biographical entity and within the scope of his immediate milieu – the social setting that is directly open to his personal experience and to some extent his willful activity. A trouble is a private matter: values cherished by an individual are felt by him to be threatened. Issues have to do with matters that transcend these local environments of the individual and the range of his inner life. They have to do with the organization of many such milieus into the institutions of an historical society as a whole, with the ways various milieus overlap and interpenetrate to form the larger structure of social and historical life. An issue is a public matter: some value cherished by publics is felt to be threatened. Often there is a debate about what that value really is and about what it is that threatens it. This debate is often unfocused if only because it is the nature of an issue that it cannot be defined by immediate and everyday environments of ordinary men.
> (Mills, 1959: 8–9)

As Mills had argued earlier (1943), the idea that social problems were like pathological problems in the human body – malfunctions in the way the body is supposed to work – and that social scientists were like physicians, analysing objective disorders, was erroneous. Human problems were outcomes of politics and power. Howard Becker's contribution to the study of social problems followed on from this argument and also owed much to the influence of the Chicago School and to Fuller and Myers. Two texts stand out as having a big impact on the promotion of a 'constructivist' view of social problems. First is his study of 'outsiders' – drug users and other varieties of deviants – in 1963. This was followed in 1966 by a book on 'modern social problems' which served as an antidote to the functionalist 'social pathology' of Merton and Nisbet (1961). The 'outsiders' study aimed to show how a 'social problem' – such as the use of marihuana – was essentially the outcome of a process of 'labelling' by one group of an activity or condition with which it disagreed or disapproved. This was in contrast to the approach adopted by Merton and Nisbet, which was concerned to show how 'dysfunctionalities' such as drug abuse were disruptive to social stability. Becker's focus is not on the causes and consequences of deviance, but on how a problem is the outcome of a political process wherein a crusade or campaign is waged by 'moral entrepreneurs' in and through the media to label a condition 'a problem':

> The central fact about deviance [is that] it is created by society … social groups create deviance by making the rules whose infraction constitutes deviance, and by applying those rules to particular people and labeling them as outsiders. From this point of view, deviance is not a quality of the act the person commits, but rather a consequence of the application by others of rules and sanctions to an 'outsider'. The deviant is one to whom the label has successfully been applied; deviant behaviour is behaviour that people so label.
> (Becker, 1963: 8–9)

In Becker (ed.) (1966) he widened this analysis to include a range of other problems, including race relations, housing, work and mental illness. The collection acknowledges its debt to the ideas of Fuller and Myers. Although he does not accept the terms they use or the stages they put forward, Becker agrees with their main idea: 'to understand a social problem fully, we must know how it came to be defined as a social problem' (Becker (ed.), 1966: 11). Social problems were essentially the result of a political process:

> a process in which opposing views are put forward, argued, and compromised; in which people are motivated by various interests to attempt to persuade others of their views so that public action will be taken to further the ends they consider desirable; in which one attempts to have the problem officially recognized so that the power and authority of the state can be engaged on one's side.
> (Becker (ed.), 1966: 11)

In the same year as the publication of Becker's *Social Problems* another important book was published which refined the arguments in favour of viewing social realities as constructed rather than objective 'facts' to be discovered through a sociology of knowledge approach: Berger and Luckman (1975). Their study of the 'social construction of reality' provided a formidable intellectual underpinning to the constructivist position. Although the book drew heavily from the same well of Mead and symbolic interactionism, Berger and Luckman also deployed a range of other approaches and ideas, including those of Marx, Mannheim, Nietzsche, Weber and Schutz, amongst others. The study rejects the 'objectivist'/'positivist' underpinnings of contemporary social science and functionalism in particular, and called for a renewal of sociology based on the investigation of how 'realities' come to be objectified and legitimated.

The 1970s: Blumer, Spector and Kitsuse

In the 1970s Herbert Blumer further developed the constructivist model of social problems by refining the 'stages' of problem formation and arguing that problems exist when they are seen as undesirable by a group of people. A problem moved through a cycle of definition, rather than 'discovery':

1   the emergence of a social problem;
2   the legitimation of the problem;
3   the mobilization of action;
4   the formation of an official plan;
5   the implementation of the official plan.
(See Blumer, 1971.)

The important aspect of these stages in the formation of a problem was that they were not objective realities, but products of 'collective behaviour': problems were formed 'in the process of being seen and defined in society (Blumer, 1971: 305–6). Social problems, he argued, were 'fundamentally the products of collective definition instead of existing independently as a set of objective social arrangements with an intrinsic make up' (Blumer, 1971: 298). Later Mauss (1975) extended this idea of social problems as subjective perception, rather than an objective reality, by maintaining that social problems were kinds of social movements which are produced by the 'behaviors of publics, interest groups and/or pressure groups' (1975: 13). Mauss argues that we may analyse the process in which social problems get established on the policy agenda in terms of the social movements which facilitate the promotion of an issue as a certain kind of problem at times when people have time, energy and resources to address social conditions: 'to define some of them as problematic and to engage in the process of collective behavior which will produce social movements' (1975: 44). A convincing argument for this position can be made by consideration of the development of social movements concerned with race, the environment and women. Were it not for the growth of such movements it is difficult to imagine how new definitions of problems could have made their way on to the policy agenda.

❖ Problems and social movements: Feminism and public policy

Ellen Boneparth and Emily Stoper (eds), *Women, Power and Policy*, 2nd edn, 1988
In this collection of papers the various authors discuss the relationship between the women's movement and the policy agenda in the US and other industrial and developing countries. The contributions cover women's relationship to public policy, women and production, reproduction and women, and public policy in a comparative perspective.

Women, it is argued, need to get into the decision-making system if they are to have a greater impact on how issues are defined and how the policy agenda is shaped. This requires a strong and well-organized social movement (p. xvi). A 'framework for policy analysis' appropriate for understanding the place of women's policies (in the US in particuar) is put forward and the variables which have influenced the agenda are set out as:

- *environmental*: social climate; economic climate; political climate;
- *systemic*: decentralized government; role of the courts; incremental policy-making;
- *political*: lobbying; political coalitions; leadership;
- *policy characteristics*: types of policy (distributive, regulatory and redistributive); and role equity versus role change.

> it is clear that policy change occurs only when groups seeking change have sufficient power to influence the policy-making process. The women's movement has come to distinguish between power over and power for. The feminist critique of power has been directed at ways of reducing the power of one group over another. The goal of women's groups in the policy-making process has been to achieve and utilize power for both equity and role change.
> (*Boneparth and Stoper (eds), 1988: 19*)

Feminism, the authors maintain, must seek to exercise more influence on the way in which problems come to be defined by policy-makers. In those societies, such as Scandinavia, where feminism has more influence, policies have reflected the feminist agenda. The possibilities of so changing the policy agenda turn, however, on the vitality of the women's movement.

Joyce Gelb and Marion Leif Palley, 'Women and interest group politics', 1979
The authors analyse what makes for success in women's policy issues. They put forward six factors. The issues:

- must be broadly supported;
- must be narrow enough not to alienate support and disturb the values of supporters;
- must have a good policy network (see 2.10.2) to provide information and access to decision makers;
- must be able to be subject to compromise during the process;
- must define success in an incremental way;

- must be an issue that focuses on equity rather than change of roles. ◆

In 1977 Spector and Kitsuse contributed to the constructivist case in a book which sought to reformulate the natural history model – as originally propounded by Fuller and Myers and by Blumer – by focusing on problem-constructing as an activity of making claims. The main addition to these frameworks is that it considers what happens after policy-makers have recognized a problem and the impact of policy implementation on the ongoing problems. Stage 2 in the Spector and Kitsuse model is where Fuller and Myers and Blumer leave off. Stages 3 and 4 involve a 'second generation' of the problem once policy has been determined and implemented.

❖ M. Spector and J.I. Kitsuse, *Constructing Social Problems*, 1977

Stage 1: Group(s) attempt to assert the existence of some condition, define it as offensive, harmful or otherwise undesirable, publicize these assertions, stimulate controversy, and create a public or political issue over the matter.

Stage 2: Recognition of the legitimacy of these group(s) by some official organization, agency or institution. This may lead to an official investigation, proposals for reform and the establishment of an agency to respond to those claims and demands.

Stage 3: Re-emergence of claims and demands by the original group(s); or by others expressing dissatisfaction with the established procedures for dealing with the imputed conditions, the bureaucratic handling of complaints, the failure to generate conditions of trust and confidence in the procedures and the lack of sympathy for the complaints.

Stage 4: Rejection by complainant group(s) of the agency's or institution's response, or lack of response, to their claims and demands, and the development of activities to create alternative, parallel or counter institutions as responses to the established procedures. ◆

Spector and Kitsuse conclude their study by conceding that examining social problems in terms of 'stages of development' is open to many criticisms, and they cite Wallerstein's summation of the problems faced by thinking in terms of stages (comments which, it must be said, also hold good for other 'stagist' modes of policy analysis):

> Not only does the misidentification of the entities to be compared lead us to false concepts, but it creates a non-problem. Can stages be skipped? This question is only logically meaningful if we have 'stages' that 'co-exist' within a single empirical framework. If within a capitalist world economy, we define one state as feudal, a second as capitalist and a third

as socialist, then and only then can we pose the question: can a country skip from the feudal stage to the socialist stage of national development without 'passing through capitalism'? But if there is no such thing as 'national development' (if by that we mean a natural history) and if the proper entity of comparison is the world-system, then the problem of stage skipping is nonsense. If a stage can be skipped it isn't a stage.
(*Cited in Spector and Kitsuse, 1977: 158*)

As we have noted earlier, metaphors are dangerous things. The notion that we can analyse problems as unfolding 'life-cycles' is of obvious analytical merit in that it enables a deconstruction of a construction process; but trying to squeeze reality into these stages, however extensively defined, only serves to create additional problems. That said, and with the health warning on the side of the packet in mind, the Spector and Kitsuse model has great merit for the analysis of the process in which problems come to be defined/invented/discovered/ constructed. It offers a framework of understanding problems in the context of the meaning which is manufactured in a political and institutional context. Problems are also, as the model suggests, things which are created by social movements and are promoted by professionals involved in analysing and dealing with problems. The dissemination of problems in the media has a major part to play in constructing problems. As the later stages illustrate, policy-makers themselves are involved in creating problems – through action and research – as well as in 'solving' problems. An advance on the stage approach is Henshel (1990), whose focus is not the stages of problem formation and policy-making, but an analysis of the role of different groups – moral entrepreneurs, victims, the mass media, professionals and experts – in defining problems, and the 'strategies of intervention' deployed by policy-makers and others.

During the 1970s and 1980s the 'objectivist' approach to social problems did not wither in the face of the constructionist arguments of Spector and Kitsuse and others (see Schneider and Kitsuse, 1984; Schneider, 1985); to some extent it thrived through the growth of 'evaluation' research. Evaluation was framed by the belief that it was possible to measure and appraise the costs and benefits, and the effects of problems and policies (see 4.5.2). Thus, although the constructivist arguments against positivist approaches to the analysis of problems formed an important critique, it is true to say that the positivist approach remains the dominant paradigm of social policy-making and analysis. Quantificationism – rather than deconstruction – still constitutes the operative ideology of policy-making in the modern state. Perhaps the main difference is that, whereas in the 1960s and 1970s the fear was that professionals, experts, technocrats, bureaucrats and others were doing the calculations and evaluations (see

2.8.1, 3.3.5, 3.3.6; Illich, 1975b; Dunleavy, 1981; Wilding, 1982; Henshel, 1990: 70–80, 223–64), in the 1990s one could argue that the power has shifted towards the four Ms: markets, managers, moralists and the media (see, for example, Loney *et al.* (eds), 1991).

❖ Whose 'problems' are they anyway?

That there are certain 'conditions' or practices does not mean that they are problems which require public action and policy. Conservatives (with small and big 'c's) have long been un-happy with the idea of using the language of 'social problems' to discuss social conditions, because the acceptance of a problem has consequences for how we view the condition in terms of the need for a 'solution'. If, for example, we characterize certain conditions as 'moral', 'personal' or 'individual' problems, then the consequences for public policy are very different.

- See Glazer (1988) for a conservative critique of the notion of social problems.
- See Davies (1991) for an argument for the 'remoralization' of social problems.
- For a more literary account, the confrontation between Scrooge and two men seeking to help the poor at Christmas time in Charles Dickens's *Christmas Carol* reveals a clash between two paradigms. For Scrooge the poor are a social condition, to the men collecting for charity they represent a problem in need of amelioration.

Projects

- A longitudinal study: select a problem that is current in the press. Show how this problem is being 'constructed'.
- Take the Fuller and Myers model, or the Spector and Kitsuse model and chart the life cycle of a problem.
- A comparative study: compare and contrast how different kinds of issues have been con-structed as policy problems.
- Imagine you work for a think tank or pressure group. You have been asked to lead a project. Develop a strategy to get your definition of a problem on to the wider agenda.
- Write a report making the case for something as being a social problem. Having constructed the problem set out some policy options.
- Make the case for why something which is regarded as an issue of public concern should be left to private or individual choice. ◆

2.2.3   The media and the construction of problems

As we noted above, the role of the media in the agenda process is, as Henshel argues (1990: 203–32), an important factor to consider in the construction of problems. We shall review the role of the media and public opinion below (2.3.1), as well as in the work of several agenda theorists (2.4 and 2.9). From the perspective of the 'constructivist' approach, the impact of the media on social problems is a key aspect of the 'labelling' process in that it 'sensitizes' and 'amplifies' (Wilkins, 1964). These ideas have had a major role in the study of deviancy, and especially in the way in which the media are seen as 'manufacturing' crime waves (Fishman, 1978; Cohen and Young (eds), 1981; Armstrong and Wilson, 1973; Chibnall, 1977).

The role of the media in defining a problem and amplifying an issue was illustrated in a classic sociological study by Cohen, *Folk Devils and Moral Panics* (1972). This was a study of the way in which the media took the issue of fighting between youth gangs in the 1960s (Mods and Rockers) and 'amplified' incidents in such a fashion as to sensationalize minor events into a major social problem, thus inducing a 'moral panic' which resulted in calls for policies to deal with a supposed threat to the social order. In the case of Mods and Rockers, Cohen argues that the press actually created a problem, distorted the issues and fashioned a 'folk devil' from what were relatively minor disturbances. In so distorting issues and creating stereotypical threats, the mass media can shape the context within which policy responses take place, and influence 'public opinion' by setting a public agenda in terms of an incident or event (see figure 2.1).

Figure 2.1   The media and public panic

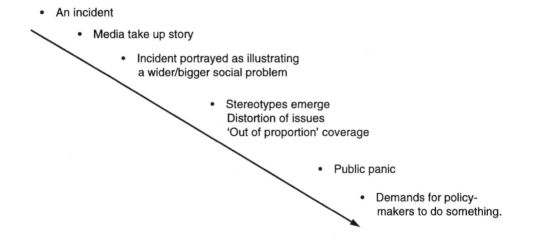

The media, therefore, by being in the business of 'manufacturing' news are also involved in the production of problems. The media select what is 'newsworthy' and in so selecting include and exclude issues, events and ideas (in Eastonian terms, they act as 'gate-keepers'). However, as Henshel (1990: 58–63) notes, the role of the media must also be viewed alongside the way in which experts use and are used by the media, the impact of bureaucratic 'propaganda', as well as the influence of drama and other TV programmes which deal with social problems.

❖ A plausible story: Trouble in Toy Town

It was a quiet news day for the Toy Town *Sunny Times*. Nothing really newsworthy had happened for days. Sales of the *ST* were not looking good, and even with the new technology and creative accounting there was pressure to sell more papers. The editor's door was suddenly flung open by Peter Pig, ace reporter.

'Boss, listen to this. Marlo Monkey, a young chimp has been arrested for the murder of Doris Doll. God, boss she was just a baby! It turns out that the young Chimp had been left alone for days on end, whilst his mother lived the life of a real swinger.'

In the following weeks the press vied with one another to get new angles on the story. Sales went up. Experts appeared on TV to give their analysis of the issue: some said it was psychological, others showed how unemployment and social disadvantage amongst chimps was the real cause. The latter thesis was a version accepted by the radical bishop of Toy Town; some politicians, on the other hand, said that it had more to do with falling moral standards.

An *ST* editorial summed up what it thought to be the 'real issue':

> We live in dangerous times. Once it was safe for any doll to play in the streets, now she's not even safe from her fellow playmates. What does it tell us about Toy Town in the nineties?
>
> - Our kids are out of control.
> - Our families are breaking up.
> - Our streets are no longer safe.
>
> The *Sunny Times* calls for:
>
> - A crack-down on young chimps.
> - More powers for the police and courts.
> - An end to the featherbedding of single-parent chimps.
> - A return to traditional Toy Town values.

Today the *Sunny Times* publishes an opinion poll which shows how concerned *the people* are about out-of-control chimps. It is their number one issue, and this paper will not rest until it is the number one priority of the government. ◆

A highly critical account of the role of the media in 'constructing' social problems, events and crises is developed in the work of Murray Edelman (see 2.9.2). In his view the media serve to obscure and manipulate, rather than illuminate social problems. The news media function in the interests of the status quo and the powerful, and construct issues so as to make democracy into a 'spectacle' which dominates the thoughts and actions of the public *qua* 'audience' (see Edelman, 1988). On the other hand, a more pluralistic version of the role of the media in public policy is that the press and TV have the capacity to bring issues to the forefront of public attention, and in so doing bring a problem which was outside the political agenda firmly into the political arena. Here the mass media may be seen as having a role in a democratic society to make problems 'visible'. A good illustration of this concept of the media as agenda-setters was Barbara Nelson's study of the way in which child abuse went from being a matter of private pain and professional interest and concern to being a public and policy issue (Nelson, 1984). She argues that although the abuse of children had long been a 'problem' it was not recognized as such until, in the 1960s, professional literature (on the 'battered child syndrome') was taken up in the media. The stories aroused public interest, which over the years was sustained by a number of newspapers and journalists. Nelson maintains that the sequence was on the lines we have outlined in figure 2.2.

Figure 2.2   Professional research and the issue of child abuse

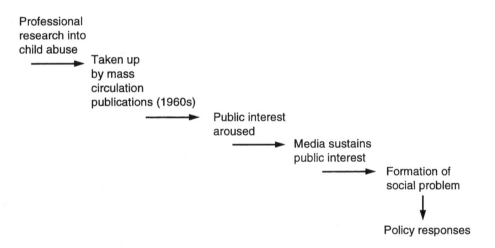

Source: Adapted from Nelson (1984)

The problem with these case studies of single issues is that they raise many questions about the broader relationship between the formation of public opinion and the formation of public policy and the role of the media in this process. We examine this interaction of public opinion and public policy in the following section.

2.3   Public opinion and public policy

❖ **Key texts**

The relationship between public opinion and policy is a fascinating field and is well supported by sources. Starting points must include the writings of Lippman (1922) and Lasswell (1972). For students of public policy, Lasswell is especially important because he was in advance of opinion research and content analysis before the likes of Dr Gallup. He also stressed that, contrary to a good deal of policy analysis post-Lasswell, the study of public opinion was a core part of policy studies. Lippman's ideas about the role of the media in forming a world outside as a picture in our heads was also an approach ahead of its time. It was not until the 1970s that the concerns of Lasswell and Lippman were developed in social science research.

As to the key text, there is only one: Protess and McCombs (eds) (1991) have in their excellent reader all the major contributions (with the exception of Lasswell) in the field. Other reading should include Rogers and Dearing (1987), who provide a comprehensive survey of agenda-setting theory. Perhaps the most extensive treatment from the point of view of the policy process is Baumgartner and Jones (1993). This takes account of work done in the field to the date of publication.

Two musts are also Nelson's (1984) study of child abuse, which was noted above (2.2.3), and Kingdon's (1984) study of agenda-setting, which will be discussed later in 2.10.3. ◆

2.3.1   Public opinion and policy agendas

As Habermas (1989), has noted, the influence of positivism has been most strongly felt in those areas of social science which have employed statistical analysis: and this most evidently in the quantification of public opinion, which developed in the 1930s in the work of Dr George Gallup. That something becomes an issue which attracts the attention of policy-makers and the media is closely tied up with the way in which that issue relates to public opinion – however that is defined and measured. Public opinion is to the political market what consumer demand is to the economic market place. In a democracy one could argue that public policy is a function of public opinion. Policy demand determines policy supply. And, the fact that opinion is measured and is treated with such attention by policy-makers gives weight to the argument that the policy agenda is set by the interplay of public opinion and public power. As liberal democracies transformed the domain of the public, so the notion of public opinion was to be transformed, and vice versa. Indeed, it is a nice point as to which came first: public policy or public opinion.

As a concept, the idea of public opinion may be said to predate that of 'policy' in its modern sense, although its modern meaning is strongly related to the growth of more collectivist modes of political life. We find observations on the character and importance of the public voice from the ancients onwards: *'Vox populi, vox dei'* (Alcuin); *'Publica voce'* (Machiavelli). But it was, as Gunn (1989) notes, in eighteenth-century Britain that the concept was developed, in the sense of being an identifiable body of views held by a defined group and to whose opinions government attached a standing and a significance. This was, as he notes, quite different to the notion that prevailed in France and other European countries. In France, for example, there was less concern about the status of public opinion, because there was 'no electorate to consult, no legislature to express indignation at irresponsible grumblings, no free comment in the press and, in sum, little that Britons would see as a political process' (Gunn, 1989: 251).

Public opinion, then, was a concept which evolved with the development of political institutions and of modes for its dissemination. In the twentieth century the main characteristic of the conceptual transformation of public opinion has been that of the desire to measure it and account for its changes and influence. Gunn argues that, in so analysing the relationship of public opinion to policy, one must be aware of the historical antecedents of the concept. The influence of public opinion on government must also be placed in the context of power to shape public opinion. This was a particular concern of commentators from the eighteenth century onwards. The concept of public opinion thereafter was central to democractic theory (Janowitz and Hirsch, 1981: 1). In the early twentieth century it was of special interest to US commentators such as James Bryce, Lawrence Lowell, Harold Lasswell and Walter Lippman (ibid.: 3–37). In the post-Second World War era, the introduction of techniques to make empirical, quasi-scientific measurements of public opinion on issues and issue identification led to the analysis of the impact of opinion on the political agenda and the manufacture of a new public opinion sphere which may be said to represent those processes of issue formation that shape public policy and public concerns, priorities and attitudes. This concern with measuring and analysing changes in public opinion could be seen in the output of *Public Opinion Quarterly* and the search for explanatory models.

❖ Agenda-setting and the media

Robert N. Mayer, 'Gone yesterday, here today', 1991
In a case study of consumer policy Robert Mayer examines the role of issues in agenda-setting in terms of two models: unidirectional (the media influencing the consumer agenda of the US government) and multidirectional (the policy agenda of government influencing media coverage and public opinion). Here is part of his conclusions:

> There is something for everyone in the data presented here. Advocates of the unidirectional view can take heart from the fact that the peak of media coverage occurred early and was followed in short order by public admiration for Ralph Nader and proconsumerist opinions ... the peak of legislative attention to consumer issues took place in the mid-1970s, several years after consumer issues reached their peak on media and public agendas.

> Advocates of the multidirectional view can also find support in the data. Most important, there is ample evidence that consumer issues reached a first peak on the policy agenda before the mass media or the general public discovered consumer problems.

> Taken together, the available evidence from the 1960–1987 period suggests that consumer issues were first raised on the policy agenda, probably because of the personal concern of presidents and congressmen. Later, after federal attention to consumer problems had become legitimized by early executive and legislative action, the unidirectional pattern took over.

S. Iyengar et al., 'The Evening News and presidential elections', 1984
This paper published the results of a group of psychologists into agenda-setting. Two experiments were set up to examine the impact of the *Evening News* on evaluating President Carter's performance. What was significant is that TV had the effect of defining the policy areas by which the President should be judged. The media set the agenda, but not the attitudes of the subjects. This capacity of the media to set out the policy areas and problems is, they argue, something which has many implications for the relationship between the public, policy and politicians as mediated by the TV. ◆

In the 1970s a new focus emerged on the impact of the media on the political process and on the relationship between the media and public policy and public opinion. The public opinion approach to agenda-setting may be said to have begun in earnest with the work of Malcolm McCombs and Donald Shaw in 1972. They hypothesized that although the role of the media in influencing the direction or intensity of attitudes was doubtful, the 'mass media set the agenda for each political campaign, influencing the salience of attitudes towards the political issues' (McCombs and Shaw, 1972: 177). They examined the capacity of the mass media to set the agenda in the 1968 presidential campaign. Later, they conducted another survey of the agenda-setting role of the media by looking at the way the media influenced the public's perception of the Watergate affair (McCombs and Shaw, 1976). McCombs and Shaw conclude that the media have had a key role in 'agenda-setting' – that is, in the power to determine what topics are discussed – in the areas that they studied: public welfare, civil rights, fiscal policy, foreign policy, and law and order (1972) and corruption (1976); and they argued that it confirmed the usefulness of the concept of agenda-setting for public opinion research. The model suggested by McCombs and Shaw was that the media orders what publics regard as important issues. The more attention that is given to an issue, the more does the public regard it as being a high agenda item, and vice versa (see figure 2.3).

Figure 2.3   The impact of media attention on the public agenda

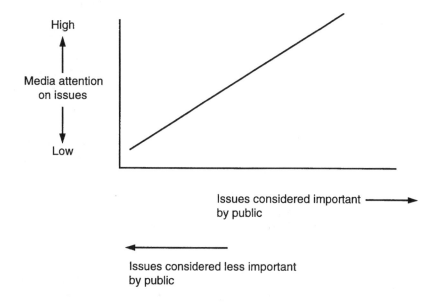

This model has not been without its critics, who have challenged its empirical standing as well as the danger of simplistic and broad application. In addition to this, commentators have also noted the lack of clarity as to influence of the media on the personal agendas of the audience; the need to take account of different kinds of agendas at work; the doubts about the relationship between the role of the media and the public in initiating concern about an issue; and the importance of power in agenda-setting (see McQuail and Windahl, 1993: 106–7). After the publication of the McCombs and Shaw paper, therefore, a large and growing body of research has emerged to examine the dynamics of agenda-setting and the interaction of media, public and policy-makers. In simple terms, the research has tended to be the study of a single issue (longitudinally), or the study of issues across different policy areas (cross-sectionally). The strength of the former is that it provides an in-depth examination of an issue and its attendant politics, but it is somewhat limited from the point of view of generating general theories and models of agenda-setting. Cross-sectional studies are perhaps better fitted to the development of more general theories or models (see 2.10). Even so, single-issue studies can yield a rich body of data which may have wide-ranging implications. For example, Protess *et al.* (1987) came to the conclusion that the influence of the media in setting policy agendas (in the case of toxic waste) was far more complex than had been thought in the 1970s. The response of policy-makers to news stories was something which had to be placed in the context of other factors. Not the least of these were: the relationship of journalists to policy-making elites and vice versa; the timing of publication; interest group pressures; political exigencies; and the costs and benefits of problems and solutions.

Another comprehensive model which focuses on the range of processes which are involved in agenda-setting has been put forward by Rogers and Dearing (1987). Rogers and Dearing argue that we must distinguish between three kinds of agenda: media; public; and policy. Their research suggests that, contrary to the McCombs and Shaw model, agenda-setting is a more interactive process. The mass media do indeed influence the public agenda, as McCombs and Shaw maintain, but the public agenda has an impact on the policy agenda, as does the media agenda. However, on some issues the policy agenda has a considerable impact on the media agenda. The media agenda is also shaped by the impact of 'real world' issues or events. The role of events on the agenda process is considered by Rogers and Dearing to be an area which requires more intensive research. McQuail and Windahl (1993) have shown what a more complete (and more complex) model of agenda-setting, which takes into account the arguments of Rogers and Dearing, looks like in a graphic form (figure 2.4).

> The model represents the different kinds of effect and of feedback ... It reminds us ... that mass media, the public, and elite policy makers all inhabit more or less the same wider environment when it comes to highly significant events and that each of the three separate worlds indicated are connected and permeated by networks of personal contacts and influenced by personal experience ... Agenda setting can be either intentional or unintentional and can be initiated by either the media or policy makers. We cannot exclude the possibility that the public itself affects the media agenda, since some media look for content selection clues in their estimation of public concerns, independently of events, other media or elite views.
> (*McQuail and Windahl, 1993: 109*)

Figure 2.4   Rogers and Dearing's model of agenda-setting

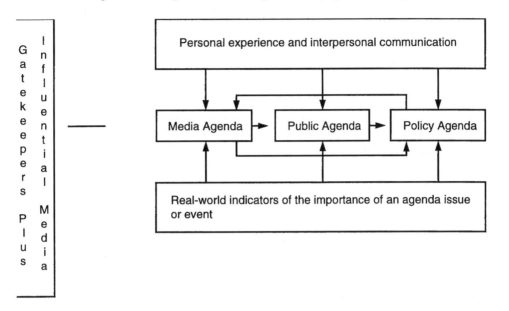

Source: Adapted from McQuail and Windahl (1993)

Issue attention cycles (IACs)

Related to this notion that the media have a role in setting issue agendas is the idea that there is a cycle in which these issues move. In 1972 Anthony Downs published a paper which had as big an impact on the subject as the piece by McCombs and Shaw (Downs, 1972).

Figure 2.5   Downs's issue attention cycle

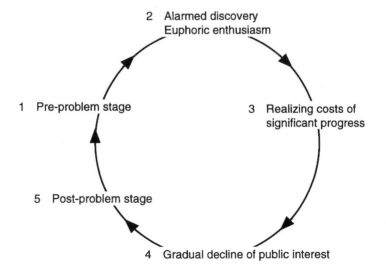

Downs set out to examine the issue process in relation to the environmental issue which was just coming to political prominence in that period. He argued that issues took the form of a cycle of attention (IAC) and that concern about the 'ecology' issue had ups and downs (see figure 2.5).

❖ The issue attention cycle: the case of the environment

Downs's model (1972)

Stage 1: Pre-problem Experts and policy-makers may be aware of the problem, and knowledge may have been produced but there is negligible public interest.

Stage 2: Alarmed discovery and euphoric enthusiasm The issue is recognized as a problem, prompted by a disaster or event which focuses concern and leads to demands for government action.

Stage 3: Counting the costs and benefits Policy-makers and the public become aware of what progress will cost.

Stage 4: Decline of public interest in issue/s

Stage 5: Quiescence A post-problem phase in which the issue slips down the public agenda. New issues replace the environment in public opinion and policy agendas.

An application of the Downs model

Timothy O'Riordan, an environmentalist, takes the Downs model and applies it to the issue in the 1980s (O'Riordan, 1991). He argues that the agenda is driven by four key factors:

- events;
- personalities;
- pressure groups;
- institutional failure.

Concern about the environment, as measured by policy and public opinion, indicates strongly that the model holds up to recent experience. He maintains that:

> Downs' model is less of a cycle and more of a spiral. The spiral moves upwards in response to changing perceptions of survivability, valuation of the quality of life, moral concerns over the disadvantaged, and the doubling disadvantaged of future generations, and recognition of the inability of technology and political management to resolve the problem. In short, environmentalism is enmeshed in changing perceptions about justice, democracy and the role of the state, plus economic performance and the proper place for humans in a degrading earth.
> (*O'Riordan, 1991: 179*)

He urges that the environmental issue should lose its distinctiveness and become embedded in other issues, such as the economy, education, defence and foreign policy. If not, the Downsian cycle will play itself out time and time again.

William Solesbury: 'The environmental agenda', 1976

Few essays have bettered Solesbury's interpretation of the agenda process than that offered by his seminal analysis of the environmental agenda in the 1970s. At the time of writing Mr Solesbury was Principal Planner in the Directorate of Planning Intelligence of the Department of the Environment (UK). Solesbury argues that the key to understanding agenda formation is the relationship between issues and institutions. An issue only begins to become important when an institution within the political system becomes associated with it. This is borne out, he argues, with respect to the environmental issue(s) in the 1970s when government took up the cause of 'the environment'. The progress of an issue was thence shaped by the degree of particularity: that is, the extent to which an issue can be exemplified by a particular occurrence or event. In the case of the environment this is very noticeable, its ups and downs coinciding with disasters and 'crises' of various kinds. Furthermore, environmental issues have three other kinds of advantages: they are visible; they are events which impact on the public as a whole; they are relatively simple to identify in terms of cause and effect.

However, particularity is not enough for an issue to get attention. It must have legitimacy. It must fit in and correspond to prevailing and dominant values, or a compatability must be established. The way in which government handles and deals with an issue is a key factor in forming the basis of legitimacy within the political system. From such legitimacy action may result. But as a civil servant he has this important observation to make:

> in moving onto those processes through which issues invoke action or inaction, one passes into the relatively closed world of the executive departments of state ... It is in this private political world that issues come, or fail to come, to final recognition through agreement and response.

Issues must then command public attention, governmental legitimacy and consideration if they are to receive public action. Even so, he argues, issues may in the end be actually lost in the decision-making phase by being suppressed or transformed into something else. ◆

Downs's model has been an influential conceptualization of the way in which issues may be seen as having highs and lows, ons and offs. Peters and Hogwood (1985), for example, argue that it has an applicability to issues other than that of the environmental agenda. They also contend that the model may also be used to understand something which Downs does not consider in any depth: the relationship between the issue attention cycle and the organizational activities of government (that is, initiating new organizations, adapting existing organizations or 'policy continuation', and abolishing organizations (or termination). (See 4.6.2 for details of this model of policy change.) In a study of the relationship between cycles of public concern and organizational activities in the US from the 1930s to the 1970s they conclude that:

- policy areas other than the environment conform to the 'cycle' pattern as set out by Downs. (They analyse over 15 areas including agriculture, welfare, education, health, and economic policy);
- the timing of peaks in issue attention varies between policy areas;
- problems which have been through the IAC will get more attention after than before the peak;
- organizational succession forms the main proportion of organizational activity after the peak in the IAC;
- peak periods of organizational activity coincide with peak periods in the IAC;
- there is a linkage between public opinion and organizational change.

Peters and Hogwood provide a linking level of analysis between the formation of issues and public attention and the response of government in terms of organizational change. We map this argument in figure 2.6.

Figure 2.6   Issue cycles and organizational activity

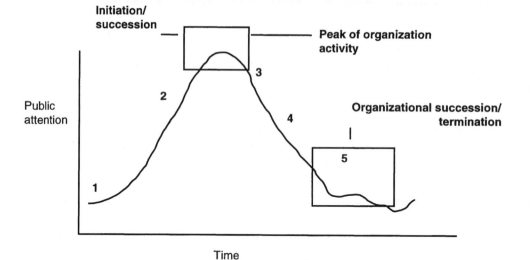

Two points need to be stressed here. First, that IACs will vary between policy areas. Thus policy makers are confronted by 'public' and 'media' agendas which have their ups and downs on different issues and policy areas.

Public policy-making is problematic not least because of the fact that IACs mean that the policy areas which are seen by public opinion to be important vary (see figure 2.7). And, as policy-makers are to be seen as 'listening to the people', the peaks of public issue attention

Figure 2.7   Public attention and policy areas

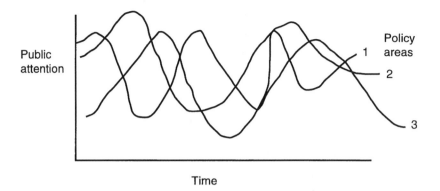

have, according to Peters and Hogwood, considerable impact on the organizational agenda of government. Indeed, they argue that the relationship between the saliency of public issues and organizational change is such that it offers 'some consolation for the supporters of responsive democratic government' (Peters and Hogwood, 1985: 251). Of course, from another (more critical perspective) such organizational change may be simply a way for policy-makers to do something to make it look as if they are actually doing something.

If we take Peters and Hogwood's analysis using organizational change as a measure or indicator, then the 'policy agenda' might be said to occur at that phase when the IAC is at its peak. At this point government must be seen to be 'doing something', 'solving problems', 'making decisions'. The second point about the IAC and organizational change is that, as Downs and Peters and Hogwood note, once an issue has been through the cycle it will be treated differently next time around: more concern in the pre-problem phase. The reasons for this are that, despite fading public interest in an issue, the organizations which have been set up or adapted to deal with it 'go on and on': bureaucracies are immortal (Kaufman, 1976) even if public interest is fickle.

Peters and Hogwood's point about the IAC and the institutional setting of public opinion and the media is important. Bureaucracy, politicians, interest groups, policy analysts and advocates of various kinds are also involved in getting issues on to and up, and down and out of the policy agenda. The formation of issues in the context of more limited policy 'communities' and 'networks' as we shall explore later (2.10) may strongly suggest that the role of policy elites is far more significant than the opinions of Joe or Josephine public (see, for example, Sabatier, 1991: 148–9; Lindblom and Woodhouse, 1993: 35–6). There can be no denying that the media have a role in shaping the policy agenda, but it may all too often have less a starring role (as in the case of child abuse or in the Watergate saga) than membership of the supporting cast of players. Cook and Skogan, for example, point out that, in an examination of the ups and downs of crime and the elderly, the demise in the saliency of the issue is due to the interaction of several factors.

Figure 2.8   Cook and Skogan's model of issue saliency

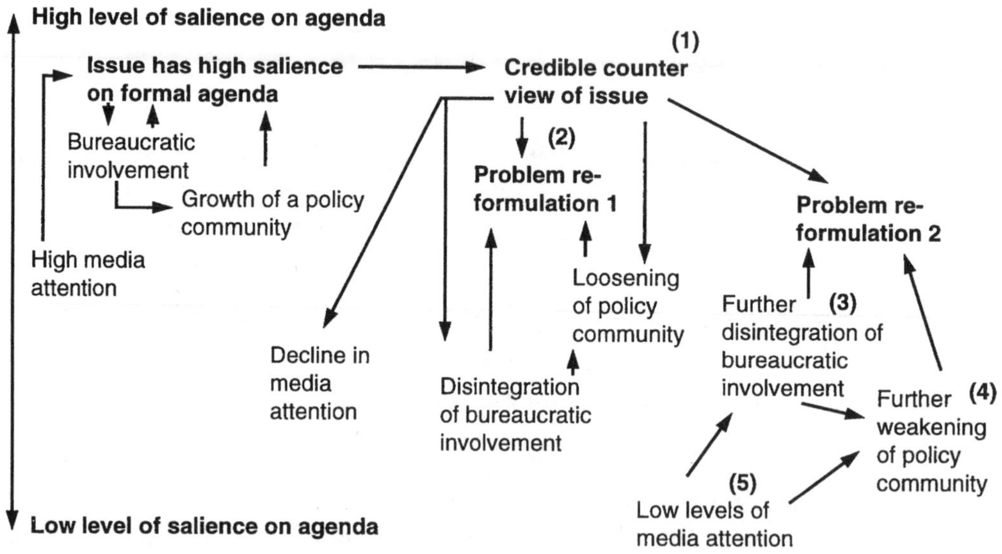

Source: Adapted from Cook and Skogan (1991)

Once riding high an issue has three main supporting factors: government bureaucracy; the media; and a policy community. The latter will be composed of persons and organizations involved or concerned about a particular issue. At a certain stage a credible counter-argument about the issue will emerge (see (1) in figure 2.8). This will propose an alternative definition of the problem, its extent or its seriousness. The result (2) is that the problem will undergo a reformulation. This process of reformulation will give rise to a greater diversity of arguments, as manifested in a disintegration of bureaucratic involvement, a decline in media attention and a looser relationship between members of the policy community. The next phase will involve a reformulation of the problem, further bureaucratic fragmentation (3), a weakening of the policy community and a low level of media interest. At this point the issue will no longer have a high position on the policy agenda. The model proposed by Cook and

Skogan is useful in that it provides a linkage between theories of problem formation which stress the constructionist nature of policy problems and theories, which we shall examine later, that deal with the policy-making process as involving 'networks' of interaction (2.10). It also links into other approaches which focus on the nature of policy arguments in the policy process (2.7.3, 3.8.8).

❖ What are the practical implications of the IAC model?

If you were a minister for the environment, how would you respond to polls showing that the public was very concerned about small furry things being washed up on the shore and about lead levels in drinking water? The model suggests that the best strategy is to respond to this concern, but in the knowledge that within a few weeks it will all be forgotten. Do you think that there is any evidence to suggest that this is indeed an accurate characterization of policy-making in environmental policy, or in other, areas?

Project

Take an issue, such as the environment, and track public concern over a given time. This may be done by consulting surveys on public opinion (such as *British Social Attitudes*, and Jowell *et al.*, 1990) or surveys of opinion in the European Community. Another method is to plot the number of citations of an issue listed in indexes to newspapers or in the *British Humanities Index* (see figure 2.9).

Figure 2.9   Measuring issue attention using newspaper citation index

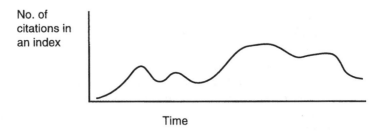

No. of citations in an index

Time

◆

2.3.2   Policy marketing and policy-making

The relationship of public opinion studies to commerce has always been close. The world of advertising and the world of public opinion research overlap in theory and in practice. Organizations and firms which specialize in opinion research produce work for commercial clients as well as for newspapers and political parties interested in what the voter thinks and what the voter wants. In understanding the issue formation we necessarily stray into the territory of how policy and issues are presented so as to make use of the information which pollsters produce. Issues and policies are increasingly approached from a marketing point of view:

> How far does *image* making determine *policy*-making? How far has our political process become captive to the demands of television, to the shaping of the audience?
> (*New Statesman, 1986*)

> In the United States, polling has become an integral part of what is called policy entrepreneurship. It is not used as a test of popularity, but as the basis for the elaboration of policy. This is not just a more scientific extension of the politician's traditional sense of what the public wants, but a qualitatively new development. Followship replaces leadership.
> (*Sir Alfred Sherman, 1987; quoted in O'Shaughnessy, 1990: 207–8*)

The relation of opinion polling to the marketing of soap powder and corn flakes is close and, many would argue, is getting closer all the time (O'Shaughnessy, 1990; Sabato, 1981; Perry, 1984). The issue which arises is to what extent does the marketing of a party or candidate actually shape the policies? Is the political process increasingly determined by the maketing people who analyse the polls and other data on voters and gear the policies and their modes of presentation to maximize the appeal of the party or candidate to the target political consumers?

❖ Political manipulation and the presentation of policy

James M. Perry, *The New Politics*, 1968

Perry's book was one of the first studies to point out that technology was changing the way in which politicians and policy-makers played the American political game. He considers the role of a new breed of political manager and the use of polls so as to ensure that the candidates' policies are geared to the target voters. Computers then were very much in their infancy but Perry shows how their use was likely to increase. The philosophy which he saw as central to this new politics was rationality:

> The idea of rational decision making is the major factor that unites all the new political technologies. Rational is the key word. Rational decisions. Rational issues. Rational campaign itineraries. Rational television. Rational literature. The technologists don't want to take a single step in the dark.'
> (*Perry, 1968: 212–13*)

Perry concluded that this trend was likely to weaken political parties and increase the power of money. He forecast a rosy future for the Republican Party who were ahead of the technological game.

Roland Perry, *The Programming of the President*, 1984.
Sixteen years on another Perry (Roland) argued that the marketing men and the pollsters had indeed taken over. His book charts the development of the so-called PINS programme which can simulate and model elections so as to help in devising a strategy for winning elections:

> Computers can compile and link the fears, hopes and aspirations, thoughts and feelings of a nation's entire population to form a picture of its mood ... This in turn gives an indication of what should be said and done ... The great weight of constantly increasing information must be filed into categories and subcategories, cross-referenced, linked, separated, grouped, and tracked ... Yet the computer's power stretches far beyond its ability to file endless facts and move them around rapidly. It can be used to program entirely a candidate's bid for political office. This is no longer some science fiction dream or a possibility for the twenty first century. It has already happened.
> (*Perry, 1984: vii*)

Robert Meadow, 'Political Campaigns', 1988
The evolving campaign technologies share a tendency to move towards demassification of the campaign communications environment ... In a sense, the new technologies seek to turn what had been public campaign messages into personal and private campaign communications. On the one hand, it can be argued that personalized campaigns are the antidote to low voter turnout and voter alienation ... On the other hand, the accompanying shift from broadly cast messages that seek to celebrate and find commonalities among voters to messages that seek to exploit differences and to fragment voters can undermine the fundamental consensus upon which stable political systems rest. Single issue politics may replace broad party politics.
(*Meadow, 1988: 270*) ◆

There is evidence to suggest that the programming of the policy agenda is a reality. O'Shaughnessy argues, for example, that in America the real power to structure the policy agenda is shifting towards the hands of the staffers and political consultants employing all the latest techniques of commercial marketing. Policies are sold like products, with the result that the policy agenda is becoming more splintered than in the past and more dominated by single issues. The implications are that the impact of ideas is becoming secondary to the impact of marketing technique. O'Shaughnessy sums up the effects of political marketing in both Britain and the USA as:

- conveying a spurious idea of the political process and the ease with which a 'solution' can be traded and implemented;
- producing a situation in which issues are selected for their dramatic appeal;
- inhibiting political and policy change;
- altering the relationship of the voter to the policy process.

Ancient and modern themes in image-making

As Brendan Bruce, a leading advertising and communications adviser, has rightly pointed out, there is nothing new in the way in which politicians and others have sought to use symbols and images to influence public sentiment. The development of the art and craft of image-making may be dated way back to the beginnings of political institutions (Bruce, 1992: 9–11). In the modern era, and with the aid of new communication technologies and psychological insights into how public opinion is formed, the 'business' has simply become more complex and sophisticated. In the post-war era in particular, sociological and psychological research greatly influenced marketing and advertising approaches of business (Galbraith, 1967; Brown, 1963). The new industrial order was one in which needs and wants were manufactured, and products positioned alongside the appropriate social and psychological type. In Britain this began with the use by the Conservative Party of a leading advertising agency to mastermind the 1951 general election (Bruce, 1992: 97). The experience of the marketing world was by the 1970s finding a renewed and strengthened applicability in politics, as the ideas of brand positioning, and functional and psychological benefits were adopted by politicians in the USA and spread thence to other countries. In this model, policies were products that had to be positioned so as to maximize their appeal to 'consumers'.

❖ Is the power of marketing exaggerated?

Bruce (1992) argues that it is. Although it helps to set the agenda, the ad men do not have the kind of power that its critics suppose. The best advertising cannot sell a product which the consumer does not want. Policies, however they are sold, cannot fool the common sense of the public. Advertising works, he argues, if people remember the product and its benefits. Far more significant, he believes, is the power to manage the news by 'spin-doctors' and others (a term which came out of the Carter–Ford debates in the 1970s).

Franklin (1994), on the other hand, argues that the situation is more critical than Bruce – and other PR/ad men – would suggest. The 'packaging of politics' has had harmful effects on the conduct of political debate in a democracy. Citizens, he believes, are becoming mere spectators in an increasingly media-dominated political system. ◆

In terms of classical notions of liberal democracy, parties advance policies upon which citizens vote. The implications of policy marketing as something which is encroaching upon (if not perhaps replacing) policy-making are profound for both the theory of liberal democracy and its practice. Policy marketing involves not simply the identification of voter needs and wants or the issues and problems which concern them, but also the use of techniques to influence, create and stimulate 'public opinion' on an issue or problem. In which case, the policy agenda is something which is less a product (*sic*) of public opinion, whatever that is, than the result of the way in which political, business and other elites choose to structure the parameters of what is actually discussed. In the brave new world in which millions are spent on marketing parties and policies, it may well be that the political process in liberal democracies is becoming more involved in manipulating the voter *qua* consumer rather than mobilizing people *qua* citizens. Such may be the inevitable result of the idea of analysing the policy agenda *as if* the voter *was* a consumer. If policies are products, then it follows that a very precise instrument indeed is required to measure the difference between a policy and a package of 'Wizzo'.

2.4   Theories of agenda control

From a pluralist perspective the definition of problems and the setting of policy agendas is essentially the outcome of a process of competition between different groups (Truman, 1951; Dahl and Lindblom, 1953; Dahl, 1958, 1961). The power to influence what issues go up and down or in and out of the policy agenda is seen as dispersed rather than concentrated, and although early versions of pluralism accepted to a greater or lesser extent that power and influence was not equally distributed, policy-making was seen as something which was open to freedom of speech and public debate. In a free society, it could be argued, all can influence the policy agenda. Structural-functionalist models, for example, represent the liberal democratic political system as one in which what comes out of the black box is a function of what goes in. However, from the 1960s onwards this notion of public policy as framed by pluralistic politics (articulation and aggregation in Almond's model) has been subject to much criticism. Critiques of this idea of the black box as open to all inputs and as being neutral have focused on the way in which public policy is made in the context of processes that are biased in favour of some groups, ideas and interests and against others. The two main sets of critique which challenge pluralist assumptions about the openness and neutrality of the policy-making process in terms of agenda-setting are:

E.E. Schattschneider, *The Semisovereign People*, 1960.
R.W. Cobb and C.D. Elder, *Participation in American Politics*, 1972.
P.S. Bachrach and M.S. Baratz, 'Two faces of power', 1962.
———, *Power and Poverty, Theory and Practice*, 1970.
S. Lukes, *Power*, 1974.

In this section we shall review the arguments of Schattschneider and of Cobb and Elder. Section 2.6 covers those of Bachrach and Baratz and of Lukes.

2.4.1   Schattschneider: determining what politics is about

E.E. Schattschneider made one of the earliest and most significant contributions to the study of bias in agenda-setting in his book *The Semisovereign People*, published in 1960. The book argues that an essential power of government is the power to manage conflict before it starts. The scope and extent of conflict is limited and framed, he argues, by the dominant players in the political game. The domain of the political is not something which is as open and pluralistic as liberal democratic theory and empirical research (by Truman, Dahl, Lindblom *et al.*) had maintained. The game we play is the game which is structured by the rules which suit the top players: pressure groups, parties and institutions. Politics as a conflict of values, beliefs and interests is thus displaced by the management of conflict:

> No regime could endure which did not cope with this problem ... All forms of political organization have a bias in favor of the exploitation of some kinds of conflict and the suppression of others because organization is the mobilization of bias. Some issues are organized into politics while others are organized out ... There is no more certain way to destroy the meaning of politics than to treat all issues as if they were free and equal. The inequality of issues simplifies the interpretation of politics. Politics becomes meaningful when we establish our priorities.
> (*Schattschneider, 1960: 71–3*)

From this model it follows that public policy is essentially an activity in which issues are included and excluded and bias is mobilized to ensure that conflict is managed and contained. The definition of issues is therefore a fundamental form of political power. And from this it follows that: 'the definition of the alternatives is the supreme instrument of power' (Schattschneider, 1960: 69). Because people cannot agree about what the issues actually are: 'He who determines what politics is about runs the country, because the definition of alternatives is the choice of conflicts' (ibid.).

The Schattschneider model of the processes wherein winners seek to contain the scope of conflict and losers expand the scale of conflict was developed further in subsequent years by Cobb and Elder (1971, 1972, 1983) and Cobb *et al.* (1976).

2.4.2   Cobb and Elder: the expansion of conflict

Cobb and Elder were concerned with the analysis of limited participation and how the agenda process provides a linking level of analysis
between the social system as a whole and decision-making. Their
focus is on the way in which conflict is expanded and managed. What
makes for an issue in their model? As a conflict between two or more
groups over procedural matters relating to the distribution of positions or resources (Cobb and Elder, 1972: 82) issues may be created by
a number of means:

- manufacture by a contending party who perceive unfairness or bias
  in the distribution of positions or resources;
- manufacture of an issue for personal or group gain and advantage;
- unanticipated events;
- 'do-gooders'.

In turn, there are internal and external 'triggering devices' which
prompt the emergence of an issue.

Internal triggers

- Natural catastrophes;
- unanticipated human events;
- technological changes;
- imbalance or bias in distribution of resources;
- ecological change.

External triggers

- Act of war;
- innovations in weapons technology;
- international conflict;
- patterns of world alignment.

The formation of an issue, however, does not depend solely on a
trigger. A link must be made between a trigger and a grievance or
problem which then transforms the issue into an agenda item. The
agenda is characterized by Cobb and Elder as being of two types:
systemic and institutional (see figure 2.10). The systemic agenda is
composed of 'all issues that are commonly perceived by members of
the political community as meriting public attention and as involving
matters within the legitimate jurisdiction of existing governmental
authority' (Cobb and Elder, 1972: 85). The institutional agenda, on the
other hand, is defined as 'that set of items explicitly up for the active

Figure 2.10   The expansion and control of agendas

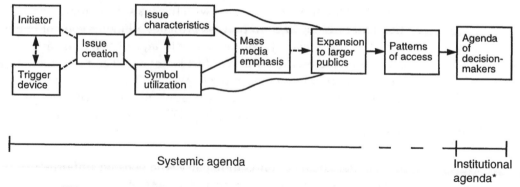

Systemic agenda   Institutional
                                                                                   agenda*

- All issues commonly
  perceived by members of
  a political community as meriting public attention
  of public authorities.
- To get access to systemic agenda an issue
  must have:
  widespread attention/awareness
  shared concern of a sizable portion of public
  shared perception that it is a matter of concern
  to a public authority

- Explicitly up for
  active and serious
  consideration by
  decision-makers.
- May be an old item
  which is up for
  regular review or
  is of periodic
  concern. Or it may
  be a 'new' item.

*or governmental/formal

Source: Adapted from Cobb and Elder (1972)

consideration of authoritative decision makers' (ibid.: 86) It is unlikely that an issue will get on to the institutional agenda if it has not first found a place on the systemic agenda.

Agenda-building occurs as a result of the expansion of an issue from a specifically concerned attention group to a wider interested or attentive public – that is, a public which is interested and informed about public affairs and which contains opinion leaders; finally an issue will reach the attention of the general public. The dynamics of this expansion depends in the first instance on the characteristic of the issue. Cobb and Elder argue that:

- The more ambiguously an issue is defined, the greater the likelihood that it will reach an expanded public (*degree of specificity*).
- The more socially significant an issue is defined to be, the greater the likelihood that it will be expanded to a larger public (*scope of social significance*).
- The more an issue is defined as having long-term relevance, the

greater the chance it will be exposed to a larger audience (*temporal relevance*).

- The more non-technical an issue is defined to be, the greater the likelihood that it will be expanded to a larger public (*degree of complexity*).
- The more an issue is defined as lacking a clear precedent, the greater the chance that it will be expanded to a larger population (*categorical precedence*).

Issue expansion has to confront various strategies of issue containment. The strategies for containing conflict involve two aspects, dealing with groups and issues:

- group strategies will focus on: discrediting the group and/or the leader of the group; appeal over the heads of the leadership; co-option of leaders;
- issue strategies will focus on: symbolic rewards or reassurance; showcasing or tokenism; creating new organizational units; symbol co-option; feigned constraint.

In the process of expansion and containment of an issue, the type of language which is used is an important dimension of agenda politics. Cobb and Elder argue that the effective use of symbols in the expansion of an issue may be related to five factors:

- *Historical precedence*: groups may use symbols with a long historical background in a political community and which can provoke strong positive or negative reactions.
- *Efficiency or credibility*: groups may use symbols well or badly. Incorrect usage may do more harm than good to the expansion of an issue.
- *Symbolic saturation*: a symbol may be so overused that it ceases to have any impact.
- *Symbolic reinforcement*: symbols must be reinforced by other symbols.
- *Urgency or portent of a symbol*: symbols which imply action are more likely to have an expansionary effect.

In the use of symbols the role of the mass media is crucial in arousing concern, provoking action, dissuading the opposition, demonstrating a strength of commitment and affirming support. Finally, the access of an issue into the formal institutional decision-making process will depend on the extent to which conflict is made visible to the various publics. The wider the audience, Cobb and Elder argue, the greater the chance that it will get into the decision-making arena:

- When conflicts are confined to identification groups, formal agenda status is most likely to be attained only when disputants threaten to disrupt the system.
- Conflicts that are confined to attention publics are most likely to be brought to the agenda by threats of imminent sanctions.
- Conflicts that are confined to the attentive public are likely to attain the formal agenda through a brokerage channel (the issue is taken up by well-informed people and groups).

Taken together Schattschneider and Cobb and Elder provide models of agenda-setting that may be used in an empirical way to show how the interests of those who have a dominant or monopolistic position in a policy field are motivated to ensure that the issue is contained within tight parameters and how an issue must be expanded if it is to impact on the decision-making process. Winners or policy-holders operate with the strategy that small is beautiful and that issues need to be privatized, whereas those who wish to challenge the dominant definitions and policies will engage in socializing and politicizing the issue, from expert to public and from a private arena to a public arena. Winners seek conflict reduction, losers conflict expansion. Agenda-setting in this sense is therefore to do with the management of conflict, and institutions and organizations have a central role:

> All forms of political organization have a bias in favor of the exploitation of some kinds of conflict and the suppression of others because organization is the mobilization of bias. Some issues get organized into politics while others are organized out.
> (*Schattschneider, 1960: 71*)

The politics of agenda-setting and bias mobilization may therefore be understood in this model as the process wherein issues and priorities are defined through the regulation of conflict. As the work of Cobb and Elder shows, the central factor to be considered is the participation in the political process and the scale of the political policy 'game'.

❖ Using agenda-setting models

Elizabeth Meehan and Selma Svenhuisjen, *Equality Politics and Gender*, 1991
This collection of papers contains two contributions, detailed below, which apply some of the ideas of Cobb, Kingdon and other agenda-setting theorists to the study of gender and public policy. (On Kingdon, see Kingdon, 1984; and 2.10.3.)

Joyce Outshoorn, 'Is this what we wanted? Positive action as issue perversion' (pp. 104–21)

Outshoorn examines the development of the positive (or affirmative) action policies in Holland in the 1970s and 1980s. She sets out a six-stage agenda cycle (pre-political; voicing of wants; issue formation or demand articulation; decision-making; implementation; evaluation), with five 'barriers' to change (breaking the silence; want-demand conversion; political agenda (demand issue-conversion); taking a decision; implementing policy). In the case of positive action policies, the cycle worked to modify the 'women question'. She concludes that:

> If one looks at the life-cycle of the issue of positive action one can discern that there has been a creeping process of issue modification ... It can emerge by broadening a demand, diluting the original content, or by a reductive process in which the original demand loses its scope. An issue can also be redefined in new terms, leading to the disappearance of the old issues. These phenomena are inherent in the policy process and it would be mistaken to see modification as the result of the conscious intention of the actors involved. One of the advantages of the agenda-setting approach is that it can show that modification is usually the result of a process in which many take part but which few can really control. (p. 118)

As far as positive action for women in Holland is concerned, she shows how:

> The life-cycle of the issue progressed from being part of a nearly all-encompassing view on women's status in society to a separate demand in terms of the redistribution of paid and unpaid work; quotas and preferential hiring were part of it. These two demands became subject to redefinition in terms of positive action in which the idea of quotas has disappeared altogether and the idea of state intervention has been abandoned. In combination with the fact that public policy on other aspects of the 'women question' is making no progress, positive action is a meagre response to the original demands of the women's movement. In this longer-term view issue modification occurs by way of reduction. If this tendency persists, one can justifiably speak of issue perversion. (p. 119)

Amy Mazur, 'Agendas and *égalité professionelle*: symbolic policy at work in France' (pp. 122–41)

Mazur examines the French policy of 'égalité professionelle' (EPP). She explains why French equal employment policies have failed to be integrated into general employment policy or enforced by the courts. Adopting Kingdon's model [see 2.10.3] of the pre-decision process, she concludes that although the gender issue was brought to the attention of government, the actual policy has been marginalized and unsynchronized with other related policies. As a consequence, the EPP policy has been largely symbolic:

> When a policy proposal comes bottom of the decision agenda, it will get short shrift in the formulation process and will not provoke significant policy feedback. As the French case shows, there are different explanations for why problem recognition, policy propositions and politics are not effectively bundled together ... Symbolic policy, at least in France, has an important role of drawing political attention to an issue that normally would not gain decision agenda status; however, the outcome of such policy can only be incremental at best. (p. 137) ◆

2.5   Typologies of policy issues

As Cobb and Elder and Schattschneider show, issues and their definition are dimensions of the policy process which require close attention. An issue will come to be placed in a context or policy setting, and
the kind of context defines its place in the arena of political conflict
and the strategy of those involved in managing the scope of conflict. A
number of scholars have suggested typologies of issues which facilitate comparison between different issues and policies.

Wilson (1973), for example, uses the criteria of costs and benefits
which may be either concentrated or dispersed. An issue which may
have very concentrated benefits to a small section of society, but whose
costs are widely dispersed is of a different kind to one that may be for
'the greatest happiness of the greatest number'. Consider, for example, the costs of the opera, which may be a benefit to a few and cost
taxpayers a good deal of money. The way in which the opera is defined as an issue is rooted in how the costs and benefits of spending
on the arts is perceived. The strategy of arts groups and bodies would
clearly involve showing how widely the benefits of the arts are dispersed, whilst those paid-up members of the Philistine Club will seek
to focus on the costs and narrow the benefits. The same might be said
of an issue such as Aids policy and spending, in which the costs and
benefits are central to the way in which that issue will be defined and
prioritized. Focusing and costs and benefits again draw our attention
to the sense in which winning and losing is involved in the agenda
process. Lowi (1964), for instance, puts forward an influential classification based upon their distributive and regulative nature (see Ripley
and Franklin, 1980, 1982). Issues, Lowi suggests, may be classified in
terms of being distributive, regulative or redistributive:

- *distributive policy issues*: the distribution of new resources;
- *redistributive policy issues*: changing the distribution of existing resources;
- *regulatory policy issues*: the regulation and control of activities.

Later, Lowi (1972) added another type: 'constituent' policy issues –
the setting-up or reorganization of institutions.

Each of these constitutes a different power arena with distinctive political characteristics. For Lowi, policies – as issue arenas – determine
politics and not vice versa. Issue arenas give rise to different forms of
politics. Although his typology has been widely adopted, the deterministic view of politics as a function of policies has been criticized as
over-simplistic and methodologically suspect (Sabatier, 1991; Heclo,

1972; May, 1986). The usefulness of the typology has also been questioned on the grounds of its assumptions and testability. Cobb and Elder, for example, note that the typology has fundamental limitations due to being based on substantive rather than analytical criteria. Thus, it does not provide a framework for understanding change as the types become less clear and more diffuse (Cobb and Elder, 1972: 96). As we have seen above (pp. 126–30), they propose an alternative classification of issues in terms of conflict rather than content.

Hogwood sets out a framework which explores the costs and benefits (see also Wilson, 1973; Ingram, 1978) from the point of view of the possibilities of differential outcomes, forms of bargaining and conflict, and a range of options. Issues of principle are those in which right and wrong, them and us are most polarized into all or nothing: moral, religious or consitutional matters. 'Lumpy' issues involve a good which cannot be divided up: airports, power stations. Issues which involve cuts or redistribution are those which involve bargaining over who gets what, who gets more, and who gets less. Issues which involve increases are those of conditions in which cakes get bigger: everyone is a winner, some win more than others (figure 2.11).

Figure 2.11   *Policy types and their costs and benefits*

	Principle	Lumpy	Cuts/ redistribution	Increases
Range of options open to government	Yes/No	Location	Finely divisible but constrained	Finely divisible
Scope for bargaining	Minimal	Minimal (except for log-rolling)	Bargaining about relative cuts (negative or zero sum)	Bargaining about relative growth (positive sum)
Outcome for participants	Win or lose	Win or lose	Differential misery	Differential menefits

Source: Adapted from Hogwood (1987: 31)

Such typologies of issues framed by costs and benefits exclude another important dimension of issue, the degree of complexity and technical or expert knowledge. From the point of view of conflict management, issues which are deemed to be 'expert' or highly technical in their nature will be more private or inner issues than the public-domain 'non-expert' variety. Gormley (1983), for example, suggests that the degree and kind of technical complexity will give rise to different forms of conflict. Technical issues which involve claims to knowledge have in the last decade or so become more 'open' to public controversy as issues have become less dominated by the power of experts and professionals to construct them in a purely scientific or technical fashion (see 2.8). Technicality of issues inherently limits the scope of conflict. It is in the interest of – in the language of Schattschneider – 'winners' to limit the scale of conflict on technical and scientific matters on the grounds that the issues are far too complex and difficult for non-experts to understand. Those excluded from this sphere engage in strategies to enlarge the issue to encompass a wider debate framed in terms other than those of the experts. Environmental groups in particular have been in the forefront of this redefinition of scientific and technical issues (Nelkin (ed.), 1992: 59–112). The more an issue is located within a definition of being technical/scientific the more is that issue defined as being 'non-political' or 'non-partisan'. The strategy of those who wish to challenge the construction of an issue as being outside the sphere of political conflict is to campaign for that issue to be seen as one which involves the public at large, or a section of the public, in asking moral and other questions. It might, for example, focus on distributive questions about the costs and benefits of a project or policy, thus challenging the power of those making knowledge claims and holding up expert issues to a wider public/political scrutiny. But who decides on what issues are defined in a 'technical' context?

2.6   Pluralism, non-decision-making and the third dimension of power

The pluralist approach to public policy tended to assume that public policy was ultimately the outcome of a free competition between ideas and interests. In Dahl, Polsby and earlier American pluralist accounts of democracy, power was seen as widely distributed and the political system so organized that the policy process was essentially driven by public demands and opinions. Dahl (1961), for example, in his famous study of New Haven could argue that :

> In the United States the political system does not constitute a homogeneous class with well-defined class interests. In New Haven, in fact, the political system is easily penetrated by anyone whose interests and concerns attract him to the distinctive political culture of the stratum ... The independence, penetrability and heterogeneity of the various segments of the political stratum all but guarantee that any dissatisfied group will find a spokesman.
> (Dahl, 1961: 91–3)

In the pluralist heaven (or Haven), participation in the great game of politics was open to all. However, this view of liberal democracy was

challenged by Schattschneider when he argued that: 'It is not necessarily true that people with the greatest needs participate in politics
most actively – whosoever decides what the game is about will also
decide who gets in the game' (Schattschneider, 1960: 105). As we
noted above (2.4.1), what Schattschneider's 'realistic' account showed
was that there was a bias which operated in favour of some and
against others. The mobilization of bias theory was greatly enhanced
by the work of Bachrach and Baratz (1962, 1963, 1970), whose approach addressed a different aspect of the pluralist case: the definition
of power. Dahl, for example, had argued that power resided in the
capacity of A to make B do something which B would otherwise not
choose to do. Power in this sense essentially involved the control of
behaviour. Dahl (1961) had shown that as power was distributed between different groups, policy-making in areas such as education and
urban redevelopment was structured by a series of minorities, rather
than a single elite. As Polsby expresses it: 'In each issue area different
actors appeared, their roles were different and the kinds of alternatives which they had to choose among were different' (Polsby, 1963:
60). However, in response to this model Bachrach and Baratz argued
that what the pluralist case had failed to appreciate was the extent to
which those with power can actually exclude issues and problems
from the policy-making agenda. Politics was not simply what Lasswell
(1936) had defined as the study of 'who gets what when and how' but
also who gets left out – when and how (Bachrach and Baratz, 1962:
105). Non-decision-making will involve the constriction or containment of decision-making so as to be focused on 'safe issues by manipulating the dominant community values, myths, and political institutions and procedures' (Bachrach and Baratz, 1963: 632). Bias against
certain interests in society may be routinized, thus making it very
difficult for certain demands to penetrate the black box of the political
system. Power is not simply the control of observable behaviour and
decisions. Bachrach and Baratz argued that it also consisted in the
non- observable realm of 'non-decisions':

> A non-decision, as we define it, is a decision that results in the suppression
> or thwarting of a latent or manifest challenge to the values and interests of
> the decision maker. To be more clearly explicit, non-decision-making is a
> means by which demands for change in the existing allocation of benefits
> and privileges in the community can be suffocated before they are even
> voiced; or kept covert; or killed to gain access to the relevant decision-
> making arena; or failing all these things, maimed or destroyed in the
> decision-implementing stage of the policy process.
> (*Bachrach and Baratz, 1970: 7*)

Non-decision-making suggests that policy-makers with power have a
capacity to keep issues off the agenda which they control. This capacity is also a function of the power and influence behind the new

issues. At the early stages in the development of social movements decision makers can largely ignore those issues they choose. 'Women's issues', for example, is an obvious case in point. The characteristics of the social movements and lobby groups is thus a major factor in the influence which new issues can have on established agendas, as are events which may force issues on to the policy agenda, an obvious example of which would be the environmental issue.

❖ Agenda-setting and non-decision-making

Peter Saunders, 'They make the rules', 1975

This was an early article which applied the ideas of Bachrach and Baratz and Lukes (see p. 142) to a case study of British local government (Croydon). He subsequently developed his arguments in a fuller form (see Saunders, 1979, 1981). His study of policy-making in Croydon seeks to show how 'the powerful selectively interpret their perceived roles, and redefine the structure in which they are embedded ... [and] how the structural context in which political action is situated may be responsive to the interests and assumptions of participants and how a largely unconscious routinization of bias, regularly favouring some interests while prejudicing others, may thereby be generated within political systems' (p. 31).

Note: On the idea that routines give advantages to some groups/interests, see Parry and Morriss (1974), one of the first reviews of the debate on non-decision-making and still essential reading.

Shamit Saggar, *Race and Public Policy*, 1991

In this study the author shows how the issue of race was kept out of politics. The liberal policy framework, he argues, effectively operated to exclude race from the political agenda at both a national and a local level. Using an empirical analysis of two London boroughs Saggar shows how the course of the race issue in public policy was largely determined by a consensus which had been established in the 1960s. Saggar terms this the race policy environment (RPE). He concludes his study by observing that:

> The story of the application of the liberal policy framework has been one of general failure accompanied by limited temporary successes. The successes centred mainly on the removal of race-specific policy debate from the RPE for a long period until the mid to late 1970s ... Radical, race-specific policy proposals were not heard largely bacause they were perceived as illegitimate threats to the established policy framework ... The result was the planting of new grievances ... The crisis was only defused through the selective and limited incorporation of race-specific demands into legitimate RPE debate, thereby transforming the recognisable character of the RPE. (pp. 162–3)

Ironically, in so attempting to take race out of the policy agenda Saggar concludes that policy-makers in Barnet and Ealing thereby facilitated the politicization of race.

Kathleen Staudt and Jane Jacquette, 'Women's programs, bureaucratic resistance and feminist organisation', 1988

The authors comment on the fact that, despite the progress in progressive laws and policies at national and international level, 'barely a dent has been made in redistributing resources and values among men and women'. One of the main reasons they contend is the bureaucratic resistance to redistributive and conflict-laden issues:

> Apparent victories are often caught up in a bureaucratic mire of inaction, avoidance and distortion ... programs to enhance women's economic integration and redistribute opportunities and resources by gender pose a special threat to male bureaucratic decision makers, a threat with which they can easily identify and stymie in myriad ways. (pp. 263–4)

The only way in which this capacity of men to stop female issues getting into the decision-making process is for women to develop autonomous international feminist movements and agendas which can challenge the dominant actions and discourse of governmental organizations. Female empowerment may also make some impact on policy-making as a pluralistic process. But a transformation in the underpinning ideology of states and bureaucracies is ultimately the only way in which female agendas can inform policy.

The disabled as a non-issue

In the 1960s the Labour MP Alf Morris was responsible for promoting the cause of the Disabled Persons Act. A quarter of a century later he recalls:

> It seems incredible and outrageous now, but from 1945 to 1964 there was no mention in party manifestos of anything specific to help disabled people. Between 1959 and 1964, there was not one debate in the Commons on disability. Westminster and Whitehall always had more pressing things than responding to the claims of people with disabilities. No one even knew how many disabled people there were in Britain. They were treated not even as second class citizens, more as non-people.
> (*Morris, 1994: 7*)

Systems approaches to 'non-decision-making'

Using the Eastonian model of the policy process one could argue that, in order to maintain the 'system', mechanisms exist to filter out, or exclude input which would be dysfunctional, or which would 'overload' the system. Easton (1965) refers to these regulators as 'gatekeepers'. These function so as to exclude from the system excessive or unacceptable demands. Interest groups, parties, opinion leaders and the mass media may serve this function. Thus a modified model incorporates the notion that the system has a bias against certain inputs that would modify the black box so as to incorporate a mediating filter which allows in supportive demands and keeps out dysfunctionality (figure 2.12).

Non-decision-making in Marxist and neo-pluralist approaches

Offe, a Marxist, has argued that, in a capitalist system, anti-capitalist demands, or demands which threaten the interest of capital, are filtered out (Offe 1974, 1976). From a different neo-pluralist perspective Nicklas Luhmann has argued that if we conceptualize systems as being

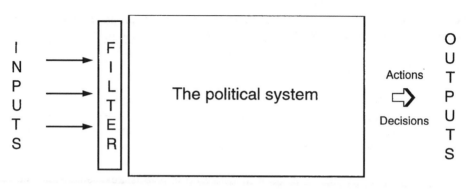

Figure 2.12   A systems model of agenda control

closed and self-regarding (or autopoietic) then the notion of such bias may be read as a process wherein change is the result of internal logic, rather than as the outcome of inputs or environmental influences. As he notes: 'Even "information" is not something that the system takes in from the environment. Information doesn't exist "out there" waiting to be picked up by the system. As selection it is produced by the system itself' (Luhmann, 1990: 4). The self-referencing policy-making system may, in this sense, be seen as driven by the logic of withinputs, rather than by the pressure of demands. And those 'inputs' which are filtered in are interpreted in terms of the system's map of the world, its frames of reference, rather than of the world outside the black box. (On self-referencing systems, see Morgan, 1986: 233–72.) ◆

The idea of agendas being shaped by non-decisional power is therefore a powerful model and a widely applied approach. However, it is not without its critics. At the behaviouralist/pluralist level the critique has been in terms of the empirical basis of studying non-events (see Merelman, 1968; Wolfinger, 1971; Polsby, 1963). An early riposte to pluralist criticism came in the form of empirical studies by Bachrach and Baratz (1970) and Crenson (1971). Bachrach and Baratz's study was an examination of poverty, race and politics in Baltimore and showed how business leaders and politicians sought to ensure that the demands of black people in the city were excluded from the decision-making processes by various means, including force, sanctions, co-options, manipulation of symbols such as the labelling of certain views as emanating from 'troublemakers' and 'communists', and strengthening 'the mobilization of bias' by new barriers or symbols. The study by Crenson of pollution in two cities, however, takes the theory a little further, and is viewed by Lukes (1974) as being on the border between the second and his own 'third' dimensional view of power. Crenson's book is of special interest to the student of public policy as it brings together several important areas of analysis: the study of issue formation; decision-making and non-decision-making; and the organizational context of issue and policy formulation. For this reason in this section we shall devote somewhat more space to Crenson than to Bachrach and Baratz or to Lukes and Gaventa.

Crenson confronts the criticism that non-events, non-issues or non-decisions are methodologically problematic, but argues that 'inaction' by policy-makers may be studied by analysing the way in which an issue penetrates the political process in one community and fails to emerge in another. The issue he considers is air pollution. Clearly, nobody wants to breathe polluted air, so if it could be demonstrated that, despite comparable levels of air pollution, some cities have been active in addressing the issue whilst others have not, a good case for 'non-decision-making' may be made on the basis of empirical evidence.

His conclusion was that the reason for the non-issue status of pollution in Gary was that it was a city dominated by a big polluter, US Steel. The way in which US Steel kept the issue off the agenda was through the exercise of power which was 'outside the range of observable political phenomena' (Crenson, 1971: 107): the power of the organization was sufficient for it to remain outside the political arena, and yet affect the scope and direction of decision-making. This assessment of the role of industry in the pollution issue in Gary is confirmed by an examination of 52 other cities, which led Crenson to conclude that where cities have powerful polluters, the issue of clean air is unlikely to emerge. Thus pluralist accounts of decision-making, he argued, were fundamentally wrong in not recognizing that although decision-making may be 'pluralistic' and fragmented, 'non-decision-making' exhibited a high degree of unity (Crenson, 1971: 179). What is not done is more important than what is seen to be done. The visible and articulate face of pluralism obscures a hidden and inarticulate process in which issues can be shut out of the political process:

> community political power may consist of something other than the ability to influence the resolution of local political issues; there is also the ability to prevent some topics from ever becoming issues and to obstruct the growth of emergent issues ... [furthermore] this power need not be exercised in order to be effective. The mere reputation for power, unsupported by acts of power, can be sufficient to restrict the scope of local decision-making. Even people and groups who do not actively participate in a community's political deliberations may influence their content. Likewise, the 'victims' of political power may remain politically invisible – indeed, invisibility may constitute their response to the power of non-decision-making ... The operation of political power, therefore, is not always revealed in observable political action ... To put it simply, there is more to local politics than meets the eye.
> (*Crenson, 1971: 177–8*)

Power resides as much in the capacity to command inaction as to command action. And the existence of such power constitutes a major challenge to the pluralist belief that the policy-making process is open and 'penetrable' as originally proposed by Dahl (1961: 93) and others. Another point of criticism advanced by Crenson is with regard to the pluralist approach to the rise and fall of issues. Crenson defines an issue as:

> any unresolved matter, controversial or non-controversial, which awaits an authoritative decision. It is a topic which has been included on a community's political agenda. The problem is to decide at just what point a topic becomes an agenda item and is therefore ripe for authoritative resolution.
> (*Crenson, 1971: 29*)

According to pluralist theory (Crenson, 1971: 161), issues (like power) are fragmented and competitive, and the linkages between one issue and another are 'few and weak'. However, Crenson argues that this is a grossly inaccurate and simplistic conception of how issues get on or are kept off the agenda. He suggests that we view issue politics in terms of an 'ecological' relationship in which the policy costs and benefits (see Lowi, Wilson, Hogwood: 2.5 above) to policy-makers and organizations are the crucial determinants:

> In general, a political issue tends to be ignored if there is a mismatch between the kinds of benefits that it is likely to create and the kinds of inducements that influential community organizations need in order to survive and grow.
> (*Crenson, 1971: 156*)

To arrive at this conclusion Crenson draws together the arguments of policy theorists such as Lowi (see 2.5) which focus on the types and kinds of public policy and their respective benefits, and theories concerned with incentives and patterns of organizational behaviour (such as Etzioni, 1961; Crenson, 1971: 156–7). He concludes that:

> Political issues ... have an organizational aspect. When policy theorists try to relate the characteristics of a policy to the pattern of political activity which it has generated, they are attempting, in effect, to establish a connection between kinds of inducements that are distributed by an informal organization and the internal practices of that organization.
> (*Crenson, 1971: 158*)

In other words, the bias of organizations in their selection of issues will translate into a wider social or community bias. (As Schattschneider, 1961: 71, puts it: 'organization is the mobilization of bias'.) The ups and downs (see Downs, 1972; and 2.3.1) of the cycle of issue attention has, therefore, as Peters and Hogwood show (1985; 2.3.1) to be related to the organizational context. (See also Kingdon in 2.10.3 for another organizational approach to issues and agendas.) According to the pluralist view:

> Different issues tend to activate different groups ... alignments ... styles. The result is a high degree of political disorder. Political issues are transitory, episodic phenomena, and because the political life of a community tends to be organized around issues, it too tends to be episodic and unordered.
> (*Crenson, 1971: 178*)

However, Crenson contends that his examination of the air pollution issue yields a very different picture. Issues, he argues, are not as random as they may appear: they have an order and a rationality. One set of demands may lead to a series of other rationally related issues. Given a certain end, issues may be deployed as means to that end. For example, concerns about air pollution may rationally lead to the issue of governmental reforms. The promotion of one issue may promote or inhibit other issues. Thus the commitment of a community to one concern will diminish its concern with issues which contradict or are antagonistic to that primary concern. In the case of the environment, it is likely that if the community is committed to 'jobs' and economic development or arresting decline, the direction of the agenda will be framed in such a way as to downplay or ignore the environmental costs. The agenda is not random, but highly ordered. The 'ups and downs' of concern may mask a more fundamental set of collective values and priorities:

> The visible political activities of a community are more ordered and inhibited than an inspection of the activities alone would lead us to believe. There are politically imposed limitations upon the scope of decision-making ... there is a general bias or direction in ... disjointedness. Decision-making activity is channelled and restricted by the process of non-decision-making. The power reputations of people and groups within the community may deter action on certain sensitive or politically unprofitable issues. Activity in one issue-area may tend to foreclose action in certain other issue areas.
> (*Crenson, 1971: 178*)

Significantly, Crenson sees this exercise of power by promoting inactivity as operating at an 'ideological' level in which 'political forms and practices' serve to 'diffuse discontent' and 'promote selective perception and articulation of social problems and conflicts' (Crenson, 1971: 23). Issues can 'create political consciousness' as well as 'shape and restrict consciousness'. And, he argues: 'The issues on a political agenda may be rationally linked, not to one another, but to some comprehensive political ideal or principle that transcends the agenda – an ideological vision of the political system' (Crenson, 1971: 173).

Steven Lukes in his essay on power (1974) extends Crenson's argument about the way elites 'exercise considerable control over what people care about and how forcefully they articulate their cares'

(Crenson, 1971: 27) by positing that power operates at a far deeper level than is considered by Bachrach and Baratz, but is implied in Crenson:

> A may exercise power over B by getting him to do what he does not want to do, but he also exercises power over him by influencing, shaping, or determining his very wants.
> (*Lukes, 1974: 23*)

Power also operates in the way in which myths and symbols are manipulated (see Edelman in 2.9.2; and Lasswell, 1930, 1935, 1948) and in the existence of an 'ideological hegemony ' (Gramsci, see 2.7.1). Power exists in the 'construction' of meaning in society (Berger and Luckman, 1975; see also 2.2.2). As Lukes notes:

> One does not have to go to the lengths of talking about Brave New World, or the world of B.F. Skinner to see this: thought control takes many less total and more mundane forms, through the control of information, through the mass media, and through the process of socialization.
> (*Lukes, 1974: 23*)

❖ Power in three dimensions

Lukes's framework
The differences between the 'pluralist', 'non-decisionist' and Lukes's view on how the distribution of power shapes the issues and agendas of public policy is summarized below (based on Lukes, 1974: 25).

Pluralist model (one-dimensional)
Method: Behavioural
Focuses on the analysis of:
(a) behaviour;
(b) decision-making;
(c) key issues;
(d) conflict which can be observed and is open;
(e) the subjective interests and preferences which may be observed in open political participation

The non-decisionist model (two-dimensional)
Method: Critical behavioural
Focuses on the analysis of:
(a) decision-making and non-decision-making;
(b) issues and potential issues;
(c) observable covert or overt conflict;
(d) subjective interests revealed by policy preferences and grievances

Lukes (three-dimensional)
Method: Radical anti-behavioural
Focuses on the analysis of:
(a) decisions and agenda control, but not just through decisions;
(b) issues and potential issues;
(c) observable and latent conflict;
(d) subjective real interests.

J. Gaventa, *Power and Powerlessness, Quiescence and Rebellion in an Appalachian Valley*, 1980

Gaventa provides another useful classification of the three dimensions of power (figure 2.13).

Figure 2.13   Dimensions of power compared

	First dimension	**Second dimension**	**Third dimension**
Power of A over B	Control of A over B through superior bargaining resources	A constructs a barrier against participation of B (non-DM and mobilization of bias)	Influencing or shaping of consciousness of B about inequalities (through myths, information control, ideology ... etc.)
Powerlessness of B to A	Defeat of B due lack of resources	Non-participation of B due to barriers and anticipated defeat	Susceptibility to myths, etc., induces sense of powerlessness; uncritical consciousness about issues of B due to influencing or shaping by A and due to maintenance of non-participation by A
Response of A to challenges by B	Open conflict with competing resources over clearly defined issues	Mobilization on issues; action upon barriers	Formulation of issues and strategies

Source: Adapted from Gaventa (1980)

W.I. Jenkins, *Policy Analysis*, 1978

At the crucial stage of Antonioni's film *Blow-Up* the central character ... struggles to find out whether he has unwittingly witnessed and photographed a murder in a London park ... In a frantic quest to find out he runs his film through the enlarger until the grains almost separate out from each other on the print. Technology, however, sets a limit on perception. Shadow or substance? Fact or fantasy? The final answer is unknown ... As a concept, non-decision is frequently much like quicksand. Both logically and empirically it poses problems. May it, at both one and the same time, mean everything and nothing? ... a focus on non-decisions is a clear way out of the dilemma described by Lowi (1970) as 'the technocratisation of policy analysis': that the analyst, in being instrumental and technocatic, becomes blinded to certain fundamental political patterns. A non-decision-making perspective is one way to clear this blindness, to gaze with Antonioni's photographer through the park railings, and to identify whether there is a figure at all and whether it is threatening. (pp. 105, 115, 116) ◆

Lukes argues that his three-dimensional view provides the basis of a sociological examination of power. This was brilliantly accomplished by Lukes's doctoral student John Gaventa in a study of power and powerlessness in the Appalachian mountains. Gaventa applied the three approaches and concluded that, contrary to critics of the 'hidden faces' of power, his study showed that:

> power can and should be viewed in its multiple dimensions, and that mechanisms or processes within each are specifiable ... a 'view from be-low' has allowed a unique perspective of power's hidden faces, as they work in the maintenance of quiescence and in the containment of rebel-lion.
> (*Gaventa, 1980: 253*)

His examination of power in an Appalachian community illustrates that it involves three dimensions: the surface mechanisms of power; participation and decision employed by pluralists; the control of agendas; the mobilization of bias; and the setting of rules, as put forward by Schattschneider, and Bachrach and Baratz; and the shaping of wants and beliefs and the manipulation of myths and symbols, as suggested by Lukes. His key point is that each dimension acts upon another:

> While each dimension of power has its mechanisms and uses, it is only through the interrelationship of the dimensions and the re-inforcing effect of each dimension on the other that the total impact of power upon the actions and conceptions of the powerless may be fully understood. What is voiced by the powerholders in the decision-making arenas may not always reflect the real conflict, but may articulate norms or myths which disguise or deflect the more latent conflict ... What does not happen or what goes unsaid in the first-dimensional arenas ... may also shape conceptions about which matters are appropriate for consideration upon the dominant agendas. Similarly, second dimensional exercises of power affect vulnerability to the shaping of wants and beliefs, as in the third dimension of power, which in turn strengthens the symbolic resources available from the second ... From this perspective, the total impact of a power relationship is more than the sum of its parts. Power serves to create power. Powerlessness serves to re-inforce powerlessness. Power relationships, once established, are self-sustaining.
> (*Gaventa, 1980: 256*)

The arguments of third-dimensional theorists have a particular relevance to the student of public policy in that they develop the line of argument which was first developed in the work of Lasswell and, later, of Edelman (as Gaventa, 1980: 12, notes). The third dimension, argues Gaventa, involves the study of 'social myths, language, and symbols and how they are manipulated in power processes ... [and] the study of communication of information' (Gaventa, 1980: 15). For Lasswell the study of such non-visible, psychological dimensions of politics was a vitally important aspect of the policy-making process. Sadly, for the greater part of its development the analysis of policy-making has tended to focus almost entirely on the first dimension, with scant attention paid to the way in which elites seek to use symbols to manipulate public opinion and the subconscious of men and women: or the person, personality, group and culture (Lasswell, 1939). An elite, he argued, 'preserves its ascendancy by manipulating symbols, controlling supplies and applying violence' (ibid.: 3). The study of policy-making therefore should, as Gaventa demonstrates, include those deeper processes whereby what Lasswell termed 'symbol specialists' (politicians) and others including the media exercise a subtle and less-visible form of power.

As we shall examine in the next section, this has also been a theme of neo-Marxist and critical approaches.

2.7   Neo-Marxist and critical approaches

2.7.1   Deep theories

The idea that 'problems' and 'agendas' are set in a dimension which is, as Lukes argues above, not observable in a behavioural way is an argument which is to be found in a broad range of what we might term 'deep' theories. In common with Bachrach and Baratz and Lukes, deep theorists argue that the exercise of power in defining problems and setting agendas is something which takes place at a deeper level than what may be seen in surface or decisional terms. Deep theorists direct our attention to the ideological or psychological processes at work in society as a whole which are not necessarily revealed in the surface level of power. Problems may be constructed and agendas set in a dimension which is not empirically observable, through systems of beliefs, values, assumptions and ideologies.

In this section we examine two groups of 'deep' theorists whose ideas have considerable importance to the analysis of problems and agendas: a group of theorists who have worked in the context of Marxist and Weberian frames and who have been identified by Ham and Hill (1984) as providing 'linking levels of analysis' (2.7.2), and a so-called 'argumentative' approach derived from sources as diverse as French post-structuralism and German critical theory (2.7.3).

❖ Sources of 'deep' approaches

Hegemony: Gramsci and unseen power

The model offered by Gramcsi constitutes a major refocusing of the Marxist idea of class rule, and echoes the psychological concerns of Freudians and the Frankfurt School Gramsci argued that the power of the ruling class was more subtle than the physical domination of one class over another. The ruling class had a 'hegemony' over the mental processes of the ruled. The real power of the dominant class was the power they had in making their view of the world pervade and dominate other views. It follows from this that the ruling class does not simply control the agenda or the definition of problems, but it also has the capacity to control the way men and women see social reality. Force and coercion are not the norm, but are used only at times of crisis. The theories of Bachrach and Baratz and Lukes are echoing Gramsci's analysis that power is not an open, but a concealed process.

Radical views of how problems are defined and agendas are set owe much to Gramsci's notion of hegemony. Indeed, from this framework, the ability of the ruling class so to control social reality means that the focus on the 'meso' level is far more important than the analysis of how decisions are made in government, or how they are implemented. Given that reality is something which is determined by the ruling class, a Gramscian analysis would be far more concerned with how that process of framing reality takes place: the role of intellectuals as mediators in the ideological control is of special significance.

The hegemonic view of the policy process is less concerned about events and the observable, than about the non-events, the ordinary and unseen power of capital:

> the proof of that power is not to be found only, or even chiefly, in the fact that capitalists make decisions. It is to be found in the fact that the decisions which both they and others – including government – make, and the sheer routine conduct of affairs even without definite decision-making, in the main have a common denominator: an everyday acceptance of private property and market mechanisms ... Power is to be found more in uneventful routine than in conscious and active exercise of will.
> (*Westergard and Resler, 1976: 143–4*)

Stewart Clegg and David Dunkerly, *Organization, Class and Control*, 1980

The authors employ a Gramscian model to show how organizations are not simply involved in making things, decisions and implementation, but are also reproducing the dominant ideologies of the ruling class. From this perspective, organizations are not black boxes which get inputs from outside, but are instruments of social, economic and political control. Thus the distinctions which are made in the phases of the policy process – formulation – decision – implementation – evaluation – may be regarded as false representations of a reality in which organizations reproduce class domination, rather than process demands.

The Frankfurt School and critical theory

The analysis of how problems become political has been dominated by what may be termed social models, that is the focus of explanation has been in terms of showing how 'problems' are products of the human conscious mind. From a Freudian perspective, however, the policy agenda is determined by the need for civilization to repress subconscious instincts. The Marxist philosopher Herbert Marcuse (1954, 1972) argued that politics was predicated on sexual repression and the development of administration which could control the sexual urges of human beings. However, Marcuse argued that this form of control was not universal or inevitable, but a product of a capitalist society, dominated by the 'performance principle' and economic goals. Whereas Freud believed repression was an inextricable part of the human condition, radical libertarian Freudians such as Marcuse (and others of the Frankfurt School) have been more optimistic in believing that a revolutionary new social order could create conditions for the liberation of the individual.

This theme of how politics in industrial societies works to control the mind and repress the individual forms an essential part of the model of problem-definition contained in critical theory: including Marcuse, and Habermas. The 'totally administered' society produces a politics which is merely 'one dimensional' (Marcuse, 1972). The trend towards the bureaucratization of life may therefore be seen as producing a political agenda which structures reality in forms which suit the interests of the capitalist system. From this position, the idea that the policy process involves a free definition of problems is erroneous. The real power of capitalism is the power which it has to influence the individual's sense of reality. The rationality which expresses itself in the public policy agenda is an instrument of domination and control.

Perhaps the most significant critical theorist for public policy is Jürgen Habermas. From the perspective of Habermas's work, the process by which problems are defined and the agenda of public policy is set should be understood in the context of deeper controls and manipulations which operate in capitalist society in the interests of maintaining the legitimacy of the state. The remedy he proposes is that of the development of 'ideal speech situations' in which there can be a genuine equality of participation in the analysis of social problems and public policy, rather than the domination of instrumental technocratic rationality. As Bobrow and Dryzek note, this has much in common with the arguments of Harold Lasswell (Bobrow and Dryzek, 1987: 174). Habermas has been highly critical of the way in which the quantification of public opinion has contributed to the distortion of politics and policy by the mass media and bureaucracy, and has served to debase and destroy the public sphere:

> Citizens entitled to services relate to the state not primarily through political participation but by adopting a general attitude of demand – expecting to be provided for without actually wanting to fight for the necessary decisions … The extent to which the public sphere as an element in the political realm has disintegrated as a sphere of ongoing participation in a rational-critical debate concerning public authority is measured by the degree to which it has become a genuine publicist sphere to begin with.
> (*Habermas, 1989: 211*)

Habermas argues that this debasement of public opinion, and the narrowing of public discussion in industrial societies may be traced to the rise of a state system in which expertise and technical knowledge has a determining role in shaping the public agenda (see 2.8.1).

French post-structuralism: Foucault, knowledge and power

The relationship of knowledge and power is a central theme of one of the most influential thinkers of modern times, Michel Foucault.

He was a philosopher at Clermont-Ferrand, Paris-Vincennes, and professor of the 'history of systems of thought' at the *Collège de France*. Power, he argued, has to be seen as strategies which function on many levels, and his writings direct the student of public policy towards analysing the networks of 'microphysics of power' that exist in knowledge rather than in centres of power. Of particular relevance are his studies of the development (or genealogies) of institutions – *Madness and Civilization* (1965); *Discipline and Punish* (1977). In the latter he shows how disciplinary institutions are central to understanding power relations in modern society. The prison is viewed by Foucault as a model of the ways in which society seeks to discipline and control its members. He rejects the structural view of power in favour of analysing the ways in which discipline becomes internalized within the individual. The growth of 'governmentality' in this sense is to be seen as the development of knowledge as a mode of personal/ political control. In 'On governmentality', for example, he points out that as detailed knowledge became available it increased the power of the state and defined a new rationale for the political process. The knowledge was called 'statistics': the science of the state. This control through knowledge extended into the micro core of the personal domain, as in the case of sexuality:

> Sex was not something one simply judged; it was a thing to be administered. It was in the nature of a public potential; it called for management procedures; it had to be taken charge of by analytical discourses ... One of the great innovations in the techniques of power in the eighteenth century was the emergence of 'population' as an economic and political problem; population as wealth, population as manpower ... It was essential that the state know what was happening with its citizens' sex, and the use they made of it, but also that each individual be capable of controlling the use he made of it. Between the state and the individual, sex became an issue, and a public issue no less; a whole web of discourses, special knowledges, analyses, and similar injunctions settled upon it.
> (*Foucault, 1984: 307*)

See also 4.5.3. ◆

2.7.2   Linking levels of analysis

Ham and Hill in their influential textbook on the policy process conclude by directing our attention to a number of theorists who provide a 'middle-range' level of analysis which links policy formulation, micro decision-making in organizations and the macro political system (Ham and Hill, 1984: 174–89). They argue that the main contributors to this middle-range approach are :

J.K. Benson (1975, 1977a, 1977b, 1982)
S. Clegg and D. Dunkerly, *Organization, Class and Control*, 1980.
G. Salaman, *Class and the Corporation*, 1981.

G. Burrell and G. Morgan, *Sociological Paradigms and Organisational Analysis*, 1979.

Although they differ in their respective frames in terms of the adoption of a Marxist or a Weberian perspective, they share a common concern to go beyond the surface of organizational and institutional power, to show how the policy process is shaped by society. As is the case with Bachrach and Baratz and Lukes, Ham and Hill's 'linking theorists' seek to analyse the deeper processes which influence the surface levels of public policy in its agenda, decision and delivery phases. Benson, drawing on Marxist ideas and the theory of social constructivism put forward by Berger and Luckman (1975: see 2.2.2), for example, provides an analysis of the 'deep' structure which shapes the way in which issues are brought into the realm of decision-making and others are kept outside the decisional processes. Policy-making, from Benson's point of view may be understood as taking place in the context of policy sectors, which compose a 'cluster' or complex of organizations connected to each other by resource-dependency relationships (see 4.3.7). This policy sector may be examined at three levels: administrative structure; interest structure; and rules of structure formation (figure 2.14). In terms of agenda-setting, Benson's framework stresses how the analysis of administrative and interest structures in given policy sectors are shaped by 'deep rules' which operate to ensure that some demands are excluded from the decision-making process, and which limit the choices and behaviour of policy-makers.

Figure 2.14   Benson's model of a policy sector

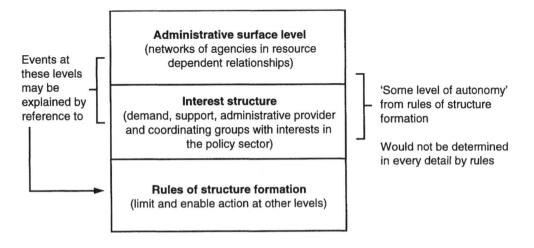

Source: Adapted from Ham and Hill (1984)

What is not clear from this model is what is the 'autonomy' enjoyed by the surface and interest structures? It is not a case of the rule base determining the superstructure above, so much as its being a predominant influence over structures and interests. Benson believes that over time and in some circumstances the 'superstructure' may well develop a large measure of independence. (Perhaps the conditions under which this autonomy could occur may best be explained in terms of so-called 'state-centred' models which argue that the state institutions in a capitalist society do have a capacity for 'relative autonomy' (2.11.6, 3.6.4).

As Ham and Hill note, the Benson model draws on the ideas of the neo-Marxist Carl Offe and has parallels with the idea of policy communities (2.10.2) and Lindblom's neo-pluralism which emphasizes the role of big business in shaping public opinion (3.4.4). In defining a 'linking' level of analysis, Ham and Hill also point to the relevance of Clegg and Dunkerly (1980) with regard to the way in which capitalism is internalized within individuals. From this Gramscian viewpoint, the idea of a free and autonomous process of problem definition and agenda-setting is a nonsense which is sustained only as a legitimating myth for the political order: the reality is that the policy process is determined by the hegemony of capitalist ruling ideas and interests.

Although this emphasis on the deep ideological processes shaping the policy process is echoed in other theorists classified by Ham and Hill as providing a linking, middle-range theory, they differ in being less deterministic than Clegg and Dunkerly. Benson, Salaman, Burrell and Morgan, and Ham and Hill themselves take a more Weberian view of the role of those involved in the policy process, especially with regard to the influence of professionals, interest groups and corporatist arrangements. Whilst acknowledging the 'agenda-setting' power of values, beliefs and ideologies in capitalist society, the Weberians are concerned with how, in Benson's sense, the 'surface' interacts with the 'deep structures'. The Weberian approaches, whilst agreeing as to the importance of the deep structural interests of capital, assign a degree of autonomy to the role of surface actors in defining problems and agenda-setting. This is especially the case when we consider those areas of policy which contain powerful professional or expert groups. Ham and Hill conclude by arguing that, although the role of capital in shaping the parameters of policy-making is central to understanding the relationship of the state to society in a capitalist system, the explanation of policy cannot be reduced to the kind of deterministic model put forward by writers such as Clegg and Dunkerly.

2.7.3   The 'argumentative' turn

The theorists considered by Ham and Hill address the issue of how the policy process may be explained, employing varieties of Marxist and Weberian analysis. Although they differ in their determinism, they have a common theme in seeking to show how power is exercised in capitalist society in ways beneath the surface levels of political institutions and bureaucratic organizations. This idea is also evident in the work of students of public policy whose theories derive from other sources. Whereas the focus of Ham and Hill's linkage theorists is on the structure of power relations, the concern of the 'argumentative' group is the way in which language shapes the world. The sources of this approach are a diverse bunch, ranging from French 'post-structuralists' such as Foucault; the ideas of German critical theorists, most notably Habermas; the British tradition of linguistic philosophy; and American pragmatism.

The focus of the argumentative approach is the study of how language comes to shape the way we make sense of the world. From this perspective, the analysis of public policy involves exploring the way in which 'policy discourse' comes to frame the arguments which form the frameworks within which problems and agendas are constructed. The starting point for the mode of analysis is the notion that the language we use to talk about policy and problems is not neutral. If, therefore, we want to understand how a 'problem' has been defined, we must endeavour to analyse the way in which its 'discourse' has been formed. The argumentative approach is concerned with the articulative dimensions of public policy, which in the structural-functionalist 'black box' is characterized as being an 'input' (see, for example, Almond and Powell, 1966). However, from the argumentative perspective, the articulative process is not an input, so much as constituting the framework within which politics and policy takes place. Drawing on the work of Unger (1987), Edelman (1988) and Sederberg (1984), Hoppe defines the 'argumentative' idea of politics as an arena:

> for conflict over the concepts used in framing political judgments and social problems, public policies and political leaders and enemies. In the case of democracies, this conflict is managed by public debate and a negotiated definition of shared meanings. Policy-making becomes the capacity to define the nature of shared meanings; it is a never ending series of communications and strategic moves by which various policy actors in loosely coupled forums of public deliberation construct intersubjunctive meanings. These meanings are continually translated into collective projects, plans, actions, and artefacts, which become the issues in the next cycle of political judgment and meaning constructions and so on.
> (Hoppe, 1993: 77)

The argumentative approach to agenda-setting and problem definition is therefore to address what is going on when an issue becomes set in a particular language or discourse. The struggle for power is a struggle for setting the discourse in which a problem is framed. Policy analysis in this sense may be conceptualized as a process of argumentation. Analysts working to influence policy seek to devise persuasive arguments (Majone, 1989) and when we are analysing the policy process, the 'argumentative' approach suggests that we understand and explain how meaning is being manufactured. Language frames and structures the policy process. Thus from this perspective, the agenda/problem phase is the determining part of the process: problems and agendas are consequently held to be matters for textual analysis.

This may suggest to the reader that the argumentative approach is less engaged with the 'real world' than is the case for the 'linkage' theorists. However, the argumentative focus has a number of contributions to make to the development of policy analysis. Fischer and Forester (1993: 5–7) note, for example that the approach offers :

- an appreciation of how practitioners formulate and construct problems;
- a focus on the claims and rhetoric of analysts;
- a recognition that policy arguments are complex exercises in agenda-setting power;
- an understanding that 'problems' may be represented in many different languages, discourses and frames and that shifts in political power involve shifts in the language in which policy issues and choices are presented, as well as shifts in elites.

❖ Cindy Patton, *Inventing Aids*, 1990

In this study the author explores the language of Aids and its representation as a problem. She analyses the discourse of Aids and the Aids industry in the 1980s by employing the social theories which frame the 'argumentative turn' in public policy. Aids discourse, she concludes, is about power in that it shapes what we think about the problem and how public policy is formulated. 'Aids words', she maintains, are never simply about 'facts' or 'truth', but 'take on a particular meaning at particular times, and are understood differently by different people' (Patton, 1990: 45). From the author's point of view, if we want to construct an Aids narrative, then we must take account of the discourse which has defined the problem and government policy. This deconstruction of the language of Aids is necessary if the power relationships in the Aids issue are to be challenged. She commends this strategy of deconstruction to Aids activists. ◆

The argumentative 'turn' in policy analysis, which has developed rapidly in the 1980s and 1990s, has made its most important contribution to directing our attention to the way in which knowledge and rationality are central to understanding the nature of power in modern (and post-modern) society. In a world ever more capable of generating knowledge, the policy process is increasingly one in which conflict takes place – or does not take place – at the level of arguments structured by information and expertise. It is to this issue that we turn in section 2.8.

❖ **The argumentative turn**

Frank Fischer and John Forester (eds), *The Argumentative Turn in Policy Analysis and Planning,* **1993**
This volume is the starting point for studying the argumentative approach. It makes an important contribution to the literature and brings together some of the leading exponents in the field. It draws on the theories of Foucault, Habermas and others to show how policy arguments are selective and are shaped by power relations. The case studies are based upon US and European experience and cover: the role of think-tanks; acid rain; ethnicity; health policy; and energy policy. It also contains several articles which provide an up-to-date analysis of current theoretical issues.

In addition to this volume, readers interested in the argumentative approach should also consult earlier contributions by McCloskey (1985), on the role of rhetoric in economics; Majone (1989), for a discussion of policy analysis as argument; Edelman (1988), on the construction of political spectacle; and Stone (1988), for a discussion of how shared meanings are created. For a review of theoretical development, Dryzek in Fischer and Forester (1993) should be consulted. On Dryzek, see also 3.10.5. ◆

2.8 Knowledge and the policy agenda

2.8.1 Experts, professionals and the policy process

As we have seen in our review of the argumentative approach, the analysis of the policy process involves considering the impact of knowledge. In this section we shall take up some of the issues raised in 2.7.3, by examining different approaches to the question of how knowledge frames agendas and problems. We shall examine the role of experts and professionals; discuss the relationship of social science to public policy; explore the growth of the 'think-tank'; and consider the role of ideas in the policy process. The rise of power based on knowledge in the form of experts or technocrats has been a key feature of the analysis of policy-making in the post-war era. It is a concern which, as we saw earlier, may be dated to the ideas of Bacon. The modern concern for the role of knowledge in the way in which societies come to define their problems may be said to have begun with the work of such people as Bell, Drucker, Ellul and Galbraith. At the philosophical level the politics of knowledge has been a concern of Foucault, Habermas *et al*. The particular focus of students of public policy has been the role of those with claims to knowledge: professions. Professional groups, including scientists and academics, are often represented as the creators and proponents of particular bodies of knowledge that play important roles in shaping both social policy and the institutions of everyday life. Thus they and their knowledge are said to have power. Knowledge becomes power, and the professional stands as the human link between the two (Freidson, 1986: ix).

❖ What does the word 'profession' mean?

This question occupies a great proportion of the literature on professionalism.

Once upon a time it was a term applied to a narrow range of occupations: the church, medicine and law. However, with the development of industrialization the concept was widened.

Studies of professionalism at first sought to define the main traits of professionals as opposed to non-professionals. One of the most cited list of traits is that put forward by Greenwood (1965). The main attributes of a profession were: systematic theory, community sanction, authority, an ethical code, and a professional culture. However, this attempt to draw up lists was criticized by those who argued that such traits were fundamentally ambiguous both empirically and analytically. More attention in the 1970s and 1980s was given to relating professionalism to economic and political power (Freidson, 1986) The main criterion of professionalism from this point of view is the ability or power of a group to define and control their work; in which case professional power resides in their essentially political capacity to use knowledge. ◆

In the construction of problems those who 'know' or have claims to know about a certain issue have a vital input into the definitional process. In terms of public policy, professionals clearly have a key role in the production and dissemination of knowledge and in the interpretation and implementation of policy at 'street level'. In social policy, for example, Wilding (1982) has argued that in welfare policy social workers and health professionals have five forms of power: in the policy-making process itself, where social workers and doctors have an input into policy-making; power to define needs and problems; power in the allocation of resources; power over people; and the power to control their own work. Professionals, he argues, 'gain power and influence as experts who are technically and politically useful to governments. Their use, and the granting of power to them, is legitimated by the technocratic rationality which is part of the ideology of advanced industrial society' (Wilding, 1982: 17).

❖ The power of professionals

Social problems

Richard L. Henshel, *Thinking About Social Problems*, 1991.

Henshel argues that the links between experts, intellectuals and professionals are stronger than the differences between them. Not the least of the reasons is the role of the university in modern society. He provides a handy (and growing) list of all those involved in the definition of social problems, including: criminologists, psychologists, social workers, sex therapists, marriage guidance counsellors, psychiatrists, psychoanalysts, labour/management mediators and geriatric specialists.

Henshel is wary of the way in which the general public and public authorities entrust experts with defining and interpreting social problems, and gives four main reasons: they have a common background and a self-imposed isolation; their motivations and ambitions have to be questioned; they operate within institutional constraints; and they tend towards 'selective blindness'.

His criticisms of the professional elites are severe, but he concludes with the view that:

> The opposite side of the coin to the problems of elitism is what the elitists of the nineteenth century called the 'sovereignty of the unqualified'. I do not argue for a return to a day in which intellectuals were ignored! But neither the intellectuals themselves nor society in general can afford to ignore the systematic tendencies we have touched on. The intellectuals ... may be in danger of assuming too much for themselves in prescribing for society's ills. (p. 87)

The unmasking of medicine

Ian Kennedy, *The Unmasking of Medicine* (the 1980 BBC Reith Lectures), 1981.

> The first step on the way to understanding modern medicine, looking behind the mask, is to unravel the rhetoric of medicine ... A choice exists whether to categorise particular circumstances as amounting to an illness. Power is vested in the doctor, and the power is not insignificant ... To analyse the word 'illness' is to explore the role of the doctor ... It is to discover that medical practice is above all a political enterprise. (p. 2)

Trust and experts

Anthony Giddens, *The Consequences of Modernity*, 1990.

Trust in experts and professional knowledge, argues Giddens, is a 'bargain with modernity', and is symptomatic of the way in which in modern cultures trust is vested in disembedded abstract systems, as opposed to the localized trust of pre-modern societies. The modes of social life which developed from the age of Bacon and the Enlightenment have resulted in the growth of trust in those who possess knowledge and technical expertise. He suggests that far from entering a post-modern world, we may be moving into a period of 'high modernity'.

Does this mean simply more experts, and new sources of professional power? Have we abandoned our faith in nuclear scientists, to trust ecologists? Have policy-makers transferred their trust from wizz-kid economists to the professional 'spin doctors', PR men and political managers? ◆

The power of professional groups to lay claim to expert knowledge and their capacity to utilize and maintain that power has been the subject of numerous studies in all the various policy areas, especially by Anglo-American researchers. So much so that Freidson (1986) has argued that perhaps the concern for the power of doctors and lawyers, social workers and teachers, and the technical professionals who work in engineering and technology, is a 'disease' which does not appear to have been so prevalent in other industrial societies.

This argument that the concern for professional power is a peculiar Anglo-American ailment is to some extent borne out by the fact that in the 1970s and 1980s there was the development of a number of powerful academic critiques of 'professionalism' and growing popular disenchantment with experts and their handiwork. Professionals no longer had the autonomy from non-professionals that they had previously enjoyed. Teachers, doctors, lawyers and scientists (not to mention practically every other occupational group that laid claim to professional status) have found themselves challenged: claims to knowledge are no longer enough for the 'customer'. The consequence of the apparent decline of professional power for the way in which problems are defined and agendas are set is considerable. Underpinning the changing impact of experts is a layer of uncertainty. For so long Western culture was uncritical about the contribution of knowledge and science to human progress. However, in the 1970s industrial societies began to feel more ambivalent towards the expert, science and technology (Nelkin (ed.), 1992: x). Not the least of the reasons for this disenchantment was the perception of the dis-utility of growth, technology and 'progress'. Public trust in public policy based upon 'scientific' reports and experts declined alongside trust in doctors and teachers *et al.*

❖ Experts and political controversy

Dorothy Nelkin (ed.), *Controversy: Politics of Technical Decisions*, 3rd edn, 1992

In this collection of papers Nelkin brings together a range of decision areas which are highly technical and scientific. These include foetal research, animal rights, surrogacy, holes in the ozone layer, the *Exxon Valdez* oil spillage, nuclear power, diet and cancer, occupational health, genetic testing, creation-evolution, Aids, and DNA research. Each case study aims to illustrate:

- the interplay of science and political factors in research, development, application, risk assessment and regulation;
- the structure of decision-making and the sources of conflict;
- the relationship of the groups involved and how they use information;
- the role of experts;
- how controversy is 'resolved'.

The case studies are all matters of intense public controversy and each shows how expert knowledge and opinion is used at a political level. Reviewing the case studies, she concludes that controversies which involve science are no different to other political issues:

> How one perceives science and technology reflects special interests, personal values, attitudes towards risk, and general feelings about authority. The general social and moral implications of a particular practice may assume far greater importance than any details of scientific verification ... Nor is there much evidence that technical arguments change anyone's mind ... In some cases, dramatic events (a major oil spill or a nuclear accident) have more effect on disputes than technical arguments ... Efforts to resolve conflicts over science and technology are confounded by intrinsic difficulties in assessing technical matters. The specialized knowledge involved in such assessments creates problems for the concerned citizen, especially in a climate of mistrust. The vagueness of the boundaries between the technical and political dimensions of policy decisions, and the problems of technical feasibility and political acceptability enhance the problems in determining who should be involved in a decision, who really represents the public interest.
> (*Nelkin, 1992: xxi–xxii*) ◆

Within the public sector professionals were also subjected to another line of attack in addition to scepticism: financial constraints. As Laffin and Young note in the case of British local government professionals in the 1980s and 1990s:

> The government's overriding commitment to reducing public expenditure has meant that most of the policy aims of the professions, involving as they do increased public expenditure, have had to be shelved. The govern-

ment's policy style [on policy style, see 2.10.2.], largely shaped by this commitment, is in sharp contrast to that of other post-war governments ... It should be added that this style is also associated with a distrust of public officials and of the professionals involved in the running of the welfare state ... These political changes have reversed the trend towards policy-making within profession-dominated policy communities [see 2.10.2 on the policy community model] ... towards one involving just ministers and their close advisers rather than opening it up to those outside governing circles ... In particular policy communities have lost importance or ceased to exist in many policy fields.
(*Laffin and Young, 1990: 35–6*)

Laffin and Young believe that a new type of professional discourse is developing in which professionals no longer make claims to 'know best', but realize that they have to 'earn their credibility' (Laffin and Young, 1990: 108). However, as a 'language' (ibid.: 3; 2.9.1) they argue that professionalism appears robust enough to adapt to these changing conditions.

This is not to say, therefore, that professionals in the 1990s no longer have a major impact on defining problems and framing policy agendas. On the one hand, knowledge has become more pluralistic: for every expert who says A, there are experts who can say B with equal claim to professional or expert authority. This inevitably means that 'expertise' or professional standing must be viewed as an integral part of the political argumentation which takes place. Thus experts and professionals should not be seen as a distinct separate class or structure within the policy-making process, but inextricably enmeshed with power and politics. They are not 'non-political' or neutral participants in the process: they may advance class and business interests as well as professional values and beliefs (see, for example, Johnson, 1972; Parry and Parry, 1976; and Dunleavy, 1981). Wilding makes the point that professionals may be seen as being granted power by government when it is in the interests of policy-makers so to do. What was given may – as has been the experience of the 1980s and 1990s – be taken away (Wilding, 1982). An instance of this is the position of social scientists in the policy process. From the 1970s onwards, the apparent damage done by academic theorists to various policy areas was seen by 'the new right' as a reason to delegitimize the professional claims of social scientists (Steinfels, 1979; Levitas, 1986). Three contributions to this attack on the damage done by social science 'experts' which are 'required reading' are those by Moynihan (1965), Banfield (1980) and Glazer (1988).

❖ **Nathan Glazer, *The Limits of Social Policy*, 1988.**

Glazer was an academic who participated in the Kennedy administration as an urban sociologist. Describing himself as a liberal in the 1960s, he was commited to social reform. The policy sciences and the journal *The Public Interest* (founded by Daniel Bell in 1964) reflected a new mood:

> it heralded a new age in which we would rationally and pragmatically attack our social problems. We could relegate the ideological conflicts between conservatives and liberals and radicals to the past because we knew more and because we had the tools, or were developing them, to do better. (p. 1)

However, by the end of the 1960s that mood changed. The new social policies 'seemed to be creating as many problems as we were solving'. Liberally inspired social policies weakened the family, ethnic and neighbourhood ties and the work ethic. The pursuit of equality had, it seemed, made matters worse and the liberal belief that 'for every problem there is a policy' proved ill-founded in practice:

> Social policy ... in almost every field, created new and unmanageable demands. It was illusionary to see our social policies as only reducing a problem; any policy has dynamic aspects such that it also expands the problem, changes the problem, generates further problems. (p. 5)

The demands from voters and experts for more spending to match that in other countries, and the professionalization of social and health services, when allied to a lack of knowledge has meant, Glazer argues, that he came to the view that, far from every problem having a solution, solutions gave rise to no less grave a set of problems. His verdict on the impact of sociology on social policy proved to be optimistic about the use of knowledge to effect social reform. In the case of America, he argues that too little attention has been paid to the big differences as between the US and Western Europe, specifically with regard to:

- the influence of federalism;
- the ethnic and religious diversity of the US;
- the unique problems and experience of US blacks;
- the individualism of US society and culture, with its emphasis on voluntarism, privatization and decentralization;
- the view that problems should not be taken care of by the state, but by autonomous, independent institutions. ◆

With the development of academic and 'professional' social sciences after the Second World War the relationship of organized knowledge and social, economic and other problems became more institutionalized. This growth of knowledge for policy was not confined within university and other academic institutions. Such was the demand for social knowledge that, by the 1970s, the range of organizations which conducted social science research had grown rapidly in all industrialized countries (Crawford and Perry (eds), 1976). The most influential of the 'policy sciences', as Lasswell termed them, was economics, not least because of the recruitment into government of economists, from the war onwards. However, if other social sciences were not to achieve this measure of incorporation into policy-making, they were to exercise influence in terms of the analysis which they offered of social problems and issues. The record, however, is rather mixed. The ideas of Goffman (1968), for example, on asylums had, as Bulmer (1990: 137) notes, an undoubted influence on changing policies towards the care of the mentally ill. On the other hand, research on the social structures of inner-city areas was totally ignored when it came to dealing with the housing and other problems of such areas.

The influence of the social sciences on public policy was a major theme in the backlash against 'sixties liberalism, especially in policies aimed at improving social welfare and increasing equality of opportunity. It was in this climate of disillusionment with reforming policy research during the 1970s and 1980s that an expansion took place in the number, kind and variety of 'think-tanks'.

2.8.2   Think-tanks

❖ Key texts

Think-tanks have attracted a growing literature. The main references in the field which deals with their general development are:

C.H. Weiss, *Organizations for Policy Analysis*, 1992.
J.A. Smith, 'Think-tanks and the politics of ideas', 1989.
J.A. Smith, *The Idea Brokers*, 1990.
F. Fischer, 'American think-tanks', 1991.
K. Hoover, 'The changing world of think-tanks', 1989.
P. Self, *Government by the Market*, 1993.
R. Cockett, *Thinking the Unthinkable*, 1994.

Studies of particular think-tanks that should also be consulted include:

RAND: Williams and Palmatier (1992); B.R. Smith (1966); T.A. Smith (1972).
Brookings: Rivlin (1992).
American Institute for Public Policy Research: Ford (1992).
The Institute of Economic Affairs: Cockett (1994).
The Centre for Policy Studies: Todd (1991).
The Adam Smith Institute: Pirie (1988); Martin (1993).

Political and Economic Planning: Pinder (ed.) (1981).
The Fabian Society: Ingis (1982); Cole (1961); Smith (1979). ◆

The most important development in the study of agendas and problem construction has been the emergence of think-tanks and research bodies which aim to influence the policy agenda through the publication of research and policy advocacy. The 1970s and 1980s were a particularly fruitful time for the think-tank business, not least because in the economic and social conditions then prevailing, policy-makers and others were in need of new ideas and policies. Non-governmental think-tanks see their role as shaping the context within which debate on issues takes place, and aim to influence the process wherein issues are formulated into 'problems'. The idea of think-tanks is, on the face of it, a modern invention. However, the idea of advisers to decision-makers is by no means a new concept, indeed it is as old as the idea of government itself. Joseph in the Old Testament is an example of an adviser who achieved great influence by his forecasting capacity, and by his ability to help his master to think and clarify his problems, opportunities, strengths and weaknesses. Throughout history princes have had their wise men and their counsellors to advise them. Francis Bacon and Machiavelli are, as we have seen, two representatives of an early form of hired thinker. Joseph, Bacon and Machiavelli were, however, all insiders: advice on tap (see Kelly, 1963).

The genesis of the modern external think-tank in Britain may be found in the establishment of the Fabian Society in 1884 by Beatrice and Sidney Webb, Bernard Shaw, Sydney Oliver and Graham Wallas. H.G. Wells was also a prominent member, as were L.T. Hobhouse and J.A. Hobson. Their aim was to promote socialism through gradual change, rather than revolution. The society was named after the Roman Emperor Fabius Cunctator – 'the gradual'. They believed that in publishing pamphlets and books, organizing seminars and stimulating discussion they could alter the intellectual climate of the times and of the Labour Party in particular (Cole, 1961; Inglis, 1982; Smith, 1979). The Fabians are a prototype of many subsequent think-tanks. Their influence was at its height before the First World War, but they continue to be active today as the 'grand old men' of the think-tank world.

In the 1920s and 1930s two other early think-tanks were to emerge: Chatham House and Political and Economic Planning. The former continues as a premier international institute for international affairs and provides an influential forum for academics, politicians and civil servants. Political and Economic Planning (see Pinder, 1981) was merged in 1976 with the Centre for Studies on Social Planning to form the Policy Studies Institute.

A major development in the post-war period was the establishment of the Institute for Economic Affairs in 1955 by Anthony Fisher and Oliver Smedley as a result of being 'converted' to the ideas of Hayek. Like the Fabian Society, it saw its mission as changing the intellectual climate – but in the opposite direction. The IEA was to have an enormous impact from the 1970s onwards, and rightly claims to have framed much of the policy agenda which was adopted by the Thatcher governments (Seldon, 1981; Cockett, 1994). It was the model adopted by Thatcher and her chief supporter Keith Joseph in their decision to set up the Conservative Centre for Policy Studies (CPR) in 1974 (see Todd, 1991). Later, in 1976, another (independent) right-wing think-tank – the Adam Smith Institute – was formed by Eamon and Stuart Butler and Madsen Pirie (Pirie, 1988). The Adam Smith Institute has been in the forefront of campaigning for ideas such as privatization (Pirie, 1988), the 'Citizens Charter' and other aspects of the 'new right' policy agenda in the 1980s (see Martin, 1993: 48–54). For a while it looked as if the 'left' in British politics had been out-think-tanked. Having really started the idea, the Labour Party decided to develop a new organization to assist the development of new left-of-centre policies. This was achieved in 1988 with the formation of the Institute for Public Policy Research headed by Tessa Blackstone, a former member of a governmental think-tank, the CPRS (see 3.8.2), James Cornford and Patricia Hewitt (see Smith, 1994). Not to be out-done, the new SDP Party led by David Owen created their own tank in 1989 in which to think up big ideas – the Social Market Foundation. The growth of new think-tanks has continued in the 1990s with the creation of the European Policy Forum (1992), headed by Graham Mather and Frank Vibert, and DEMOS in 1993, with Martin Jacques and Geoff Mulgan. The latter Trevor Smith has characterized as a quintessential product of a post-modern politics:

> DEMOS ... is avowedly post-modern, and in drawing its advisory council from across the mainstream political, academic and commercial spectrums seeks to open up the public agenda to a new set of participants and medium term objectives. In doing so, it seeks to influence the culture and context of political thought and action by taking the longer view rather than addressing the more importunate issues of the moment
> (Smith, 1994: 135)

Although Britain can claim – through the Fabian Society – to have possibly the oldest think-tank and, in DEMOS, one of the youngest, it was in America that they have been most fully developed in their modern form, and where they are most numerous. Early examples of research organizations include: the Russell Sage Foundation (1907); the Institute for Government Research (1916); the Twentieth Century Fund (1919); and the National Bureau of Economic Research (1920). (For a review of these institutions, see J.A. Smith, 1989, 1991.) However, the creation of the Brookings Institution in 1927 may be said to mark the birth of the 'think-tank' as we now know it. Brookings was founded by a successful businessman, Robert S. Brookings, who after his experience in Washington at the War Industries Board during the First World War was convinced of the need to improve government by improving understanding and knowledge. The immediate result was the Institute for Government Research. Later he created a graduate school for the study of public policy and in 1927 the activities were consolidated into the Brookings Institution (see Rivlin, 1992). Brookings is not an ideological think-tank. At various times it has been seen as 'liberal' in approach and well-disposed towards the Democrats, but the institution is in no way 'political' or 'partisan' in the sense which many other US think-tanks are. Amongst the leading 'non-political' think-tanks are the Center on Budget and Policy Priorities (est. 1981: see Schapiro et al., 1992); and the Center for Policy Research in Education (est. 1985: see Fuhrman, 1992). A foremost example of the ideologically committed think-tank was founded in 1943 to campaign for conservative pro-market ideas and policies – the American Enterprise Institute for Public Policy Research (AEI). Another 'new right' think-tank is the Heritage Foundation which was established in 1973 (Ford, 1992). As was the case in Britain with the EIA and the CPR, the AEI and Heritage Foundation were to have a significant role in shaping the US policy agenda in the 1970s and 1980s – along with other think-tanks such as the Center for Strategic Studies, the Cato Institution, the Hoover Institution, the Institute for Contemporary Studies, and the Institute for Education Affairs (see Pescheck, 1987; J.A. Smith, 1991). Again, as in Britain, non-conservatives were slow to get in on the think-tank scene. However, the Democratic response – the Center for National Policy – founded in 1981 was somewhat quicker off the mark than the IPPR.

Along with Brookings, the RAND Corporation is the other big player in the US think-tank league, founded after the Second World War in 1948:

> The RAND Corporation is sometimes called 'Mother RAND' in recognition of its status as an early think-tank and as parent, over the years, of a varied progeny of smaller think-tanks. It stands apart from the community of such institutions, however, in its stubborn independence and refusal to accept a constricting label such as 'conservative' or 'liberal'. This quality of free expression pervaded the RAND staff in the early years and still is seen, although it has yielded somewhat to stricter controls in recent times

> ... RAND in sum, began its corporate life in equipoise between the scientists of the Academy of Lagado ... in *Gulliver's Travels*, and those of Francis Bacon's *New Atlantis*. It was a community of intellectuals – young, brilliant, untiring, totally committed – that could be hardly matched anywhere in the world.
>
> (*Williams and Palmatier, 1992: 50–1*)

That said, however, it has to be noted that the RAND Corporation's brilliant young people were also responsible for a certain brand of technocratic zeal (see Smith, 1972: 61–2) which contributed in no small part to the development of a defence strategy which reached its consummation in the Cuban missile crisis (see 3.3.6).

As we can see from the review of think tanks above, the exact definition of think-tank varies from those that are large and well funded, to small and highly political, to large, well funded and political. They may be 'academic', in that they aim to produce reports and publications which assist the general level of knowledge, or they may be highly 'ideological' in their approach. Dror, for instance, rules out a whole heap of organizations when he says that 'policy research, design and analysis organizations' (think-tanks) are distinct from 'units engaging in decision improvement within government', or from 'institutes for advanced study' (Dror, 1984) A clearer way of putting it is to say that broadly there are two types of think-tank: inside and outside government. We shall deal with the former in part three (3.8.2). Outside or external think-tanks may be categorized on a left to right spectrum with those claiming to be independent or 'non-partisan' being located somewhere around the centre (see Barberis and May, 1993: 113 and below).

❖ Think-tanks

James Cornford, 'Performing fleas: reflections from a think-tank', 1990

James Cornford left the academic world in the 1970s for the policy-thinking business, the Outer Policy Circle Unit. He later went on to head one of the largest social science funding bodies in the UK, the Nuffield Foundation. In 1989 he joined a left-wing think-tank, the Institute for Public Policy Research (IPPR). His paper argues that think-tanks are small players compared to government departments, corporations, professional bodies, political parties and interest groups. They are, he suggests 'performing fleas' who are constantly seeking a moment or opportunity when they can sting the body politic. The think-tank in this performing-flea role is essentially an intermediary, living on and off others. They are significant less for the originality of their contribution to policy as for their capacity to broker and mediate ideas. How a think-tank does this will depend on its 'size, width of remit, time horizons, involvement in research, ideological commitment, and access to those in power as well as strategy of influence'. Think-tanks, he concludes, are 'committed to government by conversation, to the power of rational discussion as a force for improvement'.

A good think-tank guide

In 1991–2 *The Economist* (vol. 321, 21 December–3 January 1992, pp. 81–5) published a guide to the best-known think-tanks in the world. The journal judged them on marks out of five for being: clever, connected, canny, cushy and kooky. Here is the list with marks in the above order:

Council on Foreign Relations (New York) 4;5;3;3;0
Royal Institute of International Affairs (London) 3;5;3;2;0
Stiftung Wissenschaft und Politik (Ebenhausen, Germany) 3;4;1;4;2
Foreign Policy Association (Moscow) 2;3;4;2;0
Center for Strategic and International Studies (Washington) 3;5;5;3;1
International Institute for Strategic Studies (London) 3;4;3;1;2
Institute of Strategic Studies (Kuala Lumpur) 2;4;4;3;4
Centre for European Policy Studies (Brussels) 4;4;2;3;1
East–West Center (Hawaii) 3;3;3;5;2
Institute for International Economics (Washington) 5;3;4;3;0
Institute of Economic Affairs (London) 3;2;3;2;4
Adam Smith Institute (London) 2;3;5;2;3
Economic Policy Institute (Washington) 2;2;3;1;2
Liberty and Democracy Institute (Lima, Peru) 4;5;4;2;3
Korea Development Institute (Seoul) 4;5;2;3;1
Institute for Policy Studies (Singapore) 3;4;1;4;2
Promethée (Paris) 3;4;2;3;1
Mazingera Institute (Nairobi) 4;2;1;0;2
Brookings Institution (Washington) 4;3;3;4;1
American Enterprise Institute (Washington) 4;4;3;2;2
Cato Institute (Washington) 4;1;3;2;5
Heritage Foundation (Washington) 2;3;5;3;4
Hoover Institution on War, Revolution and Peace (Stanford University) 5;3;3;5;3

Think-tanks in the 1990s

The 1980s were the boom time for think-tanks. However, as *The Sunday Times* reported in 1994, rumours of their demise were exaggerated:

> Trevor McDonald apologised gravely. The chap who had been on *News at Ten* earlier, he said, talking about the Liberal Democrats' financial policy was not, as we had been told, Andrew Dilnot from the Institute of Fiscal Studies. No, he was Madsen Pirie of the Adam Smith Institute. Not to worry, Dilnot turned up just a few minutes later on *Newsnight* to debate Paddy Ashdown's proposals, hot on the heels of Helen Wilkinson of Demos, who was talking about the slack generation. Suddenly the airwaves are filled with the opining of the denizens of think-tanks. It is just like the early 1980s again.
>
> (*'Great minds think alike', The Sunday Times, 21 August 1994: 4.3*)

Mapping British think-tanks

Barberis and May (1993) suggest a map of the think-tanks in Britain on a left–right continuum (figure 2.15).

Figure 2.15   A framework for British think-tanks

Left	**Centre**	**Right**
	Fabian Society	Centre for Policy Studies
Labour Research Department	Hansard Society	Adam Smith Institute
Institute for Public Policy Research		
	Policy Studies Institute	Institute for Economic Affairs

Source: Adapted from Barberis and May (1993: 113)

Outside Britain and America

There has also been a proliferation of think-tanks of various kinds, as the survey in *The Economist* (above) makes clear. One of the countries where their growth has been as notable as in Britain and the US is Japan:

> Until the 1960s there had been little organized private involvement in Japanese policy-making. By the early 1970s, however, there were over 70 ... Most of Japan's think-tanks have a close corporate affiliation, and ties with universities are not as strong as in the United States.
> (*Smith, 1989: 177*)

Self (1993) describes how in Australia, New Zealand and Canada right-wing think-tanks came to have a significant impact on the policy agenda. In Australia and New Zealand, he notes 'the linkages between think-tanks and right-wing politicians are extremely close' (Self, 1993: 66). See also Marsh (1991) for a review of the role of think-tanks in Australia.

In New Zealand the Business Roundtable and in Canada the Fraser Institute have been important in framing the policy agenda in their respective countries. ◆

Carol Weiss (1992) argues that there are four major factors which have led to the development of policy analysis organizations in the USA: political fragmentation and disaggregation, the complexity of social problems and the declining influence of the civil service. These factors also apply in varying degrees to other political systems. They fill a gap which growing knowledge, growing complexity and increased pluralism creates. In the past it could be said that the 'great men' and political parties could play this role of mediating and synthesizing knowledge and ideas. Key people – opinion leaders – served as a point of entry for new ideas, standing as they did in the midst of a network of opinion, ideas and knowledge. This was a political world

inhabited by a small, relatively coherent elite who had access to decision-makers and who moved in and out of the policy and decision
domains of ruling elites. But, for all the reasons which Weiss identifies, more knowledge and more complexity and greater pluralism
now mean that ideas relate to the policy-making process very differently to the age of Keynes. The growth of think-tanks is therefore
something which may be seen as either a manifestation of pluralism at
work in a modern information society or a threat to democracy. As a
pluralist one might argue that with the proliferation of think-tanks
knowledge can be effectively presented as policy argument, and in an
open society knowledge clashes constitute a democratic way of proceeding. However, as a threat it may be said that there is an issue here
about those who do not have the power and resources to have access
to analysis. This prompts us to consider the relevance of the arguments of theorists who point out the way in which analysis can serve
to distort and manipulate debate (2.7.3). If it is to be effective, participation in the policy process must address the issue of how policy
analysis can level up rather than increase inequality of influence. As
Bobrow and Dryzek note:

> Large corporations, government bureaucracies, national interest groups,
> and professional associations are highly organized and have the resources
> to hire skilled and persuasive advocates. Community organizations, small
> businesses, and the poor typically come off worse even in a forum of
> formal equality of access (such as a legislative hearing, court case, project
> review, public hearing, or special commission). Policy analysis can act as
> an antidote to such inequality by educating participants to the ways of the
> policy process, by sponsoring informal networks, and by directing atten-
> tion to key issues.
> (Bobrow and Dryzek, 1987: 177)

Fischer (1991) suggests that the threat of think-tanks and policy analysis might be countered by returning to the experiments of the 1960s
and 1970s, when projects were set up which involved experts and
citizens working together to address problems. Another response might
be to re-examine the idea put forward by Lasswell for decision seminars (Lasswell, 1960). However, the forces for such changes are not
apparent to Fischer, or to the present author. Thus, it remains the case
that, given the fact that in order to have an impact on the policy
process interest groups and others need to make analytical arguments,
the lack of policy analysis outside those organizations and interests
that can afford it severely reduces the capacity of citizens to participate in formulating agendas and constructing problems. (This is an
issue to which we shall return when we examine policy implementation and evaluation; see 4.3, 4.5).

The growth of think-tanks, as Trevor Smith anticipated in the 1970s, has effectively filled the vacuum left by the decline of parties and parliamentary politics. Smith's (1994) argument is that we need, above all, to urgently reform the constitutional arrangements of liberal democracies such as Britain so as to revitalize the role which voting and politics – as opposed to 'analysis' – can play in framing the political agenda. Think-tanks in this sense are symptomatic of a wider 'postmodern' decline and disillusionment with 'classical' politics. The danger is, of course, that without the renewal of the democratic political process ideas will clash in 'tanks' rather than in open political – and elected – fora. And, far from being a means of expanding the range of ideas, a political agenda dominated by think-tanks may only serve in the long run to narrow the range of policy options and ideas (see the case for 'social' think-tanks, 4.4.8).

2.8.3   Ideas and the policy process

❖ **Key texts**

Several books provide excellent collections of papers on this theme. Chief amongst them are:

A. Gamble *et al.*, *Ideas, Interests and Consequences*, 1989.
P.A. Hall (ed.), *The Political Power of Economic Ideas*, 1989.
D.W. Colander and A.W. Coats, *The Spread of Economic Ideas*, 1989.

The text for much of the debate is provided in the closing two pages of Keynes's *General Theory* (1936). Parsons (1983, 1985 and 1989) discusses the Keynesian view of policy-making as driven by ideas.

The above literature is concerned with economic ideas and policy. However, attempts to develop new ways of looking at how ideas shape policy in more general terms may be seen in the work of Kingdon (1984) and Sabatier and Jenkins-Smith (1993). ◆

The growth of think-tanks in the 1970s and 1980s signalled that 'ideas' were increasingly regarded as important in the political process. Throughout history theorists and philosophers have placed great stress on the role of ideas. The notion that ideas change the world and it is great men who champion ideas was the central conceit of nineteenth-century liberalism. John Stuart Mill (in chapter 3 of his essay on Liberty) notes, for example, that:

> The mass do not now take their opinions from dignitaries in Church or State, from ostensible leaders, or from books. Their thinking is done for

them by men much like themselves, addressing or speaking in their name, or the spur of the moment.
(*Mill, 1968: 124*)

However, the initiation of new ideas and 'noble things' cannot be expected from this 'collective mediocrity' called public opinion. Progress is in the hands of the intellectual elite: people such as himself:

> No government by a democracy or a numerous aristocracy, either in its political acts or in its opinions, qualities, and tone of mind it fosters, ever did or could rise above mediocrity, except in so far as the sovereign Many have let themselves be guided ... by the counsels and influence of a more highly gifted and instructed One or Few.
> (*Mill, 1968: 124*)

It could be argued that this Victorian attitude has echoes in the arguments of policy analysts and think-tanks to this day. What counts is the influence of key people and their ideas. This is a viewpoint expressed most eloquently by the economist J.M. Keynes, who is often cited as the main proponent of the view that it is ideas that ultimately shape the policy-making process. It is expressed in the famous closing lines of his *General Theory of Employment, Interest and Money* (1936)

> the ideas of economists and political philosophers ... are more powerful than is commonly understood ... Practical men, who believe themselves to be quite exempt from any intellectual influences, are usually the slaves of some defunct economist. Madmen in authority, who hear voices in the air, are distilling their frenzy from some academic scribbler of a few years back. I am sure that the power of vested interests is vastly exaggerated compared with the gradual encroachment of ideas.
> (*Keynes, 1936: 383*)

Keynes has long been criticized for this 'naive' viewpoint (Sweezy, 1964; Buchanan *et al.*, 1978; Parsons, 1983; Gamble *et al.*, 1989; Colander and Coats, 1989). But his argument has long been a focus of a debate on the relationship between theories, ideas and policy. Keynes's ideas about policy-making were to be as influential, indeed it might be true to say that they were more influential, than his actual economic theories. Keynes believed in the essential primacy of ideas in human affairs: for good or evil it was ideas which shaped history and the policies of government. Keynes's view of the relationship between progress and knowledge was highly Baconian. Governance of society involved the use of knowledge rather than the pursuit of interest. It was in Keynes that we find the full flowering of the Baconian belief in reason and experiments: knowledge was power. And from that it followed that the world would be best ordered when those with knowledge come to a position in which they can influence the course of policy. This 'New Atlantis' located intellectually somewhere betwixt Bloomsbury and Cambridge was a model of government as becoming based more on knowledge than on the interests of a narrow class or power elite. However, although we may be critical of Keynes with respect to the 'Utopia' wherein government is run by clever people rather than in the interests of the powerful, Keynes's belief that knowledge and ideas would be the main source of governmental legitimacy was very close to the reality of modern policy-making. The world for which Keynes envisaged a greater role for information, knowledge, facts, advisers and experts was in practice to approximate to a realistic model of policy-making in the post-war era. What Keynes argued was that policy-makers should make rational decisions based on knowledge and 'reasoned experiment' (Keynes, 1971–: XXI, 289):

> it must be the avowed and deliberate business of Government to make itself responsible for the wholesale collection and dissemination of industrial knowledge. The first condition of successful control and useful interference of whatever kind from above is that it must be done with knowledge.
> (*Keynes, 1971–: XXI, 643*)

❖ Ideas and leaders

Gabriel Weimann, 'The influential: back to the concept of opinion leaders?', 1991
It has long been argued that, like Mill and Keynes, the key factor in the impact of ideas and opinions is that of leaders or influential trend-setters. This notion has led to a good deal of empirical research. In this article Weimann reviews the literature of opinion leadership and endeavours to measure opinion leadership in terms of a strength-of-personality scale (PS). This is applied to Germany and Israel.

Opinion leadership was put forward by Katz in 1957 as being a matter of personal and social factors: who one is, what one knows, and whom one knows (Elihu Katz, 1957).

Weimann's study observes that these have to be related to actual communications activity:

> The individuals identified as 'strong' on the PS scale combined personal traits, competence, and social position in their personal network, enabling them to influence others. Thus, it is not merely a unidimensional measure, but a combination of personal traits with social network positioning.

The conclusions suggest that the use of a PS scale demonstrates the existence of a group of key influentials in Germany and Israel, and furthermore that the identification of such a group has important practical implications for all who combine social research with persuasive communication. Such research by Weimann *et al.* seems to confirm the views of Mill and Keynes that ideas and opinion leaders are important. For them, of course, the idea of a network would have been rather obvious. The ruling elite in Mill's and in Keynes's times was a very narrow group. Influence really amounted to little more than shaping inner opinion.

David H. Burton, *The Learned Presidency: Theodore Roosevelt, William Howard Taft, and Woodrow Wilson*, 1988

Burton analyses three presidents in terms of how ideas shaped their presidencies, and how the pursuit of knowledge was integral to their approach to politics and policy. Roosevelt, the historian and naturalist; Taft, the legal scholar; and Wilson, the political theorist.

The influence of ideas and learning on the shape of presidential government in the later twentieth century is, the author feels, undergoing considerable change:

> Post FDR presidents have relied heavily on the mass media ... They have projected their personalities and sold their images, calling on the special devices of mass communication to win and hold office ... The results in terms of national leadership have been mixed, but the dominance of the new political specialists ... is hardly debatable ... the exact character of a neo-learned presidency remains unclear ... What elements from the past world of knowledge will be retained and in which fashion and in what combinations ... are beyond calculation. (pp. 198–9) ◆

How do ideas influence? Four approaches

Hall's approach Keynes claimed a new role for economics, economic theory and economists in government and a new belief in the capacity of policy-makers to utilize the increasing information about the economy and apply it to macroeconomic policy interventions. In the end, it was less the power of the ideas than the power of institutions to embody and incorporate them into the policy processes of western governments, not least in the economic models and assumptions which structured government policies. Keynes provided for an objectification of the public interest, and laid the foundations of the notion which was to dominate the greater part of economic – and other – policy until the 1980s, that the public interest was knowable. The Keynesian model of policy-making in which ideas rather than interests shaped decisions has long been the subject of discussion. How important ideas are to policy-making was an issue which came to special pre-eminence in the 1980s when economic policy-making in many countries was in the grip of a 'counter-Keynesian' revolution. A collection of papers edited by Hall, *The Political Power of Economic Ideas* (1989) addressed the Keynesian model on a comparative level. In his conclusion Hall suggests the model in figure 2.16 based on the relationship of new ideas to three factors which are required for a new set of ideas to influence policy-making.

In Hall's model ideas are important, but so are other factors which can make or mar its progress. For an idea to be adopted as a policy it has to have a good fit with the economic circumstances which are existing; it has to be seen as being in the interests of the dominant political

Figure 2.16   Hall's model of how ideas influence policy

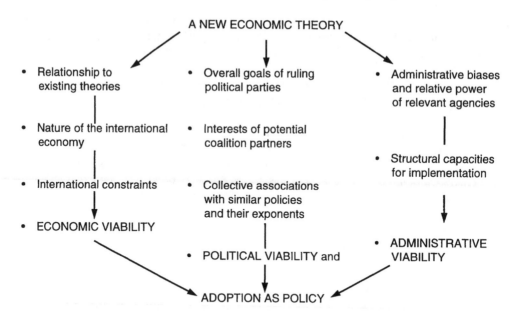

Source: Adapted from Hall (1989)

interests and it has to be judged to be feasible in administrative terms. As Hall shows, this provides a good basis on which to compare the way in which ideas (economic, in this case) come to shape policy in different countries at different times.

Coats and Colander: three models of how ideas spread   As economists, Coats and Colander are used to thinking in terms of models. In their book on the spread of economic ideas they propose three models to account for the propagation of ideas (Colander and Coats, 1989: 10–15):

1   the infectious disease model;
2   the market place for ideas model;
3   the information theory model.

Model 1 suggests that we study the spread of an idea as if it were a disease. The main focus here is contact points between those who are carrying the disease and those who are susceptible to catching it. The function of the propagandist and the popularizer is to weaken individuals and groups so as to make them more receptive to new ideas. Model 2, on the other hand, views the process in terms of ideas in a market place in which there are sellers and buyers. Does supply create its own demand, or do ideas look for buyers? What is the relationship between idea producers and consumers? How does the demand and supply change over time and space? Are some ideas better suited to one market than another? Are there conditions of monopoly, competition or oligopoly? Are there fads and fashions in the ideas market? How are ideas advertised, marketed and sold? Model 2 corresponds closely with the 'economic theory of democracy' and public choice theory (see Downs, 1957; Tullock, 1976). Model 3 applies another metaphor: that of ideas as a flow of information. What are the sources? Who are the receivers? Is the signal strong, or is it unclear? How are signals transmitted? How are signals encoded? Is the feedback efficient? Model 3 has echoes in Lasswell's (1972) study of public opinion and communications.

As Coats and Colander are aware, however, no one model can explain how ideas spread and influence. Rather, it may suggest ways of viewing the process.

'Network' and 'community' approaches to the politics of ideas   Another set of models which seek to provide more general explanations of the relationship of ideas and policy are advanced by political scientists using new metaphors for the policy process, such as 'networks', 'subsystems', 'streams' and 'coalitions'. These will be reviewed in 2.10. Of particular relevance to the study of ideas are the theories of Kingdon (2.10.3) and Sabatier and Jenkins-Smith (2.10.4). The focus of these explanations is the way in which policy networks and communities – which include politicians, civil servants, policy analysts, experts, interest groups and so on – advocate ideas in given policy areas. Thus if we want to explain how an idea has impacted (or not) on policy we have to examine the particular network or community involved. An approach which is closely related to 'policy sub-system' models of policy change is the idea of 'epistemic communities' (see Holzner and Marx, 1979; Foucault, 1973; Evan (ed.), 1981; Crane, 1972; Haas, 1990). The most developed exposition of the approach is Haas (1990) Haas considers 'epistemic communities' to be composed of professionals who 'share a commitment to a common causal model and a common set of political values. They are united by a belief in the truth of their model and by a commitment to translate this truth into public policy, in the conviction that human welfare will be enhanced' (Haas, 1990: 41; see also Young's idea of 'assumptive worlds' in 3.7.7). Haas's focus is on the role of such communities in international organizations, but his framework applies equally to national settings. He suggests that they take the form of 'invisible colleges' or 'networks of the like minded'. The success of communities in getting their ideas adopted depends on two factors:

(1) the claim to truth being advanced must be more persuasive to the dominant political decision makers than some other claim, and (2) a successful alliance must be made with the dominant political coalition. We can say that epistemic communities seek to monopolize access to strategic decision-making positions, though a few of them succeed in holding such a position for a long period.
(*Haas, 1990: 42*)

From this perspective something like the Keynesian revolution may be read as a successful monopolization of decision-making positions by 'like-minded' people. Some were to retain that power for a long time until another rival epistemic community – 'monetarist' economists, politicians, academics, journalists and others – advanced claims which proved more attractive to policy-makers than the established Keynesian community. The success of communities varies. The natural sciences, Haas argues, have had more 'spectacular' success than the social sciences because the former can lay claim to more 'certain' knowledge. Moreover, social science communities tend to lack policy 'brokers' who can inform 'political consumers of knowledge' of the relevance of their findings. The result is that (as Lynn, 1978, shows) policy-makers tend to be somewhat less interested in the use of social knowledge for decision-making (Haas, 1990: 221–2). The role of idea brokers is, from the Haas model, crucial, as without people to get ideas into the policy process an idea is unlikely to prove influential. As was the case in the Keynesian revolution and the 'counter-revolution ' in the 1970s, brokers who could mediate and translate theories into practice and get into the centre of power were of great importance (see Parsons, 1989; Barberis and May, 1993: 107–19).

The contribution of the historical approach to public policy

❖ Ideas in history

The processes of nature can therefore be properly described as sequences of mere events, but those of history cannot. They are not processes of mere events but processes of actions, which have an inner side, consisting of thought; and what the historian is looking for is these processes of thought. All history is the history of thought.
(*Collingwood, 1974: 26*)

One ventures to say that from the record of history it appears that those ideas in history which have the most force are those which speak for everyone ... It is the idea itself which is the long-lived actor on the human stage ... The great idea is ... an agent of change, a shaper of the moral order.
(*Redfield, 1968: 89–91*)

The end of history?
One of the most influential – or at least widely discussed – theories which analyses the power of ideas is that put forward by Francis Fukuyama in the wake of the break-up of the Eastern Bloc and the demise of communism in the late 1980s. Fukuyama argued in his book *The End of History* (Fukuyama, 1992a) that far from convergence having taken place, as some had argued in the 1970s, Western ideas had triumphed. We may be witnessing, he maintained, not simply the end of the cold war, but the 'end of history as such'. Ideological conflict is dead, and is being replaced by 'Common Marketization' in international relations. Reflecting on the controversy his theory had provoked (in a newspaper article) he stood by his observation that 'liberal democracy had won broad acceptance and that the trend in that direction would continue over the very long term', notwithstanding the rise of fundamentalism and nationalism in many parts of the world (Fukuyama, 1992b). ◆

The analysis of the role of ideas is a topic which is particularly suited to a historical approach. In place of simplistic and generalized theories about the impact of ideas, historical analysis of specific policy changes tends to be less clear-cut about when ideas actually influence and how they impact on policy-making. A study which illustrates this is Jose Harris's book on unemployment and politics in Britain between 1886 and 1914. She says that: 'In tracing the evolutions of a national unemployment policy it is difficult to point to the decisive influence of any single set of reforming ideas or to discover any logical sequence of institutional change' (Harris, 1972: 362). This is not to say that ideas do not have a role, but that locating the 'decisive' point at which ideas shape policy is no easy task. The political motivations of decision-makers and civil servants, and the context within which policy is being framed mean that interests and ideas are in practice difficult to prise apart. Furthermore, the relationship of policy innovation to policy continuity is not always as clear as many social scientists assume (see 4.6). Historical analysis tends to show that change in policy is difficult to define, locate and pin down. As Hartwell observes:

> Of course, ideas influence policy, but not neatly. At the micro-level of day-to-day history, it is possible to explain the evolution of a particular policy, and how ideas get translated into action, and to recognise the power at any time of a general philosophy of government to influence particular policies. But ideas ... while determining the general character of legislation [do] so along with other influences.
> (*Hartwell, 1989: 119*)

Amongst these other influences Hartwell counts social and economic conditions, changes in institutions, displacements on government activity as in times of war and the impact of policy entrepreneurs. Thus ideas have to be placed in the (complex) context of social and economic forces, and institutions as well as the motives and operations of key personalities (on the role of personalities, see 3.7.2, 3.7.7).

2.9   Policies and problems as symbols

❖ **Key texts**

The starting point for the study of language in the policy process is the work of Edelman (1964, 1971, 1977, 1985, 1988). Edelman (1985) is an excellent short introduction to his approach.

He draws on the work of Orwell, Wittgenstein, Chomsky, Derrida, Foucault, Habermas and others, including Lasswell and Burke (1945). Of special relevance to the study of public policy is Habermas (1970, 1973) and Lasswell (1930a, 1949).

A reading strategy would be to get into Orwell ('Politics and the English Language' in Orwell, 1984, and his novel *Nineteen Eighty Four*, 1954), Edelman and Lasswell (see Elshtain, 1985) and thence explore the material upon which the former has developed his arguments. In general, the best review of the way in which political language changes is Ball *et al.* (eds) (1989). ◆

2.9.1   Language, power and policy

Think-tanks and other modes of policy analysis and advocacy exist to influence and shape the policy discourse (Fischer, 1991). That is, they aim to play a role in the framing of issues and the language which we employ to discuss and analyse the problems to which policies are addressed. However, the study of this dimension of public policy is one of the least-considered areas of policy analysis. As Dye notes:

> Television has made the image of public policy as important as the policy itself. Systematic policy analysis concentrates on what governments *do*, why they do it, and what difference it makes. It devotes less attention to what governments *say*. Perhaps that is a weakness in policy analysis. Our focus has been primarily upon the activities of governments rather than the rhetoric of governments.
> (*Dye, 1987: 355*)

❖ **Same words, different meanings**

Being there: a plausible story
In Peter Sellers's film *Being There* (based on the book by Jersey Kosinski) he portrays a somewhat slow-witted TV-obsessed gardener, Chauncey, who, by a series of accidents, becomes a friend of a powerful kingmaker. Chauncey uses the language of gardening, the only language he understands, but it is a language which appeals to his powerful friend, TV and eventually the President. When Chauncey talks about the seasons in the garden that is all he means. However, his listeners believe him to be talking about the economy and the state of the nation. Such is the power of his (apparent) metaphors and because there is no information

about him at all, he is seen as an ideal candidate for the office of President of the USA. Chauncey is blissfully unaware that his words mean anything more than gardening.

The case of the 'space between words'

The fact that a definition of a problem may be agreed as a form of words does not mean that there is a consensus surrounding a policy problem. For example, in a discussion of race relations policies with regard to equal opportunities, Ken Young makes the point that:

> Discussion of equal opportunity in employment is bedevilled by ambiguities and confusions which typically characterise areas of public policy. In such areas, a shared language may mask multiple and conflicting meanings ... While these ambiguities may facilitate agreement at the symbolic level, they preclude clear specification of ends of policy and so inhibit the proper identification of feasible means for its achievement.
> (*Young, 1987: 94*)

Professionalism as a 'language'

As we noted above (2.8.1), Laffin and Young describe 'professionalism' not as a 'property of an individual, but as a language within which the individual asserts certain claims'. Politics, they note is 'a linguistically constituted "activity". That is to say, it is about language and the ideas that language expresses or elides. The language of professionalism belongs at least in part to the discourse of discretion and accountability' (Laffin and Young, 1990: 3, 7).

Rhetoric as analysis

> Too frequently rhetoric is substituted for adequate conceptualization, resulting in vagueness and lack of direction throughout the entire formulation and carrying out process. The end result is perceived to be a program which has failed to solve a problem even though no one is quite certain what the problem is ... Policy agendas reflect the mobilization of political demands rather than a rational process of evaluating needs, values, and objectives. Thus 'problems' frequently appear on the decision-making agenda without having been adequately conceptualized or thought through.
> (*Wolman, 1981: 463*)

The language which surrounds problems and policies has a strategic function. As Edelman argues, ambiguity in problem definition can be a useful device in policy-making and may be exploited for 'political' purposes. ◆

Since classical times, the importance of language in politics and power has been recognized. Rhetoric or the art of words and persuasion was a subject taught to young men as an essential part of their education. The Greek and Roman authors have much to say on the matter, and St Augustine was, before his conversion, a professor of rhetoric. Herbert Spencer and J.S. Mill in the nineteenth century both gave attention to the importance of rhetoric in human discourse (Dixon, 1990; Bailey (ed.), 1965). Yet it is only comparatively recently that the role of language in politics has once again come to occupy a place in the modern study of politics (see Wilson, 1990; Fowler, 1991). In the analysis of policy we too must be aware of the use that policy-makers make of policy talk and the underlying aspects of meaning which are located in policy presentation and discourse.

Francis Bacon, the philosopher who we considered in Part One as something of a 'founding father' of policy analysis, had much to say about the relationship of words and their distorting effects. Words, he noted, can obstruct understanding, and may be either words of things that do not exist, or of things which do exist but are ill-defined. Words are, he argues, products of 'idols of the mind'. It was a primary task of learning to expose and rid the world of such idols (Bacon, 1985: 277–85). Harold Lasswell also considered the analysis of language, symbols and 'style' in political communications to be an essential aspect of the study of politics, power and the clarification of values for policy (see Lasswell, 1936, 1949, 1972). Politicians and policy-makers, he thought, were essentially 'symbol specialists'.

However, the study of such issues has not, until comparatively recently, been central to the analysis of the policy process. As Dye (1987) notes, this neglect has been at some cost to the analysis of public policy as it has meant that analysts have largely been preoccupied with policy rationality – 'deeds' – rather than policy talk and rhetoric or 'words'. However, for Lasswell politics was best understood as the process whereby the irrational was brought into the open (Lasswell, 1930a). What followed from this was that the study of policy-making should be concerned with the construction of irrationality: how words, language, symbols, signs, myths, images are deployed by elites, since:

> Any elite defends and asserts itself in the name of symbols of the common destiny. Such symbols are the 'ideolology' of the established order, the 'utopia' of counter-elites. By the use of sanctioned words and gestures the elite elicits blood, work, taxes and applause, from the masses.
> (*Lasswell, 1959: 31*)

The study of public policy should therefore be focused on the way in which symbols are manipulated in order to shape the composition and distribution of values and exploit the sense of personal insecurity in citizens. Alas, the study of policy has, for the greater part of its history, been neglectful of this absolutely crucial aspect of public policy.

❖ Language and power

George Orwell and the politics of language

One of the most perceptive of all writers on the subject of the relationship between language and politics was the author of *Nineteen Eighty Four*, George Orwell.

In *Nineteen Eighty Four*, Orwell portrays a world in which those in power, 'Big Brother', find it necessary to restructure language, which he called Newspeak, the purpose of which was 'not only to provide a medium of expression for the world-view and mental habits ... but to make all other modes of thought impossible'.

In his essay on 'Politics and the English Language', Orwell makes the point that the debasement of a language has political and economic causes:

> The political dialects to be found in pamphlets, leading articles, manifestos, vary from party to party, but they are all alike in that one almost never finds the fresh, vivid, home-made turn of speech ... And this reduced state of consciousness, if not indispensible, is at any rate favourable to political conformity ... political language has to consist largely of euphemism, question-begging and sheer cloudy vagueness ... When there is a gap between one's real and one's declared aims, one turns as it were instinctively to long words.
> (*Orwell, 1954: 361–3*)

Brendan Bruce, *Images of Power*, 1992

Bruce was a former adviser to the Conservative Party. He stresses how important it is for politicians to invent and use languages which can 'undermine the enemies' case':

> Language is often a key determinant in winning the battle of ideas. For example, the Labour party successfully changed 'community charge' to 'poll tax', and 'self governing' to 'opt out' ... Demons are conjured up in this way so that the exorcists may arrive like the cavalry in the nick of time. 'Missing the bus', whether in the context of expansion or European integration is held unquestioningly as a bad idea. Likewise, being 'out of step' or 'isolated' is unthinkingly viewed with terror ... (p. 176) ◆

Lasswell's interest in the communicative, symbolic and distortive nature of policy-making has, thankfully, become more vital to the study of public policy since the late 1980s with the impact of Habermas, Foucault, Derrida and others on the development of a so-called 'argumentative' approach (see Fischer and Forester (eds), 1993), which we have examined earlier in this book (see 2.7.3, and also 3.9, 3.10.5). An author who has been in the forefront of the study of the symbolic and linguistic aspects of politics and policy-making since the 1960s is Murray Edelman. We examine his ideas in the next section.

2.9.2　Edelman: words that succeed and policies that fail

Edelman is the political scientist who has done most to explore the relationship between the symbolic and substantive aspects of problems and policy since Lasswell. In books such as *the Symbolic Uses of Politics* (1964), *Politics as Symbolic Action* (1971), *Political Language* (1977) and *Constructing the Political Spectacle* (1988) he has analysed the use of language by politicians and bureaucrats as involving the manufacture and manipulation of symbols as placebos to public concern. The real power in policy-making, he believes, resides in the process whereby problems are constructed and articulated, since it is through language that we experience politics: 'the language that interprets objects and actions also constitutes the subject' (Edelman, 1988: 9). Edelman has been concerned to examine the symbolic content of policy and politics and the ways in which policy-makers are involved in exploiting symbols and language. Symbols may, he suggests, be either referential, that is they may refer to something that is tangible and be related to real rewards and resources. However, given that referential symbols are a limited commodity, policy makers are more likely to be engaged in the production of condensational or emotional symbols, which reassure and give an illusion of concern or a solution. (Cf. Lasswell's argument about the relationship between personal insecurity and policy-making: Lasswell, 1930a, 1935.) In *Political Language*, for example, Edelman argues that this capacity to structure complex problems in ways and words that suit policy-makers distorts the perceptions of citizens. Problems are 'constructed' in order to justify solutions (Edelman, 1988: 20–2) rather than solve problems (see, for comparison, the 'garbage can' model: March and Olsen, 1976; see also 2.10.3).

> The various issues with which governments deal are highly inter-related in the contemporary world, though we are cued to perceive them as distinct. Because each day's news and each day's governmental announcements evoke anxieties and reassurances about specific 'problems' perceived as separate from each other ... our political worlds are segmented, disjointed, focused at any moment upon some small set of anxieties, even though each such issue is part of an increasingly integrated whole ... In place of the ability to deal with issues in terms of their logical and empirical ties to one another, the language of politics encourages us to see them and feel them as separate ... From subtle linguistic evocations and associated governmental actions we get a great many of our beliefs about what our problems are, their causes, their seriousness, our success or failure in coping with them.
> (*Edelman, 1977: 40–1*)

In his *Constructing the Political Spectacle* (1988) Edelman analyses the ways in which the more visible dimensions of the political agenda are dominated by ideas and interpretations which tend to support the status quo and the powerful, and work against change and the power-less. In particular, he focuses on the role of the media and news broad-casters, and the relationship between leaders and their audience. The definition of problems takes place in a process whereby politicians and the media manipulate meaning and symbols so as to facilitate tight control over what is discussed and how it is discussed and what significance is attached to an issue. The citizen therefore does not, as far as Edelman is concerned, face a world of facts, so much as a world of political fictions:

> The spectacle constituted by news reporting continuously constructs and reconstructs social problems, crises, enemies, and leaders and so creates a succession of threats and reassurances. These constructed problems and personalities furnish the content of political journalism and the data for historical and analytic support and opposition for political causes and policies.
> (*Edelman, 1988: 1*)

The definition of problems and policy language is therefore necessar-ily ambiguous (Edelman, 1988: 25–30). In policy talk – as in all prag-matic language and behaviour (see John Wilson, 1990) – more is meant than is said or can be said. The way in which a policy is expressed is central to understanding what is going on when issues, problems and policies are defined. Language is a key element in the making of a problem and the defining of solutions. How policy is framed is very important to the capacity of the policy to adapt to circumstances, accommodate demands and promote the compliance of the public. Hence, although a policy succeeds as a political device, it may actu-ally fail to address or ameliorate the problem – except in the terms defined by policy-makers. Edelman, in *Political Language* (1977) gives an interesting description of this phenomenon: 'words that succeed and policies that fail'. Policies may succeed at the symbolic, reassur-ance level, but fail in practice – as in the expression, 'the operation was a success, but the patient died'. Policy-making therefore may be viewed from this perspective as the manipulation of symbols (Lasswell, 1936) or the manufacture/construction of 'spectacle' (Edelman, 1988). Public policy is about 'doing something' rather than 'problem-solv-ing'. As Bacon argued long ago, the words which we use in policy become idols or symbols to define something which may not actually be there. The policy-maker may therefore think that a policy has 'solved' or a condition has been improved, when in 'reality' all that has hap-pened is that symbols have been manipulated. The public is reassured by such actions and policy-makers have enhanced or maintained their legitimacy:

> Political language can win or maintain public support or acquiescence in the face of other actions that violate moral qualms and typically does so by

denying the premises on which such actions are based while retaining traces of the premise.
(*Edelman, 1988: 116*)

While coercion and intimidation help to check resistance in all political systems, the key tactic must always be the evocation of meanings that legitimize favored courses of action and threaten or reassure people so as to encourage them to be supportive or to remain quiescent ... While most political language has little to do with how well people live, it has a great deal to do with the legitimation of regimes and the acquiescence of publics in actions they had no part in initiating.
(*Edelman, 1985: 11, 14*)

Policy-making for Edelman is essentially a form of political performance or theatre played out before an audience (citizens) in order to ensure public acquiescence. Its object is to obscure, rather than to enlighten public problems; to reduce, rather than to extend the power of the public. It benefits the privileged and disadvantages the powerless:

The limited power of the public is implicit in most language about policy formation [through] ... its depiction of policy formation as taking place in a forum that is remote from everyday life ... In this respect the political spectacle evokes something like the awe and sense of personal powerlessness characteristic of a religious posture ... Like religious myths about great events in a time and place outside everyday experience, these political accounts build an intensified appeal and an acquiescent response upon their remoteness.
(*Edelman, 1988: 98*)

For Edelman, therefore, a core task of policy analysis should be the deconstruction of policy discourses and the demystification of the myths and symbols which are deployed by policy-makers to their advantage.

❖ Policy as symbolic activity

Ken Young and Charlie Mason, 'The significance of urban programmes', in Young and Mason (eds) (1983)

The intelligent citizen has long been aware that a large part of governmental activity is symbolic rather than substantive. The basic distinction is familiar to those who have never encountered Walter Bagehot, George Sorel, Graham Wallas or Murray Edelman. Policy statements, new machinery and the allocation of fresh resources are almost self-justifying when they are decided upon in a climate of acute and rising public concern. There is little room for the iconoclast who asks for a firmer rationale than the comfort of 'doing something'.
(p. 216)

Policy-making as theatre: the presentation of policies in everyday life
Doing something, going through the motions, rather than substantive action which addresses 'reality' is, of course, a characteristic of human behaviour as individuals and groups.

This question of how we present or communicate in a public way was the subject of Erving Goffman's book *The Presentation of Self in Everyday Life* (1971).

Goffman argues that we must distinguish between regions of communication which he considers analogous to the theatre. There is communication or performance, which is a public front of stage activity, and there is the performance backstage. Performances are essentially managed behaviour and Goffman finds the language of the theatre appropriate to that of analysing social behaviour. All the world is a stage. Policy-makers in Goffman's sense have their routines and patter, their cues, entrances and exits. They have their sets and lights, they can go out as nobodies and come back stars. They can fall flat on their faces.

In the modern state, politics is largely shaped by the discourse of 'policy'. The presentation of policy is a matter of great concern. Indeed, it is not unknown for policy-makers to argue that the policy is good but the presentation has been poor: people have not 'got the real message'. If we view policy-making in this theatrical light, then it may be argued that agendas and problems are part of a relationship between the citizen as audience and the policy maker as performer. Hence:

> The key factor in this structure is the maintenance of a single definition of the situation, this definition having to be expressed, and this expression sustained in the face of a multitude of potential disruptions. A character staged in a theatre is not in some ways real, nor does it have the same kind of real consequences as does the thoroughly contrived character performed by a confidence man; but the successful staging of either of these types of false figures involves use of real techniques.
> (*Goffman, 1971: 247*)

Images as a post-modern condition

David Harvey, *The Condition of Postmodernity*, 1992

> The mediatization of politics has now become all pervasive ... The production and marketing of such images of permanence and power require considerable sophistication ... The materials to produce and reproduce such images, if they were not readily to hand, have themselves been the focus for innovation – the better the replication of the image, the greater the mass market for image making could become. This is in itself an important issue and it brings us ... to consider the role of the 'simulacrum' in post-modernism. By 'simulacrum' is meant a state of such near perfect replication that the difference between the original and the copy becomes almost impossible to spot ... We can certainly see it at work in the realm of politics as the image makers and the media assume a more powerful role in the shaping of political identities ... (pp. 288–9) ◆

2.10   Networks, streams, advocacy coalitions and punctuated equilibrium

2.10.1   New approaches to agenda analysis and policy formation

The argument that the policy agendas of liberal democratic and other countries are converging (Fukuyama, 1992a and b) adds weight to the idea that we need more overarching general models and theories to explain the processes which we have been analysing above. There is no shortage of middle-range models which explain various aspects of policy in its formative phases. Indeed, the array of ideas is quite bewildering to both the student and the professional analyst. As a consequence of this sheer proliferation in approaches one of the main features of policy analysis in recent years has been the search for models of a more comprehensive kind. This desire for a synthesis has found expression in a number of models. Here we shall consider four major approaches:

- policy networks and communities (2.10.2);
- policy streams (2.10.3);
- advocacy coalitions (2.10.4);
- punctuated equilibrium (2.10.5).

2.10.2   Networks and communities

These approaches are concerned with the more relational and informal aspects of the policy-making. As a word, 'network' may be found in use in the nineteenth century, meaning to cover with network – or a piece of net. Tulloch informs us that the term has two current usages, both of which are employed by network theorists. As a verb, to network means to take advantage of contacts, as in:

> As the feminist movement gathered momentum during the seventies, it was realised that men had always used the old boy network to get ahead, and there was no reason why women should not do the same ... By the late eighties networking was recognised as an important way of advancing all kinds of interests.

Of course, the other modern source was that of the language of computer technology which involved the idea of linking computers (*Oxford Dictionary*, 1992: 211).

In social science the term was first employed in the 1940s and 1950s to analyse and map personal relationships, inter-connectedness and dependencies (see Bott, 1957; Frankenburg, 1966). It became attractive to political scientists and others in the 1970s because it allowed a more fluid and realistic analysis of how people interact at different levels. In the case of policy-making it has clear attractions in that it draws attention to the way in which policy is the product of a complex interplay of people and organizations and provides a more informal picture of how 'real' politics takes place. By the end of the 1970s the network metaphor became, as Kenis and Schneider note, 'an appropriate metaphor for responding to a number of empirical observations with respect to critical changes in the political governance of modern democracies' (1991: 34). For Keynes in the 1930s and 1940s the policy network was relatively small. However, with the growth of both government and policy-making activity the sheer range of participants has grown both wider and more complex. Greater diversity in society and in policy programmes geared to specific targets and functions and the increase in the number of participants in the policy process has meant that the network metaphor has been seen to have a better fit with modern policy-making than pluralism, corporatism (see 3.3) and other 'traditional' models. The result has been the production of a variety of typologies which seek to define the new patterns of relationship which exist in modern societies. The strength of the network approach is that it provides a metaphor for this complexity which 'fits' with the technological and sociological changes of modern society. Against this is the weakness that the metaphor is highly diverse in its use and interpretation.

The metaphor of a network or community seeks to focus on the pattern of formal and informal contacts and relationships which shape policy agendas and decision-making as opposed to the interplay within and between the formal policy-making organizations and institutions. This is particularly important in the case of societies which are highly pluralistic and in which there are a multiplicity of influences on the policy process. Network analysis is based on the idea that a policy is framed within a context of relationships and dependencies. As David Knoke and James Kuklinski have noted, network analysis assumes that actors are participating in a social system in which other actors impact upon one another's decisions, and secondly, that the levels of structure within a social system must be a focus of investigation. In analysing the context of relations and the structures within which they take place, it is argued that it provides a 'powerful brush for painting a systematic picture of global social structures and their components' (Knoke and Kuklinski, in Thomson *et al.* (eds), 1991: 173).

In political science one of the earliest uses of the idea was by Heclo (1978) in an essay which compared 'issue networks' with 'iron triangles' in the context of the US executive. The idea was subsequently applied in Britain by Richardson and Jordan (1979), who suggested that the policy-making map of Britain was characterized by a fragmented collection of subsystems: a 'series of vertical compartments or segments, each segment inhabited by a different set of organised groups and generally impenetrable by "unrecognised groups" or by the general public' (Richardson and Jordan, 1979: 174). Rhodes has applied resource dependency and exchange theory and the idea of policy networks to the study of local–central relations (see Rhodes 1981, 1986, 1988). He follows Benson in defining policy networks in terms of a 'complex of organizations connected to each other by resource dependencies' (Benson, 1982: 148), and suggests that we may model this network in terms of different structures of dependencies (see 4.3.7).

Richardson *et al.* (1982) went on to develop the idea of policy communities on a comparative level through the idea that different countries exhibit a variety of patterns – or styles – of policy formulation and decision-making. The two main dimensions of policy style, Richardson suggested are:

- an anticipatory style (a tendency to anticipate problems) or a reactionary style (a tendency to react to events and circumstances as they arise);

Figure 2.17 Dimensions of policy style

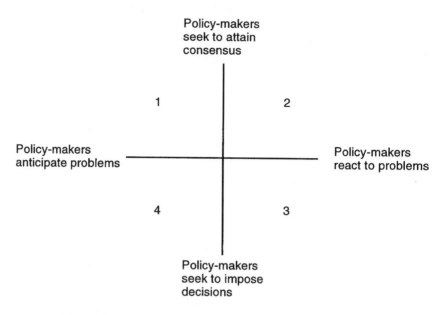

Source: Adapted from Richardson (1982: 13)

- a consensus-seeking style (a tendency to make decisions through getting agreement between interested parties) or a style which tends to impose decisions on society.

The policy style model (figure 2.17) suggests that although the modes of policy-making in industrialized countries are exhibiting a shift towards more 'community', 'network' structures, there will be considerable differences in the way in which policy communities interact. In quadrant 1, for example, the policy style will tend to be such that government seeks to plan and consult with the policy communities. In quadrant 2, we might find the style of policy-making associated with 'incrementalist' politics: pluralistic, fragmented, fire-fighting, imperfect knowledge and so on. In quadrant 3, government does not see its role as making policy through planning and consensus, so much as reacting to problems when necessary and imposing its decisions. In quadrant 4, government will lay claims to planning, rationality, prediction and so on, and assert that it has the foresight to impose its plans and solutions. (Compare this with the model put forward by Braybrooke and Lindblom, 1963: 67; see 3.4.3.)

The 'style' which frames the way in which policy communities and networks function will, of course, vary over time and between different policy sectors. Richardson, for example, argues that in Britain the policy style which predominates is in quadrant 2: that is, a tendency to negotiate with policy communities and 'react' to problems rather than anticipate them in a 'rational' way. Jordan and Richardson (1983, 1987) describe it as being essentially a system of 'bureaucratic accommodation' amongst the relevant policy communities. However, under the 'Iron Lady' (sic) the style was far more in quadrant 3: she was not a 'consensus' politician so much as an exponent of the 'confrontational style' (see Richardson, 1990). In countries where the style has tended to be in quadrants 1 and 4, policy-making usually involves some kind of planning process (France and Japan, for example). As the policy communities will vary from one policy sector to another, the style in a sector which has a well-organized and powerful policy community will be very different to one in which policy-makers face a loose, diffuse network. In the case of the former, policy-making may have to take place with a good deal of negotiation and bargaining; in the latter, government may well opt for a more 'robust' approach and impose its decisions without too much by way of consultation with a policy community. Some policy issues – such as defence – may be dealt with in secrecy and without very much consultation with a wider policy community (Jordan and Richardson, 1987: 180).

The policy style approach is an important contribution to the tool box of policy analysis as it provides a simple, but effective framework to compare policy communities both within and between political systems. However, although the approach does offer an insight into the policy-making process, it is less convincing as an explanation of what governments actually do, and with what effects and outcomes. Rose (1984b), for example, argues that in 'understanding big government', 'policy style' has little bearing on the changing patterns of government expenditure and on the allocation of resources to different programmes. Vogel (1986) also notes that although the policy styles of the UK and the USA are very different, the actual substantial outcomes of environmental regulation are not so marked as an analysis of style might suggest. Although 'style' may 'matter' in terms of how policy agendas and decisions are made, it may have but a marginal impact on policy output and outcomes. (We shall discuss this issue more fully in 4.7.) Another point of criticism is that when originally put forward (see Jordan and Richardson, 1979), the model posited the growing convergence of style because of the existence of policy communities: towards a more 'reactive' consensual form of policy-making. The Thatcher government quickly put paid to the idea that policy-making through policy communities would give rise to a highly consensual politics (although Jordan and Richardson, 1987, and Richardson, 1990, contend that the confrontational politics of the Thatcher years obscured a deeper, less public consensual style in which policy communities did exercise a predominant influence over a range of policy sectors; a view which is supported by later work on the period, which emphasizes the continuities of the Thatcher years: see, for example, Marsh and Rhodes (eds), 1992). Furthermore, as Neary (1992) argues with regard to Japan, it does not appear that a more 'reactive' style is necessarily characteristic of all contemporary industrial societies.

Another influential application of the idea of networks was put forward by Benson at around the same time as the emergence of the policy style approach (1982). Using organizational theory Benson distinguished between various types of structural interests: demand groups; support groups (resource providers); administrative groups; provider groups (who deliver the services) and co-ordinating groups (who co-ordinate in and between programmes). However, the configuration of networks and types will be different from issue to issue and from policy to policy. Studies of policy networks endeavour to explore the way in which policy is made within the context of a network of actors and organizations. Policy analysts themselves may be part of an issue network, as they are involved in the identification of 'problems', the development, and propagation of ideas and in policy evaluation and implementation (see Jenkins-Smith, 1990).

❖ Policy networks

One of the leading exponents of network analysis is Rod Rhodes. In his study of local–central relations in Britain he argues that we should investigate the structures of dependency within policy networks and identify the main variety of networks at the central and local level, including the professional, local government and producer networks and how they interact with central government. Policy networks, he suggests, have become the main feature of policy-making in Britain, and lie at the 'heart of one of the major problems of British government: policy messes, or the non-correspondence of policy systems and policy problems. The failure to appreciate that service delivery systems are complex, disaggregated and indeterminate has led to the failure of policies' (Rhodes, 1988: 85).

Whilst Rhodes addresses the structural types of network, Wilks and Wright in their work on industrial policy (1988) are more concerned with the disaggregative and inter-personal dimensions. There are, they suggest, three levels of policy: the policy area; the policy sector, and the policy issue. The 'policy universe' is big and includes all those who share a common interest, whilst the policy community is a smaller and more consensual network focused on a sectoral or sub-sectoral aspect of policy. At the level of policy issues, communities interact with one another in a network. ◆

Much discussion in this area is centred on the difference between policy networks and a more closed policy community. A policy community is a more tight-knit set of relationships between actors who share central values and attitudes towards issues and policies (see Richardson and Jordan, 1979; Rhodes, 1988). Rhodes argues that the types of network are to be distinguished by their degree of integration. At one end of a continuum are policy communities which have stable and restricted memberships. Policy communities are highly integrated within the policy-making process. Issue networks, in contrast, represent a much looser set of interests and are less stable and non-exclusive and have much weaker points of entry into actual policy-making.

❖ Networks and communities

Key texts
The literature on policy communities and networks is large and growing rapidly. Two contributions to this literature provide excellent reviews of the theories and issues.

Martin J. Smith, *Pressure, Power and Policy*, 1993
The most comprehensive account to date of the approach which is considered in the context of pluralist, corporatist and Marxist theories. The focus of the study is the relationship between state actors and groups and how these relationships shape policy outcomes in the US and Britain. He describes the notion of policy networks as a 'meso-level concept which is concerned

with explaining behaviour within particular sections of the state or particular policy areas' (p. 7). He advances six propositions about the relationship of state autonomy and networks which are suggested by the literature:

- the type of network and community relationships varies across time, policy sector and states;
- state actors have interests which shape the development of policy and policy networks;
- the autonomy of the state in making and implementing policy is affected by the types of policy networks which exist;
- types of policy networks affect policy outcomes;
- the type of policy networks provides a context for understanding the role of interest groups in policy-making. Networks are the 'enstructuration' of past policies, ideologies and processes;
- the types of network will affect the way in which policy changes.

In addition to this he sets out four propositions about the comparative context of policy networks/communities in the US and Britain (p. 10):

- policy communities are more likely to develop where the state is dependent on groups for implementation;
- policy communities are more likely to develop where interest groups have important resources they can exchange;
- issue networks will develop in areas of lesser importance to government, of high political controversy, or in new issue areas where interests have not been institutionalized;
- policy communities are more likely in Britain than in the US.

Smith shows how the idea of policy networks may be used in a range of theoretical macro frameworks which define different relationships between state autonomy and policy networks. In the case of Marxist frames, policy communities are characterized as dominated by capital; in elitist models, communities are viewed as dominated by privileged interests; state-centred theorists envisage networks as dominated by the state; and pluralists envisage networks as having no dominant group.

The author uses several case studies dealing with: agriculture; business; the power of professionals (doctors) in health policy; and consumer policy. He concludes that relations vary considerably across policy sectors. The interests of the state are a key factor in how these relationships are formed. He argues that his case studies demonstrate how policy networks do indeed affect state autonomy and structure interests in the policy process. He concludes by arguing that:

Policy communities do develop where the state needs highly resourced groups to assist in policy implementation, and issue networks develop in areas of lesser importance or where there is a high level of political controversy. Although policy communities do seem more likely in Britain than in the United States, the book did identify some policy communities in the US. Perhaps the most important point to emerge from this book is the complexity of the policy process. Notions of the state, pressure groups, state autonomy and policy networks are highly problematic. Consequently, it is difficult to make general claims about any of these concepts. The relationships between the state and groups have to be examined in a context that is historical, ideological and institutional. It also has to be remembered that the relationships between state actors and groups are relationships of dependence and therefore simplistic society- and state-centred approaches say little about empirical reality ... The state has advantages but ultimately it exists in an intricate relationship with civil society and so state actors cannot ignore group pressures. (pp. 234–5)

See also Martin J. Smith (1991), who analyses the development of food policy in the wake of the outbreak of salmonella in eggs in Britain in the late 1980s. Smith shows how the affair changed the close consensual policy community which greatly influenced food policy and politics into a more pluralistic, less consenual 'issue network'.

Michael M. Atkinson and William D. Coleman, 'Policy networks, policy communities and the problem of governance', 1992
The authors review and evaluate the network literature. They argue that the approach constitutes a significant attempt to understand the policy process in a way which takes us beyond the bureaucratic-political models. However, the authors are critical of three aspects of the approach. First, that the models have a problem with the influence of macro-political institutions and the impact of political discourse. Secondly, that they have difficulty with the issue of the internationalization of many policy domains. And thirdly, that the network/community approach has failed to address the problem of policy innovation and change. They conclude on an optimistic note, arguing that the approach offers the possibility of bridging the boundaries between disciplines:

These approaches appear to serve as a kind of conceptual crossroads for ongoing theoretical and empirical research ... they provide a useful junction for the converging fields of international political economy and comparative public policy. They also invite discussions between those studying executive and legislative structures of government, those focusing on interest intermediation, and those analysing party politics and party government. More broadly, insights from such important branches of sociology as network analysis and the sociology of ideas and from the studies in economics on industrial organisation, the structure of the firm, and institutional transactions have also been examined and, in some studies, incorporated into the analysis of networks and communities. (p. 176) ◆

The idea of policy communities and policy networks has attracted considerable support as a model of policy-making in modern society. However, it is not without its critics (see Smith, and Atkinson and Coleman, in box above). Hogwood, for example, is not entirely convinced as to its usefulness when it comes to understanding how issues are processed in the political system. Many issues, he argues, are not so neat and tidy as the 'policy community' theory claims. In practice issues tend to overlap and get mixed up with other issues. They do not remain confined in one policy community or network. This does not mean that we should abandon the concepts, but he thinks that we should be more subtle in the way in which we define the boundaries between policy communities and policy areas. Policy communities will consist of a core set of issues, but at the boundaries there will be more 'peripheral ' issues which will overlap with the interests and concerns of other communities. Furthermore, Hogwood argues that the model presents a picture of the policy process which is altogether misleading as to how issues get taken on to the policy agenda. Issues do not exist in well-defined communities, but interact with the 'solutions' which are on the look-out for problems. The 'garbage can' model paints a very different kind of picture to the one which is described in the community/network theory:

> Suppose we view a choice activity as a garbage can into which various problems and solutions are dumped by participants. The mix of garbage in a single can depends partly on the labels attached to the alternative cans; but it also depends on what garbage is being produced at the moment, on the mix of cans available, and on the speed with which garbage is collected and removed from the scene.
> (*March and Olsen, 1976: 26; quoted in Hogwood, 1987: 23*)

As Hogwood argues, this model suggests that issues are not dealt with in a neat way. They get attached to solutions and other problems in a way which is not so rational as the community/network models imply. Issues are not well packaged, but spill over one another and exist in relationship to the 'solutions' which policy-makers have to hand at the moment. And, over time, the definition of issues will change and move from one garbage can to another, rather than remain in the context of a given community or network.

This idea of a 'garbage can' process also forms a major element in one of the most interesting and developed theories of agenda-setting advanced by Kingdon: the policy streams approach.

2.10.3   Policy streams

John Kingdon made an important contribution to the study of agenda-setting with his study *Agendas, Alternatives and Public Policies* (1984). His book is concerned with how issues come to be issues; how they come to the attention of public officials and policy-makers; how agendas are set and why ideas 'have their time'. To tackle these questions he engaged in an interview programme involving 247 officials, politicians and policy activists involved in transport and health policy over the period 1976–79. He also undertook 23 case studies in these policy fields. The study employs a variety of metaphors to explain the agenda-setting process. He begins with a consideration of the notion of organizational 'garbage cans' as propounded by Cohen *et al.* (1972: 2) (see 3.4.5). The garbage can model stresses the anarchical nature of organizations as 'loose collections of ideas' as opposed to rational 'coherent structures'. Organizations discover preferences through action, rather than act out of preferences. Understanding is poor, trial and error learning operates, and membership is fluid. Organizations *qua* 'garbage cans' are collections of choices which look for problems and issues and seek decisional situations in which they may be advanced. Solutions look for problems. Choices thus compose a 'garbage can' into which 'various kinds of problems and solutions are dumped by participants as they are generated' (Cohen *et al.* 1972: 2). Kingdon finds this model an attractive framework to approach an agenda-setting process in which solutions search for problems and the outcomes are a function of the mix of problems, participants and resources. Just as organizations do not rationally relate problems and solutions, so the agenda process may be conceived, argues Kingdon, as composed of three separate and distinct streams: problems, policies and politics. The governmental agenda is set by the political stream, whilst the policy stream shapes alternatives.

The problem stream

'[F]or a condition to be a problem, people must become convinced that something should be done to change it' (Kingdon, 1984; 119). The problem stream is composed of those problems on which government policy-makers fix their attention, as opposed to those which they choose to ignore. Kingdon argues that there are three mechanisms which serve to bring problems to the attention of policy-makers:

- *indicators*: measurements which are used to assess the scale and change in problems. Government data and reports feed into government a picture of the problem and thus have a significant role in shaping governmental attitudes and positions;
- *events*: which serve to focus attention on problems: disasters, personal experience, and symbols;
- *feedback*: gives information on current performance and indicates a failure to meet goals or points towards unanticipated consequences.

The policy stream

Kingdon conceptualizes the policy stream in terms of a 'primeval soup', and draws heavily on the theories of Dawkins and other recent writers on evolution. Ideas float around, confront one another and combine. The soup changes in a process of natural selection, survival, demise and recombination. In this soup stream some ideas float to the top of the agenda and others fall to the bottom. The environment in which the soup sloshes about is composed of policy communities – specialists in certain areas – and their organization varies. Some are closed and tightly knit, whilst others are more open and fragmented. Swimming in this soup are policy entrepreneurs: 'people who are willing to invest resources of various kinds in hopes of a future return in the form of policies they favour' (Kingdon, 1984: 151). They are crucial to the survival and success of an idea. They 'soften-up' policy communities to gain acceptability for a policy. The idea itself has to satisfy a number of criteria if it is to survive and get to the top. It must be technically feasible; compatible with the dominant values of the community; and able to anticipate future constraints under which it may operate. The end result of this struggle in the soup is a list of proposals which constitute a set of alternatives to the governing agenda.

The political stream
The political stream operates quite separately from the other streams and may serve to determine the status of the agenda item. It is composed of a number of elements:

- *national mood*: public opinion, climate of opinion;
- *organized political forces*: parties, legislative politics, pressure groups;
- *government*: change in personnel and jurisdiction;
- *consensus-building*: bargaining, bandwagons and tipping.

At critical times the political, policy and problem streams come together: 'A problem is recognised, a solution is developed and available in the policy community, a political change makes the right time for policy change, and potential constraints are not severe' (Kingdon, 1984: 174). Kingdon uses another metaphor to describe this critical point when streams merge: it is like a launch window in a space flight mission. If the window is lost, then the launch has to wait for another time when conditions and alignments are appropriate. The successful launch of a policy change is the result of the opening of such a window in the interplay of streams: solutions which have been floating around become attached and coupled to a problem and policy entrepreneurs seize the opportunity to change the decision agenda. Policy windows open because of a compelling problem (a problem window) or because of something in the political stream (a political window). In such conditions the policy stream has the opportunity to push an alternative and couple it to a problem. If all three streams – problem, proposal, and political receptivity – are coupled in a single package then the item has a high probability of reaching the top of the decision agenda and may result in a spillover to a related area.

2.10.4   The advocacy coalition framework

As we noted in Part One, policy analysis has been dominated by the 'stagist' or policy cycle framework. One of the most developed alternatives to this way of thinking about the policy process has been advanced by Paul Sabatier (in conjunction with a number of other co-authors). Sabatier argues that the idea of separating the 'agenda-setting' phase from the wider policy-making process is neither realistic nor a satisfactory way of explaining how change takes place. Whereas Kingdon argues that the analytical and political streams converge now and then, thus providing a window of opportunity, Sabatier sees analysis, ideas and information as fundamentally part of the political stream and a major force for change. Sabatier maintains that we need to set out a more comprehensive and testable theory of the policy process that brings together a number of approaches and frameworks into a 'better' theory which may serve to predict policy change. The synthesis may be regarded as composed of several key ideas; these include:

- the idea that the policy process as a whole may be understood in the context of policy 'networks' and 'communities' (Heclo, 1974; Kingdon, 1984; Cook and Skogan, 1991);
- the idea that policy analysis has a long-term 'enlightenment' function. Policy analysis gradually alters the arguments surrounding policy problems (Weiss, 1977a; Nelkin, 1979; Mazur, 1981);
- the idea that beliefs, values and ideas are important and neglected dimensions of policy-making (Pressman and Wildavsky, 1973; Wildavsky, 1987; Majone, 1980);
- the idea that socio-economic factors have a major influence on the making of policy and upon its outcomes (Heclo, 1974; Hofferbert, 1974);
- the idea that elite belief systems have a 'structure' or hierarchy (March and Simon, 1958; Putman, 1976).

Figure 2.18   Sabatier's model

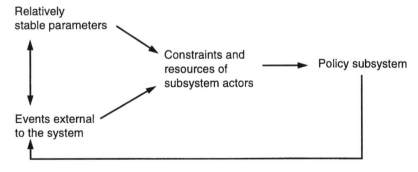

Source: Adapted from Sabatier (1988, 1991)

In place of the traditional iron triangle approach of political science, and the policy cycle beloved of policy analysts, Sabatier suggests that we conceptualize the policy process in terms of of policy subsystems (figure 2.18).

Change in the policy subsystem is a result of an interplay of 'relatively stable parameters' and external events, which frame the constraints and resources of the actors in the subsystem and the interactions within the policy subsystem itself.

The policy subsystem is composed of all those who play a part in the generation, dissemination and evaluation of policy ideas. These include the elements of the iron triangle, interest groups, bureaucracy and elected politicians, but also academic analysts, think-tanks, researchers, journalists and actors in other levels of government. A policy subsystem will comprise a set of actors who are involved with a policy problem, rather than simply formal decision-makers. Furthermore, the levels of policy-making are viewed as extending to those actors who, from a formal point of view, are charged with implementation (civil servants, professionals, 'street level' implementators) rather than the actual making of policy (see figure 2.19).

Figure 2.19   The policy subsystem

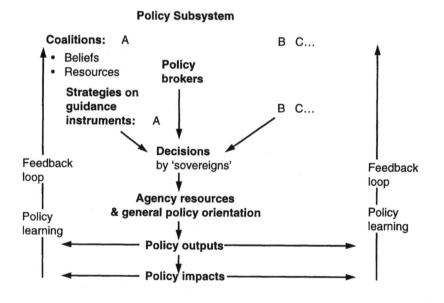

Source: Adapted from Sabatier (1986, 1988, 1991)

The policy subsystem is composed of a number of 'advocacy coalitions' (ACs) which may be distinguished from one another in terms of their beliefs and resources. The beliefs of ACs may be analysed in terms of a hierarchy with the structure shown in figure 2.20 (see also, for comparison, Young, 1977; and 3.7.7).

Figure 2.20   The structure of beliefs

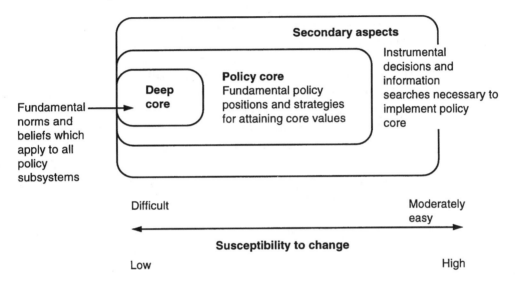

Source: Adapted from Sabatier (1988, 1991)

Whereas Kingdon and other agenda-setting theorists consider the process of defining issues and agendas in the context of wider social or environmental pressures or in terms of the relationship of 'public opinion' to public policy, Sabatier takes the view that the policy-making process, in terms of agenda-setting and other phases, is dominated by elite opinion. The impact of public opinion is, at best 'modest' (Sabatier, 1991: 148; 1993: 30). If we wish, therefore, to understand policy change, Sabatier recommends that we focus on elite opinion and the factors which make it shift over a relatively long period of time. The model predicts that when core beliefs are in dispute, the composition of allies and opponents will remain quite stable. Within ACs there will be a large measure of agreement on the policy core and less agreement on the secondary aspects. Change or modification is more likely to take place in the secondary aspects of policy rather than the policy core or at the level of deep beliefs. Changes at the level of the policy core are 'usually the results of perturbations in noncognitive factors external to the subsystem' (Sabatier, 1993: 19–20). These 'noncognitive' factors will include changes in macro-economic conditions or new systemic governing coalitions. At the 'secondary' level, change comes about as the result of 'policy orientated learning' (POL) within and between ACs. POL is defined by Sabatier as a process involving 'relatively enduring alterations of thought or behavioural intentions that result from experience and which are concerned with the attainment or revision of the precepts of the belief system of individuals or collectivities such as ACs' (Sabatier, 1993: 42).

The model predicts that in a policy subsystem there will be a multiplicity of ACs who will be competing for influence over and in the decision-making process. 'Policy brokers' are conceived of as actors who are concerned with finding reasonable or feasible compromises between the positions advocated by coalitions. These brokers may take the form of civil servants, elected officials, commissions of inquiry or the courts. Coalitions 'seek to alter the behaviour of governmental institutions in order to achieve policy objectives in their respective policy cores' (Sabatier and Jenkins-Smith, 1993: 227). They seek to bring about this change through the use of direct and indirect 'guidance instruments' (Sabatier and Pelkey, 1987; Sabatier and Jenkins-Smith (eds), 1993: 226).

The consequent influence or change as reflected in policy outputs and impacts completes the 'subsystem' through 'feedback' into the beliefs and resources of coalitions. Sabatier describes this as a process of 'policy orientated learning'. That is, policy coalitions learn from the experience of change and endeavour to reorientate their policy ideas and guidance strategies to better understand the world and their policy objectives. The policy 'subsystem' interacts with other policy subsystems, and of course with the wider social, legal, economic, resource and institutional 'system'. The parameters of this system are defined by two sets of forces: stability and change.

- Relatively stable parameters within which subsystems function comprise:
  1 the basic attributes of problems and goods;
  2 the basic distribution of natural resources;
  3 fundamental cultural and social values and structures;
  4 the constitutional rules within which policy-making takes place.
- External (system) events:
  1 change in society and economy;
  2 change in public opinion;
  3 change in the governing coalition of the system;
  4 policy decisions and impacts from other subsystems.-

Taken together these systemic 'parameters' and 'events' set or determine the wider constraints and resources within which policy subsystems function. In turn, of course, the subsystem impacts on the 'system' as a whole.

As a model it provides a powerful framework for organizing and mapping the wide range of ideas which have emerged in the study of public policy and policy analysis. It successfully provides for an integrated approach to the policy process in terms of 'network', and in placing policy analysis and beliefs in a central position. However, Sabatier's AC framework aims to go much further than mapping in a heuristic way. The AC model is promoted as a set of *testable* hypotheses and predictions.

❖ A testable model

In Sabatier and Jenkins-Smith (1993) a number of hypotheses are tested in qualitative and quantitative studies. The initial set of hypotheses cover two areas:

The behaviour of actors in the subsystem

1   On major controversies within the policy subsystem when core beliefs are in dispute. The line-up of allies and opponents tends to be rather stable over periods of a decade or so.
2   Actors within an advocacy coalition will show substantial consensus on issues pertaining to the policy core, although less so on secondary aspects.
3   An actor or coalition will give up secondary aspects of a belief system before acknowledging weakness in the policy core.
4   The core or basic attributes of a governmental programme is unlikely to be significantly revised as long as the subsystem advocacy coalition that instituted the programme remains in power.
5   The core or basic attributes of a governmental action programme is unlikely to be changed in the absence of significant perturbations external to the subsystem, that is, changes in socio-economic conditions, system-wide governing coalitions, or policy outputs from other subsystems.

Policy-orientated learning (POL)

6   POL across belief systems is more likely when there is an intermediate level of informed conflict between the two.
7   Problems for which accepted quantitative data and theory exist are more conducive to POL than those in which data and theory are generally qualitative, quite subjective or altogether lacking.
8   Problems involving natural systems are more conducive to POL than those involving purely social or political systems because in the former many of the critical variables are not themselves active strategists and controlled experimentation is more feasible.

9   POL across belief systems is most likely when there exists a forum that is: prestigious enough to force professionals to participate; and dominated by professional norms. (*Sabatier and Jenkins-Smith, 1993: 27–54*) ◆

The empirical work which tested the AC framework has broadly confirmed its usefulness as a model which explains policy change over a decade (Mawhinney, 1993; Brown and Stewart, 1993; Munro, 1993; Barke, 1993). However, although the framework lays claim to being capable of explaining change in modern industrial polyarchies (Sabatier and Jenkins-Smith, 1993: 225), it has mainly been used in an American (or North American, cf. Mawhinney, 1993) context. Thus the first criticism of this model, as far as its hypotheses are concerned, is that we need to see a good deal more use of the framework outside America and with case studies from other polyarchies if we are to come to any real conclusions as to its general applicability. Greenaway *et al.* (1992), in their examination of the UK, argue that the model does appear to be appropriate to those policy-making in areas such as Aids, nuclear power and trade union law reform. However, in the case of policy-making in areas where advocacy coalitions were not evident and where decision-making was not very pluralistic – such as in defence policy and the Falklands War – they note that the framework is less applicable. In political systems, such as Britain's, where there is much less openness and contact between actors in different institutions, the relevance of the AC framework is in doubt.

It may be that the AC model is one which has best fit where the 'policy style' (Richardson, 1982) is such that government has a disposition towards consultation with interested groups and organizations. If the policy style is highly consultative and open then the AC model offers the prospect of a comprehensive and coherent aproach to policy-making and learning. However, where government is more prone to impose policy and to plan in the longer term, rather than react to events and problems, the AC model may prove to be less useful in explaining policy change. (In such cases, of course, it may serve as a normative model of how policy-making ought to be.)

Where government does actively seek to arrive at a consensus which involves finding agreement amongst 'coalitions', and where this process is characterized by conflict or disagreement which may be described as relatively open, the AC model fits well – as in the case of Aids in the UK – however, it is more problematic when applied in circumstances and in 'policy styles' which do not correspond to pluralism *à la* American. If we apply the model to political systems which have a more étatist tradition – such as France or Italy – or a more consensual or 'democratic corporatist' style – such as the Scandinavian countries, Austria and Germany (see Lijphart, 1984; and 3.3.4) – the AC approach seems far less convincing.

At present, therefore, all that can be said is that the available evidence suggests that the AC model has considerable utility for policy styles and policy/issue areas which exhibit the kind of pluralistic characteristics which underpin Sabatier's model. In addition to policy style, there is also the matter of structures: the degree of centralization and decentralization of decision-making and implementation. Sabatier makes great play with the argument that government in modern society is characterized by 'network' forms of relationship. In the USA the federal system and the fragmentation of power in Washington certainly lends weight to the idea that policy-making is something which takes place in the context of multiple layers and interactions. However, the AC model may be less appropriate to those political systems with a tradition of greater centralization, both in terms of territorial distribution of power and the political and administrative arrangements at the level of national politics, government and administration.

Two further criticisms may also be noted. First, the model posits that there are 'events' and 'stable parameters' which set the constraints and resources for the 'subsystem' and its actors. However, we might argue that this notion is rather suspect. Do these forces exist 'out there' in the wider system ('real-world change' (*sic*)), or do they exist in the minds of the participants and in the organizations which compose the policy subsystem – as forms of 'cognitive activity'? Sabatier, for example, notes that one form of this real-world change is 'macroeconomic conditions' (Sabatier, 1993: 20). However, one could argue that these exist in the context of 'cognitive activity'. What counts as a 'macroeconomic event' is a construction: it is not 'out there' in the real world. As we noted in 2.6, above, the 'subsystem' may be 'self-referencing', rather than shaped by forces outside itself. In Part Three (3.7.5) we shall discuss the theories of Sir Geoffrey Vickers, who argues that mental activity and social process are 'indivisible' (Vickers: 1965: 15) and that the world is not a set of data, but a 'construct, a mental artifact, a collective work of art' (Vickers, 1968: 85). Such arguments point towards a much less well-defined boundary between the subsystem and its outside environment than is contained in the AC framework. Furthermore, as we shall examine in 4.6.3, John Child makes the point that it is elites within organizations who frame the image of the environment 'outside' in order to facilitate their strategic choices (Child, 1972).

A second point to note about the AC framework is that it makes claims to being a testable empirical model (what the policy-making process is), but it also contains normative implications for what the policy-making system ought to be, or could be. 'Policy learning' appears to be a process which is restricted to the subsystem actors: interest groups, think-tanks, civil servants, politicians and professionals. Thus in the original model, public opinion was subsumed under changes in socio-economic conditions and external events. The 1993 modification incorporated 'public opinion' as a distinct factor, but the AC framework still adheres to a view of non-elites as having 'neither the expertise, nor the time, nor the inclination to be active participants in the policy subsystem' (Sabatier and Jenkins-Smith, 1993: 223). A more radical idea of policy learning, such as that put forward by Lindblom, urges that this learning process should be seen as involving wider participation, a more open agenda and greater competition between ideas, as well as removing impediments such as social and economic inequality. Even more radical variants of a learning model would argue that, if policy-making is to facilitate improved learning, it must be a far more ' social ' and 'bottom-up' process (see 4.6.4).

Are successful ACs those which learn better than others? Or is it the case that learning has far less to do with it than the power (or resources) which ACs possess? Are beliefs (rather than greed, self-interest, power) the 'glue' which holds ACs and the political system together? Sabatier has little to say on the question of where this model of the policy process stands in relation to 'power' theories, such as non-decision-making, or more radical neo-Marxist frameworks. It may be that the belief systems – or ideologies – of coalitions change because of a desire to maintain and advance core interests rather than because of a rational learning process. In this respect the AC model, for all its claims to be real worldish, is prone to the kind of criticisms levelled at Keynes's assertion that it is ideas rather than interests which shape policy in the long run. Sabatier is dismissive of 'raw political power' (Sabatier, 1993: 44) because he believes that, in the long run, policy learning has a greater capacity to change the agendas and decisions of government than the exercise of power. The AC model concedes that POL is more likely in conditions where there is a high level of quantitative data, and where natural systems are involved (see hypotheses 7, 8, 9 above). This excludes a very large number indeed of policy arenas and political issues. The model puts itself forward as a more realistic framework than the 'stagist' approach, and yet in this regard the AC theory appears to be occupying a space somewhere in the land of Oz. The vast majority of social, economic and other issues with which public policy is concerned are very messy and do not have neat quantifiable characteristics. Hypothesis (9), that the existence of professional bodies and expertise is a powerful force for POL, again seems to fly in the face of the 'real-world' experience of 'de-professionalization' and the demise of professional power.

These criticisms apart, the AC framework is a notable contribution to synthesizing a range of approaches into a coherent and robust theory which links the early phases of the policy cycle – problem definition and agenda-setting with decision-making and implementation. The particular strength of the framework is that it facilitates 'mapping' the policy process in a way which illustrates how the various phases of the policy cycle have to be considered as being more fluid and interactive than stagists often imply. No doubt further research and application (especially in countries other than the US) will test the claims of the AC model to be more than a heuristic device.

2.10.5   A punctuated equilibrium model

Baumgartner and Jones's (1993) study of agenda-setting is one of the most comprehensive accounts to date of agenda-setting theory. The predominant metaphors of their inquiry are drawn from biology and computer science. From the former they derive the idea that change in policy agendas might best be understood in terms of 'punctuated equilibrium': the policy process may be characterized as having long periods of stability which are interspersed with periods of instability and major policy change. From the world of computers – and the theories of H.A. Simon – they suggest that human beings are limited in their capacity to process information, thus it is necessary for issues to be processed in parallel, rather than in a serial (one at a time) form. Policy subsystems therefore enable the political system to process issues in parallel, and only in periods of instability do they move up the agenda to be dealt with in a serial fashion. (For Simon, see 3.7.4.)

Their model of punctuated equilibrium, they believe, provides an explanation of why a political system can be both incrementally conservative, and subject to more radical phases of policy-making. During periods of stability there is a large measure of agreement on how problems are defined and where they are on the policy-making agenda. At times, issues emerge and bring about change in policy and, significantly, in institutional arrangements (cf. Peters and Hogwood's (1985) argument, discussed earlier). These new institutions create the basis for a new period of stability. Baumgartner and Jones argue that this punctuated equilibrium is driven by two interacting forces:

- how issues are portrayed: policy image; and
- the institutional context of issues: institutional policy venues.

The authors examine in some detail a number of issues, such as nuclear power, urban problems, smoking, and car safety, to test out their ideas. Their analysis of these, and other issues, over a long time period shows that they have a similar pattern of evolution: a period of equilibrium, during which an issue emerges, unsettles the way in which the issue is portrayed and the institutions which are involved in making decisions about the issue concerned; new institutions are set up; and then a period of equilibrium follows. At times, when the stability which surrounds an issue is disrupted, a policy monopoly is challenged, reconstructed or destroyed – to be replaced by another dominant set of images and institutions.

When there is instability there is access to the agenda, and the policy monopoly – composed of the dominant policy subsystem – is open to criticism or enthusiasm. Agenda access through criticism will involve an attack on the existing images and institutions and this may result in new institutions to replace the old subsystem. Enthusiasm as a source of agenda access will have the effect of creating a new set of institutions. Agenda access punctuates the equilibrium and results in a legacy of institutions which remain intact for many years after the initial wave of criticism or enthusiasm brought about change. Thus, contrary to the Downsian model of IACs, Baumgartner and Jones argue that periods when issues come to their peak of attention can have an ongoing effect through the institutions which were created in the period of highest saliency.

The role of the media in periods of instability is crucial. The authors show that the activities of the media provide a major source of instability to images and institutions. The influence of the media in promoting change in the agenda works through 'directing attention alternatively towards different aspects of the same issues over time, and by shifting attention from one issue to another' (Baumgartner and Jones, 1993: 103). However, in 'lurching' from one issue to another, the media are serving to reinforce and reflect what happens within policy-making institutions. The concerns of the media are as fitful and lurching as those of decision-makers: the one reinforces the other (ibid.: 125).

The institutional structures which sustain policy equilibrium, and which are also the source of change, are (as Sabatier and others have argued) essentially organized in modern policy-making into policy subsystems. It is the interaction of these subsystems which, along with the reinforcement and reflectiveness of the media, accounts for agenda change. Using Simon's ideas about the limits of human cognition (and a computer metaphor), the authors argue that:

> Given the myriad problems that face all complex societies, issues must normally be assigned to policy subsystems dominated by issue experts. Such specialization is the only way the system can deal with the issues in a parallel fashion, rather than serially ... this is just as true for a political system as for a large computer. From time to time, however, issues that are normally confined to policy subsystems move higher onto the political agenda, where they are processed only one or a few at a time. This period of agenda access, when new participants become interested in the debate, is when major changes tend to occur, often disrupting one or more policy sub-systems. So the political system, combining as it does systems of parallel and serial consideration of many issues, involves the continual creation and destruction of policy subsystems ... there are powerful forces of change that can sweep through the entire system. These are not controlled or created by any single group or individual, but are the result of multiple interactions among groups seeking to propose new understandings of issues ... The forces that create stability during some periods are the same that combine during critical periods to force dramatic and long-lasting changes during other periods. Rather than being controlled by any single group, institutions, or individual these forces are the result of complex interconnection of many institutions in society. When they combine to reinforce the pressures for change, their force may be unstoppable. (*Baumgartner and Jones, 1993: 236–7*)

All in all, Baumgartner and Jones put up a robust (normative) defence of liberal democracy derived from an explanatory model. Contrary to the view of policy-making as deadlocked by a 'cosy' relationship between politicians, interest groups and the media, 'punctuated equilibrium', when allied to a computerized view of the political system, provides a story in which there is a happy ending. First, because the method of lurching from one issue to the next does provide for a political evolutionary process which is far more adaptive than its critics concede: change occurs, but in bursts; policy subsystems are more fragile than theorists who stress the power of organized bias. Secondly, the pattern of lurching from one issue to the next which characterizes the agenda process of liberal democratic systems also enables policy-makers and activists to make the best use of their limited attention spans and limited information processing. In agenda access mode, the system processes serially, at times of stability the system processes in parallel through specialist sub-systems.

In using these biological and cognitive metaphors the proponents of the punctuated equilibrium model advance a coherent and convincing synthesis of agenda approaches which relates ideas about subsystems and institutions to the cognitive concerns of Simon. They show in their case studies that agenda analysis has to take account of long-term institutional consequences of changes in the way problems are defined. However, from a more critical standpoint, their model may be read as, rather, a justification of the status quo than an analysis of the agenda process. Baumgartner and Jones present agenda-setting as a way in which policy elites regulate or manage complexity through simplification, rather than through 'control'. The 'bottleneck of attention' (Simon, 1985), which is inevitable in individual and institutional decision-making, appears to have a functionality. Lurching from one issue to another enables the political system to process a 'wider variety of issues over time' (Baumgartner and Jones, 1993 : 250), whilst the subsystems exclude issues that are fragile and are subject to change, decay and replacement. Subsystems exist, but they do not exclude change: indeed, they make change more likely to happen at periods of instability. The roller coaster of attention – high saliency, low saliency – is, they argue, a successful means of systemic adaptation.

Thus, although policy sub-systems organize the mobilization of bias, they do not have a permanent monopoly on an issue: they grow up and they wither. Contrary to the position adopted by Schattschneider and other agenda theorists, Baumgartner and Jones do not believe bias means that new ideas are 'always' kept out of the policy process. At times of agenda access new ideas do get in. And yet, the authors concede Schattschneider's point that the chorus in their pluralist heaven sings with 'a strong upper class accent' (Schattschneider, 1960: 35): 'we cannot help but note that the American political system seems more devoted to the processing of issues of interest to various factions of the middle class than those of benefit to the lower class' (Baumgartner and Jones, 1993: 249). The authors therefore come very close to arguing that, although there is a substantial class bias in agenda-setting, it is necessary in order for the political system to function. And in so processing through exclusive sub-systems, 'multiple policy venues' demonstrate 'impressive parallel processing capabilities' (ibid.: 250). Critics of this capacity would, however, argue that it is far less evident in the agenda-setting which takes place in issues which are of more concern to those who do not have a powerful policy sub-system. Lurching from one issue to another may be a way of processing complexity, but it has less to recommend it as a mode of problem 'prevention' and 'solving'. As Lindblom and Woodhouse note, the agenda has worked to the distinct disadvantage of those who are politically and economically impaired. In this case it is the policy subsystems of bureaucrats, politicians, think-tanks and others who do the defining and shape the 'policy image', with little input from those with more direct experience of the problems (Lindblom and Woodhouse, 1993: 112).

Policy elites may not control the agenda process, but it is manifestly true that they have far more impact and influence over what goes up, what goes down, and what gets on the agenda than those members of society whose participation is marginal and impaired. Thus although the framework does advance a useful synthesis of what might be termed a pluralist version of agenda-setting, its failure to take account of power and class renders it less plausible an account when applied to issues which involve political and economic inequalities. What may work as an explanation of smoking, the environment and car-safety may be less convincing when it comes to explaining how the agenda is set in policy issues which involve redistributions of power, wealth or income.

2.11   Analysing the boundaries

2.11.1   The contexts of problem definition and agenda-setting

Policy-making, as the models discussed above show, does not take place in isolation. There are wider factors which set the boundaries or parameters – as Sabatier terms them – for the formulation and implementation of policy agendas. Policy-making takes place in the context of the constraints of economic, social, geographical, historical and cultural limits. Policy-makers engage in judgements (cf. Vickers, 1965; see 3.7.5) as to what these realities are. In terms of the AC model, the various coalitions are endeavouring to get their ideas or judgements about the 'real world', and aim to bring decision-makers – sovereigns – around to their values and beliefs. These 'reality judgements', as Vickers terms them, may be said to constitute the boundaries of what is possible and desirable – of what is and ought to be. The way these boundaries – such as the 'state of the economy' – are constructed manifestly sets the context within which 'subsystems' function. To paraphrase Schattschneider, whoever defines these boundaries is determining what politics and policy-making is about. Hence, as we noted earlier, the special role of the media in constructing what is seen to be the broad context within which issues and problems are perceived by the public.

In this section we shall consider the boundaries which exist within the context of the 'nation state': the economic, social and other factors which form the boundaries within which policy agendas are set and decisions made and implemented. In the final section of Part Two we shall consider those factors which, at a world or international level, shape and constrain the context within which national actors seek to operate.

2.11.2   The economic parameters of policy formulation

In macro-economics the concept of a production possibility frontier (PPF) or boundary is used to plot the combinations of goods and services that may be produced with given resources. Different societies have preferences and make choices about the distribution between public goods, such as defence, and consumer goods (see figure 2.21). Public policy decisions involve, at their most basic level, choices along the boundaries of what is possible in the context of the resources which policy-makers confront. Patterns of public expenditure are reflective of the distributions which pertain along the PPF. More of one involves less of another: more guns, less butter; more butter less guns: *bc* represents the opportunity cost of choosing to produce more guns rather than (*de*) butter.

Figure 2.21   A production possibility frontier

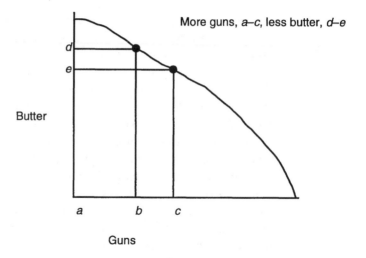

What the PPF sets out is a boundary of what kind of policy agenda is possible. For example, a country with a given productive capacity may choose (in theory) to allocate resources to *x* quantity of 'public goods' – such as guns – or to *y* goods for private consumption – butter.

Given the possible boundaries of production within a society, the parameters of choice are those which are defined by the locational positions of decision-makers. At a very simplistic and 'pure' level, public policy involves choosing between public goods and services and private goods and services. Nations arrive at the distribution by means of public policy. Command economies choose to have a high level of production of public goods and a low level of private goods:

the old USSR is an example of this. Free-market economies such as the USA operate at a lower level of public good and higher private goods, and for the greater part of this century chose to operate the public good largely in terms of defence expenditure (figure 2.22).

Figure 2.22   Choices along the curve

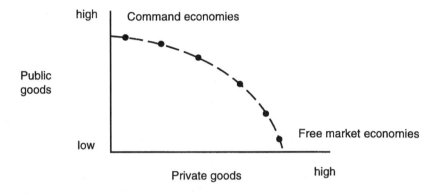

Public policy may be said to be the process whereby a society defines the relationship between the production of goods and services along the boundaries of what is possible, given the constraints of resources. Over time the levels of satisfaction with a given mix may/will change. As we have seen in the 1980s, the preferences along the PPF do indeed change. Voters and politicians may begin to express a desire to adjust the production of public and private goods. Over time it could be said, for example, that preferences in the 1980s shifted towards private and away from public. One reason for this is that, as Albert Hirschman (1983) argues, individualist and collectivist ideas may be subject to a cycle. The pattern is, says Hirschman, one of collectivism and individualism always failing to perform as promised. Bruno Frey (1978: 116) argues that a dissatisfaction with the mix of goods and services can arise because of: rises in income (or falling incomes); prices may change; new goods and services may be introduced; or preferences may change. As far as private goods are concerned the market provides a means of communicating these changes to producers. The political system provides for the transmission of changes in the demand for public goods. Costs and benefits may well be separated in the articulation of demands for public goods. Later, the costs of the goods are evaluated by the voters – in terms less of their individual than of their social utility. As a result, the government 'gains the (possibly sad) experience that, when it comes to cost, the unanimous support for the public goods policy rapidly vanishes and even turns into hostility' (Frey, 1978: 120). Thus, Frey concludes:

> The cycles of the demand and supply [of public goods] have all the same sequence. A disequilibrium arises leading to political demands and to a reaction from the government. When the problem of financing the expenditure arises a reaction sets in leading to activities even in the opposite direction. The enthusiasm for growth of the early 1960s decreased, for example, when the required cost in terms of present consumption sacrifice, and especially in terms of the negative effects on the natural environment, became apparent. The resulting enthusiam for environmental controls led to demands for zero growth. But the enthusiasm for such controls decreased when the individual taxpayers and various groups realised that the environmental policy demanded sizable income sacrifices.
> (Frey, 1978: 121)

Economic growth has been what Fred Hirsch described as a 'compelling attraction' (Hirsch, 1977: 7) to western politicians and voters. It is not difficult to understand why. The prospects of economic growth meant that it was an effective substitute for the problem of distribution along the curve. Distributions and the policy agendas that went along with them could be relatively stable if the cake was getting bigger for all, and the PPF was shifting to the right. When the good times roll, the agenda set may well be orientated more towards private goods, whereas when we expect low growth, or negative growth, it would make sense to demand greater public provision. Again, with high growth we may be prepared to forgo some part of increased economic welfare for the 'greater good', whereas in low growth times, options of *pro bono publico* may be less appealing: this has been the case with the environmental issue on the agendas of industrial societies. However, if a society has – like Sweden – chosen to frame choices largely in a 'public good' context, then lower economic growth may well have the opposite effect, namely, of pushing the distribution towards more private and less public. Over time the distribution of preferences will change, as the possibilities of economic growth frame the boundaries of choice. Agendas will shift in the light of such shifts in the possibilities, expected and real, in the production of public and private goods.

Of course, in a democracy, policy demands may exceed supply, and promised supply exceed actual delivery: hence the central place of economic growth within the political economy of modern liberal democracies. Policy-making and problem definition involve an assessment of what are the possible levels of production within society. As long as a distribution occurs along the frontiers of what is possible, then one could argue that public policy is in balance. Policy-makers move along the frontiers of what is possible, and make choices between the domains of public and private choices. These choices will be the source of much disagreement and discontent, as they will produce winners and losers; but provided that the distribution is possible, a political system may sustain its claim to be effective and legitimate. However, if the desired position is off the curve, policy-makers and voters are in trouble: we are in the zone of 'excessive expectations'.

Figure 2.23   Choices off the curve

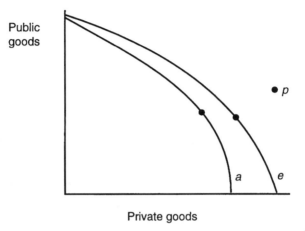

In figure 2.23, the *a* curve may be actual economic growth which permits a given position; *e* may be what is expected; and position *p*, off the curve, may be what is promised. In western liberal democracies the experience from the 1970s onwards, which impacted more harshly on some countries than others, was that there were limits to what government could deliver in the circumstances of declining growth and rising inflation. Public choices had to take place on the boundaries of the actual, curve *a* above, rather than what was desirable. And, as we know, this had considerable effects on the policy agenda of every industrial democracy.

It is this very point about which so-called 'new right' and 'overloaders' became concerned in the 1970s (onwards), as the problem seemed to be that governments were reluctant to resist more demands for spending. Demand-led theories of public policy argue that because of the pressures on government, policy-makers find it impossible to make choices between policy areas and spending priorities because, unlike a business, they do not have financial constraints. If a government runs short of money, it can print more of it; in which case, the discipline of public choice is undermined by the supply side of the equation (the desire of policy actors and programmes to maximize spending on their domain), and made even worse by the demand side (voters pressing government to spend in those areas voters want). Government ends up – so it was argued – pouring more money down a bottomless drain, rather than allocating resources in accordance with an evaluation of what can be afforded within the boundaries of what is possible (figure 2.24). (However, it needs to be emphasized again that what is portrayed as 'possible' and the 'real world' and 'economic crisis' are in themselves highly political, value-laden notions.)

Figure 2.24   Overload

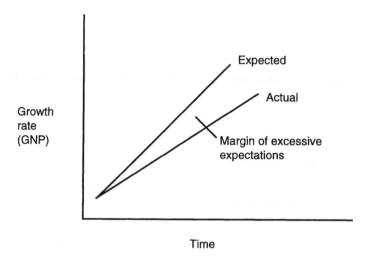

In such a situation, 'overload' theorists argued that the policy-making processes of modern government in conditions of low or negative growth place democracy in danger of political deficit because of excessive expectations (see Parsons, 1988).

2.11.3   Trends and the policy agenda

'Economic realities', or at least the construction of economic realities, as expressed in the PPF curve suggest that policy agendas exist in the context of constraints, chief amongst them being economic conditions and trends. In a review of the politics of expenditure in the US and the UK, Klein, for example, makes the point in these graphic terms:

> To discuss the political factors affecting public expenditure decisions may be to fall into the trap of discussing the illusions of policy-makers who believe in their own freedom of action when in reality they are being driven by forces outside their control ... It would be misleading to concentrate exclusively on what the men in the life boat are doing, without taking into account the sea or the direction of the wind.
> (*Klein, 1976: 402*)

From this perspective, the policy-maker is confronted by social, economic, demographic and other trends which really frame the agenda, rather than the ideas of a John Rawls or a Maynard Keynes or the rise and fall of public opinion. In which case we could better characterize the policy agenda and policy-making as driven by trends in crime, ageing, employment, divorce, sexual conduct, technology and so on, rather than by parties or think-tanks, public opinion or ideas.

A key issue here is that raised by the earlier 'constructivist' analysis in 2.2.2: what is a trend, and what does information mean? Are there trends 'out there', or are these trends something which are constructed? Are trends in crime real or actual, or is crime a 'crisis' which is constructed in a certain way in the interests of a certain class? Whosoever determines what the 'trend' is could be said to determine the form of political agenda which is considered to exist. The notion of 'social indicators' is therefore problematic. As a movement it may be said to have begun in earnest in the 1950s. By the 1970s most industrial democracies and international organizations began to produce reports which identified major trends. The criteria of key indicators are not matters which attract a large measure of commonality (Sheldon and Moore, 1968). Although, therefore, the analysis of trends is a major informational context within which problems arise and are addressed, the meaning and significance of trends is open to much controversy. Trends may be whatever you want them to be: trends may be less a determinant of public policy than an outcome of politics and policy.

❖ Trends and public policy

1   Brian W. Hogwood, *Trends in British Public Policy*, 1992
In this book Hogwood analyses the impact of trends on policy in Britain and other countries, and considers the use which politicians and others make of trends. The article by Klein, cited above, provides a metaphor and motif for the analysis of the relationship of politics and trends, and he concludes by arguing that although it is possible to predict where public policy trends will take us, it remains the case that:

> There is still plenty of scope for choice and for politicians who recognise that it can take a long time for changes to have an impact and who are more concerned about the final outcome of their decisions rather than what is apparent during their tenure in office. On crude measures used by some analysts such future consequences of decisions may show up as 'inertia', but this does not reduce the importance or the scope for strategic decisions. (p. 225)

Even so, he suggests that although decisions are not predetermined by social and economic pressures, the demands on public expenditure in the remaining part of the century will set constraints on the political system.

2   John Naisbitt and Patricia Aburdene, *Megatrends 2000*, 1990
This book is the son of *Megatrends*, published in 1982, which sold over 8 million copies. The argument of the book is that there are big 'trends' taking place and that these trends will set out the context within which individuals, businesses and governments *et al.* will make choices:

> Events do not happen in a vacuum, but in a social, political, cultural, and economic context. This book describes for you that context. You need not agree with or accept every element of this world view. But do use it to structure as a context within which to measure the news of the day, opposing viewpoints, and new information. (p. 3)

3   Keith Hope, 'Indicators of the state of society', in Martin Bulmer (ed.), 1978

> Social indicators, even well-constructed social indicators, are not good in themselves. Their value is dependent on the institutional framework within which they are used. The best guarantee I can suggest for ensuring that they are not misused is that they should be completely constructed according to public and comprehensible, even if technical, criteria. If they are, then it will be in principle possible for journalists and members of the public to bring their experience to bear in assessing the information which the indicators contain. It is imperative that, by one means or another, social indicators be kept in the public political arena. (p. 267)

4   Age and the political agenda
An area that is most clearly an issue which has been informed by the analysis of 'trends' is that of ageing. As the proportion of the world's population classified as 'aged' is recognized by all governments in the industrial world, so the implications of these trends are being considered.

See, for example, Edgar F. Borgatta and Rhonda J.V. Montgomery (eds), *Critical Issues in Aging Policy*, 1987. The book examines the relationship between trends, knowledge and policy. Of particular importance are the implications which such trends in demography and life expectancy have for the costs of health care.

A social-movement approach would argue that it is not until the 'old' get their political act together that they can begin to influence the issues and define the problems in their terms, so-called 'grey power'. In turn, the growth in 'grey power' could be read as changing other trends in voting, consumption and political demands. ◆

2.11.4   Policy as epiphenomena

Does the existence of these 'trends' in society, the economy and much else constitute the primary determinant of policy formulation? Are policy-making and politics somewhat secondary and of little real consequence? One school of thought argues that, ultimately, the policy-making process is driven less by parties, policies and ideas than by 'environmental' or demographic forces over which political actors have only a marginal influence. From this perspective, policy is essentially an epiphenomenon, that is to say, it is largely determined more by fundamental underlying conditions than by the political process. Two proponents of this argument have come to the fore in advocating this theory: Hofferbert (1974) and Wilensky (1975).

Hofferbert argues that what comes out of the policy process is, for the most part, determined by the underlying realities of a country, as opposed to the influence of what Sabatier would term advocacy coalitions. The policy agenda, and the actual outcomes of political systems are functions of three main factors:

- historic and geographical conditions;
- social and economic composition;
- mass political behaviour.

These are mediated through:

- governmental institutions;
- elite behaviour.

He employs the metaphor of the policy process as a funnel: at the broad input end we have the key determining factors and, at the end of the funnel, institutions and elites which serve to filter and mediate these forces so as to form policy output (figure 2.25).

Figure 2.25   The policy process as a 'funnel'

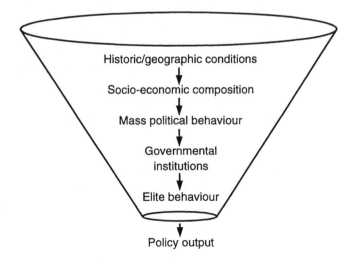

Source: Adapted from Hofferbert (1974)

In this model the way in which a political system defines its problems and formulates policy is a function of the pressure of 'macro' factors and conditions which are outside the capacity of policy makers to influence to any significant extent. What you get out depends on what goes into the funnel. The Hofferbert argument is, in all essentials, a 'black box' theory, that is, it envisages that the political process has mediating or converting devices: the inputs are historic, economic and social factors and mass political behaviour; and the institutions and elites are a black box from which drips 'output'. Like the Eastonian black box, the Hofferbert funnel greatly underestimates the role of institutions and elites. The notion of a funnel-shaped process seems to allow little by way of an interaction of elites and institutions with these forces. Inputs are one-way things, exogenous forces which the black box merely processes.

The problem with this metaphor is that in order to provide a clear map of the causal sequences which determine policy, Hofferbert neglects to consider the dynamics and interactions which take place within his variables. To begin with, here is another theory in which reality seems to take place 'out there'. Who says what the 'historic-geographical conditions' or the 'socio-economic composition' of a political system are? Government and elites are not – as Edelman, Cobb and Elder and others have demonstrated – simply processing these variables; they are involved in their manufacture. Secondly, as the 'network' theory argues, government is something which takes place at many levels, and with a multiplicity of interactions. As the AC model suggests, the existence of competing beliefs and values expresses this complexity of organizational and group perceptions (although Hofferbert subsequently modified his model to take more account of this; see Hofferbert and Urice, 1985). Although the model has proved to be attractive to students of public policy as providing a clear set of procedures with which to map policy formation, especially in the study of comparative public policy, it is perhaps an illustration of how a model can greatly distort our understanding of the policy-making process in attempting to simplify a 'reality' which is infinitely more complex than the metaphor allows.

Another theory which has had a great impact on comparative analysis is that proposed by Wilensky (1975), who argued in a book on welfare policy that if we wish to understand and explain the main determinant of how welfare policies are constructed we need look no further than affluence and economic growth. As with the Hofferbert model, therefore, Wilensky is of the view that the role of 'politics' is greatly exaggerated as compared with the impact of underlying economic and social conditions.

Wilensky argues that the development of social welfare policy is shaped less by the political factors, such as party competition and voter choices or institutions, than by economic development and its resultant social consequences and correlates. As economic growth leads to affluence, so new social and economic forces and attitudes develop and, with new affluence, a growing ability to meet the demands for more spending to deal with social and other problems. In economic terms one could argue that, as the production boundaries of what is possible increase with economic growth, the tendency is for societies to move towards greater public spending on welfare: social security, pensions, health care, etc. And as countries experience similar patterns of economic growth, with their PPFs shifting to the right, so the level of public spending will converge. In which case, according to the 'economic determinism' argument, changing economic growth brings about a changing strategy towards the level or proportion of national income devoted to public welfare provision. Fred Hirsch in his *Social Limits of Growth* (1977) made the point that this is why affluent societies are more concerned with distribution of the cake, and why, notwithstanding the demands of personal freedom of action in non-economic areas such as aesthetics and sexuality, capitalist societies have also experienced 'reluctant collectivism' along with the compulsion to distribute. From this point of view institutions and politics do not really matter very much: politics is less a cause of policy than an effect of economic and social change. This viewpoint has given rise to a heated debate between two schools of thought: those who say politics does matter and those who say it does not!

In the vanguard of the 'politics matters' brigade is Francis Castles (1982; (ed.), 1989), who argues that the data which Wilensky and his supporters use to support their argument that economic and structural variables are the main determinant of policy choices, also sustains a different interpretation, namely that the processes of political choice do indeed shape the policy agenda. Another study which has confirmed the role of parties in framing policy choice and policy mixes is the study of 20 states by Budge and Keman (1990). The authors examine a number of policy areas: social welfare; economic policy; social and economic welfare; external security; and trade-offs between welfare and security. They reach an unequivocal conclusion that, as Castles maintains, parties do affect policies:

> One could only negate these findings by arguing that the areas examined are unimportant – which they clearly are not, being central to any government programme and consuming a major share of resources – or claiming that other factors account for the seeming relationship between party participation and particular policy lines. But if so, what are they? We have explicitly allowed for the effects of world economic crises. By noting

whether parties wholly control the government or only participate in a coalition the research design also incorporates a measure of the party's ability to effect its policies. Whereas the onus at the beginning of the study was to show that parties really do make a difference (even though this has been shown before), after this demonstration it surely rests with the sceptics to show what unknown factor can be accounting for the relationships which so clearly emerge. We prefer the obvious interpretation that parties exert a strong, and even a determining, influence on government decision-making.
(*Budge and Keman, 1990: 158*)

However, this argument, although having the merit of directing our attention to the relative importance of politics and economics, poses, it seems to the present author, a rather false dichotomy. It is obvious that the economic condition of a country does determine the boundaries of what is possible. And what is possible depends on whether the PPF curve is moving right, left, or is stationary. But the distribution of choices as to public expenditure and private spending, public production of goods and services, and private production of goods and services, and the mix between them, does vary from nation to nation and over time. Shared economic growth rates and structural problems may lead to a convergence in the proportion of GNP spent on welfare, but the political choices which inform the modes of implementation do vary considerably. One could argue that, although economic factors stucture the agenda of what is possible, political processes determine how the possible is perceived, realized and implemented. As Heidenheimer, Heclo and Adams note:

> How stongly macroeconomic conditions affect public sector growth has been amply demonstrated over the past decade. Where the public sector had attracted increasing proportions of national incomes in all Western countries up to about 1975, there have been standstills and declines since then. But within these strong structural constraints governments have made very different kinds of choices.
> (*Heidenheimer, Heclo and Adams, 1990: 360*)

As they point out, the USA and the UK, for example, made very different choices as between military spending and welfare spending than other western countries. And, notwithstanding economic and structural convergences which may be discerned between nations, the modes of implementing policies – such as on the environment – has seen considerable divergence. Not only has there been divergence in the way in which policies have been implemented, there has also been wide variations in the kinds of economic 'success' which has occurred in industrial societies in the post-war era and in the mix of policies which have resulted and which frame the boundaries policy and problems. Schmidt (1989), for example, proposes that we might see this condition in terms of the contrasts in policy mixes (inflation, and

Figure 2.26   Comparing policy mixes

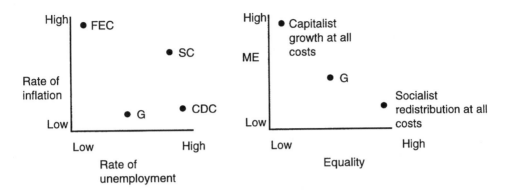

Source: Schmidt (1989)

unemployment and macroeconomic efficiency and equality) as between Germany and other industrial countries (figure 2.26).

The contrast here is between the policy mix in the full-employment
capitalist countries (FEC) with high inflation and low employment,
stagflation countries (SC) with high inflation and high unemployment, Germany with its low inflation and low unemployment (G),
and the chronic disinflation countries with high unemployment and
low inflation (CDC). At another level, it is between macroeconomic
efficiency (ME) and equality. Germany again is in the middle lane. If
we want to explain why German public policy profiles have been
different to that of other countries, Schmidt argues that we must understand the processes of political and institutional learning from historical catastrophes, and the specific compromises between economic
liberalism, conservative reformism and Social Democracy.

In other words, the positing of a politics versus the environment argument does not help us to understand why different countries set about
defining their problems and formulating policy differently. The theory
advanced by Hofferbert and Wilensky in the 1970s, that environmental factors determine politics and policy, has generally not been supported by subsequent research (Lane, 1993: 71). And furthermore, the
notion that empirical evidence can resolve matters one way or the
other is deeply suspect. The politics matters/does not matter debate,
therefore, is perhaps more important for what it tells us about the
(crass) empiricism of the 1970s than the question of the relationship of
politics, policy and economic, social and other environmental factors.
As we shall discuss in Part Four (4.6.3), a more satisfactory basis of
discussion is to grant that it is manifestly the case that the environ-

ment will impact on the policy process: however, it is also the case that the 'environment' is something which exists in the context of the values and beliefs of people (Sharpe and Newton, 1984). The 'environment' as such therefore exists within the 'assumptive worlds' (see Young, 1977/1979; and 3.7.7) of policy-makers.

2.11.5 Voters, parties and policy

Hofferbert and Wilensky regard politics as somewhat marginal in its influence on the formation of policy as compared with the larger forces of history, society and economy. However, as we have noted above, other approaches take exception to this downgrading of the role of politics and institutions. What about the role of voters in the formation of policy? In a democracy voters, in theory, are supposed to have a central position in the shaping of what government *qua* party government does. However, do voters shape agendas, or do parties shape the preferences and political agendas? Are voters, parties and their leaders motivated by self-interest, and is the policy agenda shaped by this political commerce, rather than by 'socio-economic' forces?

The relationship between voter motivation and economic calculations has been an object of study since the 1920s, but it was with the publication of Downs's *An Economic Theory of Democracy* in 1957 that the idea of analysing self-interest – or pocket-book voting – took off. What evidence has emerged concerning voter self-interest? The hypothesis as put forward by Downs regarding the primacy of self-interest as an explanation of voter behaviour *qua* consumer behaviour has been over-whelmingly refuted by empirical studies in both the US and Europe. There is little to substantiate the theory that personal self-interest is the motivation behind voter choices – even if it may be that policy-makers and politicians believe it to be the case. However, the matter of how voters see the economic circumstances of the country as a whole seems to be far more significant a factor in explaining voter attitudes and election outcomes. The work of Lewis-Beck argues that politicians do not appear from the data to be engaged in 'special bursts of vote-buying around election time. National economic output does not move to an electoral rhythm' (Lewis-Beck, 1990: 158). However, this is not to deny that self-interest plays a part, but it is apparently a self-interest that is focused on an assessment of economic performance (past, present and future) rather than a self-interest based on the pocket-book. From such researches into the relationship between economic conditions and voting, it is clear that perceptions of how the economy is doing have a major impact on framing the context within which issues are prioritized by electorates. This pattern is, posits Lewis-Beck, both cross-national and cross-temporal: 'economic issues are always on the agenda, and these days we tend to seek solutions from government. If governments deliver on their promises they are rewarded with votes. If not, they are punished' (Lewis-Beck, 1990: 100–11). Governments must deliver convincing promises as well as performances (ibid.: 151). We shall return to this question of performance and delivery in Part Four. What is clear is that economic issues are the key agenda items, and that governments may not be able to control the economy as they would like or they may not be involved in manipulating the economy, but the way in which economic perceptions are constructed is of vital importance in the study of agenda-setting (Parsons, 1989).

If it is the case that, as Tullock argues, parties use policies to win votes (1976: 66) and, as Downs postulates, 'parties formulate policies in order to win elections, rather than win elections in order to formulate policies' (1957: 28), then, according to Downs, policy-makers will conduct strategies so as to maximize votes and win elections. What follows from this is that we would expect a cycle of policies to manipulate the economy for the benefit of the government in office. Research is divided as to whether such a cycle in policy-making (or a political business cycle) exists. A leading exponent of the view that policy-makers do manipulate the economy for electoral gain is Tufte (1978). However, his study, which shows that economic policy is so geared in 19 out of 27 countries studied, has not been replicated in later studies by political scientists in various countries (Lewin, 1991: 66–74). The weight of evidence suggests that the case for vote maximization, on the lines that Downs put forward, remains at best not proven. The model manifestly overestimates less the self-interest of politicians so much as their capacity to control and influence inflation, unemployment and other issues of electoral concern. If they could perhaps (no perhaps?) they would, but the evidence indicates that they just can't! However, Downs's model is suggestive less of outcome than of intention. Policy-makers are involved in the process in which opinion and perceptions of the economy and national economic wellbeing are moulded and shaped. If we cannot say, with any measure of confidence, that politicians shape the economy to maximize votes, we can say – from a commonsense position – that they do endeavour to shape the way in which voters view the economy.

Policy choices and positions involve knowledge of the political market place, and an ability to satisfy and shape preferences. On one level, political parties have to be in the business of accommodating voter preferences, which involves identifying what the voter *qua* policy consumer wants, and delivering it. In this case, the policy programme may be seen as a function of how voter policy utility is perceived.

Hence, the increased use of polls and surveys to generate information which can serve to adjust policy and its presentation so as to maximize the appeal of the party programme. However, it is rather obvious that the idea that policy-making stands in the same relationship to 'policy production' as business response to consumer demands is somewhat unreal. In a free-market economy, business is also involved in the manufacture of new wants. The consumer demands what advertisements tell him he should want. The production or shaping of policy wants is also something which is involved in the political process. The policy agenda 'market' is not perfect: policy demands and voter preferences are as much subject to producer influence as are consumer tastes and preferences. As Galbraith argued in his *New Industrial State* (1969), the view of consumer sovereignty does not correspond with the reality in which producers are engaged in adjusting consumer preferences in the context of the demands of the industrial system. The policy market tends towards oligopoly, in which there are a few producers whose aim is to shape what preferences can be shaped, and to adapt policies to suit what voters express in terms of preferences. Competing parties – both in and out of power – are in the business of shaping the preferences of voters, although the capacity of governing parties to shape such preferences is different to that of parties out of office. Dunleavy (1991, ch. 5) identifies four main strategies of shaping preferences employed by political parties in power:

- partisan social engineering;
- adjusting social relativities;
- context management;
- institutional manipulation.

Non-ruling parties, on the other hand have, he suggests, four options:

- to shape voter preferences;
- to capitalize on social tension;
- joint institutional manipulation;
- agenda-setting.

He concludes that the strategies will vary across political systems. In Britain and other Commonwealth countries, the strategy of shaping voter preferences is possible; whilst in the USA, parties tend more towards accommodating voter preferences. As Dunleavy notes, the idea of a preference-shaping model of the relationship of parties to voter preferences offers an account which stresses the endogenous factors at work within the party/political system as opposed to a more simplistic account of voters and parties on the lines of 'consumer' and 'producer'. There is, he maintains, evidence to suggest that political parties do engage in shaping voter preferences, but that we still know relatively little about the demand and supply relationship between public opinion and party policy goods (Dunleavy, 1991: 144).

2.11.6 The institutional parameters

The development of modern political science and public policy has tended to neglect the fact that politics and policy-making take place in the context of institutions. The study of politics was until the 1960s dominated by a focus on constitutions, legislatures and executives, on the one hand, and political thought, on the other. The emergence of the policy approach marked a departure from this traditional concentration on institutions in favour of exploring the 'political system' as a whole, or the 'policy process'. However, the impact of institutional arrangements cannot be ignored in understanding the 'process' of policy formulation or how problems are defined. 'Problems' and policy 'solutions' exist in a constitutional or institutional space as much as in a wider economic or social 'environment'.

The renewed interest in institutions has taken place within a variety of frameworks. In broad terms we might define these in three major (overlapping) categories:

- *'economic' institutionalism*: which consists of theories derived from 'transaction cost' and 'principal–agent' theories. This approach will be reviewed in 3.6.3;
- *sociological institutionalism*: which has developed out of the field of organizational sociology. Several key contributions to sociological institutionalism may be noted. The first kind of institutionalism is associated with the work of Selznick (1949), and later with Di Maggio and Powell (1983, 1991) and Perrow and others. The second and more recent sociological model has been advanced by March and Olsen (March and Olsen, 1984, 1989; Olsen, 1988). In this section we shall focus mainly on March and Olsen, as the work of Selznick *et al.* will be considered in more detail in 3.6.2 and 4.6.3;
- *'political' institutionalism*: which comprises contributions that focus on the 'autonomy' of the state in policy-making and the relationship of state and society. In this section we shall examine those studies which argue that policy-making is often the outcome of the internal agenda of state institutions, rather than the result of 'external' pressures and influences. This approach will also be examined in 3.6.4.

Sociological institutionalism

March and Olsen maintain that institutions provide the important parameters within which the formulation of problems and decisions takes place. In contrast to the 'environmentalist' approach which requires that we map the wider social, economic and other forces which determine the inputs and outputs, institutionalists argue that our primary focus should be how the institutional arrangements within a society shape human behaviour. Ideas and interests, therefore, are considered as essentially framed by the institutions within which they are set. As Olsen argues:

> Institutions dispose of authority and power, but also of collective wisdom and ethics. They provide physical, cognitive and moral frames for joint action; capacity for intervention; conceptual lenses for observation; agenda, memory, rights as well as duties as well as conceptions of justice; and symbols you may identify yourself with.
> *(Olsen, 1988: 35, cited in Lane, 1993: 171)*

From this perspective, therefore, problems and solutions happen within institutions, rather than 'outside' the black box, because human activity and thought is fundamentally bounded by the institutions within which they are located. If we want to explain why a 'problem' or a 'solution' has been framed or constructed in a certain way, then March and Olsen suggest that we must analyse the development of ideas/interests in their institutional setting. The political order, as a framework of institutions and rules, provides the parameters of how conflict takes place, how participants interact, and how citizens relate to governing bodies. In other words, problems and solutions take place within the boundaries of what is deemed acceptable, legitimate, just in terms of means (strategies) and ends (outcomes). Individuals as rational actors endeavour to make choices based on their levels of information and resources, and values or preferences which are framed by the rules, interests, values and resources of the institution which they inhabit. Thus an explanation of how and why a given policy emerged in relation to a 'problem' requires that we first analyse the structure, historical development, personal networks and decisions over time of the institutions involved in finding a solution to a 'problem' (March and Olsen, 1972).

❖ Institutionalism, rational choice and public policy

The application of the kind of ideas put forward by March and Olsen about institutionalism in public policy terms has been developed most fully in the work of Larry Kiser and Elinor Ostrom (Kiser and Ostrom, 1982; Ostrom, 1986a and b, 1990). The starting point for the model advanced by Ostrom is the primacy of institutions in the policy process. 'Decision situations' will comprise three aspects:

- institutional arrangements;
- events relevant to the issue concerned;
- the community which has a stake in the outcome.

In seeking to analyse decision situations, the Ostrom model would wish to explore factors such as: the number of actors involved; who can/cannot participate; what agencies, officials, departments and political institutions are involved; what resources they have; how institutions and actors relate to one another; how rules and constitutional arrangements influence the strategies of actors. These decisional situations have to be considered as changing over time; and as rules, institutions and resources change, so, the model argues, does the behaviour of individual actors as they endeavour to adapt their strategies. The model also puts forward the idea that choice operates at three levels:

- constitutional;
- collective;
- operational.

Each level frames the institutional attributes with which successive levels work: the constitutional level frames the rules for entry and participation in governmental (collective) decision-making; and the implementation of policy decisions at the collective level frames the institutional setting of the policy in operation.

For an application and critique of the model to nuclear waste policy, see Jenkins-Smith, 1991; and on equal opportunities policy, see Stewart, 1991. ◆

We have already encountered two political science models which apply aspects of March and Olsen: Kingdon (1984) and Sabatier and Jenkins-Smith (1993). Kingdon derives a major part of his theory of agenda-setting from the so-called 'garbage can' model developed by March and Olsen. Sabatier and Jenkins-Smith have endeavoured to incorporate some of the insights of the institutionalist approach (Kiser and Ostrom, 1982; Ostrom, 1986a and b, 1990) into their AC model. In one sense, this (deterministic) emphasis on the impact of institutions in setting the frameworks within which ideas, interests and agendas happen is the flipside of the position adopted by Hofferbert (1974) Wilensky (1975) and others that politics does not matter, or alternatively, that it does (Castles) (see 2.11.4). The development of an institutional focus has served, however, to remind students of the policy process that 'agenda-setting' and problem construction is bounded by constitutions, rules, resources and institutions which shape the conduct of politics and which set out the rules of the game: who should play; what counts as winning; what is acceptable; what is a good outcome; and so on.

It also reminds us of the fact that in the last few decades the formation of policy agendas has increasingly been influenced by institutionalized policy analysis in modern think-tanks. The predominance of institutions in the making of policy, and the setting of policy agendas in particular, has meant that, as Lindblom argues, participation in policy-making has become an exclusive preserve of those interests which are powerful and well resourced (Lindblom and Woodhouse, 1993: 104–13). If ideas and interests are to have any real impact they have to become 'institutionalized'. For as Stewart comments:

> What must be kept in mind is that before actors can be rational within institutions … institutions must exist. During the headier days in Texas, television commercials advised: 'If ya' don't have an oil well, git one.' The same advice is appropriate for advocates of policy change – 'If you don't have an organization promoting change, form one.' Without such organizations/institutions policy-making is left to the institutions that have produced the status quo. And social scientists have known at least since Olsen … that organizations do not spring from the furrowed brow of anyone who has a problem. They must be created.
> (Stewart, 1991: 171–2)

However, once created, an organization set up to press for a particular cause or issue does not come into a world devoid of other institutions all of whom are eager to play their part in defining problems, setting agendas and influencing decisions. And, having been invented, institutions are, as Di Maggio and Powell (1983/1991) argue, subject to the pressures of more-powerful, better-resourced, better-connected organizations. Agendas and problems therefore have an organizational setting/environment/demography which frame the boundaries within which problems are defined and politicized – or not. The sociological approach stresses that problems have an organizational context. And organizations exist within wider environments: some may have more control over their environments than others (Perrow, 1986: 175). In this case, more-powerful organizations will have an ability to shape their own agendas, whereas the less-powerful (more dependent) will be far more the product of the external environment. The strategic choice approach (see 4.6.3 and Child, 1972) also points out that – as March and Olsen argue – institutions frame reality. The role of dominant elites in creating an image of the world outside the organization suggests that the construction of 'problems' and 'solutions' and agendas are the product of elites internal and largely autonomous from the environmental 'input'.

Political institutionalism
This theme of the autonomy of institutions from outside pressures and demands is also the main issue addressed by political institutionalism. In her review of research which has sought to 'bring the state

back in', Theda Skocpol (1985) shows how several lines of inquiry point towards the theory that, contrary to the Marxist idea of the state as an instrument of the dominant class, the state in both liberal democratic systems and the developing world has the capacity to be relatively insulated from social and economic forces. It appears from this 'state-centred' model that state institutions often display an ability to act in stable and continuous ways over long periods of time. To illustrate her point Skocpol presents several examples of how, in both liberal democracies with 'strong' states (such as France, Britain and Sweden) and 'weak' states (such as the USA), policy has been formed by civil servants and institutions. Amongst the examples she gives are:

- Heclo's (1974) study of the development of social welfare policies in Britain and Sweden. The study shows how civil servants in both countries had a major role in policy development – far more so than parties or interest groups;
- Krasner's (1978) study of the formation of US foreign policy in respect of international investmemts in the production and marketing of raw materials. Despite the apparently weak and fragmented nature of the US state, this policy was shaped by institutions and actors who were 'insulated' from 'societal' pressures.
- Skocpol and Finegold's (1982) work on the agriculture policy of the New Deal, which shows how policy was the result of administrative innovation, rather than simply farming pressure groups.

However, this capacity for autonomy is, she argues, by no means fixed or structural, but will vary over time and between policy areas. State autonomy is something which has to be related to several factors: the international position of the state concerned; the domestic order-keeping functions; and the organizational possibilities which exist for officials to formulate and conduct their own policies. Thus in bringing the state back in, Skocpol is not arguing that we abandon the analysis of social, economic and cultural factors which shape policy, but that the capacity for state autonomy should also be taken into account. Hall's (1986) analysis of economic policy-making in Britain and France continues this line of argument, but takes a broader view of what the concept of institution should encompass. We shall examine Hall's model in 3.6.4.

The arguments of the institutionalists have gained wide recognition. As Almond *et al.* (1993: 133) concede, such issues were grossly neglected in the 1960s and 1970s. The impact of March and Olsen and of Skocpol and others have done much to redress the balance in favour of taking more account of the institutional context within which problems and policy are formulated. Political institutionalism also offers a critique of the kind of arguments advanced by Sabatier and Jenkins-Smith in respect of policy-making as the product of 'advocacy coalitions'. Skocpol and Hall, for instance, argue that the analysis of policy-making must be set within the context of the capacity which state institutions have for shaping policy. Sabatier argues that this idea of state autonomy is 'highly dubious' in the case of the USA with the 'permeability' (*sic*) of its institutions, and 'misleading' in the case of countries like France with 'supposedly centralized regimes' (Sabatier, 1993: 37). However, the models advanced by political institutionalists cannot be so quickly dismissed. As we shall see later, in Hall's analysis of economic policy in Britain and France, the argument that institutions exercise a dominant role in shaping key areas of policy-making over a long period of time offers a plausible account of two political systems with very different institutional arrangements from the US – on which the Sabatier AC model is largely based. As for the US, the theory that state institutions have a relative autonomy suggests that change in key areas of American public policy is more likely to come about as a result of crises than because of 'learning' due to the very 'impermeable' characteristics of American institutions which Sabatier underestimates. Hence, in so many areas US policy-making has not demonstrated much by way of innovation; but, on the contrary, considerable conservatism. As Amenta and Skocpol maintain:

> When the autonomy of the state in the policy-making of liberal democracies is discussed, scholars point to the contribution of bureaucrats and civil servants in the creation or reworking of public policies ... these actors were less prevalent in America than elsewhere ... However, where state capacities were created [they] often influenced the later development of public policies. This chequered growth of executive state capacities across policy areas and across levels of government had a strong impact on the pattern of American public policies. Nevertheless, it was not so much the weakness of the state as the overall character of political institutions that influenced public policy-making.
> (*Amenta and Skocpol, 1989: 313–14*)

Thus the authors are not optimistic about the capacity of American policy-making to change. Even if a left-wing coalition were to come to power (an unlikely prospect indeed!), Amenta and Skocpol posit that unless it rules for a considerable period of time, 'the United States will continue to have one foot in the nineteenth century' (Amenta and Skocpol, 1989: 328).

❖ Do institutions matter?

This is the title of a volume edited by Weaver and Rockman (1993) comprising a number of case studies that deal with topics including energy policy, pensions, industrial policy, budget deficits, the environment and trade policy. The case studies address the issue of what impact institutions have had on the policy process and the policy output and outcomes in the US, Sweden, the UK, Canada, France, Germany, the Netherlands, Japan and other industrial countries. These countries have different institutional arrangements – presidential and parliamentary, unitary and federal systems, for example – and varying levels of success in dealing with problems. What has been the role of these arrangements on the policy-making capabilities of government?

The study posits a model in which policy outcomes are determined by the institutional constraints and decision-making attributes of political systems (figure 2.27).

Figure 2.27   Weaver and Rockman's model of institutional impacts

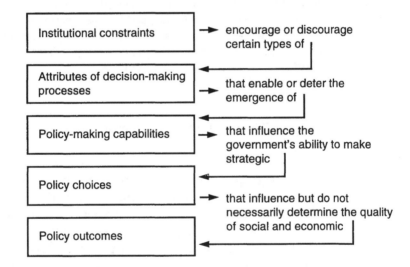

Source: Adapted from Weaver and Rockman (1993: 9)

However, the case studies reveal that in reality the impact of institutions is more complex than the model suggests. They conclude that in some cases the influence of institutions on policy outcomes is indeed as strong, direct and unidirectional as their model suggests, but for the great majority of policy areas the impact is more 'subtle or indirect and contingent in strength and direction upon the presence of other factors' (Rockman and Weaver, 1993: 446). They advance nine broad conclusions to be derived from the comparative case studies (pp. 446–53):

- Although institutions affect governmental capabilities, their effects are contingent.
- Specific institutional arrangements often create both opportunities and risks for individual governmental capabilities.
- Policy-making capabilities may also differ substantially across policy areas within a political system.

- Institutional effects on governmental capabilities are channelled through governmental decision-making characteristics.
- Differences in electoral rules and the norms which guide the formation of governments may have as much impact as institutions themselves.
- Parliamentary systems are not better than presidential systems, and vice versa.
- Divided party control of the executive or legislative branch exacerbates the problems of governance – especially that of setting policy priorities.
- Institutional arrangements involve a trade-off in capabilities.
- Governments may work around institutional constraints by generating countervailing mechanisms.

For some capabilities a concentration of power is better (for example, implementation); for some (such as trade policy), national political systems make little difference; for others, a concentration of power is highly detrimental. Thus in conclusion the study argues that the impact of institutions on policy output and outcome is best viewed in terms of the way in which institutional arrangements confer risks and opportunities, and success and failure in policy-making will often turn upon how social, political and other conditions have, in specific countries and at specific times, resulted in risks or opportunities predominating. Successful outcomes in policy-making, they suggest, involve 'matching political institutions to a set of problems that determine which capabilities are needed most and to political and social conditions in a country that determine whether particular institutional arrangements are likely to enhance or inhibit a specific cabability' (Weaver and Rockman, 1993: 461). ◆

2.11.7   The parameters set by past policy

As institutionalists argue, policy-makers have to work within the framework of given constitutional arrangements, voting systems, territorial distribution of authority, executive–legislative relationships, and so on. (Although Hall, 1986, would extend this to include the relationships of labour and capital and the international economy.) However, policy-making also takes place within the parameters of past policies and choices as well as inherited 'institutional arrangements'. When issues arise, problems being formed and policy options set out, they do so in a setting which comprises the policies and programmes and decisions of the past. These past policies will have an important role in determining how current issues will be defined, and what strategies, means and ends will be deployed. As we shall discuss in Part Four, policies and programmes have a habit of not being so easy to terminate, with the consequence that policy problems are not considered *de novo*. Events take place in a policy space (Hogwood and Gunn, 1984: 13) which structures how that event will be problemicized by decision-makers and (Sabatier's) 'advocacy coalitions'. Thinking about and debates on issues therefore inevitably are contextualized by what laws, policies and programmes already exist to deal with a given set of problems. Such policy traditions may form a considerable body of consensus which makes the development of 'new' approaches diffi-cult to achieve (see, for example, Parsons, 1988). And, such is the dominance of existing policy, it may well inhibit or prevent a more comprehensively rational review and result in a more 'incremental' policy-making process (cf. Lindblom, see 3.4.3).

Policy therefore may well be seen as its own cause (Wildavsky, 1980: 70 and ch. 3), rather than as the outcome of a 'problem'. In this sense one could argue that it is existing policies which set the agenda for 'new' problems and provide the discourse within which these prob-lems will be constructed. In many areas where the policy space is 'crowded' (Hogwood and Gunn, 1984: 13), such as social welfare policy, 'new' issues and reforms have to contend with the fact that policies (and expenditure commitments) inherited from the past constrain both the policy advocates and governmental decision-makers (Weaver and Rockman, 1993: 36–7; Pierson and Weaver, 1993: 146–7, 150; Rose, 1989: 357–8; OECD, 1987: 76; Heclo: 1974; Weir *et al.*, 1988; Marsh and Rhodes, 1992). As Rose and Davies (1994) have demonstrated, politi-cians may promise innovation but, having been elected, they inherit the decisions and commitments of previous incumbents. Agendas in government have a much longer life than appears from the political comings and goings. New policy-makers have to put their agenda into effect within the context of an ongoing set of programmes and commitments which restrict and inhibit change far more than political rhetoric suggests to voters (Rose and Davies, 1994; R. Rose, 1990).

2.12   Globalization and policy-making: the international parameters

2.12.1   The global focus of policy analysis

❖ Lasswell, world politics and the policy sciences

The idea of world politics was central to Harold Lasswell's conception of the policy sciences. However, it is a dimension of policy analysis which has only comparatively recently come into prominence with theories of 'globalization' in the 1980s and 1990s. Lasswell argued, however, that it was important for policy sciences to take account of world trends and forces when considering the context of policy problems (see, for example, Lasswell, 1935, 1951b). As Fox notes: 'Through four decades Harold Lasswell ... insisted upon the unity of the world political process ... that domestic, comparative, and international politics must be fitted into a common theoretical framework' (Fox, 1969: 367).

The policy sciences of democracy, concerned as they are with events on a global scale in our historical period, must proceed by creating world-encompassing hypotheses ... [which could] ... specify the institutional pattern from which we are moving and the pattern toward which we are going ... Indeed, one of the major tasks of the policy sciences today is to follow in detail the processes of social invention, diffusion, and restriction throughout the globe for the sake of estimating the significance of specific events.
(*Lasswell, 1951: 13–14*)

As the globe shrinks into interdependence, relying more fully on science and technology, the policy sciences gain significance ... Interdependence implies that every participant and every item in the social process is affected by the context in which it occurs ...
(*Lasswell, 1968: 184*)

Etzioni and the need for a global perspective

Etzioni, writing in the late 1960s, argued that he detected a rising interdependence between nations and economies and the emergence of 'supranational' and 'sub-global systems'. The implications of this trend for social scientists were significant:

For a social scientist, it should seem obvious, but it is not, that there is only one basis for a moral community – a global one ... Surprisingly, many social scientists tend to overplay the nation-state as the unit of societal analysis and underplay supranational bonds and controls; above all they tend to take the nationalistic moral community as the community of values.
(*Etzioni, 1968: 607*) ◆

Thus far we have been considering agenda formation and problem definition within a purely national context. However, it may be argued that one of the most important changes in the politics of the late twentieth century is the extent to which the policy agenda is no longer set and defined with purely national boundaries. The political system also operates within what has been described as a 'world system' (Wallerstein, 1974, 1979).

The implications of this notion of globalization are that the solidity of the Eastonian black box which defines the 'political system' in a rather limited and domestic way is less robust than it was in the past. The boundaries of the political system may well be atrophying and no longer impermeable to outside pressures and influences. As Karl Deutsch has argued (see also 3.7.6), the nation state may be seen as increasingly inadequate to the challenges of the late twentieth century, however:

In the present-day world, the state ... is both indispensible and inadequate. It is an indispensible instrument to get things done and to deal with many real problems. But it is inadequate to cope with an increasing number of other problems of life and death for many of its inhabitants. (*Deutsch, 1981: 331*)

❖ Globalization and globalism

The globalization of social life

'Until our day', the anthropologist Peter Worsley has written, 'human society has never existed', meaning that it is only in quite recent times that we can speak of forms of social association which spans the earth. The world has become in important respects a single social system, as a result of growing ties of interdependence which now affect virtually everyone … The general terms for the increasing interdependence of world society is globalization … The globalization of social relations should be understood primarily as the reordering of time and distance in our lives. Our lives, in other words, are increasingly influenced by activities and events happening well away from the social contexts in which we carry on our day-to-day activities.
(*Giddens, 1989: 519–20*)

Giddens identifies three major factors that make for globalism:

- transnational corporations;
- growing economic integration;
- the globalization of communications and media;

and three theories to explain the process:

- imperialism and neo-imperialism: globalism as the product of the expansion of capitalism;
- dependency: globalism as uneven development and the domination of the underdeveloped world by the industrialized world;
- world system: globalism as the product of the expansion of the world economy leading to centralization around a core, semi-periphery and periphery system of relationships.

Globalism and modernity

Anthony Giddens, *The Consequences of Modernity*, 1990
Giddens's essay on modernity argues that time and space have been reordered in the modern world, and this new order is inherently 'global' in character. Globalization has four dimensions (see figure 2.28)

Martin Albrow and Elizabeth King (eds), *Globalization, Knowledge and Society*, 1990
This collection of papers illustrates how sociologists are becoming more interested in analysing the social processes which are involved in globalization as both a 'fact' and a 'belief' or 'value'.

Albrow offers a definition of globalization set against that of universalism and globalism:

Figure 2.28   The dimensions of globalization

Nation-state system

World capitalist economy

World military order

International division
of labour

Source: Giddens (1990)

Universalism refers to those values which take humanity, at any time or place, hypothetically or actual, as the subject ... Globalism has a much shorter history. I take it to refer to those values which take the real world of 5 billion people as the object of concern, the whole earth as the physical environment, everyone living as world citizens, consumers and producers, with a common interest in collective action to solve global problems ... Globalization refers to all those processes by which the peoples of the world are incorporated into a single world society, global society. Globalism is one of the forces which assist in the development of globalization. (p. 9) ◆

The implications of global inter-connectedness for public policy are well made by Harrop when he notes that:

> The international environment forms much of the *context* of national policy-making. Policy-makers in each country share a policy context formed by the international economic cycle of prosperity, recesssion, depression and recovery ... International organizations such as the EC also form an increasingly important part of the context of national policy-making ... The policy agenda is also becoming international. Similar problems show up in different societies at a similar time and some solutions are considered though by no means implemented, throughout the liberal-democratic world. The mass media and international conferences ease this process of policy diffusion. Policy makers in one country seek to emulate the successes of colleagues overseas.
> (*Harrop, 1992: 263*)

2.12.2   The characteristics of global politics

As the world economy in particular is transformed by new modes of production and trade, and as transnational corporations and institutions come to exercise more influence and power, so the capacity of national policy-makers to frame their own agendas is diminished (see Ray, 1990). Public policy now takes place in a world system as well as in national political systems. What are the characteristics of this global system, and what impact does it have on how we analyse the agenda and problem-setting processes? McGrew (McGrew and Lewis, 1992) suggests that global politics has five distinctive features:

- *Complexity and diversity*: growing complexity and diversity in the institutions and organizations as well as in the issues on the 'global agenda'. No longer are defence and international relations the only international issues; others such as economic welfare, drugs, the environment are items on the domestic political agenda which are interlocked with global issues. This has been accompanied by growing regionalization and transnational co-operation.
- *Intense pattern of interaction*: nation states have a higher level and greater scope of interaction.
- *The permeability of the nation state*: the structural linkages between the domestic and external arenas mean that the national policy agenda is more open to developments in other countries, which in turn means that the nation state is now less able to control the agenda than it was in the past.
- *Rapid and cascading change*: not only is change rapid, but change has the capacity to spill over in an unpredictable fashion into different issues and problems. From the point of view of agenda-setting this has a major importance. Rosenau explains that:

  > issues are transformed as a cascade encounters collectivities in its flow. As a cascade gathers momentum and drags in wider circles of actors, the values it encompasses and the consequences it portends change, and each adds further complexity and dynamism to the interdependent structures that link the actors. Like the so called butterfly effect in meteorology, an event in one part of the world can ultimately have repercussions in remote places.
  > (*Rosenau, 1990: 302; quoted in McGrew and Lewis, 1992: 317*)

- *The fragility of order and governance*: the global polity is less robust and more fragile than that of nation states. Global compliance and the capacity with international institutions to gain compliance of their decisions varies considerably across issues. From the national perspective this means that the policy agenda may be more 'global' but the modes of implementation may be more local. The policy agenda may be global, but decision-making and delivery remain national. What the idea of globalization proposes is that there is a new kind of inter-play between: trans-national companies and the national and world economies; trans-governmental relations; and trans-national organizations. George Modelski (1974) expressed these new relationships in terms of a layer-cake model: global, national and local.

We might also view the agenda-setting and problem definition process in this fashion. Global issues and problems interact with national issues and problems and national issues and problems interact with the local level. Globalization posits that these layers are becoming ever more interactive and permeable and that a new trans-national public sphere or 'commons' (WCED, 1987: 261) may be emerging. In the European context, some would argue that there is evidence to suggest that a new policy level is developing in terms of a 'Europeification of national policy-making' (Andersen and Eliassen, 1993).

❖ **Sylvia Woodby and Martha L. Cottam, *The Changing Agenda: World Politics since 1945*, 1991**

The authors argue that we can view the post-war era as being dominated by three agenda frameworks:

- *Global*: issues which are perceived of interest to the world community. Issues which are seen as requiring global solutions. This would include economic relations, war, international conflict, debt, population growth, food, the environment. The global agenda was important in the early post-war period, declined in the early 1980s, and recovered in the late 1980s.
- *East–West*: the issues related to the conflict between East and West were to dominate the post-war period until the collapse of the Soviet Union in the 1990s.
- *North–South*: the issues involved in the relationship between the developed and underdeveloped world became more urgent by the 1980s as the problems of trade, debt, revolution and famine came to impact upon national politics and the proceedings of international organizations.

The classification of such kinds of agenda is useful for policy analysis since it draws our attention to the fact that the conduct of public policy in the liberal democracies has taken place within a wider international setting. For those countries with large defence budgets, the fact that the cold war necessitated such a big slice of resources had wide-ranging implications for other domestic problems and policies. At the same time as the post-war era has developed, the separation of the global, East–West and North–South agendas has become less watertight. North–South issues are leaking into the agendas of the North, and the East–West agenda is leaking into the employment concerns of western policy-makers.◆

The compression of time and space (Harvey, 1992: 284) is not a new phenomenon. The world has been getting smaller since the onset of the modern era. Policy-making and agenda-setting have long been shaped by a global or international context. The post-war world was one in which countries such as the US, Britain and France maintained a very high level of defence and military spending. This fact alone shaped the parameters within which problems were addressed in these countries, as opposed to Germany and Japan, which were not so burdened with military spending. The impact of the cold war and East–West conflict was to distort the relationship of the state to the economy and society in such countries in ways which in the late 1980s and 1990s could be seen in the consequences of the 'peace dividend' (unemployment) and the re-unification of Germany (high interest rates).

Globalization arguments pose the question of the extent to which issues and agendas (global, national and local, on the one hand, global, East–West and North–South on the other) are more permeable than others. Are there some issues such as the environment which are being defined as a *global problem* and others which are impermeable and are viewed primarily as national or local problems? How does the changing agenda of East–West relations alter the context within which priorities are allocated in a post-cold war era? Globalization suggests that the processes at work in a world system mean that more and more issues will be (and indeed have been) structured by larger forces and movements outside the nation state and outside the national framework of public policy-making.

❖ Issues on the global agenda

The environment

Gareth Porter and Janet Welsh Brown, *Global Environmental Politics*,1991
This study charts the emergence of the environment as a 'global issue' from the 1980s. It shows how the issue has involved the development of new levels of interactions among states to form a 'global environmental regime'. The book analyses the agenda-setting process within the regime and the processes of: issue definition, fact-finding; bargaining about regime creation; and regime strengthening. The authors show how these processes have led to new linkages between the environmental issue and international security, North–South relations and world trade. The environmental issue, they claim, is increasingly penetrating these and other policy issues. The authors are optimistic for change, not least because of what they consider to be the way in which the formation of a global environmental agenda and regime has met with ever-greater support in public opinion, which has pressurized policy-makers to alter their policy positions.

Our Common Future (WCED, 1987) expresses globalism in these terms:

> In the middle of the 20th century, we saw our planet from space for the first time. Historians may eventually find that this vision had a greater impact on thought than did the Copernican revolution ... From space, we see a small and fragile ball dominated not by human activity and edifice but a pattern of clouds, oceans, greenery, and soils.

Until recently, the planet was a large world in which human activities and their effects were neatly compartmentalized within nations, within sectors (energy, agriculture and trade), and within broad areas of concern (environmental, economic, social). These compartments have begun to dissolve. This applies in particular to the various global 'crises' that have seized public concern, particularly over the past decade. These are not separate crises: an environmental crisis, a development crisis, an energy crisis. They are all one.

...

The traditional forms of national sovereignty are increasingly challenged by the realities of ecological and economic interdependence. Nowhere is this more true than in the shared ecosystems and in 'the global commons' – those parts of the planet that fall outside national jurisdictions.
(*WCED, 1987: 1–4, 261*)

David Vogel, *National Styles of Regulation*, 1986
Vogel's study begins by noting that the environmental issue has taken a very similar kind of path in the two countries. However, despite these similarities in the pattern of concern for the environment, there have been significant differences in the strategies and approaches to the issue. In Britain the situation has been one of a close relationship between business and government, whereas in America the relationship has been more legalistic and hostile. Vogel shows how the styles of regulation vary: in contrast to the US, in Britain business works with government, there is a high degree of confidence and trust in public authorities, and the public at large are not suspicious of business.

As far as the styles of decision-making are concerned, the differences in the political systems of Britain and the US do make for divergences in regulation. However, Vogel's study does not lead to an unequivocal support for the 'politics matters' thesis. The divergence in regulatory style is set in the context of convergence in the environmental agendas of both polities: issues have been defined in 'strikingly similar ways'. He offers two explanations for this phenomenon:

- *socio-economic factors*: the economies of the US and the UK are dominated by the same industries and companies. Both societies have therefore to deal with the same externalities. Industrial growth places pressures on policy-makers to ameliorate the disutilities of progress;
- *international communications*: the role of the media, international scientific consensus and close ties between environmentalists have provided an exchange of information that shapes the agenda in convergent ways.

Aids

A.F. Fleming *et al.* (eds), *The Global Impact of Aids*, 1988
The conference followed a summit of world health ministers in London a few weeks earlier. Opening the conference, Antony Newton argued that:

What is needed now is to build upon the increased awareness of the need for international cooperation and national political action by turning statements of principle into specific policies and action throughout the world ... Aids is indeed a global issue. The solution to it must be a global one involving a coordinated international effort. (pp. xxvii–xxviii)

The director of the WHO's Aids programme (Johnathan Mann) made the point that Aids is bringing about a 'new paradigm of health' because of four factors: 'it is a global problem; it is understood and spoken as a global problem; and it is known worldwide; and Aids is being combated at a truly global level' (ibid.: 6–7).

Industry and the economy

Peter Dicken, *Global Shift*, 1988

As the title of this book suggests, the author argues that the changes which have occurred in industry are the result of global changes or shifts. The main sources of global shift are transnational corporations (TNCs) which organize production on a world-wide basis, the policies pursued by national governments, and the enabling technologies of transport, communication and production. As patterns of change are increasingly the outcome of forces operating on a global scale, the ability of national governments to formulate policies independently of these changes is being fundamentally weakened:

> There is a growing consensus that the world economy as a whole has become not only more volatile and more complex but also more tightly interconnected – 'a fragile and interlocking system' in the words of the Brandt Commission. In effect, this means that the well-being of nations, regions, cities and other communities depends increasingly not merely on events in their own backyards but on what happens at a much larger geographical scale ... We need a global perspective, therefore, to help understand the world economy as a whole but also to help to understand what might otherwise appear to be purely national or local problems. (p. 3)

However, Dicken is clear that this does not mean the end of the nation state, nor does it lessen its importance. But its importance is changing. National policy-makers have the task of creating the right kind of business climate for the new modes of production and trade. The global economic framework therefore interacts with the political processes and policies pursued by nation states.

The policies and the policy styles of national governments differ due to differences in the pattern of business–government relations, state traditions, institutional arrangements and the role of labour organizations (Daniels, 1992). The success of nations in economic performance will diverge notwithstanding the convergence of the global economy.

Drugs

See Woodby and Cottam (1991: 192–3).

In the early literature on drug use (see Clausen, in Merton and Nisbet (eds), 1976), drugs were considered primarily as a social problem and the focus was of seeking a national policy. However, in the 1980s the problem was increasingly defined as requiring global co-operation and action. The global concern has addressed the supply and transportation of drugs from the producer states such as Columbia, Peru, Pakistan, Bolivia and Thailand.

Globalization and uniformity: global lifestyles and cultural nationalism

John Naisbitt and Patricia Aburdene, *Megatrends 2000*, 1988

> even as our lifestyles grow more similar, there are unmistakable signs of a backlash: a trend against uniformity, a desire to assert the uniqueness of one's culture and language, a repudiation of foreign influence ... The more homogeneous our lifestyles become, the more steadfastly we shall cling to deeper values – religion, language, art, and literature. As our worlds grow more similar, we shall increasingly treasure the traditions that spring from within ... The Welsh, French Canadians and the Catalans are not anomalies; they are the bellwethers. The cultural integrity of these countries has been threatened far longer than the rest of us have experienced. As we partake of the global lifestyle, we shall begin to assert our cultural nationalism as much as they have. (pp. 103–4, 133)

The constraints of the world economic system

Helen Milner, 'Maintaining international commitments in trade policy', in Weaver and Rockman (eds), 1993

Milner examines the way in which trade policy has been made in Britain, France and the US in the 1970s and 1980s. She concludes that differences between their political systems and institutional pressure were of far less importance in shaping their respective trade policies than the constraints of international economic interdependence and the turbulence in the world economy. The three countries, she argues, as a consequence 'reacted in rather incoherent ways, protecting and promoting basically the same group of distressed industries' (p. 369).

Compare Milner's argument with Krasner's (1978) 'institutionalist' view of US trade policy: see 3.6.4.

Privatization

In a study of privatization and the shift towards new public-sector management techniques, Martin argues that national policy agendas are being shaped by the forces of global economic restructuring:

> The roles of the state in defining, protecting and promoting the public interest are being whittled away by a global campaign of privatization and public sector commercialization by the needs of transnational business ... As Lincoln Y. Rathman, managing director of invest- ment consultants Scudder, Stevens & Clark, put it [at a conference]: 'Privatization is being driven by the shift of important economic sectors to operation on a global scale.' Henrietta Holsman Fore ... has stressed the same point: 'Industries such as telecommunications, finance and energy are being restructured to respond to the needs of an integrated world economy. The global structure of these industries demands their participation in the privati- zation process.'
> (*Martin, 1993: 3–9*)

Are policy agendas driven by global economic cycles?

Kondratieff's theory of world economic cycles suggests that there are waves of prosperity, recession, depression and recovery. The theory has been widely applied to the analysis of the world economy and is of relevance for the following section. It may be that policy agendas are set in broad terms by the conditions which pertain in these long cycles (Simmie, 1990; Berry, 1991; Johnson, 1993). The policy options in a depression are very different to those which exist in times of economic recovery or prosperity. This may be a rather obvious statement to make, but it is too easily overlooked in the analysis of agenda-setting. Problems arise in a context in which economic conditions play a major role in shaping opinions and political strategies, expectations and goals, optimism and pessimism, hope and despair. The analysis of public policy itself must be placed within this context. The shifting focus of academic concern, which we examined in 1.9, is something which has to be understood in the light of the changing economic circumstances and constraints in which policy-making has taken place over the last forty or so years. As we shall see in Part Four, the concern with governmental performance and the relationship of the public and private spheres is inextricably linked with the bust, boom and bust cycle of the 1980s and 1990s.

The nation state and global change

Norman Myers (ed.), *The Gaia Atlas of Planet Management*, 1987

We are the children of the next transformation, the Third Wave. Humanity faces a quantum leap forward. It faces the deepest social upheaval and creative restructuring of all time ... we should not think of a single massive reorganization from the top, but thousands of conscious, decentralized experiments that permit us to test new models of political decision-making and new forms of development. (Alvin Toffler, p. 200)

Toffler exposes the apparent contradiction of globalization in terms of political arrangements. On the one hand, there is global change which impacts on everyone; on the other, the need to

Figure 2.29   The rise and rise of INGOs

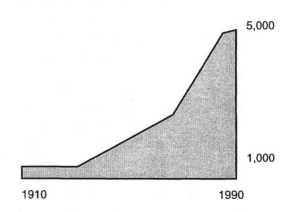

5,000

1,000

1910   1990

Source: Myers (1987)

address the problems in a manner which goes above and beneath the national policy-making structures. However, *The Gaia Atlas* notes that the nation state 'does a better job than it is given credit for' and has 'no other rival as the basis of collective living' (p. 234). Global consciousness does not mean global government so much as the development of a global agenda. The world, it argues, is becoming reluctantly internationalist, recognizing that issues of national interest are tied up with global issues: ocean and atmosphere management, nuclear war, famine, health, wildlife, energy, poverty, population, unemployment, etc. The authors believe that a key indicator of this new agenda is the growth of international non-governmental organizations (see figure 2.29). ◆

Globalization and national decision-making

The globalization argument taken at its most extreme would have us believe that the age of the nation state as the context within which policy agendas are formulated is coming to an end. Perhaps the main reason for this is that liberal democratic societies face the same issues: drugs, crime, Aids, unemployment, urban decay, an ageing population, the environment, and so forth. At the same time, the process of defining the problems may be converging because of the manner in which knowledge is now produced and disseminated as well as because a process of socio-economic convergence may be driving industrial societies to exhibit the same problems.

At the level of agenda-setting it is undoubtedly the case that, with the 'global village' a reality in terms of communications technology, and with major social, economic and environmental problems being analysed at a global level (hence the rise and rise of summits as a form of agenda-setting in these and other areas), the fact remains that the power of decision and the capacity and will to implement remains largely located within nation states. There is therefore a tension between the spillover which may be said to be occurring at a global level, wherein issues and their modes of definition are linked to other issues and tend to leak into one another, and the reality of the maintenance of national sovereignty. Because a problem is considered to be international or global does not mean that international or global institutions and policy-making (and implementation) processes will be established to facilitate a solution. The World Commission on Environment and Development (WCED) expressed this predicament as involving an 'institutional gap', whereby the 'real' problems of the world confront national institutions and agendas which fail to deal with the interlocking problems which endanger the world as a whole (WCED, 1987: 9). International policy communities and networks, which encompass governmental, non-governmental and academic participants, have undoubtedly meant that problems which confront industrial societies are more convergent, even if the modes of decision-making and implementation prove to be as divergent as they have ever been.

The compression of time and space has meant that it is possible to speak of the convergence of concerns, but this internationalization of the agenda facing policy makers is not something which necessarily makes for convergence in decision-making. Indeed, globalization may have the effect of polarizing rather than unifying responses: the more nations are compelled to accept the global forces which shape policy options, the more they may seek to retain – or obtain – their capacity to be different. Globalization may consequently lead to more decision-makers, rather than less. With the demise of the old East–West agenda, (Woodby and Cottam, 1991) the number of nation states has increased, and a relatively simple world order has been replaced by a more complex pattern of multiple decision-making centres. Against the pressure of 'global agendas', the fact remains that at times of crisis 'governments are prone to withdraw from intergovernmental co-operation and supranational policy-making rather than move positively into closer collaboration' (Metcalfe and Richards, 1987: 70). Issues and problems may well be increasingly constructed in international and global terms, but decision-making and implementation still remain domains which must be analysed within the context of nation states.

PART THREE

Decision Analysis

Analysis of the decision-making process and policy analysis for decision-making

3.1 Introduction

> Decision-making falls between policy-formation and implementation ... however [they] are closely interwoven, with decisions affecting implementations and initial implementations affecting later stages of decision-making which, in turn, affect later implementations. Decision-making is hence not to be viewed as a passive process ... decisions are processes and early decisions are often only vague directional signals, initial proddings, or trial runs for later specifications and revisions.
> (*Etzioni, 1968: 203–4*)

> the process of decision does not come to an end when the general purpose of an organization has been determined. The task of 'deciding' pervades the entire administrative organization.
> (*Simon, 1957: 1*)

Whatever the influence of 'international' or 'global' agenda-setting, the locus of decision-making remains the nation state. If we define decision-making as a process in which choices are made or a preferred option is selected then the notion of decision involves a point or series of points in time and space when policy-makers allocate values. Decision-making in this sense extends throughout the policy cycle; for example: decisions about what to make into a 'problem'; what information to choose; choices about strategies to influence the policy agenda; choices about what policy options to consider; choices about what option to select; choices about ends and means; choices in how a policy is implemented; choices about how policies may be evaluated. At each of these points decision-making is taking place. Some of these decisions involve the allocation of values and the distribution of resources by the formulation of a policy, or through the on-going conduct of a programme. Decision-making thus takes place in different arenas and at different levels. At one level there is a decision by high policy actors to make 'national' health or economic policy, at another there are the decisions of other actors who are involved in 'health' policy at the level of a hospital or local government. So too decisions about economic policy are made at a variety of levels, some more,

245

some less significant than others. As the arguments of 'network' frameworks suggest, modern government must increasingly be seen as a complex multi-layered, or multi-sphered activity in which a policy is composed of numerous decision points.

However, not only is the 'decision process' more multi-faceted, the frameworks which may be used to explain this process are equally multi-dimensional and multi-disciplinary. As Allison (1971) showed in his path-breaking study of the Cuban missile crisis, the decisions surrounding this episode may be viewed through a variety of 'lenses', each of which constructs a different story of what 'actually' took place. Thus one could argue that the decision-making which took place in that momentous 'crisis' exists at one and the same time as a series of frames, rather than as one episode. The Cuban missile crisis is therefore a kind of envelope of stories. What 'really happened' in a sense can never be known, except as constructions viewed through different 'lenses'. In this part of the book we explore five major approaches to the analysis of decision-making and review their different frameworks (3.3–3.7).

Decision analysis is concerned with what Lasswell nicely summed up as 'who gets what, when [and] how' (Lasswell, 1936). Analyses of decision-making are accounts which claim to explain or describe how a decision, or series of decisions, came to be made. Another form of decision analysis aims to provide arguments as to how it should or ought to be made. The analysis of the decision-making process (3.3–3.7) and the analysis for and in the decision process (3.8–3.9) – or knowledge of and knowledge in policy-making – are, however, not categories which are exclusive. Descriptive frameworks contain normative frameworks, and normative frameworks contain assumptions about how the decision process works. Frameworks which conceptualize what the decision-making process is or ought to be shape what we see as the role of knowledge or analysis in that process. At the same time, if we begin with beliefs about what role knowledge or rationality has or ought to have in the decision process, then this will inform what we think about the 'reality' of decision-making.

Decision analysis therefore requires that we understand the way in which facts and values interact, and the way in which 'beliefs', 'ideas', 'interests', on the one hand (what in psychology are known as 'A' variables, or the arousal system), interplay with 'information', 'facts', 'reality' (the 'K', or cognition variables), and vice versa. Thus the role which we may see 'policy analysis' having in the decision-making process will depend on what we believe to be the reality of decision-making as a process. And it will also be shaped by what we mean by a 'decision' or what we mean by 'analysis' or 'knowledge'. If this is somewhat confusing, it is because facts and values are not concepts which are intellectually watertight. Facts shape values; values shape facts ...

Policy analysis as an 'art' and 'craft' (Wildavsky, 1980) aims, as Lasswell maintained, at clarifying the values which inform both the analysis of the decision-making process and the forms of knowledge which are used in this process. Thus decision analysis may be viewed as involving two dimensions (analysis of and in) which are inextricably interwoven. Although we separate them or make a distinction between the two for purposes of exposition, it is important to be aware of the way in which these modes of analysis overlap and interweave.

3.2 Decision-making: frameworks and disciplinary contexts

Decision analysis encompasses a range of academic disciplines and frameworks. Inevitably the focus of each of these disciplines and the frameworks which they contain vary. For something as complex as decision-making by individuals and groups no one discipline or framework can possibly explain everything. In highlighting one aspect another is ignored or underestimated. Strengths are also weaknesses. There can be no one explanation of decision-making, and consequently the aim of policy analysis is to contextualize approaches, and clarify the values and beliefs which frame a given theory; thence, to arrive at an evaluation of what approach or approaches offer the most 'plausible' account of or for a particular decision. In this part of the book we examine models of decision-making drawn from a number of social sciences. These include:

- political science;
- sociology;
- organizational theory;
- economics;
- psychology;
- management.

In analysing the decision-making process we have grouped these disciplines into five major approaches and categories:

- power (3.3);
- rationality (3.4);

- public choice and its alternatives (3.5);
- institutional (3.6);
- informational and psychological (3.7).

However, in using these categorizations we are not putting ideas into neat boxes or pigeon holes. Contributions to decision analysis invariably overlap and interact. One focus serves as a critique of another, and there is often common ground between approaches and their different frameworks. One way to study decision analysis is therefore to read the core contributions – or key texts – written by the major scholars concerned, since as individuals they tend to leap across disciplinary boundaries and use varieties of theoretical frameworks. The works of Lasswell, Simon, Eztioni, Vickers, and Boulding, for example, are examples of how a theorist's ideas defy being slotted into a particular academic context or discipline.

3.3   Power approaches to decision-making

Power models view decision-making as something which is shaped and determined by the structures of power: class, wealth, bureaucratic and political arrangements, pressure goups, and technical knowledge or professionals. In this part of the book we shall comment on six such approaches and their variants:

- *elitism*: focuses on the way in which power is concentrated;
- *pluralism*: focuses on the way in which power is distributed;
- *Marxism*: focuses on class conflict and economic power;
- *corporatism*: focuses on the power of organized interests;
- *professionalism*: focuses on the power of professionals;
- *technocracy*: focuses on the power of technical experts.

3.3.1   Elitist and neo-elitist models

Elitist models of the policy process hold that power is concentrated in the hands of a few groups and individuals. Decision-making according to this model is a process which works to the advantage of these elites. As a model of decision-making, elitism purports to be founded on an analysis of how the *real* world works. In the real world there are, it is argued, those at the top with power and the 'mass' without power. The model has its origins in modern social science with the work of two Italian theorists: Mosca and Pareto. They argued that, contrary to Marx, history shows that elitism is inevitable: the classless society is a myth and democracy little more than a sham. Later Mosca modified his position to argue that democracy could be viewed as a form of politics in which elites compete for the people's vote in order to secure legitimacy for elite rule. Mosca and Pareto's ideas form the basis upon which later elitist approaches were to be formulated. Robert Michels (1915) developed Mosca's approach in a study of political parties in which he posited that there was an 'iron law of oligarchy' which operated in organizations. Over time, organizational elites generate their own interests and goals which are distinct from those of the mass members. Max Weber was also to focus on the organizational or bureaucratic context of power by showing how 'rationalization' in capitalist society leads to the formation of bureaucracy which will inevitably replace other forms of organization and, in the absence of strong parliamentary accountability, pose a threat to democratic decision-making by elected politicians.

If the arguments of Mosca, Pareto, Michels and Weber were correct, then it left the idea of 'government by the people' looking rather unreal and idealistic. The problem of reconciling the elitism of the real world with the need for democratic legitimacy was neatly resolved by the economist Joseph Schumpeter (1974). Being an economist, he applied an economic approach to the problem of legitimacy. Elitism, he argued, was legitimated in a democracy by a political market composed of competing parties and rival elites. The citizen (*qua* consumer) was involved in the decision-making process by the act of choosing between the policy programmes and promises of rival political firms. This model was to be developed most fully and taken to its logical conclusion in Downs's (1957) 'economic' theory of democracy. Schumpeter's model also provided a starting point for the pluralist theories advanced by Dahl *et al.* in the 1950s.

Lasswell and the power of elites

Another line of development in the elite approach was that put forward by Lasswell (1936) who also took the view that: 'the study of politics is the study of influence and the influential ... The influential are those who get the most of what there is to get ... Those who get the most are elite, the rest are mass' (Lasswell, 1936: 13). However, whereas for Schumpeter and Downs the functioning of 'political' markets could best serve to provide the legitimacy for elite power, Lasswell's view was that it required a more 'preventative' politics, in which knowledge could exercise more influence on decision-making. From this line of argument, of course, policy analysis was to grow.

Lasswell accepted Pareto's idea that there was a circulation of elites in democracy and argued that in the modern era a shift was taking place from class struggle to a struggle between different 'skill groups' (see

Lasswell, 1935, 1936, 1952, 1965). These skill groups included: those skilled in the use of violence (such as military and police elites); those with communication and propaganda skills; those with business and commercial skills; 'technocrats' who possess specialist technical knowledge; and bureaucrats with administrative or organizational skills. His great fear was that, when combined, these new elites posed a dangerous threat to democracy. The combination of elites with a capacity to manipulate communications and symbols with elites skilled in violence, organization and technical know-how ultimately raised the real prospect of the development of the 'garrison-state' in which military, bureaucratic and technocratic elites rule (see Lasswell, 1937, 1941). For Lasswell the key issue was how this trend could be prevented and democracy strengthened. The policy sciences, he believed, could and should have a vital role to play in enhancing democracy by seeking to promote a wider distribution and pluralism of power. In this regard – as Merelman (1981: 485) points out – he echoes the progressive liberalism of Dewey, the technocratic analysis of Thorstein Veblen, and is a precursor of the approach taken by Daniel Bell and J.K. Galbraith (see 3.3.6). Merelman believes, however, that Lasswell's prescription to prevent the 'garrison state' is pretty 'weak tea':

> Apparently Lasswell believed that in the hands of the policy scientist social science would become so compelling, so inexorable, so powerful, that the sheer strength of its ideas would sweep all before it. No advocacy or strategy is necessary when one possesses the truth; only false prophets play the advocate, the manipulator, the politician.
> (Merelman, 1981: 495)

To some extent it is true to say that Lasswell had a somewhat naive faith in the possibilities of social science and policy analysis. However, this is to read Lasswell's analysis of elites and democracy without taking into account the far more radical changes which he considered essential to curb elite power. This is understood by Bobrow and Dryzek when they note:

> The Lasswellian approach shares with critical theory a fundamental practical intent to improve the human condition with respect to freedom from coercion, want, indignity, and manipulation ...
> (Bobrow and Dryzek, 1987: 173)

Lasswell's idea for controlling elites through policy science is indeed a very weak cup of tea if we do not place it in the context of his writings on human rights and dignity (see McDougal et al., 1980) and his belief in the need to promote a critical public discourse – prototypes of which were his idea of 'decision seminars' and 'social planetariums' (see 3.10.5, 4.4.8).

Mills and the military-industrial complex

In the 1950s elitism was to be the subject of an extensive debate. The study which was to ignite much controversy about how power is distributed was that conducted by Floyd Hunter: *Community Power Structure* (1953). The book was a study of power in Atlanta based on a series of 40 interviews with key members of the business community. The 'self-evident' theory it claimed to prove was that in reality a power elite made all the important decisions in a democratic society. Another contribution to the development of the modern elitist approach was that advanced by C. Wright Mills, whose book *The Power Elite* (1956) sought to show how decision-making in the USA had become dominated by a powerful military-industrial complex. This view of a military-industrial-bureaucratic elite as the main force shaping key areas of US decision-making was to become a popular radical standpoint during the Vietnam War. The growing power of military elites in the USA and elsewhere during the cold war served to confirm Lasswell's (1937, 1941) analysis of the garrison state, and his 1941 article was consequently widely reprinted in numerous publications in the 1960s and early 1970s (see Muth *et al.*, 1990: 92; and Lasswell, 1962). Like Lasswell, Mills's analysis led him to view intellectuals, scholars, scientists and others as having a key role in checking the growth of elite power. (Mills, 1963: 246)

Dimensions of power

As we saw in Part Two (2.4; 2.6) the argument shifted ground with the models advanced by Schattschneider (1960) and Bachrach and Baratz (1962), which pointed towards the way in which power was exercised though the 'mobilization of bias', 'non-decision-making' and 'agenda-setting'. The definition of power employed by Bachrach and Baratz argued that Dahl's view constituted but one dimension of power relations, since another dimension existed when 'A devotes his energies to creating or reinforcing social and political values and institutional practices that limit the scope of the political process to public consideration of only those issues which are comparatively innocuous to A' (Bachrach and Baratz, 1962: 149). The riposte to this argument was that if the model could not be empirically demonstrated, how could one actually study something which has not happened? (Merelman 1968; Wolfinger, 1971). Work by Bachrach and Baratz (1970) and Crenson (1971) sought to provide more empirical evidence to support their theory that power had dimensions which extended beyond the open control by A over B. Power involved the control over ways of thinking and access to the agenda as well as over behaviour.

Again, as we noted in 2.6, Lukes's response was to reject the empirical/behavioural approach to 'decision-making' entirely. His 'third dimension' of power is the power which a system has to ensure that its values, beliefs and myths dominate. That this is not a theory which can be tested empirically – as it is not a surface phenomenon – is not a problem for Lukes. Gaventa (1980) endeavoured to subject the three models to empirical analysis in a study of the way in which miners in the Appalachians came to accept (or acquiesce) in their lack of power. As Gaventa notes, this study of the hidden aspects of power and domination is by far the least understood dimension of politics as it

> involves specifying the means through which power influences, shapes or determines conceptions of the necessities, possibilities, and strategies of challenge in situations of latent conflict. This may include the study of social myths, language, and symbols, and how they are shaped and manipulated in power processes. It may involve the study of the communication of information – both of what is communicated and how it is done. It may involve, in short, locating the power processes behind the social construction of meanings and patterns that serve to get A to act and believe in a manner in which B otherwise might not, to A's benefit and B's detriment. (*Gaventa, 1980: 15–16*)

Thus Lukes's argument and Gaventa's study of the hidden dimensions of elite power – as involving power over meanings – redirects our attention to the arguments advanced by 'constructivist ' theories of social problems (2.2.2) and the 'argumentative turn' (2.7.3).

3.3.2   Pluralism and neo-pluralist approaches to decision-making

The original versions of pluralism (see 2.6), as represented by such texts as Dahl's *Who Governs* (1961), came in for considerable modification in later years. The values and principles that pluralist democracy stands for have proved more resilient (the normative framework), but the analytical framework has incorporated a number of the criticisms made by Marxist and elitist critics in the 1960s.

One of the main proponents of the 'neo-pluralist' model is Charles Lindblom, whose notion of policy-making as 'muddling through' we shall consider in the following section. Lindblom has been a major figure in public policy, and the development of his arguments has been the focus of immense interest amongst students of the subject. Lindblom originally told a highly pluralist story in the 1950s: first with Dahl (Dahl and Lindblom, 1953) and later in Lindblom (1959). However, his idea of policy-making as pluralist and incrementalist and as something which *ought* to be pluralist and incrementalist had changed by the 1970s. In his *Politics and Markets* (1977) he argued that policy-making was constrained by the workings of capitalism, specifically, the interests of business and the market.

Dahl too was also to modify his view in this direction (see Dahl, 1982). Decision-making, they concluded, is not a neutral affair: the demands of business interests predominate over the demands of other groups. The decision-making process therefore is – according to their revised view – biased in favour of the powerful, and functions to the disadvantage of the less-powerful and less-well resourced. The 'key text' which displays their change of position is their preface to the second edition of their study *Politics, Economics and Welfare*, published in 1976. It is an important statement, as it reflects upon so many of the failures of policy-making which were becoming evident in the 1970s. The reality of 'polyarchy' was, they noted, far removed from the analysis which they had put forward in the 1950s. After Vietnam, Watergate, the 'imperial presidency', the growth of urban decay, and social and economic inequality, Dahl and Lindblom confessed to changing their minds on the question of who governs. Whereas their early work had neglected to take account of economic and social development, the later Dahl and Lindblom place these factors more centrally in their analysis of pluralism. Above all, they concede that pluralist politics is not played on a level playing field. Business interests have a predominant influence on the decision-making processes of liberal democracy. Whereas in the past they had believed that in a pluralist polity interests would balance and the power of business could be neutralized by other interests, by the 1970s they had concluded that liberal democracy works primarily in the interests of the capitalist system. However, the solution to this problem is not to put an end to capitalism, but to create a more participative, open and fairer democracy. Dahl, for example, in his *Preface to Economic Democracy* (1985), puts forward a list of conditions for a more effective democracy to counter the power of economic interests. Lindblom has also set out his recommendations to remove political and economic 'impairment' (see Lindblom and Woodhouse, 1993). Significantly, their arguments take on board the points which were made by agenda-setting theoristist in the 1960s: the political agenda, they argue, is narrow and deformed and is distorted by the education system and by powerful business and media interests.

A similar path was also trodden by the economist J.K. Galbraith. In the 1950s he had argued in *American Capitalism* (1953) that the dangers to democracy posed by the growth of big business could be avoided by the operation of 'countervailing power': big interests would check other big interests. However, by the late 1960s Galbraith had become far more pessimistic about the containment of corporate power. His book *The Affluent Society* (1958) showed how there was a growing gap between 'private affluence' and 'public squalor'; *The New Industrial State* (1967) argued that policy-making was now dominated by a powerful 'technostructure' in both government and the corporations. Pluralist democracy was largely a myth which, he believed, only a more radical policy agenda focused on social justice and control over the 'technostructure' could change (see 3.5.2). A similar line was put forward by another prominent liberal in this period, Michael Harrington (see his *The Other America*, 1962).

There was, however, another strand in this development of pluralism from the 1960s onwards: policy analysis. Advocates of policy analysis viewed the defects of democratic society as amenable to improvement and reform. The key to this was in a shift towards a more knowledge-based political process in which decision-making was more informed and rational. If Galbraith saw the technostructure as a problem, many policy analysts and other social scientists viewed 'technocracy' as something of a solution (see Bell, 1976). The growth of analytical approaches to public decision-making and problems was seen by many as offering a way forward for democracy. If knowledge could be harnessed to power, the contradictions which writers such as Dahl and Lindblom had identified could be resolved. Analysis by social scientists and others could thereby serve to supplement the political process and enlighten decision-making (see, for example, Weiss, 1977; Dror, 1989; Etzioni, 1968) – if it could not be a substitute for politics (see Jenkins-Smith, 1990: 39–80; Tribe, 1972). (On policy analysis, see 3.4.3, 3.4.4, 3.8, 4.5.1, 4.5.2, 4.5.4.)

Pluralist approaches have also developed new models which aim to take account of the evolution of policy-making processes and structures which have taken place in recent decades. One of the most important of these is the notion of policy networks and communities (see 2.10.2, 2.10.4, 2.10.5). Smith (1993) has argued that the idea of policy networks/communities is, however, multi-theoretic and may be applied by approaches other than that of pluralism:

> For Marxists the networks would be closed and dominated by the interests that represent capital. For elitists, networks would be closed and dominated by a small number of interest groups and state actors as in a corporatist model. For state theorists, networks could take different forms but would exist in order to pursue the interests of state actors. For pluralists, networks are continually breaking down into issue networks which makes it increasingly difficult for a small number of groups to dominate policy sectors.
> (*Smith, 1993: 74*)

Applied in this way a pluralist model might provide a common framework within which a multiplistic approach to public policy could develop. It is a promising new direction.

3.3.3   Marxism old and new: decision-making in capitalist societies

Pluralism has not been alone in undergoing significant theoretical change. As we examined earlier (2.7), the Marxist view of how issues and problems are defined have, like pluralism, evolved. As the pluralists have abandoned the simple idea of a world of decision-making which is open and competitive, so Marxists have come to accept a more complex picture than of class domination and the state as an instrument of class power.

So called 'instrumentalist' approaches have – not unlike pluralism – focused on the surface levels of decision-making. Miliband (1969, 1977), for example, argued that the state in capitalist society was an instrument of a ruling class which ruled in the interests of that class. Politicians, civil servants and business and financial elites were, he argued, people who came from the same social class, had been educated at the same schools, and operated in the interests of the capitalist system. However, 'structural' critics of this theory – such as Poulanzas (1973) – have maintained that this view of the state as an instrument of capitalism fails to take account of two factors: first, that it is not the class of civil servants, politicians and others that matters, so much as the 'structural' power of capital which ultimately structures the decision-making process; and secondly, the extent to which the state can make decisions with a measure of relative autonomy from the capitalist system. This model of the state in capitalist society as autonomous from the capitalist mode of production and from capitalist interests has been widely applied in critical or radical approaches to the study of public policy-making. It provides, in one sense, a form of Marxist pluralism in that it argues that decision-making in capitalist society is more complex than the simple instrumental model suggests. Poulanzas, for example, argues that the state is involved in a process of maintaining or managing different 'fractions' and appears as some kind of arbiter or neutral force so as to better serve the long-run interests of capital and the capitalist class. 'Functionalists' have sought to show how, in order to maintain the social order, the state promotes the interests of capital accumulation, and in order to secure legitimacy the state manages public policy through allocating resources between 'social expenses', 'social investment' and 'social consumption spending' (see O'Connor, 1973; Gough, 1979; Wolfe, 1977; for a critique, see Dunleavy and O'Leary, 1987: 252–3). The 'dual state' theory, for example, argues that the state in capitalist society seeks to structure policy-making so that those policy areas of central concern to the interests of capital are closely administered and concentrated at the higher reaches of state decision-making. However, at the lower levels, where legitimacy is of prime concern, the state will permit a more pluralistic policy-making style (Cawson and Saunders, 1983).

❖ The dual-state model

This model was developed in the light of the experience of local–central relations in the 1980s. It was argued that a two-tier decision-making process had evolved in conditions of economic crisis: a corporatist level which encompassed the production issues of the macro-economy and the non-corporatist or conflictual level of consumption of public services. Decision-making takes on a corporatist form at the level of central ruling class (producer) interests, and a more pluralist, open form at the level of working-class and middle-class (consumer) interests (see Cawson and Saunders, 1983).

Goldsmith and Wolman (1992: 15–16) conclude that although the model attracted a lot of interest in the 1980s (especially in European countries), it has a number of weaknesses. In particular:

- it is more appropriate to UK and Scandinavian circumstances than to the US;
- Saunders is wrong in assuming that the local level was not concerned with production issues and that corporatist modes of decision-making do not take place at the local level. ◆

Given the argument advanced by varieties of policy analysts that experts should have an important role in modern democracy (and by radicals such as Mills, who saw intellectuals in the forefront of challenging elite power), German and French critical thought has special relevance to contemporary policy analysis. As we noted earlier (2.7), the critiques developed by Foucault and Habermas posited that social (and other) sciences (*qua* tool or instrument of government) promote the growth of a politics dominated by technocrats and experts and which enable the state to exercise more control and discipline over society (Foucault, 1977, 1980) and to maintain its legitimacy in the face of continuing 'rationality crises' (Habermas, 1976). Habermas has also been a severe critic of a major model used in policy analysis, the 'systems' approach, and in particular its neo-pluralist reformulation by Luhmann (see Holub, 1991: 106–32). A number of students of policy analysis have endeavoured to take such criticisms into account in their reconstruction of a 'post-positivist' approach (see Fischer and Forester (eds), 1993; 3.9; and Dryzek, 3.10.5 below).

3.3.4 Corporatism

Corporatism is a term whose origins are to be found variously in the Middle Ages and in the fascist movements of the inter-war period which propounded a theory of society based on the incorporation of groups in the policy-making processes of the state as a mode of overcoming the conflicts of interest between labour and capital. As an analytical framework, however, so-called 'neo-corporatism' has been bedevilled – more than most concepts – by a failure to reach any consensus about what the term means when applied to liberal democratic societies. It became a very popular theory in the 1970s and 1980s as an explanatory model and, perhaps more significantly, as a rhetorical device employed by politicians and others. However, in the 1990s it has fared less well in the light of evidence which suggests that 'corporatist' decision-making has not been as widespread a phenomenon as its proponents originally argued and forecast. Cawson (1986) proposed a useful three-dimensional framework for understanding corporatist theory, and we shall examine some of the main approaches within this framework below.

Corporatism as a political system of interest mediation
See for example, Schmitter (1974); Schmitter and Lehmbruch (eds) (1979); Smith (1979); Middlemas (1979); Milward and Francisco (1983).

As an analytical model it may be dated back to the work of Schmitter (1974) and Lehmbruch (Lehmbruch and Schmitter, 1982), which argued that a pattern of government–business–labour interaction was developing in several European countries which was essentially corporatist in style and institutional arrangements. Corporatist forms of decision-making were different to the pluralism of the past in that the state sought to make decisions by managing the key groups and elites of which society was composed. Schmitter defined the difference between pluralism and corporatism in these terms:

> Pluralism can be defined as a system of interest representation in which the constituent units are organized in an unspecified number of multiple, voluntary, competitive, non-hierarchically ordered and self-determined ... categories which are not specially licensed, recognized, subsidized, created or otherwise controlled in leadership selection or interest articulation by the state, and which do not exercise a monopoly of representational activity within their respective categories ... corporatism (on the other hand) can be defined as a system of interest representation in which the constituent units are organized into a limited number of singular, compulsory, noncompetitive, hierachically ordered categories, recognized or licensed (if not created) by the state and granted a deliberate representational monopoly within their respective categories in exchange for observing certain controls on their selection of leaders, and articulation of demands and supports.
> (*Schmitter, 1974: 934–6*)

Wyn Grant offers another comprehensive definition of corporatism as a process which involves interest intermediation and negotiation:

> between the state agencies and interest organizations arising from the division of labour in society, where the policy agreements are implemented through the collaboration of the interest organizations and their willing-ness and ability to secure the compliance of their members.

It is these processes of negotiation and implementation which, he argues, are central to corporatist modes of policy-making:

> The arbitrary imposition of state policies through interest organizations, without any prior negotiations, does not constitute liberal corporatism ... equally, the negotiation of understanding, with no obligation on the part of interest organizations to secure the compliance of their members, does not constitute a corporatist arrangement.
> (*Grant, 1985: 3–4*)

Corporatism as an economic system
See for example, Winkler (1976); Pahl and Winkler (1974); Wolfe (1977).

This approach takes the position that corporatist arrangements exist when the state seeks to operate in the interests of capital by directing or controlling privately owned business. In order to manage economic crisis, the state will inevitably seek to develop a pattern of relations which can facilitate co-operation and reduce harmful conflict and com-petition. The corporate economy/polity would be the consummate product of this process.

Corporatism as a new form of state
See for example, Jessop (1990).

Here corporatism is viewed as that form of political arrangement which will work in the interests of capital. Parliamentary forms of politics are seen as giving way to a system of agencies in which 'functional' representation – of capital, labour and other organized interests – will replace adversarial conflict. Corporatism therefore be-comes a new form of state in a capitalist society in which the decision-making no longer takes place as a consequence of voting, legislative politics and bureaucratic rational – legal authority but through 'public corporations' in which legislative and bureaucratic power are fused.

These models saw corporatism emerging out of a decaying pluralist/capitalist system. In various ways decision-making was viewed as increasingly depoliticized and framed by bargaining and negotiation between the state and organized interests. For some (Shonfield, 1965) it offered a solution, for others, it was *the* problem (Olson, 1982; Smith,

1979). 'Successful' corporatism served as a model for those who wished to modernize policy-making (Shonfield, 1965; and see Smith, 1979, for a review of this position). However, against this view were those who argued that 'corporatism' was undermining the economic and political foundations of liberal democracy (Brittan, 1975, 1987; Smith, 1979; Olson, 1982). This was a favourite argument of the 'new right'. One of the most developed empirical analyses which employed 'corporatism' on a comparative basis was Mancur Olson's study of the 'rise and decline of nations'. Put simply, Olson argued that if you look at the successful nations in the post-war period – such as Germany and Japan – they had experienced a break with the past which reduced the power of entrenched interests. Alas, the victorious allies, Britain and America, had no such fortuitous discontinuity, with the result that they had experienced 'corporate sclerosis'. Britain in particular was held up as a model of a society stagnating because of the rise of the 'corporate state'. Proponents of 'corporatism', such as Andrew Shonfield, however, argued that British decline was due to the fact that it had failed to develop corporatist-style policy-making. Indeed, as he and later scholars subsequently pointed out, countries such as Japan and Germany experienced far less dislocation in their cosy inter-war relationships between business, industry and the state than is acknowleged by Olson (see Grant, 1989: 41; Wilson, 1985).

The contribution of the corporatist model to the analytical tool box has been most deeply undermined by the development of the 'policy-community' approach by Richardson and Jordan (1979) and others, which has provided a far more coherent framework for analysing new patterns of policy relationship in liberal democratic societies than have 'corporatist' theories. By the late 1980s corporatism as a model of public policy-making has proved somewhat anachronistic. As Wyn Grant explains:

> It is ... unfortunate that 'corporatism' is used rather loosely in the press as a term of abuse for past political failings; the academic participants in the debate must share some of the blame ... for failing to define the term more precisely. If there is a criticism which can be made of the corporatist debate it is that academic analysis responded too slowly to changes that were taking place in the relationship between the state and interest organizations ... By the time they had developed a conceptual apparatus to analyse the phenomenon, and had managed to organize large-scale research projects, the object of study was already dwindling in importance. The corporatist debate did, however, help to stimulate a new wave of theoretical and empirical work on pressure groups promoting a re-examination of pluralist theory, and thereby encouraging the development of new forms of pluralist analysis such as the idea of policy communities.
> (*Grant, 1989b: 35–6*)

As a model, therefore, 'corporatist' frameworks seem to be relevant to a limited number of countries – such as Sweden and Austria – and have increasingly been seen as having little to offer by way of an explanation of countries such as Britain and the US. As Martin Smith comments, it is an approach which only applies to 'specific and rare relationships' (Smith, 1993: 37). As a general framework for analysing decision-making and the policy processes in liberal democracy it is of doubtful value, since 'many large liberal democracies fit poorly with the imminent trend it identifies' (Dunleavy, 1991: 43). As G. Wilson (1990) argues, the problem with corporatism is that it is a relative, not an absolute phenomenon. Studies show that corporatist episodes and instances can indeed be found (see Smith, 1993: 32–7), but to apply the idea of a 'corporatist' state in general terms is not very helpful in understanding the diverse 'policy styles' which pertain in different countries, different policy areas, and at different times or at different levels. In respect of the latter – the so-called dual-state model – Cawson and Saunders, 1983, for example, argue that corporatist relations may develop at the level of the national state, but pluralism may continue to exist at the local state level. Apart from the 'consensual' democracies (see Elder, 1982) such as Scandinavia and Austria, the kinds of arrangements which theorists believed would emerge by the 1990s have clearly not developed (see Cox and O'Sullivan, 1988; Grant, 1990). Indeed, the opposite seems to have been the case in many OECD countries, where the shift towards a more market-orientated politics has been a far more significant feature of public policy-making than the predictions of the corporatists. However, as a 'normative' model, corporatism still has some life in it yet (see Streeck and Schmitter, 1985, 1991).

❖ A case for corporatism

Discussions about models of decision-making and policy delivery have largely been framed by three concepts:

- markets;
- hierarchy; and
- community.

Streeck and Schmitter (1985, 1991) argue that there is an alternative model of social order: 'associative' or 'interest governance'. This model recognizes the 'specific contribution of associations and organized concertation to social order' (1991: 228) which takes place in 'bargained' economies and societies. They argue that the associative model provides what Keynes in his essay on the end of *laissez-faire*, described as between the state and the individual. The associative model of social order is based upon the principle of interaction and allocation between organized interests which may be found in countries such as Austria, Norway, Swe-den, Switzerland and Germany (see, for example, Fitzmaurice, 1981, 1991; Elder *et al.*, 1982; Hancock, 1989). They explain their model of 'private interest' government in these terms:

> From the viewpoint of public policy, neo-corporatism amounts to an attempt to assign to interest associations a distinct role between the state and civil society (market and commu-nity) so as to put to public purposes the type of social order that associations can generate and embody. As an alternative to direct state intervention and regulation, the public use of organized interests takes the form of the establishment, under state licence and assistance, of 'private interest governments' with devolved public responsibilities – of agencies of 'regu-lated self-regulation' of social groups with special interests which are made subservient to general interests by appropriately designed institutions.
> (*Streeck and Schmitter, 1991: 235*)

Whereas market models of public policy seek to liberate individual self-interest, and 'commu-nity' models seek to mobilize 'collective other regarding interests', the corporatist 'associative' model aims to utilize 'collective self-interest' as the means for 'creating and maintaining a generally acceptable level of social order' (Streeck and Schmitter, 1991: 235). Private-interest government they see as being the attempt to make

> associative, self-interested collective action contribute to the achievement of public policy objectives. In generic terms, this is the case where it is in the interest of an organized group to strive for a 'categoric good' which is partially compatible or identical with a 'collective good' for the society as a whole ... We also maintain that the extent to which categoric and collective goods overlap depends, within limits, on two factors: on the way in which group interests are organized into associative structures and processes, and on a complex bar-gaining process between organized group interests and the state – that is, between the governments of private and public interests.
> (*Streeck and Schmitter, 1991: 236*)

They believe that such corporatist arrangements should not replace the community or the market; however, in some policy areas they see public policy through private government as a better way of making and implementing public policy and compensating for the 'dysfunctionalities' of community, market and bureaucratic approaches. The associative model will, they argue, lead to a new 'policy repertoire' for modern societies. In terms of policy style (see Richardson *et al.*, 1982; and 2.10.2) Streeck and Schmitter consider that a new 'style' is, and ought, to evolve in which policy decisions take place in a setting in which government endeavours to bargain and negotiate with an organized interest 'network' so as to develop more consensual policy-making processes. The models for this approach are the so-called 'democratic corporatist' political systems in Scandinavia, Austria and Germany. However, it is not so evident a trend within étatist (e.g. France, Italy) or 'pluralist' (e.g. UK, US, Canada) political systems where distinctive 'styles' have continued to persist and in which 'market' and 'hierarchical' modes of decision-making have predominated, rather than 'associative' private-interest government (see, for example, Hancock *et al.* (eds), 1991). ◆

A main feature of corporatist approaches to decision-making is the stress which is placed upon government bargaining and negotiating with interests. Research has shown that – as we have noted above – this has been far less frequent and significant a process than is suggested by corporatist models. Dunleavy (1981) has advanced a convincing account of why there can be an absence of bargaining and negotiation by positing the existence of an 'ideological corporatism' which does not have recourse to intermediation. He develops his theory in the context of the relationship between professionals and government, and argues that corporatism exists as a shared view of the world which leads to:

> The effective integration of different organizations and institutions ... by the acceptance or dominance of an effectively unified view of the world ... [thus the] active promotion of changes in ideas rests quite largely with individual professionals ... [and consequently] bargained or negotiated compromises will be relatively rare.
> (*Dunleavy, 1981: 8–9*)

This 'professionalization' of government and policy-making (see Dunleavy and O'Leary, 1987: 300–304) means that conflict and bargaining will be less evident and more internalized than is supposed by either neo-pluralist or corporatist approaches, at all levels or phases of policy-making: agenda-setting, decision-making and implementation:

> In the professionalized state the grassroots implementation of policy, and major shifts in the overall climate of debate in each issue area, are both influenced chiefly by individual occupational groups. Professional communities act as a key forum for developing and testing knowledge, setting standards, and policing the behaviour of individual policy makers and policy-implementers. Knowledge elites are crucial sources of innovations in public policy-making. They continuously produce a stream of specific inventions or techniques, as well as much broader models or conceptions of how policy ought to develop. In some cases these innovations may take long periods to work through input politics channels or to secure bureaucratic acceptance within government. But in areas where professions directly control service delivery the whole policy formulation process may be 'implementation skewed'.
> (*Dunleavy and O'Leary, 1987: 320–3*)

See also 4.3.2, on Lipsky.

Dunleavy's analysis of how a shared view can lead to a form of corporatism in an ideological sense draws our attention to those areas of public policy where professional expertise may well have a major role in shaping policy-making.

3.3.5 Professionalism

A vital concern in the literature of contemporary policy analysis has
been the extent to which professional elites have acquired power in
decision-making and in the implementation of public policy in liberal
democracies. The 'new right', in particular, railed against the way in
which the growth of big government had led to decision-making being determined by professional groups who were more interested in
their own gain and advantage than the public they served (see 3.5.1).
Pluralist models have tended to emphasize that professional power is
not as unified and is more fragmented than is supposed by an elitist
model of decision-making. 'Neo-elitists' have concentrated on the
power of occupational elites, as opposed to governmental elites and
shown how professional groups have a major role in the shaping of
implementation. (This theme of the ability of professionals to make or
break policy is an important theme in the literature on implementation: see 4.3.) Professionalism has been applied to those areas where
professional power (however defined) is to be found: health, education, and welfare services in particular.

❖ Professional power and public decisions

Ivan Illich, *Limits to Medicine*, 1977
Illich's writings have been immensely influential as a critique of professional power. This book,
and his other publications in the 1970s, marked a turning of the tide of opinion against
professionals, and none more so than in medicine where the god-like stature of the doctor
came under fire. Illich's controversial argument was that doctors are actually bad for you.
Medical bureaucracy created ill-health! This form of ill-health he termed 'social iatrogenesis'.
The control of the medical profession over health, and their claims to 'know' in a value-free way,
served their power at the cost of creating illness as a social condition.

R.R. Alford, *Health Care Politics*, 1975
Explaining health policy has been an important source of ideas on power. Marxist models would
maintain that it is a policy which is largely driven by the interests of capital and the dominant
class (Navarro, 1984), pluralists that it is the outcome of an interaction of a variety of interests
(Willcocks, 1967). Alford, however, in a study of health policy in New York, takes the view that it
has been shaped by the dominant structural interests within health service organizations. The
main influence on decision-making arises from the interaction of health professionals (doctors)
and corporate rationalizers (managers, planners, administrators). Decision-making in health
policy, he concludes, is dominated by doctors. (For support for this theory of doctor dominance
in Britain, see Mohan, 1990.)

Patrick Dunleavy, *Urban Political Analysis*, 1980
Dunleavy shows how urban professionals in local government have been able to resist pressures for wider participation in policy-making. Confronted with professional power, Dunleavy argues, citizens have not been able to influence decision-makers to open up the process to facilitate a more pluralistic relationship.

See also Dunleavy (1981); and Dunleavy and O'Leary (1987: 300–4 *et passim*). ◆

The power of professionals to shape decision-making processes in the interests of their particular group was a focal point in the critiques developed by both the 'left' (Illich, 1975, 1977b; Wilding, 1982; Dunleavy, 1980) and the 'right' (publications from the IEA, such as Green, 1985). As the containment and reduction of costs in those policy areas in which 'professionals' predominated – especially in the field of health – became a major issue in the 1980s, so professional power and autonomy was seen as a part of 'the problem' rather than of 'the solution' in many social and economic policy areas. As Harrop (ed.) (1992: 166–9) notes when reviewing the health policy community in the US, UK, France and Japan, the 1980s and 1990s have witnessed a noticeable shift in power away from the professionals to managers and administrators, both at the operational level and at the level of national decision-making. One of the most important innovations in this regard has been the introduction of 'market' reforms (quasi-markets, or market-type mechanisms) so as to improve the control over medical professionals and increase (supposedly) the managerial capacity and effectiveness of administrators (Degeling, 1993; Flynn, 1993; Propper, 1993). Smith (1993: 163–96) argues that this shift may be understood in terms of a changing health policy community which has arisen due to reforms in the national health service.

This assault on professional power has not been confined to the field of health. Other policy areas such as policing (Loveday, 1993; Day and Klein, 1987: 105–33); local government (Laffin and Young, 1990, and see 2.8.1); and education (Barnes and Williams, 1993) have also been the subject of reforms designed to reduce the impact that professionals have at both the operational and policy-making level and to subject them to greater managerial accountability (see Day and Klein, 1987; and 4.4.8). The attack on professional power has also extended to experts in general (see 3.3.5) and those such as planners, architects and economists, who could be held responsible for the failures and disasters which abounded in the aftermath of the social, economic and technological 'progress' heralded in the 1960s (see Perkin, 1989: 472–519). As Laffin and Young observe:

The notion of professionalism has survived from the nineteenth century into the late twentieth century. Will it survive, under the pressures for 'adaptation', into the twenty-first century? At first sight, it seems improbable. The old grandeur of the professions has been lost irretrievably. Professionals, in both the private and public sectors, no longer enjoy the social status and influence they once enjoyed. The loss of status and influence is even more marked in the case of professions associated with the welfare state. The professions no longer hold the initiative in policy formation and individual professions within the welfare state have experienced declining relative incomes and a diminution of their career prospects.
(*Laffin and Young, 1990: 107–8*)

Professionalism will, they think, persist in a much-adapted discourse in which professional knowledge, expertise and standing will have to be negotiated and argued for, rather than accepted as in the past. (In this connection, see the 'argumentative turn' theorists: Fischer and Forester, 1993; and 3.10.4.)

3.3.6   Technocracy

This model of decision-making views society as moving towards rule by scientific rationality. It is a well-explored idea in science fiction, and is an essential theme of philosophers such as Cournot, Saint Simon and Comte, and provides an underpinning to the theories of scientific management (Bell, 1976: 348–58). The argument that technicians would form the new ruling class is also to be found in the work of the economist Veblen. In the late 1950s Michael Young believed that this condition of the rise of technical knowledge would lead to a meritocratic system in which the most highly educated would form the main social elite (Young, 1958). This forecast of the year 2034 has not quite come to pass, but it is indicative of the strong belief which emerged in the post-war era that technology and science would re-shape the decision-making processes of democracy (see Smith, 1972: 57–70; Dahrendorf, 1959; Meynaud, 1968; Ellul, 1964).

As a social movement, 'technocracy' had its origins in the US before the First World War with the ideas of two engineers, F.W. Taylor (see 3.6.10) and Henry L. Gantt, and in the work of the economist Veblen. In the inter-war period, the campaign for a more rationally and scientifically administered society, inspired by the achievements and methods of engineering, was championed by Howard Scott and Walter Rautenstrauch. Their campaign reached its peak in the early 1930s, culminating in a national debate in the fall and summer of 1932–3. (Akin, 1977). In the midst of the depression the technocrats' arguments for the application of scientific and technological principles to social, political and economic organization expressed a faith in the potential of scientists and engineers to solve the problems which had so confounded politicians. If chaos were to be avoided, the technocrats believed that society had to be fundamentally reorganized so that problems could be dealt with in a scientific manner. As Akin (1977) notes, they failed not least because as a movement they did not address the conflict between technological elitism and democratic decision-making. This led to a rapid disillusionment with the movement once the implications of their ideas were explored in public debate. However, the analyses of the impact of technology on society were not lost. In 1941 James Burnham put forward the argument that, as Veblen and Scott had maintained, technocracy had indeed triumphed: experts had come to rule because they had come to know (Burnham, 1941). Technological development had brought about what Burnham termed a 'managerial revolution' in which power had shifted to the technical and managerial class. Later in the 1960s this thesis was to be up-dated in the work of J.K. Galbraith (see 3.5.2), another disciple of Veblen, with his argument that in the new industrial state real decision-making power was in the hands of the 'techno-structure'. Unlike orthodox economics, Galbraith argued that decision-making has to be understood in a group – not an individual – context. Within groups experts dominate decision-making:

> There will often be instances when an individual has the knowledge to make or change the finding of a group. But the broad rule holds: If a decision requires specialized knowledge of a group of men [sic], it is subject to safe review only by the similar knowledge of a similar group. Group decision, unless acted upon by another group tends to be absolute ... Effective power of decision is lodged deeply in the technical, planning and other specialized staff ... There is no name for all who participate in group decision-making or the organization which they form. I propose to call this organization the Technostructure.
> (*Galbraith, 1969: 75–80*)

For Jacques Ellul, the politician was (as Weber had forecast) now at the mercy of the expert as 'rationalization' gave way to 'technicization':

> There is generally only one logical and admissible solution. The politician will then find himself obliged to choose between the technicians' solution, which is the only reasonable one, and other solutions, which he can indeed try at his own peril but which are not reasonable ... In fact, the politician no longer has any real choice; decision follows automatically from preparatory technical labours ... every advance made in the techniques of enquiry, administration, and organization in itself reduces the power and the role of politics.
> (*Ellul, 1964: 258–9*)

Daniel Bell was also to deploy the technocratic case in his book *The End of Ideology* (1960). His thesis was that in societies in which the role of knowledge was dominant – the post-industrial society – decision-making would be influenced by those who possessed the technical knowledge vital to understanding the modern world. This is not to say that he thought that all ideological forms of decision-making would disappear, but that technocracy would predominate: 'in the society of the future, however one defines it, the scientist, the professional, the technician, and the technocrat will play a predominant role' (Bell, 1976: 79). This model of decision-making was fundamental to the notion that industrial societies – whatever their ideological frameworks – were set upon the road to convergence as the decision-making structures of East and West were being shaped by a common technocratic culture (Bell, 1976: 112–14). As Galbraith optimistically noted:

> the convergence between ... two ostensibly different industrial systems occurs at all fundamental points. This is an exceedingly fortunate thing. In time, and perhaps in less time than may be imagined, it will dispose of the notion of inevitable conflict based on irreconcilable difference.
> (*Galbraith, 1969: 392*)

❖ Technocracy and the science of rational war

The rational budget

Bell's model of technocratic decision-making had one major illustration: the rise of technocracy in the cold war:

> The McNamara 'revolution' of 1960–1965 transformed military logistics, and for this reason one can say that McNamara joins Saint-Simon and Frederick W. Taylor as a hierophant in the pantheon of technocracy.
> (*Bell, 1976: 357*)

Bell explains how, under McNamara, the Department of Defense was revolutionized by the introduction of rational structures of programme budgeting: PPBS (see 3.8.6). This introduction of logical functional budgeting and cost-benefit analysis was appropriate to the defence sector, where there was a large measure of agreement. But as Bell noted in other policy areas such as social policy or welfare policy, the limits of technocracy may be reached. However, it was in the military domain where the influence of technocracy was, he believed, most significant:

> Matters of foreign policy have not been a reflex of internal political forces, but a judgement about the national interest, involving, strategy decisions based on the calculation of an opponent's strengths and intentions. Once the fundamental policy decision was made to oppose the communist power, many technical decisions, based on military technology and strategic assessments, took on the highest importance in the shaping of subsequent policy.
> (*Ibid.: 364*)

War as a rational game

The technocratic mentality which Bell considers that McNamara represented in its modern incarnation was a product of a unique phase of twentieth-century history: the cold war.

The influence of the technocrat in decision-making may be dated to the commencement of the cold war in the late 1950s. After the Second World War it was decided that the talents of all the various researchers and strategists should be harnessed for the peace. In 1948 the US Air Force funded the private RAND (Research and Development) Corporation – known as the 'mother' of all think-tanks. RAND brought together mathematicians, political scientists, systems analysts, engineers, sociologists and others to develop models of how the strategy of war could be developed in the conditions of the nuclear age.

The model-builders, greatly influenced by the 'game theories' of Neuman, sought to show how, in such conditions, war would be fought as a rational game, rather than as all-out Armageddon. Out of this notion emerged the system of 'failsafe' – associated with Albert Wahlstetter – in which 24-hour vigilance would provide a rational deterrent against the Soviets, who, as they had their own war-gamesters, had systems of decision-making that were coming to resemble those of the US (convergence).

When President Kennedy was elected, he appointed Robert McNamara as Secretary of Defense (1961–8). McNamara was a leading industrial manager from the Ford Motor Corporation, who had been instrumental in the introduction of systems analysis. The Kennedy era was to see an influx of what were known as technocrats and 'Wizz kids' from RAND. The apotheosis of the rational war theory was not long in coming. The Cuban missile crisis (1962) demonstrated that the rational war was not such a logical option. However, the influence of RAND personnel in the Kennedy and, later, Johnson presidencies was evident in other areas of policy in which the application of scientific methods was seen as the way in which problems could be solved. The influence of RAND (and the Hudson Institute formed by ex-RANDer Herman Kahn) was at its most evident in the conduct of the Vietnam war. Robert McNamara resigned in 1968. The idea of the rational solving of social problems may have been abandoned in the wake of the failure of the 'Great Society' programme, but the influence of the archetypical twentieth-century technocrat, McNamara, was to be more long lived in the problems of war and peace.

On the history of RAND, see Williams and Palmatier (1992); see also 2.8.2. ◆

The classic pluralist position on experts is that they should be 'on tap' not 'on top'. However, this idea that the technocrat is merely 'on tap' to political decision makers has been widely regarded as simplistic by both radical and conservative critics of expert power (see Smith, 1972). For radicals, the rise of technocrats in the decision-making process signified the development of a new power elite allied with the forces of capitalism and the military-industrial complex (Gouldner, 1970; Chomsky, 1971). However, as Fischer (1991) has noted, this anxiety about decision-making being dominated by technocrats and technocratic frameworks and discourse was not confined to the left. In the

1970s and 1980s the so-called 'new right' became equally concerned about the impact of technocracy on decision-making and the threat it posed to liberal democratic policy-making. For American neo-conservatives, as Fischer argues, the 'Great Society' programme served as a paradigm of technocratic rule. In Part Two we considered how this threat of rule by liberal/reforming experts led to the establishment of think-tanks to advocate and campaign for a return to free-market principles of government. The notion that decision-making was increasingly framed by technical and expert opinion, and that decision-making in the modern state involved the analysis of 'problem' and the implementation of 'solutions', was most famously expressed in the words of President Kennedy at Yale in 1962:

> The fact of the matter is that most of the problems ... that we now face are technical problems, are administrative problems. They are very sophisticated judgements which do not lend themselves to the great sort of passionate movements which stirred this country so often in the past. Now they deal with questions which are beyond the comprehension of most men, most governmental administrators, over which experts may differ, and yet we operate through our traditional political system.
> (*Quoted in Fischer, 1991: 336*)

The 'traditional political system' was, from the radical and conservative perspective, in grave danger from this belief that the questions now being faced by decision-makers were 'beyond the comprehension of most men'. However, as Massey (1988, see box below) notes in the case of nuclear power – a highly technical area indeed – the actual impact of 'technocrats' on decision-making has proved to be somewhat less significant than scientists hoped or 'dys-Utopians', anxious about the dawn of a brave new world (see Gendron, 1977), feared. Indeed, the common complaint amongst erstwhile technocrats is that politicians do not pay them much heed (see, for example, Brown and Lyon, 1992; Tournon, 1992; Mills, 1993). And, notwithstanding the apparent influence of economics, economists would argue that policy decisions all too often ignore 'expert' views (Singer, 1993; Coats, 1981, 1989; Stein, 1981, 1984; Stockman, 1987). As Henderson argues, 'do-it-yourself' economics seems to predominate in decision-making, rather than expert 'technical' advice (Henderson, 1986). Politics, it seems, has been far more resistant to the onslaught on technocracy than commentators in the 1960s and 1970s believed would be the case (see Jenkins-Smith, 1990; and 3.8).

❖ **Andrew Massey, *Technocrats and Nuclear Politics*, 1988**

The power of technical professionals/experts – or technocrats – in technological and scientific areas has long been recognized. In his study of British nuclear power policy, Massey examines the influence of nuclear scientists in the policy process. He shows how the pattern of influence is more complex than simply one of nuclear scientists shaping the formation of policy by dint of their expert knowledge. Their influence resides more in their ability to mediate the requirements of politicians and civil servants with the technical options which are available. The definition of the options and issues was not purely down to expert knowledge:

> In post-war Britain the rise of the welfare state has seen the rise of professional power. It is probably no accident that the increase in the politicization of technical issues mirrors a demise in post-war corporate consensus. This leads to a consideration of the role of politics within the nuclear policy-system, a role that defines and structures professional power ... It is clear that technocrats have indeed influenced nuclear policy and will continue to do so, on terms laid down by the policy arbiters: and this is the nub of nuclear politics. (pp. 187, 190)

Massey's conclusion is therefore one which emphasizes that professional experts inhabit a political environment and an institutional context which structures their expertise in terms that are set by the state and the market. In Britain, as in other countries, the key decisions about nuclear power were made by politicians and businessmen rather than by scientists. ◆

❖ Using theories and models for analysis

S. Harrison, D.J. Hunter and C. Pollitt, *The Dynamics of British Health Policy*, 1990

As is the case in many countries, health policy in Britain has undergone a good deal of change in the last decade. In this book the authors examine the forces which have shaped British policy by clearly setting out a number of models. The authors take the following six frameworks:

- *Rational comprehensiveness*: have decisions been shaped by a rational process?
- *Incrementalism*: have decisions been shaped by 'muddling through'?
- *Neo-pluralism*: has policy been the result of group pressures and policy networks?
- *Public choice*: can we explain the changes in the health service in terms of economic models?
- *Neo-elitism*: can we explain the developments in policy in terms of the impact of a few key groups and the health professions?
- *Neo-Marxism*: how does neo-Marxist theory with its focus on the role of the state in modern capitalism explain the development of health policy?

They conclude that the best explanation of the dynamics of health policy is that of a combination of neo-elite and neo-Marxist models. The ideological shifts in the early 1980s were, they argue, the result of economic factors which led to a modification in the structure of key elites. However, they point out that the policy cannot be adequately explained by any single model. This conclusion is in line with the analysis of others in the field who have pointed out that health policy cannot be explained by one theory (see Klein, 1974: 219–20).

Debra W. Stewart, 'Women in public administration', in Lynn and Wildavsky (eds), 1990

In this paper the author examines the role of women in public administration by using three theoretical frameworks: a 'political paradigm', a 'psychological paradigm', and a 'sociological paradigm'. A political framework focuses on the relationship of participation in the political and decisional processes, the impact of the women's movement, the enactments of public policy and the entry of women into elite roles. The psychological approach focuses on the characteristics of individuals: the sex-role stereotyping, pattern of behaviour and relationships, and the importance of self-esteem and how behaviour may be modified. The sociological model is focused on the way in which organizations are structured, and the distribution of power within organizations. Each lens has a different set of strategies for improving the status of women in public life.

Andrew Bowers, *Something in the Air: Corporate Power and the Environment*, 1984

Bowers's study of environmental pollution compares and contrasts two models used in the analysis of environmental decision-making: the pluralist view and the political economy/Marxist view. In an examination of the role of corporate power as exercised by the London Brick Company (LBC), he argues that analysis has to take account of the spatial and temporal aspects of decisions. In some cases, in some places and at some times, the LBC was indeed able to exercise the kind of dominance of business interests over other interests, as the Marxist model argues. However, when economic conditions and location are such that business interests are weaker, the balance of power can well shift so that the decision process resembles the theory put forward by pluralists. In other words, in explaining the power of the LBC both models tell plausible stories and provide insights into corporate decision-making power. He suggests that as models they may be best deployed to analyse the different stages of the particular case studies, rather than as overarching theories of power. ◆

3.4   Rationality and decision-making

3.4.1   Rationality: the sociological and economic context

The rational approach to decision-making has two contexts or sources:

- the idea of economic rationality as it developed in economic theory;
- the idea of bureaucratic rationality as formulated by sociological theories of organization and industrial society.

The literature in the field has, as a consequence, been dominated by economists interested in organizations and sociologists interested in economics. A number of contributors have been pre-eminent in the study of rationality in public policy. They include Simon, Lindblom, March, Olsen, Cyert and Cohen. We shall explore their ideas in the following sections.

However, in order to understand their theories it is necessary to adumbrate the theoretical background to their work. To begin with, rationality as it has been used in public policy has its roots in the construction of 'economic man'. This holds that *Homo economicus* may be conceptualized in terms of a calculating self-interested individual. In making decisions economic man derives his choice from the acquisition of all the information necessary, comparing the information on different options, and then selecting that option which will enable him to achieve his goals and interests. Upon this foundation the edifice which is modern economics was to be built. As we shall see, rationality approaches take issue with this idea of economic rationality, and argue that individual decision-making in practice does not conform to the model or ideal.

The second context out of which the rational approach has emerged is the study of organizations. Rationality was established as a major theme in the analysis of decision-making largely as a result of the influence of the German sociologist, Max Weber (1864–1920). Whereas Marx was to see capitalism as essentially irrational and history as a story of conflict, Weber's analysis offered a model of capitalism as a high form of rationality, and in which history displayed a process of rationalization and bureaucratic 'disenchantment'. The main effect of capitalism was, he believed, its capacity to disseminate the pursuit of the kind of instrumental rationality which was manifested in machines. In industrial society the organizational analogue of the machine was bureaucracy. Industrial society had undermined 'traditional' and 'charismatic' forms of authority and had brought what Weber described as 'rational-legal' authority as the most efficient form of rule.

The basis of traditional authority is that of the idea of natural or God-given power. It is the kind of authority that is acknowledged to be legitimate because of history and succession. Charismatic authority is the authority enjoyed because of special gifts that are unique and attractive. Both of these forms of authority are less stable and much weaker than rational-legal forms. Legal-rational authority is that which derives from law, consent and rules and is 'technically superior'. It was this form of authority which was pre-eminent in capitalist society, and was the main reason for the advance of bureaucratic organization. Weber argued that the dominant trend of industrialized societies was towards authority legitimizing itself in terms of the legal-rational model. As we have seen in Part One, the fact that policy-making and policies frame political discourse of modern societies is symptomatic of the fact that, from Weber's perspective, our forms of politics have become more dominated by the legal-rational type. The best organizational form of the legal-rational society, Weber argues, is bureaucracy. Weber constructs an 'ideal-type', or model, of bureaucracy which has the following characteristics:

- specialization;
- hierarchy;
- rules;
- impersonality;
- appointed officials;
- full-time officials;
- career officials;
- the separation of public and private.

These characteristics of bureaucracy mean that it carries with it certain dangers to political authority:

> Under normal conditions, the power position of a fully developed bureaucracy is always overtowering. The 'political master' finds himself in the position of the 'dilettante' who stands opposite the 'experts', facing the trained official who stands within the management or administration. This holds whether the 'master' whom the bureaucracy serves is a 'people' ... or a parliament, ... a popularly elected president, a hereditary and 'absolute' or 'constitutional' monarch.
> (*Weber, 1991: 232*)

The idea of rationality has been central to the theory and practice of decision-making in the post-war era. Models of decision-making which focus on rationality argue that, if we wish to understand the real world of decision, we must consider the extent to which a decision has been the outcome of rational processes. The Weberian model of the rational imperative in decision-making constitutes the starting point for the analysis of rationality in public policy. A core preoccupation of this literature has been to criticize the 'ideal type' in terms of the empirical reality of decision-making, which departs substantially from Weber's model, and the limitations and boundaries of rationality in human decision-making.

3.4.2   Simon: bounded rationality

Herbert Simon's work is central to the analysis of rationality in decision-making. Sadly, as a writer it is often the case that he tends to be studied through quotations from his work, rather than through a study of them. This is, however, a very inadequate approach to someone who has had – and continues to have – such a wide impact on the social sciences. In this section, therefore, we shall outline some of the main features of his theory, but also suggest a reading strategy which

could be followed to examine his various books and articles. By setting his ideas in a developmental context we must thus avoid the
tendency to locate his work within the narrow and somewhat artificial
framework of the so-called 'rationalist-incrementalist' debate (see below, 3.4.3).

As with several other 'founding fathers' of the policy approach – such
as Lasswell – Simon is operating at a number of levels and crosses
several disciplinary boundaries. He was born in 1916 and educated at
Chicago University, took a PhD in political science, and has made
signal contributions to organizational sociology, public administration, economics, psychology, computer science as well as political science (to name but a few fields). He was awarded the Nobel Prize for
Economics in 1978. However, running through all of his work is one
dominant concern: decision-making in organizations. In this book we
shall examine Simon's contribution to the study of decision-making
by taking the following route:

- his early study of 'administrative behaviour' (1945);
- how the economic aspect of administrative behaviour was developed in subsequent work;
- how the psychological aspect of administrative behaviour was developed in subsequent work;
- how his analytical framework relates to his prescriptions or solutions.

In this section we shall focus on two aspects: the analytical framework
developed in his study of administrative behaviour and his later 'prescriptive' framework for the study of decision-making as manage-

Figure 3.1   Simon's analysis and prescription

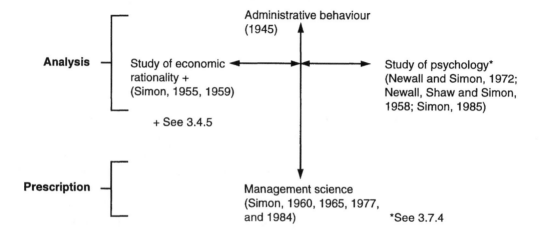

ment (figure 3.1). It is obviously the case that the analytical and normative aspects of his work interact and overlap. However, the failure
to distinguish between these has given rise to confusion (see, for
example, Smith and May, 1980). Thus although we must bear in mind
the relationship between facts and values, and analysis or diagnosis
and prescription, in order to clarify Simon's ideas it is vital that we
deploy this distinction. Again, although it is necessary to realize the
connections between the different aspects of Simon's work, for the
purposes of analysis we shall consider them in reasonably distinct
contexts. Hence, we shall examine his contribution to economic analysis in 3.4.5 and psychology in 3.7.4.

In terms of a reading strategy, therefore, the recommended approach
is to begin with *Administrative Behaviour* (1945); thence to the psychological work (e.g. Newall and Simon, 1972); followed by his 1955 and
1959 articles on economic rationality and his book with March (March
and Simon, 1958). After reading this material, round off by reading his
prescriptive ideas on management (Simon, 1960, 1965). In general
terms, read Simon's lectures on rationality in human affairs (Simon,
1983) and his paper on human nature in politics (Simon, 1985).

Administrative Behaviour

Simon's concern in his seminal book *Administrative Behaviour* is to
explain organizations in real, rather than ideal, terms. At the centre of
this is the issue of rationality. Simon argues that the problem with
social science is that, when it comes to rationality, it seems to suffer
from an 'acute case of schizophrenia':

> At the one extreme we have the economists who attribute to economic
> man a preposterously omniscient rationality ... At the other extreme, we
> have those tendencies in social psychology traceable to Freud that try to
> reduce all cognition to affect ... The past generation of behavioral scien-
> tists has been busy, following Freud, showing that people aren't nearly as
> rational as they thought themselves to be.
> (*Simon, 1957: xxiii*)

Thus, on the one hand, social science was dominated by a model of
decision-making in which, according to economists, human beings
have a set of preferences from which *Homo economicus* can select alternatives; he has perfect knowledge; no limits on his capacity to acquire
and process this knowledge; and from which he can select the best
alternative. Economic man is driven by reason and rational calculation. On the other hand, Freud, Pareto and Lasswell portray human
behaviour as driven by passions, instincts and subconscious feelings
and anxieties. Simon takes issue with this polarization and in *Administrative Behaviour* he sets out to show how human decision-making in

Figure 3.2   Simon's bounded rationality model

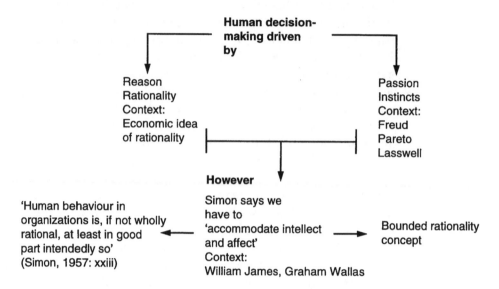

organizations is to be understood as occupying a kind of middle ground between these two extremes. Analysis should aim to 'accommodate both intellect and affect' (Simon, 1957: 200). He seeks to show how human behaviour, although not rational in the economist's sense, is 'in good part intentionally so'. The concept which he develops to explain a rationality which is limited but not 'irrational' is 'bounded rationality' (see figure 3.2).

Simon believes that we have to understand the way in which the analysis of decision-making has been framed by these rival approaches: the one promoted by economists predicated on a totally unrealistic 'ideal-type' model, and the other on a Freudian view of the human condition. Simon argues that these models do not really help us to understand the actuality of decision-making. In the case of the psychological model, Simon argues that we may trace this back to the difference between Graham Wallas and Freud on the interplay of reason and irrationality in politics. As Simon explains more fully in his paper on human nature in politics (1985), Lasswell's main influence was Freud, whereas Wallas drew his inspiration from William James:

> Although Lasswell was concerned with borderline and not-so-borderline pathology, Wallas was interested in the ubiquitous workings of instinct, ignorance, and emotion in normal behaviour ... I think that there is plenty of evidence that people are generally rational; that is to say, they usually have reasons for what they do. Even in madness, there is almost always a method as Freud was at great pains to point out. And putting madness

aside for a moment, almost all human behaviour consists of goal orientated actions.
(*Simon, 1985: 295, 297*)

Simon himself is far more attuned to the concerns of James and Wallas in that he is interested in 'normal' behaviour such as that which takes place in organizations, rather than pathological or disturbed behaviour. In his *Administrative Behaviour* he explores behaviour in terms of manifested patterns of human cognition. Later on he was to develop this in cognitive psychological research (see 3.7.4). What economists or Freudians might term 'irrationality' is not, from Simon's point of view a satisfactory explanation of the way in which rationality is limited, or bounded.

In chapter 5 of *Administrative Behaviour* Simon lays out a clear early formulation of this position:

> It is impossible for the behaviour of a single, isolated individual to reach any high degree of rationality. The number of alternatives he must explore is so great, the information he would need to evaluate them so vast that even an approximation to objective rationality is hard to conceive. Individual choice takes place in an environment of 'givens' – premises that are accepted by the subject as bases for his choice; and behaviour is adaptive only within the limits set by these 'givens'.
> (*Simon, 1957: 79*)

Human rationality is limited, therefore, in terms of:

- the incomplete and fragmented nature of knowledge;
- consequences that cannot be known, so that the decision-maker relies on a capacity to make valuations;
- limits of attention: problems must be dealt with on a serial, one-at-a-time basis, since decision-makers cannot think about too many issues at the same time; attention shifts from one value to another;
- human beings learning through adjusting their behaviour in line with purposive goals; the powers of observation and communication limit this learning process;
- limits on the storage (memory) capacity of the human mind: it can only think of a few things at a time;
- human beings as creatures of habit and routine;
- human beings with limited attention spans;
- human beings as limited by their psychological environments;
- initiated behaviour and attention that will tend to persist in a given direction for a considerable period of time;
- decision-making as also bounded by an organizational environment which frames the processes of choice. (Simon, 1957: 81–109)

As he expresses it in *Models of Man* published in 1957, the same year as the second edition of *Administrative Behaviour*:

> The capacity of the human mind for formulating and solving complex problems is very small compared with the size of the problems whose solution is required for objectively rational behaviour in the real world – or even for a reasonable approximation to such objective rationality. (*Simon, 1957a: 198*)

Given these limitations, therefore, how can decision-making be 'rational'? Simon argues that rationality is essentially procedural, that is to say, it may be viewed as selecting goals and courses of action which will best achieve the values or purposes. An individual may be said to be behaving rationally if his or her behaviour is purposive or directed at realizing the goals of expressed values. An organization may be held to be rational if it is concerned with attaining or maximizing its values in a given situation (Simon, 1957: 76). In the second edition of *Administrative Behaviour* he argues that in the intervening years he gave the issue of limits to rational decision-making more thought. These amendments were developed in papers dealing with a behavioural theory of rational choice and the psychological environment (see Simon, 1957: 241–73). Simon argues that in order to clarify what he means by rationality in organizational decision-making we have to use two models: economic man and administrative man:

> While economic man maximizes – selects the best alternative from among all those available to him; his cousin, whom we shall call administrative man, satisfices – looks for a course of action that is satisfactory or 'good enough'. Examples of satisficing criteria that are familiar enough to businessmen, if unfamiliar to most economists, are 'share of market', 'adequate profit', 'fair price'.
>
> Economic man deals with the 'real world' in all its complexity. Administrative man recognizes that the world he perceives is a drastically simplified model of the buzzing, blooming confusion that constitutes the real world. He is content with this gross simplification because he believes that the real world is mostly empty – that most of the facts of the real world have no great relevance to any particular situation he is facing, and that most significant chains of causes and consequences are short and simple. Hence, he is content to leave out of account those aspects of reality – and that means most aspects – that are substantially irrelevant at a given time. He makes his choices using a simple picture of the situation that takes into account just a few of the factors that he regards as most relevant and crucial. (*Simon, 1957: xxv*)

Thus, Simon characterizes decision-making by 'administrative man' as operating in a world of bounded rationality and as motivated by satisficing, rather than maximizing: this means that he makes decisions which are not derived from an examination of all the alternatives. And furthermore, because he sees the world as 'empty' and ignores the interrelatedness of things – complexity – he can make decisions which do not exceed his limited cognitive capacities. This idea of administrative man Simon believes may be confirmed by 'common sense': it fits the picture we have of how decision-making takes place in the real world and in our own experience. But he also argues that it is a model which can be supported by research which he has conducted into computers.

The problem as Simon describes it is one of understanding the limitations on rationality that operate in organizations. Above all it is not possible for a decision-maker to analyse all the information and options when considering a problem. Information and options may be excluded because they conflict with other more central or deep-seated attitudes, values, interests and goals. Is it really possible for decision-makers to make a calculation with regard to the outcomes of policies? In the real world of decision-making actors do not confront organizations devoid of values, prejudices, culture, history and experience. So, for Simon, rational decision-making has to be understood in terms of the organizational and psychological context within which decisions are taken. As decision-makers cannot know the outcome of decisions, and as there is no way of comparing the utility of various outcomes, there cannot be therefore in practice a straightforward relationship between the outcomes of a decision and the means which are used to achieve the goal. A decision-making process is concerned with a satisfactory outcome, as opposed to an outcome which is the maximum or optimal result. Outcomes are unknown things, so at best actors set out to pursue choices which are susceptible of a broad measure of attainment. In other words, they are concerned with what is essentially a compromise of values and goals: satisficing.

Simon sets out two tasks in decision analysis: theory and practice. At a theoretical level, analysis involves the study of the limits of human rationality in organizational contexts; whilst in practical terms it involves designing the organizational environment so that 'the individual will approach as close as practicable to rationality (judged in terms of the organization's goals) in his decisions' (Simon, 1957: 241):

> a practical science of administration consists of propositions as to how men would behave if they wished their activity to result in the greatest attainment of administrative objectivity with scarce means.
> (*Simon, 1957: 253*)

Simon and the science of management decision

In *Administrative Behaviour* Simon prefaces his observations with the comment that 'it is an attempt to construct tools', since:

> we do not yet have ... adequate linguistic and conceptual tools for realistically and significantly describing even a simple administrative organization – describing it, that is, in a way that will provide the basis for scientific analysis of the effectiveness of its structure and operation.
> (*Simon, 1957: xlv*)

He did not feel, therefore, that he had much to say by way of improving the 'effectiveness' of organizations. However, within a few years of writing these words Simon was of the opinion that the tools had advanced such as to make a 'new science of management decision' possible.

In his 1960 book, *The New Science of Management Decision*, Simon considers how decision-making might be improved in the light of new techniques and technology. He suggests that decision-making could be improved by increasing the scope of programmed, as opposed to non-programmed, decisions. Decision-making may be viewed on a continuum on which programmed decisions are placed at one end and 'non-programmed' decisions at the other (figure 3.3).

Simon argues that although organizations do not work as rationally as they might, the use of technology, training and management techniques, operations research and systems analysis could improve the situation. Rationality should, could and can be a goal in decision-making. Simon is often set up as an exponent of an optimistic rational

Figure 3.3   Programmed and non-programmed decision-making

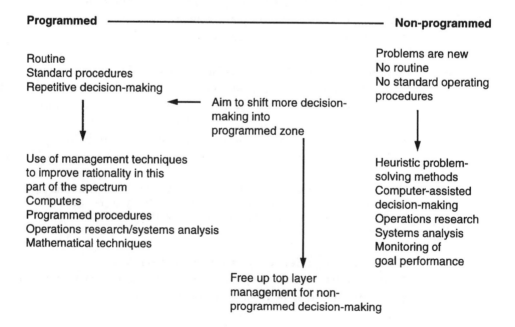

approach to human affairs. Undoubtedly, Simon's work does enthusi-astically advocate the use of rational techniques and computers in order to solve problems. However, as he notes in a series of lectures at Stanford, by 1983 this is tempered with a realism. Self-interest is, he argues, a powerful human motivator and reason can only be a media-tor and an enlightener of interests – it cannot solve conflicts (Simon, 1983: 105).

❖ A case for rationality

Psychologist Stuart Sutherland sets out to make the case for rationality in the light of all the research and evidence which is available in the 1990s (Sutherland, 1994). Irrationality, he argues, is a major fact of public and private decision-making and its results can be disastrous. Irrationality has a number of causes, including not taking enough time to think; the limitations of the capacity of the human brain to hold a large number of ideas and handle complexity; our failure to make use of 'tools' for rational thought; the way in which human beings distort reality to fit in with what they are comfortable with; and the structure of organizations. Sutherland, like Simon, believes that we should not despair. There are things that we can do to defeat 'the enemy within' (*sic*). He puts forward a package of 'morals' for improving the rationality of decision-making. Amongst them are:

- Don't make decisions on the basis of a single case.
- Think about decisions before implementing them or before obeying an order.
- In group decisions make sure counter-arguments are expressed.
- Managers should adopt a participatory and egalitarian style.
- Search for evidence which contradicts the conventional or accepted wisdom.
- Learn elementary statistics. ◆

Thus Simon is certainly a believer in rationality in decision-making, but he has modified his views over the years. In his 1983 lectures he argued that the limitations on individual rationality set the bounda-ries for the way in which institutions work and how they may be designed. The limits of institutional rationality are framed by the attention span of human beings, the existence of multiple values and the large measure of uncertainty which is confronted by decision-makers. However, although he concedes the real problems with rationality (as does Sutherland, above), Simon ultimately believes that we can do something about it. Some arrangements are 'better' than others for attaining a more rational decision-making process. Amongst them he lists:

- *specialist groups and organizations* which can deal with routine and repetitive decisions;

- *markets*: Simon argues (*à la* Hayek) that market mechanisms provide a way of restricting how much information we need to operate and reach 'tolerable', if not 'optimal', arrangements. However, he notes that markets do involve externalities and consequently 'can only be used in conjunction with other methods of social control and decision-making; they do not provide an independent mechanism for social choice' (Simon, 1983: 89);

- *adversary proceedings*: judicial or legal methods of procedural fairness, rather than evaluating outcomes, Simon suggests, is a very important method of improving the rationality of decision-making:

  > Adversary proceedings are like markets in reducing the information that participants must have in order to behave rationally. Thus they provide a highly useful mechanism for systems in which information is distributed widely and in which different system components have different goals. Each participant in an adversary proceeding is supposed to understand thoroughly his own interests and the factual considerations relating to them. He need not understand the interests or situations of the other participants. Each pleads his own cause, and in doing so, contributes to the general pool of knowledge and understanding.
  > (*Simon, 1983: 90*)

- *technical tools for decision*: Simon is a great advocate of computers and techniques developed in management science and operations research as aids to strengthening the rationality of decision-making. He concedes that there are problems in quantifying what may not be quantified, but none the less he has faith in the potential of management, mathematics and artificial intelligence:

  > If we do find solutions (as I think we shall) for the difficult problems of environment and energy – solutions, that is, that handle both sets of problems simultaneously – it will be because we are able to model the main interactions among the facets of these problems, and hence to think clearly about tradeoffs.
  > (*Simon, 1983: 92*)

- *the public information base*: although improvements in the level of public information is a key component in a more rational decision-making process, Simon has doubts about its real impact due to the distorting effects of the mass media on the one hand, and the role of experts on the other:

  > When an issue becomes highly controversial – when it is surrounded by uncertainties and conflicting values – then expertise is very hard to come by, and it is no longer easy to legitimate the experts. In these circumstances, we find that there are experts for the affirmative and experts for the negative. We cannot settle such issues by turning them over to particular groups of experts. At best we may convert the contro-

versy into an adversary proceeding in which we, the laymen, listen to the experts but have to judge between them.
(*Simon, 1983: 197*)

- *knowledge of political institutions*: Simon regards institutions as capable of changing human behaviour, but he has no prescription for how institutions may be changed, apart from better political education. Even then he is doubtful as to the prospects of a better-educated citizenry;
- *knowledge as the answer to a more rational decision-making process*: Simon is often characterized as someone who has an unbounded faith in human progress through knowledge. But this is not the case: Simon is all too aware of the limitations of knowledge as facilitating more rational problem-solving in a complex and uncertain world:

> the vigorous pursuit of research and development in the natural and the social sciences can give us important help in those areas of decision where knowledge is a prime limiting factor. But scientific knowledge is not the Philosopher's Stone that is going to solve these problems.
> (*Simon, 1983: 105*)

Reason, he argues is simply an instrument, it cannot help in selecting goals, so much as 'help us to reach agreed-upon goals more effectively' (Simon, 1983: 106). Here the contrast between Simon and Lasswell is most telling. Whereas Simon really believes that 'the new science of management' and technology can enable us to 'get better' (ibid.), Lasswell, who adopted a psychoanalytical rather than a cognitive framework, views the policy sciences as offering the prospect of greater 'freedom', rather than 'rationality':

> It is insufficiently acknowledged that the role of scientific work in human relations is freedom rather than prediction. By freedom is meant the bringing into the focus of awareness of some feature of the personality which has hitherto operated as a determining factor upon the choices made by the individual, but which has been operating unconsciously. Once elevated to the full waking consciousness, the factor which has been operating 'automatically and compulsively' is no longer in this privileged position. The individual is now free to take the factor into consideration in the making of future choices.
> (*Lasswell, 1951a: 524*)

In this respect the differences between Simon and Lasswell with regard to their cognitive and psychoanalytical orientations point towards a very clear parting of the ways. Simon's work (notwithstanding his 1983 lectures) leads inexorably to the 'management' approach to public policy, whereas Lasswell's directs us (ultimately) to a more critical form of policy analysis (see Torgerson, 1985). As Dror (1979) points out, although 'management sciences' and the 'policy sciences' are closely related, it is important that we keep in mind that they are different in respect of their values and goals and their applicability to 'programmed' or routine decisions and to 'non-programmed' or highly complex areas of decision-making (see Dror, 3.4.4). Thus although in his later work Simon waters down the technocratic spirit – that is so evident in remarks made in *Administrative Behaviour* (cited above) and in a full-blown form in his prescription for a new science of management in which computers could help us to be more rational (1960, 1965) – it is still the case that Simon does articulate an analytical and normative framework which remains central to the concerns of contemporary 'goal'- and 'objective'-setting managerialists (see Bourn, 1974; Pollitt, 1990).

3.4.3   Lindblom: Decision-making as muddling through

One of the most notable responses to the rational approach was advanced by Charles Lindblom in a series of major contributions to public policy published in 1959, 1963, 1965 and 1979. In addition, his position has been further refined in other articles and books, most notably *Politics and Markets* (1977) and in editions of his textbook *The Policy-making Process* (1968, 1980, 1993).

In his paper 'The science of muddling through' (1959), which set out his initial objections to the notion of decision-making as a 'rational' process, he has two main targets. The first is the idea of rationality, which was also the focus of Simon's analysis; and the second are prescriptions to improve the rationality of decision-making. As far as the analysis of rationality is concerned, Lindblom has much in common with Simon. However, where he departs from Simon's position is in respect of the belief that decision-making can or ought to be improved in the kinds of way which Simon's managerialism (or Lasswell's policy science approach) suggests.

In the 1959 article Lindblom seeks to criticize both the notion of rational decision-making, and also of rational analysis. It is apparent that, by the end of the piece, he has thrown the baby out with the bathwater. For, as later works show, Lindblom is not against analysis as such, but is hostile to the ideology that rational analytical techniques could in someway supplant the need for political agreement and consensus. 'Muddling through', he argues, is a method or 'science' which advocates of policy analysis ignore. For the rationalists, decision-making ought to conform to some neat set of steps in which improvements are possible by virtue of the growth in knowledge and technology. In this representation decision-making was essentially something which was about defining goals, selecting alternatives and comparing options. A good decision was one which meets the objectives. Simon's arguments had provided a manifesto for this belief in the essential improvability of decision-making. Lindblom's aim was

Table 3.1   *Lindblom's two models of decision-making*

Rational comprehensive (root)		Successive limited comparison (branch)	
1a	Clarification of values or objectives distinct from and usually prerequisite to empirical analysis of alternative policies	1b	Selection of values, goals and empirical analysis of the needed action are not distinct from one another but are closely interwined
2a	Policy formulation is therefore approached through means–ends analysis: first the ends are isolated; then the means to achieve them are sought	2b	Since means and ends are not distinct, means–ends analysis is often inappropriate or limited
3a	The test of a 'good' policy is that it can be shown to be the most appropriate means to desired ends	3b	The test of a 'good' policy is typically that various analysts find themselves directly agreeing on a policy (without their agreeing that it is the most appropriate means to an agreed objective)
4a	Analysis is comprehensive; every important relevant factor is taken into account	4b	Analysis is drastically limited: (a) important possible outcomes are neglected; (b) important alternative potential; policies are neglected; (c) important affected values are neglected
5a	Theory is often heavily relied upon	5b	A succession of comparisons greatly reduces or eliminates reliance on theory.

Source: Adapted from Lindblom (1959: 81)

to challenge the rational blueprint for a brave new politics by pointing out that there was method in the apparent 'irrationalism' of 'muddling through'. Furthermore, he wanted to show how the idea of a more rational decision-making process (through the use of new tools and techniques) was simply 'not workable for complex policy questions' (Lindblom, 1959: 81).

Lindblom summed up the differences in terms of comprehensive or root rationality as propounded by Simon and what he regarded as the operative mode of decision-making as 'rational' activity: 'successive limited comparisons' or 'root' decision-making. This comparison is set out in table 3.1.

The 'branch' method of decision-making involves a process of 'continually building out from the current situation, step-by-step and by small degrees'. In contrast, the 'root' approach as favoured by the policy analysts was to start from 'fundamentals anew each time, building on the past only as experience embodied in a theory, and always prepared to start from the ground up' (Lindblom, 1959: 81). The core idea which he advances is based on an agreement with Simon: human information capacities are limited in conditions of complex decisions in which actors cannot possibly have all the information, or know consequences, or evaluate every alternative. Lindblom proposes that 'successive limited comparison' is both more relevant and more realistic in such conditions of 'bounded rationality'. The question which Simon addresses is how information can be managed so as to enable something approximating to a more rational decision to take place. Lindlom's answer to this problem is that we do not need to search out new techniques; we need to be more appreciative of the benefits of 'non-comprehensive analysis':

> In the method of successive limited comparison, simplification is systematically achieved in two principal ways. First, it is achieved through limitation of policy comparisons to those policies that differ in relatively small degree from policies presently in effect. Such a limitation immediately reduces the number of alternatives to be investigated and drastically simplifies the character of the investigation of each ... The second method of simplification of analysis is the practice of ignoring important possible consequences of possible policies, as well as the values attached to the neglected consequences.
> (*Lindblom, 1959: 84–5*)

Decision-making, therefore, in terms of 'muddling through' exhibits the following characteristics:

- it proceeds through incremental change;
- it involves mutual adjustment and negotiation;

- it excludes by accident, rather than by systematic or deliberate exclusion;
- policy is not made once and for all;
- it proceeds through a succession of incremental changes;
- it is not theoretically driven;
- it is superior to a 'futile attempt at superhuman comprehensiveness';
- the test of a good decision is agreement and process rather than goal-attainment or meeting objectives;
- it involves trial and error.

Disjointed incrementalism

In his subsequent (1963) work with David Braybrooke, Lindblom developed his ideas on the non-comprehensive approach to decision-making and the role of policy analysis. By this time Lindblom's name had become synonymous with 'incrementalism' and in *A Strategy of Decision* (Braybrooke and Lindblom, 1963) he sought to enlarge upon and refine the idea beyond the simple use of the term: the result is the introduction of the notion of 'disjointed incrementalism'. He sees this as a method of decision-making in which comparison takes place between policies which are only marginally different from one another and in which there is no great goal or vision to be attained, so much as an amelioration of problems and policies. Objectives are set

Figure 3.4   Change and levels of understanding

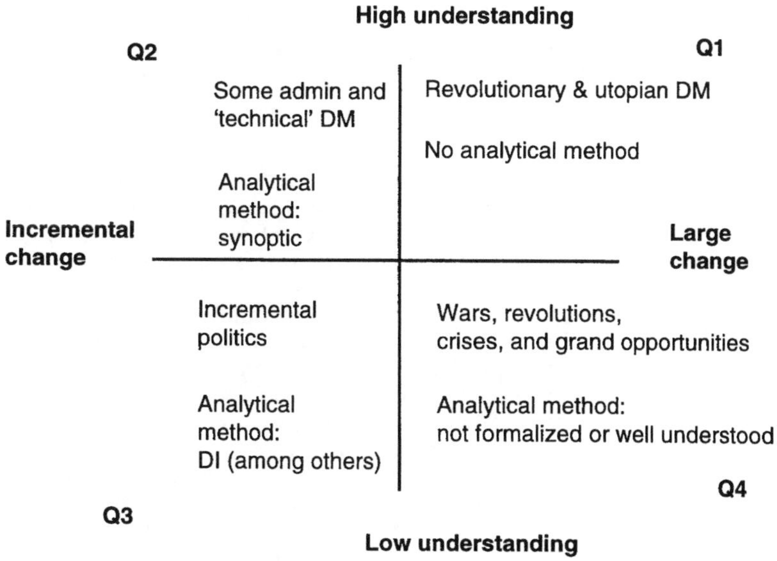

	High understanding	
Q2		**Q1**
	Some admin and 'technical' DM	Revolutionary & utopian DM
		No analytical method
Incremental change	Analytical method: synoptic	**Large change**
	Incremental politics	Wars, revolutions, crises, and grand opportunities
	Analytical method: DI (among others)	Analytical method: not formalized or well understood
		Q4
Q3		
	Low understanding	

Source: Adapted from Braybrooke and Lindblom (1963: 71)

in terms of existing means and resources, and policy-making takes place by a trial and error method. It is disjointed because decisions are not subject to some kind of overall plan, analysis, control or co-ordination. The 1963 book also places incrementalism in a continuum of understanding and a scale of change (figure 3.4).

Synoptic methods are limited to quadrant 2 (Q2), that is, circumstances in which there is a high level of understanding and small amount of change. Big change demands that decision-making (DM) be synoptical, but in such a situation (Q1) the conditions cannot be met. And in Q4 the methods of decision-making are quite different to those in peace-time and of their nature cannot be formalized. In conditions of incremental politics (Q3) we are in circumstances in which the analytical methods approximate to disjointed incrementalism (DI) in which forms of strategic analysis may enhance decision-making by improving the level of understanding.

Partisan mutual adjustment

This conceptualization of incrementalism as a decision-making method which has to be related to levels of understanding and scale of change was further refined in 1965 with the addition of a more developed analysis of how, in pluralist democracies, co-ordination takes place in conditions of disjointed incrementalism – as set out in 1963. In *The Intelligence of Democracy* (1965) he argues that decision-making involves a process of bargaining and negotiation between decision-makers: partisan mutual adjustment. In other words, decision-making is a process of adjustment and compromise which facilitates agreement and co-ordination. Partisan mutual adjustment, he argues, is the democratic and practical alternative to centralized hierarchical controls. As he argues later (1993) it is a matter of 'sensible politics':

> When bureaucrats from different programs and agencies have to come into agreement with each other, they will to some considerable extent be led to take account of a great many more angles on a problem than if left to administer their own narrow policy segment by themselves.
>
> ... policy evolves through complex and reciprocal relations among all the bureaucrats, elected functionaries, representatives of interest groups, and other participants. The outcome may be unpredictable, not fully intended by any one of the individuals who participated. It nevertheless may be a great deal more intelligent and even more democratic than normally is achieved through hierarchical coordination efforts, in the sense that a greater diversity of considerations often are brought to bear, and in the sense that no one set of participants can readily dominate others. Given all the obstacles facing centralized coordination, a high percentage of the effective coordination done in any government bureaucracy actually is achieved through decentralized mutual adjustment. That is not to say that sufficient coordination thereby is achieved.
> (*Lindblom and Woodhouse, 1993: 68*)

Strategic analysis

By the end of the 1970s Lindblom had revised his ideas to take account of his critics (such as Etzioni and Dror) as well as his own appraisal of pluralism as being not quite the system which he had described in his early writings. In 1977 *Politics and Markets* recognized that pluralist decision-making was biased: not all interests and participants in incrementalist politics were equal: some had considerably more power than others. Business and large corporations, he realized, exercised a powerful influence over the policy-making process. Furthermore, such was the 'high degree of homogeneity' in public opinion (1977: 532), many issues were (as Bachrach and Baratz had suggested) simply excluded from the agenda altogether. *Politics and Markets* thus conceded much to Etzioni's (1967) critique of Lindblom's theory of incremental pluralism: that it failed to take account of power and bias. This modification of incrementalism by Lindblom meant that he placed a new emphasis on the role of policy analysis as a way of compensating for the deficiencies of pluralism. *Politics and Markets* thus proposes the need to improve mutual partisan adjustment by 'greatly improved strategic policy-making' (1977: 346).

In 1979 Lindblom developed these arguments in a review of the 'muddling through' debate for the journal *Public Administration Review*. He makes clear that the core idea in an incrementalist approach is the belief in skill in solving complex problems, and that his aim is to suggest 'new and improved' ways of 'muddling through'. To do this he makes a clear distinction between two dimensions of incrementalism:

- incrementalism as a political pattern of small, step-by-step changes;
- incrementalism as policy analysis.

The paper endeavours to make the case for 'analytical incrementalism' as providing an alternative to the 'synoptical' or 'root' ideal conceptualization of policy analysis, and also as a method of redressing the balance of power in a pluralist polity in which business interests tend to occupy a predominant position. Lindblom argues that incremental analysis may be viewed as having three main forms:

- simple incremental analysis (SIA);
- strategic analysis (SA);
- disjointed incrementalism (DI).

Simple incremental analysis (SIA)   SIA is a form of analysis in which only those alternative policies or options which are marginally different to the existing policy are analysed. Critics of this would argue that it is simply an excuse for conservative incremental politics. Lindblom concedes that this is a danger, but argues that this need not be the case. SIA, he maintains, is a useful method of proceeding to make decisions, however, if it is not to be an excuse for a conservative approach to social change, since SIA should be 'supplemented' by political philosophy, and other

> broad ranging, often highly speculative, and sometimes utopian thinking about directions and possible features, near and far in time ... [which can] greatly raise the level of intellectual sophistication with which we think about policy.
> (*Lindblom, 1979: 522*)

In 1993 he argues that the case for SIA is still valid, since:

> Focusing on small variations from present policy ... makes the most of available knowledge. Because the new options are not terribly different from present and past policies, a great deal of what administrators and other participants already know about existing programs will be applicable to evaluating the new proposals. While uncertainty may still be substantial, errors probably will be smaller.
> (*Lindblom and Woodhouse, 1993: 27*)

Strategic analysis (SA)   SA is Lindblom's main innovation in his 1979 paper. As with *Politics and Markets*, SA may be read as a concession to his critics such as Simon, Dror and Etzioni (who we consider in 3.4.4). He argued that the synoptic or 'root' ideal of policy analysis is simply a non-starter: completeness of analysis is not possible, for all the reasons advanced by Simon's model of bounded rationality. Therefore, instead of aiming for the unattainable synoptic ideal, or being content with 'ill-considered, bumbling, incomplete' analysis, we should take a middle position: 'informed, thoughtful' use of methods to 'simplify problems' so as to make better choices (figure 3.5). These 'informed and thoughtful' methods include the very tools of the wizz-kid policy scientists, including:

- trial and error learning;
- systems analysis;
- operations research (OR);
- management by objectives (MBO);
- programme evaluation and review technique (PERT).

However, Lindblom's 'strategic' use of these techniques is informed by a different motivation. In using these tools, analysis should not aim for the 'synoptic/root' ideal, but should aspire to deploy them in the development of strategies to guide and direct: 'something' to be done, something to be studied and learned, and something that can be successfully approximated' (Lindblom, 1979: 318).

Figure 3.5   Strategic and synoptic analysis

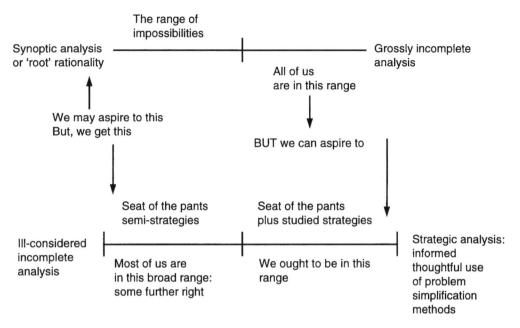

Source: Adapted from Lindblom (1979)

At the end of his outline of SA the reader is left puzzling over whether very much is left of the 1959 version of Lindblom's 'science'. The main difference, he believes, is that of choosing between 'ill-considered, often accidental incompleteness on the one hand and deliberate, designed incompleteness on the other' (Lindblom, 1979: 519). In other words, SA is realistic in its assumptions and aspirations: it does not aim for the moon, because it knows it cannot get there, so it sets out deliberately to aim for what is possible. Incompleteness is built in, rather than an accident. It claims to be a practical analytical method.

Disjointed incrementalism (DI)   DI is also considered to be a practical analytical method in which the aim is not formal completeness so much as a method of simplifying problems. DI is an analytical strategy which involves 'simplifying and focusing' problems by the following six methods:

- the limitation of analysis for a few familiar alternatives;
- intertwining values and policy goals with empirical analysis of problems;
- focusing on ills to be remedied rather than on goals to be sought;
- trial-and-error learning;
- analysing a limited number of options and their consequences;

- fragmenting of analytical work to many partisan participants in policy-making.

The modification of his position from 1977 onwards signalled an apparent *volte face* in Lindblom's arguments. In 1959 we have Lindblom the pluralist, conservative advocate of incremental decision-making as the most effective mode of policy-making. Yet in 1977 and 1979 Lindblom attacks the idea of simplistic pluralism, offers a radical critique of the power of business and comes around to the need for some kind of policy analysis not a million miles removed from his main critics. What happened? Lindblom offers an explanation of the contradictions in a collection of papers published in 1988. He argues that his pre- and post-1977 arguments should be viewed as two sets of research interests, rather than as a chronological change of mind and heart. He concedes that there was a lack of integration between his research interests, and a lack of care in resolving 'marginal' contradictions, but the conflict between the two Lindbloms is more 'apparent than real'. He believes that, as he argued from 1977 onwards, there is a need for drastic radical change in a whole range of policy areas, and that the world is in dire need of more than simply incremental change. But societies 'seem incapable, except in emergencies, of acting more boldly than in increments' (Lindblom, 1988: 11). Such are the limitations on decision-makers and on the way in which policy agendas are narrowly formulated, he doubts whether such extensive change is possible, but not that it is desirable. Thus, he contends, the case for the radical Lindblom does not contradict his analysis of incrementalism as the most operative way in which human beings can simplify complex problems. A conservative analysis does not preclude a radical prescription, nor does it follow that a 'radical diagnosis must lead to a radical prescription' (Lindblom, 1988: 15). Lindblom therefore stands by his analysis of the essential characteristics of decision-making in pluralist democracies, argues that there is need for improvement in this system, but has grave doubts as to the likelihood of 'drastic' change.

Lindblom also argues that if we wish to understand his shifting position, we need to locate his writings in the context of his professional career. The early work was written (as an economist) with a focus on the utility or usefulness of incrementalism in terms of the hidden rationalities of apparent disorder – as in markets. This economic framework and professional orientation precluded a consideration of an analysis of remedies for the defects of social organizations. In the 1960s Lindblom was to become less and less of an economist, and more and more of a political scientist. The completion of Lindblom as a political economist was signalled by *Politics and Markets* (1977). He concludes his plea of mitigation against the charge of changing his mind in terms of being not a 'conspicuous dissenter, bravely fighting the constraints of bigots', so much as someone who had a conventional academic career which involved adaptation to the demands and confines of disciplinary traditions. In his later years he found 'a willingness to disregard them growing slowly with age and security' (Lindblom, 1988: 19).

The Lindblom of the 1970s, 1980s and 1990s is indeed a more radical critic of incrementalism as a political ideology. He has held to and developed his ideas about the policy-making process as moving slowly and in small steps, but has continued to argue that it can be improved. Where he is consistent with his orginal position (1959) is in rejecting the idea that knowledge, rationality, expertise, policy analysis or social science can do very much to improve matters. The usefulness of knowledge in making better decisions or in 'solving problems' is, he stresses, very limited, if not negligible (Lindblom and Cohen, 1979; Lindblom and Woodhouse, 1993). This later work seeks to provide a more coherent account of his ideas as a whole, and is perhaps where students should begin rather than end. As we shall discuss below, the final version of Lindblom is deeply pessimistic about experts and analysts, but optimistic about the potential of wider social learning, greater participation in decision-making by citizens, and increased social justice as ways of making better decisions.

❖ Is Lindblom a 'Lindblomian'?

It is often the fate of theorists and their theories that they become victims of their success. Ideas which actually develop over an author's lifetime become 'fixed' and 'set' in a context and form which actually do little to facilitate our understanding of his/her ideas. Lindblom is very much a case in point. The important aspect of his contributions to public policy is that it developed beyond the early work, to the point that 'incrementalism' is hardly used in later work (in the 1970s, 1980s and 1990s). Taken as a whole, the focus of his work has been to explore the constraints which shape decision-making in the modern policy process. Incrementalism has therefore not been a predominant concern of his writings so much as the relationship between power, human knowledge and politics. As he notes in the preface to the 1993 edition of *The Policy Process*:

> there are sharp constraints in what can be achieved through policy analysis and other 'rational ' methods for understanding social problems; this is largely because uncertainty and disagreement are fundamental facts that cannot be wished away by the most rigorous analysis. Political interactions and flawed human judgments play a primary role in making policy, and these necessarily involve partisan disagreements that are settled by voting or other manifestations of power. Hence, anyone who wants to understand what goes wrong in the effort to use government to promote human well-being needs to comprehend how power

relations shape and misshape public policy – and to probe how power relations might be restructured to produce better policy.
(*Lindblom and Woodhouse, 1993: vii*)

Thus to cast Lindblom as a theorist who is simply concerned with deploying an 'incremental' model against 'rationality' is to miss the point of his wider arguments, which are really about power, politics and knowledge. However, that said, it must also be noted that (as with many a theorist) his terminology and arguments, over time, are not of the clearest. For a review of what Lindblom 'really said/meant', see Gregory (1989). ◆

3.4.4 Finding a middle through the muddle? Dror and Etzioni

The incrementalist position adopted by the early Lindblom sparked much debate. Two key contributors to this debate were Yehezekel Dror and Amitai Etzioni. As we shall see, although they tend to be bracketed together, their approaches are very different. We shall also be considering their ideas later in this part of the book (3.10.2) (see also 1.6, 4.4.4, 4.4.8 on Etzioni, 3.10.6 on Dror).

Dror's 'normative-optimum' model

Dror's criticism of the incrementalist model is that it is profoundly conservative and is appropriate in those circumstances where policy is deemed to be working, or is satisfactory, where problems are quite stable over time, and where there are resources available. However, in practice he believes that incrementalism can only serve to reinforce conservatism and the forces of anti-innovation. Furthermore, Dror considers it to be unfair since, where an incremental approach predominates, those with power have the upper hand, whereas those who have little power will find it difficult to bring about change (see Dror, 1964, 1989; 143–7). In place of both the incremental and rational models Dror puts foward an alternative. One way to view this alternative is in terms of a Simon–Lasswell continuum (see figure 3.6). Dror's model seeks to accept the need for rationality – within the limits as defined by Simon – and in order to enhance the rationality of decision-making at relatively low levels of decision where there is a large amount of routine he also accepts the need for the introduction of management sciences and management techniques. But Dror also accepts Lasswell's argument that complex problems require the development of decision-making at the higher levels in which the knowledge gap (Dror, 1989: 23) is filled by the policy sciences. Along with the acceptance of Lasswell's policy science approach, Dror also takes on board Lasswell's point with regard to the irrational elements in decision-making and the need to take account of values. (see also Vickers, 3.7.5). His aim is therefore to increase the rational content of government, but at the same time to build into his model the 'extra-rational' dimensions of decision-making. This 'normative optimalism', he argues, combines both an analytical and prescriptive approach since:

> What is needed is a model which fits reality while being directed towards its improvement, and which can be applied to policy-making while motivating a maximum effort to arrive at better policies.
> (*Dror, 1964: 164*)

Figure 3.6   Simon, Lasswell and Dror

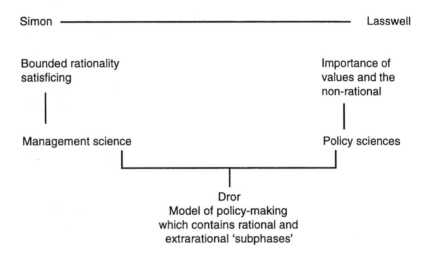

Dror thus accepts the ideal of comprehensive rationality as a goal to which we should aim, recognizes its limitations, but advocates a model which can move policy-making in a more rational direction. Instead of discounting the role of extra-rational aspects of decision-making as revealed in cognitive psychology, social psychology and psycho-analytical approaches, Dror incorporates them into an 18-phase model (see 3.10.2) which operates at two interacting levels: rational and extra-rational. For example, in phase 1, 'the processing of values', decision-making will involve 'specifying and ordering values to be a general guide for identifying problems and for policy-making'. At the rational 'subphase' this involves 'gathering information on feasibility and opportunity costs'; at the extra-rational subphase decision-making will involve 'value judgments; tacit bargaining and coalition-formation skills' (Dror, 1989: 312). Thus Dror's model envisages decision-makers using rational analysis, but also thinking creatively, using intuition, hunches, feelings and impressions. In short, he keeps the penny and the bun:

> My assumption that optimal public policy-making is not a pure-rationality process, that it involves many extrarational components, will make this model distasteful to believers in 'pure rationality' ... On the other hand, the many rational components of my optimal model will make it unacceptable to those who regard extrarational processes as the more valid ones. The model's strong predisposition toward innovation will also disturb those who believe tradition is the major embodiment of human wisdom.
> (Dror, 1989: 302)

To accomplish this transformation of decision-making predicated on a model that claims to be both descriptive (in the real world decision-making is driven by 'rational' and 'extra-rational' influences) and prescriptive (improving both the rational and extra-rational aspects), Dror envisages a radical reform of the process of public policy-making. He believes that changes need to take place in personnel (politicians, bureaucrats and experts); and in structures and process (to improve systematic thinking, feedback, and integrating experts into policy-making); as well as in the general environment of policy-making. Muddling through, he believes, is not an option, and despite the fact that 'conservative forces' are strong, Dror considers that a long-term strategy to improve public policy-making is vital for human progress. In many respects this fusion of the rational and 'extra-rational' has much in common with Lasswell's idea of the role of the policy sciences. However, there is something missing from Dror which might redeem him from being assessed as a top-down technocrat: a sense of how his model relates to the wider society. Whereas Lasswell saw the policy sciences as having a role in enlightenment, emancipation and democratization, Dror seems to have very little regard for the public in policy-making:

> Many thinkers have pointed out that democracy depends on enlightened public opinion: what they have in mind, in general, is that citizens should be familiar enough with public issues to be able to arrive at intelligent opinions on which to base their votes. Certainly, we expect this condition to be fulfilled in Utopia. But if the success of democracy depended on the people's ability to judge the main policy issues on their merits, then democracy would surely have perished by now. In a simpler world a privileged few could be familiar with all the main policy issues and know all there is to know on them. But in a complex modern society, the main problems are so diverse and so much difficult knowledge is needed to deal with them, that no one can form an enlightened opinion of his own on more than a few policy issues.
> (Dror, 1989: 289)

The role of the public in public policy is therefore marginal and restricted to 'evaluating how a policy is arrived at and what its value components are (as well as on personalities and policy-making styles) than on trying to judge specific policies on their merit' (Dror, 1989: 290). It is this theme of the relationship of policy-making and analysis to society as a whole which also contrasts with Etzioni's position.

Mixed scanning: Etzioni's third approach

Like Dror, Etzioni is not convinced that incrementalism or the rational model are either realistic or satisfactory normative accounts of decision-making. Etzioni puts forward a third approach that he believes offers a realistic model which avoids the conservatism of the incrementalist position as articulated by Lindblom. Etzioni calls his model 'mixed scanning':

> A rationalistic approach to decision-making requires greater resources than decision makers command. The incremental strategy which takes into account the limited capacity of actors, fosters decisions which neglect basic societal innovations. Mixed scanning reduces the unrealistic aspects of rationalism by limiting the details required in fundamental decisions and helps to overcome the conservative slant of incrementalism by exploring long-run alternatives. The mixed-scanning model makes this dualism explicit by combining (a) high-order, fundamental policy-making processes which set basic directions and (b) incremental ones which prepare for fundamental decisions and work them out after they have been reached. (*Etzioni 1967: 385*)

The mixed-scanning model is drawn from early weather forecasting and observation techniques. Cameras were used to record the weather picture at two levels of detail: broad scanning and more detailed images on selected areas of interest. In other words, and in the context of decision-making, it would involve a detailed examination of some areas of a problem, with a general sweep across the problem as a whole. This mix of scanning depends upon the differentiation of decisions into those that are 'fundamental' and those which are 'incremental'. This division may, of course, be less well defined in practice than in theory, and the weather forecasting model may be somewhat inappropriate to the storms and gales which beset the ship of state. However, the value of the 'third way' is that it stresses again how no one pattern of decision-making may be considered to be best in the abstract. The key, for Etzioni, is flexibility of decision-making in the light of change and uncertainty in the environment. The ability or capacity to scan has to be placed in the context of the incremental character of liberal democracy which requires consensus to be built, and thus inhibits long-run planning of the kind which has been employed in totalitarian societies.

For Etzioni the mixed-scanning approach is both an 'is' and an 'ought': it is a description of the reality of decision-making strategies as used in a variety of fields and it is also a model for better decision-making. It recognizes that decision-makers have to take into account the costs of knowledge: not everything can be scanned, thus decision makers endeavour (or should endeavour) to scan key areas fully and 'rationalistically', whilst other areas will be subject to a more 'truncated' review.

Ham and Hill note that there are problems with Etzioni's model, not least on the issues of

> whether fundamental decisions are as significant as he suggests. While in some situations fundamental decisions are important in setting broad directions, in other situations decision-making proceeds in a much less structured way ... When this occurs, unplanned drift rather than conscious design characterizes the policy process ... A futher difficulty with mixed scanning is how to distinguish fundamental and incremental decisions.
> (*Ham and Hill, 1984: 88*)

Even so, as they also note, a number of commentators have endorsed the model as being an effective prescriptive model (see ibid.).

Etzioni's idea of mixed scanning has, however, to be placed in the context of his wider intellectual concerns and in the framework of the development of his thought as a whole. After the publication of his 'mixed scanning ' paper in 1967, Etzioni published a large work on *The Active Society* (1968), and if we are to fully understand the mixed-scanning model his paper should be read in the light of his general approach. In *The Active Society* mixed scanning appears as the concluding section of Part Two which is about the 'cybernetic' aspects of the active society. In this part Etzioni examines the social context of knowledge; how the testing of reality is a collective social process; the relationship between power and knowledge; the distribution of knowledge; and 'societal consciousness'. His view is that the rational model and incrementalism are flawed, and cannot be the basis for promoting an 'active society'. This is a society in which people, through social collectivities, can become more knowledgeable about themselves and more able to transform society in accordance with its values. Like Simon, he rejects the psychoanalytical framework, but on the grounds that

> no man can set himself free without extending the same liberty to his fellow men and the transformation of the self is deeply rooted in the joint act of a community transforming itself.
> (*Etzioni, 1968: 2*)

In common with Dror, he acknowledges that there is an information gap in government (Etzioni, 1968: 10), but he does not think that this is a gap which can be bridged simply by improving decision-making. The transformation of 'post-modern society', Etzioni believes, requires a far more extensive change in the way in which society as a whole is actively involved in the process of developing a 'societal consciousness'. In this regard Etzioni's idea of 'mixed scanning' is a long way removed from Dror's technocratic managerialism. Read in context, mixed scanning is part of a theory of transformation in which decision-making is rooted in a less-alienated and more-responsive society (see 3.10.2).

The responses to the rationalist versus the incrementalist positions have in effect generated a continuum of theories which advocate ways in which decision-making might be improved. What Simon, Lindblom, Dror and Etzioni all have in common is their belief in the improvement of decision-making through changing the relationship of the political process to knowledge and information. All these ideas express a belief in the notion that there is an alternative to the unrealistic concept of comprehensive rationality. In this respect, perhaps, Simon, Lindblom, Dror and Etzioni have a great deal in common.

❖ **G. Smith and D. May 'The artificial debate between rationalist and incrementalist models of decision making', 1980**

Smith and May argue that the arguments between the rationalists and incrementalists is somewhat false. They have common epistemological features in the way in which they mix up 'is' and 'ought', descriptive and prescriptive models. It is, they argue, anomolous to presume that 'is' and 'ought' correlate. They doubt if a model which serves two functions can really hold up to methodological criticism. The two sides are in reality talking about very different things: they do not share the same idea of what decision-making is about, or what it is about for those involved. Smith and May conclude by suggesting that this kind of *a priori* model-building is not very useful to understanding and researching the actuality of decision-making. The key questions which the rational-incremental debate bypasses, they suggest, are how policy decisions are operationalized, and how actors operationalize the notion of 'decision-making' itself. ◆

3.4.5 Economics and the organizational context of decision-making

The model of the firm which predominates in neo-classical economic theory stresses a view of the firm as an organization whose decision-making processes are motivated by the rational pursuit of profit-maximization, and economic man as acting with a self-interest predicated on perfect knowledge. Herbert Simon put forward a powerful critique of economic rationality in his 'Epistle to the economists' (Simon, 1985: 293) in 1955: 'A Behavioral Model of Rational Choice' (Simon, 1957: 241–60; see also Simon, 1959).

Simon argues that the idea of a rational economic man who is assumed to have near-perfect information, a 'well organized and stable system of preferences, and a skill in computation that enables him to calculate, for the alternative courses of action available to him, which … will permit him to reach the highest attainable point on his preference scale' (Simon, 1955: 241) is no longer a satisfactory basis on which to analyse rational economic choice. Nor, he thinks, does the idea of the firm as a rational profit-maximizing organization, in the light of evidence and argument, hold much water. As he had earlier demonstrated in the case of administrative decision-making, Simon argues that there are severe limits on the capacities of rational decision-making in economic choices. Economic man, like his brother administrative man, is in need of a 'drastic revision'. He urges that we

> replace the global rationality of economic man with a kind of rational behaviour that is compatible with the access to information and the computational capacities that are actually possessed by organisms, including man, in the kinds of environments in which such organisms exist. (*Simon, 1957a: 241*)

However attractive the concept of economic man is to the economist, Simon argues that it has 'no place in the theory of organization', or indeed, in the many areas of economics, since little is left of the 'predictive power' of classical theory once we take account of bounded rationality. Economic man operating with perfect rationality is unobtainable and consequently the focus of attention should not be the study of rational choice, so much as on how goal-striving individuals in organizations adapt to their cognitive limits and environments.

In 1958 Herbert Simon in conjunction with James March (March and Simon, 1958) presented the first major account of organizations in conditions of bounded rationality. March had earlier written a paper with Richard Cyert which had applied the approach to the study of organizational structure and pricing behaviour (Cyert and March, 1955). Later March was to develop his ideas about how organizations really behave (as opposed to the assumptions made about behaviour contained in economic theories of the firm) in a collaboration with Richard Cyert in the now classic text *A Behavioral Theory of the Firm* (Cyert and March, 1963).

In their 1958 study March and Simon adopt the model of decision-making as 'problem-solving' in conditions of bounded rationality and satisficing. They argue that if we wish to understand how decision-making takes place, organizational processes must be set in the context of the limits of human cognition. The search and choice activities of actors are bounded: these boundaries they describe as 'performance programs' which are set off when people are stimulated into decision-making. An example they give of this 'programmed' behaviour is the bell ringing in a fire station which triggers a set of responses. Decision-making in organizations, they argue, is more like this performance programming than the rational maximizing activity of economic theory. Programmed responses are aimed at 'satisficing' in an uncertain world, rather than optimizing in conditions of perfect information. This theme of suboptimal decision-making is taken up in the subsequent work by Cyert and March (1963), which posits a model of the firm as an organization with a multiplicity of goals: production; inventory; sales; market share; as well as profit. In reality, the decision-making process is one in which groups within the firm bargain to secure agreement or compromise about what is deemed to be a satisfactory decision. The behavioural viewpoint therefore emphasizes how goals and policies are full of inconsistencies. It is a picture far removed from the image of rational economic man whose decision-making processes are those of setting goals and attaining them in ways which are consistent with the goals as defined. In behavioural theory goals are multiple, changing and selected to meet the demands of the coalitions of interests within the firm. These goals, like the goals of Simon's administrative man, are not optimal, but 'acceptable'/satisfactory. The analysis of alternatives is sequential, rather than comprehensive, and if the policy is meeting the goals at an 'acceptable level' there is no attempt to search for alternatives. The search for new alternatives is driven more by failure than by rational evaluation or appraisal, and decision-making is reactive and preoccupied with avoiding uncertainty through regular procedures, rather than by attempting to forecast the environment. The firm is therefore not a monolithic organization, but comprises a variety of coalitions, goals and interests. Not only is the external environment uncertain, the decision-maker also faces an uncertain and complex internal environment. Decision-making is therefore not driven along by rational choice as: the quasi resolution of conflict; the avoidance of uncertainty; the search for problems (see the garbage can analogy, below); and a process of adaptation and learning. In other words, the firm satisfices rather than maximizes, and bases its decisions on a less than full search of information and alternatives. It is an absurd, rather than a rational world.

In a subsequent paper March, along with Cohen and Olsen, developed the idea that a manifestation of this kind of decision-making was what they termed the garbage can theory (Cohen *et al.*, 1972; March and Olsen, 1976):

> Suppose we view a choice activity as a garbage can into which various problems and solutions are dumped by participants. The mix of garbage in a single can depends on partly the labels attached to the alternative cans; but it also depends on what garbage is being produced at the moment, on the mix of cans available, and the speed with which garbage is collected and removed from the scene.
> (*March and Olsen, 1976: 26*)

Summing up the idea in the second edition of their book *The Behavioural Theory of the Firm* (1992), Cyert and March observed that there is order in decision-making, but not of a conventional kind. There are many claims on the attention of participants:

> In a garbage can process there are exogenous, time-dependent arrivals of choice opportunities, problems solutions and decision makers. The logic of ordering is temporal rather than hierarchical or consequential. Problems and solutions are attached to choices, and thus to each other, not only because of their means–ends linkages but also because of their simultaneity. At the limit, almost any solution can be associated with almost any problem – provided they are contemporaries.
> (*Cyert and March, 1992: 235*)

The garbage can model argues that there is essentially a condition in which some issues will have solutions attached to them, others will not, other solutions may be roaming around looking for an issue to which to attach themselves. Decision-makers may well dump a problem or solution into whatever can they have to hand, or whatever can is empty enough to contain the problem/solution. What the garbage can idea graphically suggests is that issues, problems and solutions are messy, untidy sorts of things, whose mode of identification by policy-makers will depend on the time it was picked up, and the availability of cans to put them in. The model is deduced from the assumptions that values are complex, knowledge is uncertain, rules are complex, and that decision-making involves (as Edelman maintains) much that is symbolic (Cyert and March, 1992: 235-8). The decision-making process, when viewed through a behavioural model such as the garbage can, is therefore far less rational than traditional economic and organizational theories of decision-making suppose. They contrast their position with the rational model in the following terms:

> Classic ideas of order in organizational decision-making involve two related concepts. The first is that events and activities can be arranged in chains of means and ends, causes and effects. Thus consequential relevance arranges the relation between solutions and problems, as well as the participation of decision makers. The second concept is that organizations are hierarchies in which higher levels control lower levels, and policies control implementation. Portrayals built on such conceptions of order seem, however, to underestimate the confusion and complexity surrounding actual decision-making ... Many things are happening at once; technologies are changing and poorly understood; alliances, preferences, and perceptions are changing; problems, solutions opportunities, ideas, people, and outcomes are mixed together in ways that make their interpretations uncertain and their connections unclear; actions in one part of an organization appear to be only loosely coupled to actions in another; policies are not implemented; decision makers seem to wander in and out of decision arenas.
> (*Cyert and March, 1992: 232–3*)

Cyert and March originally proposed their theory as an account of how business decision-making takes place. However, they also consider that it provides a convincing account of how decision-making takes place in 'non-business' organizations such as government departments, political executives, hospitals, schools and professional associations. The behavioural theory of the firm, they argue, has much in common with the ideas about rational decision-making as advanced by Simon, as well as by social psychologists (such as Argyris). They also believe that their ideas on the limitations on rational decision-making have been echoed and confirmed by later work by political scientists and others (Allison, 1971; Janis and Mann, 1977). Four particular areas of research into organizations have, they suggest, enhanced their original thesis:

1   Theories which point towards the complex environments within which organizations function. 'Ecological' approaches to organizations emphasize that decision-making involves interaction between and within organizations and their environments, as opposed to a simple model of decision-making as being located in a single organization (see 3.4.6, 4.3.7, 4.6.3).
2   Network theories which show how decision-making in modern organizations is no longer a process which can be adequately described in terms of hierarchical structures. In this model decision-making is to be understood as the result of multiple interactions of components of a 'network', rather than Weberian bureaucracy (see 3.4.6 and 2.10).
3   Attention mosaics, or theories, which argue that decision-making is to be characterized as more like bedlam than an orderly sequence. Attention to problems is seen as erratic, changeable and has little which could be described as 'comprehensively rational'. Decision-making is an unstable process driven by events, people, and the claims of other problems (amongst other things) (see, for example, Kingdon, in 2.10.3).
4   Decision-making as a process involving symbolic rather than substantive outcomes (see, for example, Edelman in 2.9.2).

In the following section (and also in 4.3.7 and 4.6.3) we examine points 1 and 2 as aspects of the behavioural theory of the firm which have been developed to explore the interorganizational and intergovernmental context of public policy-making.

3.4.6   The interorganizational and intergovernmental context

Interorganizational relations

> Events of organizational life are produced by the complex ecological character of organizational existence. Modern firms are often large systems of intermeshing parts embedded in large, complex industries and markets ... Outcomes are produced not by a process of decision-making within a single firm but by complicated networks of interacting organizations and parts of organizations.
> (*Cyert and March, 1992: 233*)

This theme of interorganizational interaction has been developed in the study of 'interorganizational relations' (see Evan (ed.), 1976). Amongst its earliest contributions were behavioural theories of the firm such as Phillips (1960) and Williamson (1965, 1975, 1985) which showed how, in the words of Cyert and March (above), the analysis of decision-making had to take account of an increasingly complex pattern of relationships between organizations. Decisions in this model are to be understood as arising from 'multiple interactions' within an elaborate internal structure and environmental network.

The arguments of Williamson were to be of particular importance to the development of the study of organizational complexity as they provided a framework for the analysis of organizational change in terms of 'hierarchies' and 'markets'. The former grow, Williamson posits, as market mechanisms fail to provide an efficient mode of organization. This model is derived from Simon's concept of bounded rationality, the theory of transaction costs as propounded by Coase (1937; see 3.6.3), and a view of human nature as self-interested and opportunistic. Williamson maintained that in seeking to attain efficiency, organizations with complex structures will, in given circumstances, tend to shift from a 'U'-form pattern – in which there is a hierarchy organized on a functional 'uniform' basis – to an 'M'-form pattern – in which organization is 'multi-divisional'. The M-form structure in which organization is decentralized to relatively self-contained or quasi-autonomous operating units (organized on a U-form basis) overcomes the problems of bounded rationality in large uniform hierarchical structures, and exploits opportunistic behaviour by creating a system in which the performance of different divisions can be measured and compared – a kind of internal market within the firm. The implication of this theory for the public sector is that, in a more complex and uncertain world, efficiency (low transaction costs) involves shifting from hierarchies arranged on a uniform basis to structures which – like a large modern corporation – operated through 'multi-form' organizations in which managerial decisions take place in a decentralized internal market. From the standpoint of the Williamson model, therefore, in order to deal with the problem of limited rationality (bounded rationality), large public agencies will, like large firms, endeavour to lower the costs of transactions by adapting organizational structures to be more 'multi-form'. Furthermore, where markets can be more efficient than bureaucracies, governments should seek to use market modes of organization – by 'privatizing' or sub-contracting (see also 3.6.3; and Self, 1993).

This notion of interorganizational relations was also developed by organizational sociologists in the 1960s and 1970s to show how decision-making takes place within conditions of: interdependence (Aiken and Hage, 1968; Aldrich, 1976; Yuchtman and Seashore, 1967); 'organizational fields' (Warren, 1967); 'organizational sets' (Evan, 1972); and 'networks' (Turk, 1970; Benson, 1975). Such analysis marked a break from the study of organizations in terms of intraorganizational behaviour and sought to demonstrate that decision-making in modern society takes place in a highly complex setting. Decision-making is best understood as a process of 'joint decision-making' (Tuite, 1972) between organizations and actors sharing a common 'organizational pool' (Hjern and Porter, 1981). The more complex society becomes, the more decision-making structures manifest interorganizational characteristics (for a more detailed account of these ideas, see 4.3.7 and 4.6.3).

Intergovernmental relations
An illustration of this theory that complexity breeds interorganizational structures and interactions is found in the various approaches which go under the broad heading of 'intergovernmental' relations which have been greatly influenced by the theories we have mentioned above. The study of intergovernmental relations is concerned with how the multiplicity of types of governmental unit interact with one another. A landmark book in this field is an edited collection of papers on interorganizational policy-making by Hanf and Sharpf (eds) (1978), which surveys the rising interest in how central and local government in both unitary and federal systems interact and limit control and co-ordination. As a framework, intergovernmental relations is diverse and multi-theoretic. As Rhodes (1992: 320–2) notes, several main approaches may be discerned. They include:

- *a public/development administration approach,* which is focused on describing changing patterns, procedures and institutions of governmental decision-making (e.g. how decentralization and centralization is developing in practice; what new 'partnership' relationships are emerging in local government);

- *the 'new right' approach*, which seeks to apply 'public choice' and market models to governmental performance (e.g. making the case for privatization and contracting-out);
- *the centre–periphery framework approach*, which analyses the relations between central government, institutions and interests, and the territorial periphery (e.g. the study of how peripheral areas may be exploited and colonized by the core);
- *radical approaches*, which adopt neo-Marxist and neo-Weberian theories for the study of intergovernmental relations (e.g. the argument that local and central government form a 'dual state': see 3.3.3);
- *the intergovernmental approach*, as developed by Hanf (1978), which is concerned with the changing nature of 'neopluralist' governing 'networks' (see also 2.10.2 on policy networks).

The study of intergovernmentalism has been equally significant as a line of inquiry for both federal and unitary states in recent decades, as federal systems have become increasingly complex and fragmented in their patterns of intergovernmental relations (see Harman, 1992; Keller and Perry, 1991). A widely applied method of analysis which combines interorganizational and intergovernmental approaches is the 'resource-dependency' or power-dependency framework, which analyses interactions in terms of the way in which resource/power dependency (see Yuchtman and Seashore, 1967; Aldrich, 1976) may structure the context within which decision-making takes place (see 4.3.7).

3.5   The public choice approach to decision-making

❖ **Key texts**

A starting point is Tullock's IEA pamphlet *The Vote Motive* (1976), which gives an accessible account of the approach.

Lane (1993) contains a good review of the approach and may serve as the basis for moving on to Downs (1967); Niskanen (1971); and Mueller (1979, 1989).

Three outstanding contributions to the field are Dunleavy (1986, 1991) and Self (1993). The latter provides a review of the theories and examines public-choice theory in practice in several countries. ◆

3.5.1 Economics and public choices

Theorists of the power of bureaucracy in the decision-making process argue that one of the main characteristics of the modern state has been the manner in which bureaucratic, or technocratic power as Galbraith would have it, has increased by serving *itself* rather than the public interest. The focus on bureaucracy has been particularly important for the so-called public-choice school, whose ideas were highly influential in setting the political agenda in the late 1970s and through the 1980s. The origins of the approach may be discerned in the work of Gordon Tullock, Anthony Downs and William Niskanen. Their concern is with the rationale and motivations of administrative agencies and government departments. As a group of theories their impact on the political agenda, particularly in Britain and the USA, cannot be underestimated. Not the least of the reasons for this influence was the fact that public-choice arguments about bureaucratic inefficiencies and expansionism had considerable support from political parties via think-tanks (see Self, 1993).

Gordon Tullock's work is generally regarded as amongst the earliest contributions to the public-choice approach, although it does not contain much by way of economic theory. His critical observations on the self-serving nature of bureaucracy, based on his experience in the US State Department (Tullock, 1965), and his critique with Buchanan of party competition and its consequences (Buchanan and Tullock, 1962) may be said to have laid the basis for a debate on the dangers of the power of bureaucracy and the politicization of the economic and public policy which other theorists – such as Niskanen – were to examine from the standpoint of economic models. Later in the 1970s he published an oft-cited pamphlet for a think-tank – the Institute for Economic Affairs (Tullock, 1976). The IEA was also responsible for publishing several other 'key texts' of the public-choice school, including Buchanan (ed.) (1978) and Niskanen (1973). For Tullock the study of politics, policy-making and bureaucracy should be based on the same set of assumptions which were used to explain the behaviour of firms, business people and consumers: self-interest. From this could be deduced the following set of conclusions:

- Parties make excessive promises to win votes.
- In power politicians have to cut deals so as to secure support, and this pushes up the budget.
- Bureaucrats are just interested in maximizing their own self-interest rather than in the public interest. This means that they want ever-bigger bureaux and more and more money for their departments.

- The political processes of liberal democracy are failing to control the growth of political and bureaucratic power.

From these it followed that the solution to the problem of big government was the introduction of market forces to combat bureaucratic self-interest and the pressures of the vote motive. Tullock, in common with other public-choicers, was therefore to recommend the introduction of competition into bureaucracy through contracting-out, privatization and increasing competition between government departments by rewarding performance. The analysis and solutions he advanced in his 1976 IEA pamphlet were not to have much of an impact in the 1970s; however, in the 1980s and 1990s they came into their own (see Self, 1993; Pirie, 1988).

The most developed account of the theories which underpinned Tullock's arguments were put forward by Anthony Downs and William Niskanen.

Anthony Downs

Downs – whose work featured in Part Two (2.3.1, 2.11.5) – has also made an important contribution to the study of bureaucratic behaviour. *Inside Bureaucracy*, published in 1967, was the outcome of a grant from the US Air Force which supported research at RAND. The study aimed to 'develop a useful theory of bureaucratic decision-making' which should 'enable analysts to predict some aspects of bureau behaviour accurately, and to incorporate bureaux into a more generalized theory of social decision-making' (Downs, 1967: 1). Downs starts from the (untested) assumption that decision-making in bureaucracies is informed by the pursuit of self-interest. The structure of the book takes the form of deriving some 16 'laws' which are deduced from the initial hypotheses that: officials seek to attain goals rationally; that they are motivated by self-interest; and that the social functions of organizations are strongly influenced by its internal structure and vice versa. The laws (*sic*) which are extrapolated from these hypotheses are:

- *Law of Increasing Conservatism*: as organizations get older they become more conservative, unless they experience rapid growth or turnover.
- *Law of Hierarchy*: large-scale organizations without markets require hierarchical authority for co-ordination to be possible.
- *Law of Increasing Conserverism*: there is an inherent long-run tendency for officials to become conservers.
- *Law of Imperfect Control*: in large organizations no one can control behaviour.

- *Law of Diminishing Control*: the larger the organization the weaker is the control exercised at the top.
- *Law of Decreasing Co-ordination*: the larger the organization, the poorer the co-ordination.
- *Power Shift Law*: conflict that is unconstrained has the effect of shifting power upwards.
- *Law of Control Duplication*: attempts to control large organizations tend to result in the generation of another organization.
- *Law of Ever-expanding Control*: the quantity and detail of information required by bureaux which monitor other bureaux rise over time.
- *Law of Counter Control*: as top-level officials seek to exercise more control over subordinates they seek to increase efforts to evade or counter greater control.
- *Law of Free Goods*: the demand for free services rises to the capacity of the producer agency.
- *Law of Non-money Pricing*: when organizations do not charge money for services they develop other non-money costs to ration outputs.
- *Law of Progress Through Imperialism*: bureau aggrandisement stimulates innovation.
- *Law of Self-serving Loyalty*: officials are loyal to the organization that controls their job security and promotion.
- *Law of Interorganizational Conflict*: all large organizations are in some degree of conflict with the social agencies with which they deal.
- *Law of Countervailing Goal Pressure*: conflict develops between goal diversity and goal consensus because of the conflicting pressures of innovation, control and co-ordination.

Downs argues that the motivations of individual officials are diverse and give rise to different kinds of bureaucrat:

- *Climbers*: concerned with their power, income and prestige;
- *Conservers*: concerned with minimizing change;
- *Zealots*: highly motivated officials committed to push for a policy or programme;
- *Advocates*: who see their interests in terms of maximizing the role and resources for their bureau;
- *Statesmen*: who have a sense of the public interest which may be advanced by increasing their power so as to realize their goals.

He argues that different types of official may be motivated by different sets of general motivations, which he classifies as pure and mixed:

- Pure self-interest:
    power

money income
prestige
convenience (resistance to change that increases personal effort
and acceptance of that which reduces it)
security (low probability of loss of above)
- Mixed
personal loyalty (to work group, goals, larger organization)
pride in the performance of work
desire to serve the public interest
commitment to a specific programme of action.

As there are different kinds of bureaucrat, there are also, Downs claims, different kinds of bureaux, whose characteristics derive from where they are on the life-cycle of bureaucratic growth: old and young, small and large. Although the motivation varies as between bureaux and bureaucrats, their aim is always to maximize self-interest by growing bigger. And this quest for greater size leads to a condition of bureaucratic life in which conflict is the norm. Hence, if bureaucrats are not to be simply concerned with the pursuit of self-interest, rather than the public interest, bureaucracy requires strong supervision and control.

Downs sets out to provide a model which lays claim to a predictive power; that is, he argues that the analysis he offers shows how bureaucratic growth takes place as a result of 'laws' and how the motivations of bureaucrats and bureaux vary in the way in which they set about maximizing their interests. The criticisms which may be made of the approach turn on the assumptions he makes with regard to self-interest, hierarchy, and size as defining characteristics of bureaucratic development.

William Niskanen
Whereas Downs's model is largely dependent on a theory of psychological motivation, Niskanen's (1971) model is framed by neo-classical economics. He starts from the same assumption: self-interest maximization. Niskanen posits that we may apply theories which seek to model the behaviour of profit-maximizing firms to bureaucracies. Just as firms seek to maximize profit, Niskanen argues that those who work in bureaucracies or bureaux seek to maximize their budgets and the size of the bureau. This is the case, he maintains, because it is only by increasing the budget that they can maximize their self-interest. Budgetary and bureau growth are, in this model, regarded as the only ways in which bureaucrats can maximize their utility. Why this is possible is due, it is argued, to the way in which bureaux allocate resources

and make decisions as compared with the way in which markets make decisions and allocate resources. Markets make decisions by maximizing the difference between marginal utility and marginal cost: that is, between increasing costs and the returns which are consequent upon the supply of an additional unit. However, the bureau, unlike the firm, does not know what the gains are, and thus can only increase the marginal utility by increasing the size of the bureau's budget. They can do this because of the way in which politicians are themselves pressured to make promises to increase spending.

The approach evaluated

On the face of it, the bureau thesis is attractive. It provides a powerful model for explaining the commonly held belief that bureaucrats are not interested in anything apart from their own interests. It is a theory made popular by the television series *Yes Minister* and *Yes Prime Minister*, in which bureaucrats are seen to be operating in their own interests rather than in the public interest.

However, the model has a major difficulty in that, from a methodological point of view, it is difficult to test or falsify. Given that we know little about the utility and costs of those who work in bureaux, as compared with those who work in profit-maximizing firms, it is somewhat arbitrary to say whether a bureau is 'too large'. Empirical research on the question of budget-maximization has not yielded the kind of evidence which would support the theory. The idea that bureaucratic decision-making is motivated by selfish interests and big budgets has proved an influential model more for its normative (anti-bureaucrat) content than its empirical status. It does provide useful definitions and typologies, but as far as its explanatory power is concerned, the idea that bureaucratic decision-making is motivated by the pursuit of self-interest which can only find expression in bigger budgets and bigger bureaux is simplistic in the extreme. As Downs's model shows, the range of motivations is far more complex and diverse than self-interest of the kind which Niskanen advances as the basis for a theory of bureaucracy. Although there is evidence that 'self-interest' is a motivation towards increased budgets and bigger bureaux, as an explanation for the changes in the size of the public sector and of bureaux it is far from being adequate. As Lewin notes:

> The extensive debate over the hypothesis has exposed so many shortcomings that one is left with serious doubts about whether it captures any essential feature of Western bureaucracy at all. The lasting impression left by this research is its failure to uncover any convincing evidence. To put it briefly, the budget-maximisation hypothesis is not sustained by empirical research.
> (*Lewin, 1991: 97*)

However, this is not to say that the idea of using economic analysis to study decision-making does not have a utility for the student of public policy. The budget-maximization hypothesis, once extricated from its highly ideological context and purpose, does offer important insights and questions. As one leading critic of the school has argued:

> The gains made by public choice theory in extending the scope and methods of debate and research in political science towards new forms of logically and mathematically informed reasoning are ... undeniable.
>
> The development and refinement of institutional public choice into behaviourally realistic and theoretically diverse explanations of broad classes of political phenomena should provide a much needed antidote.
> (*Dunleavy, 1991: 259*)

The models of Downs and Niskanen were largely framed in the context of a period (post-war) in which bureaucracy was on the march. However, the 1980s were to see major changes to the way in which bureaucracies – and organizations in the private sector – would function. The size thesis was always methodologically shaky, resting as it did upon the assertion of self-interest; however, the empirical evidence which emerged in the 1980s pointed towards a serious flaw in the public-choice school. The experience of the 1980s in many industrial countries was that of a reduction in civil servants and the introduction of markets to fulfil those tasks earlier assumed to be the domain of bureaucracy. Downs himself gives a whole chapter of his book to explaining why bureaucracy is 'here to stay' because there are a range of social functions that 'must be performed by nonmarket-orientated organizations' (Downs, 1967: 32). This is not to say that they will be performed in an optimal fashion but, Downs argues, that there will remain services and functions for which hierarchies are 'necessary'.

In the 1980s and 1990s, however, the experience in many industrialized countries – and less-developed countries as well – has been to question the notion that there is a realm of 'non-market' decision-making. In Britain, for example, the experience has been that of the downsizing and radical shake-up of bureaucracy.

3.5.2   Alternatives to the public-choice model

Public-choice theory has had considerable influence on both the theory and practice of public policy (for general critiques of the approach in terms of theory and practice, see Self, 1993; Stretton and Orchard, 1994). However, there are several alternative frameworks within which to analyse the kinds of issues with which public choice theorists have been concerned. In this section we shall consider three such approaches:

- management theories;
- a bureau-shaping model;
- 'unorthodox' economics.

Management theories of human motivation and organizational behaviour

The public-choice approach is especially deficient in its conceptualization of human decision-making as essentially informed by individual self-interest. Given the impact of managerialist ideas on the analysis and reform of the public sector (Van Strien, 1982: 24), it is well to keep in mind the debate within management theory (and practice) on human motivation. Like the public-choice school, 'scientific' and 'classical' management theory begins with the same postulate about human behaviour: the individual as a self-interested maximizer.

F.W. Taylor was an engineer and he viewed the problems of human beings in organizations in engineering terms (see Taylor, 1911). Organizations were like, or should aim to emulate, machines. As with the economic model, the engineering model assumed that the cogs that made up the machine were motivated to maximize wages, and that greater efficiency was the means by which wages and production could be assured. Taylor examined old-fashioned modes of production and found them to be lacking in efficiency: the solution was to break down the organization of production into small tasks which could be carried out quickly and efficiently. Charlie Chaplin's great film *Modern Times* is perhaps the most famous representation of the logic of Taylorism.

Later, Taylor's ideas were developed in the work of Henri Fayol (1949) and other members of the so-called 'scientific management' school. Taylor and Fayol believed that they had discovered the core component in the human machine: self-interest, and that they had developed methods by which this self-interested creature could be organized so as to be efficient and productive. Because people were only interested in making money and maximizing their own interests, structures could be devised to control and utilize this so as to make more profits and bigger wage packets. It was all a matter of control. For the public-choice school the problem was also one of control. The modern government bureaucracy was populated by people who were able to make decisions without the kinds of disciplines and constraints which existed in industry or business. The problem was how could this self-interest be constrained and directed to more-efficient and effective choices in the interest of taxpayers rather than to ever-bigger budgets and ever more government. The answer which suggested itself was twofold: first, to cut down the size of bureaucracy and reduce what government did; and secondly, to run or 'manage' bureaucracy and those who spent public money in ways in which self-interest could be disciplined and controlled.

Against this view of human behaviour as driven by self-interest was the 'human relations school' which opposed the Taylorist notion that human beings were motivated by purely individualistic self-interest. The human relations school began with experiments at the Western Electric Company between 1924 and 1932 headed by Elton Mayo. The aim of the 'Hawthorne experiments' was to study and measure the effect of factory conditions on workers. The conclusions were that group behaviour was central to individual performance. Informal relationships were important and, they argued, organizations were not mechanistic and 'rationalistic', as had been thought by Taylor and 'the scientific management' school (see Mayo, 1933, 1949). Lasswell met and worked with Mayo (between 1926 and 1927, and Trahair has suggested that Mayo had a significant impact on the development of Harold Lasswell's approach (Trahair, 1981–2). However, as Muth points out, Lasswell was influenced by a great many people and it is, perhaps, somewhat erroneous to think that Mayo had more impact than Freud, Weber, Marx, Mead, Merriam or Harry Stack Sullivan (see Muth, 1990: 10). What is true, however, is that in developing the policy approach Lasswell 'took him on board'.

Later in 1937 Chester Barnard also endorsed the view that, contrary to the Taylor theory, people were not simply motivated to maximize wages and self-interest. Barnard was an executive of the Bell Telephone Company – not an academic – whose long experience in management had taught him that human motivation was a long way removed from the idea of rational, selfish, maximizing economic man. Organizations, he argued, were composed of people who had many roles and goals: as husband, wife, son, brother, member of a club or church, and so on. Inevitably, there would be conflicts between roles, and the function of leadership was to promote co-operation between people in an organization. Human beings, Barnard maintained, have a mix of motivations. If organizations are to be efficient and effective, co-operation, common purpose and communication are the primary requirements, not Taylorist control: 'The vitality of organizations lies in the willingness of individuals to contribute forces to the cooperative system' (Barnard, 1938: 82).

One of the most famous refutations of the Taylorist idea of motivation was developed by the psychologist Abraham Maslow, who proposed that the motivations of people within organizations are more varied than simply that of 'maximization of interests' (Maslow, 1943, 1968,

1970). The human motivation to work, he contended, has to be viewed as shaped by human needs. Maslow proposed a hierarchy of five needs: basic physiological needs; security and safety; belonging or affection; esteem and ego needs; and the need for self-actualization. With this critique of the Taylorist notion of human motivation developed by the human relations school in mind, one could argue that the public-choice approach is rooted in a kind of Taylorist framework which constructs a narrow definition of human behaviour that fails to take account of the possibility that human motivation is far more complex than crude 'self-interest'.

❖ Motivations and management

In place of the idea of individual self-interest which informs the public-choice approach human relations theorists have posited a variety of motivations.

Maslow (1943): a hierarchy of needs

- physiological (food, clothing, etc.);
- safety and security;
- social (the need to have contact and relationships with other humans);
- esteem (the need for respect);
- self-actualization (the need for the development of potential).

McGregor (1960)

McGregor developed two frameworks to understand how managers see people in organizations (the public-choice model is clearly marked with an *X*):

- *X theory*: assumes that people don't really want work, need to be coerced and controlled, and do not want responsibility.
- *Y theory*: assumes that people want to work, are interested in what they do and want responsibility, and are committed to the goals of the organization.

Herzberg (1966)

Herzberg argued that two kinds of factors are at work in motivation and the organizational setting within which people are located:

- *Motivation*: people want a sense of achievement, responsibility, recognition, promotion and a satisfactory job to do.
- *Hygiene*: the work context has to be maintained at a level which is acceptable in terms of

monetary reward, how the employee is supervised, the general conditions of the physical environment, and relations with superiors. ◆

A key point which may be made against the economic model, therefore, is that it fails to take account of the different needs which exist within institutions. As Dunleavy argues (below), it may well be that the bureaucrat is motivated by an interesting job or higher status, rather than by just the desire to maximize interests in terms of budget and bureau size. The Taylorist/public-choice frameworks conceptualize motivation in highly individualistic terms. However, as Mayo and Maslow and others have shown with *far* more empirical evidence on their side, the group context is a vitally important dimension of human behaviour and decision-making. Public policy does involve individual decision-making, but this takes place in a group setting. In the light of the evidence regarding the way in which groups behave, the reduction of analysis to the level of individual rationality and self-interest seems an implausible basis on which to construct a theory of human behaviour. The theme of human behaviour as involving co-operation rather than self-interest has been well developed in modern management theory and research, most notably in the work of Argyris (1957, 1965) and McGregor (1960), Likert (1961) and Herzberg (1966). In contrast to the narrow, rather low view of human nature to be found in Taylor and public-choice theory, the tradition of thought which stems from Mayo, Barnard and Maslow in the 1930s and Argyris in the 1950s and 1960s derives from a wider, more optimistic notion of human motivation.

However, it is ironic that although the human relations school provides a powerful critique of the theory of organizational behaviour contained within the public-choice model, their ideas underpin the 'new public-sector management' which has made common cause with the public-choicers in attacking 'public-sector' bureaucrats and professionals. This convergence of the human relations school with the Taylorist assumptions of public-choice theory adds weight to the argument that 'Mayoism' was little more than a refinement of the Taylorist paradigm (see Clegg and Dunkerly, 1980: 122–35; Mouzelis, 1967). New public-sector management is a derivative of the human relations approach (see, for example, Peters and Waterman, 1982; Osborne and Gaebler, 1992). It has been deployed in the public sector as a means of implementing the kind of criticisms which are at the heart of the public-choice model. The difference is that the modes of discipline are more subtle than the Taylorist approach and use the rhetoric of human relations, but their goal is the same: more control over organizations and the people within them. 'Marketization', 'contracting-out' and 'public-sector management' are, in this sense, another way of saying 'industrialization': public agencies and services become businesses and factories. Thus, management theories which might be viewed as a critique of the public-choice model have in practice been incorporated within the framework (see 4.3.5).

A bureau-shaping model

Public-choice theory has not been the sole property of the 'new right' (see Self, 1993: 16–20). One of the most important analyses which uses public-choice theory as a critique of 'new right' arguments is that put forward by Dunleavy (1986; 1991). Drawing upon the experience of the civil service in Britain in the Thatcher years, Dunleavy advances a convincing case for a model of bureaucratic behaviour which, although employing a public-choice approach, arrives at an explanation which shows how self-interest works to very different outcomes than that advanced by Downs and Niskanen. Dunleavy's critique of the public-choice approach came in the form of an analysis of the privatization boom of the 1980s (Dunleavy, 1986) and subsequently in *Democracy, Bureaucracy and Public Choice* (1991).

In explaining the privatization boom of the 1980s in Britain and the USA, Dunleavy (1986) takes issue with the model offered by the 'new right' theorists which emphasizes big budgets and big bureaux as the main object of bureaucratic self-interest. He shows that this model has some difficulties in explaining why bureaucracies have exhibited a preference for getting smaller and cutting costs. In order to develop a radical account, Dunleavy shows how we have to realize that the budget and the relationships between types of bureaucrat and differences in power are far more complex than is recognized by Niskanen *et al.* Self-interest need not be expressed through size, but in 'shaping'. In the case of privatization, Dunleavy shows how senior bureaucrats have been far more concerned with shaping their departments and budgets so as to advance their interests in the same direction as politicians and the business sector. In explaining the low resistance to privatization, therefore, Dunleavy argues that in practice it has served to advance the class interests of top civil servants at the cost of job losses and deteriorating conditions for the rank and file. Contracting-out and other forms of privatization may consequently be read as the continuation of the strategy of bureaucratic elites to maximize their own interests by shaping their organizations, rather than pursuing bigness.

Dunleavy argues that there are four reasons why budget-maximization is not the sole rational motivation of bureaucrats and bureaux:

- There are different individual and collective strategies for maximizing interests. The reality of bureaucratic politics is that the budget is not in the hands of one top official but a group of officials. This means that a bureau is involved in a competition to secure resources so that its department does not suffer a reduction in prestige relative to another department, or a budget which means it gets less. Given this, it does not follow that it is rational for officials to advocate a bigger overall budget. They will press for a bigger budget only if the returns are higher than the effort involved in advocating it. What follows from the hierarchical structure of bureaucracy is that the lower the rank, the less success is probable from an attempt to get a budget increase.
- There are different bureau strategies for maximizing utility. This is so because there are different kinds of budget: core budgets, bureau budgets, programme budgets and super-programme budgets. Dunleavy's model of the budget allows the deduction that benefits of budget increases do not fall across the board. An increase in the core budget benefits each official (salaries, buildings, etc.). However, programme budgets which involve funding which is spent by implementing agencies will come under pressure from the core and bureau budgets in their quest to increase their slice of the cake. In short, there is a conflict in budgetary interests as between the core/bureau budget and the budget which is allocated to those agencies responsible for implementing policy. The relationship between the size of the budget and its component parts will vary depending on the type of bureau concerned: delivery; regulatory; transfer; contracts; control; trading; and servicing.
- There is an optimum level at which budget-maximizing will take place in a bureau. The motivation to maximize the core and bureau budget will vary with the kind of relationship between the core and other parts of the budget which exist in a given agency. Budget-maximization will be greatest within those which have a close relationship between core, bureau and programme. In such conditions as pertain in delivery agencies, for example, the interests of different levels of seniority will be served by a bigger budget.
- The rank and seniority of officials will have a determining impact on whether an official will choose to pursue the maximization of individual welfare or collective interests. The motivation of officals will vary with rank. Those involved in senior decision-making will, argues Dunleavy, be far more interested in maximizing their own welfare than the collective interests of the department as a whole: 'Rational officials want to work in small, élite, collegial bureaux close to political power centres. They do not want to head up heavily staffed, large budget but routine, conflictual and low-status agencies' (Dunleavy, 1991: 202).

Figure 3.7   Shaping bureaux

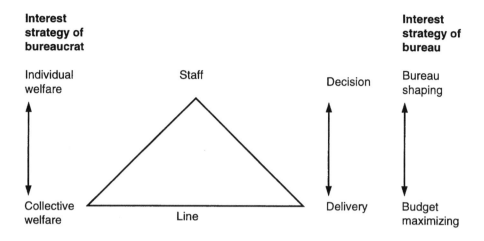

Interest strategy of bureaucrat

Individual welfare

Collective welfare

Staff

Line

Decision

Delivery

Interest strategy of bureau

Bureau shaping

Budget maximizing

Source: Adapted from Dunleavy (1991)

There are a number of strategies which bureaucrats employ in order to shape their bureaux so that it approximates to a staff rather than a line function (figure 3.7).

As it becomes more of a control, transfer or contracts agency, the interests of the bureaucratic elite become increasingly separate from the maximization of the bureau or programme budget. Dunleavy identifies five such strategies:

- Major internal reorganization: a strengthening of the role of the policy-making domain, and a separation of routine (line) functions.
- Transformation of internal work practices: thus increasing the pre-eminence of control activities.
- Redefinition of relationships with external 'partners': so as to maximize policy control and promote greater decentralization of responsibility for routine issues.
- Competition with other bureaux: so as to defend the scope of responsibilities, whilst exporting low-grade tasks elsewhere.
- Load-shedding, hiving off and contracting out: thus transferring functions which do not conform with the desired bureau shape to other agencies and tiers of government and administration.

He concludes with the argument that:

> Public choice models of bureaucracy which predict open-ended budget maximization are badly flawed. Bureaucrats typically do not embark on collective action modes of improving their welfare unless they have exhausted individual welfare-boosting strategies ... although lower-ranking

bureaucrats have most to gain from budgetary expansion, they will know that the attainment of increments is almost completely insensitive to their individual advocacy, so that even though their advocacy costs are small, campaigning for budgetary expansion is unlikely to advance their individual utility ... Higher-ranking officials ... have much less to gain from increments and confront substantial advocacy costs in seeking to push through increases in the agency's base budget ... There are major differences between the agency types in the extent to which officials associate their welfare with the growth of the program budget.
(*Dunleavy, 1991: 208*)

The arguments of Downs and Niskanen laid claim to being based on a realistic and empirically grounded analysis of the context of bureaucratic decision-making. It was an argument that has proved more powerful as a normative model than as an explanatory or descriptive one. The bureau-shaping model developed by Dunleavy, on the other hand, does have a far better fit with the experience of bureaucracy in contemporary society.

❖ Explaining privatization

- As a global trend driven by the demands of capitalism (see Martin, 1993; and 2.12.2).
- As an outcome of an agenda shift propagated by think-tanks (see Self, 1993: 64–9; and 2.8.2).
- The product of 'post-Fordism' and 'post-modernism' (see Clegg, 1990: 176–207; Burns *et al.*, 1994: 81–3; and 4.6.3).
- Part of the trend towards public-sector management (Pollitt, 1990).
- As a shift from hierarchical to contractual modes of control (Williamson, 1985; and 3.6.3). ◆

Boulding and Galbraith: the views of two 'unorthodox' economists
The predominant framework of the economic analysis of decision-making has been that of rational self-interest. However, there are a number of 'unorthodox' (Frey, 1978: 53–65) economists who have offered interpretations of decision-making which are framed by non-market models (see Monroe, 1991, for a critical assessment of economic notions of rational action and self-interest). In this section we examine two of the most prominent critics of 'orthodox' economic approaches to politics: Boulding and Galbraith.

Boulding rejects the notion that self-interest is the main motivating factor in human nature. He argues that it is wholly inadequate as an explanation of decision-making in economic and other areas of human life. He offers three categories of power:

- *threat power*, which is destructive in nature and when applied particularly to political life;
- *economic power*, which rests largely on the power to produce and exchange items – and on the constantly changing distribution of property ownership;
- *integrative power*, which is based on such relationships as legitimacy, affection, love, community and identity.

Boulding argues that it is 'integrative power' that is the most significant, in the sense that neither threat power nor economic power can achieve very much in the absence of legitimacy (Boulding, 1990: 10). Love, he argues, operates as an integrative mechanism within society. Here motivation is a desire to do good or to help. It is not based on a cost-benefit analysis, but on concern and affection. Love, in the words of the song, makes the world go round; it makes an integrated social system possible. In positing the idea of love as a motive in the calculus of decision Boulding is rejecting the basis on which economic theory has been based: self-interest. Boulding argues that decisions may be informed by an interest in the other, rather than in what the self can get out of it. Decision-making may also function through a threat: 'Do what I say, or else'. Threats operate within group decision-making, and groups may threaten one another by invoking a sanction: the threat decision scenario is one of sticks, rather than the exchange of carrots for compliance. In positing love and threat in addition to exchange as decision mechanisms, Boulding is seeking to expand economic concepts of motivation to include benevolence and co-operation, as well as the exercise of power.

Another contribution of note to the analysis of decision-making by Boulding is that of the role of image in decision-making in individuals, groups and organizations. In his book *The Image* (1956) Boulding considers how decision involves the rejection of some information and the use of other forms of information. Boulding endeavours to show that decision-making must be understood as structured by images rather than 'facts':

> We do not perceive our senses through data raw; they are mediated through highly learned processes of interpretation and acceptance ... Indeed, we only get along in the world because we consistently and persistently disbelieve the plain evidence of our senses ... What this means is that for any individual organism or organization, there are no such things as 'facts'. There are only messages filtered through a changeable value system. (*Boulding, 1956: 14*)

This does not mean that images are personal matters. Images are also shared by individuals and groups as 'public images'. Images determine behaviour and are powerful structures of thought which are resistant to change and require something of a revolution to alter (Boulding, 1956: 8).

Images act as filters and place limits on the possibilities of 'rational' decision-making processes in which, according to the rational model, all information is examined and decisions are made on the basis of the evaluation of the data. Boulding's model of decision-making is a world away from the rational economic calculating man, and has more in common with the arguments of non-decision-making (2.6) psychologists, information sciences (3.7) and 'deep theorists' (2.7) than the rational ideal beloved of his fellow economists. Dominant images and conventional wisdom are of more significance in understanding human decision-making than the rational calculation enshrined in mainline economic theory.

This theme of 'conventional wisdom' is also a central dimension of the arguments of Galbraith. One of his most famous books, *The Affluent Society* (Galbraith, 1967), claims to be aimed at the 'conventional wisdoms' which shape public policy and public opinion: those ideas and myths which sustain an economic system which tolerates private affluence and public squalor. Galbraith's notion of conventional wisdom is close to Boulding's idea of 'image'. Decision-making, he believes, was for the most part framed by the conventional wisdoms of the age, rather than by rational analysis.

Also like Boulding, Galbraith rejects the idea of self-interest as an adequate model for explaining decision-making processes, and of markets and the price system as inaccurate models of how industrial societies work. The age when markets and the price system functioned in the manner described in neoclassical economics is, Galbraith believes, long gone (Galbraith, 1969). The new order is one in which decision-making is dominated by the military-industrial complex, and one in which, as organizations become more and more complex, the power of the 'technostructure' (the managers, the experts and engineers) tends to dominate in the decision-making of government and business. Whereas the tenets of neoclassical economics hold that markets are the best decision-making mechanisms, Galbraith maintains that the real world of capitalism is shaped by the management decisions of big corporations and big producers, rather than by the interplay of owner/producers and consumers. Producers manipulate and manufacture the demands of consumers, and large corporations manipulate the decisions of politicians and bureaucrats. The decision to be a modern industrial society thus determines and shapes all other decisions in the public and private sectors. The details of this model have been subject to modification, especially with regard to the power of the big corporations and the capacities of planning against the market, but Galbraith has remained constant in his analysis of democratic decision-making as being essentially driven by the demands of the large corporations, the dominance of conventional wisdom, and the power of the technostructure.

3.6   Institutional approaches

3.6.1   Institutions matter – again: the 'new' focus on institutions

The policy approach has in large part evolved out of a dissatisfaction with looking at politics purely in terms of executives, legislatures and constitutions. David Easton's little black box offered the prospects of analysis which looked at politics and policy in ways which dispensed with institutions and constitutions in favour of the policy 'process' as a whole. However, in recent times there has been a growing awareness of the importance of placing public policy in the context of institutions. We have commented on this shift in Part One, and have given examples of this institutional analysis in terms of 'garbage can' theory and in the work of March and Olsen, Ostrom and Hall. Institutionalism encompasses a number of frameworks which are, for the most part, incommensurate (in a Kuhnian sense). As we noted in 2.11.6, we may specify three frameworks of institutional analysis:

- *sociological institutionalism*, most closely associated with the early work of David Selznick and its more recent exponents such as March and Olsen, Perrow, and Di Maggio and Powell;
- *economic institutionalism*, which has been advanced in the form of two major theories, transaction cost economics and agency theory;
- *political institutionalism*, as developed in the work of Theda Skocpol, Peter Hall and others.

The first framework is a contemporary of the structural functionalism of David Easton. Its concern was to go beyond the formal structures of institutions and examine what they did or what was their function, and how did they function in reality, as opposed to some 'ideal' rational type. As an approach it was very empirically orientated and given to communicating ideas through reasonably comprehensible English and case studies, rather than through theoretical model-building such as afflicts the economic approach. In common with Hall, sociological institutionalism had a preference for taking a historical approach to case studies and was, unlike economic institutionalism, focused on actual public institutions rather than 'firms'. Economic institutionalism, on the other hand, has developed out of theories of the firm, and has found its main applications in economic analysis. Some attempts have been made to apply the theories to both the analysis and reform of political institutions and public policy. Skocpol and Hall's approaches come from another direction – theories of state–society relations – and consequently their definition of institutions goes far beyond that of either of the two other frameworks. Thus, although they share a common focus in asserting that institutions matter, they share little else, including the definition of what the concept of 'institution' means. Each provides a different window or insight into how institutions shape the way in which decision-making takes place – and, especially in the case of economic institutionalism, how institutions ought to be arranged so as to ensure that they function 'efficiently' (*sic*).

3.6.2   Institutionalism: the functionalist framework

If David Easton's black box provided a dominant 'macro' framework within which the policy-making process was framed in the 1950s and 1960s, then Phillip Selznick was to have an equally important role in setting the agenda of 'micro' analysis in terms of a functionalist perspective of how institutions 'really worked' on the inside, as opposed to what their structures presented as their formal 'outside' rationale. On the outside, organizational life appeared to be (*à la* Max Weber) a rational machine-like 'tool'. However, Selznick argued that, by adopting a structural-functionalist model, organizations could be revealed as far more complex, 'living', 'organic' systems that adapt to their external environment in order to maintain their existence as institutions, rather than the goals and purposes for which they were established. There is, consequently, a tension in decision-making between the rational formal goals of an organization and the capacity of the human beings who actually make decisions to be concerned with the maintenance of the 'irrational' and informal goals of systems maintenance. Thus, he argues: 'as we inspect ... formal structures we begin to see that they never succeed in conquering the non-rational dimensions of organizational behaviour' (Selznick, 1948: 25). The focus of institutional analysis, he believed, should therefore be the way in which organizations interact with their environments so as to adapt, survive and thrive. The decision-making which takes place in organizations is therefore influenced by its dependence on the environment in which it is situated, rather than by purely formal, rational considerations. Having laid out the ground-work of these theories in the early 1940s, Selznick was to apply them in a justly famous study (published in 1949) of one of the most important experiments of the New Deal era in the USA, the Tennessee Valley Authority (TVA). This study was to set a benchmark for empirical work on public institutions for several decades and may be considered the text which laid the basis for later interest in the relationship of policy-making to 'implementation'. It showed how a policy could lose its way in an institution, and how, in order to ensure its survival, members of an organization could make decisions which were contrary to the defined means and ends for which it was actually established:

> All formal organizations are moulded by forces tangential to their rationally ordered structures and stated goals. Every formal organization... attempts to mobilize human and technical resources as means for the achievements of its ends. However, the individuals within the system tend to resist being treated as means. They interact as wholes, bringing to bear their own special problems and purposes; moreover the organization is embedded in an institutional matrix and is therefore subject to pressure upon it from its environment, to which some general adjustment must be made. As a result, the organization may be significantly viewed as an adaptive social structure, facing problems which arise simply because it exists as an organization in an institutional environment, independently of the special ... goals which called it into being.
> (*Selznick, 1957: 251*)

Selznick showed clearly how the notion that organizations were neutral, rational tools was far removed from the reality in which informal and environmental pressures shaped decision-making, rather than the formal structures. The TVA study offered a more realistic view of what goes on in an organization at a time when the study of public policy was largely conducted in terms of a policy/administration divide. However, the TVA study showed that, in carrying out public policy, agencies are also involved in remaking and redefining policy. One of the main reasons he offered for this relates back to the criticism we made earlier of public choice theory: that as Mayo and the human relations school argued against Taylorism, human beings have more diverse needs, not the least of these being 'self-protection' and 'self-fulfilment' (Selznick, 1949: 7–8). The existence of such needs involves the formation of an informal organization within the confines of formal structures. Decision-making by individuals and groups, therefore, must be understood as involving choices which are focused on the needs of the people who comprise an institution, as well as those who seek to advance the formal goals of the organization. People are dependent on the organization to fulfil certain needs, and in turn the organization is dependent on the environment in which it is located. Thus, as in the case of the TVA, decisions were often made that were more in the interest of the organization and its members than in advancing the formal policy goals. In other words, decision-making in organizations may be driven by an inner logic, the interests and values of its members, by its need to adapt or displace goals, rather than by rational calculation. The decision-making processes may consequently undermine and subvert formal policy and institutional arrangements.

Although the model offered considerable insight into the organizational context of decision-making, Selznick's structural-functionalist approach does suffer from a genetic defect: it does not take account of power within and around organizations. Organizations, according to the model, 'adapt' to deal with their environments. However, one could argue that this excludes the possibility that some may be powerful enough to shape their environment to suit themselves. The decision-making of some organizations may be such that its agendas are indeed set by more-powerful 'environmental ' forces outside its control. They have to adapt to survive. On the other hand, some organizations may have far more control over their decision-making, and may seek to create an environment that is conducive to its continued existence and expansion. Some organizations are better-resourced and less-dependent on their environment than others. As one critic of the Selznick model, Charles Perrow, puts it:

> The military has been able, many believe, to create, define, and shape our foreign policy ... The goals of the agencies for the blind may be displaced, but those of the American Medical Association seem very much intact – even though they do change gradually ... the dominant organizations or institutions of our society have not experienced goal displacement and have been able to institutionalize on their own terms ...
> (*Perrow, 1986: 175*)

Some organizations shape, and others are shaped. Some have the capacity/resources to set out their own agendas, make their own decisions with a measure of independence; others are constrained by their dependence on their environment – which includes more-powerful sets of decision-makers. (This issue of dependency and the capacity of powerful organizations to shape the less powerful is reviewed in Part Four, when we consider interorganizational analysis and the work of Child, and Di Maggio and Powell and others: see 4.3.7.) Furthermore, the Selznick model also neglects the way in which power operates within organizations. Elites clearly have an important role in defining the environment and in constructing an image of 'what is out there'. Selznick argues that this role is one of 'leadership' (*qua* 'statesmanship') (Selznick, 1957). But adaptation to the environment, or adaptation of the environment, may also come about by dictat, domination or tyranny. Again, as Perrow argues, the goals of the organization may simply be the goals of its leaders (Perrow, 1986: 172).

3.6.3   Economic institutionalism

❖ **Key texts**

O.E. Williamson, *Markets and Hierarchies*,1975.
O.E. Williamson, *Economic Organizations*, 1986.
A.A. Alchian and H. Demsetz, 'Production, information costs and economic organization', 1972.
E.F. Fama, 'Agency problems and the theory of the firm', 1980.
J.E. Stiglitz, 'Principal and agent', 1987.

Accounts and critiques of the theories:

T.M. Moe, 'New economics of organization', 1984.
C. Perrow, *Complex Organizations*, 1986.
D. Mueller, *Public Choice*, vols 1 and 2, 1979, 1989.
J.-E. Lane, *The Public Sector*, 1993. ◆

Whereas Selznick and his schoolfellows have emphasized (as did Mayo and Maslow and the human relations school) that human behaviour is composed of a complex set of needs and wants, with economic institutionalism we are once again back in the narrow confines of *Homo-economicus*. Whereas the sociologists envisage decision-making in institutions as involving values, interests, the impact of the environment, goal displacement, compromises, adaptation and so on, economic institutionalism returns us to a Taylorist world in which human beings are driven by self-interest and are self-regarding. We are a long way away from Boulding's view of human behaviour as motivated by love, or indeed from the possibility that, out of rational self-interest, we may adopt co-operative strategies. Efficiency is about containing self-interest and monitoring what human beings are up to. It is the world of the market place.

Transaction cost economics (TCE)
The institutionalist model(s) derived from TCE is one composed of buyers and sellers: where there is little trust, much uncertainty, duplicity and opportunism, and where contracts impose on human transactions discipline, order and control. However, notwithstanding the fact that the framework seems to have scant regard for other ideas about human behaviour and organizational theory which offer rather more convincing and comprehensive accounts, economic institutionalism has proved an attractive analytical and normative framework. Reductionism, alas, has always had an enduring appeal and, not infrequently, unfortunate consequences.

In the beginning was the market. Markets involve buying and selling. Transaction cost economics reasons that the costs of engaging in the decision to buy and sell – that is, of participating in a market – is not without costs. For example, we need to get information; we need to locate our buyers (customers) or our sellers (suppliers); we need to negotiate with them over price, terms and conditions; we need to agree contracts (*ex ante* costs) and we need to monitor them to make sure that they are being carried out (*ex post* costs). In all of this we are involved in trying to reduce uncertainty and increase control over our transactions. Neo-classical economics tended to ignore the idea that there were costs in economic transactions. However, in the 1970s this issue was taken up by the economist Oliver Williamson and developed into a theory of how firms grow.

The main elements of this theory are:

- *uncertainty*: firms confront a world of factors and forces which they cannot control or predict;
- *small-numbers bargaining*: once a contract is awarded, the firm's capacity to make decisions is limited. If the firm is dissatisfied with a supplier, a worker or its buyers, it has problems in changing the supplier, sacking the worker or getting new customers. Contracts limit the number of choices and a firm becomes dependent on a given number of contractors;
- *bounded rationality*: as with Simon, the information available is imperfect. There are limitations in what can be known about contractors;
- *opportunism*: given other factors – such as bounded rationality – and given the nature of human beings, contractors will operate in ways which maximize their interests rather than the firm's interests. Two aspects of opportunism are highlighted by TCE: adverse selection and moral hazard;
- *moral hazard*: 'when the cat's away, the mice will play'. Principals (purchasers/employers/buyers) cannot monitor their subordinates/agents/suppliers all the time. Given the opportunity, agents (providers/sellers/employees) will maximize their own utility and interests rather than that specified in the terms of the contract;
- *adverse selection*: 'telling the whole truth and nothing but ...'. As there are limits on resources, information, time, etc., principals cannot make a complete search of the type of people (or firms) they take on. Furthermore, agents (sellers/employees/providers) are aware of this and do not reveal all the aspects of their abilities, skills, honesty or industriousness to a prospective principal.

Williamson argued that there comes a point in the life of a firm when the costs of buying and selling with outside firms involves high transaction costs (TCs) which might best be reduced by buying a supplier and placing it within a hierarchy of other departments or divisions. A firm grows by incorporating firms within its structure so as to reduce all the uncertainties and difficulties of doing business in the market place. Instead, the firm adopts a 'hierarchy' of activities and divisions within itself so as to lower transaction costs by substituting an internal market or price system for an external arrangement. From this model Williamson deduces that hierarchies replace markets when the costs of transactions are such as to make for lower efficiency. Now, because the firm contains within its corporate form divisions and departments where once it did business with them as outside firms, the costs of monitoring contracts (a major component of transaction costs) falls. For Williamson the core of the theory is that lower transaction costs -- more certainty, more control, more capacity to monitor the opportunism of individuals and subordinates – will make for greater efficiency in the firm. Hierarchies grow as markets fail to keep transaction costs down. Complexity and the higher costs of dealing with factors such as uncertainty, bargaining, bounded rationality and opportunism mean that the firm must grow in order to lower the costs which impair efficiency. Given the nature of human beings as rather untrustworthy creatures, long-term contracts are a particular problem for the efficient firm. It makes sense to say, Williamson argues, that the longer the term of the contract, the greater the uncertainty involved – and the greater the costs of monitoring that contract. It may be far more efficient to replace a market relationship with a supplier with a command or authority relationship. Picture the scene: the managing director of Sprockets PLC becomes head of the sprockets division of the Megabits Corporation. Megabits no longer has the costs of monitoring the contract with an outside outfit, the business is now an 'infit' (so to speak). Of course, this does not mean that Megabits does not incur internal transaction costs with its sprockets division, but it is now under better control: there is less uncertainty, and internal contracts can be more effectively monitored and enforced.

Agency theory

Agency theory, or, to give its full title, 'principal–agent' theory (see Stiglitz, 1987; Alchian and Demsetz, 1972) focuses on the problem of the relationship between principals (purchasers), contracts and agents (providers). TCE argues that efficiency involves the idea of low transaction costs by removing as much uncertainty and maximizing the capacity to monitor and control transactions. Agency theory suggests that this is a problem within and between firms of ensuring that providers do what they are supposed to do in accordance with what the purchaser – principal – has demanded. The relationship between principal and agents in the market place is problematic for all the reasons which TCE sets out (above): as a consequence the principal is highly dependent on (and at the mercy of) agents. Employees will be after their own interests; outside firms will be more interested in their profits than those of the purchaser; cheating and an eye to the main chance (opportunism) therefore form the essential considerations of principals in monitoring their agents.

Let us pass over the somewhat contentious view of human nature in this model and focus instead on what the framework offers by way of an insight into the institutional context of decision-making. The first point is that the principal–agent theory views decision-making as being to do with calculations about implementation and enforcement. That is, the main issue at stake is that we see a world populated by buyers and sellers, the decisions of buyers involve judgements about the capacities of other members of the market – what other principals are up to and whether agents will carry out what is required of them. The costs of monitoring the relationship will, in conditions of high uncertainty, a small number of agents, poor information, an inevitably opportunistic behaviour of agents, be higher in dealing with outside agents than with intraorganizational agents. The answer to this troublesome relationship, in which agents seem to have the upper hand, is the selection of institutions – markets or hierarchies – so that contracts can be monitored at low cost.

Let us imagine, therefore, a situation in which decision-makers are framing a policy for disabled people. Part of the calculation which must be made if they are operating within this agency framework is that of institutional choice. Is policy to be enacted within the firm (governmental agencies) or outside the firm, say through the voluntary sector? On the one hand, decision-makers might make the calculation that the policy is best executed through governmental agencies, thus lowering the transaction costs relative to dealing with outside 'contractors' such as the the voluntary sector. On the other hand, decision-makers may conclude that, for reasons of cost-cutting and public-sector savings, the tasks might best be performed through the voluntary sector, thus incurring more risk, more uncertainty, and all the problems associated with monitoring an outside provider. If the decision-makers have read the agency theory, they could well reach the decision that the best course to take is to use an outside agency, thus saving money. As volunteers will do it for less, you can put them on short-term contracts so that, if they do not deliver, the relationship can be terminated, but in awarding the task of implementing the policy to outside agents the contract has to be such that it maximizes the ability of the provider to control the agent *qua* individual and 'firm'. In other words, the agency model, in claiming to have a theory of how human beings make decisions, proposes that in making decisions we should also be in the business of choosing those institutional arrangements which best provide for contractual (monitorable) relationships between purchasers and providers. Like public-choice theorists, economic institutionalists who deploy arguments based on TCE and agency theory are keen advocates of the idea that markets should be brought into play so as to improve the efficiency of the public sector (see figure 3.8).

Figure 3.8   The TCE framework

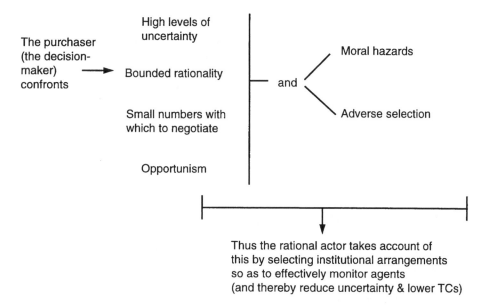

The key point about agency theory as a model of public or political decision-making is that it posits that when actors are enagaged in making decisions, an important dimension of choice is the institutional modes available in a given situation. Whereas the 'rational' view sees decision-making as involving a means/ends dichotomy, the agency model emphasizes how in making choices about goals we are making judgements about principal–agent problems. Effective and efficient decision-making (like the manufacture of sprockets in a Taylorist factory) involves a capacity to monitor the behaviour of agents. (Of course, Machiavelli had much to say about keeping an eye on friends and enemies which is in line with the agency model. He also thought that you could not trust anybody, and suckers should on no account be given an even break. Politics is politics, and business is business, after all.)

The problem of decision-making as revealed in TCE and agency theory is the way in which advantages are on the side of agents or providers rather than on principals. In the political context, this perspective suggests that the decisions of voters, politicians and bureaucrats may be seen as framed by uncertainty, inadequate information, only a few groups from which to choose, bounded rationality, and the fact that principals cannot turn their backs on agents because they will be feathering their own nests (and vice versa) – the so-called moral hazard. At the same time, if we accept this view of the political system it is likely that the whole process is riddled with adverse selection because of the fact that people are not honest about themselves and that getting more information about them is difficult and costly. For the proponents of TCE and agency theory as a model of political life, the answer appears to be to improve the way in which contractual arrangements can keep tabs on actors in the policy process and the decisions they make. One approach, of course, is to infuse public services with a consumerist ethos so that the voter/citizen is seen as a customer whose relationship to public services is mediated through quasi contracts such as performance targets and 'mission statements'. The impact of the arguments for looking at public policy in 'contractual' terms has, as we discuss in Part Four, been extensive (see 4.3.5, 4.4, 4.5.3).

❖ Public policy, TCE and agency theory

The use and critique of these frameworks in policy analysis has taken several forms. Key readings include:

Analysis of the policy process

Moe (1984); Weingast (1989); Weingast and Marshall (1988); North (1990); and Lane (1993: 166–89).

Policy-making in a democracy not only involves deciding on a programme structure as well as the ends and means of a programme. It also comprises the implementation stage, the activities of public servants as administrators or professionals. The implementation of policies gives rise to the typical double principal–agent problem within the public sector referred to by the troublesome conceptual pair: politics versus administration. In addition to the electoral cycle of picking the politicians and choosing an agenda, civil servants have to be hired by government to execute policy decisions.

The implementation stage requires a set of activities monitored by the state in order to accomplish political objectives. Contracts have to be made between the state and civil servants stipulating what the state expects in return for remuneration. Due to the transactions costs involved in hiring and monitoring public officials, the state typically employs the

bureau model for handling various state activities. Basic to the operation of the bureau is a principal–agent relationship between politicians on the one hand and civil servants on the other hand.
(*Lane, 1993: 188*)

Analysis of policy outcomes

Le Grand and Bartlett (eds) (1993: *passim*); Self (1993: 127–8, 149, 165, 199, 201, 230).

Le Grand and Bartlett, reviewing the use of quasi-markets in social policy, offer a conclusion in terms of TCE that it has pushed up TCs in the delivery of welfare services:

> if only because of the increased amount of information now required to coordinate the transactions between the now separate decision-making centres of purchaser and provider organizations ... Transaction costs may therefore be a significant problem, and one which needs to be addressed by policy makers ... Overall, the issue of appropriate institutional design to minimise transaction costs is one which will undoubtedly require a long period of experimentation and disruption in the evolving quasi-market system.
> (*Le Grand and Bartlett, 1993: 211–12*) ◆

3.6.4   Political institutionalism: institutions in the context of state–society relations

As we noted in 2.11.6, the renewal of interest in the institutional context of public policy has also taken place within what are termed 'state-centred' approaches to the relationship of the state to society. The development of this approach has been outlined by Skocpol (1985).

Hall (1986) takes a far broader concept of institutions than is employed by economic institutionalists who focus on constitutional and formal organizational practices and arrangements or the 'state-centred' approaches discussed by Skocpol. His approach is fundamentally opposed to the functionalist sociological framework of Selznick and Co., and although it shares with economic institutionalism a belief in the importance of institutions as having a determining role, it does not share the individualistic assumptions, or its belief that we can make choices about institutional arrangements as easily as is suggested by the economists. Hall's model gives a macro view of the relationships of institutions to society and state, rather than single organizations or the mechanisms of individual rational choice.

For Hall, focusing on institutions/organizations refers to an analysis of 'the formal rules, compliance procedures, and operating practices that structure the relationship between individuals in various units of the polity and economy' (Hall, 1986: 19). Whereas the IRC model (see 2.11.6) developed by Ostrom (from Moe's analysis of TCE and agency theory) rather vaguely refers to the 'attributes of the community', Hall's approach is to expand the notion of institution to include the interaction of state and society as well as of the international economy. Institutional factors in the wide sense have two main roles:

- they affect the degree of power that actors have over decision-making and its outcomes;
- the institutional position of actors influences the definition of his/her interests, responsibilities and relationships.

The institutionalist focus means that the analysis of policy-making involves taking account of the way in which the configuration of interests and ideas within an institutional context shapes and determines the conduct of policy-making. However, institutions do not exist in isolation from the wider relationship of state to society. Furthermore, Hall argues that, unlike the approach taken by economic institutionalism, a state–society approach must take account of specific historical experiences. The most developed account of Hall's institutional approach is his detailed study of economic policy-making over the post-war period in Britain and France. His conclusion is that economic policy in both countries has been the result of institutional structuring of state–society relations. In the case of Britain and France, the interaction of ideas and interests, Hall argues, means that economic policy may be explained in terms of five sets of structural variables:

- organization of labour;
- organization of capital;
- organization of state (legislative and executive institutions);
- organization of political systems (electoral practices and rules, political parties);
- the structural position of the country within the international system.

By taking a more extensive definition of institutions it offers a convincing account of the politics of economic policy-making in the two countries over a long period of time. This is an important contrast with the economic approaches which require that we abandon any analysis of the real world in building a model of institutional decision-making. Even where the model has been adapted to study public policy, such as the Ostrom model, the approach's focus on individual rational choices makes it difficult, if not impossible, to apply in an actual case study (Jenkins-Smith, 1991: 160). The strength of Hall's approach is that it provides a framework for the analysis of decision-making in historical and comparative terms. It requires that we understand how institutions constrain decision-making in government outside the formal constitutional arrangements that also shape and often determine decisions that are made. By developing a framework which is suited to examining institutions over a long period of time Hall is also able to take account of two aspects which are not considered in the analytical forms of the economic approach: ideas and personalities. In showing how institutions shape the choices which policy-makers make, Hall argues that ideas and ideologies have an important role to play:

> On the one hand, organizations can structure the very logic associated with rational action from a particular social position; and on the other hand organizations are indispensable to the diffusion of ideologies among multiple social actors ... organizational relations can alter the basic logic of political rationality for many actors by altering their relationship to other actors. Not only does organization alter the power of a social group, it can also affect the interpretation they put on their own interests, and thus the direction of their influence. In this case, the ideas or perceptions of the relevant actors are not an exogenous variable but a component of their rational action as it is situationally determined ... ideas acquire force when they find organizational means of expression. Most ideas have some power on their own: a number of people will be persuaded by them. But the social power of any set of ideas is magnified when those ideas are taken up by a powerful political organization, integrated with other ideological appeals, and widely disseminated. The likelihood of this happening may depend partly on the congruence between a new set of economic ideas and other facets of the longstanding ideology of an organization.
> (*Hall, 1986: 277–80*)

The framework demonstrates that if we want to explain how, why and when decisions were taken, and with what effects, decision-making must be placed within the context of the relationship of institutions and state–society relations, but his historical approach permits us to consider the role that (real live) people can have on decision-making. Institutions exist and have an impact on how decisions are made as they provide the context within which judgements are made, but they do not eliminate the 'free will of policy-makers' (Hall, 1986: 259).

Having said that policy-makers are free to make choices (within the constraints of institutional arrangements), Hall does not accept the central assumption of the economists, that we are free to choose and reform institutional structures. The view which runs through TCE and agency theory is that, as Chandler (1962, 1977) argues, structures follow strategy. In the case of managerial decisions about company growth, expansion is the outcome of strategic choices. The new institutional arrangements are means to those strategic ends. However, in the case of political decision-makers Hall doubts that, on the strength of historical evidence, structures follow strategy: it is more usual in politics for the structures to shape strategy. History shows that political arrangements are far less manipulable than the organization of firms – however big. At a time when reforms in the public sector are greatly influenced by the rationale contained in the economic/managerial approach, that the institutions of government and administration can be changed like those of something infinitely less complex such as a firm or a sausage factory, is a salutary warning to reformers eager to marketize and contractualize public decision-making.

3.7   Personality, cognition and information processing in decision-making

3.7.1   Decision-making: the behavioural and cognitive contexts

The study of decision-making owes much to the contribution of psychology and the 'information sciences' (such as systems analysis, cybernetics and artificial intelligence). In this section we examine how the ideas, models and metaphors advanced in these disciplines can help to analyse decision-making in and for the policy process.

The contribution of psychology to understanding decision-making has been extensive. As section 3.5.2 noted, psychologists such as Mayo and Maslow have contributed greatly to the development of management theory. However, despite the fact that the early development of the policy approach was very much concerned with incorporating the insights of psychology into public policy, the influence of psychology on the study of policy-making has not been as widespread as in management. With the rise of managerialism in the public sector, it is to be expected that the influence of psychology on the study of public policy will grow. This comparative neglect of the psychological context of policy analysis has been to the detriment of our understanding of decision-making. The notion of decision in the policy sciences has, by and large, rested on notions of rationality and self-interest which, when examined from the psychological point of view, are as the human relations school showed, grossly simplistic concepts of human motivation. As Harold Lasswell believed, the psychological dimension is absolutely central to comprehending the politics of power. And yet too much of the theory which informs policy analysis rests upon a slender and partial view of 'rational' human behaviour. This is especially true of economics which, as Boulding argues, provides a very inadequate explanation of decision-making at either a collective or an individual level.

In this section of the book we are concerned with two main approaches to the study of human decision-making which derive from psychological and informational theories:

- approaches to decision-making which focus on factors such as human emotions, personality, motivations, group behaviour, and interpersonal relationships. These derive from the insights of psycho-analytical theory and social psychology. Included in this category is the work of Harold Lasswell, who best illustrates the early use of psycho-analytical theories to analyse the impact of of personality on decision-making (3.7.2). More recently this analysis of personality and politics has been advanced by Greenstein (3.7.7); Irving Janis, on the other hand, has done most to apply theories of group psychology to the study of political decision-making (3.7.3);
- the second category of theories derives from a different, though related, source and is concerned with issues such as how human beings recognize problems, how they use information, how they make choices between various options, how they perceive 'reality' or 'problems', how information is processed, and how information is communicated in organizations. We include in this category examples of three theorists who have made important contributions to understanding the cognitive dimensions of decision-making: Simon, Vickers and Deutsch.

Herbert Simon' s approach, which developed out of his early ideas on bounded rationality and his investigations of computers and artificial intelligence, has been perhaps the most influential (3.7.4). Sir Geoffrey Vickers, whose ideas about cognition are very close to Simon's, and who is somewhat unjustly neglected by comparison, developed his ideas out of his practical experiences and his observations of 'self-regulating' systems. More than any other contributor to this field Vickers stands out as a theorist who combines practical knowledge with a concern for cognition (or reality judgements) and human values and beliefs (or value judgements). As the ideas of Simon are relatively well known and available (that is, they are still in print!) we make no apologies for devoting rather more space to Vickers than to Simon (3.7.5). Karl Deutsch, like Vickers, also draws on cybernetic models, but is concerned with how information 'flows' within organizations and how 'communication' takes place (3.7.6). Simon has been the most widely used framework; Vickers the most neglected; and Deutsch is possibly the theorist whose ideas have the closest resonance with some of the concerns about governance which have surfaced in the 1990s.

The theories we examine form a body of ideas which have, over the years, proved of most use in the analysis of public policy decision-making. It is, however, an extensive field of investigation, and readers interested in more recent developments are advised to consult Greenstein (1992), Fiske and Taylor (1991), Fischer and Johnson (1986), and Lindzey and Aronson (eds) (1985). The psychological contribution to public policy has been particularly important in evaluation research, and having read this part of the book readers would be advised to examine the work of Donald Campbell (see 4.5.2) and the guide to decision research by Carroll and Johnson (1990). Another area where psychological approaches have had an impact is in terms of learning models as applied to public policy-making: see Argyris and Schön (1978) and 4.6.4 of this volume.

3.7.2   Lasswell and the psychology of decision-makers

It is fitting that we begin our consideration of the psychology of decision-making with Harold Lasswell; first of all, because Lasswell was one of the earliest social scientists to develop a psychological approach to politics, and secondly, because two key contributors to the field, Herbert Simon and Irving Janis, were respectively his pupil and research collaborator. Prior to Lasswell the political scientist most closely associated with the development of a psychological approach was Graham Wallas (1908) whose seminars Lasswell attended whilst in London in the 1920s. Wallas was critical of the fact that the study of politics tended to be preoccupied with the rational content of politics and with the analysis of 'deliberate thought', rather than human emotions and 'irrationalities'. Lasswell's own particular focus on the non-rational aspects of human political behaviour came out of an interest in the growth of propaganda and his observations on how modern elites had developed a capacity to shape the ideas and exploit the fears and anxieties of the masses. His interest naturally extended to studying the ideas of Freud and Harry Stack Sullivan (as well as Marx), and by the late 1920s he had begun to apply these theories to analysing the role of personality in politics. His ideas about personality and power came together in his study *Psychopathology and Politics* published in 1930 (Lasswell, 1930a), and later in *Power and Personality*, published after the war in 1948 (Lasswell, 1948a). In between and afterwards there were numerous papers and other writings which elaborated his theories. The best introduction to his approach is a book whose title says it all: *Politics: who gets what, when, how* (Lasswell, 1936).

Who gets what, when and how refers to values. From the Lasswellian perspective, therefore, decision-making was a process to be analysed in terms of who gets what values, when they get them, and how they are obtained. Politics, he argued, was the process in which people

Figure 3.9   Lasswell's model of the political process

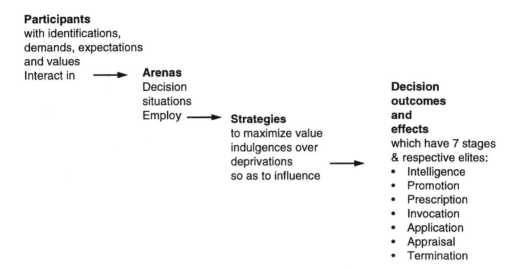

Participants
with identifications,
demands, expectations
and values
Interact in ⟶ **Arenas**
Decision
situations
Employ ⟶ **Strategies**
to maximize value
indulgences over
deprivations ⟶
so as to influence

**Decision
outcomes
and
effects**
which have 7 stages
& respective elites:
• Intelligence
• Promotion
• Prescription
• Invocation
• Application
• Appraisal
• Termination

aimed to secure and advance valued outcomes through institutions. Thus the political process could be analysed in terms of the model in figure 3.9.

The values of participants he categorized as: power; enlightenment; wealth; well-being; skill; affection; respect; and rectitude. These values are pursued through their corresponding institutions, and divided into two groups:

1 *Deference values and institutions*
   Power: governmental, legal and political institutions;
   Enlightenment: research institutions and the mass media;
   Wealth: production and market institutions.

2 *Welfare values and institutions*
   Well-being: medical/health care institutions;
   Skill: institutions which give training and skill in arts, crafts and professions;
   Affection: family and friends;
   Respect: institutions which award distinction or honour;
   Rectitude: institutions which apply religious or ethical standards.

In pursuing these values an individual's success or failure may be envisaged as a ratio of indulgences to deprivations. However, from the psychological point of view, what especially interested Lasswell was the type of person who chose 'power' values and institutions as their predominant concern as opposed to other values: in other words, what kinds of men and women choose a political career as opposed to other directions, such as a skill career (a painter or an accountant), or focused more on spending time with the family (affection).

Decision-making is something which takes place in all kinds of institutions or arenas with different participants and different perspectives. Lasswell's approach is to address how values shape decision-making. He thus studied a wide variety of institutional decision-making – including that of a mental hospital. The political type, however, wâs different to other types of human being because of the degree to which power values were to the fore in his or her personality. Thus, for example, within a church or hospital there will be priests and doctors for whom 'power' may be an indulgence necessary for them to participate in decision-making. This may be such that it places a strain on other 'welfare' values for which power is only a means. The policy analyst has to consider not just the social, environmental, world, and other contexts within which people make decisions, he/she must also understand the personalities of the individuals concerned. Decision-making for Lasswell has to be placed within the context of analysing person, personality, group and culture as a 'system' or as a whole.

His psychological approach was concerned with the way in which people related to themselves, to others, to groups and to their wider culture and society. He thus analysed the way in which national circumstances or conditions impacted upon personal security and their resulting political outcomes – as in his analysis of the rise of Hitler – but he also used individual case studies (Lasswell, 1933). Lasswell argued that the study of decision-making and political leaders reveals a wealth of psychopathic traits. His early work in this field addressed the issue of power and personality type. He argued that those who sought and maintained the exercise of political power had usually experienced a severe blow to their ego. The resulting damage to their self-esteem prompts the search for compensation in the quest for political power (Lasswell, 1948a: 37–58). Decision-makers therefore may well be seen as engaging in some kind of compensation for a sense of injured pride or self-esteem. In making decisions they also 'displace' a private motive with a public object. This idea of displacement is one of the most important aspects of Lasswell's work for the study of public policy. He expressed this in the formula:

$$p\} \, d\} \, r = P$$

(where p = private motives; d = displacement on to public objects; r = rationalization in terms of the 'public interest'; P = the political man; and } means 'transformed into'.

The political man has – like all men – private motives which are developed in his early life. At some time these private motives become 'displaced' on to public objects. Again, this he has in common with many other kinds of people. However, the political man rationalizes this displacement in terms of it being in the public interest.

Lasswell argues that there are various types of 'political man': political agitators; administrators and theorists; and various combinations of them. These types derive from the values which they place on different aspects or dimensions of political activity:

- *the agitator*: places a high value on the response of the public;
- *the administrator*: places a high value on the co-ordination of effect in continuing activity;
- *the theorist*: places a high value on abstraction.

> Political movements derive their vitality from the displacement of private affects upon public objects. The affects which are organized in the family are redistributed upon various social objects such as the state. Political crises are complicated by the concurrent reactivation of specific primitive impulses. One might suppose that when important decisions are in process of being made society would deliberate very calmly; but the disproportionality between the behaviour of man during wars, revolutions, and elections, and the requirements of rational thinking is notorious. Evidently a reactivating process is at work here; there is a regressive tendency to reawaken primitive sadism and lust.
> (*Lasswell, 1930a*: 264–5)

A Lasswellian analysis of decision-making, therefore, would be interested in how these private motives come to shape the definitions of 'public' interest, and how different types of political actor interact with the wider social system. Of particular importance in this approach to decision-making is the use of biographies (if not psychobiography; see p. 343) to understand the background and motivations of actors. This emphasis on the personal and on the impact of personalities on decision-making is something which features in historical approaches to public policy, but has been considered less important by social scientists. For Lasswell decision analysis involves both the macro levels of society, culture and institutions, and also the 'micro' level of how human beings bring their personal feelings, emotions, motivations, fears, and so on, to bear upon the problems they confront. Hence, for Lasswell the role of the policy sciences was crucial in helping decision-makers clarify their values, intentions, motives and perceptions, so as to 'prevent' the irrational impulses which we all have tending to dominate and determine the decisions we (as a society) take. Policy analysis therefore was something like psycho-analysis: a method of policy-making which aims at a clear or conscious grasp of value objectives, and their means of realization.

After Lasswell the psychological approach to politics and power was somewhat neglected until the publication of the Adorno (Adorno *et al.* 1950/1993) study of the authoritarian personality. This controversial examination of the background of authoritarian types sparked off research in the measurement of authoritarian traits in the left and right, dogmatism and Machiavellianism. A number of approaches have followed Lasswell's interests in the psychological dimensions of politics and decision. The literature which deals with how elites are subject to selective perception and bias in the face of contrary evidence, for example, is strongly supportive of Lasswell's concern with the way in which egos are liable to defend ideas and perceptions and succumb to subconscious pressures and instincts (see Fiske and Taylor, 1984; Innis, 1978. Sabatier makes use of such material to support his advocacy coalition model: see Sabatier, 1993: 33–4).

❖ The unconscious and personality in decision-making

The 'psychic prison' metaphor

Gareth Morgan (Morgan, 1986, 199–231) uses the psychological approach to organizations in terms of a 'psychic prison' metaphor. By this he means that we can view organizations and the decision-making which takes place therein as prisons created, not by the rational conscious mind which is the overwhelming concern of decision analysis, but as a product of the unconscious mind:

- What is the relationship between sexual repression and organizations?
- Are organizations forms of family?
- Are organizations a flight from our mortality?
- Are organizations expressions of anxiety?
- Do people use organizations as dolls and teddy bears: forms of comfort and security?
- Can decision-making be understood in terms of the way in which sensation, thought, intuition and feeling predominate?

Morgan notes that the use of psychological approaches enables us to examine the link between unconscious processes and the structure of organizations, and assists in identifying barriers to change. Applications to the 'psychic' metaphor include the sexual dimensions of organizational structure and behaviour; personality and management styles; and power relations (Morgan, 1986: 365–71).

Sexuality and power

One of the most important areas wherein the ideas of psychoanalysis are applied within a political context is that of sexual repression and male domination. This is, for example, a major focus of the work of Foucault (1986) and Marcuse (1954). The model of decisions as manifestations of the subconscious lends itself to radical feminist critiques of decisional power as dominated by male power and patriarchy (Mitchell, 1977).

Psychoanalytical biographies

The idea that we can explain decision-making in terms of a psychoanalytical treatment of biography provides a fascinating insight into the motives and drives of 'great men and women'. Can we explain decisions less as products of rational deliberation and power, than as outcomes of their unconscious mind and early childhood experiences? (Freud himself applied this in his book with Bullitt on President Woodrow Wilson (1967).) A number of recent politicians have been subject to a psycho-biographical treatment: see, for example, Thatcher (Abse, 1989); and Gough Whitlam (Walter, 1980). Louis Stewart has made a detailed study of US and British prime ministers from a Jungian perspective (Stewart, 1992). A rich source of material is to be found in the contributions to the *Journal of Psychohistory*. In general, see: Greenstein and Lerner (1971).

Foreign policy

This has been a field in which attention has been given to the impact of personality on decision-making. See Burke and Greenstein (1989); George (1980); Kull (1988); McClosky (1967).

Keynes and personality

Keynes was a thoughtful and provocative biographical essayist. He believed that personality had a considerable impact on decision-making. His most famous exposition of this theory was in his brilliant sketches of the main protagonists at the Paris conference of 1919, which are contained in his indictment of the Treaty, *The Economic Consequences of the Peace and Essays in Biography*. Analysing the role of Clemenceau, Lloyd George and President Wilson, for example, Keynes concludes that: 'Out of their disparities and weaknesses the Treaty was born, child of the least worthy attributes of each of its parents, without nobility, without morality, without intellect' (Keynes, 1963: 39). Thus although Keynes thought that, in the long run, it was ideas that shaped policy, he did not discount the part played by the personality of decision-makers.

The psychology of incompetent decision-making

Norman Dixon's book (Dixon, 1976) on military blunders and mishaps from the Crimea to Arnhem is a study of how organizational and personality factors interact with often tragic and costly results. It is a highly informative account of how decision-making takes place in a classic Weberian hierarchy. Perhaps it may serve as a paradigm of decision-making in hierarchical organizations in other areas of public policy. Dixon makes extensive use of history, social psychology and psycho-analysis which can be read in conjunction with Sutherland (1994) and Janis (1982). On Janis see the following section. ◆

3.7.3   Decision-making and group psychology

The ideas of Le Bon have been influential in showing how irrational individuals can be in mass groups. Le Bon argued in his book on the crowd (Le Bon, 1895) that as a member of a crowd individuals think and behave differently than they would in a state of isolation. Crowds produce a 'collective mind' which gives a feeling of invulnerability, helps to spread feelings and ideas, and makes individuals more open to suggestion. Le Bon's arguments were accepted by both Freud (1991: 98–109) and Jung (1988: 86): men in the mass are dangerous and irrational. This idea that the crowd or big group is irrational gives rise to the idea that small groups are perhaps more rational. However, this faith in the rationality of small decision-making groups may be questioned in the light of researches which demonstrate that small groups are just as prone to the condition of the crowd. The study of the effectiveness of group decision-making was developed further as a result of war. Kurt Lewin and Wilfred Bion (at the Tavistock Institute in London) and Leon Festinger, amongst others, pioneered research in the 1950s and 1960s into how highly cohesive groups make decisions and enforce group norms (de Board, 1978; Janis, 1982: 4–5, 277. On the use of Lewin to study the 'life space' of political actors, see Young, 1977/79 and 3.7.7 below).

A good deal of research has gone into investigating the influence of groups on individuals. Such research shows how powerful the group can be in distorting perceptions and judgements. A group norm can become a reference point for the decision-making and judgements of members of the group (see, for example, Muzafer Sherif, 1936; Solomon E. Asch, 1955). Experiments on group behaviour have consistently shown that individuals in groups are under pressure to conform to group norms and perception of information. A great many studies support the theory that decision-making and judgement is distorted by the influence of group pressures. Whereas the cohesiveness of a group is held to be a major factor in the achievements of tasks, the same cohesiveness can have a negative effect (Wright *et al.*, 1970: 634–43).

Janis and groupthink

One of the most recent and more relevant theories for students of public policy is that propounded by Janis, 'groupthink': 'the psychological drive for consensus at any cost that suppresses dissent and the appraisal of alternatives in cohesive decision-making groups' (Janis, 1982: 8). Rational models argue that information and the capacity of decision-makers to utilize information in an optimal way is important to explaining what is going on in a decision-making process. In

Groupthink Janis argues that because of the way in which members of a group may be loyal to a group's viewpoint or interpretation of information, consensus blinds decision makers to the realities. The pressures to conform to what the group thinks, as opposed to what other people think, can lead, as he shows in the case of the Bay of Pigs crisis, to a total misinterpretation of the signals: perfect failure. In 1961 President Kennedy and his advisers approved a CIA plan to invade Cuba. It failed in three days. The fiasco resulted, Janis argues, from the fact that the plan was based on a pile of assumptions which had not been tested or subjected to critical appraisal.

The model (simplified below, figure 3.10) suggests that there are three antecedent conditions (A, B1 and B2) which if present in decision-making may lead the group to the kind of uncritical thinking which was evident in the Bay of Pigs episode. The tendency to seek concurrence may be discerned in a variety of symptoms (C, D and E) and ultimately in a low probability of a successful outcome.

A   Cohesiveness of decision-makers:
     The primary condition for groupthink is that decision-makers have a high degree of cohesiveness:

Figure 3.10   Groupthink

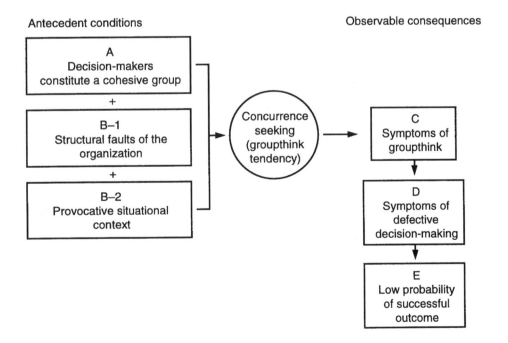

Source: Adapted from Janis and Mann (1977) and Janis (1982)

> The more amiability and *esprit de corps* among the members of an individual group of policy-makers, the greater is the danger that independent critical thinking will be replaced by groupthink. (*Janis, 1982: 245*)

The sense of being a cohesive group increases the likelihood of it developing irrational fears of those that are 'not one of us' (as Mrs Thatcher might have put it!). When a group has this sense of cohesiveness and the other conditions (B-1 and B-2) are present then Janis believes that the chances of concurrency-seeking are increased.

B-1   Structural faults of the organization:
Allied to the concurrency seeking is a potent mix of structural faults in the way the group is organized:

1   insulation of the group;
2   lack of tradition of impartial leadership;
3   lack of norms requiring methodical procedures;
4   homogeneity of members' social background and ideology.

B-2   Provocative situational context.
To this mix of organizational faults add a provocative situation or decision which involves:

1   high stress from external threats with low hope of a better solution than that advocated by group leaders;
2   low self-esteem temporarily induced by:

- recent failures that make members' inadequacies salient;
- excessive difficulties on current decision-making tasks that lower each member's sense of self-efficacy;
- moral dilemmas: apparent lack of feasible alternatives except ones that violate ethical standards.

C   Symptoms of groupthink:
The observable consequences of these conditions are seen in three types of symptoms:

Type 1: overestimation of the group:
- illusion of invulnerability;
- belief in inherent morality of the group.

Type 2: closed-mindedness:
- collective rationalizations;
- stereotypes of out-groups.

Type 3: pressures towards uniformity:
- self-censorship;
- illusion of unanimity;
- direct pressure on dissenters;
- self-appointed mindguards.

D   Symptoms of defective decision-making:
The manifestations of 'defective' decision-making which will result from groupthink encompass:

- incomplete survey of alternatives;
- incomplete survey of objectives;
- failure to examine risks of preferred choice;
- failure to reappraise initially rejected alternatives;
- poor information search;
- selective bias in processing information at hand;
- failure to work out contingency plans.

Groupthink is a model which fits well with the dynamics of small groups. Policy-making in modern government greatly relies on small working groups and committees; in this context it may be said to operate in such a way as to reinforce a view or belief. Thus groupthink has been seen to have its greatest applicability in situations in which a decision or policy is made by a group which develops a strong *esprit de corps* and commitment to a certain line such that it resists other interpretations of information and events.

❖ Case studies of groupthink

The Falklands war

Lebow (1983), Heller (1983), Gray and Jenkins (1985), and Greenaway *et al.* (1992) use the model to show that the war was an outcome of, on the one hand, 'defence avoidance', and on the other, groupthink. Lebow suggests that the war was a classic instance of defence avoidance in that decision-makers did not want to face up to the truth and all the psychological stress that would be involved. Instead, information was interpreted in a way which confirmed what they wanted to be the case – that Argentina would not invade the Falklands. Instead of trying to confront this problem the government simply persisted with negotiations which were going nowhere. Groupthink occurred when decision-makers were isolated in their beliefs about the intentions of Argentina. The decision to sink the *Belgrano* was also an illustration of how a small group operates to reinforce perceptions. These problems were made worse by the existence of an organizational structure in which the various parts of the governmental machine were not functioning in a 'systematic' way.

Excellent study material on the crisis is to be found in Cmnd 8787 (The Franks report).

The Iran hostage siege

Ridgeway (1983) and Smith (1984) provide accounts of the (Carter) Iran hostage rescue mission in terms of the groupthink model.

The *Challenger* space disaster

Aronson (1988) argues that the decision to go ahead with the ill-fated mission was the result of groupthink.

Stories of groupthink

The French at Agincourt: defeated by groupthink?

In Shakespeare's *Henry V* (III.vi) we see how the French military leaders had made up their minds that the English were a piece of brioche. One of their number is less convinced of this view, but is outnumbered:

> CONSTABLE OF FRANCE: ... Alas poor Harry of England! he longs not for the dawning as we do.
> DUKE OF ORLEANS: What a wretched and peevish fellow is this King of England, to mope with his fat-brained followers so far out of his knowledge!
> CONSTABLE: If the English had any apprehension they would run away.
> ORLEANS: That they lack; for if their heads had any intellectual armour they could never wear such heavy head-pieces.
> LORD RAMBURE: That island of England breeds very valiant creatures; their mastiffs are of unmatchable courage.
> ORLEANS: Foolish curs ...! You may as well say, that's a valiant flea that dare eat his breakfast on the lip of a lion.
> CONSTABLE: Just, just; ...

Once upon a time ...

There was a king who was fooled into buying clothes that only wise people could see. His ministers when told that only wise people could see the clothes all agreed that they were 'absolutely wonderful, Sire'. News spread, and when the king decided to show off his new clothes, it was only a foolish boy who shouted: 'But the king is naked!'

The king had relied on his advisers and was amongst the first victims of groupthink in storyland. As we all know, he was not the last. But that is another story.

The wisdom of the fool

The tendency of kings to be surrounded by 'yes men' has long been a familiar theme of fable and history. In times long gone, the fool or jester had an important political function: he was given licence to say things and to challenge the prevailing consensus in ways which might well have landed a member of the king's court in deep trouble. The most famous example of this is the fool in Shakespeare's *King Lear*, who freely and openly criticizes his master for dividing up his kingdom, whilst the Earl of Kent is banished for daring to question Lear's sanity and policy.

How to make a disaster

The ultimate cost of poor decision-making is the loss of human life. One of the most spectacular was the *Challenger* incident. S. Dennis Gouran, R.Y. Hirokawa and A.E. Martz in their paper 'A critical analysis of factors related to decisional processes involved in the Challenger Disaster' (1986) investigated the factors which may have contributed to this tragedy.

The *Challenger* disaster of 1986 led to high-level investigations into the flaws in NASA's decision-making process. In this paper the authors review the evidence which was published in the *Report of the Presidential Commission on the Space Shuttle 'Challenger' Disaster*. Five types of failure of the decision-making process were identified:

1 perceived pressure to produce a desired recommendation and concurrence with it among some of those initially opposed to the launch;
2 an apparent unwillingness to violate perceived roles;
3 a questionable pattern of reasoning among key managers;
4 an ambiguous use of language, which minimized risks;
5 failure to ask important questions.

The authors conclude that:

> no matter how carefully crafted a decision structure may appear in terms of the sequence of the analysis and choice to which it commits decision makers, its effective utilization is still reliant on the social, psychological and communicative environment in which responsible parties function.
> (*Patton* et al., *1989: 232*) ◆

Janis contrasts the examples of groupthink decisions with two instances of 'vigilant' decision-making: the Marshall Plan and the Cuban missile crisis. In these cases decision-making took place in an environment in which there was a large measure of critical appraisal and open discussion, analysis and consideration of different policy options. From these two case studies Janis derives a number of measures to combat the groupthink process (Janis, 1982: 262–71):

- Leader has a role in encouraging critical evaluation in all members and the expression of doubts and objections.
- Key leaders should not state preferences when assigning policy planning and analysis.
- Decision-making should be conducted through the setting up of several policy-planning and evaluation groups.
- From time to time the policy-making group should divide into subgroups and meet under different chairpersons.
- Members of policy-making groups should discuss deliberations with trusted associates outside the group.
- Experts and others not in the policy-making group should come in and be encouraged to challenge core members.
- Alternatives should be evaluated at every meeting. Someone should play devil's advocate.
- If the policy issue involves a rival nation or organization ample time should be given to surveying the signals and intentions of the rival. (Janis suggests scenario writing and role playing; see 3.8.7.
- After arriving at a consensus, a 'second-chance meeting' should be convened to allow the expression of outstanding doubts.

The groupthink model, and its prescriptive preventative measures as outlined above, has been widely used (and abused) in policy analysis and management. However, more than twenty years since the publication of *Groupthink*, the scientific or analytical status of the study is still somewhat unclear. Janis himself argued that, until there had been development of controlled experiments and systematic research which could test the model in a rigorous way, the theory of groupthink must perforce remain speculative (Janis, 1982: 259). In general, it may be said that the model (as it stands) has not received clear support from the work that has been done to test it empirically or systematically on the lines advocated by Janis. Perhaps, therefore, students of public policy would be well-advised to treat the model with caution, and to use it essentially as a 'speculative' theory which provides a framework of questions to ask about the psychological dimensions of decision-making, rather than as a formal model which has been 'proven' by scientific research and testing.

❖ Criticisms of the Janis model

Janis's ideas have produced a number of critical responses. The main objections to the groupthink model include:

(a) the inadequacies of the case study method for hypothesis testing (the risk of selective attention to evidence and the temptation to fit messy historical facts into neat theoretical

categories), (b) the suspiciously perfect correlation between soundness of process and the goodness of outcome (the risk of hindsight), (c) the all-or-nothing placement of decision-making episodes into the groupthink and vigilant categories (the risk of downplaying differences within a classification and of exaggerating differences between classifications), and (d) conceptual misspecification of the model (challenging the causal flow from two of the antecedent conditions – group cohesiveness and provocative situation – to concurrence seeking).
(*Tetlock,* et al., *1992: 404*)

Critiques of the Janis model have taken two main forms: detailed analyses of case studies, and the use of group experiments. The evidence provided by such research is very mixed. In general there is much sympathy for the general notion that groups can distort decision-making, but the details of the model have come in for criticism from amongst a variety of approaches and methods.

Case study approaches

- *Raven (1974)*: In a study of Watergate the author did not find cohesion or an *esprit de corps*, but a desire to maintain membership of the group. Found evidence of some symptoms: illusions of superiority and invulnerability, as well as unanimity and 'mindguards'. Suggests a reformulation of the antecedent conditions.
- *Tetlock (1979)*: Using a quantitative method the author examines Janis's case studies by analysis of the public statements of the protagonists. Finds that decision-makers had simplistic perceptions, and did have positive group references, but did not exhibit stereotyping of 'out-groups'.
- *Esser and Lindoerfer (1989)*: In a study of the *Challenger* disaster the authors found little evidence of the antecedent conditions relating to cohesion as set out by Janis. However, the authors find some evidence of illusions of invulnerability, pressures on dissenters to conform, and distortion of information.
- *Hensley and Griffen (1986)*: Found evidence supporting groupthink model in a study of the decision of Kent State University to build a gym on the site of shootings carried out by the National Guard.
- *Tetlock et al. (1992)*: Support for classification of groups (vigilant, non-vigilant); failure to find evidence of group cohesiveness or stress as predictor of groupthink symptoms; confirmed importance of structural and procedural factors; takes issue with Iran hostage rescue and Mayaguez rescue and other case studies as manifestations of groupthink.

Experimental approaches

- *Flowers (1977)*: In an early experimental test found that cohesion did not have any significant effect on the decision-making process. However, did find that groups with directive leaders proposed fewer solutions, shared less information, and used fewer facts.
- *Courtwright (1978)*: Found that group cohesion did have some impact on the number, creativity, quality, feasibility, significance and competence of solution.
- *Fodor and Smith (1982)*: Although the authors found that groups with low-power leaders discussed more facts and considered more options, group cohesiveness did not influence the solutions reached by the group.

- *Callaway and Esser (1984) and Callaway* et al. *(1985)*: Found that decision quality was unaffected by group cohesion.
- *Turner* et al. *(1992)*: Confirmed that groups attempt to maintain shared positive view of themselves in the face of threat; does not support strict interpretation of model's causal sequences, but claims that research suggests that a broad 'liberal' interpretation of model is a satisfactory basis for more-detailed empirical research on the links with antecedent conditions, the groupthink process and the consequences of groupthink.

This list of research is compiled from Turner *et al.* (1992) and Tetlock *et al.* (1992). Interested readers should start here for further discusssion of the groupthink model. ◆

❖ Concepts related to 'groupthink'

Cognitive dissonance

This theory was originally propounded by a student of Lewin, Leon Festinger (1957), as an explanation of how, even after a prophecy has failed, believers adapt their beliefs to fit with the failure of certain events to happen as predicted. He suggested that this condition is one in which there is a dissonance between one belief and another, beliefs are modified so as to reduce the dissonance by adopting strategies which involve changing one of the beliefs, downgrading the importance of a belief, or adding a new belief. As Janis notes, Festinger's ideas had a wide-ranging impact on social psychology. His earlier work had developed the theory of social comparison, in which he posited that people strive to verify their opinions and assumptions, and in group conditions people evaluate their judgements by comparing them with similar members of their group. Such comparison, Janis notes, produces considerable pressures to conformity in decision-making (Janis, 1982: 277). See also Hirschman: 4.6.2.

Simon was also interested in the dynamics of group psychology and wrote a number of papers on the issue of pressures on deviant members and uniformity. See, for example, the papers by Simon and by Simon with Guetzkow, in Simon (1957a).

Ego defence

Lasswell, applying Freudian theory to politics, was concerned with the dangers to democracy when people, as individuals or groups, sought to protect their beliefs from threatening or challenging ideas through a variety of 'ego defences': denial, projection, rationalization, regression, repression and sublimation. For Lasswell these forms of behaviour in elites were an ever-present problem for decision-making. The answer, he believed, was the development of a politics in which the illusions of ego defence could be 'prevented' from distorting the judgement of those involved in making public policy decisions.

See 'Decision seminars', below: 3.10.5. ◆

3.7.4 Simon and the cognitive dimensions of decision-making

Few figures have had such a wide-ranging influence on the development of the policy approach as Herbert Simon. As we have already
noted, his idea of 'bounded rationality' forms a central theoretical
contribution to the study of decision-making (see 3.4.2). Here we want
to look more closely at what he has to say about decision-making as a
'problem-solving activity'. This involves an understanding of his work
in cognitive psychology. His work in this field is important because it
provides a theory of how human decision-making may be conceptualized in terms of a computer metaphor (an explanatory framework),
but it also incorporates a very distinct view on how decision-making –
as 'problem-solving' – can be improved (a normative framework).
One sets out a theory of the decision-making process, the other a
framework for the role of policy analysis in that process.

Lasswell's views on decision-making and of a preventative politics
were predicated on his use of psycho-analytical theories. For Lasswell
the real 'problem' in decision-making was that elites were so often
simply using public policy-making as an opportunity to project their
personal feelings, emotions and experiences. Private problems become
'public' problems (displacement), or decision-makers may be using
power in order to compensate for a sense of hurt or damaged ego
(compensation). As we noted above (3.4.2), Simon comes at decision-
making from a very different direction: the way in which human
beings 'solve problems' within given cognitive limits. Simon (1985)
argues that this may be traced back to the fact that he – like James and
Wallas – has been more concerned with 'normal' behaviour than with
the behaviour of the mentally ill. Whereas Lasswell was inspired by
Freud, Simon is working in a more cognitive orientation which uses
experiments and computers:

> Within this new paradigm, cognitive psychology has made great strides
> towards understanding how an information processing system like the
> human brain solves problems, makes decisions, remembers and learns.
> (*Simon, 1985: 295*)

Simon believes that we need 'to listen to Lasswell and Freud as well as
to Wallas and James' (Simon, 1985: 301). This means that we need to
take account of 'passion' and 'impulse', but to realize that such behaviour in which decision-making is driven by subconscious passions is
'exceptional and not common in human behaviour' (Simon, 1985:
301). The control processes which are the focus of cognitive psychology are more the norm; even in the case of Hitler, whose behaviour
may be analysed in a psycho-analytical framework as being an exam-

ple of 'all-consuming hatred and self-hatred a large cognitive element intrudes into the behaviour':

> Hitler was not just angry; he directed his hatred towards a particular group of people, Jews, and he made decisions that were arguably rational on the premise that the Jewish people had to be extirpated to satisy that hatred. For some purposes of political analysis, it may be enough to postulate the overly expressed values and goals without seeking their deeper roots in the unconscious, or at least trying to explain how they arrived there.
> (*Simon, 1985: 301*)

Simon believes, therefore, that we should direct our attention to the behavioural manifestations of decision-making and its cognitive limits, rather than to its subconscious dimensions. Thus, although we need to take Lasswell into account, it appears that even in the case of Hitler we just need to analyse his rationality in terms of goals, means and ends! At the individual and organizational level, decision-making as a 'rational' process is limited by the human mind's capacity to store (in short-term and long-term memory) and process (one thing at a time, or serially) information. This theme has been explored by Simon in collaboration with numerous psychologists and computer specialists in a body of work which it is not really possible to explore fully within the context of an introductory textbook. Readers are advised to consult some of the many articles and books by Simon to develop a fuller understanding (see, in particular, Newell *et al.*, 1958, 1979; Newell and Simon, 1972; Simon, 1969, 1973, 1960/1977, 1979, 1981, 1985; Hayes and Simon, 1974).

Two ideas have to be remembered: Simon sees decision-making as a 'problem-solving' activity; and if we want to understand and improve on this activity we can use the computer as a model. When human beings engage in making decisions they are, from this point of view, endeavouring to fill a gap: given a goal, how may this be achieved? A problem exists because a goal exists.

Human beings face two kinds of problems: well-structured problems (WSPs) and ill-structured problems (ISPs). A classic WSP is a problem in chess. Here the goal is well-defined, the nature of the problem structured; such that a computer can be programmed to play the game. (The author can verify this because the computer upon which this book has been composed routinely beats the socks off me.) Sadly, computers are far less clever when it comes to solving the kinds of problems which are the stuff of human existence. This is because, if you did not already know it, the problems which confront decision-makers in the real world of politics and life are infinitely more messy, ill-defined and intractible. Not everything in life is as predictable and reliable as a chess problem or a German motor car.

Leaving the realm of WSP we enter into the dark domain of ISP. Here the problem is that we do not know what the problem is. ISPs are problems which require that we simplify them so that we can begin to think about them and 'solve' them. The computer, Simon believes, offers us a method – or protocol – of proceeding which involves stucturing problems (in stages) so that a complex problem becomes more manageable. How can this be done? By using the same kind of method which the computer uses: breaking down each aspect of a goal into various parts. In other words, problem-solving involves the substitution of a complex reality with a more simplified model which decision-makers can use to solve the problems of attaining their goal(s).

Human beings tend to think in wholes. Thus if I am asked to make a cup of tea, I do not start by breaking down this goal into a multitude of tasks (get off chair, stand up, walk, open door, walk into kitchen … and so on); but if a computer were asked to make a cup of tea the task would be broken down into wads of computer print-out. Complexity demands that we simplify, and reduce a goal to a series of defined stages which our limited cognitive abilities can handle. With simple problems, such as making a cup of tea, this is not necessary (for me; but of course, it may be for some), the problem is sufficiently well-structured that I do not have to think too much about it. It is a routine, repetitive task. Machines and administrative systems are good at dealing with these 'programmed' decisions. However, in decisions that cannot be easily programmed into a sequence of routine stages (non-programmed), problem-solving requires ways in which complexity can be broken down into stages which enable us to use our limited cognitive powers to their maximum. These methods are, in the language of the cognitive approach, termed 'heuristics'.

Simon and his collaborators have spent a good deal of time investigating the kinds of strategies which are used by men and machines to reduce complexity and solve problems. He has identified a number of these ways to facilitate more-effective problem-solving, and they include: well-organized and stored information; long-term commitment to the problem; a high level of motivation to solve a problem; originality in abandoning earlier constructions of the problem; the use of long-term memory to incubate a problem; the use of computer technology (to improve our information, memory and calculative capacities); and the use of techniques of analysis (such as OR). We have considered these and other methods earlier, in 3.4.2.

Decision-making is effective when the problems are well-structured, and poor when the problems are ill-structured. And the structure of problems has a lot to do with scale: they are 'well structured in the small, but ill-structured in the large' (Simon, 1973: 190). So, for Simon, the real challenge in decision-making is the division of a problem into its component parts which can be well-structured. Within Simon's framework, therefore, many problems are difficult to solve for cognitive reasons: failures are due to lack of knowledege and poor design of the problem. Decision-making should fit the structure of problems. Where a problem is well-structured, a top-down or hierarchical arrangement would suit (programmed decision-making). However, the greater the ill-structuredness of the problem, the more open, flexible and long term needs to be the decision-making process.

On the plus side, the Simon approach does offer great insights into the cognitive dimensions of decision-making. Human beings are clearly limited in their capacity to process information, and complex problems are manifestly different to those of simple problems. Simon does provide us with a model of decision-making, and a set of heuristics to improve on the way in which we approach a complex and uncertain world. However, there is a downside. Is it not rather dangerous to think about policy problems as akin to the kinds of problems which computers or chess players face? How is it possible to 'simplify' complex policy problems? Surely the great difficulty in public decision-making is that 'problems' do not have 'solutions', nor are they best served by simplification. To see decision-making as a 'problem-solving' activity is to express a kind of faith in the capacities of human beings to 'solve' the housing 'problem', or the unemployment 'problem' or whatever, when this makes no sense. What would solved 'problems' look like? At heart, Simon believes that technologies will help us to improve our cognitive capacities so as to enable us to solve our problems. In this spirit, for example, two authors of a textbook which takes the cognitive approach to decision-making conclude:

> There is substantial cause for optimism and excitement about the future of decision research. The field has seen explosive growth in the last 10 to 20 years as powerful tools have been developed for studying and aiding decision-making. We believe that behavioural decision research, as a field, can make substantial contributions to improving decision-making, ranging from small and seemingly unimportant decisions such as which brand of cereal to buy to more immediately important ones such as medical diagnoses, responses in negotiations, or choices amongst alternative public policies. Our optimism is based, in part, on what has been done in a relatively short period of time. It is also based, however, on the prospects for new developments inspired by new information technologies.
> (*Carroll and Johnson*, 1990: 123)

It is this optimistic faith which Simon invites us to share. That said, however, it is important to stress that Simon himself has made it clear that complex, ill-structured problems require commitment to the long term and to creativity, unconventionality and high levels of motivation. Of course, from Lindblom's point of view politics is a form of human activity in which qualities such as these are invariably in short supply. In which case, 'improving' decision-making has far more to do with power and participation than with 'problem solving', whilst from a Lasswellian perspective, Simon's focus on the cognitive dimensions of decision-making inevitably under-estimates the role of the personal and the irrational in public policy-making. In answer to this, one could argue that, if one adopts a behavioural point of view, the strength of the cognitive approach is that it formulates its theories of decision-making by investigating how people may be observed to make decisions within the constraints of limited memory and information-handling capacities. The cognitive approach does offer a plausible account of how decision-making takes place.

However, more questionable is the idea that such knowledge can provide the basis for improving decision-making. Here we may contrast the normative positions reached by Simon, Lasswell and Lindblom. For Simon, the prescription seems to be a variety of managerialism (see Simon 1983), with a few modifications to take account of the limits of techniques and technologies. For Lasswell, policy analysis is a political analogue of psycho-analysis: it is a means through which society can clarify its values and goals. For Lindblom, Simon's analysis of the cognitive limits of the human mind suggests that decision-making needs to be informed by a 'self-guiding society' which aims at reducing impairments to participation and competition between ideas (Lindblom, 1990).

❖ The cognitive approach

Simon contributed much to the development of an approach to decision-making which focuses on how people acquire and use information. It is an exciting and fascinating area of research and one which offers many insights to the student of public policy. It has the advantage of using empirical experiments into how people think and 'solve problems' which is missing from economic or psycho-analytical models. Whereas the model adopted by Lasswell sees decision-makers as driven by deep-seated instincts, or that of the economists by 'self-interest', the approach adopted by cognitive decision analysis takes the view that human decision-making involves people attempting to solve problems and reach their goals in a rational, albeit 'bounded' way. A key feature of the approach is the idea – which is also central to the policy approach – of breaking down the decision process into a sequence of stages (variously defined). Carroll and Johnson (1990) 'distil' these stages as commonly used into seven main stages:

- recognition;
- formulation;
- alternative generation;
- information search;
- judgement or choice;
- action;
- feedback.

This framework provides both for a way of analysing and investigating the decision process, and also of developing ways of helping people to make better decisions (heuristics).

As a framework for analysing the decision process Carroll and Johnson (1990: 21–4) suggest that we might use the framework to analyse what is going on in different stages, thus:

- *Recognition*: Who noticed the problem? When was it recognized? What had to happen in order for it to be labelled as a decision problem?
- *Formulation*: Who defined the problem? How could it be separated or combined with other problems? Did different people define it differently? What goals emerged and whose goals are they?
- *Alternative generation*: Where did the alternatives come from? How and why was it decided to stop producing alternatives?
- *Information search*: How much and what kind of information was collected? How was the search for information determined?
- *Judgement or choice*: Who made the judgements or choices? What was the informational basis of the choice made? What assumptions were made?
- *Action*: How was the decision carried out? What happened?
- *Feedback*: How was information about the decision's effects communicated to decision-makers?

Amos Tversky and Daniel Kahneman, 'Judgment under uncertainty: heuristics and biases', 1974

This paper, by two psychologists interested in how decisions are made in uncertain conditions, has been widely acclaimed. (As we shall see below, the increase in analysis of government is designed to try and increase certainty.) The authors argue that, when confronted with uncertainty, decision-makers have recourse to bypassing dubiety by employing several 'heuristics'. These guide and (often) bias decisions. The most frequent heuristics are:

- *representativeness*: how probable is it that x belongs to y or originates from y or will lead to z?
- *availability*: the ease with which instances and occurrences may be brought to mind;
- *adjustment from an anchor*: fixing on an initial value or starting point.

Such heuristics are the product of cognitive processes which may not derive from rational or logical rules of reasoning. In conditions of uncertainty, however, such heuristics and biases are the basis upon which a decision may have to be made. ◆

3.7.5   Vickers and the art of judgement

A writer who provides a framework in which the insights of communications, systems and psychological approaches are combined is Sir Geoffrey Vickers. Vickers is somewhat unique in that he was both an insider practitioner as well as someone who engaged in theorizing about decision-making. He described himself as a 'student of communication' with an interest in 'the part communication plays in the regulation of human societies' (Vickers, 1968: 73). Although he was not an engineer or a psychologist or a political scientist by training and education, Vickers applied himself to the investigation of decision-making process by using ideas and metaphors drawn from these and other disciplines. His book *The Art of Judgment*, published in 1965, remains a seminal contribution to the study of policy and decision, although it is not as well known as many other, less-sophisticated texts. In his foreword to the 1983 edition, Kenneth Boulding, whose own work was a great influence on Vickers's theories, argued that it is a classic volume, to be read by all those concerned with the analysis of policy-making, as it contains:

> critique of the more academic models of human behaviour, both from economics and from psychology, inspired by a reflection on a large and varied experience of it ... Vickers' experience taught him that the real world is an endless dynamic flux, that all goals are transient, that equilibrium is a figment, even though a useful one, and that our images of facts and of evaluations are inextricably mixed and are formed in an interactive learning process which he calls 'appreciation'.
> (*Vickers, 1983: 8*)

Vickers's model is derived from two primary sources: cybernetics and systems analysis, and psychology. Although he is convinced that the model of regulation devised by systems engineers is appropriate to the study of forms of human regulation and control, he believes that the model needs to be adapted to take account of the behaviour, cognition and psychology of human beings as individuals and groups and as part of society.

❖ The strengths and limitations of the mechanical metaphor

Vickers's idea of regulation is as it occurs in mechanical systems. Information is compared to a set course and the correction is made by comparing what is happening with what is supposed to happen. He gives the illustration of a helmsman on a ship as an instance of regulation (Vickers, 1965: 106). However, there are limitations to the notion of mechanical regulation when applied to institutional policy-making:

- the number of multiple relations and norms is more numerous and complex;

- the means of regulation are far less dependent on past experience;
- implementing responses to information/judgements requires time, because it requires agreement, trust, and co-operation between many people built-up over decades (Vickers, 1965: 107).

Furthermore:

> The indices which the political governor watches are for the most part not mere observations of the present state of critical variables but estimates of their future course, based on his latest knowledge of them (which is usually imperfect) … A more important difference is that half the skill consists in setting the standards which he shall try to attain. For unlike the engineer, who controls a system designed to be controllable, the politician intervenes in a system not designed by him, with the limited object of making its course even slightly more acceptable or less repugnant to his human values than otherwise it would be.
> (*Vickers, 1968: 77*) ◆

The study of human regulation, therefore, is an activity which must be predicated on the idea that 'The mental activity and the social process are indivisible' (Vickers: 1965: 15). Vickers saw his contribution to the study of human decision-making as covering the same kind of ground as marked out by Simon. However, although sharing a good deal in common with Simon, especially in terms of the limitations on human rationality and cognition, he sets out some significant areas in which there are major differences between himself and Simon. These differences include: the conceptualization of human decision-making in terms of 'systems' and 'subsystems'; the rejection of the notion that decision-making is about 'goal-setting' and 'best' choices, in favour of the idea that decision-making is like the way in which systems 'regulate' themselves; the belief that facts and values are 'interlinked'; the centrality of 'appreciative systems' to understanding the decision-making process; and the way in which appreciative systems are changed by the exercise of judgement (Vickers, 1965: 22).

Vickers gives a concise summary of his arguments in *The Art of Judgment* in these terms:

> An appreciation involves making judgments of facts about the 'state of the system', both internally and in its external relations. I will call these reality judgments … It also involves making judgments about the significance of these facts to the appreciator or to the body for whom the appreciation is made. These judgments I will call value judgments. Reality judgments and value judgments are inseparable constituents of appreciation … for facts are relevant only in relation to some judgments of value and judgments of value are operative only in relation to some configuration of fact. Judgments of value give meaning to judgments of reality, as a course gives meaning to a compass card. Information is an incomplete concept; for it

tells us nothing about the organization of the recipient which alone makes
a communication informative.
(*Vickers, 1965: 40*)

Thus, although Vickers is applying a mechanical metaphor in setting
decision-making in a cycle of regulation and learning, his metaphor
takes on board the fact that human (or what are now termed 'soft')
systems are different to mechanical systems because they are informed
by appreciation and the 'art of judgment'. The world is not a set of
data, but a 'construct, a mental artefact, a collective work of art'
(Vickers, 1968: 85). Facts are judgements about reality, and in themselves mean nothing without value judgements. The choices which
confront decision-makers are multi-valued, and therefore in analysing

Figure 3.11   Vickers's framework

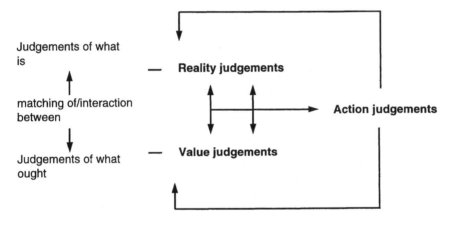

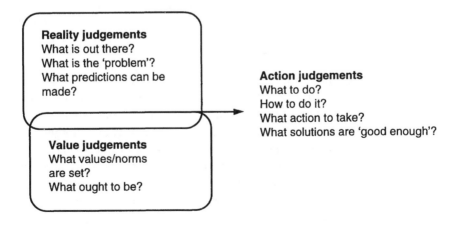

Source: Adapted from Vickers (1965)

the decision-making process Vickers's model stresses the importance of understanding the way in which 'appreciation' constructs 'reality' and 'value' and sets the context within which judgements are made about action – or judgements about what to do – as based on the reality and value judgements (see figure 3.11).

Action judgements – judgements about what should or can or ought to be done, and how, when and with what and by whom, etc., – are to be understood as the outcome of an interaction between the appreciation of reality and value. Judgements as to the outcomes of actions (evaluation) or attempts to resolve (rather than solve) problems must, from Vickers's perspective, take into account how unobjective 'objective' tests and criteria actually are, since:

> The appraisal of judgment is itself an act of judgment. In particular judgments are logically incapable of being validated by any objective test. They cannot be proved true or false. They can only be approved as right or condemned as wrong by the exercise of another value judgment.
> (*Vickers, 1991: 179*)

In so arguing, Vickers departs significantly from the idea that decision-making is essentially a process of setting goals, or of evaluating decision-making in terms of how goals have been met:

> I have described policy-making as the setting of governing relations or norms, rather than in the more usual terms as the setting of goals, objectives or ends. The difference is not merely verbal; I regard it as fundamental. I believe that the great confusion results from the common assumption that all course -holding can be reduced to the pursuit of an endless succession of goals. Some of the blame must be taken by the psychologists who have made 'goal-seeking' the paradigm of rational behaviour ... This view I believe to be fallacious ... To explain all human activity in terms of 'goal-seeking ... raises insoluble problems between means and ends and leaves the most important activities, the ongoing maintenance of our ongoing activities and their ongoing satisfactions, hanging in the air ... I believe [that] a more fundamental and more neglected aspect of our activities [is] the maintenance of relationships in time ...
> (*Vickers, 1965: 33*)

Vickers's model addresses policy-making and decision-making as a complex multi-valued activity in which values and reality judgements are adjusted and in which problems are never solved in the kind of way in which goal-setting conceptualizations suggest. Furthermore, this process is not seen as an activity of individual rationality, so much as how decision-making, in an institutional setting, involves the analysis of how shared sets of judgements about reality and values are derived and frame judgements about actions. The Vickers model consequently directs our attention to the learning processes that take place when decision-makers endeavour to regulate social, economic and political systems. And, despite the mechanical nature of its discourse, the Vickers model posits that the focus of decision analysis should be the study of the 'appreciative' dimensions of human behaviour.

❖ Using Vickers's framework

The Art of Judgment

This book is an important, if nowadays somewhat neglected framework for the analysis of policy decisions. What follows is a guide to using his ideas.

In broad terms Vickers's method is to focus on the decision-making process as the way in which norms, values and standards are set and modified, and the way in which information/facts are acquired to facilitate the making of judgements.

Vickers's methods involves what we may describe as four analytical contexts or dimensions:

- mental;
- institutional;
- situational;
- ecological.

A 'Vickerian' analysis may be viewed as a process of examining policy decisions in terms of focusing in the first instance on the psychological or inner dimension of decision, and concluding with placing the decision in the context of a wider (ecological) network of communications. These four contexts may be deployed on actual case study material which use three kinds of sources: documentary evidence; analysis of language; and personal experience. In addition to this, Vickers was also a great advocate of story-telling as a way of exploring the policy process (Vickers, 1965: 173).

Mental

The first task, using Vickers, is to map the 'appreciative system' involved in the decision. This system may be envisaged as an 'interpretative screen' through which situations are judged and acted upon. Vickers also describes this as being a 'network' of reality judgements and value judgements. Thus we may conceptualize Vickers as proposing the existence of a network of 'value' and 'reality' judgements which serve to interpret or appreciate the problems confronted by decision-makers. The analysis of the process therefore involves understanding how this network frames the 'mental artefact' (p. 115) which constitutes the world of the policy-maker (figure 3.12).

This network will reflect the interests, responsibilities, implicit and unconscious values of decision-makers (p. 67). The task of analysis therefore is to map the settings, understand how they change over time, and explain the hows and whys of the adjustment/regulative process.

Figure 3.12   The warp and weft settings of the appreciative system

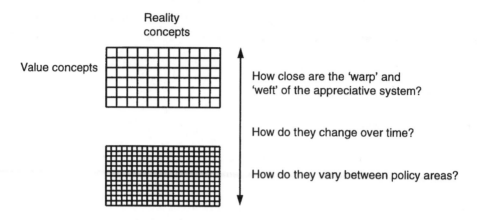

The reality 'warp' and the value 'weft' settings of the appreciative system

Source: Adapted from Vickers (1965)

The next aspect of the analysis of the appreciative system is a consideration of its key skills, namely:

*   *Prediction*: How are inferences, forecasts, estimates and conclusions about the future made, by whom, when, how, (etc.) and how are they stored? Analysis of predictive skills therefore is concerned with the way in which 'reality' judgements are constructed about what consequences will follow from action, and what the future holds in store. Who are making these judgements, and on what basis? How do value judgements influence the perception of the future?
*   *Valuation*: What are the 'ideal norms' of policy? How skilful are decision-makers in making judgements about what can and cannot be done, or about what they want and do not want to do?
*   *Innovation*: How are decisions made about what to do (action judgements)? How do decision-makers select what is 'good enough', rather than what is best? What kinds of relationship/dependencies limit action? Which bodies/groups/interests/institutions can frustrate policy implementation? How do policy-makers secure compliance/co-operation? What is the pattern of communication/dialogue?

Institutional

The next phase of analysis involves the examination of the institutional setting of the appreciative system. Key areas for consideration are:

*   the limitations and facilities of the institution;
*   how the institution changes, adapts and grows;
*   the accountabilty of the institution;
*   what the internal criteria are for defining/measuring success and failure.

Situational

Decisions have also to be placed in their situational context, that is, in the context of:

- *Ideas and events*: The relationship or interplay of ideas and events is an important aspect of Vickers's analysis. In order to understand a policy judgement it has to be placed in the context of a 'dual sequence' of ideas and events (p. 189). Policy-making therefore is something which may be seen as the outcome of a 'conjunction' of the world of ideas and the world of events: new judgements and decisions are the result (p. 169). Analysis of policy-making must seek to map and chart how such a conjunction has taken place to produce 'new' policies or decisions (figure 3.13).

Figure 3.13   The interaction of ideas and events

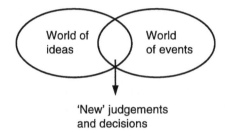

Source: Adapted from Vickers (1965)

- *Kinds of allocative decision*: may be considered to take place on a continuum from conflict, through compromise to integrative.
  — Has the decision been made as a result of conflict?
  — Has the decision been the result of compromise and bargaining?
  — Has an 'integrative' decision been reached by which the assent of all contestants has been obtained?
- Kinds of decisional situations will vary in terms of the contexts within which they take place:
  — situations of regular or vigorous growth;
  — situations of constant resources;
  — situations of sudden and severe retrenchment;
  — situations of acute threat;
  — situations of a revolutionary nature;
  — situations in which decisions are made under protest.

Ecological

- How do decisions about policy relate to the wider society?
- What role do citizens have in participating in the decision process?
- How do decisions relate to the network of communications as a whole?
- How does policy-making contribute to social learning?

Vickers and analysis for decision-making

By placing concepts such as values, judgement and appreciation at the centre of his theory, Vickers has a distinctive view about the role of rational techniques in policy-making. At the time he was developing his ideas, PPBS and cost-benefit analysis were seen by many as techniques which could improve decision-making. Vickers was very sceptical as to their potential and alert to their limitations:

> the analytic skills of the programme-budgeter reveal a dilemma inherent in the policy-making process. The more crudely simplified the objective, the more efficiently it is likely to be pursued. Given a single-valued objective and a repertory of 'means' assumed to be comparable simply by their cost in resources, it may be possible to demonstrate objectively which means is the 'best'. But no political problem can or should be stated in these terms; the more truly we present to ourselves its multi-valued nature and the multi-valued effects of all the means by which we might pursue it, the more impossible it becomes to compare either the costs or the benefits of alternative solutions.
> (*Vickers, 1968: 89*)

Costs and benefits are inadequate to the task of making decisions in the context of multiple values, since values cannot be proved correct, so much as approved or condemned (Vickers, 1965: 71). Improvements in decision-making therefore involve vastly more than techniques such as CBA (cost-benefit analysis) supposed. Policy analysis in Vickers's sense involved dealing with policy-making as a communications process. His prescription for improving this process involved a number of suggestions, including:

- developing the skills and arts of judgement, whilst recognizing that the capacities of individuals to handle, arrange and combine information vary, as do moral qualities, courage and endurance. Organizations should be schools in which all are learners and teachers (Vickers, 1991: 189–91);
- improvements in policy-making also involve a wider process: the development of society which can learn: 'learn not primarily new ways of responding ... but new ways of appreciating a situation which is new and new through our own making' (Vickers, 1965: 233);
- the use of systems analysis to improve the capacity of organizations and society as a whole to learn. Vickers's work in this respect is seen as contributing to the development of 'soft-systems' approaches (see Open Systems Group (eds), 1984; Carter *et al.*, 1984; Checkland, 1981; Checkland and Scholes, 1990). See below, 3.8.8;
- above all, Vickers's approach to policy analysis stresses the need to recognize that decisions involve multiple values. In this respect he is much closer to the ideas of Lasswell and Lindblom than to other 'systems' theorists. ◆

3.7.6   Decision-making as steering: Karl Deutsch and the cybernetics of government

Advances in the communications sciences had a great influence on thinking about decision-making processes. The science of cybernetics, which is concerned with the control of information flows, provided a powerful model for the analysis of decision-making in terms of systems. Norbert Weiner, the originator of the approach, envisaged that it would provide the basis of a new unified science of man, nature and machine. This proved to be an attractive idea to a number of social scientists schooled in Parsonian functionalism. Cybernetics showed how systems could be analysed in terms of the relationship between information inputs, outputs and feedback processes which counteracted entropy within the system by facilitating a modification of the system via inputting information about the results of its actions and the environment in which the system is located. To the young policy sciences this offered the possibility of a framework which could be used to explain decision-making without recourse to the discourse of institutions and constitutions.

Karl Deutsch put forward the most developed cybernetic model in his book *The Nerves of Government* (1963: for a summary see Deutsch, 1967). His focus was on the process of 'goal attainment' and 'enforceable decisions', and the problems of co-ordination involved in goal attainment. Deutsch argues that information and not power should be the primary concern of political analysis. Information, he maintained 'precedes compulsion' (Deutsch, 1963: 151). The political system is, from this perspective, to be conceived of as a 'network of communication channels' (Deutsch, 1963: 122) in which information flows facilitate 'self-regulation' and control. Governmental decision-making thus involves 'steering' information rather than the use of power. This control process, he argues, is one which involves the 'transmission of messages', and the understanding of control processes as a 'branch of communications engineering, not power engineering' (Deutsch, 1963: 182). Failures in decision-making may be seen as failures in steering and failures to learn and to apply learning in response to its environment. This flow of information, from the past, external environment and internal environment, permits society to be 'self-steering'. The key process which enables this to take place is feedback, which permits responsive action and the attainment of goals. Deutsch set out five key modes of feedback (Deutsch 1963: 188–9):

- *negative feedback*: information about results of decisions and which prompts the system to change in order to attain its goals;
- *load*: the amount of information which the system has;
- *lag*: the time-delay between information received and decisional response;
- *gain*: how the system responds to received information;
- *lead*: the capacity of a system to react to forecasts about the consequence of decisions and actions.

The capacity of the system to attain goals is a function of load and lag. This stress of goal attainment raises many questions about the applicability of the model to a 'real world' in which conflict over goals and how they can be measured is the stuff of government and politics. Decision-making does not inhabit this world in which goals are as clearly defined as they are for a living system or a machine. However, it is well to note that Deutsch's model is normative as well as purely descriptive. Deutsch's model is prescriptive: he is positing that governmental decision-making can learn from the model of control advanced by cybernetics. It is significant that in recent years concerns about the possibilities of governance in complex societies have made the idea of 'steering' as an effective mode of control an attractive idea in many quarters (Kooiman (ed.), 1993; Osborne and Gaebler, 1992). It may well be that *The Nerves of Government* does prove to be an 'interim report from an enterprise of thought that is still continuing' (Deutsch, 1963: xxv).

Although the cybernetic model has not been as widely used by political scientists as the Eastonian input–output 'black box', there have been a few exceptions: North (1967), Steinbrunner (1974) and Haas (1990). (On Haas, see 4.6.4.) Steinbrunner's application includes an analysis of the use of information in the context of three different cognitive patterns: grooved thinking; uncommitted thinking; and theoretical thinking. This focus on cognition is an area where cybernetics has made a considerable contribution to organizational analysis; in particular to the learning process within systems, and the activity of learning to learn (Morgan, 1986: 87–95). These ideas have been incorporated in management texts and underpin managerial approaches that were developed in the public sector in the 1980s and 1990s. Cybernetic 'learning' concepts have been particularly important in the development of managerialist approaches to implementation and evaluation (4.3.5, 4.6.4; Deutsch, 1981: 338).

3.7.7   The psychology of decision: integrative approaches

The problem for the student and practitioner alike is actually to apply and operationalize the ideas we have discussed here to the real world. Fortunately, several models have been developed to integrate the ideas we have examined into tools for analysis. In the concluding part of 3.7 we examine three such integrative approaches:

- Greenstein's model of the personality;
- Kaufman's model of decision-making and conflict;
- Young's model of the 'assumptive worlds' of decision-makers.

Greenstein (1969, 1975, 1992) argues that to historians and journalists the impact which key personalities have on decision-making is rather self-evident. However, despite the fact that an early advocate of the policy approach, Lasswell, considered the study of political personalities and biography to be a vital part of the policy sciences, policy analysis has tended to neglect the role which real people play in decisions. Simon and Deutsch's approach, for example, excludes any consideration of the impact of a particular personality on decision-making in favour of the cognitive limitations and logical contexts (Simon) or the flow of information (Deutsch). However, it is somewhat narrow to abstract from the analysis of decision-making the particular personalities involved: imagine, for example, not taking account of the distinct contributions which such people as Gorbachev or Churchill or Thatcher made to decisions. In the case of the Cuban missile crisis, or in far less important or crucial decisions, the personality of the actual people involved does matter. But, of course, to what extent it matters has long been an issue of intense debate (for example, Herbert Spencer's environmental versus Thomas Carlyle's 'great man' theory of history in the nineteenth century).

Lasswell and Kaplan (1950: 4–6) put forward a simple model to analyse the relationship between personality and environmental factors.

Figure 3.14   Greenstein's model of the personality

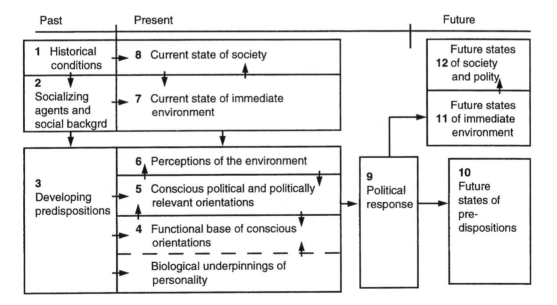

Source: Adapted from Greenstein (1992)

Political response (R), they argued was a function of the actors' environment (E) and predispositions (P): $E \rightarrow P \rightarrow R$.

Greenstein (1992) has developed a more comprehensive map for modelling this relationship between the environment, personality and political response. We outline this model in a simplified form in figure 3.14.

Greenstein sets out a map which takes account of the interaction of the environment and the personality of the decision-maker over time. The environment consists of the 'macro environment' (historical conditions) and the 'micro environment' (socializing agents and social background of actors). As in the Lasswell–Kaplan model, these environmental factors shape and interact with the predispositions of actors. The predispositions are composed of:

- (4) biological underpinnings of the personality; temperament; physiological state; genetic inheritance; and so on;
- the functional bases of the conscious orientations of the actor. This would include Simon's concerns about cognitive factors; relationships with others (Janis); and operation of ego defences (Lasswell);
- (5) the conscious, politically relevant orientations of actors: identifications, opinions, attitudes, beliefs, values, ideology, and stereotypes;
- (6) how actors perceive the micro and macro environments and the impact of these on actors.

(4), (5), and (6) in Greenstein's model broadly correspond to Vickers's notion of 'value' judgements; and the micro and macro environments are close to Vickers's idea of 'reality' judgements. Political responses or decisions in this model are, therefore, the outcome of an interaction between the environment and its perception by actors, and the predispositions (or Young's 'assumptive world') of actors. Thus whereas 'rational', 'power' and 'institutional' approaches to decision-making tend largely to ignore the factors that shape how particular people make decisions, Greenstein's model places human agency and personality in the centre of any analysis of decision-making. The analysis of the policy process should, therefore, endeavour to take account of the impact of the predisposition of actors and how they make sense of their environments, as well as how their decisions may be contextualized in a wider environmental setting. Far too much analysis of the policy process – and of particular moments of decision – has excluded the personal, and the role of actual people and personalities. However, without such considerations the analysis of policy-making can be (rightly) accused of lacking any sense of reality. Someone like

Margaret Thatcher clearly and manifestly had a major impact on how, when and why decisions were made. This is not to exclude the wider factors which shape decisions, such as limitations to rationality, power, institutional arrangements, the environment and so on, but to realize that these take place – or are mediated – in the brains of those involved. The capacity of actors to shape events is, as Greenstein argues, by no means a constant:

> The sources of variation are parallel to the determinants of success in the game of pool. The number of balls a player will be able to sink is in part a function of the location of the balls on the table. The parallel in politics is the malleability of the political environment. The second determinant of success in the pool room is the position of the cue ball. This is analogous to the actor's position in the relevant political context. Roosevelt and Gorbachev could not have had an impact from the lower-level administrative positions. The third class of variable has the same labels in the games of pool and politics – skill, self-confidence and other personal requisites of effective performance.
> (*Greenstein, 1992: 117*)

As an 'art of judgment' (Vickers) decision-making is something which is possessed in different forms by different people in different situations. Their personal life experiences, their knowledge, hang-ups, relations with others, values and beliefs, all matter. As Lasswell argued, the study of biography is, therefore, an absolutely integral aspect of understanding how, why and when decisions are made (Lasswell, 1930b). It should not be an option, but an essential tool of analysis. The 'art' and 'craft' (as Wildavsky terms it) of policy analysis involves making judgements about the impact of personalities on the decision-making process. Without a consideration of the role which different personalities play in politics and public policy, analysis can fall victim to a simplistic and dangerous determinism.

Kaufman (1991) is concerned with understanding decision-making and conflict in the context of local government, but the model has a broader applicability as it examines the 'micro' context of how individuals make choices and decisions as well as how, at the 'macro' level, agencies and organizations interact, select options and make decisions. Her model is informed by theories of cognitive psychology as well as by organizational theory (March and Simon, 1958; March and Olsen, 1976) and studies of conflict. She first sets out the main informational ingredients of a decision (figure 3.15).

Preferences include factors such as the culture, values, traditions and knowledge of decision-makers. Perceived options involve those courses of action, their timing, resource allocation and the friends and enemies of the decision-maker. External events will be those factors

Figure 3.15   Kaufman's model of decision-making

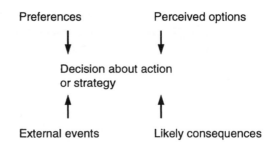

Source: Adapted from Kaufman (1991: 118)

which frame the decision process: such as a decision rule (Simon's satisficing); the state of the world; and the choices which other stakeholders in the decision process have made. Finally, the decision-maker also has to make 'reality judgments' and 'action judgments' (Vickers) as to the likelihood of certain events happening, other people's choices and the consequences of the actions of herself/himself and others.

The decision-making process, however, has an organizational and environmental context, the layers of which are structured as shown in figure 3.16:

Figure 3.16   The organizational and environmental context of decision-making

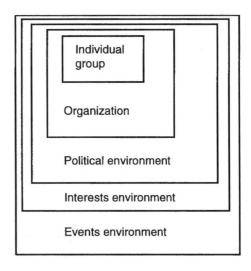

Source: Adapted from Kaufman (1991: 126)

Individual deliberation and group problem-solving, coalition formation and persuasion (as examined by Janis) take place within an organizational environment and an inter-organizational environment
(see 4.3.7 and 4.6.3) of persuasion, dictation and negotiation, etc. In
turn, of course, organizations exist in relation to political institutions,
actors and processes in which persuasion, negotiation and lobbying is
active. Politicians, managers and administrators are also subject to an
interest environment in which actors seek to influence through persuasion, negotiation and litigation. Finally, decision-makers have an
event environment which will compose events and the forecasts and
contingency plans which decision-makers have made to deal with
eventualities outside their control.

Decision-making and implementation in local government – but as we
have said, given the model suggested by network and community
theorists (see 2.10.2, 2.10.4 and 4.3.8), we can extend Kaufman's arguments more widely – involves joint action between different individuals, groups, organizations, the public and private sectors, etc. We shall
be examining Kaufman's model in relation to implementation later
(see 4.3.8, 4.6.3). Here we shall focus on her ideas to explain the

Figure 3.17 Decision-making and the management of conflict

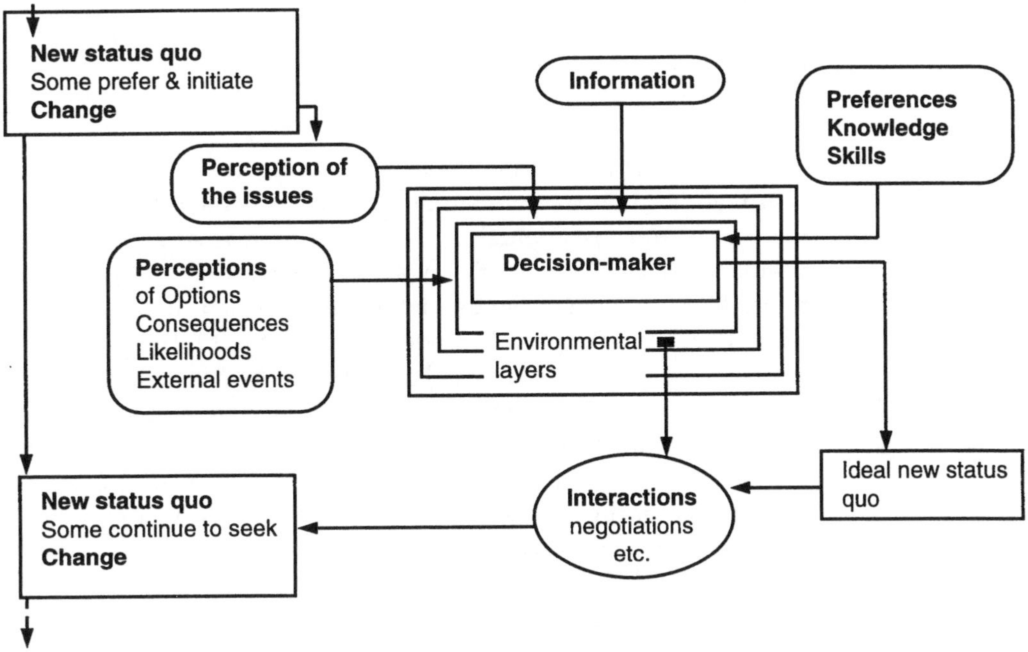

Source: Adapted from Kaufman (1991: 125)

dynamics of decision-making. However, it is important to note that her framework does work well in setting decision-making and implementation within a more unified policy-action/decision-implementation context (see, in comparison, Sabatier, 1986; 4.3.8).

Kaufman puts her models of the environment of the decision-maker and the informational ingredients of decision-making together in a single model which we have adapted in figure 3.17. She explains the key elements of decision-making in the following terms:

> The decision maker brings to any situation preferences, knowledge, skills and power deriving from position, special skills, or access to resources. He or she forms perceptions about the issues to be tackled as well as about available options, consequences of choices, likelihoods of certain events, and prevailing decision rules. The decision maker may identify some preferred outcome (an 'ideal' new status quo) that still must be negotiated with the environment on which it depends for implementation ... The decision environment is composed of individuals, groups, organizations and agencies that can affect the outcome of the decision by their choices or by their control of resources or whose interests can be affected by the decision (stakeholders).
> (*Kaufman, 1991: 124*)

The strength of Kaufman's approach is that it does enable us to use a variety of theories so as to analyse decision-making as something which takes place in conditions of conflict between different stakeholders and differences of information, perception and environments. It thus provides a useful bridge between theories of cognition and organizational behaviour and between theories of decision-making and implementation.

Young (1977/79) also provides a model which, as with Greenstein and Kaufman, enables us to integrate approaches which derive in whole or in part from psychological theories and ideas so as to develop a usable analytical framework for policy analysis. In Young's case, his model draws on cognitive psychology; the ideas of Lewin which underpin Janis's groupthink model (see above, 3.7.3); and the constructivist sociology of knowledge advanced by Berger and Luckman (1975, and see 2.2.2); Edelman on the symbolic nature of politics (1964, and 2.9.2); and it also finds echoes in the recent work of Sabatier on the structure of policy beliefs (1993, and see 2.10.4 and 4.3.8). It is, therefore, a short good-value read which enables the reader to explore a wide range of ideas old and new.

Young begins by noting that the study of values in the policy process is a 'methodological minefield' as the term 'values' has such a variety of connotations. To tackle the problem he starts from the idea put forward by Kurt Lewin (1948, 1952, 1972; see also 3.7.3) that we can view people in terms of their 'life space'; de Board notes that, for Lewin, the 'life space' is a highly subjective way of dealing with the world 'as the individual sees it' (de Board, 1978: 51) and will consist of 'his conscious and unconscious goals, his dreams, hopes and fears, his past experience and future expectations. The physical and social conditions will also be important, limiting as they do the variety of possible life spaces and creating the boundary conditions of the psychological field' (de Board, 1978: 53). The 'life space' comprises four properties or dimensions which Young argues we can use to analyse the 'life space' of policy-makers:

- *cognitive*, or existential or perceptual;
- *affective*, or evaluative;

Figure 3.18 The 'assumptive world'

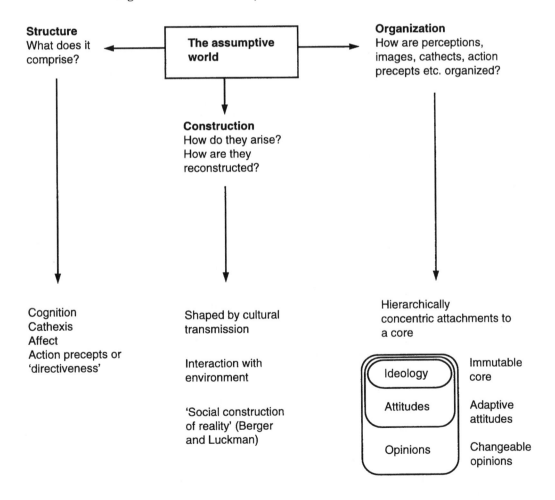

Source: Adapted from Young (1979)

- *relational*, or 'cathectic';
- *directive*, or intentional.

We shall examine these in more detail below, but Young's main point is to stress how these different aspects of the policy-maker's life space 'intermingle'. To convey the way in which these several strands co-exist in policy-making Young adopts the term 'assumptive world' (see Parkes, 1971; and Kluchhohn, 1951: 394). The assumptive world may be viewed from three aspects: its structure; its construction; and its organization (figure 3.18).

The structure of assumptive worlds is composed of cognitive and affective aspects, that is beliefs, information (cognition) and values and norms (affect). However, as Young notes, research by psychologists and others has demonstrated that the two are closely interrelated and are mutually interdependent. Actors relate to their environment by means of 'cathexis', a term which is derived from psycho-analysis, meaning the development of a sense of strong attachment:

> Without cathexis an organism would be in a state of autism. And so, like value orientation, the 'assumptive world' must 'synthesise cognitive and cathectic elements in orientations to an object world, most specifically a social object world – that is a social relationship system' (Kluchhohn, 1951: 394). With cognition joined by cathexis, the policy system recognizes and orientates itself to the environment, and in so doing, is able to invest it with value.
> (*Young, 1979: 32*)

Policy actors, Young argues, may be viewed as bringing 'aspects of their environment into focus and thereby cathect either positively, in the sense of commitment, or negatively, in the sense of rejection, itself a manner of relating to the world "out there"' (Young, 1979: 32). The structure of the assumptive world is also made up of intentionalities, precepts for action, directionality and a 'call for action'. These are, in a sense, the 'stage directions, lines and cues' or signs and symbols (see Edelman, 1964) which guide action. Young suggests that they are 'plans' – rather than images – or instructions which enable an actor to operate in his or her environment:

> Plans as representations of courses of action inhere within images ... Similarly images inhere within plans, for plans are 'written' in accordance with the cognitive map of the world out there...
> (*Young, 1979: 33*)

In acting out our plans we derive information about the world, reformulate our plans or revise our assumptive world.

The construction of the assumptive world takes place with the transmission of culture. But it is also the product of an interaction of actors and their environment. Young uses Berger and Luckman to explain that human interaction with the world makes the idea of social reality as 'concrete' deeply problematic:

> It is important to keep in mind that the objectivity of the institutional world, however massive it may appear to the individual, is a humanly produced, constructed objectivity ... man is capable of producing a world that he then experiences as something other than a human product ... man and his social world interact with each other. The product acts back upon the producer ... Society is a human product, Society is an objective reality. Man is a social product ... only with the appearance of a new generation can one properly speak of a social world.
> *(Berger and Luckman, 1966: 78–9)*

The construction of the assumptive world of the policy actor takes place therefore in a 'living system' of interaction:

> Above all, it is the tension between image and experience that produces for the actor models of the world as it might be ... 'The world as it might be' provides for individual actor and policy makers alike a call to action, a statement of purpose.
> *(Young, 1979: 36)*

Organization of the assumptive world is not a random matter. Like Sabatier (1993), Young posits that beliefs, attitudes or precepts are hierarchically arranged. At the core is ideology: 'the most generalized symbolic representation of the world and our relation to it'; then attitudes, with which we 'manage the concrete world presented to us'; and thence opinions which are forged circumstantially in day-to-day encounters with the world (Young, 1979: 34). Young's model may be presented (figure 3.19) in a similar form as that we used for Sabatier (see 2.10.4).

Actors, informed or 'armed' with judgement and discrimination, will modify opinions at the margin of their assumptive world, but the deep inner core of belief will be far less likely to change:

> Such change as occurs does so only in contact with the world. Actors and environments provide an interface between specific realities and specific assumptions. Messages travel 'up the line' and may lead (as the theory of cognitive dissonance suggests) to some adjustment in assumptions. But if the environment is sufficiently disturbing, the actor is more likely to respond by acting upon it than by conceding change.
> *(Young, 1979: 35)*

(*Note*: on this last point see Janis, 1982; Festinger, 1957, above: 3.7.3.)

Figure 3.19   The organization of the assumptive world

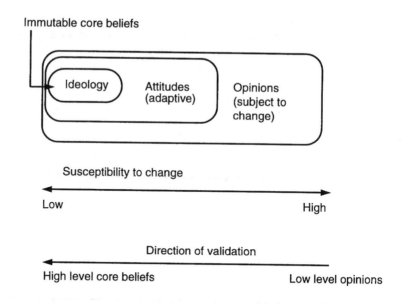

Source: Adapted from Young (1979)

Putting the various elements together we may model Young's assumptive world as illustrated in figure 3.20.

Figure 3.20   Young's assumptive world of the policy-maker

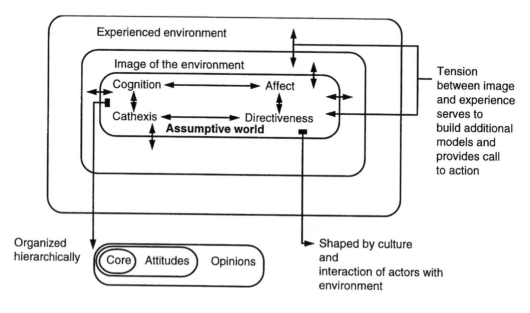

Source: Adapted from Young (1979)

This is quite a complex model of the world of policy-making, and if we were to include elements of the Greenstein approach to personality and politics we would arrive at a very comprehensive framework for exploring the psychological dimensions of decision-making in the policy process. One of the important points about the assumptive world model is that, unlike the Sabatier model, with which it has a good deal in common on the issue of the organization of beliefs, Young takes account of the fact that the 'environment' is not simply 'out there' but is also 'inside' the heads of the participants. Events in the environment which are depicted as outside the system in Sabatier are portrayed as taking place in the context of an ongoing tension between 'image' and 'experience'. (On this point compare Young with Boulding, 1956, and above, 3.5.2.)

The problem is, of course, how can we as students of public policy actually study this 'assumptive world'? As we have noted in the case of the second and third dimensions of power (see 2.6) and in our examination of the argumentative turn (see 2.7.3 and 3.10.5) 'below the surface' levels of power and politics have serious methodological difficulties. Surface, observable forms of politics are somewhat straightforward as compared with 'values', beliefs', 'assumptions', and the 'subconscious' aspects of policy-making. As Young acknowledges, there are significant problems relating to how we can gather data and explain the 'assumptive world' of actors. Young suggests that perhaps the most appropriate technique in terms of interviewing actors is the interview as used by doctors, social workers, personnel managers and counsellors. In such cases, judgement, empathy and experience are the relevant skills which are required. The search for an 'objective' interview is, he believes, rather futile. Data from interviews, observation and written documents will inevitably be biased, and so the task of the analyst is to focus on the 'action setting' of actors and decisions:

> The investigator must go, in the best traditions of participant observation, beyond the behaviour itself to tease out the assumptions upon which it was based ... [so as] to account for their meanings. And the way to do this is by frequent and searching conversation, and the close inspection and questioning of what the policy makers do. The assumptive world is a perception of a world; ultimately it can only be studied within that world. The primary mode of research on assumptive worlds in action settings must therefore be to encourage political actors to give accounts of their behaviour in the action context.
> (*Young, 1979: 41*)

❖ Related concepts

Etzioni and a 'community-of-assumptions'

Etzioni also uses the notion of a shared view of the world which may be compared with Young's conception of 'assumptive worlds' and the approach taken by Sabatier (2.10.4):

> A community-of-assumptions may be defined as the set of assumptions shared by the members of a societal unit which sets a context for its view of the world and itself ... Communities of assumptions are usually held without awareness of the hypothetical nature. Many actors assume that the world really is the way their internalized and institutionalized images depict it ...
> (*Etzioni, 1968: 178–9*)

Hence, the importance of 'public reality testing' and the role of policy analysis (see Etzioni,1968; and 3.10.2).

Haas and 'epistemic communities'

Ernst Haas uses the idea of 'epistemic communities' to describe a

> community ... composed of professionals (usually recruited from several disciplines) who share a commitment to a common causal model and common set of political values. They are united by a belief in the truth of their model and by a commitment to translate this truth into public policy, in the conviction that human welfare will be enhanced as a result.
> (*Haas, 1990: 41*)

See also Foucault (1973); Kuhn's idea of community/paradigm (1962) and (1.9); Holzner and Marx (1979). ◆

3.8   Policy analysis and public decisions

3.8.1   Knowledge and advice in the decision-making process

❖ Key texts

Despite its importance, the role of knowledge and advice in government is somewhat under-researched as compared with other aspects of decision-making. Fortunately, there are some excellent materials which provide much insight into how knowledge is used and abused. From the European perspective two volumes stand out:

Anthony Barker and B. Guy Peters (eds), *The Politics of Expert Advice***, 1992**
This book examines the way in which scientific knowledge is transmitted to governments. The book contains a number of case studies drawn from Italy, Switzerland, Britain and France, concerned with the relationship of expert advice to government decision-making. In reviewing the issues raised, Richard Topf makes the point that the various case studies reveal the changing attitudes towards scientific knowledge amongst the general populations and policy makers which is, in a 'post-materialist' world, more critical and demanding of more openness.

B. Guy Peters and Anthony Barker (eds), *Advising West European Governments***, 1993**
Another important collection of papers from Peters and Barker focuses on the relationship of government to knowledge. Again, it comprises papers from several West European countries and examines the differences and similarities in the way in which governments use policy advice: how they acquire, receive and ignore expert advice, and how the information process is used as a form of legitimation. The policy areas include: economic advice; Aids; heart disease; and land-use planning.

For American material:

- Meltsner (1976) and Majone (1989) provide interpretations of the role of analysis in government.
- Weiss (1992) surveys the role of policy analysis in outside think-tanks, inside government and in the legislature. Absolutely essential reading.
- Fischer (1990) offers a critical analysis of the role of technocracy and expertise in the political process.
- Williams (1990, 1992) reviews the 'rise of the anti-analytical (Reagan) presidency'.
- Jenkins-Smith (1990) takes a case study of oil export policy and shows how analysis was used in the Reagan administration.
- Nelson (1992), Radin (1992), and Thompson and Yessian (1992) show how policy analysis has been used in various US government departments.

More specifically on Britain:

- Blackstone and Plowden (1988) give a fascinating account of the rise and fall of an experiment in policy analysis in Britain, the Central Policy Review Staff (CPRS: 1971–83). May be read in conjunction with Williams (1990, 1992)
- Gray and Jenkins (eds) (1983), published the same year as the termination of the CPRS, review the state of policy analysis in British central government.
- Martin Bulmer is an unquestioned leader in the field, and his various studies of the relationship between social research and government decision-making are essential reading (see, for example, Bulmer (ed.), 1980, 1982, 1987 (ed.), and 1993). ◆

Thus far we have been largely concerned with the analysis of the decision-making process and models which offer frameworks in which we can explain and understand the decision-making process. As we have seen, however, a defining characteristic of modern decision-making is the extent to which it is involved with the use of information and knowledge. All the models are based in various ways on a view of the relationship between knowledge and power, and the nature of rationality. The development of information and techniques of analysis has led to a growth of research which is used by decision-makers; the generic name for this is 'policy analysis'. This may include analysis which takes place before a decision or analysis (or *ex ante*), or which takes place after (or *ex post*) to assess or evaluate policy. (Evaluation is discussed in Part Four.)

In reality, the distinction between analysis for policy-making and evaluation of policy is not well demarcated. The evaluative studies of policy feed into analysis of problems and policy issues and vice versa.

The origins of policy analysis may be said to be as old as the state itself. At one level it involves reviewing the options available and the strategy, means and ends necessary to achieve goals. When kings sat with their 'councillors' to discuss 'policy' they were engaging in a form of analysis which is, in all essentials, not too far removed from that of modern-day policy-making:

> In some measures the importance of basing policy on knowledge has been recognised in every civilization. Confucius, the most influential thinker in Chinese history, spent a lifetime preparing himself and his students to answer a call that never came to him. The idea of a secular scholar-adviser was competitive with other advisers, especially with untrained kinsmen and friends, soldiers, magicians and priests ...
> Ancient Indian civilization gave prominence to teachers and advisers of the prince who were more concerned with the invention and weighing of strategic alternatives than with religion or magic.
> (*Lasswell, 1968: 183*)

As the state grew and information became more available, particularly in the nineteenth century, so the nature of the analysis of options and strategy changed. What changed above all was not the quality of judgement, so much as the rational quality of the information which was used to come to a decision. The word 'statistic' developed out of this fact: statistics were numbers used by the state, and as the state acquired more power and control, so the need for numbers and a rational basis of decision increased. Max Weber argued that the growth of bureaucracy in industrial society was inevitable because it constituted the most rational form of rule: organized and institutionalized knowledge:

> The 'political master' finds himself in the position of a 'dilettante' who stands opposite the 'expert', facing the trained official who stands within the management of administration. This holds whether the 'master' whom the bureaucracy serves is a 'people' ... or a parliament.
> (*Weber, 1991: 232*)

In the nineteenth century, Britain, the US and other industrial democracies sought to acquire more and more knowledge about social, economic and other conditions as the basis upon which policy could be formulated. Official inquiry through committees and commissions provided the means by which the state could assemble more accurate knowledge (Clokie and Robinson, 1937; Harris, 1990). This quest for more knowledge increased in the face of growing economic and social problems (Furner, 1990; Hawley, 1990; Supple, 1990; Winter, 1990). The effect of the inter-war depression and two world wars was to greatly increase the informational requirements of governments, and the Second World War in particular was to witness a growth in scientific and economic staffs to enhance the governmental and control capacities of state institutions. In the post-war era there was an unprecedented increase in both the demand and supply of social knowledge (Crawford and Perry, 1976). This expansion in the information economy was facilitated in government by the growth of internal inquiries and investigation, but also in the use of external information gathered from official committees and commissions (Cartwright, 1975; Rhodes, 1975; Tollefson and Chang, 1973; Bell, 1966; Komarovsky, 1975).

The development of policy analysis has to be placed in this context of a changing informational environment within which decision-makers worked. In Simon's terms, some method was required whereby this filtered information was simplified and structured so as to enable more strategic or rational choices to be made. As we saw earlier, in Part Two, the development of the RAND corporation and US defence strategy based on 'MAD', showed the way in which a new breed of mathematically orientated strategists provided much of the impetus towards developing a more 'rational' US military strategy. Policy analysis was to spread out from the military sphere to other areas in the 1960s with the introduction of PPBS and other techniques. What Williams (1983) terms 'hard-edged' policy analysis was adopted with varying degrees of enthusiasm in other industrial countries. No single pattern of advice and analysis may be discerned in liberal democratic systems of government, and the 'hard' analysis which, Williams argues, typifies the American experience, is not a model that has been closely imitated. However, analysis does take place, even if the structure, organization and significance of analytical institutions varies across government and between departments and levels of government. The lack of such 'hard-edged' analysis is felt by Williams to be reprehensible and, in the case of Britain, symptomatic of a 'pre-modern central government that has not faced up to the information and analytical demands of running a complex welfare state' dominated by secrecy and lacking a process of scrutiny and challenge (Williams, 1983: 24).

'Hard analysis' seeks to represent itself as scientific and technical in approach, designed to provide decision-makers with objective maps and models of alternatives. Such a position, Majone (1989) maintains, is a false representation of what analysis actually involves. Policy analysis which seeks to provide models and techniques of a scientific type is, he argues, less like that of an engineer or a scientist, than of someone who provides arguments – such as a lawyer. Models and techniques for policy-makers are therefore from this perspective a means by which arguments are clarified, and the values and beliefs from which they are drawn are communicated effectively. From this notion of policy analysis which is involved in the construction of reasonable, acceptable and persuasive arguments, we may deduce that analysis in the decision-making process is essentially embedded in values, rather than being value-free. Experts are involved in a political process in which norms are set, decisions are legitimated, and a case made out. Analysis in the policy process is consequently a form of persuasion; techniques, a form of rhetoric.

Against this idea of policy analysis and social research as providing 'arguments' is a much older, and possibly more entrenched and institutionalized model predicated on a mechanistic view. Bulmer has termed this a five-stage 'engineering model' research utilization (figure 3.21):

Figure 3.21 Bulmer's engineering model of research

Source: Adapted from Bulmer (1990)

The model is a linear one. A problem exists; information or understanding is lacking either to generate a solution to the problem or to select among alternative solutions; research provides the missing knowledge; and a solution is reached. Typically a single study will be involved. This – with its data, analysis and conclusions – will affect the choices decision makers face.
(*Bulmer, 1990: 125*)

However, this highly positivistic model is somewhat simplistic in its conceptualization of knowledge and the relationship between information and problem-solving. Information is not the only component in solving the problems which decision-makers face. As the analysis-as-argument thesis suggests, decision-makers confront a range of interpretations or accounts of reality, and thus information is not the kind of value-free thing which the engineering model implies. As Bulmer notes, the evidence of work on the relationship of policy research and decision-making does not accord with the engineering view. Decision-makers employ analysis to frame and orientate themselves to problems, rather than solutions:

> Research provides the intellectual background of concepts, orientations and empirical generalizations that inform policy. It is used to orient decision-makers to problems, to think about and specify the problematic elements in a situation, to get new ideas. Policy makers use research to formulate problems and set the agenda for future policy actions. Much of this is not direct, but the result of long-term infiltration of social science concepts, theories and findings with the general intellectual culture of a society.
> (Bulmer, 1990: 128)

The utilization of knowledge (information, advice, analysis and research) within the decision-making process may be considered in terms of four quadrants: formal and informal and internal and external (figure 3.22).

Figure 3.22   Formal and informal sources of information

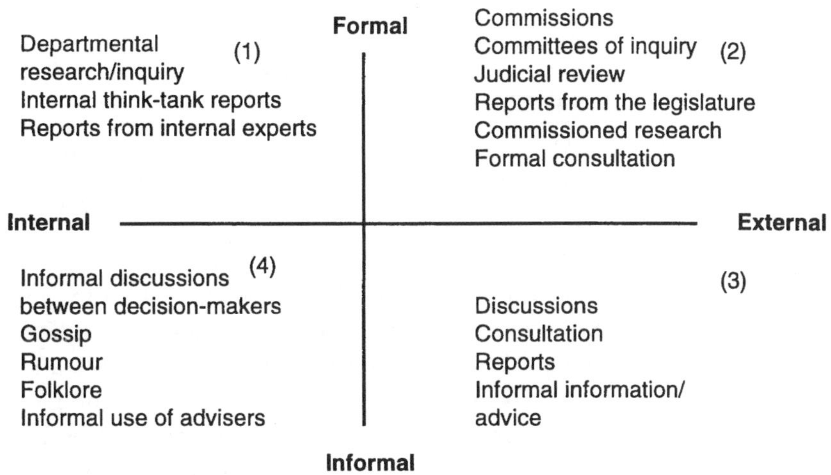

In quadrant (1) decision-making will involve the use of formal internal sources. This may or may not be made public, but essentially it is knowledge which is being generated within government. This may be the outcome of departmental research or inquiry, or through the use of special research or policy units. In-house experts or advisers may also be responsible for generating formal internal reports. In France, for example, and in several other countries, there are 'cabinets' of advisers (a mix of civil servants, academics, party activists, business people and industrialists) which support individual ministers with policy advice of a formal and informal (quadrant (4)) kind (see Searls, 1978). In quadrant (2) knowledge is generated wholly or in part outside the governmental machine. This may take the form of reports and research and evidence from commissions or committees of inquiry, panels of experts, or consultation which is required by statute. Knowledge may also be input from judicial reviews or by committees of the legislature. In quadrant (3) knowledge may be obtained through informal discussion with experts or interest groups. Government is also on the receiving end of many reports from think-tanks and policy networks and communities. Finally, in quadrant (4) decision-making may be informed by informal discussion, conversation and advice within government. This may comprise the 'theories in use' (see p. 595), rumours, intuition, gossip, departmental folklore, grapevine information.

3.8.2 The organizational context

Power has always used the clever, wise and expert. As Kelly observes of this phenomenon:

> Where a measure of centralised power exists, there too the expert, sometimes more in sun, sometimes more in shade; in harmony with the rationale of power or working to change it; sometimes the 'lion beneath the throne', sometimes the god Thoth handing the sacred letters to the temporal ruler and adding to his divinity. Leader of a priestly cult or sponsor of a busy corps of technocrats, the expert stands with a foot in knowledge and a foot in power and prepares the arcane for practical use.
> (*Kelly, 1963: 533*)

No doubt mindful of this association with the magicians and priests of old, their modern incarnation were to be called 'wizz-kids'. At first the idea of a group or body of experts – or wizz-kids – was something which grew out of the US Department of Defense under Robert McNamara in the 1960s. In a later decade the idea was to spread to other government departments and agencies. This was in part due to the introduction of PPBS. In the Nixon–Ford era the think-tank truly came of age with the setting up of an office of Planning, Research and Evaluation (PR&E) in the Office of Economic Opportunity (est. 1964) and later with the institution of a Domestic Council Staff in 1970 (see Williams, 1992). In Britain, too, the age of the think-tank was to dawn in the same period with the setting up by Edward Heath of the Central Policy Review Staff (CPRS) in 1970.

❖ Michael J. Prince, *Policy Advice and Organizational Survival*, 1983

The 1970s witnessed the growth of policy units in local and central government in most industrial societies in response to the argument that government required a greater capacity to use research so as to improve decision-making. Britain was no exception to this trend for think-tanks. In this book the author examines the role of policy and planning units in British government. It provides an excellent review of the literature on policy advice and think-tanks to this date. The author is convinced that policy units do indeed have the potential to improve the effectiveness of organizational decision-making. However, he concludes that the future of such units is in doubt. (This was confirmed by the fact that the CPRS was abolished the same year as the publication of the book.) Prince argued that there are a number of prerequisites to the survival and effectiveness of policy units:

- they must have a strong and influential patron;
- they must be taken seriously by senior officials and they must think in corporate terms;
- they must have a high-level steering group which can ensure representation of the interests of those affected;
- they must provide for reviews of planning and research to ensure effective co-ordination and close integration of steering groups, planners, researchers and line officials;
- they must be staffed by experienced and high-status personnel. ◆

The CPRS was composed of a multi-disciplinary staff whose job it was to enable government to 'take better policy decisions' by assisting the Prime Minister and ministers in the Cabinet to 'work out the implications of their basic strategy in terms of policies in specific areas, to establish the relative priorities to be given to the different sectors of their programme as a whole, to identify those areas of policy in which new choices can be exercised and to ensure that the underlying implications of alternative courses of action are fully analysed and considered' (Cmnd 4506, 1970). The CPRS was conceived at the high point of a new found belief in the need for a more rational, strategic approach to decision-making. The analysis undertaken in the unit was seen as a way of compensating for the departmentalism and short-termism of policy-making by institutionalizing policy analysis.

In the later Wilson and Callaghan administrations the think-tank approach developed with the appointment of some 25 special advisors located in Number 10 and in other government departments. In practice it met with mixed success and much opposition from ministers and civil servants eager to defend their own departments and policies (Blackstone and Plowden, 1988). In 1983 it was finally abolished by Mrs Thatcher, to be replaced by a more prime-ministerial policy unit based at Number 10. Reflecting on the experience of the CPRS, Blackstone and Plowden muse that it was far removed from the ideal type of policy unit to be found in the academic literature. Despite its very best endeavours, the CPRS found that influencing the decision-making agenda was fraught with opposition and hostility to its task of bringing a more analytical approach to bear. In reality the decision-making agenda is often forced on actors by external events and the demands of the organizations and staffs which compose the government machine:

> In this context the job of the policy analyst as adviser is to help rulers at least to influence the agenda, to elicit what is on their minds and to structure the issues for discussion and, more problematically, to infer what ought to be on their minds and to persuade them that they should discuss it.
> (Blackstone and Plowden, 1988: 195)

The 'still small voice of the policy analyst' was, therefore, not particularly effective in the face of the entrenched interests of civil servants and politicians, and the pressures of events which tended to make decision-making operate in an essentially short-term, reactive mode. The same pattern of events may also be discerned in the rise and fall of policy analysis at the White House. As Williams (1990, 1992) shows, the Reagan presidency, like the Thatcher premiership, was to mark a shift towards a more 'anti-analytical' approach to decision-making. The Domestic Policy Staff (DPS) set up under Carter was downgraded and downsized (and renamed the Office of Policy Development) with no direct line of communication to the President. The Office of Management and Budget (OMB) under David Stockman, argues Williams, became deeply ideological and antipathetic to analytical arguments (Williams, 1990: 80). The Reagan years therefore saw deep cuts in the staffs and funds allocated to non-defence-related analysis (Williams, 1992: 115–18). Thus, as was the case in Britain under Thatcher, the emphasis in the 1980s and 1990s has been to shift towards a more explicitly ideological, rather than 'analytically' informed, decision-making process. Outside think-tanks were consequently to have far more influence on the policy agenda than in the 1970s. Forms of policy analysis in the 1980s and 1990s, as we shall see, have tended towards using more explicitly 'managerial' techniques.

The aim of the CPRS and its US equivalents was to provide a more strategic, long-term analysis of problems and were located within specific and permanent units for policy analysis. In place of this central unit model the organizational setting of knowledge and advice has become far more pluralistic, as the concept of policy 'networks' and 'communities' would suggest. Government has come to rely on a mix of internal and external bodies to provide information, analysis and evaluation. Anthony Barker has mapped these sources of infor-

Figure 3.23 Barker's framework of government information

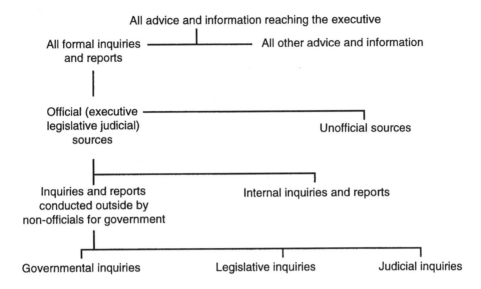

All advice and information reaching the executive

All formal inquiries ————————— All other advice and information
and reports

Official (executive ————————————————————
legislative judicial)   Unofficial sources
sources

Inquiries and reports   Internal inquiries and reports
conducted outside by
non-officials for government

Governmental inquiries   Legislative inquiries   Judicial inquiries

Source: Adapted from Barker (1993)

mation available to government in terms of a 'hierarchy of inquiries and reports' (figure 3.23).

'All other advice and information' in this schema includes a range of material which inputs into government in the form of feedback: consultation, reports and surveys in an essentially informal way. 'Unofficial sources' encompasses information which comes from non-government or local government bodies and which is offered publicly in an inquiry or in a report. 'Official sources' may be viewed as internal reports which are the result of inquiries conducted within government by officials and ministers. This category would include the work of internal think-tanks and policy units and internal (departmental or interdepartmental) working groups. This material may be published. External inquiry takes the form of offical reports which are conducted by non-governmental agents which assist government and report to the executive. These governmental forms comprise a variety of types. Barker suggests:

- government-appointed standing expert advisory committees;
- government-appointed *ad hoc* expert advisory committees;
- government-appointed *ad hoc* non-expert advisory committees.

Such reports might be concerned with a specific policy issue, or with an investigation into a disaster, scandal or a catastrophe. Legislative inquiries are those which are produced by the legislative branch. Again, these may be divided into reports which examine policy or administrative issues, or which address scandals, disasters and catastrophes. Finally, the executive is also on the receiving end of judicial inquiries and judgements.

It is useful to think of the uses of knowledge and advice moving around this hierarchy over time and space. Policy styles will vary at different times, and in different political systems' policy fields. In the case of Britain, for example, from the 1980s there has been a move away from using Royal Commissions as a means of getting 'independent' advice and information (Bulmer, 1993). Mrs Thatcher did not appoint any, whereas Mr Wilson in the 1960s and 1970s regularly used them (Bulmer, 1980). Under Mr Major they came back into favour. As a method of investigation the British commission system has been widely copied and has parallels in most liberal democracies. (In the US, for example, there are presidential and congressional commissions of inquiry.) Bulmer identifies five functions of the commission model:

• as a source of dispassionate and impartial advice;
• as a means of addressing a moral conundrum facing state and society;
• as a form of symbolic action;
• as a means of de-politicizing an issue;
• as a means of legitimizing action or inaction.

Commissions are essentially public exercises: ways of obtaining information in an open manner about a particular issue which may or may not have very much actual impact on the decisions which government takes. Another source of information may take the form of standing or *ad hoc* committees, panels or groups of 'wise men' who advise government and/or give of their expertise. Government departments may call upon committees of experts, for example, to advise in technical or scientific areas (see, for example, Street, 1993, on Aids; Mills, 1993, on heart disease).

Amongst the first of these areas of expertise to become incorporated into governmental decision-making was economics. The formal organization of this advice has varied. In Britain, for example, it has taken the form of 'inside' economic units combined with *ad hoc* forms of 'outsider' co-option. Prime ministers have appointed economic advisers to give advice, although this has not been without the kind of problems which were evident in the CPRS, whereby outside expertise conflicts with internal advice and policy. Perhaps the most famous of such clashes took place in Mrs Thatcher's government when her economic adviser, Professor Sir Alan Walters, was in considerable disagreement with the then Chancellor of the Exchequer, Nigel Lawson (see Smith, 1992; Kegan, 1989). Mr Major has operated with a team of advisers known as the 'wise men'.

❖ Economists in government

After the Second World War economists were to have a new role in the policy-making processes of most industrial societies. For example, in Britain the 1944 White Paper on employment marked the turning point for the introduction of a staff of permanent economists, the Economic Section. In the USA a Council of Economic Advisors was created in 1946 to advise the President. A similar approach was taken in Germany with the setting up of a Council of Economic Experts. In Japan key documents and institutions, such as MITI, EPA and the Finance Ministry were to have important economic staffs. A comparable pattern of growth in the economic staffing of organizations was to be found at the international level in the OECD, the EEC and GATT.

The rise and fall of economic expertise in government is a phenomenon with much significance for students of public policy. Its role has altered over the years with the changing fortunes of the economy. The 1960s were good, 1970s bad, 1980s not much better. However, in countries such as Germany and Japan, whose success has been one of the most notable developments of the last quarter of the twentieth century, the story of economic expertise in government has been somewhat different than in the Anglo-Saxon countries. And yet it is still the case that in both these countries the influence of economists was to decline.

Norbert Kloten (1989) gives these following factors that may explain the loss of influence in Germany:

1 the changing conditions of the 1970s: policies (especially the stabilization policy) were not performing as expected;
2 disappointing results from the growing proportion of GNP spent on social and welfare policies;
3 models and differences over equity and efficiency leading to a diffusion of arguments;
4 increased differences over values and beliefs, greater pluralism and 'muddling through';
5 economic prosperity tending to favour the status quo rather than reform.

Saburo Okita (1989) has given rather similar reasons for the decline in the influence of economists in Japan:

1 as Japan caught up with the West, greater differences in values led to greater dispersion of policy goals. There was less unity than in the days of the quest for economic growth;
2 traditional macroeconomic and econometric theories lost their credibility;
3 increasing influence of politicians in the distribution of 'new pie';
4 increasing international interdependence.

The model which seems to suggest itself from these and other examples is that high goal agreement, consensus and certainty, combined with theories that 'work', leads to conditions in which expert advice has a high level of influence. When circumstances give rise to uncertainty, conflict over values and goals and 'failing theories', the influence of the economist and other experts will fall, or change to one in which their expertise is one of many sets of values/ arguments to be considered. ◆

The impact of economic advice on governmental decision-making has had its ups and downs over time and between political systems. This influence has to be related to the rise and fall of economic consensus and the proliferation of economic advice within and outside government. With the erosion of Keynesian dominance in the 1970s and 1980s, policy advice has been far more pluralistic and 'unorthodox'. Thus, in the 1980s outside think-tanks in the US and the UK were to have far more impact on the economic policy agenda than official agencies and actors (Singer, 1993).

3.8.3   Academic scribblers and madmen in authority

In considering the impact of economic advice and analysis on decision-making it is important to recognize that the influence of ideas extends far beyond institutions and official channels. Keynes said as much when he argued that, in the end, decision-making owed far more to the influence of 'academic scribblers' over 'madmen in authority' than to interests. Keynes himself was one of the earliest examples of the 'academic' or the professor (although Keynes, of course, was never actually a 'professor') being brought into government to advise on policy. It was, however, not just economists who were to be employed by decision-makers in the post-war period. Academics have been drawn into the advice process in all industrial democracies, either through appointment to advisory committees, investigations of various kinds or commissions, or as personal advisers to politicians, or as advisers to legislative committees. In America academics can achieve considerable recognition, if not power, as in one of the most famous, Henry Kissinger; or notoriety, as in the case of J.K. Galbraith (Sharpe, 1975: 13–14). At times, as in the 1960s, academics have been credited or blamed for promoting significant reforms (Moynihan, 1965; Aaron, 1978; Banfield, 1980; Glazer, 1988). The influence of professors over the policy agenda continued in the 1970s with the rise of the 'new right' on the backs of economists such as Hayek and Friedman and their followers (see Parsons, 1989). In the 1990s, as we noted in Part One (1.6), so-called 'communitarians' such as Etzioni have come to the fore as agenda-setters. Thus whilst government has a habit of ignoring what academic researchers advise in particular policy or programme fields (see, for example, Bulmer (ed.), 1980; Mills, 1993; Parsons, 1988), the professor as 'guru' seems to have an enduring appeal to all mad persons in authority.

The reason why this should be the case is somewhat obvious. From the decision-makers' point of view the academic researcher can provide information and added legitimacy for a decision. Government can argue that its policy is based upon 'independent' evidence, or that its policy has met with the expert seal of approval. Academic input can therefore serve political purposes and be subject to manipulation so as to make the arguments of the expert fit with the decisions taken by government (Sharpe, 1975; Topf, 1993). Or governments may choose to use the language of the academic expert to dress up a very different kind of policy (as was the case in British 'regional ' policy: see Parsons, 1988). Thus for decision-makers, the 'model-maker' is a power resource rather than a simple source of ideas or information. The academic is also a filtering device. The expert can filter out arguments or arrange them so as to shape the policy agenda in terms which suit the policy-maker. As was the case with Mrs Thatcher and her adviser, Alan Walters, the expert may be used as a weapon in an argument. Of course, it is in the nature of such arguments that the expert confronts another expert: put two or three in a room and, as everybody knows, you get a dozen different theories. Academic scribblers – and others in the advice game – therefore cannot resolve arguments so much as provide arguments and evidence which can be deployed (as Keynes believed) to persuade (Majone, 1989). Hence, in practice, as the story of the CPRS amply demonsrates, the academic experience of policy-making has generally been somewhat more disillusioning and frustrating than the wonderful prospect which Keynes held out in the 1930s. However, as Keynes also appreciated: 'there is nothing a government hates more than to be well-informed; for it makes the process of arriving at decisions much more complicated and difficult' (quoted in Sharpe, 1975: 19).

This is not to say that scribblers cannot have a role in shaping policy, but that it may not be through direct involvement with committees, commissions and formal channels, so much as in the way in which ideas may be generally diffused or propagated. In this situation the academic may have far more impact, be less subject to organizational constraints and serve democracy by widening the terms of debate (see 2.8.1, 2.8.2, 2.8.3). As Jim Sharpe argues:

> This may sound like a restatement of the obvious, but in the long term social scientists can make a much greater contribution to policy-making ... Our measure, however, must not be so much the extent to which a direct link is established between specific research and policy, but rather, the extent to which studies by individual social scientists ... influence policy ... the roll call beginning with Bentham and Mill ... Booth, Rowntree, Geddes, the Webbs, Tawney and Beveridge to Burt, Keynes, Bowlby and Titmus is distinguished and surprisingly long. It may or may not be true ... that in the age of organization the lone wolf has had his day, but it is of no material consequence if such social science is the work of one hand or many.
>
> (*Sharpe, 1975: 28*)

This tradition of the influence of 'great books' is, he argues, more in keeping with the British policy-making process than is the US style of professors in government. And, in the long run, the 'great books' may also have far more impact than policy-related research. With the benefit of hindsight we can say that Sharpe's analysis was accurate. In the 1980s it was indeed to be the great books (of Hayek *et al.*) which really called the tune and framed the policy agenda. This may well be the case for the 1990s. However, it is also the case that these great books required the organizational backing of policy think-tanks. Whether this aided or hindered democratic discussion is, of course, a matter of debate. Not all ideas had the benefit of the money and influence which were enjoyed by the 'new right'.

3.8.4   Analysis and democracy

Keynes was an elitist. He believed that, in the best of all possible worlds, clever men should rule. However, in the post-war era this Keynesian view of an intellectual aristocracy has been subjected to growing criticism. Whereas Lasswell viewed the future of the policy sciences as being directed towards improving the practice of democracy and a fuller realization of human dignity (Lasswell, 1951b: 15), in practice the idea of policy analysis has been criticized for undermining democratic society. Experts have increasingly – so it has been argued – come to form a powerful elite within government and society, so much so that rather than saving democracy as Keynes saw it, the influence of analysts poses more of a threat to democratic decision-making than a means of improving it. Giovanni Sartori, for example, was to put forward the view in the 1960s that, given the growing complexity of issues confronting policy-makers, 'the expert's opinion must acquire much greater weight than his vote as an elector' (Sartori, 1962: 405). It was an argument which was echoed in the ideas of Jacques Ellul (1964) and Daniel Bell. In his *The Coming of Post-industrial Society* (1973/6) Bell seeks to analyse the development of post-industrial society in terms of the dominance of those institutions which process information and the changing modes of innovation, science and theoretical knowledge. The impact of theoretical knowledge on policy as signalled by the Keynesian revolution had, he argued gone further with the development of new intellectual technology:

> the methodological promise of the second half of the twentieth century is the management of organized complexity ... the identification and implementation of strategies for rational choice ... and the development of new intellectual technology which, by the end of the century, may be as salient in human affairs as machine technology has been for the past century and a half ... Since 1940, there has been a remarkable efflorescence of new fields whose results apply to problems of organised complexity: information theory, cybernetics, decision theory, game theory, utility theory, stochastic processes. From these have come specific techniques such as linear programming, statistical decision theory, Markov chain applications ...
>
> (Bell, 1976 : 29)

The developments in 'intellectual technology' offered the prospect of substituting problem-solving rules – or algorithms – for intuitive judgements and guesses. Since these arguments were first put forward, the attack on policy analysis as somehow distorting democracy have become more widely based because throughout the subsequent decades the use of experts and policy analysts of various kinds (economists, planners and scientists) has been seen as a process which has altered the nature of decision-making. Reviewing this debate as to the relationship between analysis and democracy, Jenkins-Smith argues convincingly that despite the fears that decision-making would become dominated by the expert analyst, the hopes that rational techniques would improve decision-making have been wildly misplaced. Experts and analysis, he claims, have not brought about any fundamental change to the political process:

> Analysis has been transformed as it has been integrated into the political process ... Rarely does policy analysis acquire significant independent influence in the shaping of public policy-making, although on occasion, it can alter the beliefs of policy makers ... the criticisms of policy analysis hold greatest force when applied to the use of analysis in specific contexts. When the forum is open, and many sides have cause and resources to mobilize analysis, the threat to the democratic process is slight; it is when applied in less visible and less open fora ... that advocacy analysis may do most to distort policy and mislead decision makers ... The most general effect of analysis appears to be its surprising tendency to inhibit political initiatives, thereby reinforcing the policy status quo. Critics who feared that the mobilization of analysis would lead to radical change in policy and in political institutions should be reassured. If anything the provision of another tool with which to resist political initiatives serves to reinforce the decanting and slowing of political power that for liberal democrats is so essential. Participatory democrats, on the other hand, will find little to celebrate; though policy analysis poses little threat to direct decision makers, its tendency to inhibit change on larger issues may reduce the ease

with which popular expression can work its way through the policy process to a new policy.
(*Jenkins-Smith, 1990: 217–18*)

In other words, the role of analysis in the policy process serves to
constrain or limit the capacity of decision-making to make radical
change, whilst at the same time it reduces the impact which political
participation may have on the decisions which are taken by government. Furthermore, where the decision-making process is closed, secret policy analysis is more likely to have a formative role to play.
Such arguments confirm the critiques of modern society offered by
radical theorists such as Habermas and Marcuse, and agenda-setting
theorists such as Schattschneider and Bachrach and Baratz. The knowledge–decision process seems, from the conclusion reached by Jenkins-
Smith, to enforce a kind of one-dimensionality in policy debates
(Marcuse) ; degrade discussion in the public sphere, whilst serving to
legitimate power (Habermas); at the same time because knowledge
and information is not an equal resource, the uses of knowledge by
government ensure that many issues are kept out of the decision-
making process (non-decision-making). Policy analysis in certain contexts appears to be more a form of democratic 'distortion' (Tribe, 1972)
than 'enlightenment' (Weiss, 1977).

For these and other reasons critics of policy analysis, such as Charles
Lindblom, argue that (as we shall see in 3.8.8, 3.9 and 3.10.3 below),
without addressing the wider context within which analysis takes
place, all social inquiry is impaired and fundamentally biased against
the disadvantaged and information-poor and in favour of those with
power who are information-rich. With this in mind let us now examine some of the main analytical approaches used in decision-making.

3.8.5   Analysis for decision-making

Decision-making in the modern polity may be distinguished from that
of other periods of history in one important regard: the development
of models and techniques of analysis aimed at providing a more rational basis for decisions. As we saw earlier (3.4), this belief in the
possibility and desirability of making decision-making more rational
is regarded as questionable by 'incrementalists' such as Lindblom.
However, as was noted with regard to Lindblom, even incrementalists
would acknowledge the need for some kind of 'rational' analysis in
decision-making. The key question here, therefore, is what kind of
rational analysis is compatible with the real world of decision-making
in which there are conflicts over facts and values, means and ends,
and in which there is considerable uncertainty?

As with models of the decision-making process, frameworks of rational analysis vary. At one end of a continuum there are those who would take a heavily scientistic/positivistic view as to what policy analysis is and can be (Stokey and Zeckhauser, 1978), at the other, a more pragmatic and more politically informed approach which accepts the limitations of rationality, whilst accepting the need for improving public decision-making. In this former category, for example, is Edward Quade's book *Analysis for Public Decisions* (1983) which concedes that policy analysis can never be an exact science as it is concerned with helping 'a decision-maker make a better choice than he otherwise would have made', and it thus aims to facilitate an 'effective manipulation of the real world' (Quade, 1983: 25). Quade asserts that policy analysis remains a 'reasonable strategy for discovering good solutions' despite the fact that: 'more often than not the persons for whom a study is done are no more than key participants in a decision-making process who use the results of the analysis to try and bring others to their point of view' (Quade, 1983: 45).

The strategy which frames rational policy analysis is usually expressed in terms of a cycle involving five key stages. Quade defines these stages in terms of:

- *formulation*: clarifying and constraining the problem and determining the objectives;
- *search*: identifying, designing, and screening the alternatives;
- *forecasting*: predicting the future environment or operational context;
- *modelling*: building and using models to determine the impacts;
- *evaluation*: comparing and ranking the alternatives.

Rational analysis is predicated on this framework, which maintains that a decision is the result of a series of logical steps. (Compare this with the cognitive approach discussed earlier: 3.7.4.) The role of analysis is to facilitate a rational choice of means and ends, within the limitations recognized by Quade, that in the real world decision-making is often constrained and bounded by interests and involves clashes of values and beliefs. Carley (1980) argues that the kinds of policy analysis which may take place are also constrained by policy type (figure 3.24).

Relating the possibilities of rational policy analysis to types of policy decision reveals that when considering the uses of analytical techniques, the more we are in the realm of making big strategic decisions as to resource allocation between health, education, defence, and so on, the less-precise, less-'scientific' or less-rational is the analysis. Even

Figure 3.24   Kinds of policy analysis and types of decisions

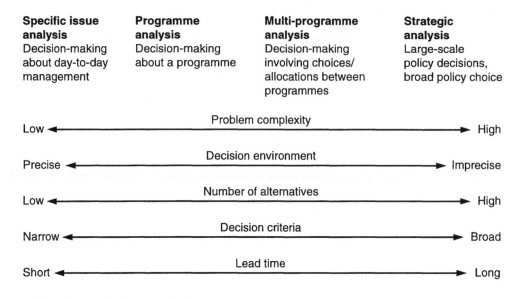

Source: Adapted from Carley (1980)

so, within programmes and 'day-to-day' decisions which are taken at 'street level', 'low' complexity or a 'low' number of alternatives does not mean that there will not be conflicts over values, beliefs and interests which do not create boundaries and limitations for rational analysis. We shall discuss this in Part Four.

Analytical techniques employed in Carley's problem types involve several areas of decision-making:

- decision-making concerning planning and budgeting;
- decision-making as to the allocation of resources within and be-tween programmes;
- decision-making involving choices between policy areas;
- decision-making about policy change, continuity or termination;
- decision-making focused on the aims and objectives, means and ends of a policy/programme;
- decision-making aimed at improving efficiency and 'value for money'.

In practice, these areas of decision-making inhabit a time dimension which means that it is difficult to prise apart analysis that takes place before (*ex ante*) a decision is made, or after (*ex post*). For example, if a decision is being made about future transport or education policy, decision-makers will obviously have recourse to evaluation research into how previous policies or programmes have worked, with what effect and at what cost/benefit. In this section of the book we are concerned with *ex ante* analysis, that is, analysis which takes place prior to a decision. This involves the utilization of *ex post* evaluation of existing policies and programmes. However, this topic will be considered in Part Four. Here it needs to be stressed that analysis for decision-making necessarily involves analysis of the existing policy space, that is, of those policies which impact upon the 'new' or future policy decisions.

The idea of rational analysis is predicated on the capacity to acquire, store, and use information. Sources of data in modern government comprise a variety of formal and informal information. Formal information consists of data on the economy and society. These are compiled in the form of official statistics. This formal data, as we noted earlier, constitutes the basis of official problem formulation. However, informal sources of information will also be employed. Non-formal channels and forms of information may in reality prove far more determining than the official data in shaping the decision-making process. Personal contacts and experience, rumours and gossip, newspapers, dinner conversations and advice all form part of the informal information which may structure the means and ends of analysis. Rational techniques are designed to organize information in a way which aids decision-making. However, it is important to note that, as we discussed in Part One, there are no 'facts' out there. Data is not neutral, but is the result of an exercise of values, beliefs and assumptions. In studying any decision-making episode it is well to remember that the first questions to ask are those which focus on the issues of how, why, when and for whom data was collected. Rational techniques are only as good as the data which is used. Garbage in, garbage out!

3.8.6 Techniques for rational policy analysis

The key techniques of rational analysis include:

- cost-benefit analysis;
- economic forecasting;
- financial planning;
- operational research, systems analysis;
- social indicators;
- impact assessment.

Cost-benefit analysis (CBA) and its offshoots

❖ **Key texts**

One of the most comprehensive books in the field is Layard and Glaister (eds) (1994). In addition to a review of theoretical issues, it also contains application of CBA in several policy areas, including health and environmental policy. An analysis of how CBA is used in environmental decision-making is Hanley and Spash (1993). Williams and Giardina (eds) (1993) provides a wide-ranging review of how CBA has been used in various European countries.

For a review of CBA as a core technique of policy analysis, see Stokey and Zeckhauser (1978: 136–8) and Jenkins-Smith (1990).

A lively attack on CBA and all its (misguided) works is found in Peter Self's now somewhat dated but still highly relevant (1975) essay.

Colvin (1985) provides a number of case studies where CBA was used in a variety of policy decisions in Britain, including health, transport and human resources. ◆

It is generally regarded that the technique of CBA first saw the light of day in the USA in the Flood Control Act (1936). This legislation set out the costs and social benefits of flood control. Subsequently the technique was developed within the context of welfare economics in the US and Europe in the 1950s and 1960s. In the USA cost-benefit analysis was to be developed most fully in the area of defence. A turning point came in the history of CBA in the Defense Department under Robert McNamara, with the introduction of PPBS (Planning, Programming and Budgeting Systems), and resulted in CBA being extended to other departments. Although PPBS was abandoned by the Nixon administration (in 1971), CBA was to continue in operation and was developed in the Carter and Reagan administrations.

The fundamental rule of CBA is that the costs of a programme can be calculated and set against benefits. The same procedure is carried out for all other options and the net benefits are compared. In a choice between options the one with the maximum net benefit will be preferred. The problem with the CBA model is the same as J.S. Mill had identified in Utilitarianism: not all pains and pleasures are equal. Putting a price on the various components of a scheme is not as straightforward as the model suggests. We may have a funadamental disagreement about the values that are being applied to the project, such as decisions which involve amenities and natural beauty. Perhaps the most famous or notorious nonsense of CBA is that of the

Roskill Commission in Britain, which considered the costs of destroying an old church to make way for an airport. The Commission decided to measure costs by attributing the costs of parishioners' travel
to find another church!

Critics of the CBA model argue that this quantification is simply politics dressed up in techniques: 'nonsense on stilts' (Self, 1975). It may
be fine in a setting in which costs and benefits are more 'objective',
such as in a factory or company trying to produce widgets at the
lowest cost and at the maximum profit; but assessing value in terms of
health or the environment or an airport or a road is a different set of
costs and benefits. Value-free it might look, but value-free it ain't.
Other problems arise from the equity and efficiency of the distributions of welfare that result from CBA. What is fair and what is efficient
are bundles of values which are deeply problematic and fill many a
bookshelf in many a library. Yet, as Colvin notes, most economists
working in the public sector 'operate as if the theoretical problems
were not there' (Colvin, 1985: 189).

But because it is so 'rational' a model – dealing as it does with numbers that can be crunched – it has long proved an attractive approach
to sorting out and ranking options. This capacity for economic models
to approach something akin to value-freeness is, of course, one of the
main reasons why other CBA techniques have been employed.

Chief amongst these are budgetary models. A budget is the most
political of things: it is a graphic illustration of the winners and losers
in a decision-making process, and there is no clearer demonstration of
how values have been allocated. Given its centrality to all policy
domains, the allocation of financial resources is where the manure
really hits the fan. The budget is where conflicts over value and priority are to be found in their most naked form. In order to create a
means by which such conflicts may be 'rationalized', budgetary techniques are employed to ensure that resources are allocated between
options in the optimal way. Amongst the more widely adopted developments of CBA technique are those employed in techniques of financial management (see pp. 406–8).

The CBA models are used with varying levels of success by governments all over the world. The attractiveness of CBA as a tool of
decision-making is somewhat obvious: it provides an apparently neutral technique for identifying goals, their impacts, and their costs and
benefits, and it creates a measurable, 'objective' statement which can
serve to aid the formulation and selection of choices and options.
However, CBA has its problems and limitations, the first of which is

that the assumptions and values of welfare economics may not be applicable to some policy decisions: the prices and costs and utility of 'good health' or 'noise' or 'deaths' may be considered to be matters which are not of the kind which may be easily calculated and measured. The maths may simply obscure the values which are fed into the analysis and therefore do not so much aid decision-making, as legitimate a decision already made.

The golden age of CBA was coincident with the consensus that government had an ever-expanding role in making decisions about social welfare. CBA provided government with a means of framing decisions in terms that were like markets. In the 1980s, however, this consensus as to the role of the state in the 'public interest' came under increasing pressure. Why simulate markets through CBA when marketizing, privatizing or de-regulation could do the job properly (see Martin, 1993; Letwin, 1988). Optimality, the public-choice school argued, could best be attained when *markets* were allowed to allocate costs and benefits. However, it still remains the case that CBA provides the essential core of rational analysis in government decision-making and in the legitimation of decisions. When governments endeavour to justify or explain a decision to do x rather than y, or to build A in B rather than C, the arguments of cost and benefit are deployed, as in: 'The costs to the environment of this road will be outweighed by the social and economic benefits to the community and country as a whole'. Decisions to spend money on one policy area rather than another are constructed in terms of the calculations which have been made about costs and benefits. Arguments may then take place as to the assumptions and values which underpin these calculations. The framing of arguments in terms of quantifiable costs and benefits is greatly to the advantage of those decisions which involve 'hard' quantifiables (economic, efficiency, effectiveness arguments) as opposed to 'soft' intangibles (ethical, fairness, quality of life arguments). As we shall see in Part Four, the use of performance indicators and other measures further strengthens the force of the quantifiable side of arguments, which turn on assessments of costs and benefits.

❖ There is no alternative?

Layard and Glaister, in the introduction to one of the standard texts on CBA (Layard and Glaister, 1994) take on board many of the criticisms which are levelled at the method by its critics. However, they argue that the fact remains that in the real world we do have to make decisions about building new airports, the location of new factories, the expansion of higher education and so on. There is no escaping the need to make informed and rational choices as to the costs and benefits of a decision.

They propose an evaluative process involving:

- the relative valuation of costs and benefits at the time when they occur;
- the relative valuation of costs and benefits occurring at various points in time;
- the valuation of costs and benefits accruing to people with different incomes.

The main stages of any cost-benefit exercise should proceed by:

- valuing costs and benefits in each year of the project;
- obtaining an aggregate 'present value' of the project by 'discounting' costs and benefits in future years to make them commensurate with present costs and benefits, and then adding them up.

At each of these stages they stress that CBA is different from a commercial project appraisal because:

- costs and benefits to all members of society are included and not only the monetary expenditures and receipts of the responsible agency;
- the social discount rate may differ from the private discount rate.
  (Layard and Glaister, 1994: 3–4)

However, as the various contributions to their book make clear, in practice CBA encounters considerable methodological and political difficulties in being used in the real world. But, is there an alternative? As another leading scholar in the field, David Pearce, argues:

> CBA remains a controversial appraisal technique. As an aid to rational thinking its credentials are higher than any of the alternatives so far advanced. That it cannot substitute for political decisions is not in question, but social science has a duty to inform public choice, and it is in this respect that CBA has its role to play.
> *(Pearce, 1989: 166)* ◆

Economic forecasting

❖ Chickens and charts, Merlin and models

All societies have methods by which they seek to know the future as a guide to decisions. An ancient method, still no doubt in use in many a tribal society, is that of consulting chickens or other animals. This may either be through reading the entrails or by giving the bird poison and then see if it lives or not.

The economist Devons in a celebrated essay (1961) suggested that the difference between consulting entrails and statistical forecasts and charts was pretty slim. It is all a matter of providing the basis for decision and has as much to do with faith as with reason.

Rulers throughout history have used wizards and magic to provide forecasts of the future. So what is new? ◆

Since the mid-1960s attempts have been made in most industrial countries to model, in a systematic way, the relationship between key macroeconomic variables which operate in an economy. The dominant approach to this has been the use of econometric models, although they have been subjected to criticism from those who maintain that non-linear time series models are more accurate as forecasts than econometric analyses (see Holden *et al.*, 1982). However, the dissenting viewpoints have made less headway in policy terms than economic modelling. The development of forecasting models was pioneered by the OECD with models of international trade in the 1960s and 1970s, and during this period national governments also made increasing use of models to forecast trends and scenarios. The models are usually housed in the finance or treasury ministry or an economic planning ministry (as is the case in Japan) and serve to inform the wider strategy and decisions across policy areas.

All governments have a model of the national economy which is used to show what the effects of policy changes and changes to economic circumstances would have on the economy and on the economic strategy which they are pursuing. With the development of computers, the use of econometric models within government, and by those seeking to analyse governmental economic policy, means that these models have a central place in economic policy-making in all industrial economies. A model sets out the assumptions which may be framed in the light of existing information and theoretical knowledge, and which allows options to be tried out. Given x, y and z, the effect of a 4 per cent increase in borrowing will be such and such on inflation, growth and employment. A model of this kind allows decision-makers to define the parameters of choice and the costs and benefits of macroeconomic options. They also provide a forecasting instrument which permits justification and explanation of policy decisions. Governments will argue that, in the light of their forecast of the rate of inflation or whatever, x will bring about y. Of course, their forecast may be completely wrong. Econometricians, however, express the hope and belief that, with the advances in computer technology, the accuracy of the forecasts which models can generate will improve. However, the old rule of garbage in, garbage out remains a powerful antidote to the idea that better technology will improve the decision-making capacity of decision-makers. Whatever the scientific merits of forecasting and models, the existence of models within government and outside – in research institutes, universities and financial institutions – means that, for better or worse, they are the source of much political and media attention. They may be used to justify economic policy and expenditure plans, and they may also be used to test and explore policy options.

Thus, notwithstanding the actual reliability or accuracy of models in forecasting the future state of national and international economy as a whole, policy-makers are increasingly dependent on such forecasts. As Llewellyn *et al.* comment:

> The policy-maker's need for an economic forecast derives not only from the delays in gathering, processing and disseminating data. Additional reasons are that policy takes time to formulate and implement, and further to take effect upon an economy ... Hence, the sum of the time that it takes to enact policy measures (often called the 'inside' lag) and the further time before significant effects are felt on the economy (often called the 'outside' lag) typically amounts to a year or more. For these reasons policy settings have to be made in response to expected, rather than actual economic circumstances.
> (*Llewellyn* et al., *1985: 76–7*)

Although faith in forecasts has declined since the 1960s, it appears that economic models are necessary tools of decision-making in the modern state as all decisions on the economy involve making policy on the basis of predicted rather than actual development. It means, however, that the policy-maker with an eye on economic growth, inflation, the balance of trade and levels of public spending and borrowing necessarily is heavily dependent on the predictions about economic numbers that may well prove wildly optimistic or pessimistic. Expenditure plans, the very stuff of the real world of decision-making, is predicated on the predictions and numbers which models generate. It can indeed be an 'unsettling' experience for the policy-maker (Llewellyn *et al.*, 1985: 77).

❖ Forecasting

'Mavericks win hands down in forecasts game', David Smith, *The Sunday Times*, 12 July 1992

Smith comments on outside economic forecasters (Patrick Minford, Tim Congdon, Wynne Godley and Alan Budd) who did better at forecasting the state of the economy than did government forecasters and other inner-circle economists who underpredicted the strength of the 1980s boom, and failed to forecast the recession of the 1990s.

Patrick Minford (University of Liverpool) comments in the article that: 'Government funded model-building is confined to a very small circle. The London Business School and the National Institute are a cartel. The LBS's forecasting record in the past couple of years has been diabolical.'

David Currie of the LBS responded to such criticisms thus: 'The argument that economic models haven't worked very well does not mean that anything else has worked any better. The one thing that has not been emphasised is that economists have had to forecast on the basis of very poor data.'

A politician's view

Denis Healey, a former Chancellor of the Exchequer:

> Like long-term weather forecasts they are better than nothing. But no one who has held office in the Treasury or, indeed, who has had the job of following Treasury activity from outside will deny that they are subject to wide margins of error. The numbers contained in the forecasts ... give a spurious impression of certainty. But their origin lies in the extrapolation from a partially known past, through an unknown present, to an unknowable future according to theories about the causal relationships between certain economic variables which are hotly disputed by academic economists, and may well in fact change from country to country or from decade to decade. The current state of our economic knowledge allows of nothing better.
> (*Quoted in Browning, 1986: 64*) ◆

That economic models have a central role in the decision-making processes of modern governments and international institutions such as the OECD and EU is beyond doubt. However, there is a wider question which we touched upon in Part Two: do economic theories actually influence policy? David Henderson, then head of economics and statistics at the OECD and a former civil servant, argued in a series of Reith Lectures for the BBC in 1985 that they matter far less than is supposed. The idea of economists and economic models shaping policy is, he argued, far removed from a reality in which policy-making is done on the hoof, flying by the seat of the pants. Henderson termed this 'Do-It-Yourself Economics'. In contrast to Keynes's belief that it is the ideas of economists which, in the end, determine the decisions which policy-makers make, Henderson makes a convincing case for the view that the economics which informs governmental decision-making in OECD countries owes very little to academic theories and models. This is due to political factors and bureaucratic traditions of thought which operate, as well as to the fact that economists have not been successful in communicating and operating their knowledge in a governmental context (Henderson, 1986).

Financial planning

In its heyday PPBS was regarded as the most important technique associated with policy analysis. Indeed, for many it was synonymous with policy analysis *per se* (Wildavsky, 1969). For its advocates in the 1960s it offered the prospect of an end to the dark ages of incrementalism and symbolized the dawn of a new era when social and economic evils could be vanquished by a rational planning of the budget (Jenkins, 1978: 160–1). As we noted above, this dream was not to be: Nixon scrapped it in 1971, and in Britain it died a slow death, being abandoned in 1979.

Figure 3.25   The PPBS approach.

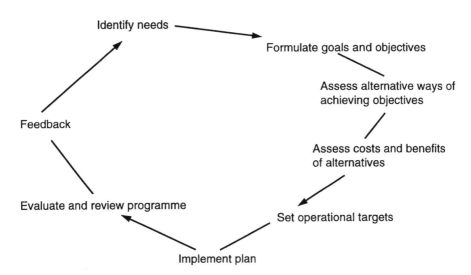

The PPBS approach sought to establish clear goals, outputs and values in the budgetary process, and to create a system of analysis and review in which the costs and benefits of a programme could be calculated over several years. PPBS aimed at locating decisions about parts of the budget in the context of the whole of government spending strategy. The philosophy behind it was a desire for a comprehensive rationality which could cut across policy areas and departmental boundaries so as to analyse the relationship of inputs to outputs, promises to performance, and government actions to their consequences. The cyclical model was derived from a classically rational approach, beginning with the identification of goals, objectives, needs and problems, and culminating in monitoring, review and feedback (figure 3.25). In the model advanced by one of its most famous proponents, Charles Schultze (1968), PPBS called for:

- careful identification and examination of goals and objectives in each area of government activity;
- the analysis of alternatives to find the most effective way of achieving programme objectives at least cost;
- forcing agencies to consider programmes as means to defined objectives;
- subjecting programmes to competition from alternative and more effective or efficient programmes.

The PPBS approach therefore aimed at setting goals and strategies, analysing their costs and benefits, focusing on objectives to be achieved, and monitoring through an ongoing review of results. As an approach it encompassed a range of techniques, apart from CBA. Most of these techniques have continued to be applied in the new forms of public-sector management which developed in the 1980s (Massey, 1993). They include:

- corporate planning;
- investment appraisal;
- management accounting;
- budgetary control.

The demise of PPBS may be accounted for in two ways: first, that it was never really tried; and second, that the whole enterprise was founded on the unrealistic and over-rational conception of the policy process and organizational behaviour. The argument that it was never really tried is, of course, familiar to students of social movements and ideology. In common with other ideologues, the PPBS brigade claim that their ideas were never given a chance to work, were implemented badly, and were frustrated by bureaucrats and politicians (see Schultze, 1968). PPBS proved ill-suited to non-technical decision-making, worked somewhat better in new programmes where there was less resistance, and in decisions involving 'pure' public goods, where market conditions did not pertain, such as defence (Frohock 1979: 176–7). The case for PPBS as a somewhat ill-conceived exercise in rationality is (it seems to the present author) more convincing. To begin with, 'goals' and 'objectives' are tricky things. PPBS was born at a time (the Cold War) and in a department (Defense) when there were clear goals and objectives, and a strategy of deterrence which laid claim to being a science. However, once applied to decision-making in environments which had far fewer clear-cut certainties and less-well-defined strategies, and in which there were conflicts and clashes over goals and multiple organizational goals, PPBS simply failed to live up to its promise (Self, 1975: 178–203). PPBS did not bring about a brave new world of rational decision-making: politics persisted. This holds true whether of the US federal government or of a local authority in Wales (Wildavsky, 1978a; Peters, 1986: 124–31; Griffiths, 1987).

However, alongside this persistence of the 'non-rational' in decision-making, it is important to stress that, although PPBS was largely a failure, it proved something of a Trojan horse. The introduction of PPBS brought into government a more comprehensive approach to CBA and the idea that the analysis for decision-making should be framed by how the inputs of government relate to outputs, and what is being achieved, in contrast to the earlier approach, which focused on how money was spent and by whom, with little attention to the issue of to what effect.

Operational research (OR) and systems analysis

As a group of techniques and approaches, OR, systems analysis and decision analysis may be said to share the following characteristics (see Dror, 1989: 237):

- a bias for action and improvement;
- the values of 'rationality' and 'efficiency';
- utilization of quantitative models;
- an holistic view and examination of all relevant variables.

OR units were established during the Second World War in Britain and the US to apply mathematics to problems considered appropriate, including search and bombing patterns, and the location of radar installations. After the war operational research (British term)/operations research (US term) was championed as a method of using science to improve peacetime decision-making. In the 1950s and 1960s, with the formation of professional OR societies and the publication of textbooks and journals, the approach spread to other countries. In this period the 'classical' concept of OR was the dominant paradigm or 'normal' science. The definition propounded by the UK's Operational Research Society in 1962, for example, notes that:

> Operational research is the application of the methods of science to complex problems arising in the direction and management of large systems of men, machines, materials and money in industry, business, government and defence. The distinctive approach is to develop a scientific model of the system, incorporating measurements of factors such as chance and risk, with which to predict and compare the outcomes of alternative decisions, strategies or controls. The purpose is to help management determine its policy and actions scientifically.
> (*Quoted in Burley and O'Sullivan, 1986: 2*)

The classical approach was firmly wedded to the belief in rational comprehensiveness, and to a procedure predicated on logical progression from one stage to another in order to arrive at the optimal decision. Rosenhead (1989: 3) defines these stages in terms of the following model:

- identify objectives, assign weights;
- identify alternative courses of action;
- predict consequences of actions in terms of objectives;
- evaluate the consequences on a common scale of value;
- select the alternative whose net benefit is highest.

Systems analysis developed out of OR and an oft-cited definition of the subject explains that it may be characterized as a 'systematic approach to helping a decision-maker choose a course of action' by investigating the problem, and 'searching out objectives and alternatives, and comparing them in the light of their consequences, using an appropriate framework – in so far as possible analytical – to bring expert judgement and intuition to bear on the problem' (Quade and Boucher, 1968: 2). The use of systems analysis has been widespread in government (Black, 1961)

The options, objectives, costs and benefits are all assigned numerical values such that they can be calculated and plotted to arrive at what is an optimal decision (Morse, 1967; Pinkus and Dixon, 1981). It is an attempt to objectify the process, rather than relying purely on value judgements. As an approach OR has a wide application in government, especially in health, social services, transport, law enforcement and taxation (Martin (ed.), 1985; Pinkus and Dixon, 1981). Readers who wish to gain a fuller understanding of these techniques and their application in private and public sector decision-making should consult one of the widely available textbooks (Mitchell, 1993; Voss *et al.*, 1985). Here we are concerned to outline the basic ideas behind the various techniques and to consider their implications for the student of public policy.

OR and systems analysis employ a standard set of techniques to aid the decision process. These include:

- linear programming;
- decision theory;
- queuing theory;
- inventory control.

Linear programming is a 'mathematical technique for utilizing limited resources to meet a desired objective ... where resource limits are expressed as constraints' (Pass *et al.*, 1988: 290). It is a technique which is applied to those decisions involving variables and constraints which interact with one another. In public policy it has wide applicability, not least in areas of economic and other forms of planning (Littlechild, 1991: 53; Stokey and Zeckhauser, 1978: ch. 11). Linear programming aims to specify a combination of variables and constraints in the context of uncertainty. The method involves developing a set of linear equations to model a problem so as to compute an optimal solution.

The steps of the method are four-fold:

- formulate objectives;
- determine the relationships of variables and constraints;
- determine alternatives by a process of step-by-step algebraic substitution such as the Simplex method;
- compute optimal solution.

Decision theory is a form of analysis used in situations where a sequence of decisions is involved. It aims to arrive at an optimal policy by the rational analysis of each phase or 'stage' of a decision process. As a technique it is particularly well-suited to decision-making which is concerned with a series of linked decisions. In business, for example, it has been extensively applied to production planning, equipment maintenance, the design and control of processes, and stock control. Computer software is available to facilitate the application of 'dynamic programming techniques' in these and other areas.

There are several techniques used in decision theory. These include:

- means–ends analysis;
- subjective probability;
- algorithms;
- Bayesian analysis;
- decision matrix;
- decision trees.

The approach also employs other OR techniques (linear programming, modelling and simulation). However, in this book we shall focus on two core approaches: matrix and trees.

In its simplest form, decision analysis takes the form of a table of decisions, options and outcomes. For analysis which involves single decisions, a 'pay-off matrix' is employed to examine the options faced by decision-makers. The use of a matrix or 'pay-off tables' is a very

Figure 3.26   Pay-off matrix

Policies	Outcomes				
A	01	02	03	04	
B	01	02	03	04	
C	01	02	03	04	

basic mode of assessing options against their outcomes (costs and benefits: figure 3.26).

Decision trees form another mode of analysis which may be employed in decisions that 'unfurl over time and are dependent on how intermediate decisions are affected by chance as we move from an initial decision to some desired end state' (Kidd, 1991a: 193). In such multi-stage decision-making, choices have to be made between alternative routes or options in conditions of uncertainty. Calculations are made to take into account the probability of chance events or the outcomes of earlier decisions. In so mapping the tree of decisions surrounding a policy or goal the technique aims to arrive at an optimal strategy for attaining the desired outcome. At a 'qualitative' level the technique does provide a framework for considering the best available options. However, the classical OR approach would contend that the calculation of costs and probabilities is difficult but not 'formidable' (Kidd, 1991a: 193). A key factor in the method is the probabilities that are assigned. These are derived from stochastic modelling, the judgement of decision-makers, the sampling of public opinion and the use of experts (Carley, 1980: 116).

A simple illustration of a decision tree would involve mapping the relationship between decision points or nodes (□), nodes of chance or uncertainty (O) and lines of probability. Thus, a decision *a* (in figure 3.27) may depend on the certain probability of chance 1, which prompts

Figure 3.27   Decision tree

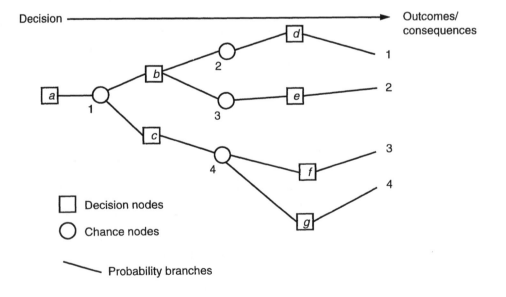

the decisions *b* or *c*. Decisions *b* and *c* in turn may result in other points of uncertainty, which suggest different decisional responses, and so on, until we arrive at the consequences or outcomes of the decisions.

The use of decision analysis techniques such as pay-off matrices and decision trees is problematic in that it makes calculations about matters which are invariably so clouded with uncertainty that probability calculations must be treated with extreme caution. Given an uncertain world and the inherent problems of calculating costs and benefits, decision analysis must be regarded as less significant for defining optimal paths than for what Carley describes as 'helping to sensitise decision makers and administrators to the problems of uncertainty and how these problems affect their preferences and management style' (Carley, 1980: 118).

Queuing Theory is concerned with the analysis of those situations which are familiar to us all: standing in line at a supermarket checkout or post office. In business the amount of time customers in a store or trucks loading-up have to wait is of obvious importance. Queuing theory developed in response to the problems of waiting in some kind of line. It is concerned with issues such as the time spent waiting, when customers arrive, how waiting time and length of queues vary. It is applied in those areas of management that are focused on the problems of demand and congestion for services which involve the use of queues. It is widely used, for example, in telephone exchanges, harbours, and the design of production schedules. In terms of public services, the approach is of special relevance to those areas of policy which involve waiting lists or waiting lines. These include health (hospital waiting lists); housing (public or social housing waiting lists); education (school waiting lists); welfare (standing in line to claim benefits); and transport (traffic management). Littlechild (1991: 155–6) sets out three main elements for consideration of queuing systems:

- Arrival of customers
  — How do customers/users arrive?
  — Is the rate of arrival deterministic?
  — Is the rate of arrival random?
  — Is the rate of arrival constant or variable over time?
- Queue discipline
  — How disciplined is the queue?
  — First come, first served/last in, first out?
  — Does the system discriminate in terms of kinds of customers?
  — Do/can people jump the queue, or jockey from one to another?
  — Is the size of the queue limited?

— Do customers leave (or renege on) the queue?
- Service mechanism
  — How effective/efficient is the service mechanism?
  — How many people are serving?
  — Do servers serve at different rates?

From the standpoint of CBA, decision-makers must make choices as to the costs of improving the waiting time and the benefits of a faster or shorter queue. A shorter queue for hospital beds may, for example, be considered too costly; policy-makers may decide that jumping the queue could be permitted, or may seek to discriminate against certain types of patients; it may decide that the optimum way of getting the queue down is to encourage (via carrots or sticks) people to leave the queue. Littlechild's framework of systems is useful for consideration of those public services which are allocated or managed by a queueing system. As we shall discuss later (4.4.8), disenchantment with the delivery of policy through such systems may result in the voicing of complaints and protests or in a higher level of exiting.

Inventory analysis is a technique which aims at making the most effective and efficient use of stock, that is the amount of goods held in store by an organization to supply internal and external demands. It is used when decisions have to be made about the quantities and kinds of goods stored for use, and in calculating the optimum time to re-order. The advances in computer technology in recent decades have greatly enhanced the approach in theory and practice. In public policy the control of stock is not simply important for office supplies of paper and pens. At a time when there is ever more pressure on the public sector to contain costs and give value for money on a par with the private sector, the use of inventory control systems is of growing importance in those policy areas which involve high levels of expenditure on goods and equipment held in store. In health, for example, stock control of medical equipment, drugs and other materials is a significant component in a nation's health budget. Improvements in stock control offer the possibility of savings which could be used to improve patient care (Lines, 1991: 130–3). Defence is another example where vast sums of money are tied up in stock. The control of the defence budget necessarily involves a much tighter approach to the stock aspects of defence policy.

❖ **What is the use of analysis?**

Marvin B. Mandell, 'Strategies for improving the usefulness of analytical techniques for public sector decision-making', in Nigro (ed.) 1984

The techniques of policy analysis such as operations research, programme evaluation and cost-benefit analysis are frequently criticized for not fulfilling their promise. As Weiss (1979) has argued, the use of analysis in decision-making is a complex process which requires that we locate the research in an organizational, social, political and intellectual setting. In this article, Mandell argues that the performance gap is a matter for concern. Applied policy research (APR) should be made more useful and its relevance to decision-making be improved. He suggests a strategy based on the identification of four stages in the process of using APR: initiation; design of the project; conduct of the project; and the transmission of the product to potential users. More attention must be paid to the strategy which decision-makers employ when they commission, conduct, design and transmit research. Each stage will involve strategy options available to management in the light of estimations of relative expense, time and effort required, and flexibility. Expert research by itself will be of little use if it is not fully and effectively enmeshed with the decision-making process. ◆

Social indicators

Social indicators (SIs) were developed in the US in the 1960s very much as the social-problem equivalent to economic indicators which had assumed such an important role in post-war public policy. In the first instance (in the 1950s), the measurement of social conditions and trends was pre-eminently an activity of international organizations, most notably the United Nations. The measurement of social change subsequently became the focus of academic and government interest in the US in the 1960s and by the 1970s, the approach had spread to most industrial and a large number of developing countries. The rise of the SI movement was indicative of the widespread belief in the 1960s and 1970s in the capacity of government to solve social problems. The advocates of SIs hoped that they would lead to a revolution in policy-making and planning on a par with the impact of economic techniques and measurements. However, as the tide of opinion moved away from state intervention in the late 1970s and 1980s, the social indicator movement was to suffer something of a decline from the heady and idealistic sixties, not least in Mr Reagan's America and Mrs Thatcher's Britain (Miles, 1985: 30–1).

As with CBA and welfare economic analysis, the use of social indicators is ridden with problems associated with value judgements. Indicators such as those which measure 'quality of life', or 'health', or levels of educational attainment or whatever, are open to criticisms about what such ideas mean, who is defining the terms, and who is selecting one problem rather than another (see constructionist arguments on social problems in 2.2.2). Much of the literature on social indicators addresses the problems of defining 'social' measures, and the difficulties of collecting and interpreting data. Such problems are particularly tricky when it comes to comparisons made between countries, when the basis of calculation, collection and definition, as well as the reliability, of the data come into question.

The ideals of the social indicator movement in the 1960s – that social reporting would help in the identification of problems and improve policy-making and problem-solving – have not been realized (Brand, 1975). Social indicators have a role in decision-making, which is to provide a broad context within which governmental agenda-setting takes place. The publication of data may also have an impact on the 'systemic' agenda processes which were discussed in Part Two. Critics of social indicators have argued that they are loaded with a bias in favour of state intervention: in setting up indicators an agenda is being set for what problems should be addressed (Henriot, 1970).

Social indicators are frequently used to plot a trend. The shape of this trend and its direction over time and other variables, thereby provide a context within which to view decisions. For example, if we discern that there is a specific trend in the demography of a country or region, that may well frame our concern about ageing or educational provision. Of course, what this trend means, or how it is derived, is ridden with values and problems of interpretation (Hogwood, 1992). The consequences for the treatment of a problem if the trend is seen in one way or another have consequences for expenditure plans and other policy areas.

Figure 3.28   Types of trend

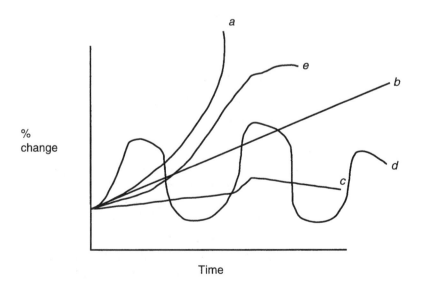

Source: Adapted from Hogwood and Gunn (1984: 134)

In figure 3.28 we can see a variety of trends, all of which indicate an upward trend over time:

a is exponential; b is linear; c is discontinuous; d is cyclical; and e is an S-curve.

The implications of different trend forecasts in a decision-making environment, where a week is a long time, are self-evident. Assuming that we are in agreement that the trend is upwards, the shape of the trend will provide for controversy within and outside government. A pressure group may support b, whilst the government might prefer c! The different trends may also be the result of different sets of data or classifications, and time periods may differ. SIs are therefore not neutral 'facts'. Understanding this point can be illustrated by the way in which social statistics are produced. Miles (1985) suggests that we might envisage this process as a 'production cycle' (figure 3.29).

Figure 3.29   The production cycle of social indicators

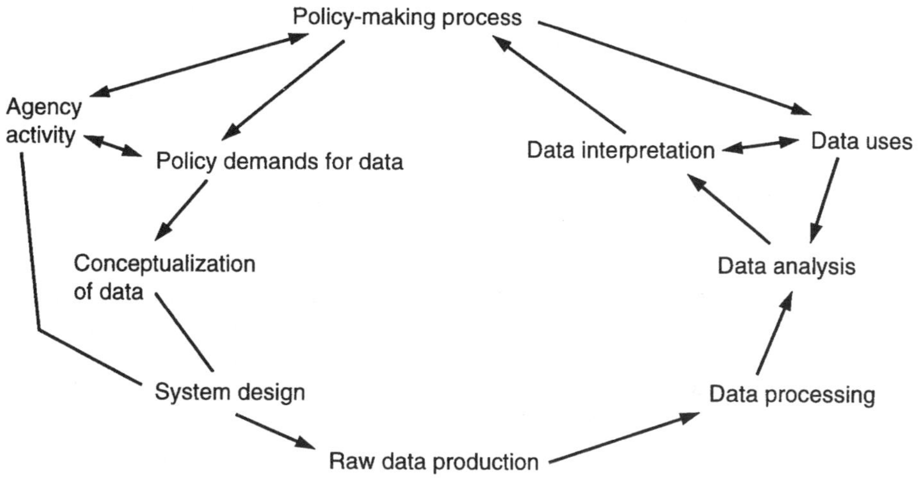

Source: Adapted from Miles (1985: 90)

The model shows how the production of SIs must be set in the context of the activities of state agencies; how data is shaped by the policy process and the demands of decision-makers for certain kinds of statistics; and the uses to which SIs are intended to be put. The division of labour in this production process is a major factor to consider when we are examining the role of SIs (and other data used in policy-making). As Miles (1985: 92) notes, although the details differ from case to case and country to country, we may distinguish between:

- senior policy-makers;
- officials who present the policy demands for data;
- those who conceptualize and interpret data;
- those who implement the system design;
- those who produce and process data;
- those who carry out data analysis.

Miles argues that the cycle model exposes several important issues for the role of SIs in public policy decision-making:

> we cannot simply take ... data at face value ... certainly we cannot treat them as neutral facts. We need to examine what *concepts* are being used, either explicitly or implicitly (through administrative agencies' practices). We need to examine what the *system design* is: in other words, what sorts of personnel are responsible for the production of raw data ... and what techniques they are using ... Less visible to the outside user of statistics will be the actual implementation of the system design in the data production (by *producing officials*).
> (*Miles, 1985: 93*)

In addition, of course, we also need to be mindful of how data is actually presented. As Miles observes, some data are not published; and what are published are the result of a process of selection and interpretation (Miles, 1985: 94).

❖ The Central Statistical Office (CSO) and its mission to inform

It began life in 1941 on the orders of the Prime Minister – Winston Churchill – who required better statistics to manage the British war economy. It was first part of the Cabinet Office (to 1989) and thence became a separate department responsible to the Chancellor of the Exchequer. It became a Government Executive Agency in 1991. The CSO issues a range of publications. Amongst the best known and most well used by policy analysts are: *The Monthly Digest*, *Economic Trends* and *Social Trends* (London, HMSO).

In keeping with the times it has a 'mission statement':

> Our mission is to improve decision making , stimulate research and inform debate within government and the wider community by providing a quality statistical service.
> (*Church (ed.), 1995: i*)

Social Trends is aimed at a wide audience: 'policy makers in the public and private sectors; marketing and advertising professionals; market researchers; journalists and commentators; academics and students; schools; and the general public' (ibid.: 3).

The 1995 edition of *Social Trends* represents a quarter of a century of social analysis and is a primary source of data on all manner of trends in: population; households and families; education; employment; income and wealth; public and personal expenditure; health; social protection; crime and justice; housing; the environment; transport; and leisure. It also lists all the analytical reports which have been included over the years. Wherever possible comparisons with 1971 are made. It is essential reading on social trends. ◆

Impact assessment

These techniques are most widely used in the field of environmental policy – Environmental Impact Assessment (EIA) and to a lesser extent Social Impact Assessment (SIA). Another type is Technological Assessment. The aim of such analysis is to create a framework within which the impact of a given decision on the environment or society can be assessed. There is a wide variety of approaches and methodologies. Assessments may involve the use of modelling and quantitative techniques:

> Each statement has to involve a wide range of considerations: the environmental impact of the proposed action, any adverse consequences which could not be avoided if the proposal were actually implemented, any irreversible resource commitment that might ensue, alternative strategies, and the relationship between local, short-term use of the environment and the maintenance of long-term productivity.
> (*Andrew Goudie, quoted in Button, 1988: 156*)

EIAs examine the potential effects of projects on the natural and social environment. The use of EIAs became compulsory in the USA in the 1960s and in many other countries for those projects which involve large-scale development. Under an EC directive of 1985, an EIA is required for all member states. The compliance with this directive is patchy: EIAs are required by law in Germany and the Netherlands, whereas it is interpreted in a flexible way in the UK. Strongly supported by the planning community and normal practice for the oil industry, yet British practice has been to ignore or avoid the directive: a policy which has brought the UK into conflict with the European Commission. However, the use of EIAs is becoming more widespread and uniform (Vogel, 1986: 1143–4), even though they are not legally required.

Two other forms of impact assessment which are less well developed and less extensively used are those of Social Impact Assessment and Technological Assessment. Social Impact Assessment is a technique which attempts to 'expand the study of natural, or biophysical, environmental impacts to include social and socio-economic impacts that may be associated with a new programme, policy or project' (Carley, 1980: 131). Technological Assessment is a decision-making aid 'used for the multiple identification, analysis and valuation of the consequences of technology and technics' (Böhret, 1987: 212), which is employed in the USA and several European countries as a method of assessing the impact of technology on society and the economy, as well as on law, ecology and demography. Its advocates claim that through this systematic analysis of the effects of technology, 'a network pattern of thought orientated towards the future', and long-run control of technological change may be 'stimulated' (Böhret, 1987: 212).

❖ The potential of EIAs

EIAs in practice have come to be forms of CBA applied to the problems of the environment. However, as O'Riordan (1976) has argued, the potential of EIAs to facilitate a more informed and participative decision-making process has largely been ignored. O'Riordan proposes a model in which EIAs are more fully integrated into internal, interdepartmental decision-making processes, and linked into wider process of conferences, inquiries and task forces to improve the political process which surrounds EIAs:

> the EIA is not an end in itself, but a guide to better political judgment and performance ... the EIA should enhance the status of the politician, place public participation in its proper perspective and generally safeguard the proper functioning of democracy. However, if the EIA is merely to be tacked on to the present institutional pattern of policy-making and decision-taking, then its function might prove detrimental to the future of democracy – and paradoxically, to our environmental well being.
> (O'Riordan, 1976: 215–16)

Alas, after now lengthy experience with EIAs, this hope expressed in the 1970s shows little sign of being realized in the practice of environmental decision-making of the 1990s. ◆

3.8.7   Qualitative techniques for decision-making

Not all problems confronted by decision-makers can be approached or resolved by purely quantitative techniques. Where problems involve wider strategic or policy decisions and raise conflicts of values, feelings, intuition, judgements, opinions, and so on, qualitative methods may be employed. The sources of such techniques are many and various. Some have been developed out of defence and foreign policy decision-making, others have their origins in private-sector management and systems approaches. With the development of 'new public-sector management' and the growing influence of techniques from the private sector applied in the public sector, managerial approaches to decision-making are becoming more relevant to students of public policy.

Amongst the most notable of the qualitative or judgemental techniques are:

- scenario writing;
- simulation, gaming and counterfactual analysis;
- cross-impact analysis;
- brainstorming;
- Delphi analysis.

Scenario writing
This involves the construction of a logical or plausible picture of a given situation and/or the likely future conditions. This may be done through a group discussion or by 'gaming' or as an exercise by individuals. Computers may be used to aid and develop the scenario. As a method it is most often associated with the name of 'futurologist' (*sic*) Herman Kahn (1965). Scenario writing has, since the early 1960s, been most often applied to defence and foreign policy decisions. It aims to promote a clearer understanding of possible futures and direct attention to the consequences of available decisions and options. The scenario can thereby provide a basis for a more formal model. However, as a technique it is inevitably subject to the criticism that it is just a flight of the imagination, and more fiction than science.

Simulation, gaming and counterfactual analysis
Gaming is a technique which has emerged from the defence and foreign policy fields. Gaming may take the form of a computer simulated exercise or a 'manual game' which involves role-playing. Gaming is designed to promote an exploration of a decision, which again may lead on to the application of more quantitative techniques. Lasswell argues that game-playing can 'shake-up' decision-making by challenging assumptions and predispositions, thereby revealing 'unrecognised expectations, demands and identifications' (Lasswell, 1971: 154). The use of games and simulations has been widely adopted in business and has found applications in decision-making in the public sector, especially in the context of urban planning (Zukerman and Horn, 1973). Lasswell argues that simulation exercises may be utilized in 'decision seminars' as they may succeed in 'conferring a vivid sense of reality' on the participants (Lasswell, 1971: 153).

Another mode of decision analysis which employs a mix of gaming and simulation (and other techniques) is that of counter-factual analysis (Baer and Fleming, 1976). In simple terms, it involves taking a given decision or situation and comparing the actual consequences with other options. The aim is to speculate on what would have happened if another decision had been taken.

Cross-impact analysis

Cross-impact analysis involves the selection of an initial list of events; probable impacts and outcomes are put before a panel, who are then asked to make their assessment of the likely impacts (if *A*, then impacts *b, c, d* ...; or: What events will happen, and in what sequence?). The method also employs computers to explore these 'cross-impacts'. Although it is in practice a very quantitative approach, it is still highly qualitative in that it extrapolates predictions from a bunch of value-based assumptions and assertions (Carley, 1980: 149–50).

Brainstorming

Brainstorming, a method which was originated by Alex Osborn (1953), came out of the wonderful world of advertising in the 1930s and was widely adopted in the 1950s. It is a method which has been a familiar aid to decision-making in the business world and has been applied in the public sector (Adams, 1987: 134–7). Whereas other approaches are 'structured', in the sense that analysis takes place within a procedure, brainstorming is based upon a deliberate break with judgements, criticism and censorship: in brainstorming anything goes (figure 3.30). The aim is to produce a quantity of ideas out of which options can emerge. It is not without its critics. Research suggests strongly that brainstorming has a number of problems which ought to be consid-

Figure 3.30   How to have a brainstorm

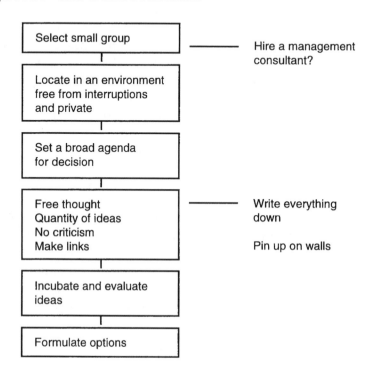

ered in appraising the value of such exercises (Huczynski and Buchanan, 1991: 245–51):

- Does it inhibit creative thought?
- Is there a danger of 'groupthink'?
- Never mind the quantity, what about the quality of ideas?
- Is creative thinking an undisciplined process?
- Do groups think more creatively than individuals?

Delphi

Delphi analysis is another technique developed at RAND in the 1960s. One of the problems of face-to-face approaches is that interpersonal and group influences may have a powerful effect on the analysis. There is, for example, no reason why brainstorming may not be subjected to 'groupthink'. A small group somewhere in a hotel in the countryside and subjected to an intense process may well experience the phenomenon of discussion dominated by one or two people; also, some people may feel inhibited from going against the general consensus. With these psychological dimensions in mind, the Delphi approach aims at analysis which is free from the problems of face-to-face contact.

A group of anonymous experts is selected. These experts correspond with a steering group and/or an on-line computer. Experts are not in direct contact with one another, but communicate with the steering group and/or the computer, which then distributes their responses to other members. Out of this process of question, response and feedback the steering group formulates a judgement. The Delphi approach is therefore an aid to decision-making which is based on an exchange of information and analysis rather than on 'discussion' of a face-to-face kind. It is a technique which is highly expert-orientated and lays great emphasis on the capacity of the steering group and the technology to produce a consensus (figure 3.31). On these and other grounds it is not without its critics. However, for many policy analysts it is regarded as a method with considerable potential in those areas of decision-making in which there are conflicts which are not resolvable through the use of formal rational methods and models (Dalkey, 1972; Linstone and Turoff (eds), 1975).

The Delphi approach has been adapted for group decision-making. Robson (1993), for example, suggests that a modified Delphi could use a process of individual judgements in a non-face-to-face way through asking a group to write down their ideas on cards. A leader then combines the ideas on a list, and members are asked to rank them in order of preference. The record of the ranking then provides the basis

Figure 3.31   The Delphi approach

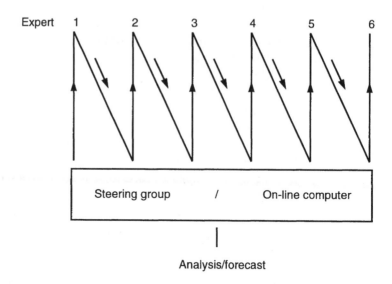

of group discussion. Robson recommends that the modified procedure should be to :

- review problem and data;
- generate ideas individually;
- combine ideas on to one list;
- individually rank ideas;
- discuss final ranking.

Finally, there is one alternative technique that was greatly favoured by the ancient Persians and Germans which sounds cheaper than a management consultancy report and a lot more fun: getting drunk. Herodotus records that before an important decision was made, Persians and Germans would frequently discuss the matter whilst drunk as skunks. Then, when they had sobered up, the decision they had reached whilst under the influence of alcohol would be re-examined. If it sounded OK, they went with it, and if they thought that it did not stand up in the cold light of dawn, they abandoned it and started the whole process again (see Mann, 1969: 138). In our own times other alternatives to rational approaches have been developed which do not (apparently) require destroying thousands of brain cells. These alternatives are reviewed in the next section.

❖ 'Mapping' as a decision-making tool

In Part One we introduced the idea of mapping as a way of thinking about models to analyse the policy process. However mapping can also be used as a tool for decision-making. Two of the most original people in the field of developing new ways of thinking about complex problems and decisions are the Buzan brothers – Tony and Barry. Their methods have been widely used by both public and private sector organizations and individuals. The Buzans' numerous books provide a fascinating introduction to the idea of 'mind mapping' as a way of improving decision-making. An excellent start is their book *The Mind Map Book* (Buzan and Buzan, 1995). The book contains a host of illustrations and applications which can be used in conjunction with many of the decision-making methods we have explored in this book. Of particular relevance to readers of *Public Policy* is their approach to group decision-making and management. They suggest a number of strategies to improve decision-making in group problem-solving, analysis, project management, training and education. Seven key stages are identified:

- define the subject;
- individual brainstorming;
- discussion in a small group;
- the creation of a preliminary mind map;
- incubation of the group map;
- the reconstruction of a second map;
- analysis of the map and decision-making.
  (Buzan and Buzan, 1995: 168–9)

These methods of mapping problems for decision are now supported by a range of computer software. (See Buzan and Buzan, 1995: 274–81.)

Is this the direction where analysis for decision-making ought to go? Should we move away from the kind of 'rational analysis' in which far too many assumptions are made about the nature of human problems, behaviour and cognition? The present author would argue yes to both questions. And so would a growing number of OR specialists. (See Rosenhead, below.)

Another book which may be read as an antidote to rational analytical methods is Morgan (1993), based on his book *Images of Organization* (Morgan, 1986). ◆

3.8.8   Alternative paradigms for rational analysis

In recent years there has been a distinct shift away from the techniques of rational analysis reviewed above. As in the case of the analysis of the decision-making process, models for decision-making have become more pluralistic and diverse. By the early 1980s, OR could be said to have a number of competing schools, including the 'official' paradigm, reformists, and more radical frameworks. In the real world, decision-making problems have been recognized as ill-structured, complex, messy and 'wicked' rather than 'tame', and full of uncertainty and conflict. Such ideas are ruled out of the 'official' rational paradigm. As one leading critic of classical rational analysis, Johnathan Rosenhead, has noted:

> the classical analytical approach asserts that an agreed organizational objective is required before analysis can start. Only in those relatively simple problems confined within the jurisdiction and competence of a unitary decision maker is this plausible. By denying or ignoring the need for mutual shaping of the problem definition, analysis renders itself largely irrelevant or even destructive to internal processes. Classical operation research fails to see the world in which decisions get taken or problems get resolved as being peopled by purposeful human beings, and by groups of such individuals aggregated by imperfectly shared interests. This is a crippling limitation on its breadth of application. It is restricted to those cases ... in which it is legitimate or feasible to treat people as if they were machines.
> (Rosenhead, 1989: 9–10)

Rosenhead suggests that the way forward for rational analysis is to be found in the development of alternative paradigms which take the real world as their starting point, rather than in a model derived from the logic of a machine. He characterizes the differences between the dominant classical paradigm, and the alternative paradigm in these terms:

❖ The dominant paradigm of rational analysis

- Problem fomulation in terms of a single objective and optimization. Multiple objectives, if recognized, are subjected to trade-off on a common scale;
- overwhelming data demands, with consequent problems of distortion, data availability and data credibility;
- scientization and depoliticized assumed consensus;
- people are treated as passive objects;
- assumption of a single decision-maker with abstract objectives from which concrete actions can be deduced for implementation through a hierarchical chain of command;
- attempts to abolish future uncertainty.

The alternative paradigm of rational analysis

- Non-optimizing; seeks alternative solutions which are acceptable on separate dimensions, without trade-offs;
- reduced data demands, achieved by greater integration of hard and soft data with social judgements;
- simplicity and transparency, aimed at clarifying the terms of conflict;
- conceptualizes people as active subjects;
- facilitates planning from the bottom up;
- accepts uncertainty, and aims to keep options open for later resolution.
  (Rosenhead, 1989: Tables 1, 2, 12) ◆

The alternative paradigm is one which is fully engaged with the messiness and unstructured nature of complex decision-making. Amongst these techniques which aim to 'enrich' the decision-making process, rather than arrive at the 'optimal decision', are:

- Cognitive mapping: Strategic Options Development and Analysis (SODA);
- Soft Systems Methodology (SSM);
- Strategic choice and the Analysis of Interconnected Decision Areas (AIDA);
- Robustness analysis;
- Metagame analysis;
- Hypergame analysis.

This is by no means a complete list of the alternative techniques now being developed in OR. There is also the development of so-called 'soft' or 'low-tech' approaches, with their stress on the need for analysis to recognize that the world does not behave like a logical machine (see Checkland and Scholes, 1990, for the application of 'soft systems' approaches in the public sector). The alternative approaches recognize that analysis must take place in the context of incomplete knowledge, and conflicts of values (the world of Captain Kirk, rather than of Mr Spock). Furthermore, the alternative approach appreciates that rational analysis, if it is to contribute to better decision-making, must seek to promote a decision-making process which is more open and more participative. Thus the models and maps which are being developed within the 'alternative' paradigm of OR have come to resemble the models and maps of the policy-making process advanced by political scientists, rather than the logical steps of the engineer. Another key difference is that the alternative approaches radically downgrade the power of expertise, something which figures prominently in the quantitative and qualitative approaches to analysis we discussed above. Whereas the 'classical' paradigm takes the view that policy analysis involves the application of 'facts', the alternative models view 'rational' decision-making as essentially a negotiated learning process. This idea of public policy as public learning will be taken up in Part Four of this book.

3.9   Rational decision-making and the quest for knowledgeable governance

What unites both areas of analysis in and of the policy process is the way in which both have stressed the role of information and knowledge. As a subject, policy analysis has, for the most part, been shaped by a neo-pluralist view of the decision-making process. Within this model the role of information is central. Theorists of the policy process focus on the mediation and filtering of ideas and information, whilst those involved in policy analysis for the policy process itself focus on the relationship between information, knowledge and 'better' decision-making.

And yet, as Lindblom and Cohen have argued:

> Information and analysis provide only one route among several to social problem-solving – because ... problem-solving is and ought to be accomplished through various forms of social interaction that substitute action for thought, understanding or analysis ... ordinary knowledge and causal analysis are often sufficient or better for social problem-solving.
> (*Lindblom and Cohen, 1979: 10*)

Policy analysis since the 1950s has, however, been dominated by the rational 'information' model. Our age has been one which has seen a quite phenomenal increase in information and in our capacity to store and process this information. Policy analysis with its variety of 'quantitative' and 'qualitative' approaches has been one response to this knowledge revolution. The use of computers has also been seen as a powerful technological answer to the quest for more rational decision-making. Nowadays we may consider that technology is part of the problem rather than the solution, but the idea that computers can improve the capacity of government to make informed and rational decisions is an enduring and endearing theme of science fiction and scientific management. Decision-making driven and directed by machines rather than by the mechanics of government is in many ways the logical conclusion of a rational view of decision-making, and indeed was in great part the inspiration behind the development of policy analysis in the post-war era.

❖ Computers and democratic decision-making

The idea of using computers to make decision-making more democratic is attractive to those who have faith in the wonders of technology. Presidential candidate H. Ross Perot (a computer salesman) made the idea a central part of his campaign for the US presidency in 1992.

C.B. Macpherson, *The Life and Times of Liberal Democracy*, 1977

> The idea that ... technology and telecommunications will make it possible to achieve direct democracy at the required million-fold level is attractive not only to technologists but to social theorists and political philosophers ... But ... somebody must formulate the questions

... as for instance, 'what per cent of unemployment would you accept in order to reduce the rate of inflation by *x* per cent', or 'what increase in the rate of (a) income tax, (b) sales and excise taxes, (c) other taxes (specify which), would you accept in order to increase by blank per cent ... the level of (1) old-age pensions, (2) health services, (3) other social services ... (pp. 97–8)

Macpherson's point is that even if decision-making were passed over to the people sitting in front of a terminal, the parameters of the questions would still have to be set by policy-makers. At the same time people might want to have their cake and be able to eat it. They may want lower taxes and more spending. Different people would want different things, and it is, he maintains, difficult to imagine a system that could somehow make these demands and interests compatible. Another big problem is formulation and implementation. It might be possible to use computers to process information on citizens' demands and preferences, but the detail of actual policy and its implementation might be beyond a referendum in a computerized village. ◆

Norbert Weiner (quoted in Roszak, 1988: 225), one of the fathers of cybernetics, was not alone when he contemplated in the 1950s the possibility of a world in which the machine could become the decision-maker and remedy the inadequacy of the human brain and the machinery of politics. In the decades which were to follow, the prospect of such new politics receded in the face of the reality that computers did not develop the kind of capacities and intelligence which some had hoped and many had feared. Even so, the myth of improving decision-making by reducing the human element is one which retains an allure for reasons both rationalistic (Simon, 1960, 1983) and radical (see Macpherson, 1977: 94–5; Lindblom and Woodhouse, 1993: 45–6; Slaton, 1991; Arterton, 1986)), and a matter of concern for sceptics (Roszak, 1988; Perry, 1984).

The appeal of computers as an aid to decision-making has remained very strong for those analysts from an OR background – whether that be from the point of view of the 'classical' or the 'alternative' school. The use of information technology (IT) in public management and planning is extensive in areas such as population, employment, land use and transport. It is evident that IT can make a major contribution to the way in which local and national government formulates policy and monitors its implementation (England *et al.*, 1985). However, it is important to note that the benefits to be derived from the costs of IT are a matter of considerable argument. One review of the use of IT in the public sector concludes, for example, that:

despite the great hopes it holds for the present and the future it must not be regarded as a panacea for coping with the ills or for solving all the problems of public sector organizations caught up in environmental turbulence. The changes and transformations necessary for effective govern-

ment and management will not automatically spring from the use of such technologies. Other factors will need to coalesce with this technological advance.
(*Isaac-Henry* et al., *1993: 110*)

Amongst these factors must be included political will and judgement, and the relationship between the structures of decision-making and the behaviour of politicians, bureaucrats and professionals involved in a policy or programme (Reinermann, 1987: 186).

❖ Harold L. Wilensky, *Organizational Intelligence*, 1967

Wilensky's book sought to relate the information explosion to the organizational revolution. He aims to explain what determines the uses of intelligence, and how the failure to use intelligence may be related to structural and ideological factors. Military decision-making (British area bombing strategy in the Second World War, Pearl Harbor, the Bay of Pigs and others) is used as an analogue for understanding the problems which confront complex organizations in non-military areas of government policy and business. The variations between countries in the use of intelligence in areas outside military and foreign policy are more divergent because of the greater impacts of national systems of law and political economy, constitutional arrangements and political institutions. Thus, although he does not suggest that there are general laws or conditions which apply in intelligence, he does argue that common factors for a poor flow and use of information do exist.

Intelligence failure has, he argues, three root causes:

1 structural attributes that maximize distortion and blockage: too much hierarchy; too much specialization and too many units involved; overcentralization of intelligence;
2 doctrines that maximize distortion and blockage: 'facts' to 'fill in the gaps' versus evaluated facts or interpretation; a conflict between intelligence-gathering (research) and clandestine operational activities; the belief that secret intelligence is superior; predication or estimate versus analysis and orientation;
3 types of problems and processes that maximize distortion and blockage: non-urgent decisions which involve heavy costs, risks, uncertainty and changes in goals and methods; problems are those of established organization; no crises in succession.

Wilensky proposes several remedies as 'organizational defences against information pathologies', which involve reforming structures and reducing hierarchy so as to reduce distortions. He concludes that the 'wiz-kids' and policy analysts may have little impact on improving the quality of information and evaluation as the sources of intelligence failures are more complex than is supposed:

Given the institutional roots of intelligence failures, scattered about like land mines, given the urgency of so many big decisions, what counts is the top executive's preconceptions – what he has in his mind when he enters the room and must act ... the symbols that surround the executive in his daily life shape his orientation. Experts and intellectuals who can write, speak and present ideas quickly and easily have a major influence on speeches and regulations, by laws and contracts, press releases and in-house organs, legal, economic, or scientific briefs and testimony. In private conferences they set the tone of policy discourse. No one who examines the history of such doctrines as 'strategic bombing' and 'massive retaliation' or the sad tale of foreign intervention in such places as Cuba and Vietnam can be impressed with 'the end of ideology', if by that we mean the end of illusions that systematically conceal social reality ... Many a brittle slogan has perpetuated a policy long outmoded.

To read the history of modern intelligence is to get the nagging feeling that the men at the top are often out of touch, that good intelligence is difficult to come by and enormously difficult to listen to; that big decisions are very delicate but not necessarily deliberative; that sustained good judgment is rare.

(*Wilensky, 1967: 190–1*) ◆

As Perrow has noted in the case of the arguments advanced by Wilensky (above), the theory that information can aid better decision-making is often made to the exclusion of other factors:

> Wilensky indicates that if information were of better quality, not distorted by the bureaucratic hierarchy, if it quickly reached the proper people, and if it were evaluated fearlessly regardless of career implications and interpersonal dependencies, our organizations would function much more in keeping with their announced goals – and much more effectively. In many cases, one can agree ... But what is striking is the number of cases where a failure of intelligence did not seem to be at stake. The information was available; it was simply not in the interests of the leaders to use it. Changing the structure, reducing the levels of hierarchy, eliminating the 'pathologies' of bureaucracy would mean little if the goals, perspectives, or prejudices of the elite were not changed. To change these might mean to change the whole structure of society and the goals of all the organizations that support that structure.
> (*Perrow, 1986: 170–1*)

The problem of the relation of knowledge to rule and decision is as old as civilization itself. In myths and legends we find stories of how wizards and viziers seek to rise above kings and queens. In Plato, we find a republic in which justice is to be founded in a state in which philosophers are kings. Francis Bacon envisaged a Utopia in which scientists would be in charge. Modern science fiction is replete with similar stories of how science and rationality lay claims to being able to make decisions better than ordinary mortals. The arguments of those such as Wilensky who suggest that it is possible somehow to make decision-making a less distorted process may be less fanciful than tales of Utopias where men in white coats rule, but it rests upon assumptions about how organizations and societies work which are equally simplistic. As Peters comments: 'Most governments do not use all the "tools" available in their tool kit. In addition there is very little theory to guide governments trying to decide what tools they should use. Thus a great deal of policy formulation is done by inertia or by intuition' (Peters, 1986: 51).

Where does this leave the idea of the policy sciences as contributing to the knowledge needs of decision-makers? What alternatives are there to the rational model of government as involving 'steering' (from the Latin *gubernare*, to steer) the ship of state by the guiding lights of science and knowledge?

❖ From knowledgeable to communicative policy-making?

What if we shift away from the idea of instrumental rationality, towards the notion that improving decision-making involves improving communication, understanding, trust, open discussion and co-operation between those involved in policy areas? A communicative form of governance may be seen as informed, not by a top-down/knowledge–solution 'process', so much as by a bottom-up kind of interactive 'learning'.

'Communicative governance'

Martin Van Vliet (1993) argues that the complexity of governing in modern society – through networks, interdependence of actors, negotiated 'games' and 'learning' processes – involves a search for alternative models to those of hierarchies or markets. He believes that a source of a new framework is to be found in the ideas of Jürgen Habermas (1984) and Dryzek (1987) (see 1.6, 3.10.5). In conditions of increasing social and economic complexity, co-operation, mutual adjustment, persuasion and dialogue may be considered to be a more rational and effective strategy than one based on conflict of interests. Vliet takes the experience of the Dutch National Environmental Policy Plan (NEPP), developed in 1989, as an example of how a 'communicative' approach to government–business relationships has been successful in bringing about a 'reasonable' and 'co-operative' pattern of policy-making in the paint and petroleum networks. *Note*: On communicative rationality in planning, see Healey, 1993.

Communication, governance and organizational co-operation: towards an ecological perspective

The study of interorganizational relationships has been largely framed by the idea that power, conflict and competition are the dominant characteristics of the way in which organizations seek to maximize their interests. The 'communicative' paradigm suggested by Habermas and Dryzek stresses that co-operation and a dialogue of mutual understanding is also a rational strategy in conditions of complex interdependencies. Boulding (1981), Vickers (1965) and Morgan (1986) show how organizations can use both co-operative, communicative and competitive strategies. ◆

3.10   Critiques of policy analysis

3.10.1   The limits of rational analysis

The use of models and techniques to improve decision-making has had mixed fortunes. The inherent messiness of politics militates against the naive belief that decision-making can somehow be made more 'rational'. There are severe limitations on the use of analytical work in real decision-making. These limitations include what several analysts (Heineman *et al.*, 1990: 62–4) have identified as:

- the sheer information overload which exists in the modern policy process;
- the use of analysis to reinforce and legitimate decisions which have already been made, rather than to enable decision-makers to choose 'rationally' between options. In other words, decision-makers make a choice and then find a plausible analytical story which will back it up;
- the subjection of analysis to considerable politicization. The idea that analysis can be neutral is a myth;
- analysts' lack a power base; thus the experience of experts in the policy process tends to be of being weak *vis-à-vis* political and bureaucratic interests;
- the fact that analysis may be strong on the diagnosis of problems and formulation of policy but weak in terms of how a policy should be implemented.

Such experience with the rational model in practice has fostered a good deal of re-evaluation of the usefulness of the idea of policy analysis as involving a series of logical stages: problem identification; setting objectives; analysing alternatives; decision-making; and implementation. The limitations of this model of analysis in the decision-making process, and the conceptualization which it contains of the decision-making process itself, has prompted the search for other approaches to the rational model and frameworks for policy analysis. Some of these we have discussed earlier in this book, and before we proceed to outline the alternative approaches to policy analysis, let us briefly review some of them.

We have seen how the dominant paradigm of policy analysis has been of an essentially positivist and rationalist kind. The 'rational framework' therefore encompasses the kinds of techniques which we have adumbrated above, most notably CBA and the tools of OR and systems analysis. However, we noted that within this paradigm there is growing dissent from the 'classical' position. In broad terms, the rationalists are working within what Simon described as 'bounded rationality'. The rationalists are aware of the bounded nature of rationality, but make claims about the possibilities of decision-making being 'more' rational or 'better'. Chief amongst their number are texts which were published in the 1970s such as: Dye (1976); Stokey and Zeckhauser (1978); and Quade (1976). However, in the 1980s this model of policy analysis as providing the basis of a more rational decision-making process began to wear a little thin. Instead of the idea of policy analysis as a science of decision which constituted a 'threat' to politics, the realization dawned that the claims for rational analysis as improving 'problem-solving' were far too extravagant. The experience of policy analysis suggested that, in reality, information, facts and figures and analytical reports were part and parcel of political arguments. Analysis was not a substitute for politics or 'anti-political' (Smith, 1972), but essentially supplementary and subordinate to the political process. Policy analysis was really about persuasion and argument rather than neutral expert advice (Meltsner, 1976; Simon, 1983: 97; Hogwood and Gunn, 1984: 266–76; Putt and Springer, 1989). As Majone (1989: 1) notes: 'As politicians know only too well but social scientists often forget, public policy is made of language. Whether in written or oral form, argument is central in all stages of the policy process.' For true believers, this notion that policy analysis was no longer the kind of scientific rational tool-set that it had been in the 1960s came as a challenge to their faith in CBA, OR and the like.

A number of frameworks take issue with this notion that policy analysis has this positivistic mission or capacity to improve decision-making. We may consider these under several headings. (However, it is important to note that, as with all such attempts to set out a 'framework of frameworks', the categories are not intended to place ideas and their authors into boxes: there are overlaps and interconnections between them.) We can describe the responses to rational policy analysis in terms of five categories:

- the critical rationalists (3.10.2);
- the political realists (3.10.3);
- the forensics (3.10.4);
- the critical theorists (3.10.5);
- the managerialists (3.10.6).

3.10.2   The 'critical rationalists'

These have taken on board the criticisms of the rational approach and offer modified models which seek to take account of the deficiencies and track a middle way. Two of the leading theorists who have maintained a critical rationalist stance are Etzioni and Dror, whose ideas we examined earlier in discussing Simon and Lindblom. Both reject the idea of incrementalism and put forward alternatives to the rational and incrementalist approaches. Amitai Etzioni's idea of 'mixed scanning' must, as we noted (3.4.4), be placed in the context of his work as a whole. Etzioni has enlarged upon his ideas in several publications (see, for example, Etzioni, 1983, 1988, 1993a, b). In the 1990s he has become most closely associated with 'communitarianism' (see 1993a, b; 1994; and 1.6). *The Active Society* (1968) remains, however, as possibly the best introduction to his ideas for the student of public policy and policy analysis. Etzioni believes that personal transformation is rooted in the 'joint act of the community transforming itself' (1968: 2). The aim of public policy is ultimately to promote a society in which people are active in their communities and in which 'political action and intellectual reflection would have a higher, more public status' (1968: 7). This is to be achieved through raising individual and societal consciousness, and a new emphasis on 'symbolization' as opposed to material wealth. The active society is one which 'knows itself' and uses that knowledge to transform the self and the public sphere. Social science and other forms of knowledge have a vital role to play in promoting the 'active society'. Thus, unlike Lindblom, he does not abandon the use of analysis to improve society (and the self). The emphasis on 'community' which has been central to his later writings has therefore to be placed in the context of his belief in the role of knowledge in bringing about a more open and more 'authentic' public policy process (1968: 635), in which knowledge and power are more widely distributed. Society as a whole should be more engaged in the 'testing' of knowledge and the 'community of assumptions' (cf. Young, 1977; and 3.7.7 above) which frame decision-making (1968: 176–80). (On this point Lindblom and Etzioni seem to converge.) An active society is one which involves the public in analysis – not excludes them. The knowledge elites – intellectuals, experts and politicians – should, in an active society, *interact* with publics in a form of 'collective reality testing' (see 1968: 155–70):

> A society that is free to test its ideas and to try out fundamentally new ones cannot be restricted to approaching the world and itself merely through the narrow political filter of elites in power; such a society must provide for fundamental criticism and be open to it. Such a self-critical society – active in its use of knowledge – cannot be brought about unless the postmodern society is transformed by a fuller exercise of the critical function.
> (*Etzioni, 1968: 189–90*)

Figure 3.32 Etzioni's 'active' society

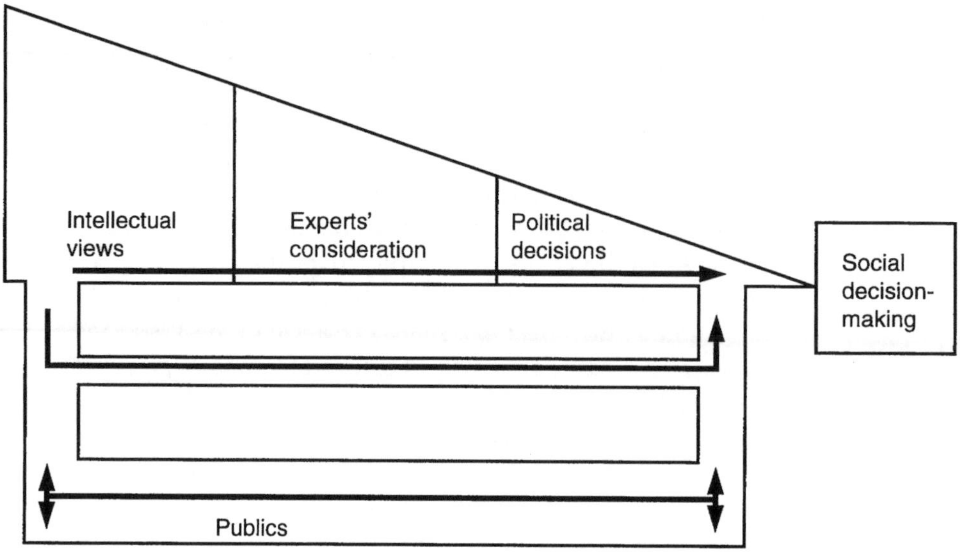

| Intellectual views | Experts' consideration | Political decisions | Social decision-making |

Publics

Source: Adapted from Etzioni (1968: 187)

This may be illustrated in a graphical way (figure 3.32).

Etzioni's views on the critical/political function of analysis and knowledge is close at a number of points to Lasswell (1951b, 1970a), Lindblom (1990) and some of the arguments of critical theorists (below). However, where he differs is in the emphasis he places on the importance of 'community' institutions and symbols as integral parts of a critical and active society. 'Rebuilding' society (see Etzioni, 1983) therefore involves both a knowledge and a moral dimension.

Another spokesman for a modified form of the rational model of policy analysis is Yehezkel Dror. Policy analysis, he argues, must acknowledge that there is a realm of extra-rational understanding founded on tacit knowledge and personal experience (Dror, 1989: 15–16). His theory of 'optimal' policy-making involves the idea that the aim of analysis is to induce decision-makers to expand their thinking and frameworks to better deal with a world which is not unlike an 'unstable casino' (Dror, 1989: 9). In contrast to the simplistic phases of a purely rational model Dror puts forward a more complex model of some 18 stages (Dror, 1989: 163–4):

- Metapolicy-making stage
    1   processing values;
    2   processing reality;

  3 processing problems;
  4 surveying, processing, and developing resources;
  5 designing, evaluating, and redesigning the policy-making sys-
     tem;
  6 allocating problems, values and resources;
  7 determining policy-making strategy.
- Policy-making stage
  8 suballocating resources;
  9 establishing operational goals, with some order of priority;
  10 establishing a set of their significant values, with some order of
     priority;
  11 preparing a set of major alternative policies, including some
     'good ones';
  12 preparing reliable predictions of the significant benefits and
     costs of the various alternatives;
  13 comparing the predicted benefits and costs of the various alter-
     natives and identifying the 'best' ones;
  14 evaluating the benefits and costs of the 'best' alternatives and
     deciding whether they are 'good' or not.
- Post-policy-making stage
  15 motivating the execution of policy;
  16 executing the policy;
  17 evaluating policy-making after executing the policy.
- 18 Communication and feedback channels interconnecting all
     phases.

The model aims to take account of the real world, which involves values and different perceptions of reality, and creates an approach which combines core elements of the rational model (such as the measurement of costs and benefits, the weighting of goals and alternatives) with 'extra-rational' factors which are excluded from the 'pure-rationality' model. As we argued earlier, Dror's analysis does lead to a very technocratic view of the role of the policy sciences and a belief in management that is at odds with the Lasswellian approach (see 3.10.6). Perhaps, however, the real strength of Dror's analysis is not in terms of the prescriptive dimension of his model, so much as in the framework it provides to analyse the policy process. As a model of the policy process, Dror's framework suggests that we should analyse public policy as being made in two interacting 'subphases'. Thus the 18 stages outlined above must be read as a cycle (figure 3.33) which has its rational and extra-rational aspects (in Vickers's sense, 'reality' and 'value' judgements).

Figure 3.33 Dror's policy cycle

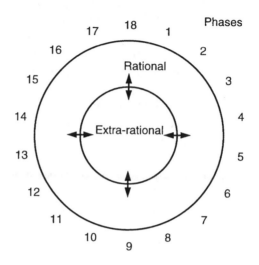

Source: Adapted from Dror (1989: appendix B)

3.10.3 The 'political realists'

These include a broad spectrum such as Charles Lindblom, Aaron Wildavksy and Hogwood and Gunn, who view policy analysis essentially as part of the political process which should aim to complement political argumentation rather than replace it. Political realists view analysis as an activity which can help to raise the level of political debate. Summing up this position, Lindblom and Woodhouse, for example, argue that:

> The quality of public policy depends on a vast network of thought and interaction, in which professional policy analysts play a small role. In a given year or decade, the actions of government are not going to be determined in main outline by analysis, reports, books, articles or pronouncements of those who make a living studying public policy. Time after time the good sense embodied in careful research is ignored, distorted, and otherwise made ineffective ... In principle, those who analyse public policy can help to challenge aspects of the policy-making process that obstructs wise policy-making, can help to broaden the range of changes under consideration, and can help to deepen political debates about problems, opportunities, and policy options.
> (*Lindblom and Woodhouse, 1993: 137*)

Dismissing the idea of rational analysis as improving decision-making, Lindblom has argued that the real issue is not rationality so much as improving the capacity of societies to cope flexibly with uncertainty, and to learn from experience (Lindblom and Cohen, 1979; Lindblom and Woodhouse, 1993). This suggests to Lindblom that the key to better decision-making is not analysis for the elite, but a more open policy-making process in which policy is shaped by a wider range of ideas, interests, analysis and social learning (see 4.6.4).

❖ The self-guiding society

In his book *Inquiry and Change* (1990), Lindblom outlines a prescriptive model of a self-guiding society as an alternative to the idea of a 'scientifically guided' society which underpins the 'textbook' approach to policy analysis. He argues that the self-guiding society may be distinguished from the scientific model in terms of the following kinds of characteristics:

- All knowledge is seen as inconclusive.
- Social science is an aid, not an alternative, to ordinary inquiry.
- Some problems are intractable to social science. Learning needs to take place amongst ordinary citizens.
- Feelings and sensitivities must be recognized as important to the way in which problems are defined.
- There are no correct solutions, only those that are 'well probed'.
- Finding solutions is a step-by-step, trial-and-error process.
- Learning needs feedback from the experience and action of citizens, functionaries, social scientists and others.
- The role of elites must be downgraded in the policy process.
- Problems must not be seen as involving issues of social 'controls'.
- Power has to be redistributed if policies are to be 'imposed'.
- Democracy and participation are vital for good problem-solving.
- The self-guiding society must leave room for problem-solving, rather than deliberately designing organizations and assigning problems to 'solvers'.
- Solutions are bound by time and space – there are no universal solutions.
- The self-guiding society has a limited faith in reason and is not motivated by general laws or 'holistic' theories.

The role of analysis in this model departs radically from the Baconian idea of knowledge improving our capacity to control, but is in keeping with the Enlightenment belief in the importance of inquiry and the need to probe and challenge the established wisdoms. Thus policy analysis should, in this brave new world, aim to open up communications by:

- challenging the policy-making process to broaden the range of ideas it includes on the agenda;
- deepen the political debate;
- adopting a thoughtful partisanship rather than an unreal 'neutrality' on issues;
- developing frameworks to cope with uncertainty and developing flexibility;
- promoting learning from experience;
- helping to accelerate the learning process;
- improving the thinking of ordinary people, rather than just of rulers. ◆

Another prominent political realist is Aaron Wildavsky, who, like Lindblom, started off as highly pluralist and very critical of analytical models such as PPBS and other rational techniques (see, for example, Wildavsky, 1969, 1971, 1975; and Heclo and Wildavsky, 1974). But in the aftermath of the 1970s he came around to accepting the need for policy analysis to provide a balance between planning and markets. Again, as for Lindblom, however, Wildavksy sees the role of analysis as contributing to the improvement of politics, rather than as a substitute for it (see Wildavsky, 1979, 1980). Policy analysis is thus an art and a craft, rather than a science. Analysis is about exercising 'imagination' and conducting 'thought experiments':

> Policy analysis, to be brief, is an activity creating problems that can be solved. Every policy is fashioned of tension between resources and objectives, planning and politics, scepticism and dogma. Solving problems involves temporarily resolving these tensions.
> (*Wildavsky, 1979: 17*)

The tasks of policy analysis in a pluralistic society are therefore:

> relating resources to objectives by balancing social interaction against intellectual cogitation so as to draw the line between scepticism and dogma.
> (*Wildavsky, 1979: 19*)

In common with Wildavksy (1979, 1980), Hogwood and Gunn (1984) also view the aim of policy analysis as supplementing politics so as to improve debate and the consideration of policy problems and alternatives. They argue that their framework assumes a multiplicity of policy actors deploying policy analysis as argument. They distance themselves from the 'sterile', 'rational comprehensive', 'muddling through' stereotypes, and reject a 'middle way' in favour of a contingent approach which recognizes that:

> Some issues will always require a highly political, pluralist, bargaining, and incremental approach. But some other issues ... will both require and lend themselves to a much more planned analytical approach ... There is no 'one best way' of making decisions, just as there is no universal prescription for 'good organization'. Among the diagnostic skills required is a very high grasp of political sensitivity and discrimination as well as a grasp of the technical skills of planning and analysis.
> (*Hogwood and Gunn, 1984: 62*)

3.10.4   The 'forensics'

The 'forensics' were discussed earlier, in the section dealing with the 'argumentative turn' in policy analysis (2.7.3). We noted that the argumentative approach focuses on the rhetorical and persuasive power of policy discourse in shaping the agenda. The forensic view of policy analysis differs substantially from the dominant paradigm associated with rational techniques. Proponents of this approach envisage policy analysis as something which is akin to the methods of legal investigation (hence the term 'forensic'). Analysis in this sense is an activity of subjecting policy arguments to the test of persuasiveness, rather than quasi-scientific proof or rational 'truth'. The policy analyst is more like a lawyer cross-examining a witness than a scientist measuring or experimenting. One of the most widely cited is Martin Rein, who proposed (in the 1970s) the idea that policy analysis is concerned with 'telling stories':

> The giving of advice and the design of social programmes is like the telling of relevant stories. Such stories resemble proverbs and metaphors, for they seek to match reality to archetypal patterns of events by drawing analogies. That is to say, they provide an interpretation of a complex pattern of events with normative implications for action ...
> (Rein, 1976: 266)

Policy analysis is therefore something which cannot be subjected to tests which determine right and wrong, truth and error, but rather, how plausible the stories are perceived as being, and which story is more plausible than another. Truth and proof of the kind which is the object of rational analysis do not really come into it at all. Some stories are more believable, or offer better insight into decisions and problems. But for Rein there are no other ways of resolving disagreements between competing views of the world, or paradigms. The task of policy analysis he expresses as being:

> to bring evidence and interpretation to bear on decision-making and social practice. This task involves not only the presentation of evidence about the consequences of pursuing alternative actions but also an interpretation of what it is we are doing in society, why we are doing what we do, and what we might do differently given our puzzlement and worry about what we do. When we consider the way we think when we analyse policy, we need to examine the interplay between theory, fact and value. This examination into the life of the mind is special because thought about policy more than other streams of mental life is grounded in action, not as an afterthought but as the essential feature of policy. When we think about the limits of what we do or about what we ought to do (policy analysis), we work from examples of policies in action. Our thought is thus a concrete expression of our experience in acting.
> (Rein, 1983: 83)

Given this intermingling of facts, theories and values, the stories which are told by policy analysts to decision-makers cannot be subjected to tests which prove one way or another. Stories in the decision-making process are bundles of facts, theories and values which cannot be disentangled by any scientific procedure or rational technique. The object of analysis is therefore the framework within which decisions about policy are made and how plausible these frameworks are. Although Rein is clear about the need to avoid a hopeless pluralism in which nothing can be refuted, it is not at all clear what prevents such a fate (or even worse, a hopeless relativism wherein everything is equal) befalling those who adopt his forensic 'storytelling' method. With this in mind we can turn to others in the 'forensic' school who adopt a more formal or logical approach to the way in which policy arguments are constructed.

Paris and Reynolds (1983), for example, take the view that policy arguments are essentially ideological constructs which lay claim to being rational in terms of: coherence (is the story, in Rein's sense, logically consistent, and consistent in the relationship of values and actions?); congruence (does the story fit well with empirical evidence?); and cogency (are its recommendations plausible?). This model provides a much clearer procedure for testing a policy argument and choosing between frames in a decision-making process than does Rein's notion of plausible and largely incommensurate stories; but it is still heavy with a relativism which claims that there is no way of deciding conclusively between ideologies. Policy analysis both for Rein and for Paris and Reynolds (see also Anderson, 1988) remains quintessentially a way of making the claims and consequences of different frameworks clearer to decision-makers and to society at large.

Others in the 'forensic' camp dissent from the position of Rein *et al.*, in that they propose sets of criteria by which truth may be tested. Using this approach, policy analysis involves the application of rules which can determine the worth of a policy argument. A prominent exponent of this 'truth test' method is William Dunn, who insists that knowledge and policy arguments can be subjected to clear tests so as to arrive at choices which are based on more than the subjectivism and relativism of a world in which all stories are equal. For Dunn, all arguments are not equal: some are more logical or more 'truthful' than others. He rejects the ideas of experimentalism, piecemeal engineering and the model of scientific explanation as the basis for policy analysis and maintains that jurisprudence provides a far more satisfactory basis on which to make choices between frameworks:

> The jurisprudential metaphor ... emphasizes that argumentation is a process of rational advocacy in which stakeholders engage in the competitive reconstruction of knowledge claims. This competitive reconstruction, in contrast to the competitive replication of experiments, leads towards a pragmatic and dialectical conception of the truth in which social discourse plays a reflective and critical role in producing new knowledge. Knowl-

edge is no longer based on deductive certainty or empirical correspondence but on the relative adequacy of knowledge claims embedded in ongoing social processes.
(*Dunn, 1993: 264*)

Dunn's work in the field relies heavily on the ideas of Stephen Toulmin (1958) on understanding 'reasoned persuasion' in knowledge claims as well as in ordinary language. Dunn (1993: 265) argues that Toulmin's 'transactional' model provides:

- a visual representation which may be used to map the arguments of analysts and decision-makers;
- a critical method of examining ideology;
- a model which may be extended to develop a typology of standards, rules and tests for assessing and challenging the truth and utility of knowledge claims.

Dunn, along with other jurisprudential analysts (Fischer, 1980; Hambrick, 1974; Macrae, 1976, 1993) have developed a variety of typologies which, they maintain, can be used to test arguments and claims in a rigorous manner so as to 'uncover the hidden standards and unexamined assumptions that shape, and often distort, the production and application of knowledge' (Fischer and Forrester (eds), 1993: 14). In brief, the model involves subjecting arguments to a series of questions which explore and map the structure of a policy argument. These questions are framed by six key elements (see figure 3.34):

Figure 3.34   Dunn's jurisprudential framework

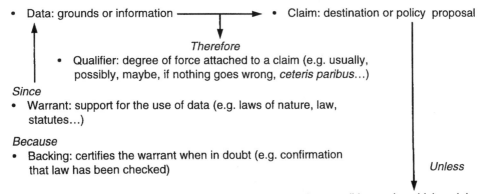

- Data: grounds or information ———→ • Claim: destination or policy proposal

Therefore
- Qualifier: degree of force attached to a claim (e.g. usually, possibly, maybe, if nothing goes wrong, *ceteris paribus*...)

Since
- Warrant: support for the use of data (e.g. laws of nature, law, statutes...)

Because
- Backing: certifies the warrant when in doubt (e.g. confirmation that law has been checked)

Unless

- Rebuttal: specifies condition under which a claim may be challenged, or warrant may be set aside

Source: Adapted from Dunn (1993: 264)

- data;
- claim;
- warrant;
- backing;
- rebuttal;
- qualifier.

This kind of model provides what Dunn believes to be a procedure or checklist by which we can test policy arguments in terms of the structure of argumentation, including types of warrants and backings, and the threats to usable knowledge in terms of cogency, relevance and adequacy. Dunn, in advocating jurisprudence as a model of policy analysis, provides a radical alternative to the 'rational' and scientific approaches. By seeing analysis as involving knowledge which is 'transacted' and negotiated, we can focus less on the problem of 'proof' than on the way in which arguments hold together when probed in a 'forensic' way. In distinction to the relativism of the kind of model put forward by Rein, Dunn's approach does assert that there are ways by which decision-making can be based upon standards for assessing theoretical and practical claims in the policy process. However, as an approach it is highly technical and in a sense substitutes one kind of expert (the purveyor of rational techniques) for another (the social scientist schooled in the philosophy of the social sciences). The arguments of Lindblom are relevant once again at this point. Would this kind of analysis/could this kind of analysis have any impact on real decision-making? It is an issue with deep resonances in the past: a few thousand years ago Plato hoped for a system of government in which philosophers were kings. Does policy analysis need to be more than simply expert power? It is the belief of those operating in the framework of critical theory that it does.

3.10.5   The 'critical theorists'

These envisage policy analysis as an activity which should be informed by a radical commitment to social change and equality as a prerequisite for improving decision-making. Critical policy analysis advocates a fundamental and far-reaching shift towards a more open decision-making process and the empowering of citizens, rather than improving the way in which decision-makers use information and knowledge. The central dimension of this approach is discussed by Dunn and Rein: the need for a more critical appraisal of frameworks and arguments. If, as Dunn argues, knowledge is something which is about 'claims' and is 'negotiated', then it follows that the arguments and assumptions which inform decision-making should be subject to vigorous criticism from as wide a range of opinion as possible. Dunn notes, for example, that: 'the transactional model may contribute to individual and collective learning capacities, and thus to emancipatory reforms' (Dunn, 1993: 284). The problem which critical policy analysis identifies as being the key to improving decision-making is: *how can this emancipation be attained?*

Two models may be cited here to illustrate the kinds of frameworks deployed in critical policy analysis: the 'integrative' and 'communicative' approaches (Dryzek, 1987). To illustrate the integrative approach, we shall consider Harold Lasswell's concept of the decision seminar, and for the communicative framework, we shall examine the ideas of John Dryzek.

One of Harold Lasswell's main preoccupations was the issue of how decision-making is subject to distortions. The policy sciences, he believed, could help to bring about a less-distorted, more rational decision-making process in conditions of growing complexity. Lasswell suggested that decision seminars could be used as a technique for developing contextual and conceptual maps for decision-making. This method he saw as a development of Freudian-inspired brainstorming techniques (see Osborn, 1957; and 3.8.7 above); role-playing exercises in law and political science; small-group therapy as suggested by Carl Rogers, Kurt Lewin and others; war-gaming techniques developed by RAND (Goldhamer and Speier, 1959); and simulation models as used by engineers. The aim of such approaches is to create situations in which 'permissive social environments' (Lasswell, 1960: 214) can create the pre-conditions for creative thinking and open communication. The decision seminar Lasswell envisaged as a way of bringing a community of concern and knowledge together in a 'collective social operation' (Lasswell, 1960: 215) that gives 'no one the last word – since the last word is spoken only as future events unfold' (Lasswell, 1960: 217).

❖ Lasswell's decision seminars approach

This is a method which aims to help decision-makers develop tools for dealing with complex problems and, above all, is a process which leads to the personal development and enlightenment of all participants. The theory of decision seminars is described in Lasswell (1960) and *A Pre-view of Policy Sciences* (1971). Accounts of its application may be found in Slonaker (1978); Cunningham (1981); Bolland and Muth (1984); Brewer (1985); Ershkowitz (1981); and Gorrell *et al.* (1993).

Requirements of the decision seminar technique

- A small nucleus of members (16–25).
- Selection of people to provide a mixed membership drawn from different academic, professional, cultural, ethnic and social backgrounds, as well as different personality groups.
- Members must have a commitment to continue with the seminar.
- High frequency of (three-hour) regular meetings (e.g.: daily, weekly, fortnightly).
- Commitment of seminar members to a disciplined and contexual programme through the application of Lasswell's models (see below).
- A seminar 'facilitator' trained in Lasswell's methods, who can develop the agenda in consultation with other members.
- A room set aside for the seminar, so that resources can be stored and displayed (a 'social planetarium').
- Develop permanent files and records of proceedings.
- Use 'selections' or records/minutes of previous meeting to set agenda for next meeting.
- Aim to produce a shared 'cognitive map' of problems, issues and affections/values.
- Audio-visual facilities and 'data synthesizers' are necessary to support the work of the seminar.
- Invite expert witnesses to give presentations to the seminar.
- There should be no restrictions on sources and methods of reporting to the seminar.
- Give priority to material that has been prepared and introduced by members of the group.
- There must be open and candid disclosure of data.
- There must be critical examination of presentations.
- Give attention to interconnections of items under discussion.
- Cultivate creativity and innovation through
    - free association of ideas (brainstorming);
    - fantasy;
    - private meditation;
    - simulations.
- Re-evaluate past constructs about the future.
- Be aware of the psychological dimensions of individual and group behaviour (ego-defence).

Lasswell's models/tools for decision seminars

Key texts: Lasswell (1936, 1956, 1965, 1970, 1971).

Lasswell proposed a framework of some 27 concepts which he arranged in four sets of ideas. Seminars should proceed by using these sets of ideas to analyse and explore problems.

The intellectual tasks
Focuses the attention of the decision seminar on five tasks designed to map out a strategy for problem-solving:

- goal clarification;
- trend description;
- analysis of conditions;
- projection of developments;
- invention, evaluation and selection of alternatives.

Decision process model
Sets out to map the decision process as comprising seven phases:

* intelligence;
* promotion;
* prescription;
* invocation;
* application;
* termination;
* appraisal.

Analysis should focus on stakeholders who are involved in intelligence elites; those who promote values/causes/interests; those who prescribe policy; those who enforce it; those who implement it; those who appraise it; and those with the power to terminate a policy. But also: what they value; how they secure their values; and when. The seven stages involve far more than just a rational sequence.

The social process model
The use of a 'social process' model is designed to map the way in which participants (stakeholders) in a decision process seek to realize their values, through institutions:

* *Participants*: Who are the relevant individuals and groups involved in a problem? Who are the official and non-offical 'value shapers and sharers'?
* *Perspectives*: What are the value demands, the expectations, identities and myths of the participants?
* *Situations*: How and where are participants located and organized?
* *Base values*: What positive/negative assets (capabilities, perspectives, values) do participants hold (see values below)?
* *Strategies*: What kinds of strategies are participants likely to employ (e.g.: coercive, persuasive)?
* *Outcomes*: What are the outcomes sought by participants in terms of values, decisions and choices?
* *Effects*: What are the actual value and institutional effects of participation?

Categories of values and institutions
Lasswell argues that human beings pursue values through institutions so as to shape and share values to effect resources. In a decision seminar the analysis of the value–institutions context of a problem is therefore a key tool. Lasswell proposes an eight-fold classification of values and their corresponding institutions. What values and what institutions are involved in problems/solutions (market, bureaucracy, community)?

* *Power*: government, law, political parties;
* *Enlightenment*: languages, mass media, scientific establishments;
* *Wealth*: farms, factories, banks;
* *Well-being*: hospitals, recreational facilities;
* *Skill*: vocational, professional, art schools;
* *Affection*: families, friendship circles;
* *Respect*: social classes and castes;
* *Rectitude*: ethical and religious associations.

Figure 3.35   Contextual mapping in a decision seminar

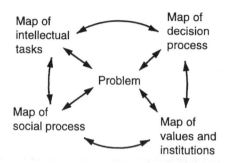

A seminar should proceed by mapping the problem at issue by applying the four sets of conceptual tools (shown in figure 3.35).

One review of the practical application of these models in decision seminars concludes:

> The genius of Lasswell's thinking is that he has anticipated and provided for the problems and issues inherent in utilizing the best of what is known. His contribution is simultaneously substantive, processual, and structural. His processes are apolitical but provide for the effective functioning of political systems. His respect for intelligence is manifest in the requirements that research and expertness be incorporated continuously through man's experience. (*Cunningham, 1981: 40*)

Dryzek (1987) refers to the decision seminar as an 'integrative' approach which :

> finds reflection in some contemporary private and public sector organizations, which responds to complexity by nurturing loose collegial groups, often isolated from the bureaucratic core. [Which] ... can expose the blind spots of any single perspective – a blindness only amplified by incorporation into large-scale systems models ... But one suspects that such integration will fall short as long as it is tied to a decision structure in which a privileged group (however intelligent, broad-minded, and unencapsulated by disciplinary and organizational socialization) manipulates – or advises the manipulators of – a system 'out there' (p. 431). ◆

Lasswell envisaged the decision seminar technique as extending into decision-making processes throughout the community in 'social planetariums' (see Lasswell, 1959; and 4.4.8).

More recently, John Dryzek has been in the forefront of the development of a more critical approach to policy analysis (see also 1.5, 2.8.2, 4.5.4). He has advanced his arguments for a policy analysis which sides with 'open communication and unrestricted participation' in several publications (see Dryzek, 1987, 1989, 1990, 1993). Here we shall examine his 1987 article, as it provides an excellent overview of policy analysis and a coherent and accessible account of the 'communicative' approach.

Dryzek argues that we can identify three main kinds of instrumental rationality – as a response to growing complexity:

- *Analytical disaggregation*: This involves the use of techniques such as CBA, decision analysis and other analytical tools that we have reviewed above which aim at 'breaking down complexity' or 'decomposing ' (Simon, 1981: 209–13) it so as to improve decision-making.
- *Systems modelling*: These approaches endeavour to model or simulate the interactions in a problem. As we have seen above, modelling is central to economic approaches and to OR and systems analysis.
- *Integrative approaches*: Lasswell's decision seminar is perhaps the most important example of the integrative approach which involves 'pooling' different people and disciplines to approach a problem in a multi-framed manner (see also Mason, 1969; George, 1980; and Brewer, 1975).

Dryzek argues that there have been two main alternatives to these forms of instrumental rationality: political rationality (Lindblom, 1959; Wildavsky, 1966); and market rationality (Hayek, 1978). Clearly, it has been the latter which has been the most significant alternative to 'rational analysis' from the 1980s onwards. However, he believes that there is a third alternative which should be considered: 'communicative rationality', which owes its philosophical origins to Arendt (1958), Gadamer (1975) and Habermas (1984). He expresses the 'communicative' approach as having a common aim in wanting to

> resurrect authentic and reasonable public discourse, eroded by centuries of instrumental rationality manifested in hierarchy, administration, and technocracy.
> (*Dryzek, 1987: 433*)

Communicative rationality is defined by Dryzek as a form of social interaction that

> is free from domination (the exercise of power), strategic behaviour by the actors involved, and (self) deception. Further, all actors should be equally and fully capable of making and questioning arguments (that is, communicatively competent). There should be no restrictions on the participation of these competent actors. Under these conditions, the only remaining authority is that of a good argument, which can be advanced on behalf of the veracity of empirical description, explanation, and understanding, and just as importantly, the validity of normative judgements.
> (*Dryzek, 1987: 434*)

(See, in relation to this, 2.7.3: the 'argumentative turn'.)

Dryzek (1987: 437–8) believes that the communicative model may not be as impossible or as Utopian as it may seem. There are, he argues, examples of 'intimations' of communicative rationality in a variety of practices in public policy, politics and international relations ('mediation of civil, labour and environmental disputes; regulatory negotiation; policy dialogue; principled negotiation; and "problem-solving" workshops in international conflict resolution'). Dryzek gives an illustration drawn from environmental policy which displays some of the characteristics of a more 'communicative' approach (see Bacow and Wheeler, 1984). However, he concludes that people will only engage in such 'rationalized interaction' if there are good reasons for so doing:

> One reason might be stalemate in other arenas of decision, such as courts. Another might be genuine desire for improved communications with protagonists. A third reason could be naked self-interest: there is more to gain from participation than abstraction. One suspects that this third calculus may dominate in a world of ubiquitous strategic pursuit of self-interest ... This explains why a third party is necessary: to ease participants over hurdles leading to an unfamiliar kind of interaction. One sign of successful dialogue is the increasing inactive role of this third party
> (*Dryzek, 1987: 440*)

As the world becomes more complex, so, Dryzek feels, the attraction of communicative rationality will increase as a practical method which can be complementary to instrumental analysis aimed at 'simple and moderately complex problems' (Dryzek, 1987: 442). Thus the communicative model retains 'analytical' tools but in the context of an open 'argumentative' process and a more participatory democracy. Dryzek is hopeful, but, as he noted in 1993:

> much remains to be done to make this combination a happy and workable one. In the meantime, the argumentative turn can strive to deliver on the promise made by Lasswell four decades ago of a policy science of democracy.
> (*Dryzek, 1993: 230*)

In addition to Dryzek, several other notable attempts have been made to explore and apply the model to improving communications and public participation in decision-making on the lines suggested by Habermas (Dallmayr, 1981; Forester, 1981; Kemp, 1985; Torgerson, 1986; Van Vliet, 1993; Healey, 1993). Nielsen (1983) provides a picture of what decision-making informed by a more radical approach might look like in practice. A 'critical' decision-maker

> would not view the future to be achieved merely by some improved, possibly a little more efficient and a little less inhumane, version of the present ... he or she would have a conception of the general direction

[changes] would take, and with a recognition that there is a causal interaction between base and superstructure, between the economic and political-legal realm, would seek to develop social policies that would help unfetter the production relations in the society ... This would consist most fundamentally in struggling to bring into being policies that would weaken capitalist-class hegemony over society. Central in such an endeavour would be (1) the articulation of policies that would futher movement in the direction of workers' control over their places of work and (2) policies that would move in the direction of achieving democratic rather than business control of the mass media and indeed the whole consciousness of industry. (*Nielsen, 1983: 157*)

Nielson believes that only by these and other measures to equalize power within society could the goals of decision-making as a genuinely 'public' activity take place.

This theme of equality as a means of improving decision-making is not, however, confined to the 'critical' framework. The position adopted by 'neo-pluralists' such as Lindblom is not too far removed from the demands of the critical theorists for a more open debate on problems, and a more active public participation in the formulation of public policy. Lindblom and Woodhouse, for example, note that although they are in agreement with much of Habermas's analysis of the causes of elite domination, they disagree with the solution he offers (Lindblom and Woodhouse, 1993: 148). The practicality of 'ideal speech' situations (and decision seminars) is a major criticism to be confronted by critical theorists. Critical policy analysis does demand that a revolution in the social order is a prerequisite for the equality of 'ideal speech situations'. Without such a social revolution it is difficult to imagine how discussion could be held on an equal footing. The pluralist model is less radical in urging that, if we want to improve decision-making, we must make pluralism work. The incrementalist view would be that only by a more active political process is it possible for the assumptions of policy elites to be effectively challenged. Lindblom and Woodhouse suggest that the strategy should involve:

- reducing the influence of business;
- reducing inequalities in the policy-making process;
- reducing the barriers to inquiry;
- a more equal competition of ideas, and a greater diversity of ideas.

Such measures would (hopefully) lead to a more motivated and thoughtful citizenry. However, the attainment of these objectives is no less fanciful than the ideals of the critical theorists. (Consider, for instance their proposal that all citizens be allocated a certain amount of media time, which they could then allocate to an organization of their choice.)

It has to be said that the ideas for tackling the issues of equality of power addressed by both the critical theorists and pluralists such as Lindblom have made (to date) little headway in the real world of policy analysis. By the 1990s the predominant accommodationist and conservative bias of the study of public policy and policy analysis (Lindblom and Woodhouse, 1993: 135–7; Dunleavy and O'Leary, 1987: 280–3) had given way to a 'new' approach to decision-making which largely excludes the problems of inequality and the wider social, political and economic factors which impair participation in the policy process in favour of a narrower managerial focus.

3.10.6   The 'managerialists'

The 'managerialists' take a view of decision-making in public policy as involving issues and problems which are like those which pertain in the management of organizations in the private or business sector. The managerialist approach may be traced back to texts such as Simon (1960) and Dror (1968) and in the practices and reforms associated with PPBS and McNamara in the 1960s. Dror (1979) imagined that in the future management sciences would merge into the policy sciences, and this has taken place to some extent. However, far more significant than the merger of policy sciences and management has been the virtual takeover of public policy by 'public sector management'. Dror thought that, although management sciences would have a key role in low-level and high-level 'sub-optimized' decision-making, the policy sciences would have centre stage in more complex policies and problems (Dror, 1979: 272). Recent experience confirms that this was somewhat optimistic, as the management orientation has been the predominant trend in public policy (see Pollitt, 1990). This position has itself promoted the search for some of the alternative critical paradigms that we have examined above. The term 'managerialist' analysis covers a wide spectrum of approaches and may be seen in texts such as Bozeman (1979) and Henry (1975). A collection of papers which illustrates the scope of the managerialist framework is that edited by Leach and Stewart (1982). Contributions in this volume range from a defence of the rational model (Leach, 1982) to a critique of the rational approach which emphasizes the limitations of the rational model as a practical method of decision-making (Stewart, 1982).

The managerialist approach does not abandon the rational model, but endeavours to develop other, more practical models and techniques derived from the experience of the world of business. Stewart's ideas about policy analysis, for example, acknowledge the centrality of the rational model in policy presentation and justification, but suggest that it needs to be modified so as to become a more effective tool of management. The role of policy analysis, he notes, is to 'break down the constraints of organizational thought' (Stewart, 1986: 81). In practice it is a means of improving decision-making by facilitating a learning process in public sector organizations. Stewart rejects the pure rational model based on problem-identification, goal-setting, analysis of alternatives, choice, decision-making and implementation, and adopts a more realistic model designed to be a tool for decision-makers in the new public sector. His model therefore is designed to help initiate thinking, rather than 'rational decision-making'. It has five key phases (Stewart, 1982; 1986: 72–92):

- know the shape of the policy area:
  — constraints and opportunities;
  — dominant assumptions;
  — conflicts and consensus;
  — patterns of behaviour;
  — stability/instability of policy over time.
- new alternatives require a change in the framework of thought:
  — challenge existing frameworks to aid new thinking;
- a new policy requires new stories:
  — 'a policy story links events, assumptions and expectations in a way that is satisfactory to the main decision makers and perhaps the main actors' (Stewart, 1982: 32);
- judgement knows no rules, but it can be encouraged:
  — judgement rather than rational calculation and evaluation is needed in many situations;
- policy achievements can be understood even if they cannot be measured:
  — not all policy achievements can be measured in terms of output.

Later versions of policy analysis and public policy in managerialist terms include Patton and Sawicki (1986), Lynn (1987) and Hughes (1994). In reviewing the state of public policy and policy analysis in the 1990s, Owen Hughes reaches the conclusion that they may have had an important impact on both theory and practice, but that its day is truly past:

> Confronted by a decision to build a dam on a river, any government or government agency would gain by commissioning empirical studies ... These could be decision trees, benefit-cost studies, path analyses, demographic and other social studies ... but what these studies cannot do is to make the decision itself. In the end the political and managerial leadership would make a decision and that is how it should be ... public policy and policy analysis have to a great extent been bypassed in the debate over managerialism. The influence of policy analysis has waned somewhat since its heyday in the 1970s, whilst new public management incorporates

> analytical techniques, instead of them having a separate existence and a separate discipline ... in the end, a part of policy analysis – that analysis could be valuable – was absorbed into public management ... As such it has become less relevant as governments and their bureaucracies found analysis being replaced by economics, allied with modern management, as applied to the public sector. In other words, they are being replaced by new public management.
> (*Hughes, 1994: 165–6*)

The adoption of a managerial framework for the analysis of policy-making and for the decision-making process which is illustrated in the kind of model put forward by Stewart *et al.* in the early 1980s is symptomatic of the changes which have come about in the theory and practice of policy analysis identified by Owen in the 1990s. Some have argued that this move away from public administration/policy towards 'public management' constitutes an entirely 'new' paradigm which has emerged as a result of the 'weaknesses' of the approaches which prevailed in the 1960s and 1970s. (Perry and Kraemer (eds), 1983: x). The traditional or classical standpoint which framed policy analysis since its inception was that public decision-making was different to decision-making in the private sector. The 'new' approach ushered in by the advocates of public management was to challenge this assumption as to the difference and uniqueness of public policy-making.

However, to say that the 'management' approach constitutes a new paradigm is to go too far. As Gunn comments, as an argument it is a little too simplistic, for 'it is difficult to see what radically new questions are being posed or novel patterns of thought are emerging from the so-called "paradigm"' (Gunn, 1987: 43). The managerialist approach is perhaps less of a new paradigm than (what is called in the music business) a re-mix. Managerialism derives many of its ideas from long-standing concerns of other approaches to policy analysis, and the 're-mix' has considerable variations across different authors and between different countries. The language of management has proved attractive because, as Perry and Kraemer note, the other approaches we have reviewed in this book have proved to be unsatisfactory in theory and practice. What managerialism shares with the rationalist mentality is a belief that *'politics'* is not an effective mode of decision-making. Managerialism (especially when allied to 'public choice' theory) in this sense represents an on-going search to take decision-making out of a world where there are conflicts over values and beliefs into a realm where decisions can be made in a more rational (non-political) way. Whether it is a new paradigm or not, or whether a new form of policy rhetoric, the analysis of public policy in terms of 'management' has come to dominate the way in which public policy is now discussed. This is especially the case when we consider the 'delivery' of public goods and services. It is to this phase in the policy cycle to which we now turn in the final part of the book.

PART FOUR

Delivery Analysis

The analysis of implementation, evaluation, change and impact

4.1 Introduction

The 'problem' focus of the policy approach has meant that, until the 1970s, policy analysis was primarily concerned with the 'front end' of the policy process. This is to say, the analysis of the policy process tended to be preoccupied with issues such as how rational, open or fair decision-making was or could be; and, from the point of view of analysis in and for the policy process, how knowledge could improve decision-making (Van Meter and Van Horn, 1975: 450–1). However, in the aftermath of policy-making in the 1960s there emerged a growing interest in what might be termed the 'post-decisional' phases of public policy. It became apparent in the 1970s that many policies and programmes had not performed as well as their advocates had hoped. Problems had not been 'solved'; indeed some had been made worse. The best-laid plans had all too often gone awry, and in place of a 'problem/solution' discourse, analysts and actors began to direct their attention to what had gone wrong, why and how. This theme of good decisions and poor or unintended outcomes had, as we noted earlier, been touched upon in Selznick's study of the great hope of inter-war liberalism, the TVA (see 3.6.2). As it became evident that policy-making in so many areas had not achieved its stated goals, or that those goals had not been well defined, so students of public policy began to shift their attention from inputs and processes towards the withinputs, outputs and outcomes.

At first, this concern with the 'delivery' end of the policy process was framed by attempts to model a rational set of sequences involved in successful implementation, thus extending the logic of the policy stage approach to a more detailed analysis of the closing phases of the decision-making cycle (4.3.2). However, this so-called 'top-down' model soon came under attack from those who argued that implementation problems were far more complex a phenomenon than the hierarchical framework suggested. In the 1970s and 1980s the study of implementation was to expand and several alternatives to the 'top-down' view were to be advanced (4.3.3–4.3.8). During the 1980s there were also important developments in the 'real world' of public policy. In Britain and America, and later in most other industrial countries, new attitudes towards the role of government and the 'public sector' as a problem-solver and service-provider came to the forefront of the political agenda (see Massey, 1993; Hughes, 1994). Market and managerial approaches offered a radical alternative to the hierarchical framework within which analysis of 'implementation' and 'evaluation' had for so long taken place. The financial constraints of the 1980s resulted in attempts by governments throughout the industrial world to tame spending and control the growth and influence of bureaucracy. As the pressure on the state to 'live within its means' and 'cut its coat accordingly to its cloth' increased, so did the demand for techniques which could facilitate more control over the fiscal crisis of the modern state. The emphasis on the delivery end of public policy signalled a revolution in the discourse of governance: the language of economics and management came to replace that of 'professionalism', 'administration' and the 'public interest' (Massey, 1993: 12–29).

This movement towards new forms of public-sector 'management' and privatization has not been confined to the Anglo-Saxon world (see Martin, 1993; Letwin, 1988). This was reflected, for example, in the decision by the OECD in the 1980s to strengthen their co-operation in matters of public management so as to facilitate an exchange of experience in the public sector. What the OECD has found is that, notwithstanding the obvious differences between member countries, the problems which they confront seem to show a remarkable convergence (see 2.12). As it reported in 1990:

> Governments of all OECD countries now recognize that improving public management is an integral part of the structural adjustments needed for better economic performance in a changing global environment. There is a growing conviction that a radical change in the 'culture' of public administration is needed if the efficiency and effectiveness of the public sector is to be improved.
> (OECD, 1990)

The framework of public policy is consequently being shaped by continuing and increasingly common concerns about cost-effectiveness, delivery of policies and services, improving human resource management, and better monitoring and evaluation (OECD, 1993a). Furthermore, as we discussed in Part Three, a key trend in policy-making in industrial societies, which many scholars have identified, is that the growth of government has taken place less in the expansion of central government bureaux – as the budget-maximization model would have it – than in the growth in new interorganizational and intergovernmental arrangements at the implementation level (see Dunleavy, 1991: 223–5). The experience of the 1980s and 1990s has thus been in marked contrast to earlier periods in Western democratic systems: whereas 'overload' (see 2.11) was claimed to be the main feature of policy-making in the 1970s, subsequent decades have witnessed a process of 'downloading' – or what Dunleavy terms 'deinstitutionalizing' – via market-type mechanisms (such as competitive tendering and contracting-out) and the expansion of the role of the voluntary 'non-profit' sector. The analysis of the delivery side of public policy therefore increasingly involves taking account of techniques (or fads) of management control developed in the private/profit sector being applied with missionary zeal in the public/non-profit sectors (Anthony and Herzlinger, 1980; Handy, 1988; Drucker, 1990.)

❖ Trends in public management

Hede (1991) surveys the trends in four Anglo-American systems towards managerial reforms. He concludes that, in the four countries surveyed, 'all are more performance-orientated, and place greater emphasis on mobility and executive development than previously. Though still disparate in size, there is a trend towards flatter structures' (p. 507). Aucoin (1990) surveys the widespread international swing of the pendulum towards a managerialist 'paradigm'. More-recent surveys, such as by the OECD, confirm that this trend is not confined to Anglo-American political systems.

David Osborne and Ted Gaebler, *Reinventing Government*, 1992

This book has proved a very popular and influential approach to government reform (especially on the Clinton administration). In its first year it went through some nine printings and was the subject of much discussion. Osborne and Gaebler attack the bureaucratic approach to delivering public policy, which they regard as being ill-suited to the late twentieth century. As they admit, the book owes a good deal to the critiques of bureaucracy put forward by Drucker, Reich, Peters and Waterman, and Toffler.

Osborne and Gaebler urge that government should be 'reinvented' to take account of the information-rich possibilities of the 1990s and exploit entrepreneurial spirit, greater decentralization and more responsive forms of public organizations. They draw on examples from the US, Britain and other industrial countries which illustrate the 'reinvention' which is actually taking place.

The reinvention should be built on a number of principles:

*   governments should steer more than they row;
*   policy-making should be about empowering communities, rather than simply delivering services;
*   governments should encourage competition in the delivery of services rather than monopoly;

- public organizations should be driven by a sense of mission rather than rules;
- funding should be focused on outcomes rather than inputs;
- the needs of the customer should be the priority, not the needs of bureaucrats;
- public organizations should concentrate on earning, not just spending;
- invest in prevention, rather than cures;
- authority should be decentralized;
- solve problems by leveraging the market place, rather than by simply creating public programmes.

OECD, *Administration as Service*, 1987

The Organization for Economic Co-operation and Development was established in 1961 to promote economic growth, employment, financial stability and living standards. Its membership is composed of all the major market economies. The publication of the report on public administration marked the degree to which concern about the management of the public sector and the citizen as 'client' had become an international phenomenon. Here is the summary of the main conclusions:

- *The root of the problem*: The public and the government want more responsive government.
- *Designing policies for impact*: Policy and programme design can affect the ability of the administration to be responsive. Particular attention must be given to the selection of policy instruments and to the specification of administrative tasks.
- *Adapting institutional arrangements*: The broad institutional arrangements of the public service at all levels must be considered as the essential context for improving administrative responsiveness.
- *Organizing for delivery*: The responsiveness of units responsible for implementation depends upon finding an appropriate balance between management components of personnel, organization, control, procedures and communications.
- *Increasing administrative responsiveness*: Administrative behaviour (organizations and individuals) is largely determined by controls and incentives which are specified through performance standards. Performance measures should be adjusted to incorporate responsiveness.

The summary for policy-makers offers words of wisdom drawn from the policies of member states:

'Engage the participation of users in the design of administrative processes' (Austria).

'Simplify and improve relations between the citizen and the administration' (France).

'The recognition of the primacy of the customer must be paramount' (Ireland).

'Public administration must respond to the public's rights, wishes and needs' (Norway).

'Lifting the burden of government [on private enterprise]' (UK).

'The success of new economic policies depends on the transparency and effectiveness of administrative operations' (Turkey). ◆

In addition to this replacement of a 'public administration' paradigm by the 'public-sector management paradigm', students of the policy process have also been busy revising their frameworks to take more account of the changing structures and institutional arrangements in modern political systems. As proponents of 'network' and 'sub-system' approaches to policy-making have noted, government is no longer a matter of triangular relationships and tiers of decision-making: new metaphors are required to explain the dynamics of policy formulation and implementation in a more complex 'post-modern' society (see 2.10). It is against this background of changing ideas and institutional forms that the study of the 'output' side of policy-making and of policy analysis must be viewed in the 1990s.

4.2   The arrangement of Part Four

The remainder of the book is divided into five sections plus conclusions (4.8):

- *Implementation* (4.3): reviews different approaches to the analysis of how policy is put into action or practice.
- *Delivery systems* (4.4): looks at how we can analyse implementation in terms of the mix of instruments, institutions and values which are used in providing public policy.
- *Evaluation* (4.5): examines how public policy and the people who deliver it may be appraised, audited, valued and controlled.
- *Change and continuity* (4.6): considers various approaches to studying the way in which policy change takes place.
- *Promise and performance* (4.7): focuses on the evaluation of policy impacts and outcomes.

4.3   Implementation

4.3.1   Approaches to implementation

> The implementation problem is assumed to be a series of mundane decisions and interactions unworthy of the attention of scholars seeking the heady stuff of politics. Implementation is deceptively simple: it does not appear to involve any great issues.
> (*Van Meter and Van Horn, 1975: 450*)

A study of implementation is a study of change: how change occurs, possibly how it may be induced. It is also a study of the micro-structure of political life; how organizations outside and inside the political system conduct their affairs and interact with one another; what motivates them

> to act in the way they do, and what might motivate them to act differently.
> (*Jenkins, 1978: 203*)

Policy-making does not come to an end once a policy is set out or approved. As Anderson nicely expresses it: 'Policy is being made as it is being administered and administered as it is being made' (Anderson, 1975: 98). Implementation is policy-making carried out by other means – (to paraphrase Clausewitz on war). However, traditionally we have tended to view the political system in a way which reinforces the problem, by demarcating between policy and administration. Administration, according to this (Wilsonian) viewpoint, takes over where policy ends. The job of the administrator is to carry out policy formulated by decision-makers, and the role of the service provider is to carry out the policy administered by the bureaucrat. The interplay and interaction between politicians, administrators and service providers has, until comparatively recently, been a neglected area of analysis and research: a 'missing link' in the policy process (see Hargrove, 1975).

To a great extent, the lack of concern about the problems of 'post-policy-making' was due to the dominance of the models and maps which structured inquiry. The black-box model, for example, provided a powerful framework to analyse policy *qua* 'system', but tended to assume much about the processes which took place within the system, and within the 'output' and 'feedback' activities. Analysts of policies tended, until the 1970s and 1980s, to bypass the impact of bureaucracy and service-providers on the effectiveness of a policy. A policy was judged in terms of the decision-makers rather than by the 'street-level' implementation of fine-sounding ideas from national and local leaders. At the same time, the tradition of Anglo-American public administration has tended to lay great stress on the different functions of the administrator and the politician. These distinctions, although a necessary part of the liberal-democratic idea of the state and accountability (see Massey, 1993: 200–1), were in practice somewhat unrealistic and bore little relation to the political reality in which bureaucrats were not just neutral servants, but also had ideas, values, beliefs and interests which they used to shape policy. This distinction between policy as politics and administration as implementation, which was fundamental to the Anglo-American notion of public administration, was perhaps less evident in other continental European political systems, where the civil servant has long been characterized as having a more dynamic 'policy' role (see Aberbach *et al.*, 1981).

❖ An outline of the development of implementation studies

Key readings
- 1940s: the work of Selznick on the TVA (1949).

Implementation stage 'discovered':

- The analysis of failure: Derthick (1972); Pressman and Wildavsky (1973); Bardach (1977).
- Rational (top-down) models to identify factors which make for successful implementation: Van Meter and Van Horn (1975); Hood (1976); Gunn (1978); Sabatier and Mazmanian (1979).
- Bottom-up critiques of the top-down model in terms of the importance of other actors and organizational interactions: Lipsky (1971); Wetherley and Lipsky (1977); Elmore (1978, 1979); Hjern *et al.* (1978).
- Hybrid theories. Implementation as: evolution (Majone and Wildavsky, 1978); as learning (Browne and Wildavsky, 1984); as a policy-action continuum (Lewis and Flynn, 1978, 1979; Barrett and Fudge, 1981); inter-organizational analysis (Hjern, 1982; Hjern and Porter, 1981); and policy types (Ripley and Franklin, 1982); as part of a policy sub-system (Sabatier, 1986a); and as 'public sector management' (Hughes, 1994).

In the sections which follow we examine several of these contributions.

Collections of readings or commissioned chapters on implementation which provide useful material are: Williams and Elmore (eds) (1976); Younis (ed.) (1990); Hill (ed.) (1993).

Williams and Elmore is essential to get a feel of the disillusionment with the reforms of the 1960s and 1970s out of which implementation was to grow. Younis is one of the few books in the field which takes a comparative perspective and includes studies of implementation from Europe, America and the developing world. Hill's collection also provides a variety of case studies drawn from European experience.

The best review of implementation theory is Sabatier (1986a). ◆

4.3.2 Top-down rational system approaches

This model was the first on the scene. The neglect of the politics of implementation was brought to an end with the publication of a study by Martha Derthick of urban policy *New Towns in Town: Why a Federal Program Failed* (1972), and *Implementation* by Pressman and Wildavsky (1973). Although Derthick's study was an important breakthrough in the development of a new focus on implementation, it was Pressman and Wildavsky's book which has had the most impact. Not least of the reasons for this is because it must hold a record for one of the longest subtitles of any book in public policy, including government reports: *Implementation: How Great Expectations in Washington Are Dashed in*

Oakland; or, Why It's Amazing that Federal Programs Work At All, This Being a Saga of the Economic Development Administration as told by Two Sympathetic Observers who Seek to Build Morals on a Foundation of Ruined Hopes! In 1968 the authors became interested in the efforts by Oakland Economic Development Administration (EDA) in California to implement a programme of economic development for the city. As they explored the programme they became aware of the fact that, although often discussed, the problems of implementation were rarely analysed. The study involved interviewing the actors concerned, and examining policy and other documents over a three-year period to find out what went wrong. A policy, they posited, is 'a hypothesis containing initial conditions and predicted consequences. If X is done at time t_1, then Y will result at time t_2' (Pressman and Wildavsky, 1973, xiii). Implementation therefore is a 'process of interaction between the settings of goals and actions geared to achieve them' (p. xv). It is essentially an ability to 'forge links' in a causal chain so as to put policy into effect. Implementation will, they argued, become less and less effective as the links between all the various agencies involved in carrying out a policy form an 'implementation deficit'. Goals have to be clearly defined and understood, resources made available, the chain of command be capable of assembling and controlling resources, and the system able to communicate effectively and control those individuals and organizations involved in the performance of tasks.

In so dissecting the mistakes of the EDA, the authors hoped that the experience of Oakland would serve as an example to other policy-makers: implementation requires a top-down system of control and communications, and resources to do the job. The moral is, that decision-makers should not promise what they cannot deliver. If the system does not permit of such conditions, then it is best to rein in the promises to a level which is more attainable for the implementation process:

> Promises can create hopes, but unfulfilled promises can lead to disillusionment and frustration. By concentrating on the implementation of programs, as well as their initiation, we should be able to increase the probability that policy promises will be realized. Fewer promises may be made in view of a heightened awareness of the obstacles to fulfillment, but more of them should be kept.
> (*Pressman and Wildavsky, 1984: 6*)

In later years the original position taken by Pressman and Wildavsky was modified to take account of the growing literature which their study had helped to stimulate. Wildavsky, in conjunction with Majone and Browne, put forward a more developed theory of implementation which form new chapters to later editions of the Oakland study:

- Majone and Wildavsky (1978): 'Implementation as evolution'
- Browne and Wildavsky (1984): 'Implementation as mutual adaption'
- Browne and Wildavksy (1987): 'Implementation as exploration'.

The main theme of these pieces is that implementation has to be understood as a more evolutionary, 'learning' process, rather than as the kind of policy-implementation sequence which was originally put forward. In the adjustments to the first edition, the study acknowledges that implementation is a process which involves implementers in making policy as well as in carrying out, or putting into effect, policy from above. These chapters written with Majone and Browne serve as a bridge between the 'top-down' model and later 'bottom-up' critiques.

The original study, however, set out an essentially 'top-down' view of implementation. Effective implementation required, they argued, a good chain of command and a capacity to co-ordinate and control which was sadly lacking in the case of the ODA. This 'top-down' notion of a rational system model – or ideal type – of implementation was later developed in the work of Andrew Dunsire (1978a, 1978b, 1990), Christopher Hood (1976) and Lewis Gunn (1978). These analysts proposed models which asked what would 'perfect' implementation 'look like'. The idea, of course, has much in common with Weber's construction of the ideal type of bureaucracy. In his book *Limits to Administration* Christopher Hood (1976) set out five such conditions for perfect implementation:

- that ideal implementation is a product of a unitary 'army'-like organization, with clear lines of authority;
- that norms would be enforced and objectives given;
- that people would do what they are told and asked;
- that there should be perfect communication in and between units of organization;
- that there would be no pressure of time.

❖ **Lewis A. Gunn, 'Why is implementation so difficult?', 1978**

In this seminal article Gunn asked a very pertinent question. He draws attention to the general neglect of the issues and sums up what the state of play was with regard to the theory and practice of implementation. Gunn then set out ten conditions (or perhaps commandments) which could be said to provide a framework of questions that might be asked about a programme:

1   Circumstances external to the implementing agency do not impose crippling constraints.

2 Adequate time and sufficient resources are made available to the programme.

3 Not only are there no constraints in terms of overall resources, but also at each stage in the implementation process the required combination of resources is actually available.

4 The policy to be implemented is based on a valid theory of cause and effect.

5 The relationship between cause and effect is direct and there are few, if any, intervening links.

6 There is a single implementation agency which need not depend upon other agencies for success. If other agencies must be involved, the dependency relationships are minimal in number and importance.

7 There is complete understanding of and agreement upon the objectives to be achieved; and these conditions persist throughout the implementation process.

8 In moving towards agreed objectives it is possible to specify, in complete detail and perfect sequence, the tasks to be performed by each participant.

9 There is perfect communication among, and co-ordination of, the various elements or agencies involved in the programme.

10 Those in authority can demand and obtain perfect obedience. ◆

This 'top-down' approach has a view of the policy-implementation relationship which is summed up in Rousseau's *Émile*: 'Everything is good when it leaves the Creator's hands; everything degenerates in the hands of man.' The rational model is imbued with the ideas that implementation is about getting people to do what they are told, and keeping control over a sequence of stages in a system; and about the development of a programme of control which minimizes conflict and deviation from the goals set by the initial 'policy hypothesis' (Pressman and Wildavsky, 1973: xiii). Andrew Dunsire (1990: 15), for example; puts forward a 'rationalist model' which deliberately excludes all considerations of 'love, hate, envy, in fact any motivational factors whatsoever'. Where implementation has failed – that is a policy objective has not been met – it may be said to be due to factors such as the selection of the wrong strategy, or wrong 'machinery' or 'instruments'; the 'programming' of the bureaucracy was incorrect; operationalization was poor; something went wrong at the 'shop-floor level'; or there was a poor response to problems. However, if we are to arrive at an explanation of what goes wrong, Dunsire argues, we must start (*à la* Weber) with the rational ideal – 'when things go right':

> We have to understand the nature of a bureaucracy, the essence of which in structural terms, is an advanced specialisation function in both horizontal and vertical planes, so that each member has a well defined function ... the essence of which, in process terms, is advanced routinisation of performance ... We have to understand the nature of 'implementation' itself, comprising, basically, a repeated and widespread exercise of a thought process called 'operationalising'; ... and secondly of an organising of 'engineering' or 'designing' ... called 'programming' ... The number of points

at which things could 'go wrong' is clearly immense … the wonder is that things ever 'go right' …
(*Dunsire, 1990: 26*)

The rational model is essentially a prescriptive theory in the sense which we may find in Taylorism and scientific management, and may be subjected to the same kind of criticisms. Too much emphasis is placed upon the definition of goals by the top, rather than on the role of the workers on the line. It assumes a great deal about goal definition and human interaction and behaviour, or, as in the case of Dunsire, it just blatantly excludes any consideration of how real people actually behave, all the better to understand the logical relationship between input, process and output. However, the distinction between 'policy' as input and implementation as the administrative output is specious. As 'bottom-up' critics argue, the implementation process involves 'policy-making' from those who are involved in putting 'it' into effect. Implementation is not a process in which x follows y in a chain of causation. Unlike a sausage factory, the output of public agencies is not so well-defined and quantified – or 'evaluated' – and what actually counts as success and failure is a matter of controversy and conflict.

4.3.3   Critiques of the rational control model

Bureaucratic 'street-level' behaviour

The top-down model has been greatly criticized for not taking into account the role of other actors and levels in the implementation process. A major source of this criticism actually pre-dates the top-down model. In an article published in 1971 Michael Lipsky argued that students of public policy had to take account of the interaction of bureaucrats with their clients at a 'street-level' (Lipsky, 1971). Later, he developed his ideas more fully for a collection of papers on urban policy (Lipsky, 1976). He concluded that:

> To better understand the interaction between government and citizens at the 'place' where government meets people, I have attempted to demonstrate common factors in the behaviour of street-level bureaucrats. I have suggested that there are patterns to this interaction, that continuities may be observed which transcend individual bureaucracies, and that certain conditions in the work environment of these bureaucracies appear to be relatively salient in structuring the bureaucrat–citizen interaction … If this analysis has been at all persuasive, it suggests that in significant respects street-level bureaucracies as currently structured may be inherently incapable of responding favorably to contemporary demands for improved and more sympathetic service to some clients. Street-level bureaucrats respond to work-related pressures in ways that, however understandable or well-intentioned, may have invidious effects on citizen impressions of governmental responsiveness and equity in performance. If, indeed, gov-

> ernment may be most salient to citizens where there is frequent interaction
> with its 'representatives' and where the interactions may have important
> consequences for their lives, then these conclusions should evoke sympa-
> thy for current proposals for urban decentralization of authority. What-
> ever their other merits or difficulties, these proposals commend them-
> selves at least for their concentration on fundamental alterations of the
> work environment of street-level bureaucrats.
> (*Lipsky, 1976: 208–10*)

Following this piece, in 1977 a study by R. Wetherley and M. Lipsky,
'Street level bureaucrats and institutional innovation: implementing
special education reform', showed how the rational model was not
effective in practice, or convincing in theory. The authors examined
the implementation of a law in the state of Massachusetts (Comprehensive Special Law, 1972), which depended on a shake-up in the
attitudes and practices of teachers, welfare workers and others in the
public sector who had direct contact with the public (service-providers). The conditions which the rational model sets out (a good chain of
command, well-defined objectives, and so on) were in large part in
place: the law was well defined; there was plenty of support; ample
resources; and a communications and monitoring system. Yet the law
was not implemented in the way which policy-makers intended: indeed, the changes actually made matters worse as the workload on
schools and staff increased dramatically. The services were maintained
by 'coping strategies' employed by the dedicated and committed people involved at the 'street level' (see Hudson, 1989, for a review and
interesting application of the Lipsky model to public policy and the
disabled). The implication of this study was that control over people
was not the way forward to effective implementation. Instead of regarding human beings as chains in a line of command, policy-makers
should realize that policy is best implemented by what Elmore (1979,
1985) termed a 'backward mapping' of problems and policy, which
involves defining success in human or behavioural terms rather than
as the completion of a 'hypothesis'. Forward-mapping – or the top-
down approach – Elmore regards as little more than a myth which
was 'increasingly difficult to maintain in the face of accumulating
evidence on the nature of the implementation process' (Elmore, 1985:
20). Elmore suggested that we should begin

> with a concrete statement of the behaviour that creates the occasion for a
> policy intervention, describe a set of organizational operations that can be
> expected to affect that behaviour, describe the expected effect of those
> operations, and then describe for each level of the implementation process
> what effect one would expect that level to have on the target behaviour
> and what resources are required for that effect to occur.
> (*Elmore, 1985: 28*)

What is really important, argue the bottom-uppers, is the relationship of policy-makers to policy deliverers. It is Alice in Wonderland in reverse. Alice says: 'Begin at the beginning and go on to the end.' The idea of backward mapping is to begin at the phase when the policy reaches its end-point, then analyse and organize policy from the patterns of behaviour and conflict which exist. The bottom-up model is one which sees the process as involving negotiation and consensus-building. These involve two contexts or environments: the management skills and cultures of the organizations involved in implementing public policy (schools, hospitals, police forces, welfare agencies, armed forces, government departments), and the political environment in which they have to work.

Bottom-up models lay great stress on the fact that 'street-level' implementers have discretion in how they apply policy. Professionals have a key role in ensuring the performance of a policy: teachers, doctors, planners, engineers, social workers, architects, all have opportunities and responsibilities of control and delivery of a service. This means that, as Dunleavy notes, the policy formulation process may be 'skewed' by policy implementation which is dominated by professionals (Dunleavy, 1981, 1982). Teachers, for example, may develop ways of teaching or implementing 'government policy' which actually result in outcomes which are quite different to those intended or desired by policy-makers. The same could be said for other professions charged with carrying out law or policy. Of course, this raises the question of analysis and prescription: street-level implementers may be shaping policy – but is it right for teachers or the police to be making up 'policy'? (See Linder and Peters, 1987.)

That this may come about is because implementation involves a necessarily high margin of discretion. The analysis of discretion in public policy is a subject addressed by students of social policy (Hill, 1969; Titmus, 1968), administrative law (Wade, 1967; Davis, 1969), law enforcement (Cain, 1973; Lambert, 1967; Wilson, 1970); and organizational sociology (Simon, 1945; Dunsire, 1978b; Gouldner, 1954). Policies, regulations, laws and procedures contain an interpretative element. As Davis expresses it: 'A public officer has discretion wherever the effective limits on his power leave him free to make a choice among possible courses of action and inaction' (Davis, 1969: 4). Whether the mode of implementation is top-down or bottom-up, those on the front line of policy delivery have varying bands of discretion over how they choose to exercise the rules which they are employed to apply. On a larger scale, the existence of discretion within international law and policy-making makes very clear the problems of differences in interpreting and applying general policy to specific circumstances. This is especially the case in the European Union, where EU law (directives and regulations) show considerable variation in how they are implemented by member countries (see From and Stava, 1993).

Implementation as a political game

Models of organizations which see policy being made and implemented in situations of human interaction, rather than as a machine or system, focus on the nature of those interactions. In the Lipsky model implementation, for example, is something which involves the recognition that organizations have human and organizational limitations, and that these must be recognized as a resource. Effective implementation is a condition which can be built up from the knowledge and experience of those in the front line of service delivery.

This theme of interaction is also the focus of models which view implementation as a process which is structured by conflict and bargaining. Rational models, of course, also recognize that conflict and deal-making will take place in implementation. However, this conflict is seen as something which is essentially dysfunctional and in need of co-ordination (Pressman and Wildavsky, 1973: 134) or resolution (Dunsire, 1978a). In these models conflict and bargaining take place within shared goals, in which case implementation is effective when groups resolve their differences and put a policy into action. An effective implementation process will have methods and systems of controlling such conflict so as to bring about compliance (Dunsire, 1978a). It is all a matter of control.

However, if we have a view of organizations which is based less upon the notion of control as of structures which are composed of groups and individuals all seeking to maximize their power and influence, we may see such conflict as an essentially political process involving different strategies for acquiring and maintaining power. Implementation from this perspective is about self-interested people 'playing games'.

This game model was advanced by Bardach in 1977 in his book *The Implementation Game*. Implementation, he argues is a game of 'bargaining, persuasion, and manoeuvring under conditions of uncertainty' (Bardach, 1977: 56). Implementation actors are playing to win as much control as possible, and endeavouring to play the system so as to achieve their own goals and objectives.

The Bardach model is essentially one which suggests that politics extends beyond the formal 'political' institutions. Politics does not stop once a bill becomes law. It does not stop in the political process, nor does it cease in the decision-making process. Models of the kind which Bardach proposes are urging us to redefine the boundaries between politics and bureaucracy, and between the decision-making process and the delivery of those decisions. Implementation is therefore simply another form of politics which takes place within the domain of unelected power.

As we noted above, the rational-control model of implementation tends to see interests as capable of being united for common goals, and conflict as a manageable source of friction. However, models of implementation which stress power, conflict and interests as the stuff of which implementation is made, divide on how it may be interpreted. The various models of power that we discussed in Part Three (3.3) would see the conflict and power struggles within and around an organization responsible for implementing policy in very different ways (for a review of these, see Morgan, 1986: 362–5).

4.3.4   Policy–action frameworks: implementation as an evolutionary process

A problem with both the top-down and bottom-up frameworks is that they tend to over-simplify the sheer complexity of implementation. Two early models which incorporated and developed the insights of both approaches were developed by Lewis and Flynn (1978, 1979) and Barrett and Fudge (1981). Lewis and Flynn, in an examination of urban and regional policy, put forward a behavioural model which views implementation as 'action' by individuals which is constrained by the world outside their organizations and the institutional context within which they endeavour to act (figure 4.1).

Figure 4.1   Lewis and Flynn's model

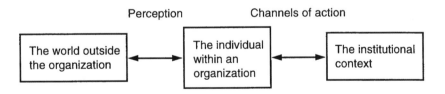

Source: Adapted from Lewis and Flynn (1978: 11)

Policy implementers inhabit a world which bears little resemblance to the rational ideal:

> In reality there are disagreements about policy goals and objectives; vague-
> ness and ambiguity about policies and uncertainty about their operation-
> alisation in practice; procedural complexity; inconsistency between pow-
> ers available and existing problems; and conflict arising from public par-
> ticipation, pressure group activity and political dissensus.
> (*Lewis and Flynn, 1978: 5*)

The interaction with the outside world, the organization and its institutional context means that policy objectives are not the source of
guides to action. In the cases they examined it was more often to be
found that

> actions result from the resolution of conflicts between two sets of priorities
> and policy areas; may precede the formulations of a procedure for dealing
> with similar cases in future and therefore the policy; or may result from
> what is feasible in the circumstances rather than the fulfilment of the
> original objectives.
> (*Ibid.*)

This theme of analysis in context is also present in the ideas of Barrett
and Fudge, who argue that implementation may be best understood
in terms of a 'policy–action continuum' (figure 4.2) 'in which an interactive and negotiative process is taking place over time, between those
seeking to put policy into effect and those upon whom action depends' (Barrett and Fudge, 1981: 25).

Figure 4.2   Policy–action continuum

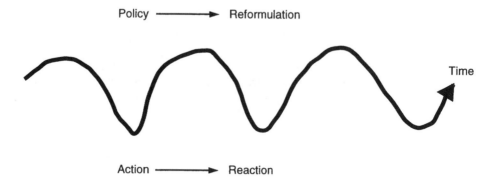

Policy ⟶ Reformulation

Time

Action ⟶ Reaction

Source: Barrett and Fudge (1981: 25)

Power is central to the dynamics of this relationship. Implementation
in this policy–action model is an iterative bargaining process between
those who are responsible for enacting policy and those who have
control of resources. In their model, 'more emphasis is placed on
issues of power and dependence, interests, motivations and behaviour' (Barrett and Fudge, 1981: 29) than in either the top-down or the

bottom-up frameworks. Furthermore, the policy–action perspective focuses on the factors which affect the scope for action and behaviour of individuals and agencies, as well as how perceptions of that scope are formed. The policy–action model shows that policy is not something that happens at the 'front end' of the policy process. Policy is something which 'evolves' or 'unfolds'. The 'front end' of policy in this sense produces potentialities and principles which change and adapt in practice. In the words of Majone and Wildavsky (1984: 116): 'Implementation will always be evolutionary; it will inevitably reformulate as well as carry out policy.'

The 'action' approach emphasizes the extent to which implementation involves more than a chain of command – it is a process which requires that we understand the way in which individuals and organizations perceive 'reality' (cf. Vickers in 3.7.5 on this point) and how organizations interact with other more-powerful or less-powerful organizations in order to attain their goals. This is an issue which is addressed in more depth in theories of interorganizational behaviour (see 4.3.7, 4.6.3). The policy–action model is also supportive of the idea in garbage-can theory that organizations do not have goals in the rational sense, but define them in the process of attaching problems to solutions (see 3.4.5).

4.3.5 Implementation in a managerialist framework

The line between the prescriptions of implementation theory – especially top-down models – and managerialist approaches to the problems associated with implementation 'failure' (*sic*) is a very fine one indeed. Sabatier and Mazmanian (1979), for example, offer a guide to perplexed managers on how to accomplish policy objectives (see 4.3.8). Many other models of implementation are redolent of the kind of advice and 'how-to' approach which is the stuff of management textbooks. Managerialist approaches to implementation have come to form the dominant 'operational' paradigm in the administration (*qua* management) of public policy. As the management of the public sector has endeavoured to become more 'business-like', so techniques which were once thought of as 'private-sector' methods have been adopted. We may consider these in terms of three kinds of approaches:

- operational management;
- corporate management;
- personnel management.

Operational management

We touched on operational management techniques when we reviewed the use of OR in decision-making (3.8.6). Operational research is also applied in the delivery process in terms of 'project management'. It is significant that the OR approach to project management developed out of the public sector. In the 1950s the US government adopted two techniques to manage the Polaris missile project (see Sapolsky, 1972):

- Critical Path Method (CPM);
- Project, Evaluation and Review Technique (PERT).

Both methods employ the idea of managing large-scale projects in terms of 'networks'; for this reason they are known as forms of 'network analysis'. The aim of CPM and PERT is to 'control' the execution of a project by controlling the network of activities and events which compose the stages of implementation. CPM is a method which aims to identify those activities which are 'critical' to the successful implementation of a project on time. A network is mapped to show the start of the project and the estimated timings involved in moving from one critical activity to another. PERT is a method which predicates that the duration of critical activities are uncertain. PERT systems are programmed on the basis of three types of calculation of this uncertainty: the most probable duration of moving from one activity to another; the most optimistic (shortest) forecast of the duration of a given activity; and the most pessimistic (longest) forecast of duration. PERT analysis is used in the implementation of large-scale projects where there is a high level of uncertainty surrounding the completion of a project. In national and local government network analysis has most applicability in construction projects which involve problems of managing a process with many areas of uncertainty, not least associated with completing the project on time and within budget, given the contingencies of weather, geology, labour relations and inflation, to name but a handful of the problems which can prevent the successful completion of roads, tunnels, power stations, buildings and the rest.

In the OR framework we must also include 'systems analysis'. This considers implementation problems as something that should be analysed in the context of the 'system' which as a whole is involved in the delivery of public goods and services. The systems analyst is interested in how a total sequence of activities, inputs and ouputs, and information flows contributes to the success or failure of projects. Implementation in human 'soft systems' (as opposed to 'hard systems' such as plant and machinery) is viewed as a problem of control and co-ordination. Effective implementation in this model is therefore dependent on such elements as:

- defining objectives and formulating a plan;
- monitoring the plan;
- analysing what has happened in terms of what should have happened according to the plan;
- implementing change so as to remedy the failure to realize a goal.

Carter *et al.* (1984: 96) suggest that a successful implementation system involves four types of control:

- co-ordination over time;
- co-ordination at particular times;
- detailed logistics and scheduling;
- defending and maintaining structural boundaries.

The systems approach lays stress on attaining good levels of co-operation within a 'soft system' by focusing on the importance of 'teamwork' for successful implementation (Carter *et al.*, 1984: 106–7).

Corporate management
Unlike OR techniques, the 'corporate management' approach to implementation is a framework which was developed in the private business sector and has been adopted by public-sector managers. As we noted in our discussion of PPBS, corporate management techniques found their way into government through the door opened by reforms to the budgetary process. The corporate management model has, therefore, much in common with PPBS, with its emphasis on the analysis of management problems in a strategic fashion proceeding

Figure 4.3   The corporate management planning cycle

through a cycle of defining objectives, planning, organizing, directing and controlling (figure 4.3).

Planning involves a process of defining objectives and thence proceeding to develop strategies to attain them. A key phase in the model is so-called SWOT analysis, that is, identifying the internal Strengths and Weaknesses of the organization, and the external Opportunities and Threats. Out of this review the objectives are then considered in terms of the strategies which are necessary in the light of SWOT. Having set the strategies, the next phase is to consider a plan to implement the objectives. A key consideration here is the relationship of strategy to the structure of the organization and its personnel. For successful implementation the adaptation of the organizational structure may be required. Strategy shapes structure, which in turn shapes strategy (Thompson, 1990: 522). The corporate approach gives a high priority to ensuring that the organization's structure, culture and style geared to the attainment of the 'mission' of the organization, and making clear to everyone in the organization what this 'mission' is, and how they relate to it (Foster, 1993). The monitoring of the implementation of the action plan provides the 'feedback' to management on how objectives are being met and what problems need to be addressed to facilitate success.

Corporate management has been an influential approach in 'new public-sector management', especially in the environment of the 1980s onwards when the pressure for cost-cutting, value for money and a more business-orientated culture has been evident in many industrialized countries (Kooiman and Eliassen (eds), 1987). As in the 1960s and 1970s, the budgetary process has been used to bring about change in the public sector. Performance measurement, for example, is advocated as a technique wherein the disciplines of financial control can be used as a way to achieve objectives more effectively (Thompson, 1990: 582).

❖ Culture as a model of implementation failure and organizational improvement

The culture model has many exponents. Amongst the more widely cited in books about public-sector management are those by Peters and Waterman (1982) and Charles Handy (1976).

Charles Handy, *Understanding Organizations*, 3rd edn, 1985

Handy argues that there are four main types of culture: power, role, task and person. These turn organizations into coherent tribes, with values, private languages, tales and heroes. And strong cultures make for strong organizations which do not suit all times, purposes and individuals. Each can, he argues, be good and effective cultures, but they can lead to ineffectiveness and failure.

Each type of culture has a patron god which symbolizes its cultural values and structures:

- *Power Culture*: a web in which decisions are the outcome of power and influence. God: Zeus who rules by impulse and whim.
- *Role Culture*: a Greek temple whose culture is one of rationality and function. Bureaucracies have come to typify these cultures. God: Apollo, the god of reason.
- *Task Culture*: a net-like culture which is concerned with getting tasks done. It is efficient, and adaptive to the demands of consumers. Handy believes it has no patron god.
- *Person Culture*: a cluster culture in which individuals predominate over structure and organization. Rarely found, save in communes. God: Dionysus, the god of the self-orientated individual.

What influences cultures?

- History and ownership;
- size;
- technology;
- goals and objectives;
- the environment;
- the people.

The Plus Programme and the Metropolitan Police

A sign of the way in which management discourse is being incorporated within what were once thought of as activities far removed from business criteria and culture is found in policing. The policing of London has been subjected to high levels of criticism in the past decades. The London bobby, an international symbol of London and 'community policing', is no longer what it was in the 'good old days'.

In response to the changing 'customer perceptions' of the police, the Commissioner of the Metropolitan Police, Sir Peter Imbert, commissioned a study by management consultants Wolff Olins. It was a decision which he later described as a 'bit of blood-letting in order to ensure that the patient becomes healthy'.

They interviewed over 250 people, examined practices, visited police stations, and surveyed all aspects of police work. What they produced was highly critical of the Met. It questioned their clearness and effectiveness of purpose, organization, management, attitudes, communication and presentation. The report argued that the police force had a job on its hands to make the service more effective. The Met had five tasks:

- to feel more united and be clear about what it is there for;
- to improve leadership as well as management systems;
- to adopt a more positive attitude towards the concept of a service;

- to improve its communication techniques, both internally and with the outside world;
- to improve its appearance in terms of buildings, uniforms, equipment and associated matters.

The report, *A Force for Change*, was distributed to all personnel and was followed up with a strategy of implementation, the Plus Programme, to make it happen. It included a 'mission statement' designed to encapsulate the aims and purposes of the police. The Commissioner's 1990 strategy statement was to make it clear to both the public (consumers) and to the police service that the Met was determined to see the report's recommendations through. Significantly, this has involved building up from the canteens, rather than down from the Plus team at Scotland Yard. For a review of changing management approaches in the police service see Loveday (1993). ◆

Personnel management

The 'cultural' aspects of the corporate management approach takes us to another important aspect of managerialism in the public sector: the management of people. The quintessential method of corporate management is the setting and the getting of objectives. How people in public organizations and services respond to these objectives which they are being asked (told) to implement is of the greatest importance. Two techniques have been utilized to improve the human side of implementation, performance appraisal and management by objectives:

- *Performance appraisal* is a method of appraising individuals in terms of his or her 'performance' as set against the objectives of the organization and in the context of the development of the potential of the individual.
- *Management by objectives* (MBO) is a technique in which objectives are agreed between manager and managed so as to set clear and well-defined goals (Drucker, 1954). The aim of MBO is to facilitate the integration of the goals of the individual and the goals of the organization (Drucker, 1964).

As methods of approaching implementation problems, appraisal and MBO are designed to address the issues associated with changing cultures by changing people. They are a mix of carrots and sticks to create an environment in which administrators/managers and 'street-level' implementers can be encouraged to modify or adapt their behaviour so as to attain corporate as opposed to departmental, individual or professional goals.

❖ The managerial approach as creating 'self-regulating' systems

The development of techniques in delivery which are no longer 'purely' public or administrative marks the predominance of managerialist values (concerned with efficiency and effectiveness) in shaping the mix of delivery instruments. Advocates of the need to 'reinvent government' argue that such changes involve a more market-driven 'decentralizing' policy process, in which there is a shift from hierarchy to participation and teamwork in order to manage a more complex society (Osborne and Gaebler, 1993). However, this remixing of government, sectors and instruments may also be viewed as measures aimed at increasing the capacity of government to maintain control (and legitimacy) in conditions of greater social, economic and political complexity and financial constraint. Decentralization in this sense may be viewed as essentially an attempt to 'download' control to more built-in, self-regulating (Kickert, 1993) delivery systems. At one level this has involved the use of new mixes of government, sectors and instruments to promote more 'self-regulating' systems (through markets), and at another level, to create more 'self-regulating' people by applying new management techniques. We may classify these controls in terms of micro and macro self-regulation.

Micro delivery controls

These controls have sought to control the discretion and to change the attitudes of providers. They include:

- human resource management;
- performance-related pay;
- appraisal schemes;
- peer review;
- limitations on tenure.

These techniques signal a move away from improving the rationality and expertise of bureaucrats and professionals as a way of improving services, to an approach which seeks to improve the methods of controlling the non-policy-making stratum so as to make it more responsive to the demands of 'taxpayers' *qua* customers. This move from rationality of production to the sovereignty of consumers and control by decision-makers may be read as subjecting bureaucrats and professionals, long held to be different from workers and managers in the private sector, to forms of control which have been familiar in the profit sector. Thus the flipside of consumerism is the 'proletarianization', deskilling and 'de-professionalization' (see Braverman, 1974; Clegg and Dunkerly, 1980) of bureaucrats and professionals.

Macro delivery controls

These techniques have sought to change the organizational and wider social and political contexts of service provision. We have reviewed these elsewhere (see 3.10.6, 4.3.5). They include:

- increasing the number of providers by measures to increase competition:
  — privatization;

— contracting-out.
- measures to create a more business-like structure of delivery:
  — internal markets;
  — charging for services.
- direct controls over costs and size of public sector:
  — incomes policies for the public sector;
  — budgetary controls through performance measurement;
  — cuts in numbers of civil servants and professionals;
  — financial management.
- monitoring and improving performance:
  — enforcement of performance indicators;
  — institutional audits;
  — departmental audits;
  — league tables of performance;
  — organizational learning.

Micro techniques aim to change the context within which individuals and groups work in the public sector, whereas the macro techniques are aimed at changing the organizational environment by bringing market, or quasi market, forces to counteract the supposed bias in bureaucratic hierarchical organizations and professional and 'street-level' discretion, whilst at the same time making policy delivery more open to the demands and requirements of 'consumers'. ◆

4.3.6   Implementation and policy type

Is implementing a missile development programme the same as a human service programme? Is it easier to put a man on the moon than put a homeless family in decent accommodation? The trouble with so much of the managerialist and 'rationalist' models of implementation is that they derive from a notion of decision-making which fails to take account of the fact that human problems are varied in their nature and complexity. Putting a man on the moon or developing a missile system does not serve as a convincing model for policy areas in which defining goals, building consensus and acquiring resources are infinitely more problematic. A more useful approach, therefore, may well be to focus on the relationship between the type of policy and the factors which may impact on the implementation process. Lowi's (1964, 1972) categorization of distributive, regulatory and redistributive policy types, for example, has been applied to implementation by several analysts (see Van Meter and Van Horn, 1975; Ingram, 1978; Ripley and Franklin, 1982; and Hargrove, 1975).

One of the first attempts to analyse implementation, by Van Meter and Van Horn (1975), took the view that the study of implementation needed to take account of the content or type of policy. Drawing on Lowi's work on policy types (see 2.5) Van Meter and Van Horn argued that the effectiveness of implementation will vary across policy types and policy issues. The key factors operating in implementation – change, control and compliance – suggested to them that where there was a high degree of consensus and a low or marginal amount of change required, policy implementation was likely to prove more successful.

Ripley and Franklin (1986) suggest that relative difficulties of success in implementation is low where distributive policies are concerned, moderate in regulative policies and low in redistributive policies. The various policy areas have different patterns of relationships, which means that in the redistributive areas there is more bargaining and politicking than in the distributive areas, where a higher measure of control may exist. Ingram (1978) has related this variation in the pattern of relationship in terms of decision-making costs, structure of statute, appropriate approach, criteria for evaluation and critical variables.

❖ Gordon Chase, 'A framework for implementing human service programmes: how hard will it be?', 1979

In the arguments of Gunn we see a general model of 'perfect implementation'. However, for the provision of human services, welfare, education, health (that is services directed at people), how can this general model be made more specific to policy types? Gordon Chase provides a framework to examine the obstacles confronting the implementation of human services: lead control, methadone maintenance, and prison health reform. Using these three examples he constructs the following framework which, he suggests, may be used by implementers as a map to enable them to identify the key problem areas for their programmes. What is significant about his analysis is that he demonstrates that in implementing human service policies, the context is complex and uncertain, even in such matters as space and equipment resources.

Difficulties arising from operational demands

1 Who are the people to be served?
2 What is the nature of the service to be delivered?
3 What are the potential distortions and irregularities in the population?
4 Is the programme controllable? Can it be measured? Are any parts not controllable?

Difficulties arising from the nature and availability of the resources required to run the programme

1 Money: what are the limits on funds, and what are the prospects for more?
2 Personnel: are they in place, and with the right qualifications? Does the programme have enough?

3   Space: has the programme got enough? Will it need more?
4   Supplies and technical equipment: are they available and usable? Is technology important?

Difficulties arising from the programme manager's need to share authority with or retain the support of other bureaucratic and political actors

1   Overhead agencies: how many will a manager have to deal with, and will they be supportive?
2   Line agencies: how many are there involved and can the personnel work together? Are lines of responsibility clear?
3   Elected politicians: can they help or hurt?
4   What higher levels of government are involved?
5   Private-sector providers: how badly will the programme manager need private-sector providers? How well will the programme manager be able to control the private contractors?
6   Special interest groups: what are their interests and political influence?
7   The press: will the programme have high visibility? Could the media do any good/harm? ◆

A key factor in policy type analysis is the issue of the organization of a policy subsystem (see Sabatier, 1986a; and 4.3.8). In the case of a simple problem – such as putting a man on the moon – the subsystem (NASA) was tightly organized, influential and well resourced. Putting a man on the moon was a triumph of rational comprehensiveness in both capitalist and communist societies. However, PERT, CPM, PPBS, Zero Budgeting and the rest, when applied to more complex social and economic problems and policies, was less than a spectacular success. Whereas putting a man on the moon was a well-defined goal and had a narrow policy subsystem, the problems of man (and woman) on earth have long exhibited fuzziness and subsystem complexity. As Mayntz (1993) notes, for example, policy sectors differ in the degree to which they have well-organized subsystems capable of resisting guidance or direction. Some organizations will be better informed, better financed, more powerful, or more independent than others. Implementation has therefore to be set in the context of types of policy and political priorities but also in terms of interorganizational relationships.

4.3.7   Inter-organizational analysis and implementation

A major focus of implementation studies has been the issue of how organizations behave, or of how people behave in organizations. However, if we accept that implementation is a process which involves a 'network' or multiplicity of organizations the question arises as to how organizations, interact with one another. Two approaches have informed and framed this debate.

Power and resource dependency

This argues that the interaction of organizations is a product of power relationships in which organizations can induce other less-powerful and more-dependent organizations to interact with them. In turn, those organizations which are dependent on other more resourceful organizations have to engage in strategies of working with more powerful organizations so as to secure their interests and maintain their relative autonomy or space within which to act (Aldrich, 1972, 1976; Kochan, 1975; Yuchtman and Seashore, 1967).

> If A cannot do without the resource mediated by B and is unable to obtain them elsewhere, A becomes dependent on B. Conversely, B acquires power over A ... dependence is an attribution of the *relation* between A and B, and not of A or B in isolation. It is thus possible that A may be dependent upon B, while having power over C.
> (*Aldrich and Mindlin, 1978: 156*)

Organizational exchange

This takes the position that organizations work with one another so as to exchange what is to their mutual benefit. Levine and White (1961) argued that the defining characteristic of exchange between organizations is that it is voluntary interaction which is undertaken for the realization of the goals and objectives of the participants. Whereas in the power-dependency model the organizational relations are based on dominance and dependence, interaction based on exchange is structured by mutual interests (Bish, 1978; Tuite, 1972; White, 1974). Even though an agency may be dependent on central resources, it may also be the case that the centre is dependent on the local agency for implementing policy goals. As Scharpf argues:

> While the seemingly dominant party may exercise hierarchical authority or control over monetary resources, it may, at the same time, be fully dependent upon the specialist skills, the clientele contacts and the information available only to subordinate units ... In short, unilateral-dependence relationships which are stable over time may be more rare, and mutual dependency more frequent, than the ubiquitous nature of hierarchical authority and unidirectional flows of budgeted resources in inter-organizational relations might suggest.
> (*Scharpf, 1978: 359*)

❖ **K. Hanf and F.W. Scharpf (eds),** *Interorganizational Policy-making*, **1978**

This book comprises a number of key readings in interorganizational analysis based on European and American case studies. At the time this book was published there was increasing concern with the apparent 'overload' taking place in liberal democracies and alarm at the prospects of 'ungovernability'. By examining the growth of organizational complexity the authors explore the structural features of policy formation and implementation which influence the capacity of governments to solve problems. The theme which the studies investigate is the way in which the existence of organizational networks of exchange and dependence impose limits on co-ordination and control in the making of policy and the attainment of policy goals. ◆

Benson (1975, 1977a, 1977b, 1982) has argued that, in order to understand the way in which interorganizational relationships operate, we need to consider the network of interests within a policy sector, which he defines in terms of: 'a cluster or complex of organizations connected to each other by resource dependencies and distinguished from other clusters or complexes by breaks in the structure of resource dependencies' (Benson, 1982: 148). Benson's approach also stresses the importance of 'deep structure' of the kind suggested by Bachrach and Baratz, which takes into account the bias which exists in a given policy sector and its constituent structures: administrative networks; interest group networks; and the rules of structure formation. Benson argues that the rules of structure formation within a policy sector – which incorporates the ideas of agenda-setting which we have encountered in non-decision-making theories and in critical theory – need to be explored in relation to the administrative and interest-group networks (see 2.7.2). (Benson's ideas have been applied by Rhodes in a network approach to central–local relations: see 2.10.2 and Rhodes, 1985, 1988.)

Applying the theories to public policy

The application of interorganizational analysis developed by Aldrich, Benson and others has been applied in the study of public policy through the work of Hjern and Porter (see also Hjern et al., 1978; and Hjern and Hull, 1982). Adopting a bottom-up framework Hjern and Porter (1981) argue that implementation should be analysed in the context of 'institutional structures' composed of 'clusters' of actors and organizations. Programmes may be conceived as being implemented in 'pools' of organizations. A programme will involve a multiplicity of organizations of various kinds: national and local, public, private and voluntary, business and labour, and so on. Programmes are not implemented by single organizations, but through a matrix or set of organizational pools (see figure 4.4):

Organizations (O1 ...) participate in parts of several programmes (P1 ...). Persons from within a single organization attempt to adjust these parts of programmes to meet overall organizational objectives. The vertical oval enclosing the parts of the three programmes implemented by O1 is the area within which an organization rationale is practiced. Persons identifying with a programme (P1) pursue a programme rationale within the horizontal oval trying to adjust the contributions of the parts of a number of organizations to meet the needs of the programme. Persons occupying

Figure 4.4   Organizational 'pools'

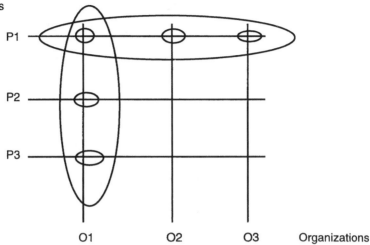

Source: Hjern and Porter (1981)

positions at any of the nine points of intersection ... have to serve 'masters' both in programmes and in organizations. Failure to identify implementation structures as administrative entities distinct from organizations has led to severe difficulties in administering the implementation of programmes. When a new programme is enacted, it is assigned to a single organization ... If there is a failure, the programme is assigned to another organization, or the department head is fired, or both ... such reactions may be inappropriate and dysfunctional.
(*Hjern and Porter, 1981: 217*)

Such arrangements whereby a programme is in the hands of a multiplicity of organizations give rise to a complex pattern of interactions which 'top-down' frameworks (and practices) fail to take into account, with the consequence that their theories do not satisfactorily explain implementation, and that in practice programmes are not successful. Implementation structures are not organizations so much as 'localized implementation structures'. Hjern and Porter believe that the implications for the theory and practice of public policy of this model are extensive, and should prompt us to revise our conceptualization of the implementation process in terms of both analytical and normative frameworks. As we shall see below (4.3.8), the theoretical implications of their model have been taken on board in more recent theories of implementation.

4.3.8   Implementation – towards a synthesis

We have already encountered Sabatier's ideas in other parts of this book. The model he advances for viewing the policy-making process may also be extended into the study of implementation. For Sabatier the policy-stages approach does not help in understanding the policy-making process because it splits it up into a series of artificial and unrealistic sections. From this point of view, therefore, implementation and policy-making become virtually one and the same process. His early contribution to the study of implementation came with a highly top-down account written with David Mazmanian (Sabatier and Mazmanian, 1979). This work has, perhaps, been more widely tested (see Sabatier, 1986) than most theories and is justifiably seen as one of the most developed top-down models. Their work endeavoured to synthesize the ideas of both top-down and bottom-up theorists into a set of six sufficient and necessary conditions for the effective implementation of legally stated policy objectives. These comprised:

- clear and consistent objectives, so that they can provide a standard of legal evaluation and resource;
- adequate causal theory, thus ensuring that the policy has an accurate theory of how to bring about change;
- implementation structures that are legally structured so as to enhance the compliance of those charged with implementing the policy and of those groups who are the target of the policy;
- committed and skilful implementers who apply themselves to using their discretion so as to realize policy objectives;
- support of interest groups and 'sovereigns' in the legislature and executive;
- changes in socio-economic conditions that do not undermine the support of groups and sovereigns or subvert the causal theory underpinning the policy.

This model has been applied in a wide range of US and European case studies which demonstrated the usefulness of the framework to empirical research. Their framework was subsequently modified in the light of this research (Sabatier, 1986: table 1), and an evaluation of the bottom-up case as developed by Hjern *et al.* Sabatier (1986) proposes that a synthesis of the two positions is possible drawing on the insights of Hjern *et al.* into the interorganizational dynamics of implemention and its network/matrix form, and the top-down focus on how institutions and social and economic conditions constrain behaviour. This is accomplished through the use of the model we have discussed in Part Two (2.10.4): implementation as taking place within the context of a policy subsystem, and bound by 'relatively stable parameters' and 'events external to the subsystem'. Central to this model of implementation is the notion that it is an ongoing part of policy-making within ACs ('advocacy coalitions'), and that the deep, near core and secondary aspects of the belief systems of implementation coalitions should be a main focus of analysis.

The model takes into account, therefore, the concerns of the bottom-up approach in that it emphasizes the network which structures implementation, whilst at the same time stressing the importance of top-down considerations within the system, including the beliefs of policy elites and the impact of external events. Implementation in this sense may be conceptualized as a learning process (Heclo, 1974: 306; cf. Browne and Wildavsky, 1984). The aim of the approach is to analyse the way in which policy learning takes place amongst ACs, and to set out those institutional conditions which are most appropriate or conducive to 'learning' and change in core beliefs.

Although the incorporation of the bottom-up concern with subsystem dynamics makes for a comprehensive model of implementation, the advocacy-coalition approach does not confront the normative dimension of the bottom-up versus top-down argument. Whereas the bottom-up approach, for example, is interested in the 'street level', the AC model is primarily focused on the policy elite. Policy learning, for Sabatier, is something which essentially takes place within 'the system' and its policy subsystems. The framework is designed to analyse institutional conditions in which such learning changes the policy core. The more radical implications of the bottom-up approach question whether success in implementation is more to do with wider social learning than policy learning by subsystem coalitions. The top-down position adopted by Sabatier and Mazmanian in their original model is concerned with the relationship of decisions to attainments, formulation to implementation, and the potential for hierarchy to confine and constrain implementers to achieve those legal objectives defined in the policy. Bottom-up approaches, however, are predicated on the significance of the relationship between actors involved in a policy or problem area and the limitations of formal hierarchy in such conditions. As Sabatier and Mazmanian (1979) make clear, their model is concerned with effective control and compliance; bottom-uppers, however, are in various ways concerned with interactions, conflict, power and empowerment. In their desire to construct a comprehensive model, the authors ignore the possibility that what they are trying to combine are, in a Kuhnian sense, incommensurate paradigms. This is most apparent when we move from using the models analytically to using them in a normative way. Top-downers are essentially working within a frame which focuses on decision and power, and the potential for decision-makers to effect change in society is regarded as a problem of developing effective modes of control and elite learning. The bottom-up models are suggestive of implementation as a process of policy-making and (possibly) empowerment of those seen as targets of decisions. The preference of the top-down models is for tiers, hierarchies, control and constraints, whereas for bottom-up models, spheres, networks or markets constitute a more desirable state of affairs.

The clash of frameworks and the values and beliefs which they contain provides competing frames of analysis and prescription. The synthesis thus serves to produce a consensus which is not there. If the aim of policy analysis is (as Lasswell argued) to clarify values, then the synthesis advanced by Sabatier only serves to muddy the waters. More satisfactory on this score is the synthesis which Sabatier (1986) commends as a guide to policy-makers, but as inappropriate as an explanatory model of the policy process (Elmore, 1985). Elmore argues that a variety of frameworks need to be deployed in analysis and implementation: 'backward-mapping' (bottom-up) and 'forward-mapping' (top-down); and that policy-making, if it is to be effective in implementation terms, must adopt multiple frameworks. What this means when applied to the study of the policy process is that analysis must aim not so much for a synthesis as a sensitivity to the frameworks (in Vickers's sense, the value, reality and action judgements) of theorists, policy elites and those at the 'street level'.

This way of looking at implementation may be derived from the kind of ideas proposed by critical policy analysis which we reviewed earlier in this book (2.7.3, 3.8.8). The use of models as 'lenses' (in Allison's sense) through which we can explore implementation is suggested by Elmore's (1978) categorization of four sorts of implementation model: systems management; bureaucratic process; organizational development; and conflict and bargaining. Elmore argues that models of implementation should not be regarded as rival hypotheses which could be empirically proved, but as ambiguous and conflicting frames of assumptions.

This idea of models as essentially incomplete, partial perspectives on complex problems and realities is an issue which has been most fully addressed in the work of Gareth Morgan (1986/1993). Morgan maintains that if we are to understand complexity, we are required to adopt a critical and creative approach to thinking in terms of models – or 'metaphors'. From this point of view an attempt to bash different models together to create a synthesis based on the strengths of two different frameworks is a somewhat misguided exercise. Developing his approach under the influence of 'postmodernist', 'constructivist' theory, Morgan takes the view that the analysis of complexity involves not a vain quest for synthesis but, on the contrary, a recognition of the differences, partiality, incompleteness and distortion which is inherent in human knowledge and discourse. Metaphors/models/ theories create insight, or ways of seeing, but also ways of not seeing. For Morgan there can be no single metaphor which provides a general theory. In terms of implementation, this means that the problems of implementation may be constructed in a variety of different ways. Each approach or theory gives some insight into a particular dimension of the reality of implementation, and, as in the case of the somewhat constrained debate on top-down versus bottom-up, both approaches and their hybrids and variants provide us with part of the picture. As students of public policy we should aim to become skilled in the art of reading the frameworks which are employed in the theory and practice of implementation in the contexts in which they occur. As Sabatier (1986) concedes, the different approaches have comparative advantages as explanations in different contexts. Applying Morgan's metaphors, for example, we should recognize that frames will disclose or illuminate various dimensions of implementation. No one metaphor provides all the answers.

In terms of the policy sciences, the approach which approximates most closely to the method which Morgan uses in organizational analysis is Lasswell's idea of contextual mapping (see p. 447). Thus, for

Figure 4.5   Metaphors of implementation failure

Machine metaphor Result of poor chain of command – problems with structures and roles	**Organism metaphor** Result of 'human relations' or the 'environment'	**Brain metaphor** Result of poor information flows – or 'learning' problems
Domination metaphor Result of labour/ management conflict	'Implementation failure'	**Culture metaphor** Result of the 'culture' of the organization
Psychic metaphor Result of subconscious forces – groupthink/ ego defences/repressed sexual instincts	**Autopoietic metaphor** Result of a 'self-referencing' system	**Power metaphor** Result of power in and around the implementation process

example, a Lasswellian approach to implementation would involve mapping the participants/stakeholders, their perspectives, situations, values and strategies, and their desired outcomes and actual effects. The method recognizes that implementation has a specific context in terms of the values and institutions involved in a given problem. Furthermore, as with the Morgan approach, the Lasswellian orientation would also stress the idea that analysis is fundamentally a 'learning' activity which should lead to the enlightenment of participants. Mapping the context of problems offers the possibility of understanding the multiple dimensions of knowledge, beliefs, power, meaning and values which frame policy-making and implementation. The quest is not for Sabatier's 'promised land' (*sic*) – a general theory – but a clarification of the values of theorists and practitioners.

❖ **Sandra Kaufman, 'Decision-making and conflict management', in Bingham *et al.*, 1991**

We examined Kaufman's ideas in 3.7.7. Her model seeks to explain decision-making and implementation in terms of theories of cognition and conflict. As we noted, her model does provide – like Sabatier's – a way of synthesizing a number of approaches to analyse implementation. Her main point is that implementation takes place in a situation in which there is necessarily conflict between numerous divergent interests, actors and organizations. This agrees with the arguments we encountered in 4.3.7. She believes that the conflict which takes place between different stakeholders can be both positive and negative. However, if such conflict is not managed, Kaufman argues that it can

> have destructive consequences on individuals, an agency, and the constituents it serves. At a minimum resources are wasted and high opportunity costs can be incurred. At its worst, conflict renders individuals and organizations dysfunctional and deprives beneficiaries of these organizations' services. The more complex a decision situation – in terms of the number of parties, issues at stake, consequences unfolding over time and affecting large groups – the more important it becomes to all involved that conflict be managed.
> (*Kaufman, 1991: 129*)

She offers a number of recommendations to improve implementation and decision-making in such conditions (see Kaufman, 1991: 131–2). ◆

4.4   Delivery systems

4.4.1 Mixes

Modes of delivery or 'systems' of policy delivery have become a central concern of analysis of and in the modern public sector. This focus on the increasingly diverse intergovernmental and interorganizational network of delivering public goods and services has been considered elsewhere in this book (see 3.4.6). As Kaufman (1991) observes (above), implementation now involves a large number of stakeholders and the potential for a good deal of conflict and 'dysfunctionalities'.

From being a neglected area of interest in the 1970s and early 1980s (see Hogwood and Peters, 1983: 165), the study of the 'technology' of delivery has come to assume a dominant position in the literature of public sector management. This is especially the case in the context of the 'complex' conditions facing modern governance (Kooiman (ed.), 1993) and the changing 'architecture' of the state in modern society (Dunleavy, 1989). As Self notes, for example, with regard to the delivery of welfare services:

> The provision of welfare can be regarded as a complex mixture of contributions from four sources: government, market, voluntary organizations and individual households.
> (*Self, 1993: 121*)

(See also Rose, 1986, on the idea of the welfare 'mix'.)

In this section of the book we examine these delivery systems in terms of the way in which public goods and services are now provided through an ever more complex and diverse set of institutions and instruments. We term these sets or combinations delivery 'mixes' to convey the idea that policy fields are composed of a plurality of actors, institutions and organizations, modes of enforcement and values. Policy fields – such as health, housing, economic development and so on – may be viewed as a mixture of relationships which change and vary over time and space – in both unitary and federal political systems. As Rhodes observes of the former:

> governments increasingly resort to a variety of instruments for pursuing their policies. Functions are not allocated to general purpose governments … but to special purpose authorities. Institutional 'adhocracy' is the order of the day, a process which generates conflicts between agencies competing for 'turf' and between central and local governments which resent being bypassed. Government has not been rolled back but splintered and politicized, a process which can only frustrate the attempt to control through

centralization. Such fragmentation not only thwarts control and fuels policy slippage (or deviancy from central expectations) but it also increases governmental complexity.
(Rhodes (ed.), 1992: 330)

This fragmentation also, as he notes, creates new problems for control and accountability in a democratic society (see 4.4.8). Citizens now confront an often bewildering array of agencies responsible for the provision of public services. Simple hierarchies and tiers have given way to delivery systems which use a mix of governmental relationships, new 'partnerships' between the public and private sectors, market mechanisms and 'marketized' public policy; and new roles are being defined for the voluntary sector and 'the community'. In place of the relatively ordered patterns of relationship which existed ten years or more ago – like a cake made of well-defined sections – industrial societies have become more jumbled up, and resemble not so much a Battenberg as a marble cake. As we take a slice through our cake we find that the arrangement or mix varies considerably between policies. Another metaphor which captures the idea of a mix is the notion of a 'field' or 'space' as used by Lewin (see 3.7.7) in which, over time, the relationship of parts of the policy field change and interact with one another.

In this section we examine four 'mixes':

- governmental mix (4.4.2);
- sectoral mix (4.4.3);
- enforcement mix (4.4.4);
- value mix (4.4.5).

The first two provide the institutional and organizational setting of policy delivery – that is, governmental forms and the interaction of the public, private, voluntary and community sectors. The enforcement mix is concerned with the mix of approaches to the problems of gaining compliance in public policy. (Making it stick!) Finally, we examine what Colebatch and Larmour express as the underlying values and framework of meaning (Colebatch and Larmour, 1993: 108), which interact with institutional, organizational and enforcement mixes. The resultant 'mix' in delivery systems may be viewed as a blend or compound of 'market', bureaucratic'/'hierarchy', and 'network'/'community' models of organization (see 1.8). By using the term 'mix', therefore, we are suggesting that thinking in terms of clearly defined sectors or modes of co-ordination is not, in practice, helpful, since in the real world there is considerable ambiguity and overlap between them. As Colebatch and Larmour point out, the world

can't be divided into 'market', 'bureaucratic' and 'community' organizations, because there are likely to be elements of all these in any organization. It will not be the same in all organizations ... and an organization in the 1990s may operate quite differently from the way that organization worked in the 1950s. The task is to identify the nature of the mix, not to place the organization into one box or another.
(*Colebatch and Larmour, 1993: 80*)

So, too, in public policy our task is not to put policies into boxes, but to analyse and map the mix of elements that make up particular policy fields. If we envisage delivery systems as a function of the mix of market, bureaucratic and community forms, we might represent them in the context of a triangular relationship which changes over time and space (figure 4.6).

Figure 4.6   The delivery mix

Thompson, *et al.* (eds) (1991: 15–16) suggest that we may envisage this in terms of three 'analytical lights' which focus on different aspects of governance (figure 4.7). In practice the mix of analytical lights overlaps and combines to provide 'hybrids' or 'plural forms' (see Bradach and Eccles, 1991).

Figure 4.7   Analytical lights on delivery

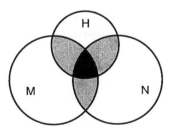

Market–Hierarchy–Network

Source: Adapted from Thompson *et al.* (1991)

4.4.2 The governmental mix

In the first instance, we must consider the territorial dimension. What part or level of government is responsible for the delivery of a programme? How is responsibility shared in terms of administrative and financial arrangements? The mix of levels will, of course, vary from policy arena to policy arena. The mix will also be determined by the political and constitutional traditions and arrangements between centralized unitary states and decentralized federal systems. Although political systems may share policy goals, the level of government which is deemed responsible for actually providing a service varies widely between:

- national;
- regional/state;
- local;
- neighbourhood.

OECD surveys (1990, 1992, 1993a), for example, which profiled the level of system delivery in its member states, illustrates that, in the case of education, health and welfare policies, a very diverse pattern of governmental responsibility exists even between countries that share unitary or federal characteristics. A service such as education may be highly decentralized, as in the USA, or highly centralized, as in France and Greece. Some countries have sub-national tiers of government and administration which may have responsibility for regions or states. The role of local government also varies considerably, from having tight control on service delivery to others where the local authorities' powers are weak. Furthermore, the delivery mix (local–public–private–voluntary) has, in the European context, long been highly diverse compared with Britain. However, as Batley and Stoker note in their review of changes in service delivery in European local government:

> the language of reform has much in common in the countries studied (France, Germany, Italy, Britain, Holland, Ireland, Denmark, Norway, Spain and Portugal) ... In different ways the issues of choice, proximity to the citizen (or customer) and reduction of bureaucratic control, complexity and uniformity are being addressed. In some cases these reforms are being pursued in the context of an ideology of efficiency of competition, market and business ... (Britain, Holland, Germany and to some extent Italy) ... In other cases the ideology is more to do with the citizen's access to a democratic state (Sweden, Norway, Spain, Portugal). Most have elements of both sorts ... the monopoly provision of certain defined, mainly social services by British local government has been unusual ... [since] in every other European state there has been a long history of partnership ... between levels of government, between communes and between the private and public sector ...
> (Batley and Stoker, 1991: 215)

An important trend in the delivery mix has been with regard to the neighbourhood and community decentralization which began in the 1980s (see Hoggett and Hambleton (eds), 1987) and has continued in the 1990s in Britain and other countries (see Carmon (ed.), 1990; Osborne and Gaebler, 1992; Batley and Stoker, 1991; Burns *et al.*, 1994). Two notable examples of this decentralization of service delivery are the London boroughs of Islington and Tower Hamlets who have under respective Labour and Liberal control developed multi-service neighbourhood offices to manage services, and forums/committees which provide for local participation, access and accountability. These two authorities have led the way in moving from centralized bureaucratic structures towards local management networks which are closer to citizens/consumers/clients/voters. At the time of writing, a considerable number of British local authorities are endeavouring to devise schemes which decentralize the management of service delivery (see Burns *et al.*, 1994). Given the experimental nature of the reforms, the range of models which have emerged is very pluralistic. The leading researchers in the field have suggested a four-point 'ideal type' of neighbourhood decentralization (see Burns *et al.*, 1994: 88):

- *localization*: the physical relocation of services from a centralized to a neighbourhood or 'patch' level;
- *flexibility*: the promotion of more flexible forms of management and work organization through multi-disciplinary team working, multi-skilling, local general and corporate management;
- *devolved management*: the devolution of decision-making powers to service delivery managers and staff;
- *organizational culture and change*: the reorientation of management and staff values to promote quality of service and local empowerment.

Hoggett (1987) has argued that this shift towards neighbourhood modes of service delivery must be viewed in the context of a wider process of 'post-Fordism' in modern society. Control through a Weberian/Taylorist/Fordist hierarchy, it may be argued, is giving way to less-bureaucratic, flatter, more-fragmented 'post-modern' structures (see Clegg, 1990: 180–207). Hoggett and his co-workers believe that in this new context public-sector organizations will go the way of business and industrial organizations:

> the conditions now exist for entirely new forms of service organization which allow both for much greater degrees of operational freedom and for centralised strategic control. The key question is how these conditions are shaped by political choices and strategies, for it is the struggle around these issues which will decide the relative weight given to internal as opposed to external decentralisation, where strategic command is to be (in

local or central government) and so on. Our vision of a reformed public
service seeks to replace complex bureaucracies with far more internally
devolved structures ... Within the context of a local authority, internal
devolution gives service managers and staff the power to deliver and
simultaneously frees the centre from absorption in administrative detail ...
In place of departmental hierarchies a new kind of organization emerges
in which there is a strong but lean centre with an outer ring of devolved
service delivery units.
(*Burns* et al., 1994: 272)

The mix of governmental levels in a given policy arena will clearly
structure the context within which interorganizational relations take
place. One level will be dependent on another for resources, and the
pattern may be such that the notion of 'levels' and 'tiers' may be
inappropriate to describe a relationship which is more akin to
'spheres' and 'networks' (Rhodes, 1981). Increasingly the pattern
which has emerged in the mix of governmental organizations involved in public policy in Europe, America and elsewhere is intergovernmental and interorganizational in form (Dommel, 1991; Batley
and Stoker, 1991; see 3.4.6, 4.3.7, and 4.6.3). As with other mixes, the
patterns of interaction and power relations between levels in industrialized societies is becoming ever more complex and diverse within
and between political systems – as the experience of multi-service
neighbourhood delivery illustrates. Indeed, it is this complexity which
perhaps constitutes the main common denominator in the experience of public policy implementation in modern (perhaps post-modern) conditions. The managerial and political pressures which influence the mix of responsibility creates some difficult and intractable
problems. As Brian Smith notes:

The managerial needs of national organizations can only be met by delegating authority to field officers. Politically, threats to integration from
culturally distinct communities can only be met by a measure of devolution ... However, having decided that an administrative presence in the
regions and localities is needed does not conclude the process of political
choice. A decision still has to be made on how the administration is to be
carried on, and whether it is to be politicized. There are too many cases of
state intervention in the fields of income maintenance, transportation,
public utilities and health care that have been centralized after a period
during which they were the responsibility of regional and local governments, and too many instances of government functions which are under
central administration in one state and local in another, to believe that
there is some politically neutral formula for the territorial allocation of
governmental powers. The distribution of power between levels of government, as well as the choice of institutions for decentralization, are the
outcomes of political conflicts at the centre which originate in group and
class interests which sometimes have a territorial identity but which also
unite and mobilize people regardless of region.
(*Smith, 1985: 201–2*)

The mix of governmental levels of responsibility is therefore an issue which prompts the need for both centralization on the one hand, to secure control – of national finances in particular – whilst, on the other, requiring decentralization in order to secure managerial benefits. Centralization in order to decentralize, and decentralization as a mode of centralization thus constitutes a key paradox in the allocation of responsibilities in the modern state (Metcalfe and Richards, 1992: 77–94). As Smith notes (above), this dilemma is not open to one neat neutral solution. In part, the reason for the attractiveness of focusing on the sectoral mix is that it provides a mode of delivery which overcomes the problem of which level of government should be responsible.

4.4.3   The sectoral mix

The mix of levels (or spheres) of government must also be considered alongside the sector which is involved in the delivery of public goods and services. Here again, the pattern is complex. The relationship between the public, private and voluntary sectors, for example, is one which has undergone considerable change in the last decade or so. Services may comprise a mix between public and private responsibility, as well as between the voluntary sector and 'community' agencies which may have a role in delivering a service.

The public–private mix: partnerships
The setting-up of partnerships between the public and private sectors (or PPPs) has occurred in a number of policy areas. These include:

- infrastructure developments;
- urban renewal;
- regional development;
- training and education;
- the environment.

The reasons for the expansion of PPPs involve understanding the advantages which government obtains in terms of private-sector finance and management expertise, and the financial and other benefits which may be gained by the private sector. Kouwenhoven (1993: 125–7) suggests that we consider the development of successful PPPs in the context of three sets of conditions:

- Start conditions for a PPP
    — interdependence between the two sectors;
    — convergence of objectives.

Given these conditions in which both sides need one another and share objectives, two secondary conditions or 'interlinking' mechanisms are required:

- Secondary (interlinking) conditions
  — the existence of a network of communication channels between the public and private sectors concerned;
  — the existence of a broker to facilitate negotiations.

- Project conditions
  In terms of the project in process, the PPP must meet a formidable list of conditions:
  — mutual trust;
  — unambiguity – and recording – of objectives and strategy;
  — unambiguity – and recording – of the division of costs, risks and returns;
  — unambiguity – and recording – of the division of responsibilities and authorities;
  — phasing of the project;
  — conflict regulation laid down beforehand;
  — legality;
  — protection of third parties' interests and rights;
  — adequate support and control facilities;
  — business- and market-orientated thinking and acting;
  — 'internal' co-ordination;
  — adequate project organization.

This model – as with models of perfect implementation – draws attention to the sheer number of things that can, do and will go wrong. The PPP is a 'learning process' for both the private and public sectors; the experience of partnerships which have not proved as successful as both sides hoped occupy a good deal of the literature on the topic. The problems which arose with the London Docklands development scheme illustrates only too well that PPPs do not present an easy route out of the apparent dead-end of top-down implementation in public policy (Massey 1993: 167–8). Even so, as long as the two sectors find mutual advantage in the risks which PPPs involve for both sides, the extension and development of partnership models of delivery will continue to grow. This is particularly the case in big projects for which partnerships are possibly the only way in which problems (such as urban regeneration) can be addressed and opportunities (such as securing the Olympic Games) may be grasped. For smaller-scale social projects, the use of partnerships in local government offer possibilities of securing additional funds and expertise from the private sector, which stand to gain in profits as well as the PR that results from the acceptance of social responsibilities and an ethical approach to business.

The voluntary sector

The involvement of the voluntary sector in social and other policy areas is a matter of growing interest. The voluntary sector has been historically very important in the history of the welfare state. Voluntary groups seeking to do good works for the poor and needy have a long and distinguished history (Butler and Wilson, 1990: 9–14). Religious organizations in particular have made an enormous contribution to the development of charitable institutions which, until the emergence of the welfare state, served as a principal provider of many 'social services' as well as education. Some services have remained in the voluntary sector: notably fire services and sea rescue services in a number of countries, and religious institutions have retained their involvement in education and other social activities. The growth of the welfare state and mass education made the existence of the voluntary sector apparently less necessary in the twentieth century. However, in recent years, the role of the voluntary sector has come to the fore as the state is no longer capable or no longer desires to provide the range of services that was once expected of it (Mellor, 1985).

As a sector the terms 'voluntary' and 'non-profit' are something of a misnomer. Their role has been described more extensively and more accurately in terms of being private agents of public policy (Streeck and Schmitter, 1985). Voluntary organizations employ people on a permanent basis, and they have to 'make' money and run on a sound financial footing. Charity is big business. This has led some to propose that the idea of the 'voluntary sector' should be replaced by the notion of a 'third sector' (Osborne and Gaebler, 1992: 44) which is recognized as having a major role in the delivery of goods and services. The responsibilities which have been devolved to this sector as a result of cuts and anti-welfare-state policies mean that it composes a key ingredient in the mix of delivery systems in the modern state, even in those societies which have traditionally had a large welfare state, and even more so in those (such as the USA) where state welfare programmes are less developed.

How this restructuring of the welfare state and the role of the voluntary sector is interpreted depends on where analysts and commentators are located on the ideological spectrum. On the 'right', the rise of the welfare state and the demise of voluntary services and self-help was a detrimental development, and from this viewpoint the future of social policy turns upon the growth of a less state-dominated system in which the voluntary sector has a wider role in actually delivering services under contract (see Gutch, 1992). On the 'left', the growth of voluntary organizations as agents or instruments of government policy is seen as symptomatic of the crisis of the liberal state in capitalist society (Loney *et al.* (eds), 1991: 206–13). 'Communitarians' would view the use of the voluntary sector as contributing to a greater sense of community and personal responsibility (Willets, 1994).

Whatever the framework used to explain the rise of voluntary organizations as service-providers, the fact remains that in designing the delivery of public services, the contribution of the voluntary sector is a factor which cannot be excluded from an analysis of the development of modern delivery systems. The mix of voluntary to private and public sectors and the 'partnership' forms is diverse. Private-sector finance may support activities of voluntary groups in association with government; government may choose to deliver via the voluntary sector and fund through grants; or there may be a web of funding and support which facilitates an exchange of finance, expertise and commitment. The model which best approximates to an explanation of such a mix is that of interorganizational analysis (4.3.8), with its stress upon the dependency of organizations such as voluntary groups on the resources of funding bodies in the public and private sectors. In the British context, for example, Butler and Wilson (1990) propose that the relationship gives rise to a neo-corporatist pattern of interaction between the state, the National Association of Voluntary Organizations, local government and charities (figure 4.8).

Figure 4.8   Government–voluntary relationships

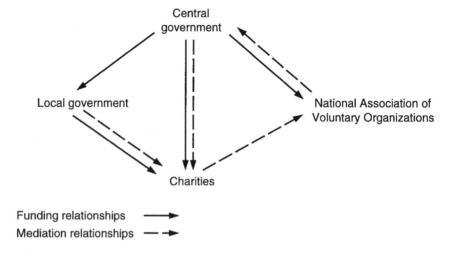

Funding relationships ⟶
Mediation relationships ⤍

Source: Adapted from Butler and Wilson (1990)

In this relationship state agencies and government have considerable influence over the strategic decision-making of the voluntary sector through its funding and mediating powers.

Contracting-out services to voluntary sector organizations has expanded rapidly in the UK, the USA and elsewhere, with the consequence that we are witnessing the emergence of

> a new type of relationship between governments and private organizations, which changes the behaviour of both parties, increases their interdependency and blurs the traditional distinctions between them.
> (*Self, 1993: 124*)

Voluntary agencies seek to raise finance from the public by fund-raising campaigns so as to minimize their dependency on governmental and non-governmental funding. The growth of the voluntary sector has raised issues as to the role of 'management' in the organization and strategies of 'non'-business/profit organizations (Butler and Wilson, 1990; Handy, 1988; Drucker, 1990b). In becoming more dependent on private-sector expertise and resources it may be that the voluntary sector will come/has come to resemble the resourcing organizations in their field (Di Maggio and Powell, 1991; 4.3.8, figure 4.9).

Figure 4.9   Voluntary sector funding and activities

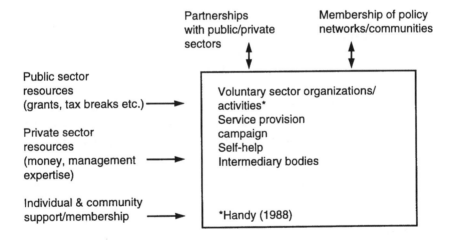

At the same time, public agencies may become dependent on the voluntary sector to deliver services which they find either difficult to provide or have not the resources to provide or which have traditionally been provided by the voluntary sector. The level of dependence of the private sector on the voluntary sector is comparatively small.

However, the participation of the private sector in sponsorship of voluntary organizations indicates that the private sector does see that such activities offer PR opportunities and advertising potential which can only do the ethical image of the organization a power of good. The spillover effects of private-sector management involvement in the voluntary sector may also be seen as having a wider benefit to a company or business (see Lloyd, 1993).

However, as Knight (1993) argues, the danger is that the close relationship which increasingly exists between the state and the private and voluntary sectors will have a damaging effect on the independence of voluntary agencies *qua* service-providers competing for resources. In recent years the voluntary sector has, argues Knight, taken a 'safety first' approach and opted for a cosy relationship with the public and private sectors. The consequence of this cosiness has been a loss of direction, and a preoccupation with financial opportunities and managerialist values with the result that it feels 'a strong sense of ... low morale and spoiled self-worth' (Knight, 1993: xi). The contribution which they have to make in terms of being important critics of government is gravely undermined by the existence of a 'contract culture' in which criticism may result in the loss of funds and contracts (see Gutch, 1992).

Furthermore, if voluntary sector organizations become ever more entwined in the state and the private sector, there is also the question of whether they can serve as the kind of intermediate bodies envisaged by the various advocates of 'communitarianism'. The voluntary sector has long had a vital role in providing 'mediating structures' which can stand between the individual and large state and business institutions (Berger and Neuhaus, 1977). If delivery mixes continue to use the voluntary sector as a service-providing instrument, their role in acting as means of 'citizenship' and 'empowerment' or 'social learning' and their critical function in society may well be put at risk.

❖ Community

'Communitarianism'

This is a theory which has proved attractive across the political spectrum: Clinton, Gore, the Labour Party in Britain; the 'new right', Helmut Kohl and Jacques Delors! As we noted in 1.6, communitarians argue that modern society has seen the destruction of a sense of community and voluntary organizations, and an over-development of the demand for individual rights at the cost of a sense of responsibility and obligation. In policy terms it suggests that policy-makers should seek to build up intermediate social institutions so as to foster social cohesion, civic pride, and counter the effects of individualism and social fragmentation. Think-tanks such as Demos and the Social Market Foundation have been widely credited with advancing the cause of 'communitarianism' in Britain. See, for example, Willetts (1994) and Etzioni (1968, 1993). Dave Willetts, a leading 'think-tanker', makes the 'new right' case by arguing for 'civic conservatism' which looks to strengthen community and voluntary organizations:

> Conservatives understand that intrusive and overweening government poses far more of a threat to our traditions and institutions than the free exchange of goods and services ... Looking back we can see that the destruction of old communities and the building of enormous housing estates ... did more damage. The insidious expansion of regulation ... has clearly become a threat to local communities, imposing unacceptable burdens on a host of independent groups, from local charities to childcare providers and lunch clubs ... The weakening of our civic institutions, as government has encroached on them ... is responsible for many of our social discontents ... A concern with the strength of Britain's institutions ... is at the heart of the Tory tradition.
> (*The Times, 17 June 1994*)

The 'community' as an alternative to markets and bureaucracies

The concept of community has a diverse theoretical background. The concern for the loss and renewal of 'community' has been an enduring theme of social and political thought in industrial societies (see Nisbet, 1974). The idea of 'community' as providing an alternative mode of governance may be seen at its most developed form in the work of M. Taylor (1982, 1987), who has formulated a philosophy of community derived in part from anthropological observations. Laver (1983: 147–66) considers the community as the basis of an anarchic society.

A 'community approach' to public policy may be traced back to the colonial administration of Britain, France and Belgium, whereby administrators aimed at making a community more self-reliant and responsible for problems in their locality. In the 1960s the idea was taken up in the USA through the Economic Opportunity Act, 1964, and the Model Cities Program (amongst others), which aimed at increasing ('maximizing', *sic*) the participation of the community in solving its social and economic problems (see Marris and Rein, 1967). In Britain the 1969 Community Development Act initiated a range of schemes to promote the community and 'neighbourhood' approach (on the development schemes of the late 1960s and 1970s in Britain, see Loney, 1983). By this time, of course, much of the damage to communities – such as East London – had already been done in the name of 'redevelopment' (see Young and Willmott (1957) for a timely, but sadly unheeded sociological warning). Significantly, the newest wave of 'community'-based public policy in the 1990s has come in the aftermath of the massive destruction of communities in the industrial regions and inner cities which had taken place in the previous decade. ◆

The 'community' and public policy

Another important component in a sectoral delivery mix is the 'community' – as opposed to 'the market' or 'the state' or 'hierarchy'. As we noted above (see 4.4.2), community-based public policy strategies have been a significant development in new approaches to local policy-making and implementation in the 1980s and 1990s. As a concept, the idea of 'community' is notorious for the variety of constructions which are deployed by policy-makers and academics. As Willmott notes:

> Those advocating a new initiative, or those attaching or defining a particular point of view, may invoke the community in support of their case, without making it clear which community they mean, in what sense they refer to it or how far they have established what its opinions or interests are.
> (*Willmott, 1989: 5*)

Hillery (1968) suggests that there are some 94 definitions. So whenever two or three social scientists or policy-makers are gathered together to discuss 'community', there are probably many more definitions than people! In general terms, the idea refers to groups who share a location or physical space or who have common interests, traits or characteristics. Thus, in 'community policy' the concept is applied in either a 'territorial' or a 'non-territorial' sense. Community policy may, for example, be directed at a neighbourhood or a part of a town, or it may be directed at a group of people who share a problem or an interest: 'young people', the 'gay community', the 'disabled community', or the 'arts community'. Forms of community policy can be divided into three major approaches (Glen, 1993):

- *community development*: this approach is concerned with helping the community to help itself. A good example would be that of programmes designed to promote the economic development of a community or to improve housing. The aim is to create a 'bottom-up' process in which people 'in the community' participate in voicing (defining) and meeting their needs and goals;
- *community service*: this is an approach which is directed at improving the relationship between the outputs of a service-provider and its users or clients. The aim is to make a service more responsive to the community, and increase the involvement of the community in the way in which services are delivered. Example of a 'service' community approach is the idea of Neighbourhood Watch schemes which are designed to improve the relationship between the police and the public, and to involve the community in policing their immediate environment;
- *community action*: is an approach which is focused on the problems of power and the mobilization of interests. Community action is a form of 'voicing' which is concerned to campaign for the interests of and policies for those who feel excluded from the political agenda/process. An instance of the 'action' approach is the way in which the 'gay community' has sought to engage in campaigns to

get their views about Aids to the attention of the public and into the policy-making process.

As there are numerous definitions of 'community', it is only to be expected that there are many frameworks within which we may understand the notion of 'community policies'. Butcher and Mullard (Butcher *et al.*, 1993: 217–37) suggest that we can differentiate between three main approaches to 'community policy' by focusing on their different attitudes towards 'citizenship':

- *the public citizen framework*: which places an emphasis on participation and rational judgement, rights and obligations. In this framework community policy is seen as a way of enhancing democratic participation, extending democracy and devolving power beyond the decision-making processes of bureaucracy, legislatures and political executives. More democracy, at a 'community'/neighbourhood level is seen as a way of involving people in the decision-making processes which impact on their lives. This view of community policy covers 'liberal', 'pluralist' strategies to improve local democracy and increase participation, as well as more radical policies which relate to the 'entitled citizen' model;
- *the entitled citizen framework*: here the emphasis is on the distribution of outcomes in a fairer way. The thrust of 'community policy' in this sense is towards greater social and economic justice through the use of strategies to empower the weak and marginal members of society. The entitled framework is committed to a radical view of the 'community' as an agent of social change and reform/revolution. The strategy is to use the community as a means of defending the interests and rights of individuals and groups who are threatened by the power of bureaucracy, capitalism and professionals;
- *the dutiful citizen framework*: in this approach the prime values are those of order, tradition and the organic nature of society. The aim of community strategies is therefore to strengthen the intermediate organizations and bodies in society and strengthen traditional social institutions as an alternative to state intervention. This is a framework favoured by the conservative right, which sees the use of community as a means of combating the growth of state interference and 'nannying'. The aim of policy is therefore seen as the encouragement of a sense of civic or public duty, community service, mutual aid, self-help, and voluntary work.

Butcher *et al.*, (1993) propose a synthesis of community policy which incorporates these frameworks (see figure 4.10).

Figure 4.10 The community and public policy

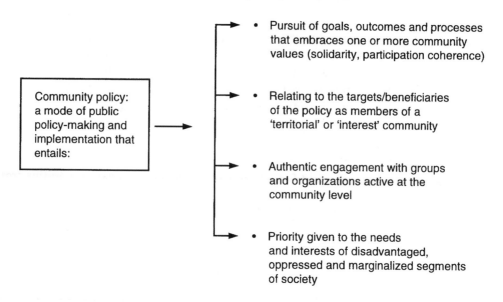

Community policy: a mode of public policy-making and implementation that entails:

- Pursuit of goals, outcomes and processes that embraces one or more community values (solidarity, participation coherence)

- Relating to the targets/beneficiaries of the policy as members of a 'territorial' or 'interest' community

- Authentic engagement with groups and organizations active at the community level

- Priority given to the needs and interests of disadvantaged, oppressed and marginalized segments of society

Source: Adapted from Butcher (1993)

Examples of the 'community' as an instrument of policy-making which display some potential for realizing this model include:

- community policing (Osborne and Gaebler, 1992: 49–52; Weatheritt, 1993);
- community health care (McNaught, 1987);
- community care for the mentally ill and physically handicapped, people with learning difficulties, child care (Walker, 1982; Hoyes and Means, 1993; Bornat *et al.*, 1993; Dallos and Boswell, 1993, Nixon, 1993; Fimister and Hill, 1993);
- community development programmes (Higgins *et al.*, 1983; Loney, 1983; Broady and Hedley, 1989; Roberts, 1979; Robinson and Shaw, 1991; Smith and Jones (eds), 1981; Rasey *et al.*, 1991; McShane, 1993);
- neighbourhood and decentralization of government (Smith, 1985: 166–84; Sharpe (ed.), 1979; Habeebullah and Slater, 1993; Hoggett and Hambleton (eds), 1987; Burns *et al.*, 1994);
- local economic development policies (Lynn, 1993; MacFarlane and Mabbot, 1993; Young and Mason (eds), 1983; Community Development Foundation, 1992; Bennett and Krebs, 1990);
- the community and race relations (Hill and Issacharoff, 1971; Saggar, 1991).

The community dimension of policy delivery adds to the 'network' and interorganizational character of the 'mix' which may pertain in a given policy field. It is also a development which further subverts and challenges the power/autonomy of professionals, such as social workers, in their relationship with the service users as more active 'partners' (Cochrane, 1993b).

❖ Alternative delivery systems: a menu for change

Osborne and Gaebler (1992) suggest that there are (in the US context) over 30 alternatives to service delivery by public employees:

1   creating legal rules and sanctions;
2   regulation or deregulation;
3   monitoring and investigation;
4   licensing;
5   tax policy;
6   grants;
7   subsidies;
8   loans;
9   loan guarantees;
10 contracting;
11 franchising;
12 public–private partnerships;
13 public–public partnerships;
14 quasi-public or private corporations;
15 public enterprise;
16 procurement;
17 insurance;
18 rewards, awards and bounties;
19 changing public investment policy;
20 technical assistance;
21 information;
22 referral;
23 volunteers;
24 vouchers;
25 impact fees;
26 catalysing non-governmental efforts;
27 convening non-governmental leaders;
28 jawboning;
29 seed money;
30 equity investments;
31 voluntary associations;
32 co-production or self-help;
33 *quid pro quos*;
34 demand management;
35 sale, exchange, or use of property;
36 restructuring the market.

In one of the most comprehensive surveys (OECD, 1993a) of the trends in public-sector management the OECD reported that the most popular initiatives amongst member states (to 1992) comprised:

- deconcentration of central government (6);
- development of 'agencies' (7);
- reorganization of public enterprises (9);
- limits to the public sector (9);
- privatization (10);
- decentralization (14);
- new role of central management bodies (18);
- market-type mechanisms (18)

What is driving this re-mixing of structures and instruments? The OECD argues that the new forms of public management are, for the most part, the consequence of economic conditions which are bringing about a 'heightened awareness, both in governments and by citizens, of the size and performance of the public sector' and growing pressures to reform the structures of the public sector so as to make it 'leaner and more competitive'. Thus, throughout the OECD countries, the picture is of a panoply of policies designed to make the public sector emulate the private sector and bring the delivery of public services closer to citizens (OECD, Survey, 1993a: 9).

OECD, *Managing with Market-type Mechanisms,* 1993

The OECD's review of the use of 'market-type mechanisms' (MTMs) is one of the most comprehensive analyses of its kind. The use of MTMs in 17 member countries is reviewed. It focuses on several of the main instruments in widespread use in those countries, including:

- vouchers (US and UK);
- contracting-out (Australia, Canada, France, Finland, Netherlands, Sweden, USA and UK);
- internal markets (Australia, Denmark, Ireland and UK).

The report notes that the practice of MTMs is very broad and varied between member states, and that, as a consequence, generalizations are somewhat dangerous. However, the authors come to three general conclusions as to the experience of MTMs:

- in the design of MTMs, the deliberate inclusion of as many basic features of competitive markets as possible is likely to maximize efficiency gains. Opting for MTMs that closely resemble market arrangements is a less-risky strategy than grafting on only a few aspects of market arrangements or private-sector policies;
- obtaining improvements through MTMs is never automatic, fast or painless. Implementation is not easy;
- fears of the distributive effects between different income and wealth groups seems less than many have anticipated.

In the light of the somewhat limited experience of MTMs, the OECD report believes that they can serve to increase efficiency in the public sector, but that it requires investment in the design, resourcing and implementation of the methods. They conclude that:

Public administrators should be encouraged to introduce MTMs in order to improve resource allocation and make savings on public expenditure. But if MTMs are poorly planned, under-funded and, as a consequence, badly implemented, they will almost certainly fail to achieve their objectives. Devoting the necessary financial, human and technical resources to the design of MTMs has to be considered a sound investment, but it needs to be complemented by campaigns to inform the public and stakeholders about their nature and operation. (*OECD, 1993b: 103*) ◆

4.4.4 The enforcement mix

Policy is all very well, but without an enforcement or compliance capability, the delivery of public policy is unlikely and uncertain. We only have to consider, for example, the difficulties which European Union policies (and other international agreements and laws) have encountered to realize that a good policy, if it is to be carried out, must have effective means of enforcement. The mix of enforcement methods may range from brute force and fixed bayonets to information broadcasts which seek to change behaviour. Markets, bureaucracy and community, for example, may be viewed in terms of different ways of enforcing. The market does it through supply and demand, prices, and the interaction of buyers and sellers; bureaucracy relies on rules; whilst community enforcement relies on such modes as shared values, reciprocity, trust, and gossip (see Colebatch and Larmour, 1993: 23). Here we shall examine four approaches to the mix of enforcement modes. One approach focuses our attention on enforcement and power (Boulding); another examines forms of administrative enforcement and their effectiveness (Hood); and a third provides a framework for analysing the relationship of enforcement to policy type and regime (Burch and Wood). Finally, we examine Etzioni's schema for analysing kinds of power as providing a link between the enforcement of public policy, and the problem of compliance within the organizations responsible for implementing it.

Boulding
We have already discussed the work of Kenneth Boulding (3.5.2). As an economist, his ideas about power have great relevance to understanding the enforcement 'costs' of delivery and the 'boundary possibilities' of different mixes of enforcement strategies. Boulding distinguishes between three kinds or categories of power: threat; exchange; and love (figure 4.11). He then considers these against their consequences: destruction; production; and integration. The consequence of destructive power is to destroy people and valued things. The consequences of productive power is to be seen in the 'fertilized egg', blueprints, ideas, tools and machines, and the activities of construc-

Figure 4.11   Boulding's categories of power

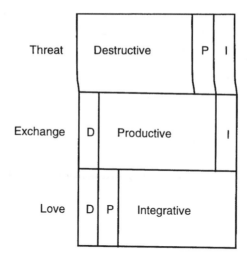

D (Destructive)
P (Productive)
I (Integrative)

Source: Adapted from Boulding (1990)

tion and manufacture. Integrative power 'may be thought of as an aspect of productive power that involves the capacity to build organizations, to create families and groups, to inspire loyalty, to bind people together, to develop legitimacy' (Boulding, 1990: 25).

Significantly, Boulding does not see his categories of power as 'pure' forms: as in the case of 'love', threat and exchange have the quality of being 'fuzzy sets', in that they contain elements of other types of power consequences. Enforcement through threats can have productive and integrative consequences, as in the case of the exercise of threats by income tax authorities or policemen. The threat carries destructive consequences, but if successful may be socially productive and 'integrative'. The use of exchange power to enforce is productive in that for *x*, *a* gets *y* from *b*, and *b* gets *z* from *a* (reciprocal) or it may be contractual: *a* gets *b* if he does *c*. It may involve bargaining to establish a satisfactory rate of exchange or terms of trade. However, it also contains elements of destruction – to enforce contracts – and trust and courtesy (integrative traits), to make exchange possible. The power of love is such that it calls for compliance on the basis of 'respect' and 'legitimacy', out of social and personal responsibility. The use of 'love' as a mode of enforcement involves an appeal to a moral sense or a sense of community or citizenship. It is the request for compliance not based on a threat, or on 'if you do *x*, you will get *y* (exchange)' but on the appeal to a social sense or loyalty to the nation. However, as with the other categories of power, love also contains a capacity to generate its destructive opposite: to create enemies, to alienate people; it has a destructive as well as a productive aspect. And also as a power, the integrative consequences of 'love' as a mode of enforcement may prove highly productive: compliance takes place because of concern, care or a sense of duty, rather than for money or avoiding the long arm of the law.

As a model for a delivery strategy, Boulding's classification points towards the mix of enforcements which societies seek to use to gain compliance (integrative enforcement), or to force compliance (threat enforcement), or to produce compliance (exchange enforcement). Some policies may contain more threat than exchange, others more love than threat.

Hood
Hood (1986: 48–60) identifies four options or modes of enforcement:

- *set aside/modify rules*: in cases of non-compliance, government may choose either to set the rules aside or to modify the rules in order to bring about compliance;
- *spread the word*: government may choose to use publicity and persuasion. This amounts to a kind of 'please keep off the grass' notice: an attempt to gain compliance by giving information or advice which aims at modifying behaviour;
- *pursue and punish rule-violators*: the use of legal and police action to deter non-compliance;
- *make it physically difficult, impossible, inconvenient to break rules*: in this case, the enforcement method is not to use notices to inform people about the grass, but involves making the grass physically difficult or inconvenient to get at in the first place. Hood examines the problems of different modes of enforcement in different conditions. We have simplified this in figure 4.12.

In the case of incompetent (1A) non-compliance, the application of mode 1 enforcement has no effect on non-compliance. Mode 2 may change behaviour, whilst mode 3 is unlikely to diminish an incompetent form of non-compliance. However, modes 3 and 4 (3B and 4B) may depend on whether the prevention of non-compliance is feasible and affordable. In the case of an opportunist non-compliance, mode 1 is likely to increase the opppportunities for non-compliance; mode 2 is unlikely to have much effect on an opportunist; modes 2 and 3, however, are more likely to have an effect on the opportunist, through fear of getting caught (3B) or inability to do it (4B). In the realm of princi-

Figure 4.12   Hood's model of enforcement

Type of non-compliance	Enforcement response			
	Soft		Hard	
	(1)	(2)	(3)	(4)
Incompetent	A	A	A	A
Opportunist	B	B	B	B
(a) Specific rule/law	C	C	C	C
(b) Authority in general	D	D	D	D

Incompetent, Opportunist ⎤ Unprincipled

(a) Specific rule/law, (b) Authority in general ⎤ Principled

Enforcement response options:
1   Set aside / modify rules.
2   Spread the word.
3   Pursue and punish rule violators.
4   Make it physically difficult, impossible, inconvenient to break rules.

Source: Adapted from Hood (1986)

pled objection to a rule or a specific application, mode 1 may influence dissent, without doing too much damage to basic rules. Mode 2, in conditions of an objection in principle, is unlikely to change behaviour (2C); 3C may lead to 'martyrdom', whilst 4C may make matters worse. In the case of a principled objection based on a rejection of authority in general, 1D amounts to admitting defeat, 2D is unlikely to change behaviour, 3D has a potential for martyrdom, and 4D is again dependent on the feasibility and affordability of the preventative measures.

❖ Evaluating the effectiveness of campaigns

With the growth of mass communications and the use of information campaigns in many areas of social and environmental policies, an increasing emphasis is placed on individual responsibility for problems. Campaigns on road safety, for example, urge that we take responsibilty for crossing roads which are becoming more dangerous because there are more cars. Why there are more cars is not something which such campaigns tend to address. If, for example, we take the view that road deaths are essentially due to public policies which favour cars against public transport, then the road-safety issue is less a problem of personal fault or carelessness than an inevitable consequence of public policy.

Lawrence Wallack, 'Mass communication and health promotion: a critical perspective', in Rice and Atkin, 1988

Wallack notes that the way in which society sees problems has a great impact on how it responds in terms of public policy. The media presentation of health issues and government campaigns have, he argues, a distorting effect on this process. Chauncey Gardner, in the film *Being There*, is all too typical of the growing trend for citizens in Western societies to receive most of their information about the world via the TV screen. Public health is a complex problem which is bound up with a wider social and political context, and yet this context is ignored by the presentation of health issues on TV:

> One of the ways to ignore the debate and take what appears to be meaningful action is to talk about life-style factors as being significant influences on health status. This is a basic marketplace concept that suggests that health problems are 'purchased' as a by-product of goods consumed. (p. 360)

He points out that the evidence strongly suggests that

- life-style changes do not have long-term effects on health status;
- large segments of the population have little chance to participate in changes;
- health status is determined far more by external factors (such as economic status) than by life-style;
- the TV images of health and medicine may be bad for your health.

The manufacture of illness as a personal/knowledge problem rather than as a complex public problem may therefore be actually making for a less-healthy population as a whole because it results in the fundamentals of health status being ignored!

In many areas of government policy the aim is to change attitudes and behaviour. This is particularly the case in areas such as health and crime, where government seeks not so much to provide a 'service' as to alter life-styles through information and persuasion. In a sense it is a form of public policy which lays the burden of change on individual behaviour rather than on public choices. Life-style campaigns stress the responsibility of the individual for problems which we may well argue are essentially social. Aids, smoking, drugs and crime prevention are some of the most common forms of campaign as instruments of public policy.

Evaluating the impact of such campaigns is fraught with difficulties, and there are a variety of models on offer. For reviews of this material, see Rice and Atkin (eds) (1988).

It may be argued that such campaigns must be viewed as forms of social learning. But how that can be measured is even more problematical. ◆

Two crucial aspects for Hood are: how much enforcement should take place? and by whom? In the enforcement of a policy, government has to make a decision about what levels of enforcement they consider to be acceptable – 100 per cent, or 20 per cent, say – and what standard or quality should be enforced. The delivery of policy will vary in terms of what levels and standards will be enforced. It may not be cost-effective to put extra resources into enforcement for a marginal improvement deemed not worth the effort. Delivery agencies may decide that enforcement will take place to attain a given level of compliance. Or they may choose to hunt down and prosecute every case of non-compliance. Standards of compliance may be low in some areas and very high in others. The levels and standards of enforcement may be related to who is doing the enforcement, and on what basis. For instance, we may decide that the enforcement of policy in one area is a matter for public bureaucrats; in another, 'professionals' may be responsible for ensuring compliance; it may be left to a private-sector agency; or enforcement may be policed internally (self-policing); or may be implemented via the community.

The issues of how much compliance and by whom adds a further layer of complexity in the mix of delivery systems. The low levels of enforcement (say of measures to counter racial discrimination or sexual harassment or social security fraud) or the low standards of enforcement (in health and safety, for instance), and the fact that the enforcement is in the hands of professionals (who use their expertise to make judgements), or that enforcement is in the hands of insiders rather than outsiders (in the police force, or in the medical and legal professions) may generate new issues and problems. Who does the enforcement is a contentious matter. Here again we must examine the other dimensions of a delivery mix. If government chooses to move a public-sector service out of the hands of professionals into the hands of private-sector businesses – such as prisons or policing – then we as citizens may complain that the standards of enforcement in the delivery of these services is driven by 'profits' rather than 'the public interest'. Yet again, as we have seen elsewhere in this book, the process of deprofessionalization and a distrust of professionals reflects a broad-based social concern with the power of professional groups.

Burch and Wood
Burch and Wood (1990) provide a framework on which to map the choices of enforcement methods in terms of 'negative sanctions' which prevent people doing things. This corresponds with the 'hard' sanctions in Hood and the use of 'threat' power in Boulding. At the other extreme is the use of 'positive' sanctions, which are more indirect: they are aimed at inducing a change in behaviour. Positive sanctions include the 'soft' sanctions of Hood, and the use of 'love' and 'exchange' in Boulding. Against these Burch and Wood set modes of controls in terms of 'formal' and 'informal' controls. The modes of control which are employed in policies are set in the context of forms

of political regime. The domain of positive sanctions and informal controls permit of a political regime which is pluralistic and in which enforcement takes place through bargaining. The domain of formal controls and positive sanctions may be characterized as being highly legalistic, but manipulated to induce compliance. (This is the domain of Hood's mode 1: set aside and manipulation.) The domain of formal controls and negative sanctions is an area of authoritarian legalism, in which rules are rules, and enforcement takes place in the use of law and policing and threat; whilst the domain of negative sanctions and informal controls takes us into the areas of tyranny and autocracy. Discretion is high in the domain of positive sanctions and informal controls, and low in the domain of negative sanctions and formal controls (figure 4.13).

Figure 4.13   Enforcement and regime type

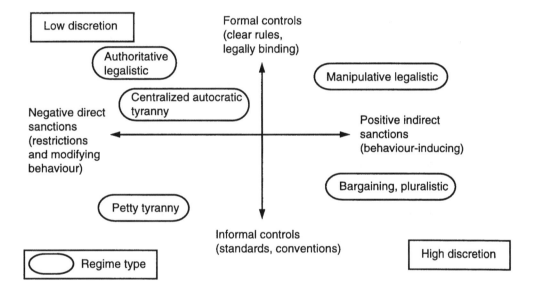

Source: Adapted from Burch and Wood (1990)

As the authors admit, such attempts to classify the complexity of the interaction of control, sanctions, discretion and types of regime is invariably 'crude'. However, this said, Burch and Wood do provide a way of understanding the mix of factors which shape the delivery process. As they observe:

> In the top left quarter, we see the combination of formal and negative systems. This can produce policies that fail to take proper account of local needs and changing circumstances and that are highly unpopular and so carried out by the use of force or directives. Citizen allegiance to the regime and its policy products may be undermined. By contrast, the bot-

tom right quarter illustrates the mixture of informal and positive powers. Those who carry out policies have great powers, but at the cost of their not being fully accountable for their actions, which will not necessarily meet the objectives of the original policy makers. And the treatment of individual cases will vary from official to official, from place to place, and from day to day. Possibly the worst of all is the bottom left quarter combination of negative sanctions and informal controls. In such 'petty tyrannies', harsh and unpredictable behaviour by uncontrollable officials results in neither allegiance to the regime nor the effective carrying out of policy.
(Burch and Wood, 1990: 184)

The Burch and Wood classification also brings out the fact that the mixes of enforcement vary across policy areas, and types of political systems.

❖ Enforcing environmental policy

The problems of enforcement come into prominence when we consider the issues relating to the implementation of environmental policy. This is a field which is not short of good intentions and legal regulations. However, making them stick is quite another matter. Vogel notes, for example, that in the case of the EU's environment policy:

as the scope of Community regulations has grown, the problem of enforcing them has become more acute. The increased number of Community regulations not only makes the monitoring of their enforcement more difficult, but also more urgent, since significant variations in national compliance threatens to disadvantage industries in some EC member states. The Community itself has no police or enforcement powers. It only knows of a violation if someone complains. If it finds the complaint is justified, its final legal recourse is to sue the member state in the European Court. This, however, is a time-consuming procedure ... The problem of enforcement is further complicated by the fact that while EC Directives are intended to bind national governments, in many cases it is local governmental officials who are responsible for enforcing them.
(Vogel, 1993: 124–5)

The case of the EU's enforcement of environmental policy in the context of Burch and Wood's highly pluralistic and discretionary quadrant (figure 4.13) illustrates that enforcement has to be viewed in terms of 'negotiation' rather than top-down command. From the perspective of nation states, the experience of 'top-down' enforcement in environmental policy has not proved a spectacular success (Downing and Hanf (eds), 1983). Hanf (1993) suggests that we ought to revise conceptions of enforcement to take more account of the way in which the practice of enforcment involves forms of 'co-production':

In real terms it is not legislation that determines what deviant behaviour is, but rather the inspectors and investigative officials who do. It is these officials who create cases of violation of environmental law. Consequently, the process of regulation is not simply one where the regulators command and regulated obey.
(Hanf, 1993: 91)

From the perspective of an interorganizational framework it might be argued that enforcement in a policy area (network) involves notions of 'co-operation' and 'negotiation' as well as formal ideas such as legal authority, 'command' and 'obedience'. ◆

Etzioni: mixing love, fear and money

Etzioni (1961) takes the view that there are three basic reasons why people in organizations comply with rules, disciplines, orders or policies: to begin with, they may do so out of a sense of agreement, love, or morality. They do not need to be forced into doing something: they do it because they want to do it. Secondly, people may comply because of fear. If they do not do what they are asked/told they fear the consequences of non-compliance. Finally, they may comply because it is in their monetary or remunerative interests. Although they may disagree on moral grounds, or hate what they have to do, they do so because of the monetary reward which compliance will bring. Enforcement may therefore be the result of normative, coercive or remunerative power. As we have seen from the other theorists above, in seeking to make sure a policy is carried out, implementation will require a mix of different enforcement modes. A policy may rely on coercion or monetary rewards/sanctions, or it may ask people to exercise a moral choice (sticks, carrots or kisses). When we consider that, in order for a policy to be carried out, the implementing agencies must also comply, we realize that enforcement has an organizational as well as a 'public' context. In making policy, decision-makers have to choose a mix of instruments which it is hoped, will ensure that a bureaucrat or professional actually does what is required. As we shall see in 4.5.3, this is the problem which has been addressed in public-sector reforms which draw on the techniques of human resource management (HRM).

Etzioni argues that there will tend to be a balance between different kinds of power and kinds of involvements:

- coercive–alienative;
- remunerative–calculative;
- normative–moral.

Effective organizations, argues Etzioni, are those which attain a balanced mix between low levels of 'fear' (coercion and alienation) and high levels of 'money' (remuneration and calculation) and 'love' (normative and moral) involvements. Significantly, from the perspective of HRM and recent management reforms in the public sector, Etzioni posits that organizations with 'similar compliance structures tend to have similar goals, and organizations that have similar goals tend to have similar compliance structures' (Etzioni, 1961: 71). As goals become more congruent, so do the compliance structures of organizations (see Clegg, 1990: 42–4, for a review of Etzioni).

We could argue on this basis that, as schools, hospitals, universities and other 'public' organizations come to share similar goals to that of the 'private sector' – efficiency and profit for example – so the compliance structures will shift to resemble the structures found in business and industry. As Clegg notes, the evidence to support Etzioni's model is 'considerable' and has withstood much empirical scrutiny (Clegg, 1990: 43). The model would predict, therefore, that as institutions and organizations which deliver public goods and services become more 'businesslike', their mix of compliance structures will increasingly resemble those in the 'profit' sector. The public and private sectors may well come to look and behave in such a similar way that the distinction may become quite meaningless (see, for example, Malkin and Wildavksy, 1991; see also the arguments regarding institutional isomorphism: 4.6.3).

Enforcement and organizational context

The enforcement or compliance mixes which are used have, of course, an organizational setting. The choice of market modes of organization, for example, will perceive the problem of gaining compliance as one which is rooted in self-interested behaviour (figure 4.14). Policy in a market model may be viewed as being enforced through market-type arrangements, the benefits of exchange, the incentive of remuneration or the use of contracts to ensure that 'agents' do what they are contracted to do by principals (see 3.6.3, on agency theory).

Hierarchy or bureaucratic modes involve the notion that enforcement will require effective methods of command and the use of coercion or

Figure 4.14   Modes of enforcement and modes of organization

Modes of organization	Modes of enforcement/compliance			
	Rigby (1964/1990)	Etzioni (1961)	Boulding (1990)	Bradach & Eccles (1991)
Market	Contract	Remunerative	Exchange	Price
Hierarchy/ bureaucracy	Command	Coercive	Threat	Authority
Network/ community	Custom	Moral	Love	Trust

threat to ensure compliance with authoritative rules. The selection of 'network' or 'community' organizational forms will rely on the operation of custom, tradition, common moral codes, values and beliefs, love, a sense of belonging to a 'clan' (see Ouchi, 1991), reciprocity, solidarity and trust.

The selection of enforcement mix is therefore a matter of values, and it is this issue of the mix of values that shape and inform choices which we examine next.

4.4.5 The value mix

❖ The value dimension

Key texts

On the problems of equity, see Le Grand (1991); Le Grand and Bartlett (eds) (1993); Rawls (1971). For the utilitarian approach, see Sen and Williams (eds) (1982); Smart and Williams (1987); Allison (ed.) (1990). The case for a minimal state is addressed in Nozick (1974); Buchanan (1977).

In general, see Frohock (1974, 1979); Beauchamp (1975); Lane (1993: 205–19); Bobrow and Dryzek (1987: 101–16); Weale (1983); Miller (1990).

On the role of values in general, see the work of Vickers (3.7.5) and Young (3.7.7). ◆

The final mix to be considered in our analysis of delivery systems should really go first: what is the distribution of values which frame and inform the delivery mix of a given policy or programme? The governmental, sectoral and enforcement mixes are ultimately manifestations of the values – or the 'assumptive world' – (see Young, 1977; 3.7.7) of policy-makers. In Vickers's terms, 'action' judgements are the outcome of the interaction of reality judgements and value judgements. The value mix will involve choices and priorities regarding the allocation of resources between policy and problem areas as well as between different programmes directed at common problems and policies. These choices in the distribution of resources between policy/problem areas will have a major impact on the other choices of mix between governmental, sectoral, instrumental and enforcement. Resource distribution reflects values and beliefs, power and interests, and, as we have seen in 4.3.7, will shape the way in which organizations within policy fields relate to one another. As Colebatch and

Figure 4.15   Institutions, values and meanings

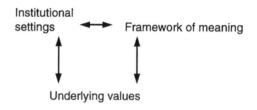

Source: Adapted from Colebatch and Larmour (1993: 108)

Larmour point out with regard to organizational mixes, we have to understand the choices between market, bureaucracy and community as an interactive process involving institutions, values and meanings (figure 4.15).

The framework of meaning they define as 'the way people make sense of the organizational activity; what action is appropriate and why' and how 'underlying values' form a pattern which 'informs the frameworks of meaning people employ and the institutional settings within which they operate' (Colebatch and Larmour, 1993: 108–9). These different dimensions interact and frame meaning for participants and what institutional or organizational mix they think is appropriate for dealing with a problem or delivering a policy response and valuing the outcome:

> For instance, a state's youth unemployment is recognized as a major policy problem, and it is argued by some that the best way to combat it is to remove the statutory restraints on the employment of young people ... this claim is hotly contested, and the conflict reflects the clash between the market and hierarchical models. The market model contains a framework of meaning which sees life as a set of self-interested exchanges between rational actors, an institutional setting where these exchanges can take place ... (market place and law and police) ... and a way of valuing outcomes ... (agreement between employer and young person) ... The hierarchical models rest on a different set of values, seeing the young person as not having bargaining power ... to preserve his/her best interests, and therefore needing protection of a set of institutions ... In other words each model offers a distinct way of organizing the employment of young people.
> (*Colebatch and Larmour, 1993: 110*)

Colebatch and Larmour's model may be combined with two models we have encountered in Part Three: Vickers's judgement approach and Young's idea of the assumptive world. Colebatch and Larmour's dimensions of organizing are illustrations of Young's assumptive world (see 3.7.7). They may also be read as the products of an interaction

Figure 4.16   Values, reality and action

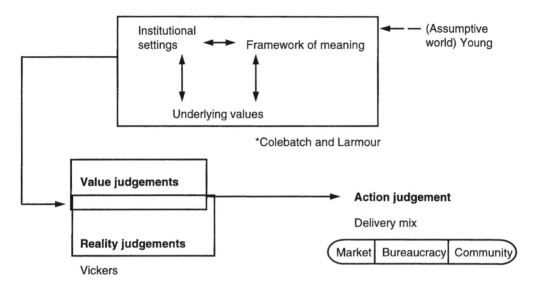

*Colebatch and Larmour

Vickers

Source: Adapted from Colebatch and Larmour (1993), Vickers (1965) and Young
(1977)

between Vickers's 'value', 'reality' and 'action' judgements. We combine these ideas in figure 4.16.

Philosophy and public affairs

The approach which has been most commonly used to explore the value or normative aspects of public policy may be broadly stated in terms of one its leading journals: *Philosophy and Public Affairs*. The philosophical approach to delivery systems would, in the context of the mix between markets, hierarchies and networks, ask questions about the assumptions, values and beliefs which underpin policy choices:

- utilitarian analysis would be concerned with whether a given mix in a policy area is 'efficient';
- analysis which is concerned with issues of social justice would ask questions about whether the implementing of a public policy is done in a fair or equitable way and/or whether the outcome of a given mix is just;
- an analysis predicated on the ideas of a 'minimal state' might be more interested in the issue of whether individual rights have been extended or reduced.

For example, a policy may be geared to the attainment of greater 'efficiency' rather than greater 'equality' or 'equity', in which case, it may be argued that markets (real or quasi) best deliver efficiency or value for money. Even though a policy may include a concern about issues such as equality, the mix of delivery techniques may be biased more towards securing efficiency than equality. A programme may well endeavour to distribute values by setting as the primary value greater efficiency, but it may also take account of the demands for equality and equity. How policies are delivered – or their organizational mix – will consequently reflect the priorities and values of policy-makers. An instance of this might be the way in which a value setting in health policy may place 'efficiency' at a higher priority than equality of access or equity of treatment (Bartlett and Le Grand, 1993: 18). A delivery system in this sense is composed of a bundle of values, and the choice of a mix is the result of the way in which policy-makers have designed or selected a mix to realize one set of values over another. Using Lasswell's idea of 'enlightenment' as a value in public policy, we might argue that 'community'-based delivery may well be predicated on a belief in developing or using institutions in which people can learn about problems. On the other hand, although the use of quasi-market mechanisms may include values of enlightenment, those of learning, of participation, and so on, will be ranked fairly low in evaluating the 'effectiveness' or 'efficiency' of the delivery system.

At the same time, the mix between efficiency and equity may vary within and between policies and programmes. Equality, for example, may be defined in terms of equality of opportunity and access, rather than equality of outcome or consumption. Freedom in the context of policy delivery may be framed in positive terms: that is, delivery should be motivated to make users free from conditions such as 'want, ignorance and disease'. On the other hand, the delivery of a policy may be more constrained by the negative sense of freedom as the absence of constraint. The former (positive) clearly involves the idea that the delivery process should be concerned with outcomes and provision; whereas the latter (negative) suggests that the delivery process should be designed to provide a procedure which is just and which 'enables' rather than provides. The theories of Rawls and Nozick which address the questions of fairness in outcome and procedural justice advance rival philosophical frameworks within which the choices of delivery systems may be understood in a normative context. For example, in the case of the decentralized systems chosen by Islington and Tower Hamlets (see 4.4.2), the actual mix of organizational arrangements and policy instruments has been framed by the different values which have informed their respective policies. As Burns et al., note:

> it is the values of the political parties and not the organizational structures
> ... that have determined the outcomes which the decentralization pro-

duces ... The Labour Party in Islington has a universalistic conception of social justice (Rawls, 1971). Hence their stress upon equal opportunities and anti-poverty ... The Liberals in Tower Hamlets, on the other hand, have a conception of rights founded on historical relationships to territory and property – which would not be uncomfortable with the radical libertarian philosophy of Robert Nozick (1974). Thus their stress on 'sons and daughters schemes' and endorsement of council house sales alongside their enthusiasm for decentralization.

(*Burns* et al., *1994: 219*)

❖ Whose costs and benefits?

What is optimal in the distribution of resources between one policy/programme/option and another? The economist Pareto (1848–1923) provided an important model to explain and explore welfare problems. His argument was this. An optimal distribution of welfare is when everyone is better off: costs = benefits / benefits exceed costs. Cost and benefit analysis was framed in terms of this notion of being able to make calculations as to the optimal distribution of costs and benefits. Does the wonderful world of public policy inhabit this domain of Pareto optimality? The answer is that it depends on a number of factors. If the size of the cake is bigger over time, then it is possible for everyone to have an increase in resources for their policy/programme. And, if decision makers believe in equity across the board (or horizontal equity) then a bigger cake means everyone is better off. However, if policy-makers do not believe in equality of welfare then the allocation of the cake will be vertical, and unequal. Bigger cakes do not mean bigger slices for all: costs and benefits are not distributed equally. It depends on the nature of the distributional values which inform the allocation. Of course, the really bloody position is where the cake is getting smaller. If the decision-makers have a horizontal welfare position then the model will be equality of misery: everyone is worse off. However, if they are of the view that equality should not be applied, there will be a vertical allocation in which case, there will be winners and losers (although according to the so-called Kaldor–Hicks modification of Paretian optimality, winners may compensate losers to satisfy an optimal distribution). The problem of the distribution of welfare in CBA raises the issue of the relationship between what is efficient and what is equitable. It may be that the budget or a series of policy decisions represents an 'efficient' use of resources, but they may not result in an equitable allocation. This problem has been addressed in John Rawls's *A Theory of Justice* (1971). Rawls argues that the values we should apply to resource allocation are not those of costs and benefits, but that of 'fairness'. His argument uses the metaphor of a veil of ignorance under which we are placed to consider what kind of world we would choose to live in. Under this veil we know all about the world, but nothing about who we are. What, asks Rawls, would we vote for? The answer, he says, is that we would opt for a situation in which gains for the best off could only take place if the least well off were in a better position after the winners had gained. Obviously this notion has many implications for the way in which we see the aims and purpose of public policy as a whole. If we take the view that such an arrangement would make for a fair society or a fair decision, then the policy process would be structured by the principles that winners can be allowed to win only if they benefit the least well off. In figure 4.17, the 45 degree line (*e*) provides for equality. Every increase in A's income is met with the same increase in B's. The distribution here is positive: y_1 represents a position in which A's increase (1) is matched by B's. However, in the case of the negative (*i*) line, an increase in A's income actually makes B worse off (y_2 to y_3). In a Rawlsian sense, we may see public policy as to do with ensuring line *f*,

Figure 4.17   Fairness and public policy

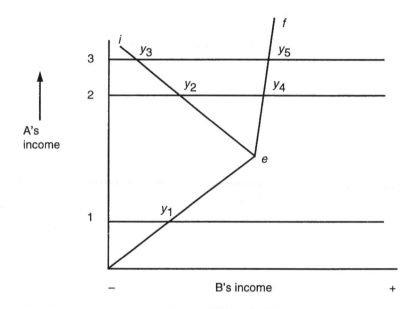

or fairness provides the context of decision-making. Here we allow A to increase his income, but as it rises, so does that of B (y_4 to y_5). The more we move the *f* line to the right, the greater the advantage to B. It may therefore be necessary to keep a programme or a policy going, even though it is not efficient or cost-effective so to do in order to be 'fair'. A Rawlsian view of the provision of public goods will mean that changes to policies, or the development of new policies will have to be set against the need to maintain existing allocations for reasons of equity rather than for reasons of efficiency. ◆

The desire for 'positive freedom', 'equality of outcome' and 'fairness' has long been regarded as strongly biased towards bureaucratic or hierarchical systems, as opposed to negative freedom, procedural justice and 'efficiency', which have been viewed as conditions best delivered by markets. However, this polarization of markets as more suited to 'efficiency', and hierarchy as more fitted to provide equality and equity, is grossly simplistic. In practice, market forms of public management often aim to arrive at a mix in the delivery process which utilizes a range of instruments to improve 'efficiency', whilst seeking to balance these values against the demands for 'equity' and 'equality' (and enlightenment) (Osborne and Gaebler, 1992: 348).

From a Lasswellian perspective, what is at issue here is how a delivery system may be mapped in terms of the values which institutional and organizational arrangements seek to promote. In this context, there will be inevitable conflicts in values between the different agencies involved in the organizational matrix (see Hjern and Porter, 1981), and between the values of high-level policy-makers (at the Ministry of Health) and the values of 'street-level' implementers (health professionals) who may well disagree with the delivery mix within which they have to do their job. In analysing the way in which values are distributed in the delivery of public policy we are therefore concerned with power: whose values predominate, when, and how (Lasswell, 1936)?

As we argued in 4.3.8, one of the problems with a 'general' or synthetic theory of implementation is that it serves to make very distinctive sets of values which operate in the delivery of public services less clear. Bottom-up approaches are, in the main, predicated on values which stress openness, decentralization, participation and so on. Thus if the value which predominates in a given delivery mix is 'control', the institutional arrangements and the modes of enforcement will reflect this value. If, on the other hand, the delivery of a policy is viewed in terms of 'social learning' (4.6.4) or as a means of 'community development', the values which shape the choice of implementation are likely to be far more predisposed to a bottom-up framework.

4.4.6   Evaluating delivery systems: exit, voice and loyalty

The ultimate test for a delivery system is whether citizens are satisfied with the goods and services which it provides. They may feel unhappy with the value outcomes and be concerned about the falling standards of service. When this happens, what options do citizens have? This issue of response to deterioration was the subject of an influential study by the economist Albert Hirschman (1970b). Hirschman's arguments as to the response of firms, organizations and states to decline provides a framework and the language uses both economic and political concepts to explore the relationship between policy-makers and implementers and those who are actually on the receiving end. As with other economic analyses, Hirschman employs the notion of rational actors; however, his model also has a cognitive dimension which is suggestive of other theories of group behaviour which we reviewed in Part Three which address the 'non-rational' dimensions of decision-making (3.7.1, 3.7.2). For this reason, the Hirschman model provides a useful integrative framework for the analysis of organizational behaviour and the interaction of members within and outside groups.

As a theory it also has a special relevance in those situations in which policy-makers have sought to make public goods and services more like those in a market place. The model illustrates the problems and issues which may arise in market-driven public policy. Hirschman argues that there are two options which may be considered available to the consumer in the face of a decline in the quality of goods and services: exit and voice.

Exit

The capacity to exit is the essential ability of the consumer in a market place. If the consumer is no longer satisfied with the goods or service, he or she can choose to buy from another firm or use another organization. For the exit mechanism to work, firms should have a mix of inert and alert customers; alert customers provide feedback on the quality of goods and services, whilst the inert provide the 'cushion' needed for recuperation to take place.

Voice

Voice corresponds to the articulation of interest and protest in a political sense. Hirschman notes: 'To resort to voice, rather than exit, is for the consumer or member to make an attempt at changing the practices, policies, and outputs of the firms from which one buys or the organization to which one belongs' (Hirschman, 1970b: 30). Just as alert customers who opt to exit serve to improve quality (although not always: Hirschman, 1970b: 27), so active, articulate customers may serve to improve the quality of output: 'Voice has the function of alerting the firm or organization to its failings, but it must give management, old or new, some time to respond to the pressures that have been brought to bear on it' (Hirschman, 1970b: 33). The readiness to resort to voice will depend on the extent to which the certainty of exit advantages can be traded off against all the uncertainties of changing things through voice. It will also depend on the strength of voice in terms of number and organization. The greater the capacity to exercise an exit, the louder and more effective will be the voice option.

Voice may serve to complement the capacity to exit, or it may be an alternative – and the only alternative for some – to exiting. Hirschman argues that in general, however, the capacity to exit drives out voice. If alert customers have alternatives, they are likely to take the option to exit rather than to express dissatisfaction. However, the efficacy of exit as a response to decline may not have a beneficial effect in counteracting decline: the firm may simply be content with its inert customers and their reluctance or inability to exit. The exit option may not be exercised for several reasons, including the customer's belief that voice may have the effect of changing the situation, or the customer/member/citizen may have a sense of loyalty to the organization and its output. The exercise of loyalty constrains the exit option, and strengthens the voice option.

In the case of public goods and services, the exit from a public good – such as transport, education or health services – does not mean that the citizen gives up voice: he or she still has a vote and may express dissatisfaction about the service from which he or she has been constrained to exit. At the same time, public goods in a pure sense cannot be exited from in the sense in which consumers of private goods can 'vote with their feet' (although public-choice theorists would argue that by marketizing public services consumers will be free to choose: see Tiebout, 1956). Citizens cannot move out of society; although, of course, they may ultimately leave and seek membership of another country – assuming that they are fit and healthy and sufficiently well-resourced to do so, and that immigration laws let them move about (see Soysal, 1993).

Loyalty

Loyalty is clearly a primary factor in the choice between exiting and voice. Loyalty restricts and retards exit and increases the propensity to choose voice as the mode of response to decline. Even though a citizen may have the capacity to exit from a public programme, he or she may decide that to leave it would be disloyal and 'wrong'. They may reason that if 'everybody' exited from the service, society as a whole, which includes them, would be worse off, and thus they choose voice, rather than exit. Another factor is the cost of exiting set against the costs of entry. The higher the costs of entry the lower the disposition to exit; and the greater the loyalty, the lower the desire to exit. This aspect of the model was subjected to a number of tests by psychologists who examined the relationship between severe initiation procedures for admittance into groups and the degree of self-deception. The more severe the initiation, the greater the group loyalty and exercise of voice, and the lower the rate of exiting (Hirschman, 1970b: 146–55).

This finding is parallel to the idea of cognitive dissonance observed by Festinger, whereby facts which disprove belief do not serve to disprove, but to reinforce, beliefs. Even when beliefs are disconfirmed, believers become even more vigorous in proselytizing (Festinger, 1957). Loyalty, therefore, may well predominate in conditions where there are high initial costs and high exit costs: in which case citizens may choose to exercise loyalty and voice, rather than exit completely. Or they may choose to exit for a temporary period in order to bring pressure to bear – by the use of a boycott as an instrument of voice. Loyalty, Hirschman argues, 'holds exit at bay'.

❖ McPublic sector

George Ritzer, *The McDonaldization of Society*, 1993

Ritzer is a sociologist interested in the process of Weberian 'rationalization'. He argues that the McDonalds chain of fast-food outlets constitutes a model of the contemporary process of rationalization. He describes the spread of this as 'McDonaldization'. Max Weber believed that the process of bureaucratic rationalization would result in an 'iron cage' from which industrial societies cannot escape. McDonaldization, however, represents less the triumph of an 'iron cage' so much as a 'velvet' or 'rubber' cage. In this world, people, especially those born since the advent of McDonalds, 'like, even crave' McDonaldization:

> This is the world they know, it represents their standard of good taste and high quality, and they can think of nothing better than an increasingly rationalized world. They prefer a world that is not cluttered by choices and options. They like the fact that many aspects of their lives are highly predictable. They relish an impersonal world in which they interact with human and even non-human robots. They seek to avoid, at least in the McDonaldized portions of their world, close, human conduct. For such people, and they probably represent with each passing year an increasingly large proportion of the population, McDonaldization represents not a threat but nirvana.
> (*Ritzer, 1993: 160–1*)

Things to do!

Go and buy a hamburger, and while you are dining (*sic*) make a list of what you regard as the key features of the McDonalds approach to delivering your yummy repast. This might include:

- training people to do a limited task, rather than to be 'cooks';
- a limited product range;
- application of assembly-line principles;
- quick turn-over of customers;
- making customers do some work;
- an emphasis on speed of delivery;
- the same wherever you go;
- an emphasis on calculation and measurement;
- a stress on 'quality' (*sic*) and 'quantity' (illusion of?);
- customer-driven (illusion of?).

Next, think of a public-sector service and consider how it might be made to be more like a McDonalds. Invent a McHospital, a McSchool, a McUniversity or a McPolice service. Then, after this flight of fancy, check out the reality: books which suggest that McDonalds may have a lot to teach the public sector (Osborne and Gaebler, 1992: 114, 167, 182–3, 229; Wilson, 1989: 135–6).

A plausible story

Once upon a time, in a land where generations had grown up with McDonalds as an icon of rationality, it was decided to 'Ronaldize' the education system. Over a period of five years all teachers were sacked and fast-food chains were given the job of delivering education policy. In place of public education, private-sector-funded schools were set up. McTeachers were trained in a limited range of skills and dispatched to McSchools, where the range of subjects taught was restricted to reading, writing and 'rithmetic.

The schools were identical, and the subjects were prepared and delivered in the same way. Schools employed McCentre-trained staff, motivated by the award of 'golden apples' which were displayed on the rather fetching McUniform. These 'McInstructs' used key McTexts designed (by a team of 25 experts) to give lessons on a programmed, predictable, efficient and controlled basis.

Where possible, computers were heavily involved in teaching. The parents of customers, or stunits, were encouraged to participate in the 'fun' of the school by helping to keep it clean, and could register for a McTeaching Unit qualification. The school Manager's task was to ensure that the quality and quantity of output conformed with the *McManagers Manual*. To this end each teacher had to complete a *Star Date Manual* on the completion of a task, such as meeting a reading target. Attainment measures (McTargets) were evaluated by the area manager and published on a weekly basis; they were also displayed on a screen outside the school.

A drive-thru service was available for parents who wanted to have a 'take-out teach' (or McHome video, CD, floppy etc.). Parents could choose (in a 'Customers' Conference') another company for the next franchise period. Or, if they had the capacity, they could simply drive to another educational outlet in the (vain) belief that another 'fast-education' school might do better. ◆

4.4.7   The limits of consumerism

The ability to exit from a public service is manifestly limited by other factors which Hirschman does not consider: economic and financial. Take the cases of private medical insurance and private education. If I consider that state provision is deteriorating to the point at which I review options, I may decide that enough is enough and I am going private. However, not everyone is able to do so. The capacity to exit from a public service to private provision is limited by financial resources and socio-economic status.

In such conditions the capacity to exercise exit is unequally distributed. Those who find themselves in such a position may view their captivity, in which they have little or no exit force and in which voice may not be effective (Hirschman, 1970b: 44–54), as nothing to do with loyalty to the national health service, so much as an expression of their dependency upon the service. They might want to go private, but they cannot afford to do so. In this case dependency/loyalty results in driving out exit and a total reliance on voice: the vote, political parties, interest groups, the use of the media. Even so, the voice option is one which, as Lindblom argues, suffers from considerable impairment (Lindblom and Woodhouse, 1993: 104–13).

The problem with exit as a mode of response is that, whereas formally all citizens have equality of voice, although their effectiveness will not be so equally distributed, exit is a response which is not available so readily to all, and, in many instances of public policy, may not be available to anyone except the very, very rich. There may, therefore, be no alternatives, or the alternatives may be too expensive for all but relatively few. In some instances, it may be impossible to exit from the 'externalities' of a public good: some goods and services impact on all, even if some members of the community choose not to use them. I may have a private security force, but I cannot exclude myself from crime in society as a whole or riots which erupt on my doorstep, even if that doorstep is two miles away behind a security fence.

Two issues arise from this. The first is that policy-makers may seek to increase the capacities of citizens to get the best out of the public sector. They may see the 'marketization' of services in this light. Markets, it could be argued, are more responsive to voice than are hierarchies. The strategy here will be to make the citizen a more effective 'consumer' and create a relationship in which a 'consumer' voice is enhanced by improving 'access' to public agencies (Lamb and Schaffer, 1981). Measures to improve the 'access' of citizens as a means of enhancing voice could include:

- citizenship (Ranson and Stewart, 1989; Hall and Held, 1989; Coote (ed.), 1992);
- consumerization of public services (Gyford, 1991; Stewart and Clarke, 1987; Winkler, 1987; Martin, 1993);
- equal opportunities policies (Lupon and Russell, 1990).

The effectiveness of access and voice may, however, still be ineffective in communicating the responses of citizens to the values and instruments of policy. Policies to improve access may, in Edelman's sense, be simply rhetoric which does little more than window-dress rather than deal with the substance of the problems. In this case, the failure of voice and conditions of dependence (rather than loyalty) may induce disillusionment: inert exiting from the political process (figure 4.18). In these conditions citizens do not vote with their feet: they may (cf. Lindblom and Woodhouse, 1993) simply not bother to vote. The

Figure 4.18 '*Active' and 'inert' exit*

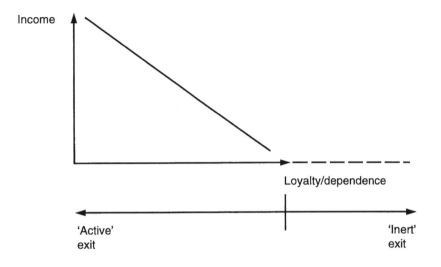

perception that public policy is not something which has much to do with them may well induce apathy and non-participation. Thus at two ends of the spectrum exiting may take place: those who can, 'opt out'; and those who cannot, 'drop out'. All of which puts further strain on those members of the community who stay put!

The problem of an optimal mix
In concluding his study, Hirschman draws attention to the elusive mix: a balance between exit and voice:

> In order to retain the ability to fight deterioration those organizations that rely primarily on one of the two reaction mechanisms need an occasional injection of the other. Other organizations may have to go through regular cycles in which exit and voice alternate as principal actors. Finally, an awareness of tendencies toward instability of any optimal mix may be helpful in improving the design of institutions that need both exit and voice to be maintained in good health.
> (*Hirschman, 1970b: 126*)

The challenge of policy-making in today's world is to arrive at a balance between the need to facilitate choices that work in market conditions where exit and voice can be effective, and the use of modes of delivery in which the provision of services to 'customers' can also be equitable. Furthermore, in addition to the arguments about whether consumers (*sic*) can opt out of public goods and whether the resultant distributions are fair, there are a number of other objections which may be made to the model of consumer sovereignty (see Potter, 1988). Hood (1986: 173–80) , for example, puts foward the following limitations on the powers of exit and voice:

- Is there a choice of suppliers? The lack of choice of suppliers does significantly reduce the power of voice.
- Is there a choice of brands and quality?
- Is the consumer or user the best judge of his/her own interests? They may not know enough to make informed choices. Some wants may have more merit than others.

Clearly, consumer sovereignty has its limitations. The market for public goods and services is different to that for pork pies and toothpaste, and such limitations do restrict the possibility of realizing a pure consumer model. In practical (as well as in theoretical) terms citizenship is more than consumership. Hood (1986: 181–6) suggests that we can identify a number of other lines of arguments against the consumer model:

- paternalist arguments that we cannot let the average citizen make choices on things about which he or she knows little or nothing;
- competition, it may be claimed, will drive down standards to the lowest quality and level of safety;
- stress and strain on providers as a result of consumer sovereignty will make life more difficult, if not impossible, for those involved in providing services;
- average costs of production will be driven down to make the product uniform.

These objections to the theory and practice of operationalizing a consumer model of delivery prompts consideration of what we know about how new modes of delivery actually work in practice. This brings us to the issue of policy evaluation. How can we evaluate the success or failure of new modes of delivery? In a study of change in the provision of public services in Britain, Le Grand and Bartlett offer the following framework for evaluating 'quasi-markets' in social policy (the health service, community care, education and housing). The goals of 'quasi-markets' in welfare services, they suggest, are a mix of values: improving efficiency, responsiveness, choice and equity. If these improvements are to be attained they propose that they must meet the following conditions, some of which have already been covered earlier:

- *market structure*: if quasi-markets are to achieve their goals, there should be a situation of competition between many providers and purchasers. If there is a monopoly, then it should be broken up, but where this is impossible, there should exist a countervailing power;
- *information*: there should be accessible independent information about costs (for providers) and quality (for purchasers);

- *transaction costs and uncertainty*: transaction costs, especially with regard to uncertainty, should be kept to a minimum. Extra transaction costs must not be higher than they would be in the administrative systems they are replacing;
- *motivation*: providers ought to be informed by financial motives. They must be motivated to respond to market signals. Purchasers ought to be motivated to pursue the welfare of users;
- *cream-skimming*: there should be no incentives for providers or purchasers to discriminate between users in favour of those who are least expensive (Le Grand and Bartlett (eds), 1993: 33–4)

The conclusions reached by the contributors to the project are, as we might expect, mixed:

> The quasi-market reforms are in their infancy and it is too early to predict their long-term consequences ... but we could summarise the argument so far by saying that reforms which involve the district health authority as a purchaser of health care and the social service department as a purchaser of social care do not seem to hold out much prospect of gains in terms of efficiency, choice and responsiveness, but may not have much adverse impact on equity either; whereas the housing, education, GP fundholding and care-management reforms seem to hold out the prospects of real improvements in efficiency, responsiveness, and choice, but, unless the incentives for cream-skimming are reduced, may have a detrimental effect on equity.
> (*Le Grande and Bartlett (eds), 1993: 218–19*)

However, as they point out, evaluation of this kind is problematic. It involves comparisons with other imperfect systems, and is constrained by the fact that reforms take time. State or hierarchical systems of providing health, housing and education have a much longer time period in which they may be judged. To be fair and methodologically sound, the evaluation of new systems of delivery needs more time to see if they work better or worse – or the same. But as a former British Prime Minister (Harold Wilson) once noted: 'a week is a long time in politics'. To which may be added Keynes's dictum that 'in the long run we are all dead'! Thus, although we need to make evaluations of policy and programmes, the business of evaluation is riddled with difficulties, not the least of which is time. It is to an examination of the difficulties of evaluation to which we turn in 4.5.

4.4.8   The control–consensus mix

In analysing the mix of instruments, mechanisms and modes of government which may compose a given policy field, an important consideration is the relationship between two sets of goals and values: the desire for control and the formation of social consensus. Etzioni (1968) defines this problem in the following terms:

> Control – The process of specifying preferred states of affairs and revising on-going processes to reduce the distance from these preferred states. Consensus formation – the process by which perspectives of the members of a societal unit are transmitted to the controlling overlayers and the differences among them are reduced. (p. 668)

> While there is no simple, straight line substitution, by and large, increasing one element reduces the other. (p. 481)

The different mixes we have discussed above may in practice be said to represent formulations along this line of substitution. The development of market-type mechanisms and other public-sector reforms from the 1980s onwards were the result of increasing pressures to control the costs of public goods and services and increase the efficiency and effectiveness of their delivery. New public-sector management has been primarily control-orientated in its preference for 'hands-on management', measurement of performance, output control, breaking up units, competition, discipline and cost-cutting (see Hood, 1991: 4–5). A major feature of this control process has been the move to create a relationship between the citizen and public services and agencies similar to that which pertains between the consumer and a market place.

As we have noted above, there are limitations to this notion that the consumer of health or education can be like a shopper in a store. The danger may well be that the new public-sector mix, in achieving control, has undermined and subverted the other aspect of the mix: the building of a social, civic or political consensus. In emphasizing control through quasi-market approaches, the issue of how citizens relate to the political or public order has been somewhat neglected. Etzioni himself has argued that this problem needs to be addressed through policies which rebuild the role of community, family and associations in an active society (see Etzioni, in 1.6; and 1993a, 1993b, 1994).

Public policy is not only concerned with the three Es – economy, efficiency and effectiveness – it is also about the two Ps – participation and politics. It is also not simply to do with 'exit, voice and loyalty', but also 'voice, ear and respect' (see Healey, 1993). It is through the promotion of democratic skills and a 'societal consciousness' (Etzioni, 1968: 224), however, that consensus-building may take place in the policy mix. The development of individual and community political education has, however, been absent from so much of what has passed for the re-mixing or 'reinvention' (Osborne and Gaebler, 1992) of public policy. The 'community' approach to local government is perhaps an exception to this rule, but in so many other policy fields and delivery systems, the relationship of the citizen to policy process *qua* politics is neglected in favour of managerialist controls, rather than political accountability and consensus-building.

Citizens' juries

However, there are some indications that the control–consensus-building mix could evolve in a way which allows public policy to be a source of public learning. An example of this is the growth in several countries – especially Germany and the USA – of 'people's juries' in which citizens participate in decision-making by subjecting witnesses – experts, politicians, bureaucrats, managers, interest groups and others – to judicial-style cross-examination. The end result is a report which can make a valuable input into the policy process (see Stewart *et al.*, 1994). As John Stewart points out:

> It is often argued that the public are not interested in participating. Apathy is the enemy and many in government will tell tales of frustrated initiatives in public participation. But these initiatives have too often worked against the grain of how people behave. Citizens' juries build on familiar and robust institutions. A local authority could use a citizens' jury to test out propositions on a school closure or a planning issue ... Problems of law and order could be explored ... mediation groups which bring together conflicting interests, deliberative opinion polls, and consultative referendums and electronic town meetings – all of these, as well as citizens' juries, can be seen as part of a strategy to strengthen democracy.
> (*Stewart, 1994*)

Decision seminars and the case for social think-tanks

Another approach which can build on familar and robust institutions is suggested by Lasswell's decision seminar technique and his idea of 'social planetariums' (see Lasswell, 1959, 1960, 1970b; Cunningham, 1981; Ershkowitz, 1981; Gorrell *et al.*, 1993; and 3.10.5). Citizens in this model are not on the end of a delivery line, but are active in guiding choices and selecting and evaluating the mix. The centre point of this process should – in an information age – be the library or another knowledge institution, such as a museum, in which the society/community/region or whatever social unit, can think about where it has been, its present realities, the likely trends in the future, and what kinds of guidance or control they would like to exercise over their problems and opportunities, strengths and weaknesses. Lasswell suggested that there should be exhibitions which can facilitate this open exchange of values, ideas, beliefs, information, fears, hopes and dreams. The social planetarium would be a place where a community could observe itself, imagine possibilities and explore problems. It could become a place where the schools, churches, voluntary organizations, community groups, universities, and so on, in a locality present arguments, images, ideas and schemes. The aim would be to increase the self-knowledge and awareness of society so as to create a forum in which to enrich the political agenda.

Citizens would be encouraged to use this information-rich environment for such purposes as citizens' juries; town planning; discussions on social and economic problems; neighbourhood forums and so on. Policy-making will thereby become a way of politicizing and analysing: a process of enlightenment rather than a delivery and consumption nexus. Now, more than ever before, we have the capacity to utilize public institutions such as the jury system, libraries and museums as 'prototype' (see Lasswell, 1963) *social* 'think-tanks' in which men and women, young and old, are engaged and are active in thinking about their society, making choices, shaping values and building consensus.

❖ The idea of social think-tanks or 'planetariums'

Lasswell envisaged that 'social planetariums' could extend the use of decision seminars (see 3.10.5) to the community as a whole.

Using the idea of a planetarium where people can observe the sky, Lasswell argued that we should adapt it for social or self-observation (cf. Etzioni's 'societal consciousness' and Lindblom's 'self-guiding society'):

> Participants are liberated from the perceptual caves of the present. The planetarium technique makes it feasible to give proportionate weight to alternative versions of the future or the past ... In principle, every community can build its own social planetarium where stress is put upon local objectives, local history, and local prospects ... [It is] ... a means of giving importance to institutions that in many places are struggling feebly for public recognition. I refer, for example, to art museums, museums of local history, and museums of natural history. The contextual frame of reference – the orientation towards the future and toward decision-making – is a 'shot in the arm'. It makes the past pertinent to the present and the future ... In many circumstances ... it will prove expedient to amalgamate the social planetarium with a program that encompasses all the museums and related cultural resources of the capital of the locality, city, region, nation, or the transnational areas involved ... Gradually society can be changed until people learn to live as much in imagination of the future as in reminiscence of the past ... In such a configurative setting ... individual choices can be made at a respectable level of rationality.
> (*Lasswell, 1959: 106–12*)

What might they look like, bearing in mind the approach taken to policy analysis by those influenced by Habermas and other critical theorists (see 2.7.3, 3.10.4, 3.10.5) and in the light of the experience of 'citizens' juries'?

- a building complex in a community, which could house rooms in which citizens' juries would sit to examine and contribute to policy-making;
- offices for the clerk of the citizens' jury system;
- an office for the director and staff to administer the think-tank;
- facilities for researchers engaged on research in and with the community (see, for example, Rice *et al.*, 1994; Phillimore and Moffatt, 1994);
- offices for people seconded from other organizations (such as universities, planning departments, and business) to work in the think-tank;
- exhibition space to promote community thinking;
- video, film and drama facilities;
- communication (computer and video) technology to provide for networking between think-tanks;
- rooms for decision seminars in which policy-makers, people and policy professionals could engage in sustained long-term analysis and discussion of issues and problems;
- library resources;
- technical support facilities to support activities;
- community advice facilities and personnel to act as citizen 'advocates';*
- rooms for political surgeries (for elected politicians to meet citizens).

* A prototype for such a system is the idea of improving the advocacy capabilities of citizens. For example, Bill Montgomery reports in the author's own neck of the woods on such a scheme in the London Borough of Barnet :

The highlight of the well attended annual meeting was the signing of a three-way agreement between Barnet Council's new administration, the Barnet Health Authority, and Choice. It means a new and improved advocacy service will be operated by Choice in the borough ... Choice works to ensure that all users of community services have a voice in how they operate. In particular it assists disabled people and others to establish their needs and aspirations. And it will represent their interests in a way they may not be able to do themselves. In Barnet it plans to support advocacy for all users of services, with the long-term aim of establishing an entirely independent system owned and managed by the users. (Edgware and Mill Hill Times, *24 November 1994: 20*) ◆

Social think-tanks or 'planetariums' could contribute to the growth of a society which thinks about itself, clarifies its values and is aware and informed, rather than passive and ignorant. Social think-tanks could help to widen and enliven the policy agenda and counter the influence of other organizations in the ideas business. In such an 'active society', Etzioni suggests:

a higher ratio of assets would be invested in political action, and intellectual reflection would have a higher, more public status. The status of political and intellectual activity combined would approximate to the status of economic processes in modern society.
(*Etzioni, 1968: 7*)

In other words, the 'public and its problems' (as Dewey, 1927, expressed it) may over time become more directly connected and engaged in forms of 'communicative rationality' (see Dryzek, 1987; and 3.10). The citizen could become less a 'consumer' than a co-producer of public policy. Hupe, for instance, reports that in the development of forms of 'co-production' in the delivery of social services in the Netherlands: 'clients ... can be seen no longer merely as calculating citizens, but rather as integral parts of the implementation structure of public policy' (Hupe, 1993: 149). The 'co-production' of policy is a phenomenon which has also been noted elsewhere (Bouckaert, 1993; Mattson, 1986), and is being spurred on by reforms in the public sector which have introduced more market and network forms of organization and less Weberian-style bureaucracy. A communicative approach to public policy may therefore develop out of or build on the changing and increasingly complex mix of delivery systems which have emerged over the last decade and more. The policy sciences should – as Lasswell long ago hoped – function so as to facilitate this interaction between the public and its problems by helping to clarify values, formulate arguments, undertake research in and for communities (see, for example, Rice et al., 1994; Phillimore and Moffat, 1994; Lincoln and Guba, 1985; and 4.5.4), and inform and widen public debate. That is, it should assist in the production of what Stacey (1994: 89) terms 'people knowledge', as in the production of professional and policy knowledge.

The citizen – unlike the consumer – is both a producer and consumer. The model of exit, voice and loyalty therefore omits another quality of political life in a democracy: input. The citizen should be seen as someone who can be involved in making a productive input to public policy. This requires that the state should aim to be as concerned about the promotion of what Etzioni (1968: 24) terms a societal consciousness as it has been in recent years with the promotion of efficiency, effectiveness and economy.

In re-mixing the relationship between control and consensus-building we also address another crucial area of public policy: evaluation. As we shall see below, the evaluative process has been primarily framed by managerial or technical values. However, if we regard control as having a political and wider social dimension, then evaluation should provide a significant opportunity for social learning and the promotion of democratic skills (see, 4.5.4, 4.6.4) or active 'citizenship' (Coote (ed.), 1992; Warren et al., 1992). Citizens in this model should be actively involved in making an input to the evaluation of public policy in ways which are more meaningful than voting either through the ballot box or with their feet. It should not be the monopoly of the manager, expert or bureaucrat (see Lindblom, 1990). In practice, of course, it has been ever thus (for critiques of the dominant evaluative paradigm, see 4.5.4).

Control and accountability

An essential aspect of the control–consensus mix are the modes and methods of accountability. This has two dimensions: political and managerial (see Hughes, 1994: 240–55). In the last decade or so the main feature of the accountability mix is the extent to which managerial approaches have been seen as applicable to the public sector. The politics/administration divide, as framed by Wilson, Weber and others, posited that the primary task of the political process was to hold the bureaucratic workings of the state to account for its activities. A strong legislature and party competition was viewed as the primary way in which bureaucracy could be kept under control and steered (see Weber, 1991: 43). However, the arguments of those advocating privatization and managerialist reforms of the public sector in the 1980s cast doubt on the effectiveness of politics as a means of controlling bureaucracy. Day and Klein (1987: 51) argue that as society and government have become more complex, so the relatively simple notion that voters elect representatives who hold civil servants to account has become a less-convincing theory. In surveying accountability in five different public services (health, police, water, education and social services), they conclude that for accountability to be a reality it requires a mix of political/community accountability supplemented with the use of managerial techniques which focus on the performance of those who actually deliver public services. They conclude that accountability

> must be seen in terms of individual institutions but as a system which is woven into the fabric of political and social life as a whole ... [however] this may, in turn, bring about excessive complexity in the machinery of accountability and at the same time create dead ends. So, why not concentrate less on formal links or institutions and engage more in a civic dialogue to recreate at least something of the high visibility and directness of the face-to-face accountability with which the story of the word began. (*Day and Klein, 1987: 248*)

In practice this weaving of accountability into the social and political fabric has taken place through privatization and the introduction of management systems, forms of budgetary control, and performance appraisal and measurement in most OECD countries (see Hughes, 1994: 247; OECD, 1991, 1992, 1993a and b). Allied to this has been the idea of cultivating a 'client' or 'customer' orientation/culture in public-sector agencies and personnel (see Hughes, 1994: 248–50; OECD, 1987). However, the notion that we should also develop a more Athenian, 'face-to-face' form of accountability in which citizens can engage in a 'civic dialogue' has been far less in evidence than managerialist reforms. As we have discussed above in this section, control also has to address the issue of how citizens can make a real and meaningful input into the process, so as to improve the political or civic dimensions of accountability. Indeed, it may be argued that in seeking to 'improve' on the political model of control, managerialism may well be undermining representative government, thus leaving little grounds for hope in terms of a more participatory – or in Etzioni's sense, 'active' – democracy. As Andrew Massey eloquently puts it:

> Public administration cannot be judged by the same standards reserved for retailers, nor can it be run along the same lines. There are no generic laws of management that apply equally to the public and private spheres ... Managerialism is a very weak bulwark to defend democratic government against malpractice, however many citizens' charters may be invented. The difficulty for observers in assessing the worth of the New Right's reforms is that of timescale and information. Government's own performance indicators have changed, becoming more managerial, whilst questions regarding morale, integrity and public service will take years to answer ... The emphasis of the New Right has been on management and control as a way to ensure the accountability of the state, devolving power out to the market and individual consumers. In short it has been an attempt to get the state to wither away. This is not the way to protect liberty. The wisdom of America's Founding Fathers was clear upon this point: if only men were angels we could do away with government.
> (Massey, 1993: 200)

The danger is, as Massey maintains, that managerial controls which aim at eroding the state will end in destroying the very foundations of political systems (such as those of Britain and the USA) which have provided liberty for generations:

> To the New Right with their obsession with efficiency, accountability may appear like Aristo's serpent, 'a hateful reptile' that hisses and stings. Yet it is the foundation upon which the two countries have avoided overbearing government: accountability may be inefficient, 'but woe to those who in disgust shall venture to crush her'.
> (Massey, 1993: 200–1)

With this resounding defence of the theory of representative government ringing in our ears, let us now examine the issue of how public policy in practice may be evaluated.

❖ **Linking policy delivery, evaluation, research and people knowledge**

J. Popay and G. Williams (eds), *Researching the People's Health*, 1994

This book provides an excellent link between the kinds of issues which we have been discussing in 4.4.8 with regard to the relationship of people, as 'consumers' and citizens, to service production, delivery and evaluation. It should also be read in the context of 4.5.4 and 4.7.

The book examines two main issues: the role of social research in health policy, and the relationship of lay and expert knowledge to the shaping and evaluation of health care policy.

In the case of the role of research, the authors draw attention to the fact that social science has an important contribution to make to health policy, yet it has been grossly underused, under-funded, undervalued and underfinanced (Klein, cited p. 19). Although several official pro-nouncements have argued that social scientists do indeed have a major part to play, in practice research into policy outcomes has had a relatively insignificant impact on the policy process. Hunter, for example, says that there is an urgent need for more interaction between policy analysts, practitioners and policy-makers – in Britain as in other countries (Hunter, 1994: 26–9).

One of the problems is that actually evaluating the outcomes of health policy is a complex methodological issue. As Andrew Long comments:

> Although outcomes are high on the policy-making agenda, progress will not be straightfor-ward. Despite the ultimate goal of health services to improve the health of patients, it is still difficult to measure health outcomes. Indeed, there is no agreed taxonomy. This is partly due to an underdeveloped theoretical framework and a paucity of people equipped to develop, apply and interpret outcomes measures ... Evidence on effectiveness and outcomes and an emphasis on health gain and health outcome provide an apparently value neutral, rational approach and means of rationing health and social care. Beneath the range of technical issues in assessing the outcomes are political and social values that need to be explicit.
> (*Long, 1994: 162, 175*)

The long-term agenda, he believes, should be focused on the clarification of such values involved in evaluating whether a policy leads to improvements or to deterioration. This issue of clarification as an aim of research is taken up by the other theme of the book: the role of lay knowledge and participation, which has been discussed in 4.4.8. A number of contributors stress how getting more input from users/customers/citizens has increasingly been seen as a vital part of new research designs.

An interesting example of this is the Glasgow (Corkerhill) study into child accidents, which involved local people. Instead of doing research on a community, researchers worked with lay people to analyse the problem of child accidents, and developed recommendations to reduce them. The contribution written for the volume is jointly authored, and includes one of the local people involved in the project – Cathie Rice. They conclude that, although their work does not provide a 'knitting pattern' to improve child safety: 'The combination of the research and the parents' action group is one we feel may be an effective way of producing local data and exploring ways of making communities safer for children' (Rice *et al.*, 1994: 132).

Another example of designing research so that people are participants and producers, rather than objects or guinea pigs, is the use of Rapid Appraisal (RA) methodology – a method of identifying and prioritizing community health needs. The authors argue that we ought to rethink the relationship between decision-makers and users, and make citizens an integral part of the evaluative process. This rethink will involve, they believe, a 'a paradigm shift whereby the community perspective will be used as the guiding principle for setting priorities in health care' (Ong and Humphris, 1994: 80).

As the editors of the book argue, there is a growing body of opinion that in health policy research and evaluation there ought to be provision for real participation by lay people (Popay and Williams (1994a): 2, 6). Such a conclusion, it seems to the present author, has an urgent relevance to other policy fields. This means that – as we note above in 4.4.8 – the lay voice should be taken seriously and that the enhancement of that voice should be a matter of concern for both policy analysts and policy-makers. ◆

4.5   Evaluation

❖ Key texts

The textbook in the field is Rossi and Freeman (1993). This gives the essentials of 'traditional' evaluation research. It is also supported by an excellent workbook.

In order to develop a good grasp of the development of the subject the reader need go no further than a variety of books published by Sage publications (including Rossi and Freeman), such as:

- Dolbeare (ed.) (1975) for a review of the field in the mid-1970s;
- Saxe and Fine (1981) on experimentation;
- Palumbo (ed.) (1987) for a collection of papers reviewing the changes in evaluation and the new frameworks.

On new approaches to evaluation, see:

- Lincoln and Guba (1985);
- Guba and Lincoln in Palumbo (ed.) (1987) give an account of their 'naturalistic' approach;
- Miller (1984) and Bobrow and Dryzek (1987) for the 'design' approach;
- Cook (1985) on multiplism;
- Rita Mae Kelly's essay on the politics of research methods in Palumbo (ed.) (1987) is an important read on the development of new approaches to evaluation. The section on the alternative approaches (4.5.4) draws on her article.

For the impact of audit, see Henkel (1991) and Power (1994). ◆

❖ Policy evaluation: linking theory to practice

Rist (ed.), (1995) is one of the most comprehensive surveys of evaluation available and is an essential reference book for studying the role and impact of evaluation in policy cycle terms. It contains some of the most important articles in the field published in the US and Europe. It is divided into three parts:

- Policy evaluation in the policy arena
  Theoretical perspectives
  Policy evaluation and policy instruments
  Policy evaluation and utilization
  Policy evaluation and governance

- Policy cycle
  Policy formulation
  Policy implementation
  Policy accountability

- Sectoral policy evaluation
  The environment
  Health insurance
  Education
  Economic development
  Industrial relations
  Energy
  Child support
  Housing ◆

4.5.1   The modes and phases

Evaluation has two interrelated aspects:

- the evaluation of policy and its constitutent programmes;
- the evaluation of people who work in the organizations which are responsible for implementing policy and programmes.

In this section of the book we shall examine evaluation in the context of two dominant frameworks: as a form of rational analysis (4.5.2); and as a tool for the management of 'human resources' (4.5.3). We shall also review critical and alternative views of evaluation in the formation and execution of public policy (4.5.4). These sections follow, in broad terms, the phases in the historical development of evaluation over the last thirty years or so:

- 4.5.2   The 1960s and 1970s saw the emergence of the subject in its modern form, as marked by the publication of books such as those by Campbell and Stanley (1966) and Suchman (1967) and the setting-up of the journal *Evaluation Review* in 1976. As Henshel notes with reference to the US, where the expansion of evaluation was most extensive, 'In the 1970s the basic message of evaluation research suddenly attained cult status of common sense, and governments at the state and federal level rushed to mandate the evaluation of many programmes' (Henshel, 1990: 214).

- 4.5.3 In the following decade, when there was a growing sense that, as Robert Martinson put it, 'nothing works' (in Lipton *et al.*, 1975), the notion of evaluation in public policy widened to encompass ideas and techniques developed in the business world, most notably with the incorporation into public-sector management of MBO, HRM and Audit. Indeed, some would argue that the emergence of evaluation and 'audit' in government has, in many senses, brought about a new 'evaluative state' and the dawn of an 'audit society' (Neave, 1988; Power, 1994).
- 4.5.4 However, alongside the conversion of government to managerialist methods of evaluation in the 1980s, there emerged a growing unease amongst some analysts about the claims and uses of social science and managerialist-inspired evaluation.

❖ **Mary Henkel, *Government, Evaluation and Change*, 1991**

In this book the author analyses the changing culture of management in the British public sector, based on economy, efficiency and effectiveness. She takes three kinds of institutions: the developing role of the Audit Commission; the Social Services Inspectorate in its transition to a more managerial body; and the Health Advisory Service concerned with peer review in the health service.

Henkel shows the importance of the links between traditions of knowledge, values and patterns of authority that largely shape the way in which evaluation impacts on organizations. She concludes that the picture which emerges is of a shift from professional assumptions and values towards more institutional and managerial modes of evaluation. This move towards managerial notions of evaluation has developed into the promotion of market forces. The boundaries between politics, management and the market are, she argues, fast being eroded.

Underpinning this process is, however a tension between evaluation theory, which had moved away from positivism, and evaluation in practice, which has sought to be highly positivist in believing that things could be measured. This signals, she argues, that the manager is superseding the professional. The emergence of the evaluative state therefore reflects a changing order of values, but not the dawn of an age of new objectivity. In practice, political and technical arguments break down and spill over. Evaluation, she believes, has made the need for judgement and sensitivity more urgent, rather than less so. ◆

4.5.2 Evaluation as rational analysis

Definitions of evaluation abound. Thomas Dye offers an excellent broad definition when he notes that policy evaluation is 'learning about the consequences of public policy' (Dye, 1987: 351):

> Policy evaluation research is the objective, systematic, empirical examination of the effects ongoing policies and public programmes have on their targets in terms of the goals they are meant to achieve.

Another leading scholar of evaluation research, Carol Weiss (1972: 6), has argued that it may be distinguished from other forms of policy analysis in some six respects:

- It is intended for decision-making, and it is geared to analysing the problems as defined by decision-makers rather than researchers.
- It is judgemental in character. The research aims at evaluating in terms of programme goals.
- It is research which is embedded in a policy setting rather than an academic setting.
- It often involves conflict between researchers and practitioners.
- It is usually not published.
- It may involve researchers in problems of allegiances to funding agencies and improving social change.

Evaluation research addresses two dimensions: how a policy may be measured against the goals it sets out to attain, and the actual impact of the policy. In this part of the book we shall be concerned with the analysis of evaluation as an activity involved in the measurement of goal performance. Impact studies, on the other hand, address the effect of a policy as a whole or the process by which implementation has taken place. We shall examine impact/process analysis in 4.7.

Evaluation analysis has a number of main approaches or techniques:

- techniques which measure the relation of costs to benefits and utility;
- techniques which measure performance;
- techniques which use experiments to evaluate policy and programmes.

Palumbo (1987) suggests that we may better understand the role of these techniques by relating the 'policy cycle' to the information cycle. In figure 4.19 we have modified this model to show how the policy cycle relates to evaluative information and analysis. In the agenda-

Figure 4.19   The policy cycle and the information cycle

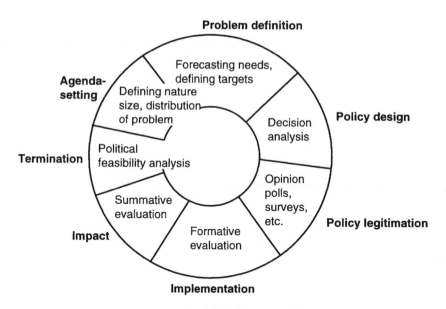

Source: Adapted from Palumbo (1987: figure 1.1)

setting/problem-definition phases, evaluation research is involved in defining the size and distribution of a problem, the forecasting of needs and the defining of target groups and areas (see Rossi and Freeman, 1993: 57–103).

The 'policy design' phase involves techniques of decision analysis in 'identifying alternative means of achieving program ends with the purpose of achieving the cost-effective alternative' (Palumbo, 1987: 40). The use of techniques to measure the relationship of costs to benefits and the 'efficiency' and effectiveness of policies and programmes has an obvious application to the evaluation stage in the policy process. A wide variety of budgetary techniques – such as PPBS, MBO and Zero Based Budgeting – derive from the impact of CBA. In particular, these techniques stress the need to build into budgetary processes cost and benefit calculations.

Palumbo's next phase, policy legitimation, involves a political evaluation as to the acceptance of a policy or programme by the public and stakeholders. This is, on the face of it, a distinctly non-rational or technical exercise (as compared to the theory and practice of CBA). However, as Palumbo notes, the use of measurements of support/ antipathy as reflected in opinion polls is an approach greatly favoured by modern decision-makers. This 'rationalization' of public opinion in forms which allow policy-makers to make judgements/evaluations about the legitimacy of policy and programmes may be regarded as consistent with the logic which is embedded in CBA: that all factors in a decision can and ought to be quantified so as to provide a more rational basis for decision-making. This measurement of opinion may also be incorporated into programmes through the introduction of published tables of 'customer' satisfaction/dissatisfaction with the delivery of public services (as with the UK's Citizen's Charter). Legitimizing evaluation information will also come in the form of legislative inquiries and judicial review and adjudication (Hogwood, 1987: 190–222; Peters, 1986: 63–76).

Formative evaluation

The evaluation which takes place when a policy/programme is being implemented involves analysis of 'the extent to which a program is being implemented and the conditions that promote successful implementation' (Palumbo, 1987: 40). The implementation phase therefore requires 'formative' evaluation, which monitors the way in which a programme is being administered or managed so as to provide feedback which may serve to improve the implementation process. Rossi and Freeman (1993: 163) describe this mode of evaluation as being directed at three questions:

> (1)   the extent to which a program is reaching the appropriate target population, (2)   whether or not its delivery of services is consistent with program design specifications, and (3)   what resources are being or have been expended in the conduct of the program.

Increasingly, this monitoring of the process of implementation provides policy-makers, stakeholders and managers with tools for evaluating the way in which a programme is being delivered, so that this information may be used to correct and/or control the policy delivery process more effectively. This takes the form of various kinds of 'management information systems' (MISs) to provide a centralized information system which can routinize the collection of information (Isaac-Henry, 1993: 97). (This has been greatly enhanced by the use of computers. MIS facilitates an ongoing accumulation and organization of information which can feed into the managerial decision-making process. In the UK the approach was introduced in the 1980s with the development of Management Information Systems for Ministers (MINIS) to give better and more regular information to ministers about what was going on in their departments. This was followed by the Financial Management Initiative (FMI) (1982) which was designed to provide managers with information so that objectives could be met more effectively (see Massey, 1993: 46–51).

A core technique of the MIS approach to evaluation is that of using performance measurement as a primary source of information about the effectiveness and efficiency of policy delivery. This is a form of evaluation which has come to a pre-eminent position since the late 1970s, when there was a growing demand for efficiency measured by inputs over outputs, due to pressures on public finances. Performance measures vary, but a key feature is their aim to arrive at a ratio of input to service outputs. Where this is inappropriate, a performance measure may be expressed as how efficient the use of given resources has been: how many/much could have been or should have been achieved, and how much was actually achieved. This is a common form of performance measure in cases such as public transport or hospitals.

The development of performance evaluation must therefore be understood in the context of the need to control public finances and attain higher levels of value for money, efficiency and effectiveness. This control is not, however, a neutral or purely technical technique – although those of a highly positivist disposition might put forward such an argument. PIs are heavily loaded with values, politics and power. As with welfare-economics-derived CBA, big questions must be asked about who sets up the criteria for measurement, how it is calculated, who asks the questions and what time period is selected for assessment. Who determines what counts as efficient and effective, or what is value for money? PIs may tell us about quantity, but we may be less convinced that more of x is of a quality which may or may not be measurable. At the same time, is it 'fair' or methodologically sound to compare measures of performance? Can one school or hospital be compared to another on the basis of a selected PI? There are limits to quantification. The simple assertion that a given service has increased by x per cent means little without a consideration of the non-quantitative dimensions; nor does it take account of the fairness or equity problems. More of x does not mean that x has been distributed fairly between users. More may be another way of saying worse. It may satisfy those who have demanded the data, but not those actually delivering and using the data in real life.

Measures of performance in themselves mean nothing. The policy analyst is concerned with the values and politics which have constructed the measures and the interpretation which is placed upon the data. The case for PIs would contend that they have a number of benefits: they determine progress in moving towards goals; identify problem areas; and contribute to improving personnel management. However, a more critical perspective would maintain that PIs simply increase the capacity of the state to control organizations and people. For advocates of PIs as part of an audit measurement of performance, the key issue is that of the integrity and professionalism of those who devise and implement audit (Flint, 1988). For critics, however, the emergence of PIs signals a shift in power within government and delivery organizations, from professionals and administrators to auditors and accountants (Power, 1994; Carter, 1989).

❖ A case for measuring performance in the public sector

The use of measures and indicators of performance in areas of human activity where there is no 'bottom line' as in business is problematic. In a paper published in 1988 the economist Peter Jackson confronts the critics of PIs by arguing that if the quality of the service provided in the public sector is to improve, then the use of measures of performance is absolutely vital. Jackson argues that the view that there are massive differences between the public and private sectors is somewhat overstated. Measures of performance can provide an effective substitute for profits so as to improve the management of schools, hospitals, local government and other services. He identifies a range of roles they can play in making for better management:

- PIs can increase accountability;
- they can provide a basis for policy planning and control;
- they can provide important information to monitor organizational activities;
- they can provide information for ex-post strategic management post mortems;
- and they can provide the basis of a staff appraisal system.

However, to work well as 'mirrors' reflecting activities PIs should ideally have nine characteristics:

- they should be consistent over time and between units;
- they should be comparing like with like;
- they should be clear and well defined;
- they should only measure what is the responsibility of the manager;
- they should not be independent of the environment in which the decisions are made;
- they should be comprehensive and reflect important areas of concern;
- they should be limited to key areas of performance;
- they should be relevant to the specific needs and conditions of the organization;
- and they should be realistic in the targets they set.
  (Jackson, 1988: 12)

Although there are dangers in too mechanical an interpretation of PIs, difficulties of definition, problems of measuring output, and of ensuring that a PI will not produce undesirable outcomes, Jackson believes that well designed and implemented measures can improve value for money (economy, efficiency and effectiveness) and have a part to play in improving the delivery of public services. That said, in his conclusion he stresses their limitations.

> Performance indicators are a means of assisting responsible management to make efficient decisions. They are not, however, a mechanical substitute for good judgment, political wisdom or leadership.
> (*Jackson, 1988: 15*)

Of course, a cynic (or a realist) might point out that good judgement, and wise leadership have been somewhat thin on the ground in a couple of thousand years of recorded human history. ◆

Summative evaluation

In the next phase of Palumbo's policy cycle (impact), the evaluative information is 'summative'; that is, it is seeking to measure how the policy/programme has actually impacted upon the problems to which it was addressed. We have already noted the role of impact assessment (IA) in reviewing tools for decision analysis in Part Three. These included IEA and Technology Impact assessment. In undertaking IA at the post-implementation phase of the cycle, evaluation seeks to arrive at an estimate of the net and gross effects of intervention. This is essentially a comparative mode of inquiry: comparing, for example, before and after; comparing the impact of intervention on one group and another, or between one group who were the subject of intervention and another who were not (a control group); comparing what happened with what might have happened without intervention; or comparing how different parts of the country experienced different impacts from the same policy. Whatever measurement is used, the quantificationism cannot disguise the fact that evaluating impact is an activity which is knee-deep in values, beliefs, party politics and ideology, and makes 'proving' that this policy has had this or that impact a notion which is deeply suspect. As we shall see in terms of 'termination', the idea that the policy process is driven by a rational calculation of costs and benefits of an impact is not borne out by real life. De Leon (4.6.1) argues for example, that termination is essentially a politically, rather than 'rationally', informed decision which is the outcome of 'evaluation' of impact.

One of the most important models of impact evaluation is the idea of measuring impact by conducting something like an experiment. Experimental approaches in evaluation research involve the attempt to apply the principles of experimentation to social and other problems. This involves a variety of techniques. An experiment may seek to study a problem before and after intervention. It may use a control group and an experimental group, which may then be compared with one another so as to measure the effectiveness of an intervention in relation to a (control) situation in which no intervention took place.

The 'textbook' example is that of the experiment in the USA in the late 1960s to test the effect of negative income tax on the willingness to work. A sample of 1,300 families in five cities in New Jersey and Pennsylvania were divided into experimental and control groups to test the effect of a guaranteed income on the work habits of disadvan-taged groups. Data were collected over a three-year period. At first the data were interpreted as demonstrating that a negative income tax had no real effect on the motivation to work (Watts, 1969). However, the same data, when later re-worked by RAND, arrived at very differ-ent conclusions (Dye, 1987: 368–9). All this suggests that experimenta-tion does not produce conclusive data: interpretation is all. Experi-mentation has a number of problems as a mode of evaluation:

- Society is a complex thing. How can an experiment be conducted which excludes so many factors? What judgements are involved in setting the parameters of which factors will be examined?
- Given the above, how can research be designed to obtain 'good' results when experiments have cash limits and time constraints?
- Not only are there cost and time constraints, the experiment also depends on management and implementation problems.
- Can social experiments be conducted which involve comparing groups which may, in all probability, be very different to one an-other?
- In social experiments people may be/will be conscious of being experimented upon (the so-called Hawthorne effect).
- What of moral issues? Is it right that one group will be deprived of resources or another may be a guinea pig? People may not like the idea of being experimented upon.
- From a political point of view, experiments take time. Policy-makers may not have the time, and when at last an experiment is com-pleted, the situation may have changed.

Critics of experimental evaluation would add more to this list (Edwards *et al.*, 1975; Scioli and Cook, 1973). However, experimentation may well be appropriate and 'scientifically' sound in some circumstances. Bobrow and Dryzek (1987: 148) suggest that such conditions are that 'there must be a well structured, reasonably static, and highly decom-posable policy problem at hand, with consensus on the criteria to be applied to it. Such circumstances are increasingly rare in today's world.'

Even so, quasi-experimentation by government in highly complex problems (such as urban policy) is something which continues to prove an attractive option. Dye makes a strong case based on practi-calities: 'It is exceedingly costly for society to commit itself to large-scale programs and policies in education and welfare, housing, health and so on, without any real idea about what works' (Dye, 1987: 372). This Popperian view (see 1.6), that change should be piecemeal so as to test the efficacy of change, has its supporters (Rivlin, 1971; Campbell, 1969, 1973, 1982; Saxe and Fine, 1981).

❖ The case for experimentation

Donald Campbell has been an influential advocate of experimentation as a means of improving evaluation. Campbell has argued for a more widespread use of experimental methods and advances the idea of an 'experimenting society' in which 'dialectic of experimental arguments' (Campbell, 1982: 330–1) would create a policy process which was committed to idealism in means as well as ends. In the experimenting society experimentation would permit a high level of learning and a focus on problems, rather than the advocacy of solutions. In enlarging on Campbell's vision, Saxe and Fine (1981) argue that in shifting from policy advocacy to policy experimentation policy-making would accord a larger role for science and research, and more-active participation by citizens. The experimenting society is also, he maintains, a response to the limited resources facing policy-makers and public, and a way of addressing the problem of inequity in access to power. Harold Lasswell was also a great advocate of experimenting as a way of assessing the worth of policy innovations (see Lasswell, 1963). He termed this method of small-scale experimentation 'prototyping'. He took part himself in two such 'prototype' experiments concerned with introducing democratic decision-making: the Vicos project in Peru and at the Yale Psychiatric Institute. The former was concerned with the Vicos Indians in Peru (see Dobyns *et al.* (eds), 1964) and the latter was an experiment in participation in a psychiatric hospital (see Rubenstein and Lasswell, 1966). For Lasswell, small-scale (official/unofficial) experimentation was not only a way of trying out ideas and evaluating reforms, it was also a way of building skills and knowledge in the people involved:

> The prototype experience is not only a means of improving institutional practice and scientific knowledge in general; it creates a new body of assets and liabilities that can be utilized to spread or block the specific innovation. Successful prototype situations tend to create an elite of knowledgeable and skilled individuals who can gain further advantages by continuing their activity on behalf of the goal (the 'cause').
> (*Lasswell, 1963: 122*)

For a review of Lasswell's prototyping, see Merelman (1981: 492–6); and Lasswell (1963). ◆

4.5.3   Evaluation and the management of human resources

❖ Some key ideas, terms and texts

'Evaluation' in public policy also involves control through the appraisal/assessment/performance-measurement/monitoring of the people who work in the public sector at both 'street level' and at policy/managerial levels. It is important for students of public policy to understand the sources of these approaches and their underlying values and ideology because they have had a major role in framing the discourse of public-sector 'management'. Essential reading is the work of prominent management theorists, most notably Peter Drucker, the father of 'Management by Objectives' (MBO). In general, one of the most useful surveys of the field to date is Beardwell and Holden (eds) (1994).

A leading textbook in this field, published by the Institute of Personnel Management, Thomason (1988) defines 'performance evaluation' in 'Human Resource Management' (HRM) as involving:

1   The identification of tasks to be performed, together with the criteria to be used to measure successful performance.
2   The evaluation of the performance given, by assessment either of the results where these are measurable, or of input of relevant effort or behaviour where they are not.
3   The determination of the amount of reward, remuneration, or 'reinforcement' to be given to improve, maintain, or advance the current level of performance.
   (*Thomason, 1988: 328*)

On the origins of HRM, see Collin (1994a).

The main contribution of MBO to this model has been in terms of making appraisal less top-down by introducing a more 'participative' approach. Superior and subordinate are involved in a dialogue and negotiation to set targets. Alongside MBO is another range of techniques which come under the banner of Organizational Development (OD). This has been a particularly important field in the making of popular management texts, such as those by Peters and Waterman (1982). The OD approach is aimed at dealing with the uncertainty which faces organizations. If they are to survive and thrive in this chaos, organizations need to achieve a 'good fit' with their environment. OD therefore aims to change the internal environment so as to allow organizations to better master their 'external' environment. The 'people variables' (*sic*) are the main focus of OD consultants brought in to improve the 'flexibility', 'learning' capacities of 'stakeholders' and the 'health' of the organization:

> Instead of top-down approaches to the definition of tasks and other requirements, emphasis is placed on a partnership in decision-taking. Instead of a training approach, a learning facility is provided ... Instead of a bureaucratic structure, a system of cooperation is aimed at.
> (*Thomason, 1988: 494*)

As a learning approach the OD method employs a variety of strategies to develop commitment, self-direction and self-control in the people variables. Thomason (1988: 473–4) expresses these as including:

- decentralization of decision-taking: moving away from centralized systems of control to ones which emphasize decisions close to the point of action and delivery;
- co-operation rather than competition: aiming at less conflict between people in the organization;
- developing systems where conflicts can be brought into the open;
- making people more responsive to the real needs of the situation;
- increasing communication between individuals, groups and departments;
- changing structures and procedures that impede performance;
- improving and developing the capacities of people in the organization.

The 'quality' movement may also be understood as a new form of people evaluation. The idea of Total Quality Management (TQM) is to stress the importance of quality at every level of decision-making and delivery. The aim is to set up systems in which service-providers are driven by 'customer needs' and 'customer satisfaction', rather than by internal needs and assessments. Orginally developed for the production line and mechanical systems, TQM has been adopted in the public sector as a way of building in an ongoing evaluative process in which 'getting it right' is implemented through systems of monitoring and checking, and developing more responsive attitudes amongst staff towards customer complaints. The OECD reported that in 1992 over a dozen countries were adopting quality programmes: Canada, France, Japan, the Netherlands, Finland, Greece, Turkey, Portugal, Spain, Denmark, the UK and the USA (OECD, 1992: 13).

The British Standards Institution (BSI) defines the approach in terms of establishing and maintaining a system 'which will demonstrate to your customers that you are committed to quality and are able to supply their quality needs'. The BSI's standard 5750, published in 1979, became a benchmark for other countries in the 1980s. In 1987 the International Organization for Standardization (ISO) published its ISO 9000 series, which provides a set of internationally recognized quality standards. As developed in the public sector the TQM approach emphasizes steps such as:

- knowing the 'customer';
- designing 'products' and services to meet these needs;
- performance should be backed by a 'guarantee';
- services and products should come with clear instructions;
- delivering on time;
- providing back-up services;
- using customer feedback to check on quality;
- acting on this information.
  (Local Government Training Board, 1989: 42)

Although there are severe limitations on the notion that public services can be driven by 'customer' satisfaction in the same way as the activities of firms in the private sector producing goods and services in a market place (Flynn, 1990: 108–9), the theory of using systems which build in continuous evaluation of the people and programme aspects of the delivery process has proved an attractive addition to the tools of management in the public and 'non-profit' sector (see Stewart and Walsh, 1990; Flynn, 1990; De Sario *et al.*, 1991; Osborne and Gaebler, 1992; Drucker, 1990b; for a critique from the standpoint of labour, see Martin, 1993). ◆

Evaluation literature in public policy is for the most part concerned with the evaluation of programmes and policies. However, in a managerialist framework it also encompasses the evaluation of people *qua* 'human resources'. Alongside the development of MIS evaluation techniques there has also been a growth in the adoption of so-called 'Human Resource Management' (HRM) and Organizational Development (OD) techniques in the public sectors of most industrial countries (OECD, 1992: 11). These techniques of 'people' (as opposed to programme and policy) evaluation drawn from HRM and OD include:

- performance-related pay schemes;
- personnel assessment and appraisal;
- organizational development strategies.

The aim of an HRM strategy is, as one textbook (Thompson, 1990: 307) has it, to change people so as to become more

- committed (commitment can be improved);
- competent (competences can be developed and bring improved product quality and productivity);
- cost-effective (ideally costs should be low and performance high ...);
- in sympathy with the aims of the organization (are the values and expectations of all parties in agreement?).

A key feature of the approach is to integrate 'personnel' management into the corporate strategy by decentralizing the management of human resources (sic) to the level of line managers, rather than separating it off into tasks which are performed by specialist personnel officers and managers. The HRM approach stresses that the aim is to improve 'performance' by developing a sense of commitment in each employee, rather than just compliance to hierarchical command or instruction (Storey, 1989). This increase in commitment is to be achieved through:

- recruiting the right kind of people (see Wright and Storey, 1994);
- an emphsasis on training at all levels (see Holden, 1994);
- regular staff appraisal (see Roberts, 1994);
- rewarding performance (see Roberts, 1994).

The idea of rewarding performance in practice has meant the attempt to link the carrots and sticks of training and appraisal to monetary incentives. As the OECD reported in 1992:

> In New Zealand, performance-based pay regimes have been operating since 1988 with the establishment of a system of ranges of rates for remuneration, but some concern has been expressed about the resulting problems of wage drift and administrative complexity. In Norway, a new pay system has been implemented which permits positions at the same level to have different salary alternatives depending upon performance and other factors. In Switzerland, new legislation was introduced to allow 'due account to be taken of the performance of the civil servant'. In the United Kingdom, the Government is in the process of renegotiating most civil service pay agreements, one aim of which is to provide a more direct link between individuals' pay and their performance. And in the United States, a new act was implemented which includes amongst its major features a requirement to develop and institute systems that strengthen the link between pay and performance.
> (OECD, 1992: 11)

Performance-related pay systems are designed to create a framework in which individuals and/or groups can be evaluated in terms of the extent to which they have met defined and measured goals and objectives. It is a standard tool in the kit of MBO and TQM approaches in the private sector where there exist clear 'bottom lines' of performance in terms of output and profits. Applied in the context of public bureaucracies and services, however, there are problems as to the philosophy that money (and self-interest) is the best kind of motivator. An early advocate of performance pay, Niskanen, thought that by introducing the system into the public sector, self-interest in lowering costs and increasing 'profits' would serve to undermine the desire of public officials to maximize interests by bigger budgets, in preference for bigger pay packets (Niskanen, 1973). So much for the theory.

In practice, however, rewarding by 'performance' is riddled with difficulties. Is money the best motivator of civil servants and professionals in the public service? Who is doing the evaluation? What measures do you take to evaluate performance? How can the 'increased' performance of teachers, nurses or the police be measured? Do you reward individual performance, with all the inherent dangers of creating divisions and resentment? Do you reward groups and 'teams' (*sic*)? Experience suggests that performance evaluation and reward is a political minefield (Osborne and Gaebler, 1992: 156–8) as well as problematic at a level of personnel management (Thomason, 1988: 328–99; Roberts, 1994). None the less, as the OECD survey indicates, it is a minefield which policy-makers across the world are endeavouring to traverse in their quest for greater financial discipline and control over the public sector. Viewed in an historical context, the adoption of HRM techniques such as performance-related pay by the ' new' public sector is the latest in a long line of experiments with rational techniques which began in the 1960s with PPBS, corporate planning and MIS. The main difference is that, whereas the analytical, managerial and corporate planning techniques of previous decades were focused on improving the rationality of decision-making and of the 'system', HRM is concerned with improving rationality (in terms of performance) by changing the motivation, culture and attitudes of the 'humans' who work in the black box of public policy.

❖ Government and the management gurus

The agenda of new public-sector management has been set by two main sources of ideas: economics (public choice) and management. The role of the former in shaping the agenda of public policy has been widely acknowledged, but the impact of management theorists and 'gurus' has been of equal importance. Their influence has been particularly prominent in the way in which the 'people' dimension of evaluation has developed both in practice and in terms of the rhetoric and 'buzz words' which are used in talking about 'human resource' issues. For accounts of the ideas of many of the leading gurus, readers should consult Clutterbuck and Crainer (1990) and Kennedy (1991). Leading management theorists whose ideas have had a role in framing the discourse of public management include:

- **Peter Drucker** (1946, 1954, 1964, 1969, 1974, 1985, 1990b). Without question, the most important modern management theorist. He developed the ideas of MBO in 1946 and has anticipated a number of important trends in the public sector – not the least of which was privatization. Drucker's emphasis on the need to orientate an organization to its customers forms a central tenet of 'new public sector management', as is the idea that structures must follow strategies. Drucker has argued for decentralized structures and self-control as vital to improving management, discipline and (top-down) control. MBO's essential philosophy is that of measurement of performance and quality and the setting of clear objectives to units and individuals.
- **Peters and Waterman** (1982). Without doubt, the single most important source of the ideas which have formed the agenda of public management. Their book *In Search of Excellence* was a publishing sensation and is perhaps one of the most widely read books in the field. By studying some 43 successful companies they arrived at eight characteristics of excellence. The book introduced ideas about culture, flatter and more decentralized organizations, quality, mission, performance and leadership to an audience in the public sector unfamiliar with the management literature from which such notions were derived.
- **Charles Handy** (1976, 1986, 1988). As is the case with Peters and Waterman, Handy is a writer whose books have made management theory and theorists (such as Argyris, Schein and Bennis) popular and comprehensible to 'managers' in the public (and 'voluntary') sector.
- **Rosabeth Moss Kanter** (1977, 1983, 1989). Kanter has been one of the most popular of the modern gurus, and is perhaps best known for the ideas about 'empowerment' in organizations as a strategy for improving performance. She is a severe critic of bureaucratic hierarchy and has stressed the need to decentralize authority, link pay to performance, the importance of creating an enterprise culture and the encouragement of individual enterprise. Staff are not to be viewed as overheads, but as sources of value. Organizations should be seen as partnerships, and in so empowering people and valuing people, the 'post-entrepreneurial' business can become more, rather than less, manageable.
- **W. Edwards Demming** (1982). An American statistician who is credited with laying the foundations of Japanese economic success by preaching his methods of Quality Circles to a receptive post-war generation of managers. The circle – planning, implementation, check and action – was ignored in the US and elsewhere until it became apparent in the 1970s and 1980s that Japan was overhauling the US and other countries. Questions were asked about why Japan had pulled off an economic miracle, and the 'Demming Circle' with its emphasis on the management of quality was identified as being a key part of the answer. In the 1980s the ideas of TQM, or Total Quality Management, became very fashionable and the 'quality' approach quickly found its way into the new agenda shaping the public sector (see, for example, Gaster, 1991). ◆

Evaluation and control

The emergence of HRM in the 'evaluative state' may be seen from a critical perspective as the extension of the power of the state to survey and control organizational processes and their target 'customers' and 'clients'. Viewed in this manner, the development of new techniques can be interpreted as improvements in the capacities of the state to perform what Dandeker (1990: 37) has classified in terms of three key activities:

• information collection, storage and retrieval;
• the supervision of people;
• the monitoring and control of behaviour.

The new managerialism therefore represents a considerable shift in organizational power from the administrator and professional to the 'manager' and the 'accountant' (Miller and O'Leary, 1987) and from 'personnel management' to 'human resource management' (Storey, 1989; Storey (ed.), 1989). This shift signifies that evaluation techniques are essentially modes of altering 'culture' and behaviour, rather than 'systems' or organizational mechanisms. The trend in evaluation has been to move increasingly towards modifying the behaviour of people in organizations, rather than organizations as systems. In this respect the evaluative state is a more developed form of the Tayloristic surveillance. As Dandeker notes:

> as surveillance involves a deliberate attempt to monitor and/or supervise objects or persons, it is to be found in its most developed form in formal organizations which possess an explicitly stated goal(s), together with a formal administrative structure for achieving these goals ... This is one indication of the long-term process of the rationalisation of social action observed by Weber.
> (*Dandeker, 1990: 38*)

Weber's concern was with domination in the various stages of human history. The form which characterised the modern era was that of the rise of 'rational-legal' social domination as opposed to charismatic or traditional forms. With the development of bureaucracy Weber argued that: 'the performance of each individual is mathematically measured, each man becomes a little cog in the machine and, aware of this, his one preoccupation is whether he can become a bigger cog (Weber, in Mayer, 1956: 126–7).

From a Weberian point of view we might argue that the evaluative state is a consummate product of industrial rationalism. Modes of quantifiable information about performance and output are developments which have followed on from the rationalistic foundations of bureaucratic and Benthamite organization. A radical organizational model would argue that the evaluative state is simply a more sophisticated and developed form of surveillance and exploitation (see, for example, Giddens, 1987, 1990; Morgan, 1986; Burrell and Morgan, 1979; Clegg and Dunkerly, 1980).

❖ Control and domination: radical views

HRM and MBO as 'panopticism'?

From the standpoint of Foucault's theories, the development of HRM and MBO may be read as the extension of forms of discipline and control. Foucault took as his model of control Bentham's plan for a prison in which cells were arranged in a 'panopticon' so that people could be kept under constant surveillance. Prisoners would be subjected to a routinized form of control in which every action could be observed. Eventually the power which the guard has over the prisoner becomes internalized, and the prisoner becomes his own gaoler. For prisoners there is no escape from the watch tower, and as they never know if they are being watched, they will be constrained to behave as required all the time:

> the Panopticon must not be understood as a dream building: it is the diagram of a mechanism of power reduced to its ideal form ... it is in fact a figure of political technology that may and must be detached from any specific use ... It is a type of location of bodies in space, of distribution of individuals in relation to one another, of hierarchical organization, of disposition of centres and channels of power ... Whenever one is dealing with a multiplicity of individuals on whom a task or a particular form of behaviour must be imposed, the panoptic schema may be used. It is ... applicable to all establishments whatsoever, in which, within a space not too large to be covered or commanded by buildings, a number of persons are meant to be kept under inspection.
> (*Foucault, 1977: 205–6*)

The main feature of panoptic discipline is that power is not exercised on the 'outside', but is internalized by those who are the objects of control. Are performance indicators, peer review, audit, appraisal and so on, variants of the panoptic 'dream'? Is the 'audit state' a refinement of Bentham's model of a more rational system of controlling people in institutions? Is this why, as Foucault notes: 'prisons resemble factories, schools, barracks, hospitals, which all resemble prisons' (Foucault, 1977: 228)?

Anthony Giddens and organizational surveillance

The issue of how organizations are improving their capacity to control people is an important theme in the work of Giddens:

> Surveillance refers to the supervision of the activities of subject populations in the political sphere ... Supervision may be direct (as in many of the instances discussed by Foucault, such as prisons, schools, or open work places), but more characteristically it is indirect and based upon the control of information.
> (*Giddens, 1990: 58*)

The collation of information is vital for the generation of administrative power, because of the control over the timing and spacing of the activities of individuals whose behaviour is then made a part of the organization. One of the most important connections between the two forms of surveillance is the relation between the accumulation of 'organizational history' and that of personal histories or personal data.
(*Giddens, 1987: 154*)

Stewart Clegg and David Dunkerly, *Organization, Class and Control*, 1980

Applying a hegemonic definition of power (see Gramsci, 2.7), Clegg and Dunkerly argue that management education has been successful in reproducing the ideology of scientific techniques in modern organizations which, they argue, constitutes a powerful form of repression in capitalist societies that controls the supervisory and professional strata, as was achieved by Taylorism and its modern applications for workers in the factory.

Nikolas Rose, *Governing the Soul: The Shaping of the Private Self*, 1990

Rose's book is a critical examination of the growth of forms of organization in which feelings, desires and relationships are the target of new forms of power. Amongst these 'technologies of control' Rose includes the management and accounting techniques which are designed to control and coax ways of thinking and acting which conform to the goals of the organization, but in ways far more subtle than Taylorism and human relations. He marks out for special note the new managerialism heralded by the publication of Peters and Waterman's *In Search of Excellence* in 1982. In this new vision:

> Man is 'waiting for motivation'. Action, innovation, entrepreneurship, excellence, initiative and the rest can be released by a company that fosters autonomy, values, experimentation, creativity, and learns by innovations and evolution ... No longer is there an antithesis between the motives of the individual and those of the organization. The citizen, at work as much as outside it, is engaged in a project to shape his or her life as an autonomous individual driven by motives of self-fulfilment.
> (*Rose, 1990: 115*)

J.A.C. Brown, *The Social Psychology of Industry*, 1986

When originally published in 1954, Brown's book fast became a classic textbook. It reviewed all the developments in the subject and has not been out of print. It displayed great hope that psychology could help in humanizing industry, and that modern industry could function to develop, not repress, the individual. However, in a postscript to the 1986 edition, Hedy Brown concedes that human relations approaches can be subjected to the criticism that they simply ameliorate power relationships, do not consider the conflict of interests, have a narrow production-based idea of psychological needs, and that they view these needs in a closed context.

Michael Power, *The Audit Explosion*, 1994

Commenting on the growth of financial and management audits in Britain, as in other industrial countries, Power argues that we are in the midst of an 'audit explosion'. The author is doubtful about the claims made for audit techniques – such as BS5750, quality circles, value for money, appraisal systems and the like – to actually improve efficiency or quality. The evidence suggests to Power that the most significant aspect of this explosion is the way it has ominously improved the policing and control capabilities of management. He urges that we change course away from systems of quantitative control towards approaches (such as are evident in Japan) which stress qualitative judgements and accountability based on trust.

Stanley Cohen, *Visions of Social Control*, 1985

Like Rose's book, Cohen's analysis of the way in which new and more-invasive methods of control are being developed in the public and private sector has considerable relevance to the development of a critique of the 'evaluative state'. Power (1994) uses it effectively in his discussion of the 'audit society' (see Cohen, 1985: 155–60).

Lenin and Taylor

Taylorism has proved as attractive to the left as to the right. Writing in 1918 Lenin, for example, viewed communism as having much to learn from Taylor:

> We must organize in Russia the study and teaching of the Taylor system and systematically try it out and adapt it to our own ends ... we must take into account ... on the one hand ... the socialist organization of production ... and on the other hand ... the use of compulsion ... (*Lenin, 1972: 25*)

Critical theory and organizations as instruments of domination

Robert Denhardt has done much to apply Habermas's critique of instrumental rationality and the case for 'unfettered discourse' to develop a critical approach to public administration. See, for example, Denhardt (1981a and b); Denhardt and Denhardt (1979); and Degeling and Colebatch (1984). ◆

At the core of evaluation which is focused on 'people' rather than policies or programmes is the belief that more control is needed over bureaucrats and professionals to ensure that, individually and collectively, the objectives which are defined by policy-makers are implemented efficiently and effectively. From a critical standpoint we can read this kind of managerialism as the extension and continuation of Taylorist 'madness' to those 'white-collar' and professional domains which were for so long considered to be different to the factory or the profit-driven office (Doray, 1988). The use of methods of 'evaluation' which had previously been used in the private sector may be said to confirm the theory that what is really at work in capitalist society is a process of Taylorist de-skilling (see Braverman, 1974), which began in the factories of Victorian Britain and continues apace in contemporary 'post-industrial'/'post-entrepreneurial' public institutions in which professional autonomy and bureaucratic rationality are being challenged and eroded.

❖ Evaluating managerialist reforms

Given the emphasis on performance and result assessment under the new managerialism, it remains disappointing that, even while recognizing the difficulties associated with evaluation, many member countries continue to report no formal or systematic monitoring or evaluation of their public sector management reform exercises. The United States observes that many reforms are regularly monitored and that progress is reported publicly, but there is less concern with the level/extent of management improvement than with evaluation of the outcomes and results of programmes; and even the use of programme evaluation and cost/benefit analysis as an integral part of policy-making is more exception than the rule ...
(*OECD, 1993a: 16*)

Approaches to the evaluation of management reforms vary widely between countries; however, there are a number of problems in evaluation which the OECD identifies as commonly associated with the exercises:

The lack of easily quantifiable data:
- difficulties of measuring progress in productivity, efficiency and service delivery fields;
- problems of collecting and analysing data on the gap between aims and results, and finding causes;
- difficulties in setting meaningful objectives and measuring outputs;
- high costs of evaluation.

The difficulty of determining direct impacts
- problems of establishing what factors influenced outcomes;
- the political setting of evaluation;
- different priorities and expectations of the groups involved;
- the orientation of evaluation to experimental projects rather than broad reform.

Do performance targets and appraisal actually work?

There is growing evidence to suggest that performance targeting and appraisal may not be all that its advocates promised. A major survey (British Psychological Society, 1994) of the effects of performance techniques argues that performance-related pay and appraisal systems have made a questionable contribution to innovation and creativity. Performance targeting and staff appraisal, the authors suggest, may do far more harm than good by stifling, rather than stimulating, creativity. In other words, the public sector may be moving in the wrong direction entirely. At a time when serious questions may be asked as to the efficacy of MBO/HRM techniques in changing organizations and improving individual and corporate performance in the 'private' sector, it appears that policy-makers all over the world are seeking to reform their arrangements to imitate the 'motivational' (*sic*) approach adopted in the business world.

For a review of research on the success of performance appraisal see Roberts (1994). ◆

4.5.4 Alternative frameworks for evaluation

The analysis of evaluation and the techniques and methods used in evaluation has, like so much else in public policy, been framed by positivist assumptions about knowledge and methods. The fundamental predicate of evaluative techniques is that it is possible to obtain measurements of performance in an objective fashion. These data are then utilized to plan, monitor, control, report and 'evaluate'. However, at the very time when policy-making has been more informed by the ideas derived from managerial evaluation and by the urge to quantify and control, the core principles of evaluation have come under fire from policy analysts. For those who first came to the study of evaluation in the 1970s (as did the present author), the developments of the 1980s and 1990s are somewhat bewildering. As Palumbo and Nachimas (1983: 1) noted:

> The field of evaluation is undergoing an identity crisis. From its initial surge in the 1960s when evaluation research was dominated by a single methodology and evaluation researchers believed that its potential was unlimited, it has undergone a metamorphosis. Rather than a single orientation, a number of alternative approaches to evaluation have sprung up and a nagging doubt about its future has crept into a number of publications.

These doubts about the dominant (positivist, scientistic, quantitative) paradigm were to grow, so that by the mid-1990s the field bears little resemblance to the textbooks of the 1960s and 1970s. It is more fragmented and more alive to the political, value-based nature of the activity. The analysis of a programme or a problem is seen by many critics of the dominant paradigm as essentially a political process, full of values rather than some kind of scientific quest for truth or an objective answer. We have already considered aspects of this critical approach in earlier sections of the book (2.7.3, 3.3.8, 3.10.4, 3.10.5), and readers would be advised to study this section in parallel with the material in those sections (on Paris and Reynolds *et al.*, in particular). In this section we want to take this analysis of critical approaches further by examining the ideas which advance a radically different view of what evaluation – and policy analysis – can be and ought to be in a democratic society. To do this we shall take three approaches to illustrate the themes and methodologies of what can be broadly termed 'post-positivist' evaluation:

- the multiplist approach (Cook, 1985);
- the design approach (Miller, 1984; Bobrow and Dryzek, 1987);
- the naturalistic approach (Lincoln and Guba, 1985; Guba and Lincoln, 1987; Lincoln, 1990).

The multiplist approach

Cook's arguments typify the disillusionment with the methods and politics of evaluation as a form of rational analysis. Cook maintains that as there can be no 'correct' policy option or evaluation we should seek to use multiple measures from several different approaches and methods. As reality is multi-faceted, so the modes of analysis used to evaluate the 'real world' faced by policy-makers must aim to use a wide variety of options and data. Selection will involve 'triangulating' between those which are most useful or most likely to be true. Explanations or options are not 'proved' but pitted against one another so as to 'see which one is superior' or most useful as opposed to which one is 'true'. Social science, Cook believes, is 'concerned not with guaranteeing truth or utility, but with offering defensible interpretations of what is in the outside world' (Cook, 1985: 45). Evaluation in this sense involves testing arguments and claims to knowledge, rather than advancing 'the truth' or 'the correct solution'. As there is no way of proving what is correct, the evaluation process, and the policy process in general, should be predicated on the importance of securing a pluralistic, multi-disciplinary, and open exchange of knowledge: let a thousand flowers bloom, and cross-pollinate!

The design approach

This theme of multiple frameworks is also central to the 'design' approach which may be illustrated by the ideas of Trudi Miller and Bobrow and Dryzek. The design approach may be traced back to the idea that Simon (1969) put forward regarding the way in which a design is both a means for understanding reality as well as acting upon it. 'Design science' is consequently a field of inquiry in which what is made is also what is studied. The design approach begins with this notion that policy-making is an activity which is about the pursuit of values or goals. In this sense it is not unlike the activity of the engineer or the architect. Human beings 'design' the 'reality' which surrounds policy-making, and thus the idea that we can be 'objective' towards a product of human values is an erroneous basis upon which to 'evaluate' a reality which is ever-changing and shaped by the meanings which human beings create and impose on the world. The design approach rejects the idea of analysis as neutral, or the belief that the policy problems can be studied in a positivistic way. If, therefore, we cannot 'observe' in a scientific, value-free sense, we should acknowledge that policy-making is about values and how they may be clarified and achieved. Miller's paper on improving public-sector performance (1984), written from this perspective, constituted a radical departure from the literature concerned with 'performance'. For Miller, improving public performance was a desired goal whose values should be made clear, all the better to apply them in specific circumstances in order to reach the desired goal. Instead of the (bogus) claims that performance measures are 'objective' and 'value-free', Miller argues that we should seek to design the goals in a way which involves the articulation (rather than the obfuscation) of values which can be achieved in different circumstances. In other words, let us clearly define what values we want to attain, rather than dress up goals with the jargon of pseudo-scientific analysis concerned with human behaviour or predictions about the future. By rejecting the whole ethos of 'performance measurement' as a scientific or rational approach to improving the performance of the public sector, Miller provides a much-needed critique of one of the most significant developments in public policy in recent decades: it is essential reading.

A more developed general account of the 'design' approach is put forward by Bobrow and Dryzek (1987). It takes on board several other contributions to the design framework. Other expositions of this approach may be found in Dryzek (1987, 1989, 1990, 1993). Let us begin with a general statement of Dryzek's position:

> one cannot conduct defensible policy analysis without attending also to the political process with which analysis and policy are involved … the myth of neutrality is exploded. Analysts cannot avoid taking sides on very basic issues of political structure. They can choose to side with authoritarian technocracy or with liberal democracy. My own position is that defensible policy analysis must side with open communication and unrestricted participation: in other words, with participatory and discursive democracy.
> (Dryzek, 1993: 229)

The 'design' approach is fundamentally rooted in the apprehension of the political and value-loaded multiple-reality and multi-framed context of policy-making and analysis. In the words of Bobrow and Dryzek, policy design 'like any kind of design, involves the pursuit of valued outcomes through activities sensitive to the context of time and place. These activities revolve around factors that can be affected by the volitions of human beings' (Bobrow and Dryzek, 1987: 19). However, unlike the designer in engineering or architecture, the policy analyst and policy-maker confront a far more complex, messy world in which there are many values and interests and little control. They propose a schema or procedure for policy analysis by design (Bobrow and Dryzek, 1987: 200–11). It is important to note that they do not present this as a mechanical linear set of stages, but as a 'recursive process, in which the latter stages can both advance upon and reopen earlier phases' (p. 211):

1　Address values
  Clarify the values being sought: their complexity, timing, quantity, priority and so on.
2　Capture context
  That is, the milieu external to the policy process, and the policy process within which policy will take effect:
  • complexity;
  • uncertainty;
  • feedback potential;
  • control;
  • stability;
  • audience (who will hinder/advance a policy).
3　Select appropriate approaches
  What frameworks may be used to analyse a problem/policy/programme?
4　Apply the appropriate approaches
  Interpretation of problem and performance goals from the perspective of different frameworks:
  • identification and collection of needed information;
  • invention and stipulation of policy alternatives;
  • assessment and comparison of policy alternatives.

> What is the best (/worst) result an alternative can produce in terms of valued outcomes? How likely is each? What is the range of probable error in these judgements? To what extent will an alternative yield a clear and prompt feedback? Is an alternative robust (that is, capable of doing well across a wide range of future conditions and developments) or is it fragile (easily derailed if the future does not unfold according to expectations)? Finally, how clear or murky is the promise of competing alternatives? (p. 209)

The aim in this process is not to 'evaluate' in the textbook sense, but to examine different ways of looking at problems from the perspective of different frameworks of values and methodology. The focus is on the construction of arguments and the improvement of the 'quality of debate'. Ideally this clash of views will lead to a consensus and synthesis which can inform decisions. Frameworks are tools for discussion and critical dialogue rather than techniques to generate or provide 'answers', 'facts', 'costs or benefits'.

The naturalistic approach

This idea of the development of a critical dialogue between a range of different frameworks is also central to the most radical model of evaluation developed by Guba and Lincoln (1987). Of the three approaches we are considering in this section of the book, Lincoln and Guba are most closely associated with 'evaluation' as a distinct phase of the policy cycle. Cook's and Bobrow and Dryzek's observations really apply to the policy-making process as a whole and the role of social science and policy analysis in that process, whereas Lincoln and Guba have set their arguments very much in the context of evaluation research. They set out what they regard as the four 'generations' of evaluation:

- *Technical*: after the First World War, with the development of intelligence, aptitude and achievement tests, evaluation was seen as a technical exercise of measurement. The role of the evaluater was seen as that of a 'technician'.
- *Descriptive*: during the 1940s a second generation emerged which was focused on describing 'patterns, strengths and weaknesses' of stated objectives. The evaluater's role was, in addition to a technician, a 'describer'.
- *Judgement*: in the 1960s and 1970s evaluation developed into a judgemental science in which objective research and standards were used to measure the efficiency and effectiveness of programmes. The role of the evaluater was now that of a judge.
- Finally, Guba and Lincoln (1987: 208) argue that we are now in the midst of a 'fourth generation' of 'responsive' models of evaluation:

  these models take as their point of focus not objectives, decisions, effects, or similar organizers, but the claims, concerns, and issues put forth by members of a variety of stakeholding audiences, that is, audiences who are in some sense involved with the evaluation.

They include in this movement illuminative evaluation (Parlett and Hamilton, 1972); utilization-focused evaluation (Patton, 1978, 1987) and adversarial evaluation (Wolf, 1979) – as well as their own 'naturalistic' evaluation. What they share is a belief in value-pluralism and the idea that evaluation is a form of negotiation, rather than a search for objective 'truth'. Evaluation in the fourth-generation sense views the constructions of 'stakeholders' as being a primary focus of inquiry, and that in any given evaluation there will be a multiplicity of constructions. It is, therefore, fundamentally a political process in which knowledge is the result of negotiation. It follows from this that evaluation has to be predicated upon wide and full collaboration of all programme stakeholders: agents (funders, implementers); beneficiaries (target groups, potential adopters); and those who are excluded 'victims'; and that there should be an opportunity for all stakeholders to contribute their input to all stages of evaluation, from defining the terms of investigation, its goals, and design; to data collection, analysis and interpretation. Evaluation in this sense is a learning/teaching process and the role of the evaluater is to mediate and facilitate learning and teaching and change. It should be an open, pluralistic and divergent process in which 'realities' are constructed, rather than one in which 'a' reality is being discovered. The aim is for evaluation to provide a dialectical discussion between all concerned parties which ultimately should lead to a consensus or synthesis.

They recognize that there are problems with introducing the fourth-generation approach into a real world (Guba and Lincoln, 1987: 255–7). It is not an approach which can be readily co-opted into existing 'legitimate' approaches. The implications of the naturalistic-qualitative-negotiated evaluation they advocate are that social inquiry involves power relations, which are not so easily changed. The open-endedness and democratic character of the process also raises the issue of time and cost: 'fourth generation evaluations end when time and money run out, and not when some full complement of questions have been asked' (Guba and Lincoln, 1987: 277). All of this suggests that the fourth generation of evaluation research is really offering a critique of liberal democracy and suggesting that new forms of social inquiry can form the basis of a new kind of politics. As Rita Mae Kelly has perceptively observed:

> Politics and policy inquiry are intertwined. Once we have replaced the positivistic foundations of the applied social science approach to policy inquiry with postpositivist multiplism or naturalistic inquiry have we not assumed a new type of politics? ... these new logics of inquiry seem to me to be quite compatible with developing notions of a society of individuals with shared, balanced interests rather than separable, hostile, competitive interests *à la* Thomas Hobbes ... At the moment our methodological foundations for policy inquiry are moving ahead of our ontological understandings of politics and human nature. One consequence of this anomaly is that when the politics of meaning is not recognized in our evaluations and inquiries, elites or their surrogates dominate. Neither truth nor democracy is served.
> (*Kelly, 1987: 294*)

4.6 Change and continuity in policy-making

4.6.1 After evaluation

In terms of a simple policy stage approach, evaluation involves some kind of 'feedback' into the policy process which results in change in policy and programmes. However, we do not have to think too long about this model to appreciate that, to say the least, it is somewhat naive. As Charles Lindblom argues, the policy process is just not that kind of rational machine. Change in policy can rarely be put down to the impact of a rational 'evaluation', or due to the impact of inquiry. As Carol Weiss notes, at best, knowledge about policy problems does not supply answers which change policy directly, so much as

> a background of data, empirical generalizations and ideas that affect the way that policy-makers think about problems. It influences their conceptualization of the issues with which they deal ... Often it helps them to make sense of what they have been doing after the fact ... sometimes it makes them aware of the over-optimistic grandiosity of their objectives in light of the meagreness of programme resources. At times it helps them reconsider the entire strategies of action for achieving wanted ends ...
> (Weiss, quoted in Lindblom, 1990: 270)

Evaluation – as rational inquiry – may shape the way in which the terms of debate are framed, and may well be deployed by participants in order to advance their cause, or their interests, or their definitions of what the problems are. However, there is no convincing story to tell about evaluation as an engine of policy change. The evidence for this rational 'economizing' process (Bardach, 1976) does not support the idea that termination is the result of the kind of evaluative procedures and methods detailed in Rossi and Freeman (1993). As they admit, the role of rational analysis in policy decisions is somewhat limited: 'An evaluation is only one ingredient in a political process of balancing interests and coming to decisions. The evaluater's role is close to that of an expert witness, furnishing the best information possible under the circumstances; it is not the role of judge and jury' (Rossi and Freeman, 1993: 454).

Given this, therefore, one could argue that the criticism of the stagist approach to the policy cycle as unrealistic and misleading is entirely justified. Change in the policy process is infinitely more complex than the 'black box' and 'stagist' models imply. In this section we focus on two aspects of analysing change:

- Change in the 'policy space': how does change in policy goals, values, beliefs, purposes, priorities take place?
- Change in the 'organizational space': what is the relationship between changing values, beliefs, goals, etc. and the organizational or institutional context of policy – and vice versa?

In order to examine these dimensions of policy change we shall use three kinds of approach:

- policy cycle approaches (4.6.2);
- organizational approaches (4.6.3);
- policy change and policy learning (4.6.4).

4.6.2   Policy cycle approaches

❖ Key texts

A good point to start is at the end: Bardach (1976) on termination, and Kaufman (1976) on why government organizations are immortal; then May and Wildavsky (eds) (1978) on the policy cycle. This latter volume contains the important article by de Leon (1978) on termination.

Thence to Brewer (1978); de Leon (1983); Brewer and de Leon (1983); Peters (1986); Hogwood and Peters (1983); de Leon (1987); Hogwood and Peters (1985); Hogwood and Gunn (1984); Hogwood (1992). ◆

For some time the policy cycle approach was somewhat vague about the closing stages of the policy process. After 'evaluation' came feedback, followed by adaptation or termination. However, in the late 1970s more attention was focused on the issue of the 'post-evaluative' stage. In particular, attention was focused on the question of termination: was there termination after evaluation; did policies or organizations die? Two early contributions raised doubts about the problem of death after life. Kaufman (1976) looked at governmental organizations and came to the conclusion that they manifested all the characteristics of immortality. Bardach (1976) examining termination of policies equally found that killing off a policy was not as easy or as frequent as the concept of a policy cycle implied. Later, work by de Leon (1978) also argued that there was a need for a more developed theory of organizational and policy termination. We shall examine these ideas below. In the 1980s the 'stagist' approach was greatly extended and much improved with the contribution of Brian Hogwood and Guy

Peters (1983), who put forward a more complete model of the post-evaluative phase. In this section we shall use their model as providing a 'vocabulary' or framework for analysing policy change.

Their starting point is that change is constantly taking place in the policy process. This may be as the result of a policy evaluation, but it is far more likely to be the consequence of changes in the policy environment, political and bureaucratic learning, or the development of existing ideas and organizational structures (Peters, 1986: 142). Furthermore, change in industrialized democracies is more often the outcome of earlier policies. As the OECD points out: 'With the maturing of the Welfare State, most administration is devoted to implementing policies that were decided upon by previous governments. Public policy has become a crowded field, with complex, overlapping and even competing programmes addressing increasingly closely specified or targeted categories of client' (OECD, 1987: 26). This means that problems and policy changes take place in an existing policy space, with the result that, as Wildavsky noted, policy is often its own cause, rather than something which has been prompted by a new 'problem' (Wildavsky, 1979: 70). (In a sense this is similar to the idea in Popper and Kuhn: see 1.6, 1.8, that problems occur within the framework of a theory/paradigm, rather than outside them.) 'New' policy, therefore, most frequently emerges from existing policy or overlaps with established programmes. Policy change will also be the result of earlier policies which may have changed the conditions, made them worse, or proved inadequate. The constraints of economic growth and public finances will also define the latitudes of manoeuvre in policy change.

Hogwood and Peters propose that we can understand the varieties of change in terms of the following types of change:

- *Policy innovation*: when government becomes involved in a problem or an area which is 'new'. Given the fact that the modern policy space is very crowded, 'new' policy is likely to be framed within the context of existing related policies.
- *Policy succession*: involves the replacement of existing policies by other policies. The change does not involve any fundamental change in approach, but is continuous with existing policy.
- *Policy maintenance*: is the adaptation of policies, or adjustments to keep the policy 'on track'.
- *Policy termination*: is the flip-side of innovation. In termination a policy or programme is abandoned, 'wound down', and public expenditure on that policy is cut. It is (with apologies to Monty Python) a dead policy, a policy that has ceased to be: an ex-policy.

Figure 4.20   Hogwood and Peters's model of policy change

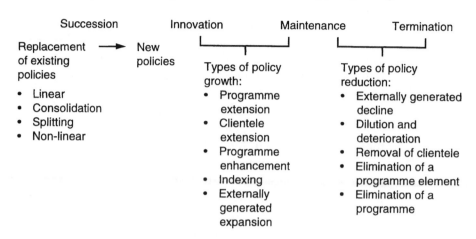

Innovation and termination (new life and death) are on the extremes of a continuum. New policy and the termination of policy are rare events. It is more likely that policy change will occur within the context of policy succession and in a domain between innovation and maintenance, maintenance and termination (figure 4.20).

Let us look at these types of change more closely. The characteristics of policy succession are to be seen in the 'extent to which the policy actors, the process, and the substantive outcomes of the policy succession process are all shaped by the existing policies which succession is intended to replace' (Hogwood and Peters, 1983: 131). They argue that there are four types of succession:

- *Linear*: the direct replacement of one policy/programme/organization by another.
- *Consolidation*: re-packing a number of policies/programmes/organizations into a unified arrangement.
- *Splitting*: unpacking a policy/programme/organization into a number of separate component parts.
- *Nonlinear*: a complex combination of other types of succession.

Succession and innovation are both responses which involve a deliberate (purposive) attempt to make a change. Succession, however, is where policy-makers aim to maintain a large measure of continuity in the means and ends of a policy, and engage in a degree of innovation in goals or organizational arrangements to secure this. Taken to its logical conclusion, succession may end up closer to the policy innovation type. Innovation

involves the entry of government into an activity in which it has not previously been involved. Such a change is purposive in nature, since governments do not normally enter into new fields of activity by accident. Because an area is new, there is no previous organization, law, or public expenditure. All of these have to be established from scratch.
(*Hogwood, 1992: 18*)

However, in this pure (ideal-type) form, innovation is rare. As we discussed in Part Two, the problem for 'new' issues is to mobilize enough support to get them on to the agenda. 'New' issues tend to be framed within the context of existing policy and institutions. Of course, a 'new' policy may be in fact an example of policy 'reincarnation'. On the other hand, policy-makers may choose to dress up an innovation in old clothes in order to get the policy accepted (and vice versa). It is more likely that innovation will involve 'new' mixes in policy instruments. Peters (1986: 7–10) has identified several types:

- laws;
- services;
- money;
- taxes;
- economic instruments;
- suasion.

Innovation in policy may involve moving from 'suasion', as in the case of health education on smoking, to the use of higher taxes, to more spending on health education services, to laws which prohibit smoking in certain places. Innovation therefore may be viewed as a process of change on a continuum with policy maintenance (Hogwood, 1992: 21–3). An existing programme may be extended, broadening its scope – as in the case of the growth of welfare policies. A programme may be extended to a new set of clients, or developed to cover new periods of time or geographical areas. Policy growth may occur as a result of an improvement in the quality or standards of an existing programme. A programme may be maintained by indexing, through automatic adjustments, or be expanded because of externally generated demands (as a result of demographic factors).

❖ Innovation

There is nothing more difficult to take in hand, more perilous to conduct, or more uncertain in its success than to take the lead in the introduction of a new order of things.
(*Machiavelli*, The Prince)

He that will not apply new remedies must expect new evils; for time is the greatest innovator. (*Bacon*, Essays, '*Of Innovation*') ◆

The other dimension of policy maintenance is that of its relationship to policy termination, that is when a policy is being maintained in the context of cutbacks and reductions in scale or resources (Hogwood, 1992: 23–5). Policy on a downward track may be greatly influenced in the first instance by external decline – such as falling numbers of children of school age; policy may decline through dilution or deterioration – fewer staff, holes in the road, poor quality buildings; cutbacks may be effected by taking groups of clientele out of a programme; or a particular part of a programme may be cut. And ultimately this results in the total elimination of a programme (termination) and the introduction of a policy which wholly reverses the previous policy (reversal).

Full circle in the life-cycle: termination

Problems are born, policies grow up, and then wither and die. However, although policy genesis is easy enough to identify, the moment of policy death is less certifiable. Old policies, like old soldiers, never seem to die, and their fading away requires a very sensitive device to measure their demise and final extinction.

❖ Eugene Bardach, 'Policy termination as a political process', 1976

Interest in the termination phase of the policy cycle was expressed most fully in a series of articles in *Policy Sciences* in 1976. In this contribution, Bardach (the editor) sets out to place termination within the context of a political process in which vested interests advance claims of inequity or unfairness against attempts to axe programmes, policies or bureaux. This distinction is, he argues, an important one as too much can be lumped within the concept of termination. He distinguishes between several kinds of termination processes: bangs or long whimpers. Those who advocate termination he sees as falling into three types: oppositionists, who see the policy as a bad policy; economizers, who are concerned with resource allocation; and finally, reformers, who argue for the termination of *x* in order to adopt *y*.

Why is termination rarely attempted? Bardach gives five main reasons:

- Policies are designed to last a long time. Massive investments have been made in them.
- Conflicts over termination are brutal affairs. Anti-termination coalitions are powerful things and policy-makers may not have the stomach for the fight and the blood on the carpet. Change is difficult for publics and processes.
- Who wants to admit they got it wrong?
- The costs of termination may be seen in terms of the damage it may do to other programmes.
- There are no political incentives to terminate policies. Politics rewards innovation.

When can it be done? Summing up the material in the issue, Bardach argues that five conditions are conducive to termination:

- When new governments/administrations come to power.
- Delegitimation of the ideological matrix in which the policy is embedded. The example he gives is of the way in which opinion turned against what Goffman termed 'total institutions'.
- Turbulence, which weakens attachment to existing policies.
- Policies may have been designed to terminate at a certain time.
- Cushioning the blow. Policy termination can be designed so as to lessen the injuries to those affected. ◆

Termination will involve several aspects of policy and organization, which Hogwood and Gunn (1984: 242–5) specify:

- *Functional*: the end of a service or responsibility. This could be where government ceases to have any involvement in the provision of health services, public transport, energy production and distribution. This is a category which may be most closely observed in forms of privatization, where government relinquishes all or some control of a service to the private sector.
- *Organizational*: in this instance policy-makers may choose to abolish an organization. However, as Kaufman (1976) observed back in the 1970s, organizations tend to have immortal qualities about them, and it is likely that, rather than be abolished, organizations will be adapted, merged or split.
- *Policy*: this form of termination occurs when policy-makers abandon an existing approach and adopt a new strategy or definition of the problems.
- *Programme*: policies will incorporate measures or instruments to implement a policy goal. A specific programme or instrument may be axed as part of a wider policy succession, innovation or maintenance.

As we noted earlier, perfect implementation is problematic, and so too is perfect termination. Hogwood and Gunn (1984: 247–8) set out nine factors which make for difficulties in the implementation of termination:

- intellectual reluctance;
- lack of political incentive;
- institutional permanence;
- dynamic conservatism;
- anti-termination coalitions;
- legal obstacles;

- high start-up costs;
- adverse consequences;
- procrastination and refusal.

The interpretation of these factors may be viewed through several frameworks which we have already encountered. For example:

- *Psychological or behavioural*: groupthink (3.7.2), for example, would lead us to conclude that a policy may inhabit a world in which fundamentals are not questioned. A psychological model may argue that the reason termination does not take place is because a policy or programme may come to be a comforter (or 'transitional object') which creates an 'area of illusion' to protect policy-makers from the real world: a doll, an old blanket or teddy bear. A challenge to a policy may be seen as a challenge to a loss of individual or collective identity (Morgan, 1986: 220–3). A policy may fail, but the information about its failure may be ignored, as in the case of cognitive dissonance (3.7.2). The failure may result in even more strident commitment to the policy, not unlike that of a sect whose response to the failure of prophecy is to believe even harder!
- *A power model*: frameworks which focus on power would argue that the factors identified above are the outcome of the interplay and distribution of organizational power and interests within the state and society. A decision to terminate a programme or a policy completely would involve confronting all the interests of those who have much to gain by the status quo. If an innovation means that something has to be cut, which in a zero-sum world is more than likely, political conflicts within government and outside government are inevitable in a liberal democratic society. Thus politics will manifest itself in different forms in different societies, and may be interpreted widely according to the model of power being employed.

Evaluation or ideology as sources of termination?

In practice, therefore, as Cameron (1978) and De Leon (1978, 1982, 1983, 1987) argue, the picture which emerges from actual case studies of termination in government is that termination is not a frequent occurrence, and that when it does happen it is more likely to be the result of ideology and 'reformers' than of evaluation and rational economizers. Values, beliefs, ideology have, they maintain, the dominant role in termination decisions. De Leon (1987: 181) sums up the arguments for the ideological view thus:

> policy termination must be viewed as an exercise in political rather than analytical decision-making, that is, as an exercise in values with most 'adjustments' being made on the margin ... ideology – either revealed or

hidden – is the motivating and defining force behind termination activities...

For this reason, termination (either partial or complete) has invariably been directed towards individual programmes, rather than at whole policies or 'immortal' organizations, because individual programmes are politically much softer targets (De Leon, 1978; Behn, 1978). However, the evidence, even from highly ideologically driven policy change, is that termination – even of a partial kind – is more rhetoric than reality in core areas of public policy. A case in point, for example, is the Thatcher government's actual record on the reform of social security, as compared to its rhetorical claims. As Bradshaw (1992: 98) notes, structures were changed, but 'at the end of the day ... it is really not much different from what it was'. At best, government 'tampered' at the margins in line with what Hogwood and Peters would classify as various combinations of policy maintenance and succession. Policy termination, or partial termination, is not a precise or objective reality. As Bradshaw argues, how the changes to welfare policy in the Thatcher years may be interpreted is a matter of opinion, values or ideology. One man's policy maintenance may be another's 'death of the welfare state'.

Change and continuity are frames of value. In this sense, therefore, although the policy-cycle approach to change provides a convincing structure within which to conceptualize post-evaluative policy-making, by definition the concepts of innovation, succession, maintenance and termination are loaded to the brim with values. What counts as what depends on the kind of value judgements we employ. To a member of the 'new' (sic) right, a radical reversal of policy or a cutback in programmes may be characterized as changing very little – just a bit of policy succession; by another it may be interpreted as the death of social policy, regional policy, health policy, or whatever. In the case of 'market' reforms in health services, we might take the position that such changes have fundamentally subverted the 'core beliefs' of health policy (to the point of termination), or argue that they have served to adapt policy to the demands of the late twentieth century (policy succession). Where you stand depends, invariably, on where you sit – or where you are on a waiting list!

❖ Ramesh Mishra, *The Welfare State in Capitalist Society*, 1990

Mishra argues that, contrary to the expectations of many commentators, the welfare state has not been dismantled in the last decade. Despite the rhetoric, governments have in practice been reluctant, unwilling, unable to go much beyond partial termination of programmes instead of more wholesale change. In his analysis of selected European countries, the US, Canada and Australia, he concludes that the dominant pattern has been of varying degrees of 'retrench-ment' in countries where neo-conservative ideology has been operative, and 'maintenance' in countries where more corporatist modes of policy-making exist. In the case of the US and Britain, where there has been a high level of ideological motivation for change, the termination of welfare policies has been very partial and largely focused on cuts in expenditure and programmes, rather than more widespread and fundamental changes in policy objectives and key organizations. This conclusion, with other analyses of the welfare state, has stressed the continuity of welfare policy rather than the rhetoric of termination which has frequently accom-panied change. However, Mishra contends that this 'unravelling' and 'erosion' of the welfare state must be considered in terms of the longer-term impact of partial termination and fiscal retrenchment. This is strongly suggestive of an incrementalist approach to termination; that is, it may take place over a longer time period than can be discerned in an analysis of a relatively short-run period (death by a thousand cuts).

The literature on the welfare state is instructive for the study of termination, as it illustrates the impact of ideology (as noted by De Leon) and demonstrates that, even when there is a high level of ideological commitment/rhetoric, the capacity of policy-makers to terminate policy in a more 'complete' manner is constrained. It is also apparent that, as De Leon and others have maintained, those programmes that are terminated are those where termination is politically feasible and meets with relatively low opposition from (weak) affected groups. Programmes which benefit the more affluent and more articulate middle-class people may make more 'economic sense' to cut, but are left alone, for fear of upsetting electoral support (Mishra, 1990: 42). ◆

❖ Termination for beginners: some tips

Given that termination appears to be somewhat tricky, what tips can we put together for would-be terminators? The best read on this is Behn (1978), who gives a list of some 12 hints. Hogwood and Gunn, drawing on de Leon, Behn and others, offer five strategies. The clear message from the literature is that the terminator must focus on the political dimensions, rather than on the technical or rational aspects of a 'target'. It is unlikely in the extreme that a devastating piece of analysis will do for a policy, a programme or an organization. So, if termination stands some kind of chance, what factors have to be kept in mind?

- The terminator's best friend is Machiavelli. He has much to say about when to use the knife, axe or poison, against whom, at just the right time, with just the right amount of violence. Don't leave home without him.
- As Machiavelli knew, the best time to terminate is when first coming to power, or when there is a crisis going on. If there is no election due, or no crisis is in sight, then a good terminator will construct a crisis.
- Redefine the problems. Agenda-setting approaches tell us much about how important it is to define the discourse and terms of debate. In terminating, this is a big weapon in the arsenal. If the problems for which a policy/programme/organization was created can be held 'no longer to exist' or to exist in a different form than in the past, the whole rationale and legitimacy of a policy can be subverted.

- Do you do it fast, or slow? Again, Machiavelli has much to teach the student prince. There are advantages and disadvantages to both strategies. If slow, you can build up support and consensus. But it's a long, long way to termination and you may find that, over time, the plan gets derailed. Machiavelli's view was that if it has to be done, do it with the minimum bloodshed. Be economical and be quick. Machiavelli, however, did not live in a pluralist democracy. Slow 'death by a thousand cuts' can be effective in the long term because it can turn the screw a bit at a time. It might even be sold as getting value for money or greater efficiency. However, you know that the policy is not safe in your hands.
- Be nice and caring whilst you are wielding the axe. Termination will cause pain and hardship to people. Show that you are aware of the problems and have plans to minimize them. This, of course, will cost time and money.
- Devolve termination so that there will be incentives for organizations to do their own cutting – in line with your policy – then reward those who make the deepest cuts. Let them keep some money.
- Devise policies with built-in 'sell-buy' dates in the first place. That is, give policies/pro-grammes/organizations a specific length of life (Sun-set laws).
- Discredit the opposition. Again, Machiavelli is a great help on this one. Instead of playing the ball, play the man. If, for example, an 'anti-termination' coalition sets out to wreck the plans, undermine their position by pointing out that they are a self-interested lot who are putting their personal or professional interests before 'THE PUBLIC INTEREST'.
- Divide and terminate: a favourite of the Romans, and of Machiavelli. Exploit the organiza-tional and institutional divisions – or organizational pool – which surrounds a policy or programme. With any luck, they will go for one another in order to secure resources and save you the trouble of having to do the job.
- Go for the weakest. The programmes which are most vulnerable to a termination attack are those which have weak levels of support, or which are aimed at the least powerful in society. If you want to terminate in order to cut expenditure, do not get bogged down in middle-class organized opposition – go for the poor, the disabled, the homeless. This may raise a few ethical problems, but as Machiavelli would advise, in politics it is best to keep morality out of it. ◆

4.6.3 Organizational approaches

Change, as the policy cycle approach recognizes, has an organiza-tional dimension. Policy change may be a consequence of organiza-tional change, or it may be that organizational change itself constitutes a change in policy, through succession, innovation, maintenance or termination. However, how we explain or frame 'change' in organiza-tions is something which requires sensitivity to the fact that there is a multiplicity of models/metaphors which may be deployed to explore what change means, or how and why it has come about. In consider-ing organizational change, therefore, the student of public policy faces, as Golembiewski (1990: 127) observes, 'a complex and contradictory body of analysis' covering the field of public sector organization and behaviour. If we begin by asking a 'simple' question, such as 'What forces bring about change in public sector organizations?', we confront an array of competing accounts of how we should set about answering this question.

From a Weberian point of view, the triumph of bureaucratic modes of organization followed inevitably from the development of modern industrial capitalism. In this model, organizational change was determined by the competition between firms; competition between states, and increasing state control; and the demands for equality under the law. The forms of organizational change in this model may be accounted for in the changes which take place in the drive of industrial societies to attain greater rational efficiency. As capitalism changes, so its modes of organizational rationality also change. As a model it seems to explain the decline of the 'public administration' paradigm and the rise of the 'management' paradigm. For Weber, the drive towards rationality would produce a capitalism composed of large bureaucratic state and market organizations. The fate of mankind was thus to be imprisoned in an 'iron cage' of bureaucracy until, as he put it in his essay 'The Protestant Ethic and the Spirit of Capitalism', the 'last ton of fossilized coal is burnt' (Weber 1930: 181–2).

The relationship between organizational change and industrial society raises the issue of what impact a 'post-industrial' society may have on the pattern of organizational change. What happens when the last ton of coal is burnt, or when the last coal miner is made redundant? Analysis of organizational change from a 'post-industrial' perspective would contend that in the conditions of a 'post-modern' world, organizations will become and are becoming more diverse. Stewart Clegg (1990), for example, argues that a main characteristic of 'post-Fordist' capitalism is that organizations are tending to exhibit less convergence, and more divergence in how they respond to the new conditions of the late twentieth century. No one model, he argues, can satisfactorily explain the changes which have taken place to modern, or rather 'post-modern', organizations. Far from capitalism producing similar organizational forms around the world, as some believed it would (Chandler, 1962), the reality of modern capitalist organizations is that there is a great variation in the ways in which different cultures construct and reproduce organizations. Clegg argues that the 'post-modern' organization is tending towards change in directions such as less 'bureaucracy', less hierarchy, more emphasis on markets and 'empowerment', greater flexibility and intra-organizational interactions (Clegg, 1990: 203). Using the ideas of 'post-Fordism', Hoggett (1987) maintains that changes in modes of production which point towards a 'post-Fordist' world, in which there is a shift from mass production, centralized organizations and standardized products, towards 'networked' and decentralized organizational structures are impacting upon the public sector. Local government, he contends, is changing its modes of organization as these 'post-Fordist' forces bring about organizations which are staffed by fewer people; less hierarchical and 'flatter'; more decentralized; multi-tasked; based on 'team' work; more flexible; more information-driven; and more responsive to citizens *qua* 'customers'.

Critics of these kinds of arguments advanced by the 'post-modernists' *et al.*, contend that the idea that modern society is 'post' is a matter of opinion. As Christopher Hood argues with respect to new public-sector management (NPM) in Britain and elsewhere:

> Skeptics may doubt whether there really is a strong link between change in the government sector and changing technologies in the wider world … if 'post-Fordism' explains NPM, what needs to be explained is why NPM has developed in countries which were never really 'Fordist' in the first place – particularly New Zealand, as the country which has perhaps taken NPM the furthest.
> (*Hood, 1990: 207*)

Sayer (1989), on the other hand, takes issue with the notion that modern industry is 'post-Fordist', and asks whether the term itself is not very helpful for understanding change. 'Regulationists' dispute the theory that change in the organization of the state is the result of technological forces, maintaining that the adoption of so-called 'post-Fordism' in the public sector has more to do with the response of politicians to economic crisis by regulating the state so as to facilitate the survival of capitalism. (For a review of this debate, see Cochrane, 1993a: 81–93.)

From the present author's point of view, I tend to agree with Harvey (1992) as to the unsatisfactory nature of post-industrialism/Fordism/modernism as a framework for explaining organizational change. If we examine the sources of organizational reform in the public sector it is clear that they spring from very industrial/Fordist/modernist approaches, most notably MBO and TQM. This is not to say that organizational change has incorporated or 'quoted' elements of post-industrialism/Fordism/modernism, such as 'flatter' organizations and 'decentralization'. But this has taken place (like McDonaldization) in the context of the dominant paradigm: Taylorism (cf. Ritzer, 1993).

Change and contingency

Contingency theorists would argue that the fact that McDonalds does not conform to the 'ideal type' of the post-Fordist/modern/industrial organization confirms that what is important in understanding organizational change is the way in which organizations change in or-

Figure 4.21   Change and contingency

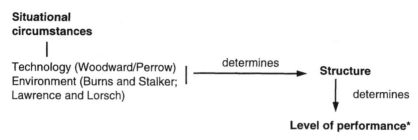

der to meet the demands of different environments and technologies. Approaches which focus on the impact of technology on organizations (Woodward, 1965; and Perrow, 1965) would therefore expect variations in the way in which they develop a 'good fit'. Although deterministic – as with some post-Fordist arguments – the contingency approach would expect no common pattern or type of post-Fordist (or whatever) public-sector organization. This would also be the case if we employ contingency theories which point to the importance of the organization shaping itself to fit its wider environment (Burns and Stalker, 1961; Lawrence and Lorsch, 1967; see figure 4.21).

However, from the point of view of the public sector, these theories of how firms and businesses change to fit their environments or are shaped by technology are somewhat deficient. They do not consider the issue of power, something which is vital in the analysis of organizations which are not as free to change as are firms in the private sector. The main source of change in the public-sector organization comes from decision-makers who have the power and legitimacy to bring about change – or at least to attempt to bring about change. Here two critiques of the contingency theories of Woodward and of Lawrence and Lorsch have a greater relevance to understanding and explaining how and why change comes about in the organizations which compose the public sector: strategic choice and population ecology.

Strategic choice and change   The strategic choice theory, associated with John Child, argues that organizations are not the kind of powerless things which contingency models suggest. The key dimension missing from their analysis is the way in which those with power *perceive* the environment, and thence make strategic choices as to the criteria of performance and organizational structure which they believe will best fit the environment as they see it. As he notes, change in an organization is

[an] essentially political process in which constraints and opportunities are functions of the power exercised by decision makers in the light of ideological values.
(*Child, 1972: 2*)

This model, in which power and ideology have the central role in framing the perception of the environment and choices about structures, has a clear applicability to the public sector wherein decision-makers – top bureaucrats and politicians who form the 'dominant coalition' – shape (in Dunleavy's sense) the organization's structure and objectives in the context of how they construct the reality of the environment (figure 4.22).

Figure 4.22   Strategic choice and change

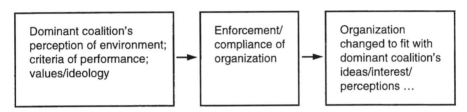

In addition to this construction of the image of the environment, decision-makers also have the capacity to select the kinds of environment in which they choose to operate. (Business decision-making involves choosing what markets to enter; educators decide which courses they teach; trade unions decide what kind of members they want.) Decision-makers in large organizations (such as government) also 'command sufficient powers to influence the conditions prevailing' by manipulating the environment (Child, 1972: 40).

❖ **Is the environment 'outside' or 'inside' an organization?**

Hall's definition of the 'environment' (1977: 304–12) includes the following dimensions or conditions:

- technological;
- legal;
- political;
- economic;
- demographic;
- ecological (physical and organizational);
- cultural.

But where are these conditions? Contingency theory assumes that the environmental conditions are essentially 'external' to the organization. The aim of change is to bring about a better 'fit' with these conditions.

However, the strategic-choice model raises the issue of how environments are also manufactured and manipulated by decision-makers. This idea is suggestive of the argument put forward by Morgan (1986: 235–45). Organizations have images of themselves which they project on to the 'environment'. As 'self-referencing' they may be said to be shaping their image of environmental reality in order to fit the goals, objectives, values, beliefs, ideologies that frame decision-making (figure 4.23).

Figure 4.23   The organization and the environment

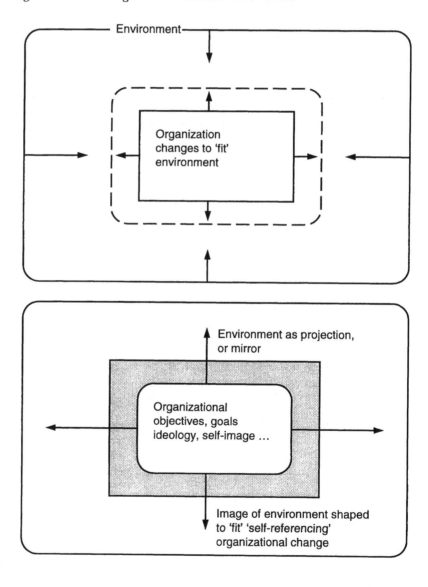

In this case, organizational change involves understanding the power of the dominant decision-makers to frame an image of 'the real world'. Thus, if the 'real world' is held to be a set of conditions (technological, legal, political, economic, etc.) by the 'dominant coalition', change takes place to fit this analysis/ideology of the supposed 'real world'. ◆

An ecological perspective The critique offered by the population ecology model is informed by the kind of determinism which is rejected by Childs, but none the less it offers a framework which does take more account of factors which have considerable relevance to the experience of change in public-sector organizations. Population ecology rejects the idea that organizations have the power to fit themselves to the environment, which is central to the model put forward by the contingency school. The population ecology model focuses on the power of the environment to determine organizational change (Aldrich, 1979; Freeman, 1982; Hannan and Freeman, 1977). The model is essentially informed by the idea that evolution in the organizational world is like that which takes place in the natural world: it's a jungle out there. In this jungle the fittest survive, natural selection takes place, organizations compete, survive, adapt or decline and die. In this fight for survival the environment itself picks winners and losers, and organizations have to secure the necessary resources in order to exist. This approach has had a major impact on the analysis of organizations in the public sector in the use of 'resource dependency' theory (Pfeffer and Salancik, 1978). We have examined this approach earlier

Figure 4.24 A population ecology model

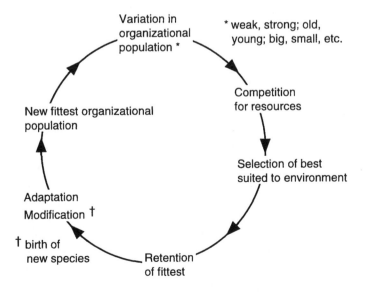

(4.3.6). As with strategic choice, the population ecology model is one which lends itself to explaining the way in which organizations change in the context of power relations (figure 4.24).

These frameworks provide coherent stories of the hows and whys of modern organizations. However, for the student of public policy, explanations and theories of organizational change are perhaps less significant than the fact that 'new' forms of organizational rationality, efficiency, calculability and control in business and industry have served as models for change in the public sector. As Morgan (1986) notes, important examples of the sort of theories which were to influence public-sector changes in many countries in the 1980s and 1990s were conducted outside the context of organization theory, even though they did confirm a good deal of the contingency approach. Much change has therefore come about in theory and practice as a result of imitation. In theoretical terms it has meant that 'public-sector management' has been driven by ideas borrowed from management in the private sector (Metcalfe, 1993), and consequently as a subject it has manifested a large measure of eclecticism (Gunn, 1987).

In the practice of modern government it means that change has largely been inspired by what are seen as examples of 'excellence' (*sic*) and success in the business world from around the world. The institutionalist approach provides a convincing explanation of why this imitation of success and excellence has been the source of major change in public-sector organizations. A Weberian analysis of the changes which have taken place in the public sector might argue that it is a manifestation of the bureaucratic imperative towards co-ordination and control. Meyer and Rowan (1977) offer a different framework, which posits that change comes about as organizations incorporate the legitimating 'myths' and 'ceremonies' which are present in their environment (composed of an organizational network) in order to secure success, survival and resources.

New public-sector management techniques and reforms, therefore, may be seen as myths and ceremonies which, if adopted and performed, will lead to added legitimacy, stability and resources. These myths and ceremonies over time will tend to make institutions more alike as they become isomorphic with their environment. Change in this sense may be seen as less the outcome of Weberian rationality, so much as adopting to adapt: performing those ceremonies which the organization must be seen to do, and going along with the myths which construct and legitimate what 'efficiency' means. Conformity means success, departure from dominant myths and ceremonies spells failure (figure 4.25).

Figure 4.25   Change and the enactment of myth

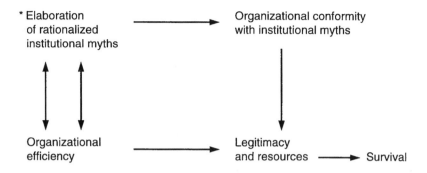

* eg: market myths; Performance Indicator ceremonies

Source: Adapted from Meyer and Rowan (1977)

Di Maggio and Powell (1983, 1991) also developed this idea of 'institutional isomorphism' as an explanation for organizational change. Their isomorphic model supposes that organizations exist in a 'field' of 'suppliers, resource and product consumers, regulatory agencies and other organizations that produce similar services or products' (Di Maggio and Powell, 1991: 65). Fields are the result of a four-fold process of 'structuration' involving the emergence of structures of interorganizational domination and coalition; an increase in the information load of organizations in a field; and the development of a mutual awareness of participants in that field. Once organizations are structured into a field, either because of competition, the state or by professions, forces emerge which make them increasingly like one another. Isomorphism is that process wherein organizations are shaped to resemble other units which face the same conditions. This change may take place through three mechanisms (Di Maggio and Powell, 1991, 61–4):

- *Coercive*: formal and informal pressures which are exerted on organizations by other organizations upon which they are dependent. It also includes cultural expectations in the society within which organizations are located.
- *Mimetic*: in conditions of uncertainty, the change may be the result of copying or imitating other organizations which are seen as offering a solution or model.
- *Normative*: professionals operating in organizations may change their organizations so as to ensure that they resemble the preferred or dominant organizational pattern in the field.

The model has two levels of prediction: organizational and field:

- *Organizational level* (Di Maggio and Powell, 1991: 74–6)
    1   The greater the dependence of an organization on another organization, the more similar it will become to that organization in structure, climate and behavioural focus.
    2   The greater the centralization of organization A's resources supply, the greater the extent to which organization A will change isomorphically to resemble the organization on which it depends for resources.
    3   The more uncertain the relationship between means and ends, the greater the extent to which an organization will model itself after organizations it perceives as successful.
    4   The more ambiguous the goals of an organization, the greater the extent to which the organization will model itself after organizations that it perceives as successful.
    5   The greater the reliance on academic credentials in choosing managerial and staff personnel, the greater the extent to which an organization will become like other organizations in its field.
    6   The greater the participation of organizational managers in trade and professional associations, the more likely the organization will be, or will become, like other organizations in its field.

- *Field level* (Di Maggio and Powell, 1991, 76–7)
    1   The greater the extent to which an organizational field is dependent upon a single (or several similar) sources(s) of support for vital resources, the higher the level of isomorphism.
    2   The greater the extent to which the organizations in a field transact with agencies of the state, the greater the extent of isomorphism in the field as a whole.
    3   The fewer the number of visible alternative organizational models in a field, the faster the rate of isomorphism in that field.
    4   The greater the extent to which technologies are uncertain or goals are ambiguous within a field, the greater the rate of isomorphic change.
    5   The greater the extent of professionalism in a field, the greater the amount of institutional isomorphic change.
    6   The greater the extent of structuration of a field, the greater the degree of isomorphism.

The virtue of the institutional approach offered by this isomorphic model is that it provides a framework with which we can analyse the interaction of processes of internal and external change. In terms of the themes addressed in this book, it offers a plausible explanation of how important changes have come about in the structure and behaviour of the modern public sector, and its relationship to the private and voluntary spheres. Of particular importance are the predictions about the role of uncertainty and ambiguity leading to the adoption of models which are seen to be successful. The changes which have taken place in the public sector in various countries towards a more 'managerial' approach to decision-making, and especially to delivery, is supportive of the idea that in conditions of uncertainty and ambiguity models of success will be powerful shapers of organizational change.

The fad for 'excellence' in the 1980s is one example of how public sectors in conditions of considerable uncertainty were quick to fix upon models which offered a successful alternative. Another aspect of the isomorphic model which we may consider a convincing interpretation of what has happened in the public sector is the way in which organizational dependence within a field is a powerful force for convergence. The three mechanisms for isomorphism also provide a useful frame to examine the dynamics of change in the delivery of public policy. Much has been the result of coercion; that is, governments have sought to change the structure, culture, goals and mission of public bureaucracies and professionals. Alongside this coercion has been a good deal of imitation: the public sector has sought to copy from 'best practice' and successful approaches and techniques from the private sector.

In all this the normative pressures have also been of significance. Professionals have a natural interest in ensuring that organizations have a uniformity and similarity which facilitates movement and professional standards. Professionals act to shape organizations so that universities become like one another, and hospitals and schools have common procedures, career paths and reward structures. Competition between organizations that employ large numbers of professionals ensures that they will seek to become more like one another so as to attract staff and customers/users/clients.

The model also provides a framework for understanding the pressures which are shaping the relationship between the voluntary and public and private sectors, in which the voluntary sector is coming under pressure to 'learn' from and shape itself in the image of those organizations upon which they are dependent for resources (Butler and Wilson, 1990). The strategic choice and resource-dependency approaches, therefore, are not entirely incommensurate with this institutionalist position adopted by Di Maggio and Powell. Strategic choice would argue that it is the decision-making coalitions that have the power to bring about isomorphism and construct an image of the environment. Resource dependency would also suggest that this process is one which takes place in an environment in which there are powerful shaping and determining forces as well as powerful organizations, and weak organizations which are highly resource-dependent and are more likely to be shaped in line with a dominant organizational model.

❖ Promoting and managing change

The managerial approach to change is concerned with 'making it happen', that is, how change may be achieved and how resistance to change may be overcome (see Hogwood and Gunn, 1984: 256–8). How this is approached will clearly depend on the operative management 'metaphor'. For the public sector in recent years managerial approaches to change have come to have an important place in discussions of change. For the most part debates on change have come to be framed by the discourse of private-sector management (for a review of management approaches to change, see Wilson, 1992).

As we noted earlier, the Peters and Waterman (1982) book on excellence is generally considered to be the most influential of texts in the development of approaches to change in the public sector. For a review of the managerial frames for understanding and achieving change, readers are recommended to consult any of the well-established texts used in management courses (see Huczynski and Buchanan, 1991: 520–46). Within this framework two central ideas tend to predominate: culture and leadership.

The managerial approach has laid great stress on changing the 'culture' in the public sector so that it is more business-like, and less bureaucratic in a Weberian (ideal-type) sense (see Metcalfe and Richards, 1987). The genesis of the cultural approach may be dated to the early 1980s with the publication of Peters and Waterman (1982) and Deal and Kennedy (1982). The cultural approach stressed the importance of beliefs, values, attitudes, norms and assumptions in the analysis of how organizations work, rather than environmental or structural factors. At a time when the public sector was coming under fire – especially from the public-choice school – the appeal of the cultural approach was that it offered models of successful organizational cultures which could serve to shape new forms of public-sector organization/management. From the cultural perspective, change is less a process which involves the structures of the public sector so much as the assumptions and attitudes (or rites, ceremonies and rituals) which underpin those structures (Huczynski and Buchanan, 1991: 466), from which it follows that change may be read as a 'learning process' which enables the organization to adapt and innovate (Schön, 1971).

Allied to this cultural perspective on change is the role of leadership in bringing about change. As Lane (1987: 47) has noted, the call for 'leadership' in the public sector from the 1980s onwards contrasts strongly with the demands for participation as a mode of change in the 1970s. The managerialist approach has laid considerable stress on the role of leadership in facilitating change. Again, students are referred to the sections on leadership in management texts for the varieties of approach to the issue of leadership (Huczynski and Buchanan, 1991: 477–519). This emphasis on leadership in the managerialist paradigm raises important questions as to the differences between change in the public and private sectors. Lane (1987: 61), for example, suggests that although the lines of demarcation between leadership in the public and private sectors is problematic in a modern mixed economy, there remain great differences in the goals and environments of the two sectors. The private-sector leader's goals are those of private interests, whereas the leader in a public-sector organization has a wider 'public interest'; at the same time, the public sector environment is less subject to sudden change than is the leader in the private sector business. However, the arguments of Clegg (1990) point towards conditions in which the stability of the environment for both the public and private sectors in conditions of post-modernity is such that rapid change is a common fact of life for both the leader in the public sector organization and the leader in a business. And in such conditions of rapid change and uncertainty, the public sector's imitation of the private sector in managing change in terms of culture and leadership seems to confirm the predictions of the isomorphic model advanced by Di Maggio and Powell (1983 and 1991).

Kaufman (1991; see also 3.7.7 and 4.3.8) argues that we have to understand the relationship between change and conflict if we are to manage change successfully. She posits the model which we illustrate in figure 4.26.

Figure 4.26   Change and conflict

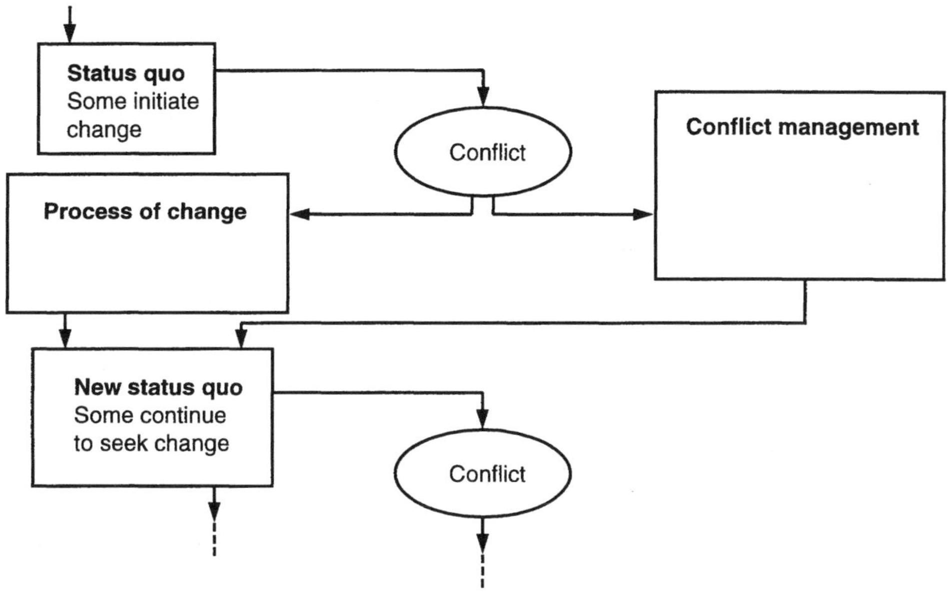

Source: Adapted from Kaufman (1991: 130)

The process of change will, she argues, involve different stakeholders, with varying levels of power, representation, resources and kinds of relationship. It will be shaped by the environment, and decision rules over time (see 3.7.7). In order to manage conflict, stakeholders will engage in unilateral moves (litigation, press releases and appeal to rules) and joint moves (communication, negotiation, and mediation). ◆

4.6.4   Policy change and policy learning

In our discussion of the policy cycle approach to change (4.6.2) we observed that the categories used to examine 'types' of change are problematic in terms of how they may be defined. Termination, succession, maintenance and succession, we suggested, were concepts whose meaning could vary from one value or belief system to another. Does the use of such a framework of 'ideal types' of change constrain our understanding of a process which could be viewed as essentially about how beliefs change? Is it not, perhaps, *beliefs* about policy which need to be analysed rather than the 'types' of change? The approach developed by Sabatier and Jenkins-Smith (eds) (1993), to which we have frequently referred, strongly suggests that the key to understanding (and predicting) policy change is the dynamics of beliefs and policy learning:

> Policy-orientated learning involves relatively enduring alterations of thought or behavioural intentions that result from experience and which are concerned with the attainment or revision of the precepts of the belief system of individuals or of collectivities ...
> (Sabatier and Jenkins-Smith (eds), 1993: 42)

Their approach to learning – and indeed the 'network' approach in general – owes much to Heclo, who argued that:

> The challenge is not to decompose process or content but to find relationships which link the two, not to reify collectivities into individual deciders but to understand the networks of interaction by which policy results. A perspective which views policy in terms of learning and adaptation offers, I believe, the greatest promise for advances in policy studies which will be both analytic and realistic.
> (Heclo, 1972: 106)

Sabatier and Jenkins-Smith argue that it is the belief system which is 'the template against which change in policy coalitions and policy content is to be measured ' (Sabatier and Jenkins-Smith (eds), 1993: 54). The AC framework, therefore, directs our attention from thinking in terms of stages from evaluation to termination towards a view of change as a process informed and driven by the interaction of a policy subsystem and external events and stable parameters. Change within this model is conceptualized as involving the way policy subsystems 'learn'. Applied to the evaluation–termination literature, the model successfully predicts what appears to be a common conclusion of stagist analysis: that a policy core will not change signficantly over time except at those times when there is a major shift in the beliefs of dominant subsystem coalitions. Change, it predicts, is more likely to take place at the level of secondary aspects of policy belief. (This theme of significant change as a rare event is also borne out in the 'punctuated equilibrium model'.)

The learning models provide an integrative framework for viewing change in the policy process. This may provide a new common ground for students of public policy and organizations, concerned with questions such as: how do policy-makers 'learn'?; how can public policy facilitate a process of organizational learning? how can public policy promote a wider social learning? and how can learning be 'speeded up'? These questions have been addressed in a wide variety of forms.

Two overlapping models may be identifed here: the organizational model, and the social learning model.

❖ Policy learning in organizations

Organizational models of policy learning focus on the way in which people and policy-makers in organizational contexts learn. (For the HRM perspective on learning, see Collin, 1994b.) The key texts for the debate (in addition to Sabatier and Jenkins-Smith (eds), 1993) in public policy include the following, roughly in order of date of publication:

- Deutsch (1963)
- Vickers (1965, 1968, 1983)
- Beer (1966, 1975)
- Etzioni (1968)
- Schein (1969)
- Schön (1971)
- Hampden-Turner (1971)
- Argyris and Schön (1978)
- Argyris (1985)
- Etheridge (1981, 1985)
- Metcalfe (1978, 1981, 1993)
- Browne and Wildavsky (1984, 1987)
- Morgan (1986)
- Metcalfe and Richards (1992)
- Lindblom (1990)
- Lindblom and Woodhouse (1993)
- Haas (1990)
- Collingridge (1992) ◆

In public policy terms, the learning approach has been most developed by Sabatier and Jenkins-Smith. Deutsch and Vickers (see 3.7.5, 3.7.6) were among the first to apply ideas about learning to the policy process. Stafford Beer's work was an influential source of the cybernetic approach to learning about learning from living (and man-made) 'self-organizing' systems. Etzioni's (1968) book *The Active Society* – which has come into its own in the 1990s – argued for a learning polity in which apathy could give way to a more active involvement of citizens in the formation and execution of public policy. In order to foster this increase in participation, he recommended major reforms in the organization of government.

Schein and Hampden-Turner developed their ideas about the organization as involving the idea of learning from a business/management background and broke new ground in raising the issue of how learning takes place and how it might be improved. Schein as a business consultant argued that ideally the relationship between client and consultant should be one in which a process of 'mutual learning' can grow. Hampden-Turner advocated a shift towards 'cellular' organizations in which interactive learning could take place more effectively. One of the key books for the 1970s and beyond was Schön's study of the stable state, and later his work with Argyris. This joint study initiated a renewed interest in applying the concept of learning to organizational behaviour.

The 'managerialist' perspective in public policy, which drew on the ideas of the period, was first provided by Metcalfe in the 1970s, and he has continued to develop his ideas on the relevance of the learning model to define a distinctive form of public-sector management in the 1990s. Another early application of a learning model was Etheridge (1981 and 1985), who was greatly influenced by Maslow's theories. Etheridge (1981) focuses on learning in terms of individual decision-makers in governmental organizations, and later (Etheridge, 1985) defines governmental learning as involving 'changes in intelligence and effectiveness'. Changes in intelligence are, he argues, operationalized through: growing realism; intellectual integration; and the growth of a reflective perspective (Etheridge, 1985: 66).

Browne and Wildavksy advanced a theory of evaluation and implementation as an on-going learning process: the organization as a self-evaluating process. Lindblom has used the concept to extend his ideas on the reduction of impairment in the policy-making process. Collingridge applies the learning model (and Lindblom's incrementalism) to the study of 'big' decisions in Europe and America. An application of learning models to decision-making in international organizations is advanced by Ernst Haas, who argues, using Deutsch and other approaches (Argyris and Schön, and Etheridge), that it is possible to redesign international institutions (such as the UN and the World Bank) so as to improve their performance.

❖ Learning and change

C. Argyris and D. Schön, *Organizational Learning*, 1978

This book is a key source for the learning model – along with Schön (1971). Argyris and Schön argue that there is a paradox in organizational life: the pressures for stability and the necessity for change. This creates a complex and confusing environment within which individuals work. On the one hand, they have to think defensively and competitively; on the other, they have to function co-operatively and in the interests of the whole. Although the 'espoused theory' is that organizations are open, communicative and participative, the reality (the theory in use) is that they tend to operate in accordance with so-called model 1 behaviour:

- *Model 1, single loop*: In this model individuals are driven by the desire to pursue their goals, reduce their dependence on others, keep their ideas and feelings to themselves and protect themselves from change. Learning in this model is self-contained and self-orientated. Its aim is to defend the position of the individual. It is a mode of learning which produces conformity, mistrust, inflexibility and 'self-sealing'. Hardly a model to facilitate change and adaptation. (But all too often it is the model which predominates in public organizations.)

Argyris and Schön propose, therefore, a new theory in use which provides for a 'double loop' learning process:

- *Model 2, double loop*: This model involves the cultivation of decision-making based upon openly obtained information, taking action with others. Model 2 involves joint inquiry and a restructuring of organizational norms, strategies and assumptions to foster an organization responsive to change.

In model 1, learning is unlikely to do more than provide a defensive strategy. Model 2, they argue, provides the conditions for change and adaptation. The defensive model 1 'pollutes' (Argyris, 1985) the decision-making system, makes it inflexible and hostile to change. The aim of management should be to promote an environment in which 'double-loop' learning can take place.

Les Metcalfe, 'Public management: from imitation to innovation', in Kooiman (ed.), 1993

Metcalfe was among the first to apply the learning model – in the 1970s. In the 1990s he makes this assessment:

> In the political environment of public management learning processes are especially difficult to create and maintain. Individual learning is a psychological process. Organizational learning is a political process. A critical task of public management is to build institutional learning capacities at the macro level to manage the environment in which private management operates. But, conventional political processes often block learning because ideology overrides evidence or vested interests resist policy evaluation and change ... public management reforms are better regarded as management by design rather than by direction. It should be concerned with designing adaptable systems rather than producing blueprints for specific reform. (pp. 107–8)

Metcalfe argues that the new agenda for public policy research should focus on learning capacities of interorganizational networks, and the design of such networks so as to improve the delivery of services.

David Collingridge, *The Management of Scale*, 1992

Is it all a matter of scale? Is incrementalism a model of learning which is inappropriate for big decisions which involve large strategic planning, and for which more comprehensive systems models are better suited?

In this book the author examines a number of grand strategic cases: the space shuttle; nuclear power; North Sea oil; VideoText; large-scale irrigation schemes; and high-rise building systems. Intelligent learning, he argues, is a trial-and-error process. In the case studies he shows how the trial-and-error method was not used, with the consequence that errors and mistakes occurred, and projects 'failed to deliver the promised benefits ... or if they did it was more by luck than management' (p. 186). The rules of the trial-and-error method are:

- trials are kept to a minor nature, thus being expensive even when they fail;
- changes are marginal in nature;
- trials have a rapid result;
- the energy of critical scrutiny is to be proportional to the cost of mistakes;
- many diverse interest groups take part in the decision process;
- political power is shared among these groups;
- choice is through compromise amongst these groups;
- actions are co-ordinated by mutual interaction rather than planned from the centre. ◆

The criticism of the stagist approach is at its most telling in the implementation–evaluation–termination framework. Neither concept appears to provide a satisfactory account of what is happening in the post-decisional phase of policy-making. The learning approach as developed by Sabatier and Jenkins-Smith (eds) (1993) in this regard is a considerable advance over the heuristic policy cycle model. As Browne and Wildavksy (1974) argue, implementation and evaluation are better explained as a continuous, endless evolution which is more accurately analysed as a fluid process in which no clear stages can be discerned. The learning model also offers a distinct normative framework: policy-making ought to be about improving/speeding up learning in the policy-making process (cf. Lindblom, Metcalfe) as well as facilitating a wider 'social learning'.

Social learning models
The social process approach to learning takes a far wider (and more critical) view of the role of learning in human development and problem-solving. Whereas the organizational model is, for the greater

part, focused on the policy elite as individuals (see, for example, Etheridge, 1981) or as organizations (see, Haas, 1990), the social learning approach is concerned with the way in which learning takes place in society as whole, and how this learning can be advanced. The sources of this approach are to be found mainly – but not exclusively – in the fields of planning and development studies.

❖ Key texts

- Mumford (1938)
- Dunn (1971)
- Friedmann (1973, 1979, 1984, 1992)
- Friedmann and Hudson (1974)
- Friedmann and Abonyi (1976)
- Michael (1973)
- Ackoff (1977)
- Korten (1980)
- Korten and Klauss (eds) (1984: the main reader which contains many key contributions)

In addition, it is important to place these texts in the context of Etzioni (1968), Schein (1969) and Hampden-Turner (1971), and the ideas of Schön and Argyris. ◆

The history of the ideas may be outlined briefly. (This account draws on the story as told by John Friedmann, and by Parsons, 1976.) The 1970s witnessed a growing disillusionment with technology, technocracy, bigness and centralism. There duly arose prophets who pointed the way towards alternative social and economic arrangements which stressed the values of smallness, human scale, community and conviviality: chief amongst them were Kohr (1957, 1973, 1975) ; Schumacher (1973) and Illich (1975a). Although they had attractive visions of what ought to be, they were far less convincing about how this brave new world should come about. The 'social learning' approach was developed in the context of these concerns about community and the need for new forms of planning to facilitate social and economic development as well as out of cybernetic ideas and systems theory. Two people shaped the debate more than most: Edgar Dunn and John Friedmann. The tradition within which they can be placed goes back, with some large breaks in time, to the work of Dewey (1927, 1938) and Mumford (1938), and through Mumford to Ebenezer Howard, and thence to the anarchist Prince Peter Kropotkin, the father of 'mutual aid'.

The starting point for an examination of the learning approach should be the study of Dewey and Mumford – especially the latter – for, as Friedmann (1984: 190) notes, their works foreshadowed much of the concerns of post-war theorists. Dewey's ideas about the need for a scientific and open approach to planning, and Mumford's advocacy of planning as a form of democracy and human liberation, however, were not really taken further until the 1970s with the publication in 1971 of Edgar Dunn's book on economic and social development as a process of social learning. An economist, Dunn's work was very much in the spirit of Dewey's pragmatic/experimentalist philosophy. Dunn argued that much social science was built on a misguided premise derived from the classical physical sciences. The idea that knowledge could be developed and applied to social problems, as to problems in physics, failed to take account of the fact that human learning is fundamentally social. Human knowledge is not external to the social system, it is deeply embedded in it. If, therefore, we are to successfully ameliorate social and economic problems we have to realize that it is at the social level that learning can best take place. Dunn called for the development of forms of organizations which could facilitate evolutionary social experimentation through which social learning could be improved.

The implications of using small 'cells' for experiment and innovation as the basis for public policy-making – and for planning and development strategies – was investigated by later scholars. Perhaps the most significant contribution to the paradigm was John Friedmann's *Retracking America* (1973) which extended the model into the field of planning theory. Planning from this standpoint is to be understood as a learning process rooted in 'social innovation' and 'mutual learning'. The aim is to plan through pooling the personal knowledge of people with different skills and abilities who face a common task. Planners and experts should abandon their claim to 'objective' knowledge and work by adopting clear value commitments. Mutual learning can best take place in a dialogue of trusting relationships – ideally in small groups so that everybody's ideas can be included. The political implications of this model are a radical departure from the organizational learning approach:

> The social learning approach is a model of politicized planning. It is also a model of how to bring about innovative changes 'from below'. Decentralized, unco-ordinated, and often with only minimal financial support, innovative social practice may seem peculiarly weak and ineffectual. Yet ... cellular organization encourages the formation of networks, social movements, and loose coalitions which can be very potent forces in the struggle for structural change in basic institutional arrangements, including those of governance ... States have almost always feared a genuine grassroots politics: the preferred term is participation, not empowerment. But a po-

> liticized planning requires a community that is active, that exercises some control over the conditions of its livelihood, and that can hold the state accountable ... The social learning approach to planning can make its greatest contribution ... toward the transformation of the structures of political governance. The ultimate terms of this struggle would be this: that planning 'from below' might accurately reflect the genuine interests of the people engaged in the social production of their lives.
> (*Friedmann, 1984: 194*)

As Friedmann admits, it is a Utopian project, but the approach does offer important insights into the real world of public policy in the 1990s. The model provides an alternative framework to the dominant paradigm of public policy as a input–output, producer–consumer process. The social learning approach argues that men and women are involved in the production of their lives in society: they are not just consumers at the end of a delivery process. Democracy, power, politics, and participation are the means by which people can learn about themselves and about social, economic and other problems. 'Problem-solving' is therefore a process of public learning and, as Dunn argued in 1971, if we are to make a better job of ameliorating the human condition in the future than we have in recent history, finding ways of improving the capacities and opportunities of people to learn through public policy – rather than just consume public policy – is essential. The implications for the way in which policies are delivered and co-produced form, perhaps, the agenda for the next millennium for both the developed and the less-developed world.

❖ An alternative paradigm?

Korten (1984) put forward a more 'people-centred' framework for development. The main features of this are:

- substantial decentralization of decision-making processes;
- non-expert-dominated decision-making, and multiple approaches;
- creating 'enabling' settings in public policy which encourage and support people in solving their own problems;
- developing organizational structures and processes that are 'self-organizing';
- developing modes of production and consumption which are based on local ownership.

In the 1990s has this agenda been 'translated' into managerial/market terms? Compare this with Osborne and Gaebler (1992).

For a more recent account of Friedmann's concept of empowerment and development, see Friedmann (1992). ◆

4.7   Promise and performance: evaluating impact and outcomes

❖ **Brian W. Hogwood, *Trends in British Public Policy*, 1992**

Looking at how policy has changed over time obviously involves using measures that are available ... However, many of the key issues about the quality and content of public policy cannot be regularly captured by the main statistical series ... There is a danger that measuring what is readily available and quantifiable misses some of the most important questions that need to be considered and may actually conceal more than it reveals. Especially in the last thirty to fifty years, many important activities of Western governments have taken forms that are not measurable by such standard indicators as expenditure and the size of bureaucracy ... (p. 5)

David Marsh and R.A.W. Rhodes (eds), *Implementing Thatcherite Policies*, 1992

There have been few 'revolutions' in modern British politics like that which has been labelled the 'Thatcher revolution'. In this collection of papers a number of policy areas are examined from the point of view of evaluating change and continuities. Did the Thatcher effect have much impact on actual outcomes?

The answers are mixed. At one level, the Thatcher revolution did mark a radical change in the ideology of government. Policies and organizations did change. The authors of the various papers argue that, in great part, rhetoric and reality did not match up.

The editors conclude that the Thatcher effect has been overestimated because of the concentration on legislation rather than outcomes:

it was only in the area of housing that her Government achieved its policy and political aims. In the other three areas of fundamental change – industrial relations, privatisation and local government – a great deal changed in terms of legislation but much less changed in terms of outcomes. If we take industrial relations as an example; the legislation severely reduced the immunities which unions and unionists enjoy but it did not transform shopfloor industrial relations which was, of course, the crucial area, given that a key aim of Thatcherite policy was to change the balance between unions and employers in favour of the latter. (p. 186)

The non-consultative (strong government) style of policy-making, they argue, fundamentally undermined the effectiveness of policy implementation. ◆

After birth, life and death, an equally problematic aspect of the policy cycle is 'does policy make a difference?'. From the standpoint of Joe or Josephine Public of Anytown, Someplace, one of the issues which might shape how they see the value of their participation in the political process is their assessment of whether policy-makers actually deliver the goods. They make output judgements (see Almond and Verba, 1989). And, as we saw in Part Two, studies of voting behaviour in the industrial democracies indicate strongly that electorates have tended to focus on the relationship between economic promises and performance come election time (see Lewis-Beck, 1990: 151). Those who feel that the political system can do nothing for them are also making judgements about whether participation is worth the effort, given the probable outcomes (Lindblom and Woodhouse, 1993: 104–13). It is, therefore, as far as the citizen *qua* consumer is concerned, the 'bottom line'. How has health policy impacted on the actual health of society? How has education policy improved education? How has environmental policy made a difference to the environment? Has 'law and order' policy made the streets safer and reduced crime? In other words, has the policy process improved, solved problems or made matters worse? When asked these questions, the well-trained policy analyst will probably reply that it depends on how you evaluate policy outcomes, and what the 'goods' are held to be. As Weiss (1972: 32) notes: 'different people looking at the same data can come up with different conclusions' about how a policy has worked, or what impact it has actually had.

❖ Impact assessment

As defined by Rossi and Freeman (1993: 215):

> Impact assessments are undertaken to estimate whether or not interventions produce their intended effects. Such estimates cannot be made with certainty but only with varying degrees of plausibility ... The basic aim of an impact assessment is to produce an estimate of the 'net effects' of an intervention – that is, an estimate of the impact of the intervention uncontaminated by the influence of other processes and events that also may affect the behaviour or conditions at which the social program is being evaluated is directed.

Methods include:

- comparing a problem/situation/condition with what it was like before the intervention;
- experiments which test the impact of a programme on an area or group against what has happened to an area or group which has not been the target of intervention;
- measuring costs against the benefits which have taken place as a result of an intervention;
- using models to understand and explain what has happened as a result of past policies;
- qualitative and judgemental approaches to evaluating success/failure of policy and programmes;
- comparing what has happened with the specified goals or targets of a policy or programme;
- using performance measurements to assess if goals or targets have been met. ◆

As with all such simple questions, to answer what effects policy has had is complex and deeply political. Assessing the impact of a policy programme on the 'quality of life', for example, turns on what the idea of 'quality of life' means. Outcomes are the product of the political 'incomes': expectations, values, beliefs and culture. Analysis of the effects of government policies may therefore be said to be contingent on 'where you sit'. James Q. Wilson has formulated two laws to explain variations in the analysis of the effects of policy. The first law states that if the research is carried out by those implementing the policy (or their pals), then the research will show that it has delivered the right results. If (the second law states) the research is carried out by independent analysts it will show negative effects:

> Studies that conform to the First Law will accept an agency's own data about what it is doing and with what effect; adopt a time frame ... that maximizes the probability of observing the desired effect; and minimize the search for variables that might account for the effect observed. Studies that conform to the Second Law will gather data independently of the agency; adopt a short time frame that either minimizes the chance for the desired effect to appear or, if it does appear, permits one to argue that the results are temporary ... and maximize the search for other variables that might explain the effects observed.
> (Wilson, 1973: 132–4)

In other words, the evaluation of the actual impact of policy on problems is something which is essentially a matter of values rather than facts: numbers mean whatever policy-makers want them to mean. This may translate into the assessment of impact being invariably biased towards research which is less than comprehensive. Rossi (in Rossi and Freeman, 1993: 446) suggests that this may be because of the 'iron law' of evaluation studies, which states that the better the evaluation study the less likely it is to show positive effects! Quantitative analysis of how a policy has impacted on a problem may therefore just be a way of legitimating the policy-making process, rather than providing any satisfactory assessment on whether a policy or programme has worked and with what effect. When policy-makers deploy research as to the impact of their policies on crime, homelessness, unemployment, health, standards of education and so on, they are engaged in shaping the context and agenda within which problems are being defined and constructed. In this sense, therefore, impact assessment takes us back to the start of the policy cycle – problem definition and agenda-setting. The aim of assessment is to show how a given programme or policy has 'worked/not worked', met the policy/programme goals or not met the goals, so as to sustain the construction of the problem and claims for policy advanced by government. Such impact claims and constructions have to confront the assessments which are deployed by other political parties, interest groups, think-tanks, researchers and so on, who seek to show how a policy/programme is not working in order to make the case for their claims, definitions and constructions. For critics of the quantitative approach to impact assessment, the political nature of evaluating the impact of a policy/programme means that more 'qualitative' forms of evaluation are necessary (observation and working with people and their problems) in order to counteract the distorting and dehumanizing effects of apparently objective facts and figures (Lincoln and Guba, 1985); (see also discussion of control–consensus mix, 4.4.8).

The problems of assessing the impact of policies are compounded when we compare countries. Different nations produce and use different data, and those data have specific contexts, which makes comparing sets of statistics a very dubious exercise. However, even though there are such obvious methodological problems with the idea of comparing policy outcomes, it is the case that in the modern world outcomes are compared by the use of data produced by international organizations such as the EU and OECD. Policy analysts, politicians and policy-makers want to know why different political systems differ in terms of the actual outcomes: why does growth in GDP vary? why do countries spend certain proportions of their GDP on health, education, and so on? why do the performance and effective implementation of policies diverge from country to country? As we noted earlier in this book, theories of comparative public policy which seek to explain such patterns offer contradictory explanations.

Politics, parties and policy outcomes
Research in the early 1960s with regard to the impact of party politics and participation in the policy process on the actual outcomes in terms of economic development offered convincing evidence based on the USA that policy outcomes have little to do with party politics. In 1963, for example, Dawson and Robinson (1963) made a study of party competition and economic and welfare outcomes in a number of US states. This indicated that levels of inter-party competition had a negligible effect on economic development in the states concerned. Following this, Herbert Dye in 1966 demonstrated with the use of a multiple regression model that consideration of a range of output measures in a number of policy areas pointed towards the unequivocal conclusion that economic development variables were of far greater significance to policy outcomes than the political process (Dye, 1966, 1972: 244; Jenkins, 1978: 51–62). Summing up much of this literature concerned with output studies, Fried argued in the early 1970s that the case against politics and policy having any significant impact was overwhelming:

> Somehow, the nature of the socio-economic environment seems more important than the nature of politics in the community shaping community policies ... The socio-economic constraints are such, it would appear, that it makes little difference for urban policy who controls urban government ...
>
> (Fried, 1972: 71)

If we consider subsequent research, however, we find that the conclusions to be reached in respect of policy-making outside the US are far more supportive to the view that politics does indeed matter in the outputs of urban policy-making (Sharpe and Newton, 1984). In the case of economic policy, however, there is a large literature which argues that the impact of government policies on various aspects of economic and industrial outcomes (GNP, employment, productivity, inflation, etc.) is at best marginal compared with wider factors, such as the impact of the international economy and national 'culture' (Weiner, 1981; Gomulka, 1979; Caves, 1980; Rose, 1984a; Grant, 1990). Furthermore, as we noted in 2.11.7 and 4.6, the fact is that policy-making and implementation take place in the context of past policy and the inheritance of earlier decisions, which severely restrict and limit choices and innovation (see R. Rose, 1990; Rose and Davies, 1994).

❖ Parties and outcomes

Parties may well have an important impact on policy (see Budge and Keman, 1990: 132–58), and in this sense they may make a difference (see Burns et al., 1994, on decentralization), but to what extent do they make much of an impact on policy outcomes? Parties may well introduce different policies reflecting their differences in values and beliefs, yet does it really matter from the point of view of 'solving' or ameliorating problems?

The rhetoric of politics is framed around the idea that the election of a party can indeed make such a difference. Is this a naive viewpoint? Richard Rose (1984a, 1989) thinks that it is. There are, he argues, severe limitations upon a party in power actually bringing about policy change, notably: the commitments of the past; public opinion; bureaucracy; and international constraints on national economic policy. In the case of the UK economy, he argues, the evidence points towards the conclusion that: 'At best, a party can make a marginal impact on the economy; economic models demonstrate that the size of this marginal change is less than voters or politicians would like it to be' (Rose, 1989: 289). These constraints on economic policy are not unique to the UK, argues Rose, and may also be seen to operate in other countries such as France, the USA, Sweden and Germany. He nevertheless believes that parties are not necessarily unimportant to policy and outcomes:

> Examining the impact of parties upon government produces both good and bad news: parties make less of a difference in reality than they claim in their rhetoric. The worst that parties threaten to do is unlikely to come to pass – as well as the best they aspire to. Neither

voters nor politicians can will everything that they want ... To say that parties make less difference than they claim is not to denigrate parties, and certainly not to denigrate the choice of government by free elections. Competition between parties is the principal means for stimulating a Moving Consensus, in which the need for movement to deal with problems is as important as consensus. In favourable circumstances, any fool could govern a country – and some have. But when times are difficult, then the need for movement is important ...
(*Rose, 1984a: xxxi–xxxii*)

See also Rose and Davies on the impact of policy 'inheritance': Rose (1990); Rose and Davies (1994). ◆

Economic policy-making, as is the case for other policy areas, does not take place in a vacuum. In particular there are considerable institutional and international constraints which shape what is done, by whom, when and how. This role of institutional contexts as having a greater influence on what happens to the economy than anything policy-makers say or do is emphasized in the 'institutionalist' arguments of Hall (1986), who maintains that policy needs to be explained in terms of policy-making institutions, social and economic factors and the international context, rather than in terms of political/ideological policy differences as suggested by the 'politics matters' school. (For a review of the different approaches, see Heidenheimer *et al.*, 1990: 7–9.) The present author considers that the impact of politics/ideology and policy differences on outcomes must be seen in terms of the way in which they come to structure the discourse of discussion and analysis which encompasses policy-making and decision-making, rather than in the effects they have on problems 'out there' in the real world.

❖ Do regulatory styles make a difference to the outcomes of environmental policy?

Countries differ in how they choose to engage in environmental regulation. Do these differences have consequences for what actually happens to the environment? Research suggests that, despite the divergences and variations in regulatory processes and approaches, the outcomes of policy-making tend to be more convergent and alike. One of the most extensive surveys of environmental regulation reported in 1983 that examination of levels of sulphur dioxide emissions in ten (European) countries demonstrated that, notwithstanding the differences in processes (open, participative enforcement in Germany, Belgium, France and Holland versus more closed administrative procedures in Italy, Switzerland and UK), an analysis of the output of sulphur dioxide did not vary between countries so much as between different regions within the same countries (Knoepfel and Weidner, 1983). This conclusion is in line with earlier studies of environmental policy and outcomes:

- Lennart Lundquist (1980) shows how the differences in patterns of regulation between the US and Sweden apparently have little or no impact on air pollution, as air pollution in those countries fell in the 1970s to similar levels.
- Brickman *et al.* (1982) demonstrate that, as far as the control of vinyl chloride in the UK, France, the US and Germany is concerned, the processes of regulation tend to be far more divergent than the actual levels of control achieved.

In a major review of the impact of regulatory style and environmental policy agendas and outcomes, David Vogel (1986) reaches a similar conclusion in an analysis of the US and the UK. The distinctiveness of decision-making, implementation and enforcement between the two countries is in marked contrast to the similarities in the policy agendas and policy outcomes. The agenda convergence, he argues, is due to the comparable levels of industrial development in both Britain and the USA, combined with the effects of the international nature of the environmental debate, information and communication. As to the convergence of outcomes, Vogel suggests that one reason why this may be the case is that

> policy makers in both capitalist democracies operate under similar sets of constraints. For while economic growth both creates externalities and provides the available resources to ameliorate them, it also constrains the amount of resources that can be committed to such efforts ... in the long run, the severity of enforcement is strongly influenced by the interests of policymakers, industrial workers, and the public as a whole in keeping their nation's industries internationally competitive ... regulation is only one factor among many that affect environmental quality or public health and safety. To the extent that the actual quality of the environment varies in Great Britain and the United States, the difference appears to be due less to their systems of regulation than to geographical conditions and industrial and technical factors.
> (*Vogel, 1986: 223–4*) ◆

Democracy and performance

The quantitative analyses of this relationship between politics and performance has been extensive in the 1970s and 1980s and continues to generate much research interest. Reviewing the state of play on the relation between political systems and policy outcomes Lane and Ersson, for example, advance the following conclusion:

> Democracy delivers, in a direct sense, by offering human rights as parts of the democratic procedures themselves. However, there is empirical support for the theory that a democratic regime delivers indirectly by means of policy outputs and outcomes. Democracies have a more pronounced welfare effort than other types of regimes. The hypothesis that political systems would converge towards a similar pattern of welfare expenditures is not substantiated. The welfare efforts in non-democratic polities have not been sufficient to match those in several democracies ... It also seems to be the case that there is a better likelihood for more equality in the distribution of resources in a democracy. On the other hand, we find no evidence of any impact of democracy on economic growth, size of the state, inflation, or war experience.
> (*Lane and Ersson, 1990: 74*)

Politics in democratic societies, on the other hand, is about the belief that policy-making can and will make differences. The danger is that this belief leads to the formation of an illusion in the mind of both voter and politician which assumes that the possibilities of control and manoeuvre are bigger than they actually are (Klein, 1976: 402). In a review of France, Japan, the UK and the USA and their respective industrial, health, ethnic minorities, and law and order policies, Martin Harrop concludes that the impact of public policy is in reality far more limited than is generally supposed:

> liberal democratic governments exert only limited control over developments. Whether impact is for good or ill it is limited ... Changes within sectors are driven by more fundamental forces than government policy. In health, current improvements in the population's health owe more to changing lifestyles than to publicly funded treatment. In law and order, the crime rate responds more to trends such as urbanisation than to policing strategies. In minorities policy, improved life-chances for minorities owe more to changing attitudes than to legislation. And in industry, governments are just one of many influences on economic competitiveness. In short, liberal democratic governments operate at the margin, seeking to react to developments they do not control and which often they cannot foresee.
> (*Harrop (ed.), 1992: 277*)

Thus the main characteristic of policy-making appears to be that it is all too frequently driven less by moving towards objectives than by reacting to what de Bono terms the 'rear-end' objectives. Policy-making in many circumstances may be better understood as involving less

Figure 4.27   Middling through

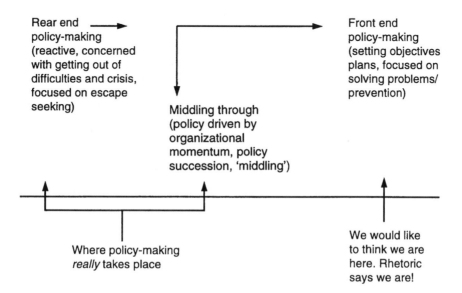

Rear end policy-making (reactive, concerned with getting out of difficulties and crisis, focused on escape seeking)

Front end policy-making (setting objectives plans, focused on solving problems/ prevention)

Middling through (policy driven by organizational momentum, policy succession, 'middling')

Where policy-making *really* takes place

We would like to think we are here. Rhetoric says we are!

moving towards policy objectives and goals which are destinations out in front, than as escaping from 'uncomfortable' positions which come up from behind: and 'when you are pulling yourself out of a swamp you do not consult a road map' (de Bono, 1981: 89). (Compare this argument with the 'policy style' model advanced by Richardson, 1982; see 2.10.2.) Or, of course, policy may be the result of what might be termed (*à la* Lindblom) 'middling' through (figure 4.27).

However, this operating at the margin, either in a front-end (preventive, objective setting) or rear-end (reactive, escapist or perhaps policy as own cause: Wildavsky, 1980: 62–85) manner, is not without significant consequences. Government may not be in as much control as it (and we) would or might like, but this does not mean that policy-making is of no importance.

The debate between 'politics matters' versus 'socio-economic determinism' does not help much in understanding or explaining what kind of influence policy has on outcomes. To argue that policy outcomes are the result of one factor rather than another is to render the issues into a somewhat meaningless debate. As Sharpe and Newton (1984: 206–8) comment in their defence of politics against the theory that it is economic and social factors which are decisive:

> To see economic or demographic variables as competing with political variables is rather like assuming that yeast, flour, sugar, and baking are all competing determinants of bakery ... But, however necessary to all forms of baking an ingredient may be ... it is still only an ingredient, and therefore for it to play any part in the final product is dependent on a series of human volitions we call baking ... Viewed as the whole process of policy-making, the political factor embraces not just the determination of public policy outputs, but also the selection and processing of the inputs of the political system ... per capita income, age structure, and population density are simply inert descriptive statistics, with the same objective status as religious affilation, eye colour, or left-handedness, until they are given policy significance by the political system. In other words they are not inputs until they are made so by a set of political values and actors ... The political system is to public policy what an individual's perceptual set is to his cognition: it abstracts some features of the social and economic environment and gives them political salience. We may all be able to agree as to the facts of a situation, but how we interpret and respond to such facts is always in the realm of value.

The distinction between politics and economy and society, and between the 'environment' and the Eastonian black box needs to be revised to take account of the argument that the world of 'facts' and social and economic forces is not simply 'out there'. As we noted in 4.6.4, it may well be that external environments are better understood as mirrors or projections of the values, beliefs and assumptions which frame the internal policy-making process. Social and economic forces

Figure 4.28   Factors shaping policy outcomes

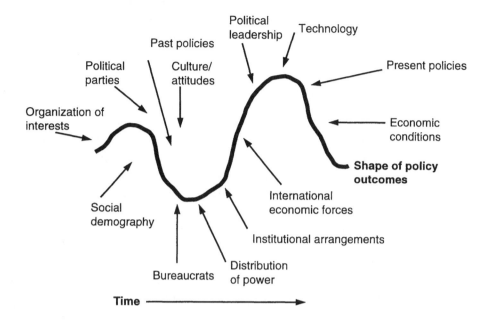

are values within the policy process, as much as they are variables which may 'determine' outputs and outcomes. Over time, therefore, the shape or path of policy outcomes must be set in the context of a multiplicity of factors (figure 4.28).

The outcomes in health, law and order, the economy, and so on, may be viewed as formed by an array of inputs and forces, of which 'policy' is but one and possibly not one of the most influential of forces at work on 'real-world' problems. At an analytical level, the exact balance and profile of these forces will depend on the framework or model being deployed which will emphasize one or more of these factors as having a determining/prominent/major/dominant (or whatever) role in framing the outcomes of public policy and will vary between countries due to differences in history, culture, demography and so on, as well as between particular policy sectors. In view of this complex interaction of forces, the value of taking an historical approach to policy problems and policy outcomes is to be especially recommended (see, for example, Castles (ed.), 1989; Vinovskis, 1988; Fee and Fox (eds), 1988).

In addition to this, the impact of policy choices is something which cannot be understood except in the long term. As Hall (1986: 282) comments from his 'institutionalist' perspective: 'economic experimentation entails long-term institutional renovation whose design is difficult and whose effects may take some time to emerge'. Even so, such an analysis does not mean that economic performance is just down to 'fate' or some 'iron laws': 'The institutions that affect the performance of the economy and distribute power in society are ultimately arte-facts of political action. They were constructed out of political strug-gles, and from time to time, we may recast them (ibid.: 283).

Operating at the margin, more effectively and efficiently and with an understanding of the forces which are shaping society and the economy can mean lives saved, jobs 'created', increasing even further life ex-pectancy and the quality of life for the elderly and infirm, or a cleaner environment. It *can* mean greater social justice and the advancement of human freedom and dignity. From a comparative perspective, for example, it is clearly the case that some countries have indeed made better choices than others in the management of their economies (see Wilks, 1986), and some have made choices which have done more harm than good. In practical terms this implies that policy-making is more successful when it is tailored to the particular contexts (histori-cal, institutional, technological, sectoral and so on) in which 'problem-solving' takes place (cf. Lasswell, 1970a, on contextual mapping). National policy 'styles' (Richardson, 1982) or 'paths' (Weaver, 1985) consequently do shape outcomes, for, as Weaver (1985: 3) argues, 'national variations in political constraints give countries differing comparative advantages in pursuing particular governmental actitivies, just as variations in economic resources create comparative advantage in specific sectors'. And, as Hancock *et al.* (1993: xix) argue:

> Without question, many aspects of system performance – including those measured by basic indicators such as annual rates of economic growth, inflation, and unemployment levels – are influenced by external economic and other factors beyond the control of national policy actors. None the less, national policy-making structures and processes mediate the domes-tic economic and social consequences of exogenous trends and events.

The experience of Eastern Europe, as they remind us, illustrates well enough how policy choices and outcomes are structured by ideology, institutional arrangements and power, the role of parties and the ac-cess of interest groups. Furthermore, as Porter (1990: 617) argues in his study of the competitive advantages of nations:

> At one extreme, some view government as at best a passive participant in the process of national competition. Because the determinants of national advantage are so deeply rooted in a nation's buyers, its history and other unique circumstances, it could be argued that government is powerless. Its proper role would then be to sit back and let market forces work. My theory and the evidence from our research, does not support this view. Government policy does affect national advantage, both positively and negatively.

More recently, work which has developed out of games theory (by Harsanyi, John Nash and Reinhard Selten who were awarded the Nobel Prize for Economics in 1994) has strongly suggested that government policy can promote improvements in economic growth by fostering greater trust and co-operation. As Will Hutton (1994: 11) comments, the economic 'miracles' of Japan and East Asia have been deliberately created by government policies and institutions which, over time, have facilitated a high level of trust between firms and with government: 'Growth, in short, can be stimulated by acts of governmental will.' (See also Hutton, 1995.)

So in focusing on the capacity of policy to impact both on and at the margin, the issue arises as to what means and mix can best operate and deliver marginally better education, health, facilities for the elderly, employment, international competitiveness and so on, in conditions of increasing complexity and rapid change (Kooiman (ed.), 1993): state, market, networks, community, or the private, public or voluntary sectors? The fact that public policy may be operating at the margin, and within possibly ever-narrower and costlier limitations and constraints, makes the debate about the means and ends of policy-making more, not less, important than in the days when the 'policy space' of liberal democracy was less crowded, or when relatively small interventions could have massive consequences for the public good – such as the public health measures of the nineteenth and early twentieth centuries which dramatically raised life expectancy. However, simply borrowing from 'successful' policies and/or institutional arrangements from other countries, without taking account of the different social, economic and historical contexts of policy-making, is invariably doomed: there is no magic formula to cure economic ills or any other problems which may be dispensed as a general cure-all. Thus, although countries can learn from each other's experience of policy-making, the record shows that copying does not have a good track record. The experience of Britain in particular has amply demonstrated that borrowing successful models from countries very different to Britain (see Smith, 1979) confirms the fact that if government has it in its power to make things a little better, it has an equal, if not greater, capacity to make things a good deal worse!

Policy-making as a symbolic activity
However, as Harrop (1992: 278) points out, the symbolic nature of policies should not be discounted in evaluating their outcomes and impacts. Indeed, it may well be that policy outcomes are best understood as involving 'symbolic' rather than purely 'substantive' outcomes. As Dye argues:

> Policies do more than effect change in societal conditions; they also hold a people together and maintain an orderly state. For example, a government 'war on poverty' may not have any significant impact on the poor, but it reassures moral persons, the affluent as well as the poor that government 'cares' about poverty.
> (*Dye, 1987: 355*)

As a social 'ritual', policy-making might be thought of as a process in which 'symbol specialists' (as Lasswell termed them: see 1948a: 11; 1971: 215) endeavour to use policies as symbols of intervention and 'doing something' which provide stability and security in an uncertain and insecure world. Although we are happy with large measures of irrationality in our personal lives, we judge public decision-making and desire 'policy' as a way of imposing rationality on an irrational, unpredictable world. This desire for policies is perhaps an expression of a fear of the irrational and uncertain: a defence against a real world which is not so easily governed, and in which problems are never 'solved'. Policy and politics therefore may have more to do with our personal and collective need for security and order than with our desire for solutions:

> The prerequisite of a stable order in the world is a universal body of symbols and practices sustaining an elite which propagates itself by peaceful methods and wields a monopoly of coercion which is rarely necessary to apply to the uttermost. This means that the consensus on which order is based is necessarily non-rational ... A sufficient concentration of motive around efficacious symbols must be elicited in order to inaugurate and stabilize ... adjustment. These symbols must have enough potentialities for the production of deference to permit an elite to ... inaugurate and conventionalize a stable order ...
> (*Lasswell, 1935: 237*)

For Lasswell, the power of elites to use symbols to 'dissipate hostility', provide scapegoats and saviours (Lasswell, 1948a: 128) in order to maintain the social order posed the kind of dangers to democracy which are implicit in Harrop's observation that policy-making has more of a symbolic than substantive impact. Policy-making as a symbolic activity involves the risk that it remains largely a reactive process, dealing with issues when they become problems, rather than anticipating them, and which can so often lead to dangerous levels of disillusionment and frustration (as Pressman and Wildavsky (1973) feared in their study of implementation). That government in practice tends to be reactive, rather than pro-active, and more likely to give first aid than to address fundamental causes, are telling comments and indictments of the actuality of public policy in the 1990s as compared with the aims and hopes of the policy sciences as set out by Lasswell in the early days of the discipline: the formation of a preventive politics in which the policy sciences have a central role in mapping the context of problems and clarifying values. The apparent marginality of public policy and politics in the face of larger social, economic, cultural and other factors and forces therefore makes the role of the policy sciences more important than ever. However, the role of the policy sciences in the 1990s is very different to that of the 1960s. As Howard Newby comments:

> Twenty years ago social science would have made the arrogant claim that it alone could produce solutions to social and economic problems according to some rational model of social engineering. However, as we now know all too well, social science does not provide solutions for policy makers in this way ... Policy 'problems' are highly contextual and contingent; they are defined and framed by certain historical circumstances and configurations. Any 'solution' has, therefore, to take into account this contingency, which includes the way in which 'problems' are perceived, interpreted and also manipulated by actors in the policy process ... To assume 'problems' are clear cut and unequivocal is to mistake society for a purposefully constructed machine with clearly designed functioning parts which can be controlled. People are not cogs in a machine and it is no part of modern social science's brief to treat them as though they were.
> (*Newby, 1993: 370*)

Social science and other policy-orientated fields of inquiry must therefore form a new relationship with society and government so that public policy is seen less in terms of 'output' and 'outcomes' than as participation and communication; and citizens less as 'consumers' than as 'shapers' of values and institutions; 'co-producers' rather than mere points at the end of 'delivery' process (see 4.4.8). And, as Newby (1993: 371) argues, the possibilities of new information and communication technologies for changing the role (and relationship) of social scientists and citizens in the policy-making process should be exploited to the full.

4.8   Conclusion: Beyond delivery and towards democratization

The delivery of goods and services is important, but as Kirlin (1984: 164) notes, 'it is not the critical role of government. Government is the institution of society with singular obligations to facilitate societal choice-making and action. Its ability to make decisions and to act are the dominant dimensions by which governmental performance should be judged.' The wider purposes of public policy as involving enlightenment, the fuller development of individuals in society, and the development of consent, consensus, social awareness and legitimacy, rather than simply the delivery of goods and services, is a theme which has preoccupied the work of leading scholars in the field of public policy and policy analysis, such as Lasswell, Lindblom, and

Etzioni. It is a theme which, in the context of the appearance of public-sector 'management' and of the notion of the citizen as customer, we do well to remember and articulate today. As Burns *et al.* (1994) argue, decentralization of service delivery needs to be allied to greater local democratic control, 'empowerment' and increased citizen participation. Public policy involves improving the democratic or political capacities of people, and not simply the efficiency and effectiveness of the delivery of services. This means extending democratic control over the managerialist arrangements – consultants and quangos – which have thrived in market-driven public policy through reinvigorating and reforming constitutional arrangements (see Smith, 1994); and more bottom-up accountability and evaluation (see 4.8.8). Where the study of public policy and policy analysis has an important role is in education. As Burns *et al.* observe:

> How striking it is that many of our children are now schooled in the art of 'setting up a business' but receive little or no education in organizing democracy … As Keane (1988: 144–5) notes, a truly democratic alternative to either statism or the market requires that … political parties abandon the false assumption that social development is necessarily decided by parties, business or states. Specifically, parties would need to explicitly recognise the necessity *and* limits of parties. They would be forced to acknowledge openly that within a democracy the fundamental source of energy and strategic protection lies in the non-party realm of civil society. (*Burns* et al., *1994: 278–9*)

For Lasswell, public policy as public education (see Lasswell, 1960, 1963, 1970a) was vital if democracy was not to fall prey to the interests and manipulations of powerful elites. The ultimate aim of policy-making, he believed, was therefore the formation of values which could shape the full development of individuals and society as a whole. Thus 'public' policy and policy analysis has (as Lasswell understood) its true source and focus in the personal and in the self. However, as we have noted above (4.4.5), some of the most important developments in public policy *qua* 'public management' have taken place in the realm of the personal, through the increasing use of modes of evaluation and audit which aim to 'improve' accountability via policing, controlling and quantifying human relationships and activities.

Public policy should, above all, be concerned with values other than those promoted by managerialism, the most important of which are the transmission and application of knowledge and democratic skills to as wide a public as possible. The goal of policy analysis should be to facilitate a policy-making process which is informed by enlightenment and emancipation and which can keep 'alive the pluralism of authority and control that prevents the absolutization of political power' (Lasswell, 1980: 533). As we have seen, there are models emerging that are more concerned with public policy as public learning and which stress values such as 'participation', 'co-production', 'communication', 'decentralization' and 'community'. These alternative models offer (perhaps) the prospect of using dialogue, communication, co-operation and social learning as modes of both policy 'production' and 'delivery' so as to promote a more 'operationalized citizenship' (Warren *et al.*, 1992) and active participation in the making of public choices. This may well require a radical shift away from the so-called 'realistic' conceptualization of representative (Schumpeterian) democracy towards an openly idealistic vision of public policy as public education and, as Pateman once noted: 'educative in the widest sense, including both the psychological aspect and gaining of practice in democratic skills and procedures' (Pateman, 1970: 42).

This re-orientation of public policy as a mode of public learning will also involve the re-design of the institutional context of policy-making so as to build on and develop existing social institutions – such as the jury system – and exploit the potentialities of new communication technologies. As we have suggested, this could be done by the adaptation of Lasswell's ideas with regard to decision seminars and social planetariums (4.4.8). As 'institutionalists' convincingly argue, 'institutions do matter' (2.11.6, 3.6.4), and the challenge for the future will be to design and adapt political and social institutions so as to improve the communicative – rather than the instrumental – rationality of democratic societies. Thus, whereas the predominant focus of policy analysis in the 1960s was speaking truth to rulers, the mission of policy analysis in the next decade must be to help in fostering a genuine dialogue between policy-makers, policy specialists and an 'active' society.

The contribution of the policy sciences in this process of re-politicizing and democratizing public policy is of great significance and requires that students and practitioners develop a critical appreciation of the limitation of instrumental analytical methods (such as CBA, orthodox OR, experimentation and evaluation); the 'management' paradigm; and market mechanisms. A critical policy analysis should explore the relevance of alternative 'integrative' and 'communicative' methods for both the analysis of policy and the policy process, and as modes of analysis for policy-making (see, in general, Dryzek, 1987; Bobrow and Dryzek, 1987; Fischer and Forrester (eds), 1993; 3.10.4). This also means that policy analysis must cease to be the preserve of the powerful and the organized and endeavour to reach as wide a public as possible so as to enrich and enlarge political argument and debate, and promote competition between ideas and values (see

Lindblom, 1990; 2.8.2; Hogwood and Gunn, 1984: 268–70). If so, then the aims of public policy in liberal democratic societies may accord in the future more closely with what Lasswell believed was the fundamental and constant goal of policy-making and policy analysis: 'the progressive democratization of mankind'. As he commented in the late 1940s:

> Today mankind has a common, though dimly seen, task which is the discovery of ways and means of realizing human dignity. There is a world community which is sufficiently well-developed to endanger itself and not sufficiently developed to release the full value-shaping and sharing potentialities of a democratic commonwealth.
> (*Lasswell, 1948a: 221–2*)

It is the clarification, shaping and sharing of values so as to extend and enhance democratization which still remains the core and vital task of the theory and practice of public policy.

Bibliography

Aaron, H. (1978) *Politics and Professors: The Great Society in Perspective*, Brookings Institution, Washington, D.C.

Aberbach., J.D., R.D. Putnam and B.A. Rockman (1981) *Bureaucrats and Politicians in Western Europe*, Harvard University Press, Cambridge, Mass.

Abse, L. (1989) *Margaret, Daughter of Beatrice*, Cape, London.

Ackoff, R.L. (1977) 'National development planning revisited', *Operations Research*, **25**(2): 212–18.

Adams, J.L. (1987) *Conceptual Blockbusting: a Guide to Better Ideas*, Penguin Books, Harmondsworth, Middx.

Adorno, T.W., E. Frenkel-Brunswik, D.J. Levinson and R.N. Sanford (1993) *The Authoritarian Personality*, W.W. Norton, New York, 1993 (abridged from 1950 edition).

Aiken, M. and J. Hage (1968) 'Organizational interdependence and intra-organizational structure', *American Sociological Review*, **33**: 912–30.

Akin, W.E. (1977) *Technocracy and the American Dream: The Technocrat Movement, 1900–1941*, University of California Press, Berkeley, Cal.

Albrow, M. and E. King (eds) (1990) *Globalization, Knowledge and Society: Readings from International Sociology*, Sage, London.

Alchian, A.A. and H. Demsetz (1972) 'Production, information costs and economic organization', *American Economic Review*, **62**: 777–95.

Aldrich, H.E. (1972) 'An organization-environment perspective on cooperation and conflict in the manpower training system', in A. Negandhi (ed.) *Conflict and Power in Complex Organizations*, CARI, Kent State University, Ohio.

Aldrich, H.E. (1976) 'Resource dependence and inter-organizational relations; local employment service offices and social services sector organizations', *Administration and Society*, **7**(4): 419–54.

Aldrich, H.E. (1979) *Organizations and Environments*, Prentice-Hall, Englewood Cliffs, N.J.

Aldrich, H.E. and S. Mindlin (1978) 'Uncertainty and dependence: two perspectives on the environment', in L. Karpik (ed.), *Organization and Environment*, Sage, London.

Alford, R.R. (1975) *Health Care Politics*, University of Chicago Press, Chicago, Ill.

Allison, G.T. (1971) *The Essence of Decision: Explaining the Cuban Missile Crisis*, Little Brown, Boston, Mass.

Allison, L. (ed.) (1990) *The Utilitarian Response*, Sage, London.

Almond, G.A. and G.B. Powell (1966) *Comparative Politics: A Developmental Approach*, Little, Brown, Boston, Mass.

Almond, G.A. and S. Verba (1989) *The Civic Culture: Political Attitudes and Democracy in Five Nations*, Sage, Newbury Park, Cal.

Almond, G.A., G.B. Powell and R.J. Mundt (1993) *Comparative Politics: A Theoretical Framework*, Harper Collins, New York.

Amenta, E. and T. Skocpol (1989) 'Taking exception: explaining the distinctiveness of American public policies in the last century', in Castles (ed.), 1989.

Andersen, S.S and K.A Eliassen (1993) *Making Policy in Europe: The Europeification of National Policy-making*, Sage, London.

Anderson, C.W. (1988) 'Political judgment and theory in policy analysis', in E.B. Portis and M.B. Levy (eds), 1988.

Anderson, J. (ed.) (1988) *Communications Yearbook*, 11, Sage, Newbury Park, Cal.

Anderson, J.E. (1975) *Public Policy-making*, Holt, Praeger, New York.

Andrews, G. (1991) *Citizenship*, Lawrence & Wishart, London.

Anthony, R.N. and R.E. Herzlinger (1980) *Management Control in Nonprofit Organizations*, Richard D. Irwin, Homewood, Ill.

Appleby, P.H. (1949) *Policy and Administration*, University of Alabama Press, Tuscaloosa, Ala.

Arendt, H. (1958) *The Human Condition*, University of Chicago Press, Chicago, Ill.

Argyris, C. (1957) *Personality and Organization*, Harper & Row, New York.

Argyris, C. (1965) *Organization and Innovation*, Irwin, Toronto.

Argyris, C. (1985) *Strategy, Change and Defensive Routines*, Pitman, London.

Argyris, C. and D.A. Schön (1978) *Organisational Learning: A Theory of Action Perspective*, Addison-Wesley, Reading, Mass.

Armstrong, G. and M. Wilson (1973) 'City politics and deviance amplification', in I. Taylor and L. Taylor (eds), 1973.

Aronson, E. (1988) *The Social Animal*, W.H. Freeman, New York.

Arterton, F.C. (1986) *Teledemocracy: Can Technology Protect Democracy?* Sage, Beverly Hills, Cal.

Asch, S.E. (1955) 'Effects of group pressure upon the modification and distortion of judgements', in H. Guetzkow (ed.), *Groups, Leadership and Men*, Carnegie Press, New York.

Ascher, C. (1987) 'Editorial comment: Policy Science in the postpositivist era', *Policy Science*, 19: 1.

Atkinson, M.M. and W.D. Coleman (1989) 'Strong states and weak states: sectoral policy networks in advanced capitalist economies', *British Journal of Political Science*, 19: 747–67.

Atkinson, M.M. and W.D. Coleman (1992) 'Policy networks, policy communities and the problems of governance', *Governance*, 5(2): 154–80.

Aucoin, P. (1990) 'Administrative reform in public management: paradigms, principles, paradoxes and pendulums', *Governance*, 3: 115–37.

Bachrach, P.S. and M.S. Baratz (1962) 'Two faces of power', *American Political Science Review*, 56: 1947–52.

Bachrach, P.S. and M.S. Baratz (1963) 'Decisions and non-decisions: an analytical framework', *American Political Science Review*, 57: 641–51.

Bachrach, P.S. and M.S. Baratz (1970) *Power and Poverty, Theory and Practice*, Oxford University Press, New York.

Bacon, F. (1900) *New Atlantis*, ed. G.C. Moore Smith, Cambridge University Press, Cambridge.

Bacon, F. (1973) *The Advancement of Learning*, ed. G.W. Kitchin, Introd. Arthur Johnson, Dent, London.

Bacon, F. (1985) *The Essays*, ed. John Pitcher, Penguin, Harmondsworth, Middx.

Bacow, L.S. and M. Wheeler (1984) *Environmental Dispute Resolution*, Plenum Press, New York.

Badcock, C. (1988) *Essential Freud*, Blackwell, Oxford.

Baer, W.C. and S.M. Fleming (1976) 'Counterfactual analysis: an analytical tool for planners', *Journal of the American Institute of Planners*, 42: 243–52.

Baier, V.E., J.G. March and H. Saetren (1986) 'Implementation and ambiguity', *Scandinavian Journal of Management Studies*, 2: 197–212.

Bailey, D. (ed.) (1965) *Essays on Rhetoric*, Oxford University Press, New York.

Bales, K. (1991) 'Charles Booth's survey of life and labour of the people in London 1889–1903', in Bulmer *et al.* (eds), 1991.

Ball, T., J. Farr and Russell L. Hanson (eds) (1989) *Political Innovation and Conceptual Change*, Cambridge University Press, Cambridge.

Banfield, E. (1980) 'Policy science as metaphysical madness', in Goldwin (ed.), 1980.

Barbalet, J.M. (1988) *Citizenship*, Open University, Milton Keynes, Bucks.

Barberis, P. and T. May (1993) *Government, Industry and Political Economy*, Open University Press, Buckingham, Bucks.

Bardach, E. (1976) 'Policy termination as a political process', *Policy Sciences*, 7: 123–31.

Bardach, E. (1977) *The Implementation Game*, MIT Press, Cambridge, Mass.

Barke, R.P. (1993) 'Managing technological change in federal communications policy: the role of industry advisory groups', in Sabatier and Jenkins-Smith (eds), 1993.

Barker, A. (1993) 'Patterns of decision advice processes : a review of types and a commentary on some recent British practices', in Peters and Barker (eds), 1993.

Barker, A. (ed.) (1982) *Quangos in Britain*, Macmillan, London.

Barker, A. and B.G. Peters (eds) (1992) *The Politics of Expert Advice: Creating, Using and Manipulating Scientific Knowledge for Public Policy*, Edinburgh University Press, Edinburgh.

Barnard, C. (1938) *The Functions of the Executive*, Harvard University Press, Cambridge, Mass.

Barnes, C. and K. Williams (1993) 'Education and consumerism: managing emergent market culture in schools', in Isaac-Henry *et al.* (eds), 1993.

Barrett, S. and C. Fudge (eds) (1981) *Policy and Action*, London, Methuen.

Bartlett, W. and J. Le Grand (1993) 'The theory of quasi-markets', in Le Grand and Bartlett (eds), 1993.

Batley, R. and G. Stoker (1991) *Local Government in Europe: Trends and Developments*, Macmillan, London.

Bauer, R.A. and K.J. Gergen (eds) (1968) *The Study of Policy Formation*, The Free Press, New York.

Bauer, W.C. and S.M. Fleming (1976) 'Counterfactual analysis: an analytical tool for planners', *Journal of the American Institute of Planners*, 42: 243–52.

Baumgartner, F.R. (1987) 'Parliament's capacity to expand political controversy in France', *Legislative Studies Quarterly*, 12: 33–54.

Baumgartner, F.R. and B.D. Jones (1991) 'Agenda dynamics and policy subsystems', *Journal of Politics*, 53: 1044–74.

Baumgartner, F.R. and B.D. Jones (1993) *Agendas*

and Instability in American Politics, University of Chicago Press, Chicago, Ill.

Beardwell, I. and L. Holden (eds) (1994) Human Resource Management: A Contemporary Perspective, Pitman, London.

Beauchamp, T. (1975) Ethics and Public Policy, Prentice-Hall, Englewood Cliffs, N.J.

Becker, C.C. (1936) Progress and Power, Stanford University Press, Stanford, Cal.

Becker, H.S. (1963) Outsiders: Studies in the Sociology of Deviance, Free Press, New York.

Becker, H. S. (ed.) (1966) Social Problems: A Modern Approach, John Wiley, New York.

Beer, S. (1966) Decision and Control, John Wiley, London.

Beer, S. (1972) Brain of the Firm, Allen Lane, London.

Beer, S. (1975) Platform for Change, John Wiley, London.

Beetham, D. (1991) 'Models of bureaucracy', in Thompson et al. (eds), 1991.

Begg, D., S. Fisher and R. Dornbush (1991) Economics, McGraw-Hill, London.

Behn, R.D. (1978) 'How to terminate a public policy: a dozen hints for the would-be terminator', Policy Analysis 4(3): 393–413.

Bell, D. (1960) The End of Ideology, Free Press, New York.

Bell, D. (1966) 'Government by commission', Public Interest, 3: 3–9.

Bell, D. (1976) The Coming of Post-industrial Society: A Venture into Social Forecasting, Penguin Books, Harmondsworth, Middx (first published 1973).

Bendor, J. and T. Hammond (1992) 'Rethinking Allison's models', American Political Science Review, 86(2): 301–22.

Benn, S.I. and G.F. Gaus (1983) Public and Private in Social Life, Croom Helm, London.

Bennett, R.J. and G. Krebs (1990) Towards a Parnership Model of Local Economic Development Initiatives in Britain and Germany, Anglo-German Foundation, London.

Benson, J.K. (1975) 'The interorganizational network as a political economy', Administrative Science Quarterly, 20: 229–49.

Benson, J.K. (1977a) 'Innovation and crisis in organisational analysis', Sociological Quarterly, 18: 3–16.

Benson, J.K. (1977b) 'Organizations: a dialectical view', Administrative Science Quarterly, 22 (3): 1–21.

Benson, J.K. (1982) 'A framework for policy analysis', in D.L Rogers and D. Whetten (eds), Interorganisational Coordination: Theory, Research and Implementation, Iowa State University Press, Ames.

Berger, P.L. and T. Luckman (1975) The Social Construction of Reality: A Treatise on the Sociology of Knowledge, Penguin Books, Harmondsworth, Middx (first published 1966).

Berger, P.L. and R.J. Neuhaus (1977) To Empower People: The Role of Mediating Structures in Public Policy, American Enterprise Institute for Public Policy Research, Washington, D.C.

Berry, B.J.L. (1991) Long-wave Rhythms in Economic Development and Political Behaviour, Johns Hopkins University Press, Baltimore, Md.

Bertsch, G., R. Clarke, and D. Wood (1992) Comparing Political Systems: Power and Policy in Three Worlds, Macmillan, New York.

Beuret, K. (1991) 'Women and transport', in MacLean and Groves (eds), 1991.

Beveridge, W. (1944) Full Employment in a Free Society, Allen & Unwin, London.

Beyme, von K. (ed.) (1974) German Political Studies, vol. 1, Sage, London.

Bingham, R.D. et al. (1991) Managing Local Government, Sage, Newbury Park, Cal.

Bish, R.L. (1978) 'Intergovernmental relations in the United States: some concepts and implications from a public choice perspective', in Hanf and Scharpf (eds), 1978.

Black, G. (1961) The Application of Systems Analysis to Government Operations, National Institute of Public Affairs, Washington, D.C.

Blackstone, T. and W. Plowden (1988) Inside the Think-Tank: Advising the Cabinet, 1971–1983, Heinemann, London.

Blowers, A. (1983) 'Master of fate or victim of circumstance – the exercise of corporate power in environmental policy-making', Policy and Politics, 11: 393–415.

Blowers, A. (1984) Something in the Air: Corporate Power and the Environment, Harper & Row, London.

Blumer, H. (1969) Symbolic Interactionism, Prentice-Hall, Englewood Cliffs, N.J.

Blumer, H. (1971) 'Social problems as collective behaviour,' Social Problems, 18: 298–306.

Bobrow, D.B. and J.S. Dryzek (1987) Policy Analysis by Design, University of Pittsburgh Press, Pittsburgh, Pa.

Böhret, C. (1987) 'The tools of public management', in Kooiman and Eliassen (eds), 1987.

Bolland, J.M. and R. Muth (1984) 'The decision seminar: a new approach to urban problem solving', Knowledge: Creation, Diffusion, Utilization, 6: 75–88.

Boneparth, E. and E. Stoper (1988) Women, Power and Policy: Towards the Year 2000, 2nd edn, Pergamon Press, New York.

Borgatta, E.F. and R.J.V. Montgomery (eds) (1987) Critical Issues in Aging Policy: Linking Research and Values, Sage, Newbury Park, Cal.

Bornat, J. et al. (1993) Community Care: A Reader, Macmillan, Basingstoke, Hants.

Bossard, J.H.S. (1941) 'Comment', *American Sociological Review*, **6**: 320–9.

Bosso, C.J. (1987) *Pesticides and Politics: The Life Cycle of a Public Issue*, University of Pittsburgh Press, Pittsburgh, Pa.

Bosso, C.J. (1989) 'Setting the agenda: mass media and the discovery of famine in Ethopia', in M. Margolis and G. Mauser (eds), *Manipulating Public Opinion*, Brooks-Cole, Pacific Grove, Cal.

Bott, E. (1957) *Family and Social Network*, Tavistock Publications, London.

Bouckaert, G. (1993) 'Governance between legitimacy and efficiency: citizen participation in the Belgian fire services', in Kooiman (ed.), 1993.

Boulding, K. (1956) *The Image*, University of Michigan Press, Ann Arbor, Mich.

Boulding, K. (1962) *Conflict and Defence: A General Theory*, Harper & Row, New York.

Boulding, K. (1968) *Beyond Economics: Essays on Society, Religion and Ethics*, University of Michigan Press, Ann Arbor, Mich.

Boulding, K. (1970) *Economics as a Science*, McGraw-Hill, New York.

Boulding, K. (1981) *Evolutionary Economics*, Sage, Beverly Hills, Cal.

Boulding, K. (1990) *Three Faces of Power*, Sage, Newbury Park, Cal.

Bourn, J.B. (1974) 'The administrative process as a decision-making and goal-attaining system', Block 2, Part 2 of D331, *Public Administration*, Open University Press, Milton Keynes, Bucks.

Bowers, A. (1984) *Something in the Air: Corporate Power and the Environment*, Harper & Row, London.

Bozeman, B. (1979) *Public Management and Policy Analysis*, St Martin's Press, New York.

Bradach, J.L. and R.G. Eccles (1991) 'Price, authority and trust: from ideal types to plural forms', in Thompson *et al.* (eds), 1991.

Bradshaw, J. (1992) 'Social security', in Marsh and Rhodes (eds), 1992.

Brand, J. (1975) 'The politics of social indicators', *British Journal of Sociology*, **26**: 78–80.

Braverman, H. (1974) *Labour and Monopoly Capital*, Monthly Review Press, New York.

Braybrooke, D. and C.E. Lindblom (1963) *A Strategy of Decision*, Free Press, New York.

Brewer, G.D. (1975) 'Dealing with complex social problems: the potential of the "Decision seminar"', in G.D. Brewer and R.D. Brunner (eds), *Political Development and Change: A Policy Approach*, Free Press, New York.

Brewer, G.D. (1978) 'Termination: hard choices, harder questions', *Public Administration Review*, **38** (3): 338–44.

Brewer, G.D. (1983) 'Some costs and consequences of large scale social systems modeling', *Behavioral Science*, **28**: 166–85.

Brewer, G.D. (1985) 'Methods for synthesis: policy exercises', in W.C. Clarke and R.E. Mann (eds), *Sustainable Development of the Biosphere*, International Institute for Applied Systems Analysis, Laxenburg, Austria.

Brewer, G.D. and P. de Leon (1983) *The Foundations of Policy Analysis*, Dorsey, Ridgewood, Ill.

Brickman, R., S. Jasanoff and T. Ilgen (1982) *Chemical Regulation and Cancer: A Cross-National Study of Policy and Politics*, Cornell University, Program on Science, Technology and Society, Ithaca, N.Y.

British Psychological Society (1994) *Fostering Innovation: A Psychological Perspective*, BPS, Leicester.

Brittan, S. (1975) 'The economic contradictions of democracy', *British Journal of Political Science*, **5**: 129–59.

Brittan, S. (1987) *The Role and Limits of Government*, Wildwood House, Aldershot, Hants.

Broady, M. and R. Hedley (1989) *Working Partnerships: Community Development in Local Authorities*, Bedford Square Press, London.

Brown, A.E. and J. Stewart (1993) 'Competing advocacy coalitions, policy evolution, and airline deregulation', in Sabatier and Jenkins-Smith (eds), 1993.

Brown, J.A.C. (1963) *Techniques of Persuasion: From Propaganda to Brainwashing*, Penguin Books, Harmondsworth, Middx.

Brown, J.A.C. (1986) *The Social Psychology of Industry*, Sidgwick & Jackson, London.

Brown, M.S. and K.A. Lyon (1992) 'Holes in the ozone layer: a global environmental controversy', in Nelkin (ed.), 1992.

Browne, A. and A. Wildavsky (1984) 'Should evaluation become implementation?', in Pressman and Wildavsky, 1984.

Browne, A. and A. Wildavsky (1987) 'What should evaluation mean to implementation?', in Palumbo (ed.), 1987.

Browning, P. (1986) *The Treasury and Economic Policy, 1964–1985*, Longman, London.

Bruce, B. (1992) *Images of Power: How the Image Makers Shape our Leaders*, Kogan Page, London.

Bryant, C.G.A. and H.A. Becker (eds) (1990) *What has Sociology Achieved?* Macmillan, London.

Buchanan, J.M. (1968) *Demand and Supply of Public Goods*, Markham, Chicago, Ill.

Buchanan, J.M. (1977) *Freedom in Constitutional Contract*, Texas A&M Press, College Station, Tx.

Buchanan, J.M. (ed.) (1978) *The Economics of Politics*, Institute of Economic Affairs, London.

Buchanan, J.M. (1989) *Explorations into Constitutional Economics*, Texas A&M University Press, College Station, Tx.

Buchanan, J.M. and G. Tullock (1962) *The Calculus*

of Consent, University of Michigan Press, Ann Arbor, Mich.

Buchanan, J.M., R.E. Wagner and J. Burton (1978) *The Consequences of Mr Keynes*, Institute of Economic Affairs, London.

Budge, I. and H. Keman (1990) *Parties and Democracy: Coalition Formation and Government Functioning in Twenty States*, Oxford University Press, London.

Bulmer, M. (1981), 'Applied social research? The use and non-use of empirical social inquiry by British and American governmental commissions', *Journal of Public Policy*, 1: 353–80.

Bulmer, M. (1982) *The Uses of Social Research: Social Investigation in Public Policy-Making*, Allen & Unwin, London.

Bulmer, M. (1990) 'Successful applications of sociology', in Bryant and Becker (eds), 1990.

Bulmer, M. (1993) 'The Royal Commission and departmental committee in the British policy-making process', in Peters and Barker (eds), 1993.

Bulmer, M. (ed.) (1978) *Social Policy Research*, Macmillan, London.

Bulmer, M. (ed.) (1980) *Social Research and Royal Commissions*, Allen & Unwin, London.

Bulmer, M. (ed.) (1987) *Social Science Research and Government*, Cambridge University Press, Cambridge.

Bulmer, M., K. Bales and K.K. Sklar (eds) (1991) *The Social Survey in Historical Perspective, 1880–1940*, Cambridge University Press, Cambridge.

Burch, M. and B. Wood (1983) *Public Policy in Britain*, Martin Robertson, Oxford (later editions, 1986 and 1990 published by Basil Blackwell, Oxford).

Burke, J.P. and F.I. Greenstein (1989) *How Presidents Test Reality: Decisions on Vietnam, 1954 and 1965*, Russell Sage Foundation, New York.

Burke, K. (1945) *A Grammar of Motives*, McGraw-Hill, New York.

Burley, T.A. and G. O'Sullivan (1986) *Operational Research*, Macmillan, London.

Burnham, J. (1941) *The Managerial Revolution*, Indiana University Press, Bloomington, Ind.

Burnham, J. (1943) *The Machiavellians: Defenders of Freedom*, Putnam, London.

Burns, D., R. Hambelton and P. Hoggett (1994) *The Politics of Decentralization: Revitalizing Local Democracy*, Macmillan, London.

Burns, T. and G.M. Stalker (1961) *The Management of Innovation*, Tavistock Publications, London.

Burrell, G. and G. Morgan (1979) *Sociological Paradigms and Organisational Analysis*, Heinemann, London.

Burton, D.H. (1988) *The Learned Presidency: Theodore Roosevelt, William Howard Taft, Woodrow Wilson*, Fairleigh Dickinson Press/Associated University Presses, London.

Butcher, H. (1993) 'Introduction: some examples and definitions', in Butcher *et al.* (eds), 1993.

Butcher, H., A. Glen, P. Henderson and J. Smith, (eds) (1993) *Community and Public Policy*, Pluto Press, London.

Butler, R.J. and D.C. Wilson (1990) *Managing Voluntary and Non-profit Organisations: Strategies and Structures*, Routledge, London.

Button, J. (1988) *A Dictionary of Green Ideas*, Routledge, London.

Buzan, T. and B. Buzan (1995) *The Mind Map Book*, British Broadcasting Corporation, London.

Cabinet Office, Office of the Minister for the Civil Service (1988) *Service to the Public*, Occasional Paper, HMSO, London.

Cain, M.E. (1973) *Society and the Policeman's Role*, Routledge & Kegan Paul, London.

Callahan, D. and B. Jennings (1983) *Ethics, the Social Sciences and Policy Analysis*, Plenum Press, New York.

Callaway, M.R. and J.K. Esser (1984), 'Groupthink: effects of cohesiveness and problem-solving procedures on group decision making', *Social Behaviour and Personality*, 12: 157–64.

Callaway, M.R., R.G. Marriott and J.K. Esser (1985) 'Effects of dominance on group decision making: towards a stress-reduction explanation of groupthink', *Journal of Personality and Social Psychology*, 49: 949–52.

Cameron, J.M. (1978) 'Ideology and policy determination: restructuring California's mental health system', in May and Wildavsky (eds), 1978.

Campbell, D.T. (1969) 'Reforms as experiments', *American Psychologist*, 24: 409–29.

Campbell, D.T. (1973) 'The social scientist as methodological servant of the experimenting society', *Policy Studies*, 2: 72–5.

Campbell, D.T. (1981) 'Getting ready for the experimenting society', in Saxe and Fine (eds), 1981.

Campbell, D.T. (1982) 'Experiments as arguments', *Knowledge: Creation, Diffusion, Utilization*, 3: 327–37.

Campbell, D.T. and J.C. Stanley (1966) *Experimental and Quasi-experimental Designs for Research*, Rand McNally, Skokie, Ill.

Capra, F. (1985) *The Tao of Physics*, Fontana, London.

Carley, M. (1980) *Rational Techniques in Policy Analysis*, Policy Studies Institute/Heinemann, London.

Carmines, E.G. and J.A. Stimson (1986) 'On the structure and sequence of issue evolution', *American Political Science Review*, 80: 901–20.

Carmines, E.G. and J.A. Stimson (1989) *Issue Evolution: Race and the Transformation of American Politics*, Princeton University Press, Princeton, N.J.

Carmon, N. (ed.)(1990) *Neighbourhood Policy and Programmes*, Macmillan, London.

Carroll, J.S. and E.J. Johnson, (1990) *Decision Research: A Field Guide*, Sage, Newbury Park, Cal.

Carter, N. (1988) 'Measuring government performance', *Political Quarterly*, 59 (3): 369–75.

Carter, N. (1989) 'Performance indicators: "backseat driving", or "hands off control"?', *Policy and Politics*, 17: 131–8.

Carter, R., J. Martin, B. Mayblin and M. Munday (1984) *Systems, Management and Change: A Graphic Guide*, Paul Chapman, for Open University, London.

Cartwright, T.J. (1975) *Royal Commissions and Departmental Committees in Britain*, Hodder & Stoughton, London.

Castles, F. (1982) *The Impact of Parties*, Sage, London.

Castles, F. (ed.) (1989) *The Comparative History of Public Policy*, Polity Press, Oxford.

Caves, R.E. (1980) 'Productivity differences among industries', in R.E. Caves and L.B. Krause (eds), *Britain's Economic Performance*, Brookings Institution, Washington, D.C.

Cawson, A. (1986) *Corporatism and Political Theory*, Basil Blackwell, Oxford.

Cawson, A. (ed.) (1985) *Organized Interests and the State: Studies in Meso-corporatism*, Sage, London.

Cawson, A. and P. Saunders (1983) 'Corporatism, competitive politics and class struggle', in R. King (ed.) *Capital and Politics*, Routledge & Kegan Paul, London.

Chanan, G. (1991) *Taken for Granted: Community Activity and the Crisis of the Voluntary Sector*, Community Development Foundation, London.

Chandler, A.D. (1962) *Strategy and Structure: Chapters in the History of the American Industrial Enterprise*, MIT Press, Cambridge, Mass.

Chandler, A.D. (1977) *The Visible Hand: The Managerial Revolution in American Business*, Harvard University Press, Cambridge, Mass.

Charlesworth, J.C. (ed.) (1967) *Contemporary Political Analysis*, Free Press, New York.

Charlesworth, J.C. (ed.) (1972) *Integration of the Social Sciences through Policy Analysis*, Monograph 14, American Academy of Political and Social Science, Philadelphia, Pa.

Chase, G. (1979) 'A framework for implementing human service programmes: how hard will it be?', *Public Policy*, 27: 387–435.

Checkland, P.B. (1981) *Systems Thinking and Systems Practice*, John Wiley, London.

Checkland, P.B. and J. Scholes (1990) *Soft Systems Methodology in Action*, Wiley, London.

Chew, G.F. (1968) 'Bootstrap: a scientific idea', *Science*, 161: 762–5.

Chew, G.F. (1970) 'Hadron bootstrap: triumph or frustration', *Physics Today*, 23: 23–8.

Chibnall, S. (1977) *Law and Order News*, Tavistock Publications, London.

Child, J. (1972) 'Organization structure, environment and performance: the role of strategic choice', *Sociology*, 6: 1–22.

Chomsky, N. (1971) *American Power and the New Mandarins*, Vintage, New York.

Church, J. (ed.) (1995) *Social Trends 25*, HMSO, London.

Clausen, J.A. (1976) 'Drug use', in Merton and Nisbet (eds), 1976.

Clegg, S.R. (1990) *Modern Organisations: Organisation Studies in the Postmodern World*, Sage, London.

Clegg, S. and D. Dunkerly (1980) *Organization, Class and Control*, Routledge & Kegan Paul, London.

Clokie, H.M. and J.W. Robinson (1937) *Royal Commissions of Inquiry*, Stanford University Press, Stanford, Cal.

Clutterbuck, D. and S. Crainer (1990) *Makers of Modern Management: Men and Women who Changed the Business World*, Macmillan, London.

Cmnd 4506 (1970) *The Reorganization of Central Government*, HMSO, London.

Coase, R.H. (1937) 'The nature of the firm', *Economica*, 4: 386–405.

Coats, A.W. (1989) 'Economic ideas and economists in government', in Colander and Coats (eds), 1989.

Coats, A.W. (ed.) (1981) *Economists in Government: An International Comparative Study*, Duke University Press, Durham, N.C.

Coats, A.W. and D. Colander (1989) 'An introduction to the spread of economic ideas', in Colander and Coats (eds), 1989.

Cobb, R.W. and C.D. Elder (1971) 'The politics of agenda-building: an alternative perspective for modern democratic theory', *Journal of Politics*, 33: 892–915.

Cobb, R.W. and C.D. Elder (1972) *Participation in American Politics: The Dynamics of Agenda-building*, Johns Hopkins University Press, Baltimore, Md.

Cobb, R.W. and C.D. Elder (1981) 'Communications and public policy', in Nimmo and Sanders (eds), 1981.

Cobb, R.W. and C.D. Elder (1983) *The Political Uses of Symbols*, Longman, New York.

Cobb, R.W., J.-K. Ross and M.H. Ross (1976) 'Agenda building as a comparative political process', *American Political Science Review*, 70: 126–38.

Cochrane, A. (1993a) *Whatever Happened to Local Government?*, Open University Press, Buckingham, Bucks.

Cochrane, A. (1993b) 'Challenges from the centre', in J. Clarke (ed.), *A Crisis in Care? Challenges to Social Work*, Sage for Open University, London.

Cockburn, C. (1977) *The Local State*, Pluto Press, London.

Cockett, R. (1994) *Thinking the Unthinkable: Think Tanks and the Economic Counter-Revolution, 1931–1983*, Harper Collins, London.

Cohen, M., J. March and J. Olsen (1972) 'A garbage can model of organisational choice', *Administrative Science Quarterly*, **17**: 1–25.

Cohen, S. (1972) *Folk Devils and Moral Panics*, Paladin, London.

Cohen, S. (1985) *Visions of Social Control*, Polity Press, Cambridge.

Cohen, S. and J. Young (eds) (1981) *The Manufacture of News: Social Problems and the Mass Media*, Sage, Beverly Hills, Cal.

Colander, D. and A.W. Coats (1989) *The Spread of Economic Ideas*, Cambridge University Press, Cambridge.

Cole, M. (1961) *The Story of Fabian Socialism*, Heinemann, London.

Colebatch, H. and P. Larmour (1993) *Market, Bureaucracy and Community*, Pluto Press, London.

Collin, A. (1994a) 'Human resource management in context', in Beardwell and Holden (eds), 1994.

Collin, A. (1994b) 'Learning and development', in Beardwell and Holden (eds), 1994.

Collingridge, D. (1992) *The Management of Scale: Big Organizations, Big Decisions, Big Mistakes*, Routledge, London.

Collingridge, D. and C. Reeve (1986) *Science Speaks to Power: The Role of Experts in Policy Making*, Frances Pinter, London.

Collingwood, R.G. (1974) 'Human nature and human history', in Gardiner (ed.), 1974.

Colvin, P. (1985) *The Economic Ideal in British Government: Calculating Costs and Benefits in the 1970s*, Manchester University Press, Manchester.

Community Development Foundation (CDF) (1992) *Mind the Gap: The Community in City Challenge*, CDF, London.

Connerton, P. (ed.) (1976) *Critical Sociology*, Penguin, Harmondsworth, Middx.

Connolly, W. (1983) *The Terms of Political Discourse*, Princeton University Press, Princeton, N.J.

Cook, F.L. and W.G. Skogan (1991) 'Convergent and divergent voice models of the rise and fall of policy issues', in Protess and McCombs (eds), 1991.

Cook, T.D. (1985) 'Postpositivist critical multiplism', in R.L. Shotland and M.M. Mark (eds), *Social Science and Social Policy*, Sage, Newbury Park, Cal.

Coote, A. (ed.) (1992) *The Welfare of Citizens*, Institute for Public Policy Research, London.

Cornford, J. (1990) 'Performing fleas: reflections from a think tank', *Policy Studies*, **11** (4): 22–30.

Courtwright, J. (1978) 'A laboratory investigation of groupthink', *Communication Monographs*, **45**: 229–46.

Cox, A. and N. O'Sullivan (eds) (1988) *The Corporate State*, Edward Elgar, Aldershot, Hants.

Crane, D. (1972) *Invisible Colleges*, University of Chicago Press, Chicago, Ill.

Crawford, E. and N. Perry, (eds) (1976) *Demands for Social Knowledge: The Role of Research Organisations*, Sage, London.

Crenson, M.A. (1971) *The Unpolitics of Air Pollution: A Study of Non-decision Making in the Cities*, Johns Hopkins University Press, Baltimore, Md.

Cunningham, L.L. (1981) 'Applying Lasswell's concepts in field situations: diagnostic and prescriptive values', *Educational Administrative Quarterly*, **17** (2): 21–43.

Cyert, R.M. and J.G. March (1955) 'Organizational structure and pricing behavior in an oligopolistic market', *American Economic Review*, **45**: 129–39.

Cyert, R.M. and J.G. March (1963) *A Behavioral Theory of the Firm*, Prentice-Hall, Englewood Cliffs, N.J.; Basil Blackwell, Oxford, 1992.

Dahl, R. (1956) *A Preface to Democratic Theory*, University of Chicago Press, Chicago, Ill.

Dahl, R. (1957) 'The concept of power', *Behavioural Science*, **2**: 201–15.

Dahl, R. (1958) 'A critique of the ruling elite model', *American Political Science Review*, **52**: 463–9.

Dahl, R. (1961) *Who Governs?: Democracy and Power in an American City*, Yale University Press, New Haven, Conn.

Dahl, R. (1971) *Polyarchy: Participation and Opposition*, Yale University Press, New Haven, Conn.

Dahl, R. (1982) *Dilemmas of Pluralist Democracy: Autonomy versus Control*, Yale University Press, New Haven, Conn.

Dahl, R. (1985) *A Preface to an Economic Theory of Democracy*, Polity Press, London.

Dahl, R. and C.E. Lindblom (1953/1976) *Politics, Economics and Welfare*, Harpers, New York.

Dahrendorf, R. (1959) *Class and Class Conflict in Industrial Society*, Routledge & Kegan Paul, London.

Dalkey, N.C. (1972) *Studies in the Quality of Life: Delphi and Decision Making*, Lexington Books, Lexington, Mass.

Dallmayr, F.R. (1981) 'Critical theory and public policy', *Policy Studies Journal*, **9**: 522–34.

Dallos, R. and D. Boswell (1993) 'Mental health', in R. Dallos and E. McLaughlin (eds), *Social Problems and the Family*, Sage, London.

Dandeker, C. (1990) *Surveillance, Power and Modernity*, Polity Press, Cambridge.

Daniels, P. (1992) 'Industrial policy', in Harrop (ed.), 1992.

Davies, S. (1991) 'Towards the remoralization of society', in Loney *et al.* (eds), 1991.

Davis, K.C. (1969) *Discretionary Justice*, Louisiana State University Press, Baton Rouge, La.

Davis, N.J. and C. Stasz (1990) *Social Control of Deviance: A Critical Perspective*, McGraw-Hill, New York.

Dawson, R.E. and J.A. Robinson (1963) 'Interparty competition, economic variables and welfare policies in American States', *Journal of Politics*, **25**: 265–89.

Day, P. and R. Klein (1987) *Accountabilities in Five Public Services*, Tavistock Publications, London.

Deal, T.E. and A.A. Kennedy (1982) *Corporate Cultures*, Addison-Wesley, Reading, Mass.

de Board, R. (1978) *The Psychoanalysis of Organizations: A Psychoanalytic Approach to Behaviour in Groups and Organizations*, Tavistock Publications, London.

de Bono, E. (1981) *Atlas of Management Thinking*, Temple Smith, London.

Degeling, P. (1993) 'Policy as the accomplishment of an implementation structure: hospital restructuring in Australia', in Hill (ed.), 1993.

Degeling, P. and H. Colebatch (1984) 'Structure and action as constraints in the practice of public administration', *Australian Journal of Public Administration*, **43**: 320–31.

de Grazia, J. (1991) *DEA: The War against Drugs*, BBC Books, London.

de Haven-Smith, L. (1988) *Philosophical Critiques of Policy Analysis*, University of Florida Press, Gainesville, Fla.

de Jouvenal, B. (1967) *The Art of Conjecture*, Basic Books, New York.

De Leon, P. (1978) 'Public policy termination: an end and a beginning', *Policy Analysis*, **4**(3): 369–92.

De Leon, P. (1982) 'New perspectives on program termination', *Journal of Policy Analysis and Management*, **2** (1): 108–11.

De Leon, P. (1983) 'Policy evaluation and program termination', *Policy Studies Review*, **2** (4), 631–47.

De Leon, P. (1987) 'Policy termination as a political phenomenon', in Palumbo (ed.), 1987.

Demming, W.E. (1982) *Quality, Productivity and Competitive Position*, MIT, Center for Advanced Engineering Study, Cambridge, Mass.

Denhardt, R.B. (1981a) 'Toward a critical theory of public organisations', *Public Administration Review*, **41** (6): 628–35.

Denhardt, R.B. (1981b) *In the Shadow of Organization*, Regent Press, Lawrence, Kansas.

Denhardt, R.B. and K.G. Denhardt (1979) 'Public administration and the critique of domination', *Administration and Society*, **11**(1): 107–20.

Derthick, M. (1972) *New Towns in Town: Why a Federal Program Failed*, Urban Institute, Washington, D.C.

Derthick, M. (1979) *Policymaking for Social Security*, Brookings Institution, Washington, D.C.

De Sario, J., J.D. Slack, C.A. Washington and K.L. Ender (1991) 'Management of human resources in local government', in Bingham *et al.*, 1991.

Deutsch, K.W. (1963) *The Nerves of Government: Models of Political Communication and Control*, Free Press of Glencoe, New York.

Deutsch, K.W. (1967) 'Communications and decision making systems', in Charlesworth (ed.), 1967.

Deutsch, K.W. (1981) 'The crisis of the state', *Government and Opposition*, **16**(3): 331–43.

Devons, E. (1961) 'Statistics as a basis for policy', in E. Devons, *Essays in Economics*, Allen & Unwin, London.

Dewey, J. (1927) *The Public and its Problems*, Holt, New York.

Dewey, J. (1935) *Liberalism and Social Action*, Putnam, New York.

Dewey, J. (1938) *Experience and Education*, Collier, New York.

Dewey, J. (1939) *Freedom and Culture*, Putnam, New York (reprinted 1963).

Dicken, P. (1988) *Global Shift: Industrial Change in a Turbulent World*, Paul Chapman, London.

Dierkes, M., H. Weiler and A. Anatal (eds) (1987) *Comparative Policy Research*, Gower, Aldershot, Hants.

Di Maggio, P. and W. Powell (1983) 'The iron cage: institutional isomorphism and collective rationality in organizational fields', *American Sociological Review*, **48**(2): 147–60.

Di Maggio, P. and W. Powell (1991) 'The iron cage revisited: institutional isomorphism and collective rationality in organizational fields', in Powell and Di Maggio (eds), 1991.

Dixon, N. (1976) *The Psychology of Military Incompetence*, Jonathan Cape, London.

Dixon, N. (1987) *Our Own Worst Enemy*, Jonathan Cape, London.

Dixon, P. (1990) *Rhetoric*, Routledge, London.

Dobyns, H., P. Doughty and H.D. Lasswell (eds) (1964) *Peasants, Power and Applied Social Change*, Sage, Beverly Hills, Cal.

Dolbeare, K.M. (ed.) (1975) *Public Policy Evaluation*, Sage, Beverly Hills, Cal.

Dolman, A.J. (ed.) (1980) *Global Planning and Resource Management: Toward International Decision Making in a Global World*, Pergamon Press, New York.

Dommel, P.R. (1991) 'Intergovernmental relations', in Bingham *et al.*, 1991.

Doray, B. (1988) *From Taylorism to Fordism: A Rational Madness*, Free Association Books, London.

Downing, P. and K. Hanf (eds) (1983) *International Comparisons in Implementing Pollution Laws*, Kluwer-Nijhoff, Boston, Mass.

Downs, A. (1957) *An Economic Theory of Democracy*, Harper & Row, New York.

Downs, A. (1960) 'Why the government budget is too small in a democracy', *World Politics*, **12**: 541–63.

Downs, A. (1967) *Inside Bureaucracy*, Little, Brown, Boston, Mass.

Downs, A. (1972) 'Up and down with ecology: the issue attention cycle', *Public Interest*, **28**(1): 38–50.

Doyal, L. (1979) *The Political Economy of Health*, Pluto, London.

Dror, Y. (1964) 'Muddling through – "science" or inertia?' *Public Administration Review*, **24**: 153–7.

Dror, Y. (1967) 'Policy analysis: a new professional role in government service', *Public Administration Review*, **27**(3): 197–203.

Dror, Y. '(1979) 'From management science to policy sciences', in Pollitt *et al.* (eds), 1979.

Dror, Y. (1984) 'Required breakthroughs in think tanks', *Policy Sciences*, **16**: 199–225.

Dror, Y. (1989) *Public Policymaking Reexamined*, 2nd edn, Transaction Publishers, New Brunswick, N.J.; 1st edn, 1968.

Drucker, P.F. (1946) *The Concept of the Corporation*, John Day, New York, 1946.

Drucker, P.F. (1954) *The Practice of Management*, Heinemann, London.

Drucker, P.F. (1964) *Managing for Results*, Heinemann, London (2nd edn, 1989).

Drucker, P.F. (1969) *The Age of Discontinuity*, Heinemann, London.

Drucker, P.F. (1974) *Management Tasks, Responsibilities and Practices*, Heinemann, London.

Drucker, P.F. (1985) *Innovation and Entrepreneurship*, Heinemann, London.

Drucker, P.F. (1990a) *The New Realities*, Mandarin, London.

Drucker, P.F. (1990b) *Managing the Non-profit Organisation*, Butterworth-Heinemann, Oxford.

Dryzek, J.S. (1987) 'Complexity and rationality in public life', *Political Studies*, **35**: 424–42.

Dryzek, J.S. (1989) 'Policy sciences of democracy', *Polity*, **22**: 97–118.

Dryzek, J.S. (1990) *Discursive Democracy : Politics, Policy and Political Science*, Cambridge University Press, Cambridge.

Dryzek, J.S. (1993) 'Policy analysis and planning: from science to argument', in Fischer and Forester (eds), 1993.

Duncan, C. (ed.) (1992) *The Evolution of Public Management*, Macmillan, London.

Dunleavy, P. (1980) *Urban Political Analysis*, Macmillan, London.

Dunleavy, P. (1981) 'Professions and policy change: notes towards a model of ideological corporatism', *Public Administration Bulletin*, **36**: 3–16.

Dunleavy, P. (1982), 'Quasi-governmental sector professionalism', in Barker (ed.), 1982.

Dunleavy, P. (1986) 'Explaining the privatization boom: public choice versus radical approaches', *Public Administration*, **64**: 13–34.

Dunleavy, P. (1989) 'The architecture of the British central state, parts 1 and 2', *Public Administration*, **67**(3): 248–75; **67** (4) 391–417.

Dunleavy, P. (1991) *Democracy, Bureaucracy and Public Choice: Economic Explanations in Political Science*, Harvester Wheatsheaf, Hemel Hempstead, Herts.

Dunleavy, P. and B. O'Leary (1987) *Theories of the State: The Politics of Liberal Democracy*, Macmillan, London.

Dunn, E.S. (1971) *Economic and Social Development: A Process of Social Learning*, Johns Hopkins University Press, Baltimore, Md.

Dunn, W.N. (1981) *Public Policy Analysis: An Introduction*, Prentice-Hall, Englewood Cliffs, N.J.

Dunn, W.N. (1993) 'Policy reforms as arguments', in Fischer and Forester (eds), 1993.

Dunsire, A. (1978a) *Implementation in a Bureaucracy*, Martin Robertson, Oxford.

Dunsire, A. (1978b) *Control in a Bureaucracy*, Martin Robertson, Oxford.

Dunsire, A. (1990) 'Implementation theory and bureaucracy', in Younis (ed.), 1990.

Durkheim, E. (1964) *The Rules of Sociological Method*, Free Press, New York.

Dye, T.R. (1966) *Politics, Economics and the Public*, Rand-McNally, New York.

Dye, T.R. (1972) *Understanding Public Policy*, Prentice-Hall, Englewood Cliffs, N.J. (2nd edn, 1987).

Dye, T.R. (1976) *What Governments Do, Why they do it, What Difference it Makes*, University of Alabama Press, Tuscaloosa, Ala.

Easton, D. (1953) *The Political System*, Alfred A. Knopf, New York.

Easton, D. (1965) *A Framework for Political Analysis*, Prentice-Hall, Englewood Cliffs, N.J.

Eatwell, J., M. Milgate and P. Newman (eds) (1987) *The New Palgrave: A Dictionary of Economics*, Macmillan, London.

Edelman, M. (1964) *The Symbolic Uses of Politics*, University of Illinois Press, Urbana, Ill.

Edelman, M. (1971) *Politics as Symbolic Action*, Academic Press, New York.

Edelman, M. (1977) *Political Language: Words that Succeed and Policies that Fail*, Institute for the Study of Poverty, New York.

Edelman, M. (1985) 'Political language and political reality', *PS*, **18**(1): 10–19.

Edelman, M. (1988) *Constructing the Political Spectacle*, Chicago University Press, Chicago, Ill.

Edwards, W., M. Guttentag and K. Snapper (1975)

'A decision theoretic approach to evaluation research', in E.N. Streuning and M. Guttentag (eds), *Handbook of Evaluation Research*, vol. 1, Sage, Beverly Hills, Cal.

Elder, N., A. Thomas and D. Arter (1982) *The Consensular Democracies? The Government and Politics of the Scandinavian States*, Martin Robertson, Oxford.

Ellul, J. (1964) *The Technological Society*, Vintage Books, New York.

Elmore, R. (1978) 'Organizational models of social program implementation', *Public Policy*, **26**: 185–228.

Elmore, R. (1979) 'Backward mapping', *Political Science Quarterly*, **94**: 601–16; reprinted in Williams (ed.), 1982.

Elmore, R. (1985) 'Forward and backward mapping', in K. Hanf and T. Toonen (eds), *Policy Implementation in Federal and Unitary Systems*, Martinus Nijhoff, Dordrecht, Holland.

Elshtain, J.B. (1985) 'The relationship between political language and political reality', *PS*, **18**(1): 20–6.

England, J.R., K.I. Hudson, R.J. Masters, K.S. Powell and J.D. Shortridge (1985) *Information Systems for Policy Planning in Local Government*, Longman, with BURISA, London.

Ershkowitz, M. (1981) 'Lasswell and teaching', *Bureaucrat*, **10**(1): 50–1.

Esser, J.K. and J.S. Lindoerfer (1989) 'Groupthink and the space shuttle Challenger accident: towards a quantitative case analysis', *Journal of Behavioural Decision Making*, **2**: 167–77.

Etheridge, L.S. (1981) 'Government learning', in S. Long (ed.), *Handbook of Political Behavior*, Plenum Press, New York.

Etheridge, L.S. (1985) *Can Governments Learn?*, Pergamon Press, New York.

Etzioni, A. (1961) *A Comparative Analysis of Complex Organizations*, Free Press, New York.

Etzioni, A. (1964) *Modern Organizations*, Prentice-Hall, Englewood Cliffs, N.J.

Etzioni, A. (1967) 'Mixed scanning: a "third" approach to decision-making', *Public Administration Review*, **27**: 385–92.

Etzioni, A. (1968) *The Active Society: A Theory of Societal and Political Processes*, Free Press, New York.

Etzioni, A. (1983) *An Immodest Agenda: Rebuilding America Before the Twenty-First Century*, Free Press, New York.

Etzioni, A. (1988) *The Moral Dimension: Toward a New Economics*, Free Press, New York.

Etzioni, A. (1993a) *The Spirit of Community: Rights, Responsibilities and the Communitarian Agenda*, Crown Publishers, New York.

Etzioni, A. (1993b) *The Parenting Deficit*, Demos, London.

Etzioni, A. (1994) 'Who should pay for care?', *The Sunday Times*, 3 July.

Evan, W.M. (1972) 'An organizational-set model of interorganizational relations', in Tuite *et al.* (eds), 1972.

Evan, W.M. (ed.) (1976) *Interorganizational Relations*, Penguin, Harmondsworth.

Evan, W.M. (ed) (1981) *Knowledge and Power in a Global Society*, Sage, Beverly Hills, Cal.

Evans, P.B., D. Reuschemeyer and T. Skocpol (eds) (1985) *Bringing the State Back In*, Cambridge University Press, Cambridge.

Fama, E.F. (1980) 'Agency problems and the theory of the firm', *Journal of Political Economy*, **88**: 288–305.

Fay, B. (1975) *Social Theory and Political Practice*, Allen & Unwin, London.

Fayol, H. (1949) *General and Industrial Management*, Pitman, London.

Fee, E. and D.M. Fox (eds) (1988) *Aids and the Burdens of History*, University of California Press, Berkeley, Cal.

Feldman, E. (1978), 'Comparative public policy: field or method?', *Comparative Politics*, **10**: 278–305.

Festinger, L. (1957) *A Theory of Cognitive Dissonance*, Row, Peterson, Evanston, Ill.

Fimister, G. and M. Hill (1993) 'Delegating implementation problems: social security, housing and community care in Britain', in Hill (ed.), 1993.

Fischer, F. (1980) *Politics, Values, and Public Policy: The Problem of Methodology*, Westview Press, Boulder, Col.

Fischer, F. (1987) 'Policy expertise and the "new class": a critique of the neoconservative thesis', in Fischer and Forester (eds), 1987.

Fischer, F. (1990) *Technocracy and the Politics of Expertise*, Sage, Newbury Park, Cal.

Fischer, F. (1991) 'American think tanks: policy elites and the politicization of expertise', *Governance*, **4**(3): 332–53.

Fischer, F. and J. Forester (1993) 'Introduction', in Fischer and Forester (eds), 1993.

Fischer, F. and J. Forester, (eds) (1987) *Confronting Values in Policy Analysis*, Sage, Newbury Park, Cal.

Fischer, F. and J. Forester, (eds) (1993) *The Argumentative Turn in Policy Analysis and Planning*, Duke University Press/UCL Press, London.

Fischer, G.W. and E.J. Johnson (1986) 'Behavioural decision theory and political decision making', in Lau and Sears (eds), 1986.

Fishman, M. (1978) 'Crime waves as ideology', *Social Problems*, **25**: 531–43.

Fiske, S. and S. Taylor (1984) *Social Cognition*, Addison-Wesley, Reading, Mass.

Fitzmaurice, J. (1981) *Politics in Denmark*, Hurst, London.

Fitzmaurice, J. (1991) *Austrian Politics and Society Today*, Macmillan, London.

Fitzpatrick, M. and D. Milligan (1987) *The Truth about the Aids Panic*, Junius Publications, London.

Fleming, A.F., M. Carballo, D.W. FitzSimons, M.R. Bailey and J. Mann (eds) (1988) *The Global Impact of AIDS*, Alan R. Liss, York.

Flint, D. (1988), *Philosophy and Principles of Auditing: An Introduction*, Macmillan, London.

Flowers, M.L. (1977) 'A laboratory test of some implications of Janis's groupthink hypothesis', *Journal of Personality and Social Psychology*, **25**: 888–96.

Flynn, N. (1990) *Public Sector Management*, Harvester Wheatsheaf, Hemel Hempstead, Herts.

Flynn, R. (1993) 'Restructuring health systems: a comparative analysis of England and the Netherlands', in Hill (ed.), 1993.

Fodor, E.M. and T. Smith (1982) 'The power motive as an influence on group decision making', *Journal of Personality and Social Psychology*, **42**: 178–85.

Ford, P. (1992) 'American enterprise institute for public policy research', in Weiss (ed.), 1992.

Forester, J. (1981) 'Questioning and organising attention: towards a critical theory of planning and administrative practice', *Administration and Society*, **13**: 161–205.

Forester, J. (ed.) (1985) *Critical Theory and Public Life*, MIT Press, Cambridge, Mass.

Foster, T.R.V. (1993) *101 Great Mission Statements: How the World's Leading Companies Run their Businesses*, Kogan Page, London.

Foucault, M. (1965) *Madness and Civilization: A History of Insanity in the Age of Reason*, trans. Richard Howard, Random House, New York.

Foucault, M. (1973) *The Order of Things*, Vintage Books, New York.

Foucault, M. (1977) *Discipline and Punish: The Birth of the Prison*, Penguin, Harmondsworth, Middx.

Foucault, M. (1980) *Power/Knowledge: Selected Interviews and Other Writings 1972–1977*, ed. Colin Gordon, New York, Harvester Wheatsheaf.

Foucault, M. (1986) *The Foucault Reader*, ed. P. Rainbow, Peregrine, Harmondsworth, Middx.

Fowler, R. (1991) *Language in the News: Discourse and Ideology in the Press*, Routledge, London.

Fox, W.T.R. (1969) 'Harold Lasswell and the study of world politics : configurative analysis, garrison state, and world commonwealth', in Rogow (ed.), 1969.

Frankenburg, R. (1966) *Communities in Britain*, Penguin Books, Harmondsworth, Middx.

Franklin, B. (1994) *Packaging Politics: Political Communications in Britain's Media Democracy*, Edward Arnold, London.

Frazer, E. and N. Lacey (1993) *The Politics of the Community*, Harvester Wheatsheaf, Hemel Hempstead, Herts.

Freeman, J. (1982) 'Organizational life cycles and natural selection processes', in B.M. Shaw and L.L. Cummings (eds), *Research in Organizational Behaviour*, JAI Press, Greenwich, Conn.

Freeman, J. and M.T. Hannan (1983) 'Niche width and the dynamics of organizational populations', *American Journal of Sociology*, **6**: 1116–45.

Freidson, E. (1986) *Professional Powers: A Study of the Institutionalization of Formal Knowledge*, University of Chicago Press, Chicago.

Freud, S. (1991) *Group Psychology, Civilization and its Discontents*, Penguin Freud Library, vol. 12, Penguin, Harmondsworth, Middx.

Freud, S. and W.C. Bullitt (1967) *Thomas Woodrow Wilson: A Psychological Study*, Weidenfeld & Nicolson, London.

Frey, B.S. (1978) *Modern Political Economy*, Martin Robertson, Oxford.

Fried, R.C. (1972) *Comparative Urban Performance*, European Urban Research Working Paper, no. 1, University of California, Los Angeles, Cal.

Friedmann, J. (1973) *Retracking America*, Rodale Press, Emmaus, Pa (2nd edn, 1981).

Friedmann, J. (1978) 'Innovation, flexible response, and social learning: a problem in the theory of meta-planning', in R.W. Burchell and G. Sternlieb (eds), *Planning Theory in the 1980s: A Search for Future Directions*, Transaction Books, New Brunswick, N.J.

Friedmann, J. (1979) *The Good Society*, MIT Press, Cambridge, Mass.

Friedmann, J. (1984) 'Planning as social learning', in Korten and Klaus (eds), 1984.

Friedmann, J. (1992) *Empowerment*, Blackwell, Oxford.

Friedmann, J. and G. Abonyi (1976) 'Social learning: a new model for policy research', *Environmental Planning*, **A8**: 927–40.

Friedmann, J. and B. Hudson (1974) 'Knowledge and action: a guide to planning theory', *Journal of the American Institute of Planners*, **40**: 2–16.

Frohock, F.M. (1974) *Normative Political Theory*, Prentice-Hall, Englewood Cliffs, N.J.

Frohock, F.M. (1979) *Public Policy: Scope and Logic*, Prentice-Hall, Englewood Cliffs, N.J.

From, J. and P. Stava (1993) 'Implementation of community law: the last stronghold of national control?', in Andersen and Eliassen (eds), 1993.

Fuhrman, S.H. (1992) 'The Center for Policy Research in Education', in Weiss (ed.), 1992.

Fukuyama, F. (1992a) *The End of History*, Hamish Hamilton, London.

Fukuyama, F. (1992b) 'The end of history is still nigh', *Independent*, 3 March: 21.

Fuller, R.C. (1937) 'Sociological theory and social problems', *Social Forces*, **15**: 496–502.

Fuller, R.C. (1938) 'The problem of teaching social problems', *American Journal of Sociology*, **44**: 415–35.

Fuller, R.C. and R.R. Myers (1941) 'The natural history of a social problem', *American Sociological Review*, 6 (June): 320–8.

Furner, M.O. (1990) 'Knowing capitalism: public investigation and the labour question in the long progressive era', in Furner and Supple (eds), 1990.

Furner, M.O. and Barry Supple (eds) (1990) *The State and Economic Knowledge: The British and American Experiences*, Cambridge University Press, Cambridge.

Gabor, D. (1963) *Inventing the Future*, Lechhner & Warburg, New York.

Gadamer, H.-G. (1975) *Truth and Method*, Seabury, New York.

Galbraith, J.K. (1953) *American Capitalism and the Concept of Countervailing Power*, Houghton Mifflin, Boston, Mass.

Galbraith, J.K. (1967) *The Affluent Society*, Penguin, Harmondsworth, Middx.

Galbraith, J.K. (1969) *The New Industrial State*, Penguin, Harmondsworth, Middx.

Gamble, A. *et al.* (1989) *Ideas, Interests and Consequences*, Institute of Economic Affairs, London.

Gardiner, P. (ed.) (1974) *The Philosophy of History*, Oxford University Press, Oxford.

Gaster, L. (1991) *Quality at the Front Line*, School for Advanced Urban Studies, University of Bristol.

Gaventa, J. (1980) *Power and Powerlessness, Quiescence and Rebellion in an Appalachian Valley*, Clarendon Press, Oxford.

Gelb, J. and M.L. Palley (1979) 'Women and interest group politics: a comparative analysis of federal decision-making', *Journal of Politics*, 41: 362–92.

Gendron, B. (1977) *Technology and the Human Condition*, St Martins Press, New York.

George, A.L. (1980) *Presidential Decisionmaking in Foreign Policy: The Effective Use of Advice and Information*, Westview Press, Boulder, Col.

Giddens, A. (1987) *Social Theory and Modern Sociology*, Polity Press, Cambridge.

Giddens, A. (1989) *Sociology*, Polity Press, Oxford.

Giddens, A. (1990) *The Consequences of Modernity*, Polity Press, Cambridge.

Glazer, N. (1988) *The Limits of Social Policy*, Harvard University Press, Cambridge, Mass.

Glen, A. (1993) 'Methods and themes in community practice', in Butcher *et al.* (eds), 1993.

Glynn, J., A. Gray., M. Murphy *et al.* (1989) 'Human resource management audit in government', *Public Money and Management*, 9 (4): 35–41.

Goffman, E. (1968) *The Asylums: Essays on the Social Situation of Mental Patients and Other Inmates*, Penguin, Harmondsworth, Middx.

Goffman, E. (1971) *The Presentation of the Self in Everyday Life*, Penguin, Harmondsworth, Middx (first published 1959).

Goldhamer, H. (1978) *The Adviser*, Elsevier, New York.

Goldhamer, H. and H. Speier (1959) 'Some observations on political gaming', *World Politics*, **12**: 71–83.

Goldsmith, M. and H. Wolman (1992) *Urban Politics*, Blackwell, Oxford.

Goldsworthy, D. (1991) *Setting Up Next Steps*, HMSO, London.

Goldwin, R. (ed.) (1980) *Bureaucrats, Policy Analysts, Statesmen: Who Leads?* American Enterprise Institute, Washington, D.C.

Golembiewski, R.T. (1990) 'Public sector organization behaviour and theory: perspectives on nagging problems and on real progress', in Lynn and Wildavsky (eds), 1990.

Gomulka, S. (1979) 'Britain's slow industrial growth: increasing inefficiency versus low rate of technical change', in W. Beckerman (ed.), *Slow Growth in Britain: Consensus and Consequences*, Clarendon Press, Oxford.

Gordon, I., J. Lewis and K. Young (1977) 'Perspectives on policy analysis', *Public Administration Bulletin*, **25**: 26–35.

Gorges, I. (1991) 'The social survey in Germany before 1933', in Bulmer *et al.* (eds), 1991.

Gormley, W.T. (1983) *The Politics of Public Utility Regulation*, University of Pittsburgh Press, Pittsburgh, Pa.

Gorrell, J., R.C. Kunkel, and D.M. Ossant (1993) 'Using Lasswell decision seminars to assure appropriate knowledge-base in teacher education', *Journal of Teacher Education*, **44**(3): 183–9.

Gough, I. (1979) *The Political Economy of the Welfare State*, Macmillan, London.

Gouldner, A.W. (1954) *Patterns of Industrial Bureaucracy*, Free Press, New York.

Gouldner, A.W. (1970) *The Coming Crisis of Western Sociology*, Avon, New York.

Gouran, S.D., R.Y. Hirokawa and A.E. Martz (1986) 'A critical analysis of factors related to decisional processes involved in the Challenger disaster', *Central States Speech Journal*, **37**(3) : 119–35; reprinted in Patton *et al.*, 1989.

Grant, W. (1989a) *Government and Industry: A Comparative Analysis of the US, Canada and the UK*, Edward Elgar, Aldershot, Hants.

Grant, W. (1989b) *Pressure Groups, Politics and Democracy in Britain*, Philip Allan, London.

Grant, W. (1990) 'Industrial policy', in J. Simmie and R. King (eds), *The State in Action*, Frances Pinter, London.

Grant, W. (ed.) (1985) *The Political Economy of Corporatism*, Macmillan, London.

Gray, A. and W. I. Jenkins (1985) *Administrative Politics in British Government*, Wheatsheaf Books, Brighton.

Gray, A. and B. Jenkins (eds) (1983) *Policy Analysis and Evaluation in British Government*, Royal Institute of Public Administration, London.

Gray, J. (1986) *Hayek on Liberty*, Blackwell, Oxford.

Graymer, L. (1978) 'Profile of the program at the Graduate School of Public Policy, University of California at Berkeley', *Public Administration Bulletin*, no. 26: 4–11.

Green, D. (1985) *Which Doctor? A Critical Analysis of the Professional Barriers to Competition in the Health Service*, Institute of Economic Affairs, London.

Greenaway, J., S. Smith and J. Street (1992) *Deciding Factors in British Politics: A Case Studies Approach*, Routledge, London.

Greenstein, F.I. (1969) *Personality and Politics: Problems of Evidence, Inference and Conceptualization*, Markham, Chicago, Ill.; 2nd edn, Princeton University Press, Princeton, N.J., 1987.

Greenstein, F.I. (1975) 'Personality and politics', in F.I. Greenstein and N.W. Polsby (eds), *The Handbook of Political Science, vol. 2: Micropolitical Theory*, Addison-Wesley, Reading, Mass.

Greenstein, F.I. (1992) 'Can personality and politics be studied systematically'?, *Political Psychology*, **13**: 105–28.

Greenstein, F.I. and M. Lerner (1971) *A Source Book for the Study of Personality and Politics*, Markham, Chicago, Ill.

Greenwood, E. (1965) 'Attributes of a profession', in M. Zald (ed.), *Social Welfare Institutions*, John Wiley, London.

Gregor, A.J. (1971) *Metapolitics: A Brief Inquiry into the Conceptual Language of Political Science*, Free Press, New York.

Gregory, R. (1989) 'Political rationality or "incrementalism"?. Charles E. Lindblom's enduring contribution to public policy making theory', *Policy and Politics*, **17**: 139–53.

Griffiths, P. (1987) 'Mid-Glamorgan County Council', in H. Elcock and G. Jordan (eds), *Learning from Local Authority Budgeting*, Avebury, Aldershot, Hants.

Guba, E.G. (ed.) (1990) *The Paradigm Dialog*, Sage, London.

Guba, E.G. and Y.S. Lincoln (1987) 'The countenances of fourth-generation evaluation: description, judgment and negotiation', in Palumbo (ed.), 1987.

Gunn, J.A.W. (1989) 'Public opinion', and 'Public interest', in Ball *et al.* (eds), 1989.

Gunn, L. (1978) 'Why is implementation so difficult?', *Management Services in Government*, **33**: 169–76.

Gunn, L. (1987) 'Perspectives on public management', in Kooiman and Eliassen (eds), 1987.

Gusfield, J.R. (1981) *The Culture of Public Problems*, University of Chicago Press, Chicago, Ill.

Gutch, R. (1992) *Contracting Lessons from the US*, National Council of Voluntary Organisations, London.

Gyford, J. (1991) *Citizens, Consumers and Councils*, Macmillan, London.

Haas, E.B. (1990) *When Knowledge is Power: Three Models of Change in International Organisations*, University of California Press, Berkeley and Los Angeles, Cal., and Oxford.

Habeebullah, M. and D. Slater (1993) 'Community Government', in Butcher *et al.* (eds), 1993.

Habermas, J. (1970) 'Toward a theory of communicative competence', *Inquiry*, **13**: 360–75.

Habermas, J. (1971) *Towards a Rational Society*, Heinemann, London.

Habermas, J. (1973) 'A postscript to Knowledge and Human Interests', *Philosophy of the Social Sciences*, **3**: 157–85.

Habermas, J. (1976) *Legitimation Crisis*, Heinemann, London.

Habermas, J. (1984) *The Theory of Communicative Action, vol. 1: Reason and the Rationalization of Society*, Beacon Press, Boston, Mass.

Habermas, J. (1989) *The Structural Transformation of the Public Sphere: An Inquiry into a Categorisation of Bourgeois Society*, Polity Press, London.

Hall, P.A. (1986) *Governing the Economy: the Politics of State Intervention in Britain and France*, Polity Press, Cambridge.

Hall, P.A. (ed.) (1989) *The Political Power of Economic Ideas*, Princeton University Press, Princeton, N.J.

Hall, R.H. (1977) *Organizations, Structure and Process*, Prentice-Hall, Englewood Cliffs, N.J.

Hall, S. and D. Held (1989) 'Left and rights', *Marxism Today*, June: 16–23; reprinted as 'Citizens and citizenship', in S. Hall and M. Jacques (eds), *New Times: The Changing Face of Politics in the 1990s*, Lawrence & Wishart, London.

Ham, C. and M. Hill (1984) *The Policy Process in the Modern Capitalist State*, Harvester Wheatsheaf, Brighton, Sussex.

Hambleton, R. (1978) *Policy Planning and Local Government*, Hutchinson, London.

Hambrick, R.S. (1974) 'A guide for the analysis of policy arguments', *Policy Sciences*, **5**: 469–78.

Hampden-Turner, C. (1971) *Radical Man: The Process of Psycho-social Development*, Anchor, Garden City, N.Y.

Hancock, M.D. (1989) *West Germany: The Politics of Democratic Corporatism*, Chatham House, Chatham, N.J.

Hancock, M.D., J. Logue, and B. Schiller (eds) (1991) *Managing Modern Capitalism: Industrial Renewal and Workplace Democracy in the United States and Western Europe*, Greenwood, Westport, Conn.

Hancock, M.D., D.P. Conradt, B.G. Peters, W. Safran and R. Zariski (1993) *Politics in Western Europe*, Macmillan, London.

Handy, C. (1976) *Understanding Organizations*, Penguin Books, Harmondsworth, Middx; 3rd edn, 1985.

Handy, C. (1986) *Gods of Management*, Souvenir Press, London.

Handy, C. (1988) *Understanding Voluntary Organisations*, Penguin, Harmondsworth, Middx.

Hanf, K. (1978) 'Introduction', in Hanf and Scharpf (eds), 1978.

Hanf, K. (1993) 'Enforcing environmental laws: the social regulation of co-production', in Hill (ed.), 1993.

Hanf, K. and L. O'Toole (1992) 'Revisiting old friends: networks, implementation structures and the management of inter-organisational relations', *European Journal of Political Research*, **21**: 163–80.

Hanf, K. and F.W. Scharpf (eds) (1978) *Interorganisational Policy Making : Limits to Coordination and Central Control*, Sage, London.

Hanley, N. and C.L. Spash (1993) *Cost-benefit Analysis and the Environment*, Edward Elgar, Aldershot, Hants.

Hannan, M.T. and J.H. Freeman (1977) 'The population ecology of organizations', *American Journal of Sociology*, **82**: 929–64.

Hargrove, E.C. (1975) *The Missing Link*, Urban Institute, Washington, D.C.

Harman, G. (1992) 'Intergovernmental relations: federal systems', in Hawkesworth and Kogan (eds), 1992.

Harrington, M. (1962) *The Other America: Poverty in the United States*, Macmillan, New York.

Harris, J. (1972) *Unemployment and Politics, 1886–1914*, Oxford University Press, London.

Harris, J. (1990) 'Economic knowledge and British social policy', in Furner and Supple (eds), 1990.

Harrison, S., D.J. Hunter and C. Pollitt (1990) *The Dynamics of British Health Policy*, Unwin Hyman, London.

Harrop, M. (ed.) (1992) *Power and Policy in Liberal Democracies*, Cambridge University Press, Cambridge.

Hartwell, R.M. (1989) 'The political economy of policy formation: the case of England', in Gamble *et al.*, 1989.

Harvey, D. (1992) *The Condition of Postmodernity: An Inquiry into the Origins of Cultural Change*, Blackwell, Oxford.

Hawkesworth, M. (1988) *Theoretical Issues in Policy Analysis*, SUNY Press, Albany, N.Y.

Hawkesworth, M. and M. Kogan (eds) (1992) *Encyclopedia of Government and Politics*, vols 1 and 2, Routledge, London.

Hawley, E.W. (1990) 'Economic inquiry and the state in New Era America', in Furner and Supple (eds), 1990.

Hayek, F.A. (1944) *The Road to Serfdom*, Routledge, London.

Hayek, F.A. (1960) *The Constitution of Liberty*, Routledge, London.

Hayek, F.A. (1978) *New Studies in Philosophy, Politics, Economics and the History of Ideas*, Chicago University Press, Chicago, Ill.

Hayes, J.R. and H.A. Simon (1974) 'Understanding written problem instructions', in L.W. Gregg (ed.), *Knowledge and Cognition*, Lawrence Erlbaum, Potomac, Md.

Hayward, J.E.S. and M.M. Watson (eds) (1975) *Planning, Politics and Public Policy: The British, French and Italian Experience*, Cambridge University Press, Cambridge.

Hazelrigg, L.E. (1985) 'Were it not for words', *Social Problems*, **32**: 232–7.

Healey, P. (1993) 'The communicative turn in planning theory', in Fischer and Forester (eds), 1993.

Heclo, H. (1972) 'Review article: Policy analysis', *British Journal of Political Science*, **2**: 83–108.

Heclo, H. (1974) *Social Policy in Britain and Sweden*, Yale University Press, New Haven, Conn.

Heclo, H. (1978) 'Issue networks and the executive establishment' in King (ed.), 1978.

Heclo, H. and A. Wildavsky (1974), *The Private Government of Public Money*, Macmillan, London.

Hede, A. (1991) 'Country report: trends in the higher civil services of Anglo-American systems', *Governance*, **4**: 489–510.

Heidenheimer, A. (1986) 'Politics, policy and polizey as concepts in English and continental languages: an attempt to explain divergences', *Review of Politics*, **48**(1): 3–30.

Heidenheimer, A., H. Heclo and C.T. Adams (1975) *Comparative Public Policy: The Politics of Social Choice in America, Europe and Japan*, St Martin's Press, New York; 2nd edn, 1983; 3rd edn, 1990.

Heineman, R.A., W.T. Bluhm, S.A. Peterson and E.N. Kearney (1990) *The World of the Policy Analyst: Rationality, Values and Politics*, Chatham House, Chatham, N.J.

Heller, F. (1983) 'The danger of group-think', *Guardian*, 31 January.

Henderson, D. (1986) *Innocence and Design: The Influence of Economic Ideas on Policy*, Blackwell, Oxford.

Henkel, M. (1991) *Government, Evaluation and Change*, Jessica Kingsley, London.

Henriot, P.J. (1970) 'Political questions about social indicators', *Western Political Quarterly*, **23**: 235–55.

Henry, J. (ed.) (1991) *Creative Management*, Sage, London.

Henry, N.L. (1975) *Public Administration and Public Affairs*, Prentice-Hall, Englewood Cliffs, N.J.

Henry, N.L. (1990), 'Root and branch: public administration's travail towards the future', in Lynn and Wildavsky (eds), 1990.

Henshel, R.L. (1990) *Thinking about Social Problems*, Harcourt Brace Jovanovich, New York.

Hensley, T.R. and G.W. Griffin (1986) 'Victims of groupthink: the Kent State University board of trustees and the 1977 gymnasium controversy', *Journal of Conflict Resolution*, **30**: 497–531.

Herzberg, F. (1966) *Work and the Nature of Man*, Staples Press, New York.

Herzberg, F., B. Mauser and B. Snyderman (1960) *The Motivation to Work*, John Wiley, New York.

Higgins, J., N. Deakin and J. Edwards (1983) *Government and Urban Poverty*, Blackwell, Oxford.

Hill, M.J. (1969) 'The exercise of discretion in the National Assistance Board', *Public Administration*, **47**: 75–90.

Hill, M.J. (ed.) (1993) *New Agendas in the Study of the Policy Process*, Harvester Wheatsheaf, New York.

Hill, M.J. and G. Bramley (1986) *Analysing Social Policy*, Blackwell, Oxford.

Hill, M.J. and R. Issacharoff (1971) *Community Action and Race Relations*, Oxford University Press, London.

Hillery, G.A. (1968) *Communal Organizations*, Chicago University Press, Chicago, Ill.

Hirsch, F. (1977) *Social Limits to Growth*, Routledge & Kegan Paul, London.

Hirschman, A.O. (1970a) 'The search for paradigms as a hindrance to understanding', *World Politics*, **22**: 329–43.

Hirschman, A.O. (1970b) *Exit, Voice and Loyalty*, Harvard University Press, Cambridge, Mass.

Hirschman, A.O. (1983) *Shifting Involvements*, Blackwell, Oxford.

Hjern, B. (1982) 'Implementation research – the link gone missing', *Journal of Public Policy*, **2**(3): 301–8.

Hjern, B. and C. Hull (1982) 'Implementation research as empirical constitutionalism', *European Journal of Political Research*, **10**: 105–16.

Hjern, B. and D.O. Porter (1981) 'Implementation structures: a new unit of administrative analysis', *Organization Studies*, **2**: 211–27.

Hjern, B., K. Hanf, and D. Porter (1978) 'Local networks of manpower training in the Federal Republic of Germany and Sweden', in Hanf and Scharpf (eds), 1978.

Hodgson, G.M. (1988) *Economics and Institutions: A Manifesto for a Modern Institutional Economics*, Polity Press, Oxford.

Hofferbert, R. (1974) *The Study of Public Policy*, Bobbs Merrill, Indianapolis, Ind.

Hoggett, P. (1987) 'A farewell to mass production? Decentralization as an emergent private sector paradigm', in Hogget and Hambleton (eds), 1987.

Hoggett, P. (1992a) *Partisans in an Uncertain World: The Psychoanalysis of Engagement*, Free Association Books, London.

Hoggett, P. (1992b) 'A place for experience: a psychoanalytic perspective on boundary, identity and culture', *Environment and Planning D: Society and Space*, **10**: 345–56.

Hoggett, P. and R. Hambleton (eds) (1987) 'Decentralization and Democracy', Occasional Paper 28, School for Advanced Urban Studies, University of Bristol.

Hogwood, B.W. (1984) 'The dangers of oversophistication', *Public Administration Bulletin*, **44**: 19–28.

Hogwood, B.W. (1987) *From Crisis to Complacency? Shaping Public Policy in Britain*, Oxford University Press, London.

Hogwood, B.W. (1992) *Trends in British Public Policy*, Open University Press, Buckingham, Bucks.

Hogwood, B.W. and L.A. Gunn (1984) *Policy Analysis for the Real World*, Oxford University Press, London.

Hogwood, B.W. and B.G. Peters (1983) *Policy Dynamics*, Wheatsheaf Books, Brighton, Sussex, and St Martin's Press, New York.

Hogwood, B.W. and B.G. Peters (1985) *The Pathology of Public Policy*, Oxford University Press, London.

Holden, K., D.A. Peel and J.L. Thompson (1982) *Modelling the UK Economy: An Introduction*, Martin Robertson, Oxford.

Holden, L. (1994) 'Training', in Beardwell and Holden (eds), 1994.

Hollis, M. and S. Smith (1992) *Explaining International Relations*, Clarendon Press, Oxford.

Holub, R.C. (1991) *Jürgen Habermas: Critic in the Public Sphere*, Routledge, London.

Holzner, B. and J.A. Marx (1979) *Knowledge Application: The Knowledge System in Society*, Allyn & Bacon, Boston, Mass.

Hood, C.C. (1976) *The Limits of Administration*, John Wiley, London.

Hood, C.C. (1986) *Administrative Analysis: An Introduction to Rules, Enforcement and Organizations*, Wheatsheaf Books, Brighton, Sussex.

Hood, C.C. (1990) 'De-Sir Humphreyfying the Westminster model of bureaucracy: a new style of governance? ', *Governance*, **2**: 205–14.

Hood, C.C. (1991) 'A public management for all seasons?', *Public Administration*, **69** (4): 3–19.

Hoover, K. (1989) 'The changing world of think tanks', *PS: Political Science and Politics*, **22**: 563–72.

Hope, K. (1978) 'Indicators of the state of society', in Bulmer (ed.), 1978.

Hoppe, R. (1993) 'Political judgement and the policy cycle: the case of ethnicity policy arguments in the Netherlands', in Fischer and Forester (eds), 1993.

Hoyes, L. and R. Means (1993) 'Quasi markets and the reform of community care', in Le Grand and Bartlett (eds), 1993.

Huczynski, A. and D. Buchanan (1991) *Organizational Behaviour*, Prentice-Hall, London.

Hudson, B. (1987) 'Collaboration in social welfare: a framework for analysis', *Policy and Politics*, **15**: 175–82.

Hudson, B. (1989) 'Michael Lipsky and street-level bureaucracy: a neglected perspective', in L. Barton (ed.), *Disability and Dependency*, Falmer Press, London.

Hughes, O.E. (1994) *Public Management and Administration: An Introduction*, St Martin's Press, New York.

Hunter, D. (1994) 'Social research and health policy in the aftermath of the NHS reforms', in Popay and Williams, 1994.

Hunter, F. (1953) *Community Power Structure*, University of North Carolina Press, Chapel Hill, N.C.

Hupe, P. (1993) 'The politics of implementation: individual, organisational and political co-production in social services delivery', in Hill (ed.), 1993.

Hutton, W. (1994) 'Why Clarke shrank from growth', *Guardian*, 17 October: 11.

Hutton, W. (1995) *The State We're In*, Jonathan Cape, London.

Illich, I. (1975a) *Tools for Conviviality*, Fontana/Collins, London.

Illich, I. (1975b) *Disabling Professions*, Boyars, London.

Illich, I. (1977) *Medical Nemesis: The Expropriation of Health*, Penguin, Harmondsworth, Middx.

Inglis, F. (1982) *Radical Earnestness: English Social Theory 1880–1980*, Martin Robertson, Oxford.

Ingram, H. (1978) 'The political rationality of innovation', in A. Friedlander, *Approaches to Controlling Air Pollution*, MIT Press, Cambridge, Mass.

Innis, J.M. (1978) 'Selective exposure as a function of dogmatism and incentive', *Journal of Social Psychology*, **106**: 262–5.

International City Management Association (ICMA) (1989) *The Citizen as Customer*, ICMA, Washington, D.C.

Isaac-Henry, K. (1993) 'The management of information technology in the public sector', in Isaac-Henry *et al.*, 1993.

Isaac-Henry, K., C. Parry and C. Barnes (1993) *Management in the Public Sector: Challenge and Change*, Chapman & Hall, London.

Iyengar, S., D.R. Kinder, M.D. Peters and J.A. Krosnick (1984) 'The evening news and presidential evaluations', *Journal of Personality and Social Psychology*, **46**: 778–87.

Jackson, P.M. (1982) *The Political Economy of Bureaucracy*, Philip Allen, Oxford.

Jackson, P.M. (1988) 'The management of performance in the public sector', *Public Money and Management*, **8**(4): 11–16.

Jackson, P.M. (1990) 'Public choice and public sector management', *Public Money and Management*, **10**(4): 13–21.

Jackson, P. and B. Palmer (1989) *First Steps in Measuring Performance in the Public Sector: A Management Guide*, Public Finance Foundation, London.

James, W. (1970) *Pragmatism*, Meridian Books, New York; first published 1907.

Janis, I.L. (1972) *Groupthink: Psychological Studies of Policy Decisions and Fiascos*, Houghton Mifflin, Boston, Mass.

Janis, I.L. and L. Mann (1977) *Decision Making: A Psychological Analysis of Conflict, Choice, and Commitment*, Free Press, New York.

Janowitz, M. and P. Hirsch (1981) *Reader in Public Opinion and Mass Communication*, Free Press, New York.

Jasper, J.M. (1992) 'Three nuclear energy controversies', in Nelkin (ed.), 1992.

Jay, A. (1987) *Management and Machiavelli: Power and Authority in Business Life*, Business Books, London.

Jenkins, R. and J. Solomos (eds) (1987) *Racism and Equal Opportunities Policies in the 1980s*, Cambridge University Press, Cambridge.

Jenkins, W.I. (1978) *Policy Analysis: A Political and Organisational Perspective*, Martin Robertson, London.

Jenkins-Smith, H. (1990) *Democratic Politics and Policy Analysis*, Brooks/Cole, Pacific Grove, Cal.

Jenkins-Smith, H. (1991) 'Alternative theories of the policy process: reflections on research strategy for the study of nuclear waste policy', *PS: Political Science and Politics*, June: 157–66.

Jervis, R. (1968) 'Hypothesis on misperception', *World Politics*, **20**: 454–79.

Jessop, B. (1990) *State Theory: Putting Capitalist States in their Place*, Polity Press, Cambridge.

Johnson, N. (1990) 'Sir Geoffrey Vickers', in Lord Blake and C.S. Nicholls (eds), *The Dictionary of National Biography 1981–1985*, Oxford University Press, London.

Johnson, R.J. (1993) 'The rise and decline of the state', in Taylor (ed.), 1993.

Johnson, T.J. (1972) *Professions and Power*, Macmillan, London.

Jones, C.O. (1970) *An Introduction to the Study of Public Policy*, Wadsworth, Belmont, Cal.

Jones, J.A. (1971) 'Federal efforts to solve contemporary social problems', in Smigel (ed.), 1971.

Jordan, A.G. (1981) 'Iron triangles, woolly corporatism or elastic nets: images of the policy process, *Journal of public policy*, 1: 95–123.

Jordan, A.G. and J.J. Richardson (1983) 'Policy communities: the British and European style', *Policy Studies Journal*, 11: 603–15.

Jordan, A.G. and J.J. Richardson (1987) *British Politics and the Policy Process: An Arena Approach*, Unwin Hyman, London.

Jordan, A.G. and K. Schubert (1992) 'A preliminary ordering of policy networks labels', *European Journal of Political Research*, 21: 7–27.

Jowell, R., S. Witherspoon and L. Brook (eds) (1990) *British Social Attitudes: 8th Report*, Gower, Aldershot, Hants.

Judson, H.F. (1980) *The Search for Solutions*, Holt, Rinehart & Winston, New York.

Jung, C.G. (1988) *Essays on Contemporary Events*, Ark, London.

Kahn, H. (1965) *On Escalation, Metaphors and Scenarios*, Praeger, New York.

Kanter, R.M. (1977) *Men and Women of the Corporation*, Basic Books, New York.

Kanter, R.M. (1983) *The Change Makers: Corporate Entrepreneurs at Work*, Simon & Schuster, New York; published Allen & Unwin, London, 1984.

Kanter, R.M. (1989) *When Giants Learn to Dance*, Simon & Schuster, New York.

Kaplan, Fred (1983) *The Wizards of Armageddon*, Simon & Schuster, New York.

Katz, E. (1957) 'The two-step flow of communication: an up-to date report on an hypothesis', *Public Opinion Quarterly*, 21: 67–78.

Katz, E. (1988) 'Communication research since Lazarsfeld', *Public Opinion Quarterly*, 51: S25–S45.

Kaufman, F.X., G. Majone and V. Ostrom (eds) (1986) *Guidance, Control and Evaluation in the Public Sector*, de Gruyter, Berlin and New York.

Kaufman, H. (1976) *Are Government Organizations Immortal?*, Brookings Institution, Washington, D.C.

Kaufman, S. (1991) 'Decision making and conflict management processes in local government', in Bingham *et al.*, 1991.

Keane, J. (1988) *Democracy and Civil Society*, Verso, London.

Kegan, W. (1989) *Mr Lawson's Gamble*, Hodder & Stoughton, London.

Keller, L.F. and D.C. Perry (1991) 'The structures of government', in Bingham *et al.*, 1991.

Kelly, G.A. (1963) 'The expert as historical actor', *Daedalus*, 92(3): 529–48.

Kelly, R.M. (1987) 'The politics of meaning and policy inquiry', in Palumbo (ed.), 1987.

Kelman, S. (1981) *Regulating America, Regulating Sweden: A Comparative Study of Occupational Safety and Health Policy*, MIT Press, Cambridge, Mass.

Kemp, R. (1985) 'Planning, public hearings and the politics of discourse', in Forester (ed.), 1985.

Kenis, P. and V. Schneider (1991) 'Policy networks and policy analysis: scrutinizing a new analytical toolbox', in Marin and Mayntz (eds), 1991.

Kennedy, C. (1991) *Guide to the Management Gurus*, Century Business, London.

Kennedy, I. (1981) *The Unmasking of Medicine*, Allen & Unwin, London.

Kershen, A. (1993) 'Henry Mayhew and Charles Booth: men of their times?', in G. Alderman and C. Holmes (eds), *Outcasts and Outsiders, Essays in Honour of William J. Fishman*, Duckworth, London.

Key, V.O. Jr. (1967) *Public Opinion and American Democracy*, Alfred A. Knopf, New York.

Keynes, J.M. (1926) *Essays in Persuasion*, Macmillan, London.

Keynes, J.M. (1936) *The General Theory of Employment, Interest and Money*, Macmillan, London.

Keynes, J.M. (1963) *Essays in Biography*, W.W. Norton, New York.

Keynes, J.M. (1971–) *The Collected Writings of John Maynard Keynes*, vols 1–30, Macmillan, London.

Kickert, W. (1993) 'Complexity, governance and dynamics: conceptual explorations of public network management', in Kooiman (ed.), 1993.

Kidd, J.B. (1991a) 'Decision analysis', in Littlechild and Shutler (eds), 1991.

Kidd, J.B. (1991b) 'Project management', in Littlechild and Shutler (eds), 1991.

King, A. (ed.)(1978) *The New American Political System*, American Enterprise Institute, Washington, D.C.

Kingdon, J.W. (1984) *Agendas, Alternatives and Public Policies*, Little, Brown, Boston, Mass.

Kirlin, J.J. (1984) 'A political perspective', in Miller (ed.), 1984.

Kiser, L. and E. Ostrom (1982) 'The three worlds of political action', in Ostrom (ed.), 1982.

Klein, R.E. (1974) 'Policy problems and policy perceptions in the National Health Service', *Policy and Politics*, 2(3): 216–36.

Klein, R.E. (1976) 'The politics of public expenditure: American theory and British practice', *British Journal of Political Science*, 6: 401–32.

Kloten, N. (1989) 'West Germany', in Pechman (ed.), 1989.

Kluchhohn, C. (1951) 'Value orientation in the

theory of social action', in T. Parsons and E. Shils (eds), *Towards a General Theory of Action*, Harvard University Press, Cambridge, Mass.

Knight, B. (1993) *Voluntary Action*, Centris, London, 1993.

Knoepfel, P. and H. Weidner (1983) 'Implementing air quality programmes in Europe: some results of a comparative study', in Downing and Hanf (eds), 1983.

Kochan, T.A. (1975) 'Determinants of power boundary units in an interorganizational bargaining relation', *Administrative Science Quarterly*, **20**: 435–52.

Kohr, L. (1957) *The Breakdown of Nations*, Routledge & Kegan Paul, London; 2nd edn, Christopher Davies, Swansea.

Kohr, L. (1973) *Development without Aid*, Christopher Davies, Swansea.

Kohr, L. (1977) *The Overdeveloped Nations*, Christopher Davies, Swansea, 1977.

Komarovsky, M. (1975) *Sociology and Public Policy: The Case of the Presidential Commissions*, Elsevier, New York.

Kooiman, J. (ed.) (1993) *Modern Governance: New Government–Society Interactions*, Sage, London.

Kooiman, J. and K.A Eliassen (eds) (1987) *Managing Public Organizations: Lessons From Contemporary European Experience*, Sage, London.

Korten, D.C. (1980) 'Community organization and rural development: a learning process approach', *Public Administration Review*, **40**: 480–510.

Korten, D.C. (1984) 'People-centered development: towards a framework', in Korten and Klauss (eds), 1984.

Korten, D.C. and R. Klauss (eds) (1984) *People-centered Development: Contributions toward Theory and Planning Frameworks*, Kumarisna Press, West Hartford, Conn.

Kosinsky, J. (1980) *Being There*, Corgi Books, London.

Kouwenhoven, V. (1993), 'Public–private partnership: a model for the management of public–private cooperation', in Kooiman (ed.), 1993.

Krasner, S.D. (1978) *Defending the National Interest: Raw Materials Investments and US Foreign Policy*, Princeton University Press, Princeton, N.J.

Kuhn, T. (1962) *The Structure of Scientific Revolutions*, Chicago University Press, Chicago, Ill.

Kukathas, C. (1989) *Hayek and Modern Liberalism*, Clarendon Press, Oxford.

Kull, S. (1988) *Minds at War: Nuclear Reality and the Inner Conflict of Defence Policymakers*, Basic Books, New York.

Lacey, N. and E. Frazer (1994) 'Blind alleys: communitarianism', *Politics*, **14**(2): 75–81.

Laffin, M. (1986) 'Professional communities and policy communities', in M. Goldsmith (ed.), *New Research in Central–Local Relations*, Gower, Aldershot, Hants.

Laffin, M. and K. Young (1990) *Professionalism in Local Government*, Longman, London.

Lamb, G. and B. Schaffer (1981) *Can Equity be Organised?*, Gower, Farnborough, Hants.

Lambert, J.R. (1967) *Crime, Police and Race Relations*, Oxford University Press, London.

Landau, M. (1961) 'On the uses of metaphor in political analysis', *Social Research*, **28**: 331–53.

Landau, M. (1977) 'The proper domain of policy analysis', *American Journal of Political Science*, **21**: 423–7.

Lane, J.-E. (1987) 'Public and private leadership', in Kooiman and Eliassen (eds), 1987.

Lane, J.-E. (1990) *Institutional Reform: A Public Policy Approach*, Dartmouth, Aldershot, Hants.

Lane, J.-E. (1993) *The Public Sector: Concepts, Models and Approaches*, Sage, London.

Lane, J.-E. (ed.) (1987) *Bureaucracy and Public Choice*, Sage, London.

Lane, J.-E. and S. Ersson (1990) 'Comparative politics: from political sociology to comparative public policy', in Leftwich (ed.), 1990.

Lane, R.E. (1966) 'The decline of politics and ideology in a knowledgeable society', *American Sociological Review*, **31**: 649–62.

Larkey, P.D., C. Stolp and M. Winer (1981) 'Theorising about the growth of government', *Journal of Public Policy*, **1**: 157–220.

Larkey, P.D., C. Stolp and M. Winer (1984) 'Why does government grow?', in Miller (ed.), 1984.

Lasswell, H.D. (1930a) *Psychopathology and Politics*, University of Chicago Press, Chicago, Ill.

Lasswell, H.D. (1930b) 'The scientific study of human biography', *Scientific Monthly*, **30**: 79–80.

Lasswell, H.D. (1933) 'The psychology of Hitlerism', *Political Quarterly*, **4**: 373–84.

Lasswell, H.D. (1935) *World Politics and Personal Insecurity*, Whittlesey House, New York.

Lasswell, H.D. (1936/1958) *Politics: Who Gets What, When, How*, Meridian Books, Cleveland, Ohio.

Lasswell, H.D. (1939) 'Person, personality, group, culture', *Psychiatry*, **2**: 533–6.

Lasswell, H.D. (1941) 'The garrison state', *American Journal of Sociology*, **46**: 455–68; reprinted in Lasswell, 1948b; Marvick (ed.), 1977.

Lasswell, H.D. (1948a) *Power and Personality*, W.W. Norton, New York.

Lasswell H.D. (1948b) *The Analysis of Political Behaviour: An Empirical Approach*, Kegan Paul, London.

Lasswell, H.D. (1949) 'Style in the language of politics', in H.D. Lasswell *et al.*, *The Language of Politics: Studies in Quantitative Semantics*, George Stewart, New York.

Lasswell, H.D. (1951 a) 'Democratic character', in

The Political Writings of Harold D. Lasswell, Free Press, Glencoe, Ill.

Lasswell, H.D. (1951b) 'The policy orientation', in Lerner and Lasswell (eds), 1951.

Lasswell, H.D. (1956) *The Decision Process: Seven Categories of Functional Analysis*, University of Maryland, College Park, Md.

Lasswell, H.D. (1959) 'Strategies of inquiry: the rational use of observation', in Lerner (ed.), 1959.

Lasswell, H.D. (1960) 'The technique of decision seminars', *Midwest Journal of Political Science*, 4: 213–36.

Lasswell, H.D. (1962) 'The garrison-state hypothesis today', in S.P. Huntington (ed.), *Changing Patterns of Military Politics, International Yearbook of Political Behaviour Research*, vol. 3, Free Press, New York.

Lasswell, H.D. (1963) 'Experimentation, prototyping, invention', in H.D. Lasswell, *The Future of Political Science*, Atherton, New York.

Lasswell, H.D. (1965) 'Introduction: The study of political elites', in Lasswell and Lerner (eds), 1965.

Lasswell, H.D. (1968) 'The policy sciences', in *The Encyclopedia of the Social Sciences*, vol. 12, Macmillan/Free Press, New York.

Lasswell, H.D. (1970a) 'The emerging conception of the policy sciences', *Policy Sciences*, 1: 3–14.

Lasswell, H.D. (1970b) 'The library as a social planetarium', *American Librarian*, 1: 142–3.

Lasswell, H.D. (1971) *A Pre-view of Policy Sciences*, Elsevier, New York.

Lasswell, H.D. (1972) 'Communications research and public policy', *Public Opinion Quarterly*, 36: 301–10.

Lasswell, H.D. (1980) 'Must science serve power?', and 'The future of world communications and propaganda', in H.D. Lasswell, D. Lerner and H. Speirer (eds), *Propaganda and Communication in World History*, University Press of Hawaii, Honolulu.

Lasswell, H.D. and A. Kaplan (1950) *Power and Society*, Yale University Press, New Haven, Conn.

Lasswell, H.D. and D. Lerner (eds) (1965) *World Revolutionary Elites: Studies in Coercive Revolutionary Movements*, Massachusetts Institute of Technology Press, Cambridge, Mass.

Lasswell, H.D. and M.S. McDougal (1992) *Jurisprudence for a Free Society: Studies in Law, Science and Policy*, Martinus Nijhoff/New Haven Press, New Haven, Conn.

Lau, R.R. and D.O. Sears (eds) (1986) *Political Cognition*, Lawrence Erlbaum, Hillsdale, N.J.

Laver, M. (1983) *Invitation to Politics*, Penguin, Harmondsworth, Middx.

Lawrence, P.R. and J.W. Lorsch (1967) *Organizations and Environment: Managing Differentiation and Integration*, Harvard University Press, Cambridge, Mass.

Layard, R. and S. Glaister (eds) (1994) *Cost-benefit Analysis*, Cambridge University Press, Cambridge.

Leach, S. (1982) 'In defence of the rational model', in Leach and Stewart (eds), 1982.

Leach, S. and J. Stewart (eds) (1982) *Approaches to Public Policy*, Allen & Unwin, London.

Le Bon, G. (1895) *The Crowd: A Study of the Popular Mind*, Cherokee, Atlanta, Ga; reprinted 1982.

Lebow, R.N. (1983) 'Miscalculation in the South Atlantic : the origins of the Falklands war', *Journal of Strategic Studies*, 6: 5–35.

Leftwich, A. (ed.) (1990) *New Developments in Political Science: an International Review of Achievements and Prospects*, Edward Elgar, Aldershot, Hants.

Le Grand, J. (1991) *Equity and Choice: an Essay in Economics and Applied Philosophy*, Harper Collins, London.

Le Grand, J. and W. Bartlett (eds) (1993) *Quasi-Markets and Social Policy*, Macmillan, London.

Lehmbruch, G. and P.C. Schmitter (eds) (1982) *Patterns of Corporatist Policy-making*, Sage, London.

Lekachman, R. (1964) *Keynes' General Theory: Reports of Three Decades*, Macmillan, London.

Lekachman, R. (1976) *Economists at Bay: Why Experts Will Never Solve Your Problems*, McGraw-Hill, New York.

Lemert, E.M. (1968) 'Social problems', in *International Encyclopedia of the Social Sciences*, vol. 14, Macmillan, New York.

Lenin, V.I. (1972) *On the Development of Heavy Industry and Electrification*, Progress Publishers, Moscow.

Lerner, D. (1975) 'From social science to policy sciences: an introductory note', in Nagel (ed.), 1975.

Lerner, D. (ed.) (1959) *The Human Meaning of the Social Sciences*, Meridian Books, New York.

Lerner, D. and H.D. Lasswell (eds) (1951) *The Policy Sciences*, Stanford University Press, Stanford, Cal.

Letwin, O. (1988) *Privatising the World*, Cassell, London.

Levine, S. and P.E. White (1961) 'Exchange as a conceptual framework for the study of interorganizational relationships', *Administrative Science Quarterly*, 5: 583–601.

Levitas, R. (ed.) (1986) *The Ideology of the New Right*, Polity Press/Basil Blackwell, Oxford.

Lewin, K. (1948) 'Experiments in social space', in G.W. Lewin (ed.), *Resolving Social Conflicts*, Harper & Row, New York.

Lewin, K. (1952) 'Defining the field at a given

time', in D. Cartwright (ed.), *Field Theory in Social Science: Selected Theoretical Papers*, Tavistock Institute, London.

Lewin, K. (1972) 'Need, force and valence in psychological fields', in E.P. Hollander and R.G. Hunt (eds), *Classic Contributions to Social Psychology*, Oxford University Press, London.

Lewin, L. (1991) *Self Interest and Public Interest in Western Politics*, Oxford University Press, London.

Lewis, J. and R. Flynn (1978) *The Implementation of Urban and Regional Planning Policies: Final report of a feasibility study for Department of the Environment*, London.

Lewis, J. and R. Flynn (1979) 'Implementation of urban and regional planning policies', *Policy and Politics*, 7: 123–42.

Lewis-Beck, M.S. (1986) 'Comparative economic voting: Britain, France, Germany, Italy', *American Journal of Political Science*, 30: 315–46.

Lewis-Beck, M.S. (1990) *Economics and Elections : The Major Western Democracies*, University of Michigan Press, Ann Arbor, Mich.

Lijphart, A. (1984) *Democracies: Patterns of Majoritarian and Consensus Government in Twenty-One Countries*, Yale University Press, New Haven, Conn.

Likert, R. (1961) *New Patterns of Management*, McGraw-Hill, New York.

Likert, R. (1967) *The Human Organization: Its Management and Value*, McGraw-Hill, New York.

Lincoln, Y.S. (1990) 'The making of a constructionist: a remembrance of transformations past', in Guba (ed.), 1990.

Lincoln, Y.S. and E.G. Guba (1985) *Naturalistic Inquiry*, Sage, Newbury Park, Cal.

Lindblom, C.E. (1958) 'Policy analysis', *American Economic Review*, 48: 298–312.

Lindblom, C.E. (1959) 'The science of muddling through', *Public Administration Review*, 19: 78–88.

Lindblom, C.E. (1965) *The Intelligence of Democracy*, Free Press, New York.

Lindblom, C.E. (1968) *The Policy-making Process*, Prentice-Hall, Englewood Cliffs, N.J.

Lindblom, C.E. (1977) *Politics and Markets*, Basic Books, New York.

Lindblom, C.E. (1979) 'Still muddling through', *Public Administration Review*, 39(6): 517–25.

Lindblom, C.E. (1988) *Democracy and Market System*, Norwegian University Press, Oslo.

Lindblom, C.E. (1990) *Inquiry and Change: The Troubled Attempt to Understand and Shape Society*, Yale University Press, New Haven, Conn.

Lindblom, C.E. and D.K. Cohen (1979) *Usable Knowledge*, Yale University Press, New Haven, Conn.

Lindblom, C.E. and E.J. Woodhouse (1993) *The Policy-making Process*, 3rd edn, Prentice-Hall, Englewood Cliffs, N.J.

Linder, S.H. and B.G. Peters (1987) 'A design perspective on policy implementation: the fallacies of misplaced prescription', *Policy Studies Review*, 6(2): 459–76.

Lindzey, G. and E. Aronson (eds) (1985) *Handbook of Social Psychology*, vol. 1, Random House, New York.

Lines, A.H. (1991) 'Inventory control: theory into practice', in Littlechild and Shutler (eds), 1991.

Linestone, H.A. and M. Turoff (eds) (1975) *The Delphi Method: Techniques and Applications*, Addison-Wesley, Reading, Mass.

Lippman, W. (1922) *Public Opinion*, Macmillan, New York.

Lipsky, M. (1971) 'Street-level bureaucracy and the analysis of urban reform', *Urban Affairs Quarterly*, 6: 391–409.

Lipsky, M. (1976) 'Towards a theory of street-level bureaucracy', in W.D. Hawley *et al.*, *Theoretical Perspectives on Urban Policy*, Prentice-Hall, Englewood Cliffs, N.J.

Lipsky, M. (1979) *Street Level Bureaucracy*, Russell Sage Foundation, New York.

Lipton, D., R. Martinson, and J. Wilkes (1975) *Effectiveness of Correctional Treatment: A Survey of Treatment Evaluation Studies*, Praeger, New York.

Lister, R. (1991) 'Concepts of poverty', *Social Studies Review*, 6(5): 192–5.

Littlechild, S.C. (1991) 'Linear programming', in Littlechild and Shutler (eds), 1991.

Littlechild, S.C. and M.F. Shutler (eds)(1991) *Operations Research in Management*, Prentice-Hall, London.

Llewellyn, J., S. Potter and L. Samuelson (1985) *Economic Forecasting and Policy – the International Dimension*, Routledge & Kegan Paul, London.

Lloyd, T. (1993) *The Charity Business: The New Philanthropists*, John Murray, London.

Loney, M. (1983) *Community against Government: The British Community Development Project, 1968–1978*, Heinemann, London.

Loney, M., R. Bocock, J. Clarke, A. Cochrane, P. Graham and M. Wilson (eds) (1991) *The State of the Market: Politics and Welfare in Contemporary Britain*, Sage, London.

Long, A. (1994) 'Assessing health and social outcomes', in Popay and Williams, 1994.

Loveday, B. (1993) 'Management accountability in public services: a police case study', in Isaac-Henry *et al.* (eds), 1993.

Lowi, T.J. (1964) 'American business, public policy, case studies and political theory', *World Politics*, 16: 677–93.

Lowi, T.J. (1970) 'Decision-making vs public policy: towards an antidote for technocracy', *Public Administration Review*, 30: 314–25.

Lowi, T.J. (1972) 'Four systems of policy politics and choice', *Public Administration Review*, **32**: 298–310.

Lowi, T.J. (1979) *The End of Liberalism*, 2nd edn, W.W. Norton, New York.

Luhmann, N. (1979) *Trust and Power*, John Wiley, New York.

Luhmann, N. (1990) *Essays on Self Reference*, Columbia University Press, New York.

Lukes, S. (1974) *Power: A Radical View*, Macmillan, London.

Lundberg, G.A. (1959) *Can Science Save Us?*, 2nd edn, Longmans, Green, New York.

Lundquist, L. (1980) *The Hare and the Tortoise: Clean Air Policies in the United States and Sweden*, University of Michigan Press, Ann Arbor, Mich.

Lupon, C. and D. Russell (1990) 'Equal opportunities in a cold climate', in S. Savage and L. Robins (eds), *Public Policy under Thatcher*, Macmillan, London.

Lynn, J. (1993) 'Community enterprise', in Butcher *et al.* (eds), 1993.

Lynn, J. and A. Jay (1987) *Yes Prime Minister: The Diaries of the Rt Hon. James Hacker*, vols 1 and 2, BBC Books, London.

Lynn, L. (1981) *Managing the Public's Business*, Free Press, New York.

Lynn, L. (1987) *Managing Public Policy*, Little, Brown, Boston, Mass.

Lynn, L.E. (ed.) (1978) *Knowledge and Policy: The Uncertain Connection*, National Academy of Sciences, Washington, D.C.

Lynn, L.E. (1980) *Designing Public Policy: A Casebook on the Role of Policy Analysis*, Goodyear, Santa Monica, Cal.

Lynn, N.B. and A. Wildavsky (eds) (1990) *Public Administration*, Chatham House, Chatham, N.J.

MacFarlane, R. and J. Mabbott (1993) *City Challenge: Involving Local Communities*, NCVO, London.

Mack, R. (1971) *Planning and Uncertainty*, John Wiley, New York.

MacLean, M. and D. Groves (eds) (1991) *Women's Issues in Social Policy*, Routledge, London.

MacLeod, M. and E. Saraga (1991) 'Child sexual abuse: challenging the orthodoxy', in Loney *et al.*, 1991.

Macpherson, C.B. (1977) *The Life and Times of Liberal Democracy*, Oxford University Press, Oxford.

MacRae, D. (1976) *The Social Function of Social Science*, Yale University Press, New Haven, Conn.

MacRae, D. (1993) 'Guidelines for policy discourse: consensual versus adversarial', in Fischer and Forester (eds), 1993.

Magee, B. (1973) *Popper*, Fontana/Collins, London.

Majone, G. (1980) 'Policies as theories', *Omega*, **8**: 151–62.

Majone, G. (1989) *Evidence, Argument and Persuasion in the Policy Process*, Yale University Press, New Haven, Conn.

Majone, G. and A. Wildavsky (1978) 'Implementation as evolution', in H. Freeman (ed.), *Policy Studies Review Annual, 1978*, Sage, Beverly Hills, Cal.; reprinted in Pressman and Wildavsky, 1984.

Malkin, J. and A. Wildavsky (1991) 'Why the traditional distinction between public and private goods should be abandoned', *Journal of Theoretical Politics*, **3**(4): 355–78.

Mandell, M.B. (1984) 'Strategies for improving the usefulness of analytical techniques for public sector decision making', in Nigro (ed.), 1984.

Mann, L. (1969) *Social Psychology*, John Wiley, Sydney.

Mansfield, H.C. (1989) *Taming the Prince: The Ambivalence of Modern Executive Power*, Free Press, New York.

March, D. and R. Rhodes (1992) *Policy Networks in British Government*, Allen & Unwin, London.

March, J.G. (1988) *Decisions and Organizations*, Blackwell, Oxford.

March, J.G. (ed.) (1965) *Handbook of Organizations*, Rand-McNally, Chicago, Ill.

March, J.G. and J.P. Olsen (1984) 'The New Institutionalism: organizational factors in political life', *American Political Science Review*, **78**: 734–49.

March, J.G. and J.P. Olsen (1989) *Rediscovering Institutions: The Organizational Basis of Politics*, Free Press, New York.

March, J.G. and J.P. Olsen (eds) (1976) *Ambiguity and Choice in Organizations*, Universitetsforlaget, Oslo.

March, J.G. and H.A. Simon (1958) *Organizations*, John Wiley, New York.

Marcuse, H. (1954) *Eros and Civilization: A Philosophical Inquiry into Freud*, Beacon Press, Boston, Mass.

Marcuse, H. (1972) *One-dimensional Man*, Abacus Books, London.

Marin, B. and R. Mayntz (eds) (1991) *Policy Networks: Empirical Evidence and Theoretical Considerations*, Westview Press, Boulder, Col.

Marris, P. and M. Rein (1967) *Dilemmas of Social Reform*, Routledge & Kegan Paul, London.

Marsh, D. and R.A.W. Rhodes (1992) 'The implementation gap: explaining policy change and continuity', in Marsh and Rhodes (eds), 1992.

Marsh, D. and R.A.W. Rhodes, (eds) (1992) *Implementing Thatcherite Policies: Audit of an Era*, Open University Press, Buckingham, Bucks.

Marsh, I. (1991) *Globalization and Australian Think Tanks*, Committee for Economic Development of Australia, Canberra.

Martin, B. (1993) *In the Public Interest: Privatisation*

and Public Sector Reform, ZED Books/Public Services International, London.

Martin, D. (ed.) (1985) *Operational Research: The Science of Decision-making in Business, Industry, Government and Society*, Operational Research Society, Birmingham.

Martin, J. (1992) *Francis Bacon, the State and the Reform of Natural Philosophy*, Cambridge University Press, Cambridge.

Marvick, D. (ed.) (1977) *Harold D. Lasswell on Political Sociology*, Chicago University Press, Chicago, Ill.

Maslow, A.H. (1943) 'A theory of human motivation', *Psychological Review*, 50(4): 370–96.

Maslow, A.H. (1968) *Toward a Psychology of Being*, Van Nostrand, New York.

Maslow, A.H. (1970) *Motivation and Personality*, Harper & Row, New York.

Mason, R.O. (1969) 'A dialectical approach to strategic planning', *Management Science*, 15: B403–B414.

Massey, A. (1988) *Technocrats and Nuclear Politics*, Avebury, Aldershot, Hants.

Massey, A. (1993) *Managing the Public Sector: A Comparative Analysis of the United Kingdom and the United States*, Edward Elgar, Aldershot, Hants.

Mattson, G. (1986) 'The promise of citizen coproduction: some persistent issues', *Public Administration*, 40: 51–6.

Mauss, A.L. (1975) *Social Problems as Social Movements*, Lippincott, Philadelphia, Pa.

Mawhinney, H.B. (1993) 'An advocacy coalition approach to change in Canadian education', in Sabatier and Jenkins-Smith (eds), 1993.

May, J.V. and A. Wildavksy (eds) (1978) *The Policy Cycle*, Sage, Beverly Hills, Cal.

May, P. (1986) 'Politics and policy analysis', *Political Science Quarterly*, 101(1): 109–25.

Mayer, J.P. (1956) *Max Weber and German Politics*, Faber & Faber, London.

Mayer, R.N. (1991) 'Gone yesterday, here today: consumer issues in the agenda-setting process', *Journal of Social Issues*, 47(1): 21–39.

Mayntz, R. (1993) 'Governing failures and the problem of governability: some comments on a theoretical paradigm', in J. Kooiman (ed.), *Modern Governance: New Government–Society Interactions*, Sage, London.

Mayo, E.W. (1933) *The Human Problems of an Industrial Civilization*, Macmillan, London.

Mayo, E.W. (1949) *The Social Problems of an Industrial Civilization*, Routledge & Kegan Paul, London.

Mazur, A. (1981) *The Dynamics of Technical Controversy*, Communications Press, Washington, D.C.

Mazur, A. (1991) 'Agendas and *égalité professionnelle*: symbolic policy at work in France', in Meehan and Svenhuijsen (eds), 1991.

McCaskey, M.B. (1991) 'Mapping: creating, maintaining and relinquishing conceptual frameworks', in Henry (ed.), 1991.

McCloskey, D. (1985) *The Rhetoric of Economics*, University of Wisconsin Press, Madison, Wis.

McCloskey, H. (1967) 'Personality and attitude correlates of foreign policy orientations', in J.N. Rosenau (ed.), *Domestic Sources of Foreign Policy*, Free Press, New York.

McCombs, M.E. and D.L. Shaw (1972) 'The agenda setting function of the mass media', *Public Opinion Quarterly*, 36: 176–87.

McCombs, M.E. and D.L. Shaw (1976) 'Structuring the "unseen environment"', *Journal of Communication*, 26(2):18–22.

McDougal, M.S., H.D. Lasswell and L.-C. Chen (1980) *Human Rights and World Public Order: The Basic Policies of an International Law of Human Dignity*, Yale University Press, New Haven, Conn.

McGregor, D. (1960) *The Human Side of Enterprise*, McGraw-Hill, New York.

McGrew, A.G., P.G. Lewis *et al.* (1992) *Global Politics: Globalisation and the Nation-State*, Polity Press, Oxford.

McNaught, A. (1987) *Health Action and Ethnic Minorities*, Bedford Square Press, London.

McQuail, D. and S. Windahl (1993) *Communication Models for the Study of Mass Communications*, Longman, London.

McShane, L. (1993) 'Community care', in Butcher *et al.*, 1993.

Meadow, R. (1988) 'Political campaigns', in R.E. Rice and C. Atkin (eds), *Public Communication Campaigns*, 2nd edn, Sage, Newbury Park, Cal.

Meehan, E. and S. Svenhuijsen (eds) (1991) *Equality Politics and Gender*, Sage, London.

Meier, K.J. (1987) *Politics and the Bureaucracy*, Brooks/Cole, Monterey, Cal.

Mellor, H. (1985) *The Role of the Voluntary Organisations in Social Welfare*, London, Croom Helm.

Meltsner, A.J. (1976) *Policy Analysts in the Bureaucracy*, University of California Press, Berkeley, Cal.

Meltzer, B.N., J.W. Petras and L.T. Reynolds (1975) *Symbolic Interactionism: Genesis, Varieties and Criticism*, Routledge & Kegan Paul, London.

Merelman, R.M. (1968) 'On the neo-elitist critiques of community power', *American Political Science Review*, 62: 451–60.

Merelman, R.M. (1981) 'Harold Lasswell's political world: weak tea for hard times', *British Journal of Political Science*, 11: 471–97.

Merton, R.K. and R. Nisbet (eds) (1961) *Contemporary Social Problems*, Harcourt Brace Jovanovich, New York; 2nd edn, 1971; 3rd edn, 1976.

Metcalfe, L. (1978) 'Policy making in a turbulent environment', in Hanf and Scharpf (eds), 1978.

Metcalfe, L. (1981) 'Designing precarious partnerships', in P.C. Nyström and W.H. Starbauck (eds), *Handbook of Organizational Design*, vol. 1, Oxford University Press, Oxford.

Metcalfe, L. (1993) 'Public management: from imitation to innovation', in Kooiman (ed.), 1993.

Metcalfe, L. and S. Richards (1987) 'Evolving public management cultures', in Kooiman and Eliassen (eds), 1987.

Metcalfe, L. and S. Richards (1992) *Improving Public Management*, Sage, London.

Meyer, J.W. and B. Rowan (1977) 'Institutionalized organizations: formal structure as myth and ceremony', *American Journal of Sociology*, 83(2): 340–63.

Meynaud, J. (1968) *Technocracy*, Faber & Faber, London.

Michael, D. (1973) *On Learning to Plan and Planning to Learn*, Jossey-Bass, San Francisco, Cal.

Michels, R. (1915) *Political Parties*, trans. Eden and Cedar Paul, Constable, London; reprinted 1959.

Middlemas, K. (1979) *Politics in Industrial Society*, André Deutsch, London.

Miles, I. (1985) *Social Indicators for Human Development*, United Nations University/Frances Pinter, London.

Miliband, R. (1969) *The State in Capitalist Society*, Weidenfeld & Nicolson, London.

Miliband, R. (1977) *Marxism and Politics*, Oxford University Press, Oxford.

Miliband, R. (1982) *Capitalist Democracy in Britain*, Oxford University Press, Oxford.

Mill, J.S. (1968) *Utilitarianism, Liberty and Representative Government*, Everyman, London.

Miller, D. (1990) *Market, State and Community*, Oxford University Press, Oxford.

Miller, P. and T. O'Leary (1987) 'Accounting and the construction of the governable person', *Accounting, Organizations and Society*, 12(3): 235–66.

Miller, T.C. (1984) 'Conclusion: a design science perspective', in Miller (ed.), 1984.

Miller, T.C. (ed.) (1984) *Public Sector Performance: A Conceptual Turning Point*, Johns Hopkins Press, Baltimore, Md.

Mills, C.W. (1943) 'The professional ideology of social pathologists', *American Journal of Sociology*, 49: 165–80.

Mills, C.W. (1956) *The Power Elite*, Oxford University Press, New York.

Mills, C.W. (1959) *The Sociological Imagination*, Oxford University Press, New York.

Mills, C.W. (1963a) 'Culture and politics', in Mills, 1963.

Mills, C.W. (1963b) *Power, Politics and People*, Oxford University Press, New York.

Mills, M. (1993) 'Expert advice to the British government on diet and heart disease', in Peters and Barker (eds), 1993.

Milner, H. (1993) 'The constraints of the world economic system', in Weaver and Rockman (eds), 1993.

Milward, H.B. and R.A. Francisco (1983) 'Subsystem politics and corporatism in the United States', *Policy and Politics*, 11: 273–93.

Mishra, R. (1990) *The Welfare State in Capitalist Society: Policies of Retrenchment and Maintenance in Europe, North America and Australia*, Harvester Wheatsheaf, Brighton, Sussex.

Mitchell, G. (1993) *The Practice of Operational Research*, John Wiley, London.

Mitchell, G.D. (1968) *A Hundred Years of Sociology*, Duckworth, London.

Mitchell, J. (1977) *Sexual Politics*, Virago, London.

Modelski, G. (1974) *Principles of World Politics*, Free Press, New York.

Moe, T.M. (1984) 'New economics of organizations', *American Journal of Political Science*, 28: 739–77.

Moe, T.M. (1990) 'Political institutions: the neglected side of the story', *Journal of Law Economics and Organization*, 6: 213–53.

Mohan, J. (1990) 'Health care and the state in "austerity capitalism"', in Simmie and King (eds), 1990.

Monroe, K.R. (1991) *The Economic Approach to Politics: A Critical Reassessment of the Theory of Rational Action*, Harper Collins, New York.

Morgan, G. (1986) *Images of Organization*, Sage, Newbury Park, Cal.

Morgan, G. (1993) *Imaginization: The Art Of Creative Management*, Sage, Newbury Park, Cal.

Morris, A. (1994) 'Paying for the Bill', *Guardian*, 26 October: 7.

Morse, P.M. (1967) *Operations Research for Public Systems*, MIT Press, Cambridge, Mass.

Moseley, P. (1984) *The Making of Economic Policy: Theory and Evidence from Britain and the United States since 1945*, Harvester Wheatsheaf, Hemel Hempstead, Herts.

Moser, C. (1973) 'Social indicators: systems, methods and problems', *Review of Income and Wealth*, 19: 133–41.

Mouzelis, N. (1967) *Organization and Bureaucracy*, Routledge & Kegan Paul, London.

Moynihan, D.P. (1965) 'The professionalisation of reform', *Public Interest*, 3: 26–32.

Moynihan, D.P. (1969) *Maximum Feasible Misunderstanding: Community Action in the War on Poverty*, Free Press, New York.

Mueller, D. (1979) *Public Choice (1)*, Cambridge University Press, Cambridge.

Mueller, D. (1989) *Public Choice (2)*, Cambridge University Press, Cambridge.

Muir, R. (1910) *Peers and Bureaucrats*, Constable, London.

Mumford, L. (1938) *The Culture of Cities*, Harcourt-Brace, New York.

Munro, J.F. (1993) 'California water politics: explaining policy change in a cognitively polarized subsystem', in Sabatier and Jenkins-Smith (eds), 1993.

Musgrave, R.A. (1959) *The Theory of Public Finance*, McGraw-Hill, New York.

Muth, R. (1990) 'Harold Lasswell: a biographical profile', in Muth *et al.*, 1990.

Muth, R., M.M. Finley and M.F. Muth (1990) *Harold D. Lasswell: An Annotated Bibliography*, New Haven Press, New Haven, Conn., and Kluwer, Dordrecht.

Myers, N. (ed.) (1987) *The Gaia Atlas of Planet Management*, Pan Books, London.

Nagel, S.S. (ed.) (1975a) *Policy Studies and the Social Sciences*, Lexington Books, Lexington, Mass.

Nagel, S.S. (ed.) (1975b) *Policy Studies in America and Elsewhere*, Lexington Books, Lexington, Mass.

Nagel, S.S. (1980) *The Policy Studies Handbook*, Lexington Books, Lexington, Mass.

Nagel, S.S. (1990) 'Conflicting evaluations of policy studies', in Lynn and Wildavsky (eds), 1990.

Naisbitt, J. and P. Aburdene (1990) *Mega-Trends 2000*, Sidgwick & Jackson, London.

Nakamura, R. (1987) 'The textbook policy process and implementation research', *Policy Studies Review*, 7: 142–54.

Navarro, V. (1984) 'The crisis of the international capitalist order and its implications for the welfare state', in J.B. Mckinlay (ed.), *Issues in the Political Economy of Health Care*, Tavistock Publications, London.

Neary, I. (1992) 'Japan', in Harrop (ed.), 1992.

Neave, G. (1988) 'On the cultivation of quality, efficiency and enterprise: an overview of recent trends in higher education in Western Europe, 1968–1988', *European Journal of Education*, 23(1–2).

Nelkin, D. (ed.) (1979) *Controversy: Politics of Technical Decisions*, Sage, London; 3rd edn, 1992.

Nelson, B.J. (1984) *Making an Issue of Child Abuse*, University of Chicago Press, Chicago, Ill.

Nelson, R. (1987) 'The economics profession and the making of public policy', *Journal of Economic Literature*, 25: 42–84.

Nelson, R.H. (1992) 'The Office of Policy Analysis in the Department of the Interior', in Weiss (ed.), 1992.

Newall, A. and H.A. Simon (1972) *Human Problem Solving*, Prentice-Hall, Englewood Cliffs, N.J.

Newall, A., J.C. Shaw and H.A. Simon (1958) 'Elements of a theory of human problem solving', *Psychological Review*, 65: 151–66.

Newall, A., J.C. Shaw and H.A. Simon (1979) 'The processes of creative thinking', in Simon (ed.), 1979.

Newby, H. (1993) 'Social science and public policy: the Frank Foster Lecture', *RSA Journal*, May: 365–77.

Nielsen, K. (1983) 'Emancipatory social science and social critique', in Callahan and Jennings, 1983.

Nigro, L.G. (ed.) (1984) *Decision Making in the Public Sector*, Marcel Dekker, New York.

Nimmo, D. and K. Sanders (eds) (1981) *Handbook of Political Communications*, Sage, Beverly Hills, Cal.

Nisbet, R. (1974) *The Social Philosophers: Community and Conflict in Western Thought*, Heinemann, London.

Niskanen, W.A. (1971) *Bureaucracy and Representative Government*, Aldine-Atherton, Chicago, Ill.

Niskanen, W.A. (1973) *Bureaucracy: Servant or Master?*, Institute of Economic Affairs, London.

Nixon, J. (1993) 'Implementation in the hands of senior managers: community care in Britain', in Hill (ed.), 1993.

North, D.C. (1990) *Institutions, Institutional Change and Economic Performance*, Cambridge University Press, Cambridge.

North, D.C. and B.W. Weingast (1989) 'The evolution of institutions governing public choice in 17th century England', *Journal of Economic History*, 49: 803–32.

North, R.C. (1967) 'The analytical prospects of communication theory', in Charlesworth (ed.), 1967.

Nozick, R. (1974) *Anarchy, State and Utopia*, Basic Books, New York.

O'Connor, J. (1973) *The Fiscal Crisis of the State*, St Martin's Press, New York.

Offe, C. (1974) 'Structural problems of the capitalist state', in Beyme (ed.), 1974.

Offe, C. (1976) 'Political authority and class structures', in Connerton (ed.), 1976.

Offe, C. (1984) *Contradictions of the Welfare State*, Lexington Books, New York.

Offe, C. (1985) *Disorganized Capitalism: Contemporary Transformations of Work and Politics*, Polity Press, Cambridge.

Okita, S. (1989) 'Japan', in Pechman (ed.), 1989.

Olsen, J.P. (1988) *Statsstyre og institusjonsutforming*, Universitetsforlaget, Oslo.

Olson, M. (1982) *The Rise and Decline of Nations*, Yale University Press, New Haven, Conn.

Ong, B.N. and G. Humphris (1994) 'Prioritizing needs with communities: rapid appraisal methodologies in health', in Popay and Williams, 1994.

Open Systems Group (eds) (1984) *The Vickers Papers*, Harper & Row, London.

Organization for Economic Co-operation and Development (OECD) (1987) *Administration as Service: The Public as Client*, OECD, Paris.

OECD (1990) *Public Management Developments: Survey, 1990*, OECD, Paris.

OECD (1991) *Public Management Developments: Survey, 1991*, OECD, Paris.

OECD (1992) *Public Management Developments: Survey, 1992*, OECD, Paris.

OECD (1993a) *Public Management Developments, Survey, 1993*, OECD, Paris.

OECD (1993b) *Managing with Market Type Mechanisms*, OECD, Paris.

O'Riordan, T. (1976) 'Beyond environmental impact assessment', in O'Riordan and Hey (eds) 1976.

O'Riordan, T. (1991) 'Stability and transformation in environmental government', *Political Quarterly*, **62**(2): 167–85.

O'Riordan, T. and R. Hey (eds) (1976) *Environmental Impact Assessment*, Saxon House, Farnborough, Hants.

Orwell, G. (1954) *Nineteen Eighty Four*, Penguin Books, Harmondsworth, Middx.

Orwell, G. (1984) *The Penguin Essays of George Orwell*, Penguin Books, Harmondsworth, Middx.

Osborn, A. (1953) *Applied Imagination: Principles and Procedures of Creative Thinking*, Charles Scribner's Sons, New York.

Osborne, D. and T. Gaebler (1992) *Reinventing Government: How the Entrepreneurial Spirit is Transforming the Public Sector*, Addison-Wesley, Reading, Mass.

O'Shaughnessy, N.J. (1990), *The Phenomenon of Political Marketing*, Macmillan, London.

Ostrom, E. (1986a) 'An agenda for the study of institution', *Public Choice*, **48**: 3–25.

Ostrom, E. (1986b) 'A method of institutional analysis', in Kaufman *et al.* (eds), 1986.

Ostrom, E. (1990) *Governing the Commons*, Cambridge University Press, Cambridge.

Ostrom, E. (ed.) (1982) *Strategies of Political Inquiry*, Sage, Beverly Hills, Cal.

Ostrom, V. and P. Sabetti (1975) 'Theory of public policy', in Nagel (ed.), 1975b.

Ouchi, W.G. (1991) 'Markets, bureaucracies and clans', in Thompson *et al.* (eds), 1991.

Outshoorn, J. (1991) 'Is this what we wanted? Positive action as issue perversion', in Meehan and Svenhuijsen, 1991.

Oxford Dictionary of New Words, The (1992), compiled by S. Tulloch, Oxford University Press, Oxford.

Page, B. and R. Shapiro (1983) 'Effects of public opinion on policy', *American Political Science Review*, **77**: 175–90.

Page, E. and M. Goldsmith (eds) (1987) *Central and Local Government Relations*, Sage, London.

Pahl, J. (ed.) (1985) *Private Violence and Public Policy: The Needs of Battered Women and Responses of the Public Services*, Routledge & Kegan Paul, London.

Pahl, R. and J. Winkler (1974) 'The coming corporatism', *New Society*, 10 October.

Palumbo, D.J. (1987) 'Politics and evaluation', in Palumbo (ed.), 1987.

Palumbo, D.J. (ed.) (1987) *The Politics of Program Evaluation*, Sage, Newbury Park, Cal.

Palumbo, D.J. and D. Nachimas (1983) 'The preconditions for successful evaluation: is there an ideal type?', *Policy Sciences*, **16**: 67–79.

Parekh, B. (1982) *Contemporary Political Thinkers*, Martin Robertson, Oxford.

Pareto, V. (1966) *Sociological Writings*, ed. S.E. Finer, Pall Mall Press, London.

Paris, D.C. and J.F. Reynolds (1983) *The Logic of Policy Inquiry*, Longman, New York.

Parkes, C.M. (1971) 'Psycho-social transitions: a field for study', *Social Science and Medicine*, **5**: 101–15.

Parlett, M. and D. Hamilton (1972) 'Evaluation as illumination: a new approach to the study of innovatory programs', Occasional Paper no. 9, Centre for Research in the Educational Sciences, University of Edinburgh.

Parry, G. and P. Morriss (1974) 'When is a decision not a decision?', in I. Crew (ed.), *British Political Sociology Yearbook*, vol. 1, Croom Helm, London.

Parry, N. and J. Parry (1976) *The Rise of the Medical Profession*, Croom Helm, London.

Parsons, D.W. (1976) 'The idea of size and decentralization in the anarchist tradition', unpublished MSc Econ thesis, University of Wales, Swansea.

Parsons, D.W. (1982) 'Politics without promises: the crisis of overload and governability', *Parliamentary Affairs*, **35**: 421–55.

Parsons, D.W. (1983) 'Keynes and the politics of ideas', *History of Political Thought*, **4**(2): 367–92.

Parsons, D.W. (1985) 'Was Keynes Kuhnian? Keynes and the idea of theoretical revolutions', *British Journal of Political Science*, **15**: 451–71.

Parsons, D.W. (1988) *The Political Economy of British Regional Policy*, Routledge, London.

Parsons, D.W. (1989) *The Power of the Financial Press*, Edward Elgar, Aldershot, Hants.

Parsons, T. (1937) *The Structure of Social Action*, McGraw-Hill, New York.

Parsons, T. (1951) *The Social System*, Free Press, New York.

Pateman, C. (1970) *Participation and Democratic Theory*, Cambridge University Press, Cambridge.

Pateman, C. (1983) 'Feminist critiques of the public/private dichotomy', in Benn and Gaus (eds), 1983.

Patton, B.R., K. Giffin and E.N. Patton (1989) *Decision Making Group Interaction*, 3rd edn, Harper & Row, New York.

Patton, C. (1990) *Inventing Aids*, Routledge, London.

Patton, C.V. and D.S. Sawicki (1986) *Basic Methods of Policy Analysis and Planning*, Prentice-Hall, Englewood Cliffs, N.J.

Patton, M.Q. (1978) *Utilization-focused Evaluation*, Sage, Newbury Park, Cal.

Patton, M.Q. (1987) 'Evaluation's political inherency: practical implications for design and use', in Palumbo, 1987.

Pearce, D. (1989) 'Cost-benefit analysis', in A. Kuper and J. Kuper (eds), *The Social Science Encyclopedia*, Routledge, London.

Pechman, J.A. (ed.) (1989) *The Role of the Economist in Government: An International Perspective*, Harvester Wheatsheaf, New York.

Perkin, H. (1989) *The Rise of Professional Society: England since 1880*, Routledge, London.

Perrow, C. (1965) 'Hospitals: technology, structure and goals', in March (ed.), 1965.

Perrow, C. (1986) *Complex Organizations: A Critical Essay*, Random House, New York.

Perrow, C. and M.F. Guillén (1990) *The Aids Disaster: The Failure of Organizations in New York and the Nation*, Yale University Press, New Haven, Conn.

Perry, J.L. and K.L. Kraemer (eds) (1983) *Public Management: Public and Private Perspectives*, Mayfield Publishing, Palo Alto, Cal.

Perry, J.M. (1968) *The New Politics: The Expanding Technology of Political Manipulation*, Weidenfeld & Nicolson, London.

Perry, R. (1984) *The Programming of the President: The Hidden Power of the Computer in World Politics Today*, Aurum Press, London.

Pescheck, J.G. (1987) *Policy-planning Organizations*, Temple University Press, Philadelphia, Pa.

Peters, B.G. (1982) *Public Policy in America: Process and Performance*, Franklin Watts, New York; 2nd edn, Macmillan, London, 1986.

Peters, B.G. and A. Barker (1993) *Advising West European Governments: Inquiries, Expertise and Public Policy*, Edinburgh University Press, Edinburgh.

Peters, B.G. and B.W. Hogwood (1985) 'In search of an issue-attention cycle', *Journal of Politics*, **47**: 238–53.

Peters, T. and R.H. Waterman (1982) *In Search of Excellence*, Harper & Row, New York.

Pfeffer, J. and G.R. Salancik (1978) *The External Control of Organizations: A Resource Dependence Perspective*, Harper & Row, New York.

Phillimore, P. and S. Moffatt (1994) 'Discounted knowledge: local experience, environmental pollution and health', in Popay and Williams, 1994.

Phillips, A. (1960) 'A theory of interfirm organization', *Quarterly Journal of Economics*, **74**: 602–13.

Pierson, P.D. and R.K. Weaver (1993) 'Imposing losses in pension policy', in Weaver and Rockman (eds), 1993.

Pinder, J. (ed.) (1981) *Fifty Years of Political and Economic Planning*, Heinemann, London.

Pinkus, C.E. and A. Dixon (1981) *Solving Local Government Problems: Practical Applications of Operations Research in Cities and Regions*, Allen & Unwin, London.

Pirie, M. (1987) *Privatization in Theory and Practice*, Adam Smith Institute, London.

Pirie, M. (1988) *Micropolitics*, Wildwood House, Aldershot, Hants.

Plant, R. (1991) *Modern Political Thought*, Blackwell, Oxford.

Plowden, W. (ed.) (1987) *Advising the Rulers*, Blackwell, Oxford.

Polanyi, M. (1967) *The Tacit Dimension*, Doubleday-Anchor, Garden City, N.Y.

Pollitt, C. (1986) 'Performance indicators in the longer term', *Public Money and Management*, 9(3): 51–5.

Pollitt, C. (1990) *Managerialism and the Public Sector*, Blackwell, Oxford.

Pollitt, C., L. Lewis, J. Negro and J. Pattern (eds) (1979) *Public Policy in Theory and Practice*, Hodder & Stoughton/Open University Press, Sevenoaks, Kent.

Polsby, N. (1963) *Community Power and Political Theory*, Yale University Press, New Haven, Conn.

Popay, J. and G. Williams (1994) *Researching the People's Health*, Routledge, London.

Popay, J. and G. Williams (1994a) 'Introduction', in Popay and Williams, 1994.

Popay, J. and G. Williams (1994b) 'Researching the people's health: dilemmas and opportunities for social scientists', in Popay and Williams, 1994.

Popper, K. (1957) *The Poverty of Historicism*, Routledge & Kegan Paul, London.

Popper, K. (1959) *The Logic of Scientific Discovery*, Hutchinson, London.

Popper, K. (1963) *Conjectures and Refutations*, Routledge & Kegan Paul, London.

Popper, K. (1966) *The Open Society and its Enemies*, Routledge & Kegan Paul, London.

Popper, K. (1976) *Unended Quest: An Intellectual Autobiography*, Collins/Fontana, London.

Porter, G. and J. Welsh Brown (1991) *Global Environmental Politics*, Westview Press, Boulder, Col.

Porter, M. (1990) *The Competitive Advantage of Nations*, Macmillan, London.

Portis, E.B. and M.B. Levy, (eds) (1988) *Handbook of Political Theory and Policy Science*, Greenwood, New York.

Potter, J. (1988) 'Consumerism and the public

sector: how well does the coat fit?', *Public Administration*, **66**: 149–64.

Poulanzas, N. (1973) *Political Power and Social Classes*, New Left Books, London.

Poulanzas, N. (1978) *State, Power, Socialism*, New Left Books, London.

Powell, W.W. (1991) 'Neither market nor hierarchy: network forms of organization', in Thompson, *et al.* (eds), 1991.

Powell, W.W. and P.J. Di Maggio (eds) (1991) *The New Institutionalism in Organizational Analysis*, University of Chicago Press, Chicago, Ill.

Power, M. (1991) 'Auditing and environmental expertise: between protest and professionalisation', *Accounting, Auditing and Accountability*, **4**: 30–42.

Power, M. (1994) *The Audit Explosion*, Demos, London.

Pressman, J. and A. Wildavsky (1973) *Implementation*, University of California Press, Berkeley, Cal.; 2nd edn, 1984.

Prince, M.J. (1983) *Policy Advice and Organizational Survival: Policy Planning and Research Units in British Government*, Gower, Aldershot, Hants.

Propper, C. (1993) 'Quasi-markets, contracts and quality in health and social care: the US experience', in Le Grand and Bartlett (eds), 1993.

Protess, D.L. and M. McCombs (eds) (1991) *Agenda Setting: Readings on Media Public Opinion and Policymaking*, Lawrence Erlbaum Associates, New Jersey.

Protess, D.L., F. L. Cook, T.R. Curtin, M.T. Gordon, D.R. Leff, M.E. McCombs, and P. Miller (1987) 'The impact of investigative reporting on public opinion and policy making: targeting toxic waste', *Public Opinion Quarterly*, **51**: 166–85; reprinted in Protess and McCombs (eds), 1991.

Putman, R. (1976) *The Comparative Study of Political Elites*, Prentice-Hall, Englewood Cliffs, N.J.

Putt, A.C. and J.F. Springer (1989) *Policy Research: Concepts, Methods and Appreciations*, Prentice-Hall, Englewood Cliffs, N.J.

Quade, E.S. (1976) *Analysis for Public Decisions*, Elsevier, New York; 3rd edn, 1983.

Quade, E.S. and W.I. Boucher (1968) *Systems Analysis and Policy Planning: Applications in Defence*, Elsevier, New York.

Radin, B.A. (1992) 'Policy analysis in the Office of the Assistant Secretary for Planning and Evaluation in HEW/HHS: institutionalization and the second generation', in Weiss (ed.), 1992.

Rainey, H.G. (1990) 'Public management: recent developments and current prospects', in Lynn and Wildavsky (eds), 1990.

Ramsey, J.B. (ed.) (1980) *Economic Forecasting – Models or Markets?*, Cato Institute, San Francisco, Cal.

Ranney, A. (ed.) (1968), *Political Science and Public Policy*, Markham, Chicago, Ill.

Ranson, S. and J. Stewart (1989) 'Citizenship and government: the challenge for management in the public domain', *Political Studies*, **37**: 5–24.

Rasey, K.P., W.D. Keating, N. Krumholz and P.D. Star (1991) 'Management of neighborhood development : community development corporations', in Bingham *et al.*, 1991.

Raskin, M. (1973) *Being and Doing*, Beacon Press, Boston, Mass.

Raven, B.H. (1974) 'The Nixon Group', *Journal of Social Issues*, **30**: 297–320.

Rawls, J. (1971) *A Theory of Justice*, Harvard University Press, Cambridge, Mass.

Ray, J. (1990) *Global Politics*, Houghton Mifflin, Boston, Mass.

Redfield, R. (1968) *The Primitive World and its Transformations*, Penguin Books, Harmondsworth, Middx.

Rein, M. (1976) *Social Science and Public Policy*, Penguin Books, Harmondsworth, Middx.

Rein, M. (1983) 'Value-critical policy analysis', in Callahan and Jennings, 1983.

Rein, M. and D.A. Schön, '(1977) 'Problem setting in policy research', in Weiss (ed.), 1977.

Rein, M. and D.A. Schön (1993) 'Reframing policy discourse', in Fischer and Forester (eds), 1993.

Reinermann, H. (1987) 'Information and public management', in Kooiman and Eliassen (eds), 1987.

Rhodes, G. (1975) *Committees of Inquiry*, Allen & Unwin, London.

Rhodes, R.A.W. (1979) *Public Administration and Policy Analysis*, Saxon House, Farnborough, Hants.

Rhodes, R.A.W. (1981) *Control and Power in Central–Local Government Relations*, Gower, Aldershot, Hants.

Rhodes, R.A.W. (1985) 'Power-dependence, policy communities and intergovernmental networks', *Public Administration Bulletin*, **49**: 4–31.

Rhodes, R.A.W. (1986) *The National World of Local Government*, Allen & Unwin, London.

Rhodes, R.A.W. (1988) *Beyond Westminster and Whitehall: The Sub-Central Governments of Britain*, Unwin Hyman, London.

Rhodes, R.A.W. (1992), 'Intergovernmental relations: unitary systems', in Hawkesworth and Kogan (eds), 1992.

Rhodes, R.A.W. (ed.) (1992) *Policy Networks in British Government*, Oxford University Press, Oxford.

Rice, C., H. Roberts, S.J. Smith and C. Bryce (1994) '"It's like teaching your child to swim in a pool full of alligators": lay voices and professional research on child accidents', in Popay and Williams, 1994.

Rice, R.E. and C. Atkin (eds) (1988) *Public Communication Campaigns*, 2nd edn, Sage, Newbury Park, Cal.

Richardson, J.J. (1982) 'The concept of policy style', in Richardson (ed.), 1982.

Richardson, J.J. (1990) 'Government and groups in Britain: changing styles', Strathclyde Papers on Government and Politics, no. 69, University of Strathclyde.

Richardson, J.J. (ed.) (1982) *Policy Styles in Western Europe*, Allen & Unwin, London.

Richardson, J.J. and A.G. Jordan (1979) *Governing Under Pressure: The Policy Process in a Post-Parliamentary Democracy*, Martin Robertson, Oxford; 2nd edn, 1985.

Ridgeway, C.L. (1983) *The Dynamics of Small Groups*, St Martin's Press, New York.

Rigby, T.H. (1964) 'Tradition, market and organizational societies and the USSR', *World Politics*, 16(4): 539–57.

Rigby, T.H. (1990) *The Changing Soviet System: Mono-organisational Socialism from its Origins to Gorbachev's Restructuring*, Edward Elgar, Aldershot, Hants.

Riker, W.H. (1986) *The Art of Political Manipulation*, Yale University Press, New Haven, Conn.

Ripley, R. (1985) *Policy Analysis in Political Science*, Nelson-Hall, Chicago, Ill.

Ripley, R. and G. Franklin (1980) *Congress, the Bureaucracy and Public Policy*, Dorsey, Homewood, Ill.

Ripley, R. and G. Franklin (1982) *Bureaucracy and Policy Implementation*, Dorsey, Homewood, Ill.

Rist, R.C. (ed.) (1995) *Policy Evaluation: Linking Theory to Practice*, Edward Elgar, Aldershot, Hants.

Ritzer, G. (1993) *The McDonaldization of Society*, Pine Forge Press, Newbury Park, Cal.

Rivlin, A.M. (1971) *Systematic Thinking for Social Action*, Brookings Institution, Washington, D.C.

Rivlin, A.M. (1973) 'Forensic social science', in *Perspectives on Inequality, Harvard Educational Review*, Reprint Series no. 8, Harvard University Press, Cambridge, Mass.

Rivlin, A.M. (1992) 'Policy analysis at the Brookings Institution', in Weiss (ed.), 1992.

Roberts, H. (1979) *Community Development: Learning and Action*, University of Toronto Press, Toronto.

Roberts, I. (1994) 'Remuneration and rewards', in Beardwell and Holden (eds), 1994.

Robinson, F. and K. Shaw (1991) 'Urban regeneration and community involvement', *Local Economy*, 6(1).

Robson, M. (1993) *Problem Solving in Groups*, Gower, Aldershot, Hants.

Rogers, D. and D. Whetten *et al.* (1982) *Interorganisational Coordination: Theory, Research and Implementation*, Iowa State University Press, Ames, Iowa.

Rogers, E.M. and J.W. Dearing (1987) 'Agenda setting research: where has it been, where is it going?', *Communications Yearbook*, 11: 555–94.

Rogow, A.A. (ed.) (1969) *Politics, Personality and Social Science in the Twentieth Century: Essays in Honor of Harold D. Lasswell*, University of Chicago Press, Chicago, Ill.

Rose, N. (1990) *Governing the Soul: The Shaping of the Private Self*, Routledge, London.

Rose, R. (1973) 'Comparing public policy: an overview', *European Journal of Political Research*, 1: 67–94.

Rose, R. (1984a) *Do Parties Make a Difference?*, Macmillan, London.

Rose, R. (1984b) *Understanding Big Government: The Programme Approach*, Sage, London.

Rose, R. (1986) 'Dynamics of the welfare mix in Britain', in R. Rose and R. Shiratori (eds), *The Welfare State East and West*, Oxford University Press, Oxford.

Rose, R. (1989) *Politics in England: Change and Persistence*, Macmillan, London.

Rose, R. (1990) 'Inheritance before choice in public policy', *Journal of Theoretical Politics*, 2: 263–91.

Rose, R. and P.L. Davies (1994) *Inheritance in Public Policy: Change Without Choice in Britain*, Yale University Press, New Haven, Conn.

Rosenau, J. (1990) *Turbulence in World Politics*, Harvester Wheatsheaf, Hemel Hempstead, Herts.

Rosenhead, J. (1989) *Rational Analysis for a Problematic World: Problem Structuring Methods for Complexity, Uncertainty and Conflict*, John Wiley, London.

Rossi, P.H. and H. Freeman (1979) *Evaluation: A Systematic Approach*, Sage, Newbury Park, Cal.; 2nd edn, 1993.

Rossi, P.H. and W. Williams (1972) *Evaluating Social Programs*, Seminar Press, New York.

Roszak, T. (1988) *The Cult of Information: The Folklore of Computers and the True Art of Thinking*, Paladin Grafton Books, London.

Rubenstein, R. and H. Lasswell (1966) *The Sharing of Power in a Psychiatric Hospital*, Yale University Press, New Haven, Conn.

Rule, J.B. (1978) *Insight and Social Betterment: A Preface to Applied Social Science*, Oxford University Press, New York.

Sabatier, P.A. (1978) 'The acquisition and utilization of technical information by administrative agencies', *Administrative Science Quarterly*, 23: 386–411.

Sabatier, P.A. (1986) 'What we can learn from implementation research?', in Kaufman *et al.* (eds), 1986.

Sabatier, P.A. (1986a) 'Top-down and bottom-up

approaches to implementation research: a critical analysis and suggested synthesis', *Journal of Public Policy*, **6**: 21–48.

Sabatier, P.A. (1987) 'Knowledge, policy-orientated learning and policy change', *Knowledge: Creation, Diffusion, Utilization*, **8**: 649–92.

Sabatier, P.A. (1988) 'An advocacy coalition framework of policy change and the role of policy-oriented learning therein', *Policy Sciences*, **21**: 129–68.

Sabatier, P.A. (1991) 'Toward better theories of the policy process', *PS: Political Science and Politics*, **24**: 147–56.

Sabatier, P.A. (1993) 'Policy change over a decade or more', in Sabatier and Jenkins-Smith (eds), 1993.

Sabatier, P.A. and H. Jenkins-Smith (1988) Symposium volume: 'Policy change and policy orientated learning', *Western Political Quarterly*, **21**: 123–277.

Sabatier, P.A. and H.C. Jenkins-Smith (eds) (1993) *Policy Change and Learning: An Advocacy Coalition Approach*, Westview Press, Boulder, Col.

Sabatier, P.A. and D. Mazmanian (1979) 'The conditions of effective implementation: a guide to accomplishing policy objectives', *Policy Analysis*, **5**: 481–504.

Sabatier, P.A. and N. Pelkey (1987) 'Incorporating multiple actors and guidance instruments into models of regulatory policy making: an advocacy coalition framework', *Administration and Society*, **19**: 236–63.

Sabato, L. (1981) *The Rise of Political Consultants: New Ways of Winning Elections*, Basic Books, New York.

Saggar, S. (1991) *Race and Public Policy*, Avebury, Aldershot, Hants.

Salaman, G. (1981) *Class and the Corporation*, Fontana, London.

Samuelson, P.A. (1954) 'The pure theory of public expenditure', *Review of Economics and Statistics*, **37**: 35–46.

Sandel, M. (ed.) (1984) *Liberalism and its Critics*, New York University Press, New York.

Sapolsky, H.M. (1972) *The Polaris System Development: Bureaucratic and Programmatic Success in Government*, Harvard University Press, Cambridge, Mass.

Sartori, G. (1962) *Democratic Theory*, Wayne State University Press, Detroit, Mich.

Saunders, P. (1975) 'They make the rules: political routines and the generation of political bias', *Policy and Politics*, **4**(1): 31–58.

Saunders, P. (1979) *Urban Politics*, Hutchinson, London; also Penguin Books, Harmondsworth, Middx, 1980.

Saunders, P. (1981) *Social Theory and the Urban Question*, Hutchinson, London.

Saward, M. (1979) 'The civil nuclear network in Britain', in D. Marsh and R.A.W. Rhodes, *Public Administration and Policy Analysis*, Saxon House, London.

Saxe, L. and M. Fine (1981) *Social Experiments: Methods for Design and Evaluation*, Sage, Beverly Hills, Cal.

Saxonhouse, A. (1983) 'Classical Greek conceptions of the public and private ', in Benn and Gaus (eds), 1983.

A. Sayer, (1989) 'Postfordism in question', *International Journal of Urban and Regional Research*, **13**(4): 171–85.

Schapiro, I., K.H. Porter and R. Greenstein (1992) 'The Center on Budget and Policy Priorities', in Weiss (ed.), 1992.

Scharpf, F.W. (1978) 'Interorganizational policy studies: issues, concepts and perspectives', in Hanf and Scharpf (eds), 1978.

Schattschneider, E.E. (1960) *The Semisovereign People*, Holt, Rinehart & Winston, New York.

Schein, E.H. (1969) *Process Consultation*, Addison-Wesley, Reading, Mass.

Schmidt, M.G. (1989) 'Learning from catastrophes: West Germany's public policy', in Castles (ed.), 1989.

Schmitter, P.C. (1974) 'Still the century of corporatism?', *Review of Politics*, **36**: 85–131.

Schmitter, P.C. and G Lehmbruch (eds) (1979) *Trends towards Corporatist Intermediation*, Sage, Beverly Hills, Cal.

Schneider, J.W. (1985) 'Social problems: the constructionist view', *Annual Review of Sociology*, **11**: 209–29.

Schneider, J.W. and J.I. Kitsuse (eds) (1984) *Studies in the Sociology of Social Problems*, Ablex Publishing, Norwood, N.J.

Schön, D.A. (1971) *Beyond the Stable State*, Temple Smith, London; and Random House, New York.

School for Advanced Urban Studies (SAUS), Decentralisation Research and Information Centre (1984 to date) *Going Local*, School for Advanced Urban Studies, University of Bristol, irreg.

Schultze, C.L. (1968) *The Politics and Economics of Public Spending*, Brookings Institution, Washington, D.C.

Schumacher, E.F. (1973) *Small is Beautiful: Economics as if People Really Mattered*, Blond & Briggs, London.

Schumpeter, J.A. (1974) *Capitalism, Socialism and Democracy*, Allen & Unwin, London.

Schur, E.M. (1980) *The Politics of Deviance: Stigma Contests and the Uses of Power*, Prentice-Hall, Englewood Cliffs, N.J.

Scioli, F.P. and T. J. Cook (1973) 'Experimental design in policy impact analysis', *Social Science Quarterly*, **54**: 271–91.

Searls, E. (1978) 'The fragmented French executive', *West European Politics*, May: 161–76.

Sederberg, P. (1984) *The Politics of Meaning: Power and Explanation in the Construction of Social Reality*, University of Arizona Press, Tucson, Ariz.

Seldon, A. (1981) *The Emerging Consensus*, Institute of Economic Affairs, London.

Self, P. (1975) *Econocrats and the Policy Process: The Politics and Philosophy of Cost-benefit Analysis*, Macmillan, London.

Self, P. (1993) *Government by the Market: The Politics of Public Choice*, Macmillan, London.

Selznick, P. (1948) 'Foundations of a theory of organization', *American Sociological Review*, 13: 23–35.

Selznick, P. (1949) *TVA and the Grass Roots*, University of California Press, Berkeley, Cal.

Selznick, P. (1957) *Leadership in Administration*, Row & Peters, Evanston, Ill.

Sen, A. and B. Williams (eds) (1982) *Utilitarianism and Beyond*, Cambridge University Press, Cambridge.

Sharkansky, I. (1970) *Public Administration: Policy Making in Government Agencies*, Markam, Chicago, Ill.

Sharpe, L.J. (1975) 'The social scientist and policy-making: some cautionary thoughts and transatlantic reflections', *Policy and Politics*, December: 7–34.

Sharpe, L.J. (1978) 'The social scientist and policy making in Britain and America: a comparison', in Bulmer (ed.), 1978.

Sharpe, L.J. (1985) 'Central coordination and the policy network', *Political Studies*, 33: 361–81.

Sharpe, L.J. (ed.) (1979) *Decentralist Trends in Western Democracies*, Sage, Beverly Hills, Cal.

Sharpe, L.J. and K. Newton (1984) *Does Politics Matter? The Determinants of Public Policy*, Oxford University Press, Oxford.

Shaw, D.L. and M.E. McCombs (eds) (1977) *The Emergence of American Political Issues*, West, New York.

Sherif, M. (1936) *The Social Psychology of Group Norms*, Harper & Row, New York.

Shibutani, T. (ed.) (1970) *Human Nature and Collective Behaviour: Papers in Honor of Herbert Blumer*, Prentice-Hall, Englewood Cliffs, N.J.

Shonfield, A. (1965) *Modern Capitalism*, Oxford University Press, Oxford.

Simmie, J. (1990) 'Varieties of state action', in Simmie and King (eds), 1990.

Simmie, J. and R. King (eds) (1990) *The State in Action: Public Policy and Politics*, Frances Pinter, London.

Simon, H.A. (1945) *Administrative Behaviour*, Free Press, New York; 2nd edn, 1957; 3rd edn, 1976.

Simon, H.A. (1957a) *Models of Man: Social and Rational*, John Wiley, New York.

Simon, H.A. (1957b) 'A behavioral model of rational choice', in Simon, 1957a.

Simon, H.A. (1959) 'Theories of decision-making in economics and behavioral science', *American Economic Review*, 49(3): 245–83.

Simon, H.A. (1960) *The New Science of Management Decision*, Prentice-Hall, Englewood Cliffs, N.J.; 2nd edn, 1977.

Simon, H.A. (1969) *The Sciences of the Artificial*, MIT Press, Cambridge, Mass.; 2nd edn, 1981.

Simon, H.A. (1973) 'The structure of ill-structured problems', *Artificial Intelligence*, 4: 181–201.

Simon, H.A. (1981) 'Cognitive science: the newest science of the artificial', in D. Norman (ed.) *Perspectives on Cognitive Science*, Lawrence Erlbaum, Hillsdale, N.J.

Simon, H.A. (1983) *Reason in Human Affairs*, Stanford University Press, Palo Alto, Cal.

Simon, H.A. (1985) 'Human nature in politics: the dialogue of psychology with political science', *American Political Science Review*, 79: 293–304.

Simon, H.A. (ed.) (1979) *Models of Thought*, Yale University Press, New Haven, Conn.

Simon, H.A. with H. Guetzkow (1957a) 'Mechanisms involved in pressures towards uniformity in groups', in Simon, 1957a.

Simon, H.A. with H. Guetzkow (1957b) 'Mechanisms involved in group pressures on deviate members', in Simon, 1957a.

Singer, O. (1993) 'Knowledge and politics in economic policy making: official economic advisors in the USA, Great Britain and Germany', in Peters and Barker (eds), 1993.

Skidelsky, R. (1977) *The End of the Keynesian Era*, Macmillan, London.

Sklar, K.K. (1991) 'Hull House maps and papers: social science as women's work in the 1890s', in Bulmer *et al.* (eds), 1991.

Skocpol, T. (1985) 'Bringing the state back in: strategies of analysis in current research', in Evans *et al.* (eds), 1985.

Skocpol, T. and K. Finegold (1982) 'State capacity and economic intervention in the New Deal', *Political Science Quarterly*, 97: 255–78.

Slaton, D. (1991), *Televote: Expanding Citizen Participation in the Quantum Age*, Praeger, New York.

Slatter, S. (1984) *Corporate Recovery: Successful Turnaround Strategies and Their Implementation*, Penguin, Harmondsworth, Middx.

Slonaker, L.L. (1978) *The Decision Seminar: A Strategy for Problem Solving*, Merschon Center, Columbus, Ohio.

Smart, J.C. and B. Williams (1987) *Utilitarianism: For and Against*, Cambridge University Press, Cambridge.

Smelser, N.J. (ed.) (1988) *Handbook of Sociology*, Sage, Beverly Hills, Cal.

Smigel, E.O. (ed.) (1971) *Handbook on the Study of Social Problems*, Rand-McNally, Chicago, Ill.

Smith, B.C. (1985) *Decentralization: The Territorial Dimension of the State*, Allen & Unwin, London.

Smith, B.R. (1966) *The RAND Corporation: Case Study of a Non-Profit Advisory Corporation*, Harvard University Press, Cambridge, Mass.

Smith, D. (1992) *From Boom to Bust: Trial and Error in British Economic Policy*, Penguin, Harmondsworth, Middx.

Smith, G. and D. May (1980) 'The artificial debate between rationalist and incrementalist models of decision making', *Policy and Politics*, 8: 147–61.

Smith, J.A. (1989) 'Think tanks and the politics of ideas', in Colander and Coats (eds), 1989.

Smith, J.A. (1990) *The Idea Brokers: Think Tanks and the Rise of the New Policy Elite*, Free Press, New York.

Smith, L. and D. Jones (eds) (1981) *Deprivation, Participation and Community Action*, Routledge & Kegan Paul, London.

Smith, M.J. (1991) 'From policy community to issue network: salmonella in eggs and the new politics of food', *Public Administration*, 69: 235–55.

Smith, M.J. (1993) *Pressure Power and Policy: State Autonomy and Policy Networks in Britain and the United States*, Harvester Wheatsheaf, Hemel Hempstead, Herts.

Smith, S. (1981) 'Allison and the Cuban missile crisis', *Millennium*, 9(1): 21–40.

Smith, S. (1984) 'Groupthink and the hostage rescue mission', *British Journal of Political Science*, 15: 117–26.

Smith, T.A. (1972) *Anti-politics: Consensus, Reform and Protest in Britain*, Charles Knight, London.

Smith, T.A. (1979) *The Politics of the Corporate Economy*, Martin Robertson, Oxford.

Smith, T.A. (1994) 'Post-modern politics and the case for constitutional renewal', *Political Quarterly*, Summer: 128–37.

Snow, C.P. (1961) *Science and Government*, Oxford University Press, London.

Solesbury, W. (1976) 'The environmental agenda: an illustration of how situations may become political issues and issues may demand responses from government or how they may not', *Public Administration*, 54: 379–97.

Sontag, S. (1989) *AIDS and its Metaphors*, Penguin, Harmondsworth, Middx.

Soysal, Y.N. (1993) 'Immigration and the emerging European polity', in Andersen and Eliassen (eds), 1993.

Spector, M. and J.I. Kitsuse (1977) *Constructing Social Problems*, Cummings, Menlo Park, Cal.

Stacey, M. (1994) 'The power of lay knowledge: a personal view', in Popay and Williams, 1994.

Staudt, K. and J. Jacquette (1988) 'Women's programs: bureaucratic resistance and feminist organisations', in Boneparth and Stoper (eds), 1988.

Stein, H. (1981) 'The chief executive as chief economist', in W. Fellner (ed.), *Essays in Contemporary Economic Problems: Demand, Productivity and Population*, American Enterprise Institute, Washington, D.C.

Stein, H. (1984) *Presidential Economics: The Making of Economic Policy from Roosevelt to Reagan and Beyond*, Simon & Schuster, New York.

Steinbrunner, J.D. (1974) *The Cybernetic Theory of Decision: New Dimensions of Political Analysis*, Princeton University Press, Princeton, N.J.

Steiner, J. (1991) *European Democracies*, Longman, New York.

Steinfels, P. (1979) *The Neoconservatives*, Simon & Schuster, New York.

Stewart, D.W. (1990) 'Women in public administration', in Lynn and Wildavsky (eds), 1990.

Stewart, J. (1982) 'Guidelines for policy derivation', in Leach and Stewart (eds), 1982.

Stewart, J. (1986) *The New Management of Local Government*, Allen & Unwin, London.

Stewart, J. (1994) 'Voice of the people', *Guardian*, 10 November: 24.

Stewart, J. and M. Clarke (1987) 'The public service orientation: issues and dilemmas', *Public Administration*, 65: 161–77.

Stewart, J.D. and K. Walsh (1990) *The Search for Quality*, Local Government Training Board, Luton, Beds.

Stewart, J., E. Kendall and A. Coote (1994) *Citizens' Juries*, Institute for Public Policy Research, London.

Stewart, J. Jr (1991) 'Policy models and equal opportunities', *PS: Political Science and Politics*, 24: 167–73.

Stewart, L.H. (1992) *Changemakers: A Jungian Perspective on Sibling Position and the Family Atmosphere*, Routledge, London.

Stier, S. (1975) 'Psychology and public policy', in Nagel (ed.), 1975a.

Stiglitz, J.E. (1987) 'Principal and agent', in Eatwell et al. (eds), 1987.

Stimson, J.A.(1991) *Public Opinion in America: Moods, Cycles and Swings*, Westview Press, Boulder, Col.

Stockman, D. (1987) *The Triumph of Politics: The Inside Story of the Reagan Revolution*, Avon, New York.

Stoker, G. (1989) 'Creating a local government for a post-Fordist society: the Thatcher project', in G. Stoker and J. Stewart (eds), *The Future of Local Government*, Macmillan, London.

Stokey, E. and R. Zeckhauser (1978) *A Primer for Policy Analysis*, W.W. Norton, New York.

Stone, D.A. (1988) *Policy Paradox and Political Reason*, Scott, Foresman, Glenview, Ill.

Stone, D.A. (1989) 'Causal stories and the formation of policy agendas', *Political Science Quarterly*, **104**: 281–300.

Storey, J. (1989) 'Human resource management in the public sector', *Public Money and Management*, Autumn: 19–24.

Storey, J. (ed.) (1989) *New Perspectives on Human Resource Management*, Tavistock Publications, London.

Streeck, W. and P.C. Schmitter (1991) 'Community, market, state – and associations? The prospective contribution of interest governance to social order', in Thompson *et al.* (eds), 1991.

Streeck, W. and P.C. Schmitter (eds) (1985) *Private Interest Government*, Sage, London.

Street, J. (1993) 'Policy advice in an established official advice structure: Aids advice through the British Department of Health', in Peters and Barker (eds), 1993.

Stretton, H. and L. Orchard (1994) *Public Goods, Public Enterprise, Public Choice*, St Martin's Press, New York.

Stringer, J.K. and J.J. Richardson (1980) 'Managing the political agenda: problem definition and policy making in Britain', *Parliamentary Affairs*, **23**: 23–39.

Stringer, P. (ed.) (1982) *Confronting Social Issues: Applications of Social Psychology*, Academic Press, London.

Suchman, E. (1967) *Evaluative Research*, Russell Sage, New York.

Supple, B. (1990) 'Official inquiry and Britain's industrial decline: the first fifty years', in Furner and Supple (eds), 1990.

Sutherland, S. (1994) *Irrationality: The Enemy Within*, Penguin Books, Harmondsworth, Middx.

Sweezy, P.M. (1964) 'John Maynard Keynes', reprinted in Lekachman, 1964.

Tallman, I. and R. McGee (1971) 'Defining a social problem', in Smigel (ed.), 1971.

Tawney, R.H. (1921) *The Acquisitive Society*, Bell, London.

Tayar, G. (ed.) (1971) *Personality and Power: Studies in Political Achievement*, British Broadcasting Corporation, London.

Taylor, C. (1985) 'Atomism', in *Philosophy and the Human Sciences: Philosophical Papers*, vol. 2, Cambridge University Press, Cambridge.

Taylor, F.W. *Scientific Management* (1911) Harper & Row, New York; reprinted 1947.

Taylor, I. and L. Taylor (eds) (1973) *Politics and Deviance*, Penguin, Harmondsworth, Middx.

Taylor, M. (1982) *Community, Anarchy and Liberty*, Cambridge University Press, Cambridge.

Taylor, M. (1987) *The Possibility of Cooperation*, Cambridge University Press, Cambridge.

Taylor, M. (1992) *Signposts to Community Development*, Community Development Foundation, London.

Taylor, P.J. (ed.) (1993) *Political Geography of the Twentieth Century: A Global Analysis*, Belhaven Press, London.

Tetlock, P.E. (1979) 'Identifying victims of groupthink from public statements of decision makers', *Journal of Personality and Social Psychology*, **37**: 1314–24.

Tetlock, P.E., R.S. Peterson, C. McGuire, S. Chang and P. Feld (1992) 'Assessing political group dynamics: a test of the groupthink model', *Journal of Personality and Social Psychology*, **63**: 403–23.

Thomason, G. (1988) *A Textbook of Human Resource Management*, Institute of Personnel Management, London.

Thompson, G., J. Frances, R. Levacic and J. Mitchell (eds) (1991) *Markets, Hierarchies and Networks: The Coordination of Social Life*, Sage/Open University Press, London.

Thompson, J.L. (1990) *Strategic Management: Awareness and Change*, Chapman & Hall, London.

Thompson, P.R. and M.R. Yessian (1992) 'Policy analysis in the Office of Inspector General, US Department of Health and Human Services', in Weiss (ed.), 1992.

Tiebout, C. (1956) 'A pure theory of local expenditure', *Journal of Political Economy*, **64**: 416–24.

Titmus, R.M. (1968) *Commitment to Welfare*, Allen & Unwin, London.

Todd, M.J. (1991) *The Centre for Policy Studies: Its Birth and Early Days*, Essex Papers in Government no. 81, Department of Government, University of Essex, Colchester.

Tollefson, A.M. and A.M. Chang (1973) *Bibliography of Presidential Commissions, Committees, Councils, Panels and Task Forces, 1961–72*, University of Minnesota Library, Minneapolis.

Tomlinson, J. (1981) *Problems of British Economic Policy, 1870–1945*, Methuen, London.

Topf, R. (1993) 'Advice to governments: some theoretical and practical issues', in Peters and Barker (eds), 1993.

Torgerson, D. (1985) 'Contextual orientation in policy analysis: the contribution of Harold D. Lasswell', *Policy Sciences*, **18**: 241–61.

Torgerson, D. (1986) 'Between knowledge and politics: three faces of policy analysis', *Policy Sciences*, **19**: 33–59.

Toulmin, S. (1958) *The Uses of Argument*, Cambridge University Press, Cambridge.

Tournon, J. (1992) 'Blind investor: the state and fundamental research – advice to the French government on the European synchrotron radiation facility', in Barker and Peters (eds), 1992.

Trahair, R.C.S. (1981–2) 'Elton Mayo and the early political psychology of Harold D. Lasswell', *Political Psychology*, **3**: 170–88.

Tribe, L. (1972) 'Policy science: analysis or ideology?', *Philosophy and Public Affairs*, **2**: 67–110.

Truman, D. (1951) *The Governmental Process*, Alfred A. Knopf, New York.

Tufte, E.R. (1978) *Political Control of the Economy*, Princeton University Press, Princeton, N.J.

Tuite, M.F. (1972) 'Toward a theory of joint decision-making', in Tuite *et al.* (eds), 1972.

Tuite, M.F., M. Radnor and R.K. Chisholm (eds) (1972) *Interorganizational Decision-making*, Aldine-Atherton, Chicago, Ill.

Tullock, G. (1965) *The Politics of Bureaucracy*, Public Affairs Press, Washington, D.C.

Tullock, G. (1976) *The Vote Motive: An Essay in the Economics of Politics with Applications to the British Economy*, Institute of Economic Affairs, London.

Turk, H. (1970) 'Interorganizational networks in urban society: initial perspectives and comparative research', *American Sociological Review*, **35**: 1–19.

Turner, M.E., A.R. Pratkanis, P. Probasco and C. Leve (1992) 'Threat, cohesion and group effectiveness: testing a social identity maintenance perspective on groupthink', *Journal of Personality and Social Psychology*, **63**: 781–96.

Turner, R.H. (1970) 'Determinants of social movement strategies', in Shibutani (ed.), 1970.

Tversky, A. and D. Kahneman (1974), 'Judgment under uncertainty: heuristics and biases', *Science*, **185**: 1124–31.

Unger, R.M. (1987) *Social Theory: Its Situation and Its Task*, Cambridge University Press, Cambridge.

United States Congress, Joint Economic Committee (1969) *The Analysis and Evaluation of Public Expenditures: The PPB System*, vol. 3, 91st Congress, 1st Session, US Government Printing Office, Washington, D.C.

Van Meter, D. and C. Van Horn (1975) 'The policy implementation process: a conceptual framework', *Administration and Society*, **6**: 445–88.

Van Strien, P.J. (1982) 'In search of an emancipatory social psychology', in Stringer (ed.), 1982.

Van Vliet, M. (1993) 'Environmental regulation of business: options and constraints for communicative governance', in Kooiman (ed.), 1993.

Van Warden, F. (1992) 'Dimensions and types of policy networks', *European Journal of Political Research*, **21**: 29–52.

Vass, A.A. (1986) *Aids a Plague in Us: A Social Perspective – the Condition and Social Consequences*, Venus Academica, St Ives.

Vickers, G. (1965) *The Art of Judgment: A Study of Policymaking*, Chapman & Hall, London; 2nd edn, 1983.

Vickers, G. (1968) *Value Systems and the Social Process*, Tavistock Publications, London.

Vickers, G. (1983) *Human Systems are Different*, Tavistock Publications, London: Harper & Row, New York.

Vickers, G. (1991) 'Judgment', in Henry (ed.), 1991.

Vinovskis, M.A. (1988) *An 'Epidemic' of Adolescent Pregnancy? Some Historical and Policy Considerations*, Oxford University Press, New York.

Vogel, D. (1986) *National Styles of Regulation: Environmental Policy in Great Britain and the United States*, Cornell University Press, Ithaca, N.Y.

Vogel, D. (1993) 'The making of EC environmental policy', in Andersen and Eliassen (eds), 1993.

von Mises, L. (1944) *Bureaucracy*, Yale University Press, New Haven, Conn.

Voss, C., C. Armistead and B. Johnson (1985) *Operations Management in the Service Industries and the Public Sector: Texts and Cases*, John Wiley, London.

Vroom, V.H. (1964) *Work and Motivation*, John Wiley, New York.

Wade, H. (1967) *Administrative Law*, Clarendon Press, Oxford.

Walker, A. (1982) *Community Care*, Blackwell, Oxford.

Walker, J. (1989) 'Introduction: Policy communities as global phenomena', *Governance*, **2**: 1–4.

Walker, J.L. (1969) 'Setting the agenda in the US Senate: a theory of problem selection', *British Journal of Political Science*, **63**: 423–45.

Wallack, L. (1988) 'Mass communication and health promotion: a critical perspective', in Rice and Atkin (eds), 1988.

Wallas, G. (1948) *Human Nature in Politics*, Constable, London; first published 1908.

Wallerstein, I. (1974) *The Modern World System: Capitalist Agriculture and the Origins of the European World-economy in the Sixteenth Century*, Academic Press, New York.

Wallerstein, I. (1979) *The Capitalist World Economy*, Cambridge University Press, Cambridge.

Walter, J. (1980) *The Leader: A Political Biography of Gough Whitlam*, University of Queensland Press, St Lucia, Queensland.

Walsh, K. (1991) 'Citizens and consumers: marketing and public sector management', *Public Money and Management*, **11**(2): 9–16.

Walzer, M. (1983) *Spheres of Justice: A Defence of Pluralism and Equality*, Martin Robertson, Oxford.

Warren, R.L. (1967) 'The interorganizational field as a focus for investigation', *Administrative Science Quarterly*, **12**: 396–419.

Warren, R., M.S. Rosentraub and L.F. Weschler (1992) 'Building urban governance: an agenda for the 1980s', *Urban Affairs Quarterly*, **14**(3/4): 399–422.

Watts, H.M. (1969) 'Graduated work incentives: an experiment in negative taxation', *American Economic Review*, 59: 463–72.

Weale, A. (1983) *Political Theory and Social Policy*, Macmillan, London.

Weatheritt, M. (1993) 'Community policing', in Butcher *et al.* (eds), 1993.

Weaver, R.K. (1985) *The Politics of Industrial Change*, Brookings Institution, Washington, D.C.

Weaver, R.K. and B.R. Rockman (1993) 'Assessing the effects of institutions', in Weaver and Rockman (eds), 1993.

Weaver, R.K. and B.R. Rockman (eds) (1993) *Do Institutions Matter? Government Capabilities in the United States and Abroad*, Brookings Institution, Washington, D.C.

Weber, M. (1930) *The Protestant Ethic and the Spirit of Capitalism*, Allen & Unwin, London.

Weber, M. (1991) *From Max Weber: Essays in Sociology*, ed., with an introd. H.H. Gerth and C. Wright Mills, Routledge, London.

Weimann, G. (1991) 'The influential: back to the concept of opinion leaders?', *Public Opinion Quarterly*, 55: 267–79.

Weiner, M.J. (1981) *English Culture and the Decline of the Industrial Spirit, 1850–1980*, Cambridge University Press, Cambridge.

Weingast, B.R. (1989) 'The political institutions of representative government', *Journal of Institutional and Theoretical Economics*, 145: 693–703.

Weingast, B.R. and W.J. Marshall (1988) 'The industrial organization of Congress; or why legislatures, like firms, are not organized as markets', *Journal of Political Economy*, 96: 132–63.

Weir, M., A.S. Orloff and T. Skocpol (eds) (1988) *The Politics of Social Policy in the United States*, Princeton University Press, Princeton, N.J.

Weiss, C.H. (1972) *Evaluation Research: Methods of Assessing Program Effectiveness*, Prentice-Hall, Englewood Cliffs, N.J.

Weiss, C.H. (1977a) 'Research for policy's sake: the enlightenment function of social research', *Policy Analysis*, 3: 531–46.

Weiss, C.H. (1977b) 'Introduction', in Weiss (ed.) 1977.

Weiss, C.H. (ed.) (1977) *Using Social Science Research in Public Policy-making*, D.C. Heath, Farnborough, Hants.

Weiss, C.H. (ed.) (1992) *Organizations for Policy Analysis: Helping Government Think*, Sage, Newbury Park, Cal.

Westergaard, J. and H. Resler (1976) *Class in a Capitalist Society*, Penguin, Harmondsworth, Middx.

Wetherley, R. and M. Lipsky (1977) 'Street-level bureaucrats and institutional innovation: implementing special education reform', *Harvard Educational Review*, 47(2): 171–97.

White, P.E. (1974) 'Intra and interorganizational studies', *Administration and Society*, 6: 105–52.

Whitehead, A.N. (1925) *Science and the Modern World*, Macmillan, New York.

Whitely, R. (1984) *Intellectual and Social Organisation of the Sciences*, Oxford University Press, London.

Wildavsky, A. (1966) 'The political economy of efficiency: cost-benefit analysis, systems analysis and program budgeting', *Public Administration Review*, 26: 292–310.

Wildavsky, A. (1969) 'Rescuing policy analysis from PPBS', *Public Administration Review*, 29: 189–202.

Wildavsky, A. (1971) 'Does planning work?', *Public Interest*, 24: 95–104.

Wildavsky, A. (1975) *Budgeting: A Comparative Theory of Budgetary Processes*, Little, Brown, Boston, Mass.

Wildavsky, A. (1978a) 'A budget for all seasons? Why the traditional budget lasts', *Public Administration Review*, 6: 501–9.

Wildavsky, A. (1978b) 'Principles for a graduate school of public policy', *Public Administration Bulletin*, 26: 12–31.

Wildavsky, A. (1979) *Speaking the Truth to Power: The Art and Craft of Policy Analysis*, Little, Brown, Boston, Mass.; published in UK as *The Art and Craft of Policy Analysis*, Macmillan, London, 1980.

Wildavsky, A. (1986) 'Schools of public policy in poor countries', *Policy Studies Journal*, 14(3): 407–13.

Wildavsky, A. (1987) 'Choosing preferences by constructing institutions: a cultural theory of preference formation', *American Political Science Review*, 81: 3–22.

Wilding, P. (1982) *Professional Power and Social Welfare*, Routledge & Kegan Paul, London.

Wilensky, H.L. (1967) *Organisational Intelligence: Knowledge and Policy in Government and Industry*, Basic Books, New York.

Wilensky, H. (1975) *The Welfare State and Equality*, University of California Press, Berkeley.

Wilensky, H. *et al.* (1987) 'Comparative social policy', in M. Dierkes, H. Weiler and A. Anatal (eds), *Comparative Policy Research*, Gower, Aldershot, Hants.

Wilkins, L.T. (1964) *Social Deviance: Social Policy, Action and Research*, Tavistock Publications, London.

Wilks, S. (1986) 'Has the state abandoned British industry?', *Parliamentary Affairs*, 39: 31–46.

Wilks, S. and M. Wright (1988) 'Conclusion. Comparing government–industry relations: states, sectors and networks', in Wilks and Wright (eds), 1988.

Wilks, S. and M. Wright (eds) (1988) *Comparative Government–Industry Relations*, Clarendon Press, Oxford.

Willetts, D. (1994) *Civic Conservatism*, Social Market Foundation, London.

Williams, A. and E. Giardina (eds) (1993) *Efficiency in the Public Sector: The Theory and Practice of Cost-benefit Analysis*, Edward Elgar, Aldershot, Hants.

Williams, B.R. and M.A. Palmatier (1992) 'The RAND Corporation', in Weiss (ed.), 1992.

Williams, W. (1983) 'British policy analysis : some preliminary observations from the US', in Gray and Jenkins (eds), 1983.

Williams, W. (1990) *Mismanaging America: The Rise of the Anti-analytical Presidency*, University of Kansas Press, Lawrence, Kan.

Williams, W. (1992) 'White House domestic policy analysis', in Weiss (ed.), 1992.

Williams, W. (ed.) (1982) *Studying Implementation*, Chatham House, Chatham, N.J.

Williams, W. and R. Elmore (eds) (1976) *Social Program Implementation*, Academic Press, New York.

Williamson, O.E. (1965) 'A dynamic theory of interfirm behaviour', *Quarterly Journal of Economics*, 79: 579–607.

Williamson, O.E. (1975) *Markets and Hierarchies*, Free Press, New York.

Williamson, O.E. (1979) 'Transaction-cost economics: the governance of contractual relations', *Journal of Law Economics*, 22: 233–61.

Williamson, O.E. (1985) *The Economic Institutions of Capitalism*, Free Press, New York.

Williamson, O.E. (1986) *Economic Organizations*, Harvester Wheatsheaf, Brighton, Sussex.

Willcocks, A.J. (1967) *The Creation of the National Health Service*, Routledge & Kegan Paul, London.

Willmott, P. (1989) *Community Initiatives: Patterns and Prospects*, Policy Studies Institute, London.

Wilson, D.C. (1992) *A Strategy of Change: Concepts and Controversies in the Management of Change*, Routledge, London.

Wilson, G. (1985) *Business and Politics: A Comparative Introduction*, Macmillan, London.

Wilson, G. (1990) *Interest Groups*, Blackwell, Oxford.

Wilson, J. (1990) *Politically Speaking: The Pragmatic Analysis of Political Language*, Blackwell, Oxford.

Wilson, J.Q. (1970) *Varieties of Police Behaviour*, Atheneum, New York.

Wilson, J.Q. (1973) *Political Organizations*, Sage, Beverly Hills, Cal.

Wilson, J.Q. (1989) *Bureaucracy*, Basic Books, New York.

Wilson, W. (1887) 'The Study of Administration', *Political Science Quarterly*, 2: 197–222.

Winkler, F. (1987) 'Consumerism in health care: beyond the supermarket model', *Policy and Politics*, 15: 1–8.

Winkler, J. (1976) 'Corporatism', *Archives Européennes de sociologie*, 17: 100–36.

Winter, J.M. (1990) 'Population, economists, and the state: the Royal Commission on Population, 1944–1949', in Furner and Supple (eds), 1990.

Wolf, R.L. (1979) 'The use of judicial evaluation methods in the formulation of educational policy', *Educational Evaluation and Policy Analysis*, 1: 19–28.

Wolfe, A. (1977) *The Limits to Legitimacy*, Free Press, New York, 1977.

Wolfinger, R.E. (1971) 'Nondecisions and the study of local politics', *American Political Science Review*, 65: 1063–80.

Wolman, H. (1981) 'The determinants of program success and failure', *Journal of Public Policy*, 1: 433–64.

Woodby, S. and M.L. Cottam (1991) *The Changing Agenda: World Politics since 1945*, Westview Press, Boulder, Col.

Woodward, J. (1965) *Industrial Organization: Theory and Practice*, Oxford University Press, London.

World Commission on Environment and Development (WCED) (1987) *Our Common Future*, Oxford University Press, Oxford.

Wright, D.S., A. Taylor, D.R. Davies, W. Sluckin, S.G.M. Lee and J.T. Reason (1970) *Introducing Psychology: An Experimental Approach*, Penguin Books, Harmondsworth, Middx.

Wright, M. (1988) 'Policy community, policy network and comparative industry policies', *Political Studies*, 36: 593–612.

Wright, M. and J. Storey (1994) 'Recruitment', in Beardwell and Holden (eds), 1994.

Young, K. (1977) 'Values in the policy process', *Policy and Politics*, 5: 1–22; reprinted in Pollitt *et al.* (eds), 1979.

Young, K. (1987) 'The space between words', in Jenkins and Solomos (eds), 1987.

Young, K. and C. Mason (1983) 'The significance of urban programmes', in Young and Mason (eds), 1983.

Young, K. and C. Mason (eds) (1983) *Urban Economic Development: New Roles and Relationships*, Macmillan, London.

Young, M. (1958) *The Rise of the Meritocracy, 1870–2033*, Thames & Hudson, London.

Young, M. and P. Willmott (1957) *Family and Kinship in East London*, Routledge & Kegan Paul, London.

Younis, T. (ed.) (1990) *Implementation in Public Policy*, Dartmouth, Aldershot, Hants.

Yuchtman, E. and S. Seashore (1967) 'A system resource approach to organizational effectiveness', *American Sociological Review*, 32: 891–903.

Zukerman, D.W. and R.E. Horn (1973) *The Guide to Simulations: Games for Education and Training*, Information Resources, Lexington, Mass.

Index